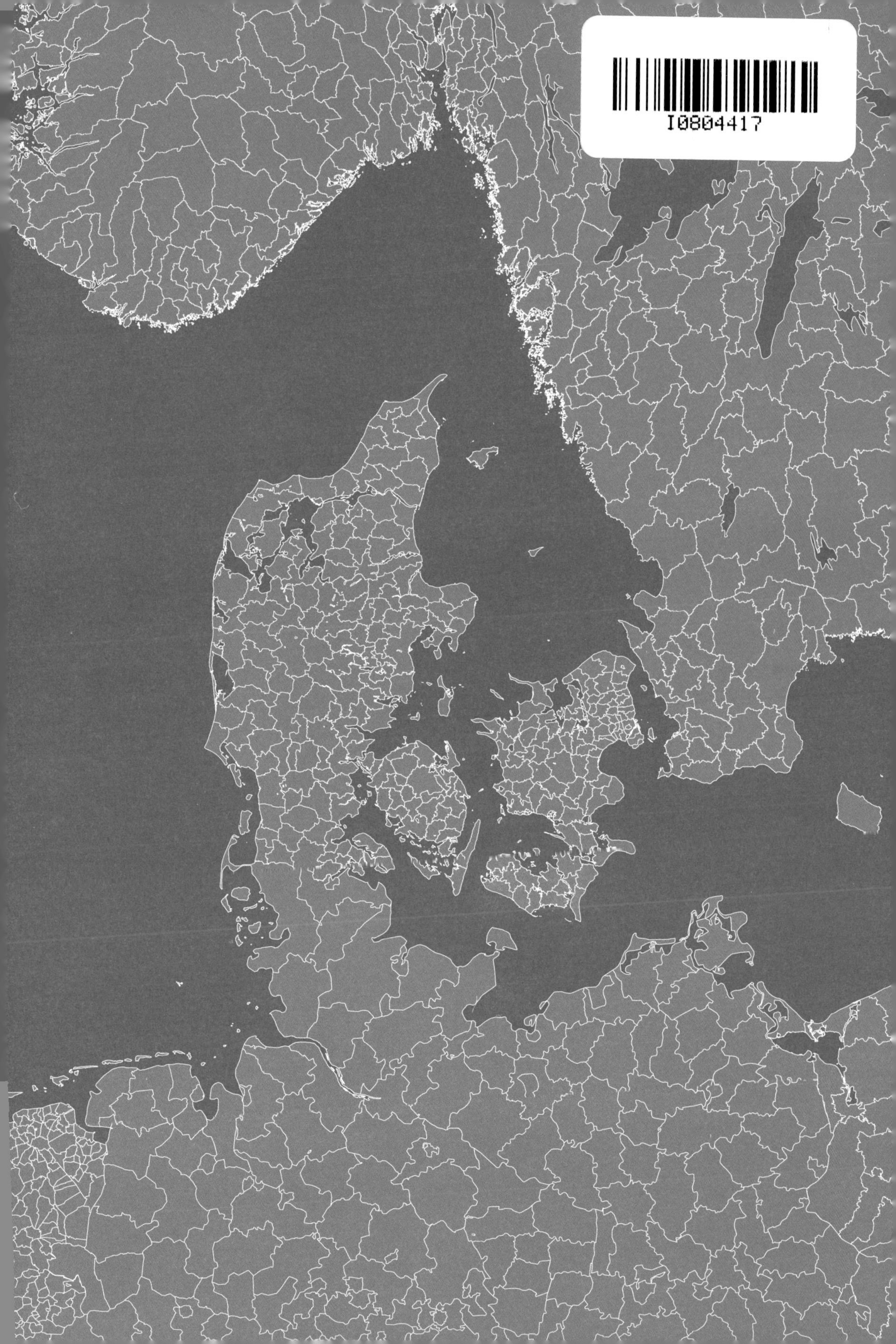

1 Kindergarten in Frederiksberg, Copenhagen, 1971.
2 The Black Square, Baggesensgade as a playground, February, 1975.
3 Senior citizens at a longtable party, Salem Old People's Home, Copenhagen, 1982.
4 Junk playground in Tingbjerg, 1970s.
5 Demonstration in connection with the Danish Maastricht Treaty referendum, Nørrebro, Copenhagen, May 18, 1993.
6 Tinggården low-rise housing, Herfølge, designed by Vandkunsten Architects, 1971–78.
7 Senior citizens planning their own senior cooperative housing, Nørrebro, Copenhagen, 2014.
8 Superkilen urban space, Nørrebro, Copenhagen, designed by BIG, Topotek 1 and Superflex, 2021.
9 Gellerupplanen public housing estate, Aarhus, designed by Knud Blach Petersen and Mogens Harbo, 1968–72. New park designed by SLA and Effekt, 2019. Urban renewal, "The Golden Gate," designed by Vandkunsten Architects and Transform Architects, 2019.

1

3

4

46

Architectures of Dismantling and Restructuring

Spaces of Danish Welfare 1970–Present

Kirsten Marie Raahauge, Deane Simpson, Martin Søberg, Katrine Lotz (eds.)

Lars Müller Publishers

Foreword:
Exploring Spaces of Danish Welfare 26
Kirsten Marie Raahauge
Principal Investigator of Spaces of Danish Welfare

Introduction:
The Welfare-Space Nexus 30
Niels Grønbæk, Runa Johannessen, Katrine Lotz,
Kirsten Marie Raahauge, Deane Simpson, Martin Søberg

Visualizing Welfare 44
Bastian Feltgen, Aleksander Nowak

Children as Symbolic Figures in Welfare Space Photography 50
Martin Søberg

1 Security

From Architecture of the Architect to the Architecture
of *Salus Populi* and the Architecture of Security 78
Lars Bo Kaspersen

Spaces and Measures between Welfare State
and Security State 94
Deane Simpson

Between Technologies of Power and Notions of Solidarity:
A Response to the Danish *Ghetto Plan* and Swedish
Vulnerable Areas Documents 148
Heidi Svenningsen Kajita, Jennifer Mack,
Svava Riesto, Meike Schalk

Holes in the Spaces of the Welfare State: Media Coverage
and Residents' Responses in the So-Called Hardest
Ghettos in Denmark 160
Mette Mechlenborg, Marie Stender

Are We Caring? Dilemmas Between Home and Institution
in Architectures for the Elderly 174
Louise Dedenroth Høj

2 Adaptability

A Welfare Situation in Tønder 218
Kirsten Marie Raahauge

From Purgatory to District Heating: Extending the Last Journey
within the Danish Welfare State 250
Niels Grønbæk

Are We All Here? Inclusion and Spatial Restructurings
in the Danish Primary School 1993–2020 282
Katrine Lotz

Healing Architecture and the Crisis of Care — 310
Runa Johannessen

Exploring Health Promotive Spaces of New Welfare: A Transdisciplinary Approach — 340
Sten Gromark
Interviewed by Louise Dedenroth Høj and Max Pedersen

Design and Decolonization in the 1970s: Beyond Spaces of Danish Welfare — 346
Alison J. Clarke

3 Community

Anthropological Perspectives on Housing as Welfare and Everyday Welfare Practices — 360
Maja Hojer Bruun

The Social Omnipotence of Neighborship — 370
Max Pedersen

Ideology of the Welfare State in Solidified Concrete for Housing — 400
Claus Bech-Danielsen

New Housing Economics — 412
Silje Erøy Sollien

On the Battle for Amager Common: A Power Play of Housing Politics in Copenhagen — 422
Jesper Pagh

Postscript — 444
Niels Grønbæk, Runa Johannessen, Katrine Lotz, Kirsten Marie Raahauge, Deane Simpson, Martin Søberg

Author Biographies — 451
Acknowledgements — 453
Image Credits — 455
Visualization Index — 459
Imprint — 464

0.01 Municipal borders, 1970s 22
0.02 Municipal borders, 2020s 24
0.03 Global events, 1970–2022 72
0.04 Events in Denmark, 1970–2022 74

1 Security

Spaces and Measures between Welfare State and Security State
1.01 Copenhagen's historical fortification development 118
1.02 Copenhagen/international securitization, 2001–22 120
1.03 Copenhagen inaccessible and secure spaces, 1970 122
1.04 Copenhagen inaccessible and secure spaces, 2022 123
1.05–07 Nine [terror-]protected zones recommended by PET to Copenhagen municipality and Copenhagen Police, 2017 124, 125, 126
1.08–09 Copenhagen physical security measures 127, 128
1.10 Copenhagen physical security measures, detail 130
1.11 Securitized public space case studies 131
1.12–13 Securitized public space: Kongens Nytorv, ca. 1970/2022 132, 134
1.14 Securitized public space: Kongens Nytorv, ca. 1970 135
1.15–16 Securitized public space: Nyhavn, ca. 1970/2022 136, 138
1.17 Securitized public space: Nyhavn, ca. 1970 139
1.18–19 Securitized public space: Amagertorv, ca. 1970/2022 140, 142
1.20 Securitized public space: Amagertorv, ca. 1970 143
1.21–22 Securitized public space: Christiansborg Slotsplads, ca. 1970/2022 144, 146
1.23 Securitized public space: Christiansborg Slotsplads, ca. 1970 147

Are We Caring? Dilemmas Between Home and Institution in Architectures for the Elderly
1.24 Distribution and size of care homes, 2020 188
1.25 Distribution of somatic care and specialized dementia care, 2020 189
1.26 Distribution of public and private care homes, 2020 190
1.27 Percentage of inhabitants older than 65 years, 1972–2017 191
1.28 Number of care dwellings per 1,000 inhabitants older than 65 years, 1972–2017 191
1.29 Percentage of inhabitants older than 65 years, 1972 192
1.30 Percentage of inhabitants older than 65 years, 2017 193
1.31 Number of care dwellings per 1,000 inhabitants older than 65 years, 1972 194
1.32 Number of care dwellings per 1,000 inhabitants older than 65 years, 2017 195
1.33 Distribution and size of care homes in the municipality of Copenhagen, 1972 196
1.34 Distribution and size of care homes in the municipality of Copenhagen, 2020 197
1.35 Distribution and size of care homes in the municipality of Høje Taastrup, 1972 198
1.36 Distribution and size of care homes in the municipality of Høje Taastrup, 2020 199
1.37 Distribution and size of care homes in the municipality of Tønder, 1972 200
1.38 Distribution and size of care homes in the municipality of Tønder, 2020 201
1.39 Development of architectures for the elderly 202
1.40 Development in the number of care home dwellings for the elderly 204
1.41 Layout of outdoor spaces, Tornhøjhaven 206
1.42 Layout of common areas in the housing units, Tornhøjhaven 208
1.43 Layout of resident apartment, Tornhøjhaven 210
1.44 Apartment ceiling plan, Tornhøjhaven 212
1.45 Apartment floor plan, Tornhøjhaven 213
1.46–47 Appropriation of the apartment by residents, Tornhøjhaven 214, 215

2 Adaptability

A Welfare Situation in Tønder
2.01 National center-periphery dynamics, 2020 233
2.02 Distribution of welfare institutions, 1970s 234
2.03 Redistribution of welfare institutions due to centralization and structural reforms, 2020 235
2.04 Routes to welfare institutions, 1970/2020 236
2.05 Welfare institutions in Tønder, 1970s 238
2.06 Tønder, urban context, 2020 240
2.07 Presence of welfare institutions in Tønder, 1970s 242
2.08 Absence of welfare institutions in Tønder, 2020 243
2.09 Construction dates of buildings that housed selected welfare institutions in Tønder in relation to the territorial changes 244
2.10 Presence and absence of selected welfare institutions in Tønder 246
2.11–12 Tønderstierne, a landscape of experience in addition to a landscape of farming, 2020 248, 249

From Purgatory to District Heating: Extending the Last Journey within the Danish Welfare State

2.13 Fælleskrematoriet, floor plan 265
2.14 Distribution and catchment area of crematoria in Roskilde Stift, 1970s 266
2.15 Distribution and catchment area of the new Fælledkrematorium in Roskilde Stift, 2022 267
2.16 Route of a dead body in Nakskov, 1970s 268
2.17 Route of a dead body in Nakskov and beyond, 2022 269
2.18 Traditional versus centralized cremation process 270
2.19 Cremations per year and per crematorium, 1890–2020 272
2.20 Location of the new crematorium Fælleskrematoriet 274
2.21 Context of the new crematorium Fælleskrematoriet 275
2.22 Traditional hearse versus modern multicoffin hearse 276
2.23 Fælleskrematoriet, section perspective 278
2.24 Catalogue of all Danish crematoria, by construction date 280

Are We All Here? Inclusion and Spatial Restructurings in the Danish Primary School 1993–2020

2.25 Inclusion rate per municipality, 2017 295
2.26 National distribution of special schools, 2017 296
2.27 National distribution of schools, 2017 297
2.28 Distribution of schools in Vordingborg, before 2013 298
2.29 Distribution of schools in Vordingborg, after 2013 299
2.30–31 A fifth-grade classroom at the Svend Gønge-School 300, 301
2.32 The activity center at the Svend Gønge-School 302
2.33 The Svend Gønge-School and its immediate environment 304
2.34 Inclusion-exclusion nexus, 1990–2022 306
2.35 Change in inclusion rates across Danish municipalities, 2008–20 308

Healing Architecture and the Crisis of Care

2.36 Key events in Danish hospital development, 1990–2022 324
2.37 Multisensorial delivery room, DNV-Gødstrup, 2020 326
2.38 Conventional delivery room, Thisted, 2020 328
2.39 Bed ward in pavilion, Bispebjerg Hospital, 1913 330
2.40 Nature as a healing element: hospital garden (exterior), Bispebjerg Hospital, 1913 332
2.41 Nature as a healing element: visual projections (interior), DNV-Gødstrup, 2020 333
2.42 Geographical distribution of hospitals and number of beds, 1970 334
2.43 Geographical distribution of hospitals and number of beds, 2020 335
2.44 Extended hospital geography: pre-hospital transport and telemedicine 336
2.45 Number of hospitals and beds, 1930–2020 338

3 Community

The Social Omnipotence of Neighbourship

3.01 Distribution of senior housing by building types, 2017 384
3.02 Distribution of senior housing by ownership types, 2017 385
3.03 Overview of nineteen Danish collective housing projects 386
3.04 Number of apartments, 1950–2021 388
3.05 Number of apartments in collective housing projects, 1950–80 390
3.06 Silkeborghus and its immediate environment 392
3.07 Major social hot spots in Silkeborghus 394
3.08 Silkeborghus space allocation 396
3.09 Silkeborghus residents profile 398
3.10 Residents engagement in three types of social interaction 399
3.11 Percentage of residents having helped neighbors within last month 399

On the Battle for Amager Common: A Power Play of Housing Politics in Copenhagen

3.12 Amager Common, key events, 1990–2021 434
3.13 Copenhagen urban development areas, metro lines and natural areas, 2017/2020 436
3.14 Ørestad Fælled Kvarter and replacement sites, size and anticipated profit, 2017/2020 437
3.15 Ørestad Fælled Kvarter and replacement sites, size and anticipated profit, 2017 438
3.16 Ørestad Fælled Kvarter and replacement sites, size and anticipated profit, 2020 439
3.17 Søringen protest signs, 1970s 440
3.18 Amager Common protest signs, 2018–21 441
3.19 Amager Common demonstration, 2021 442

Municipal borders, 1970s

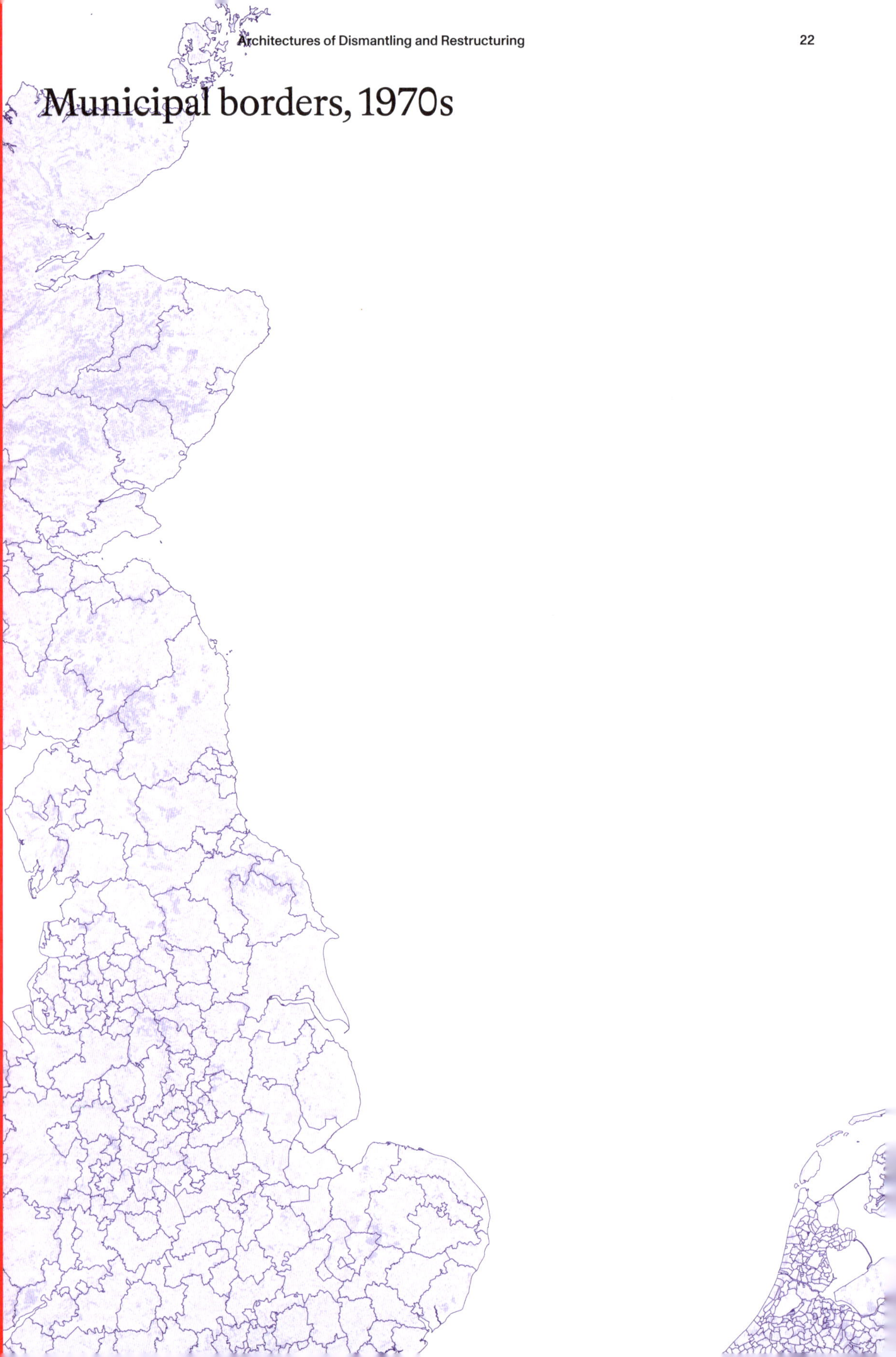

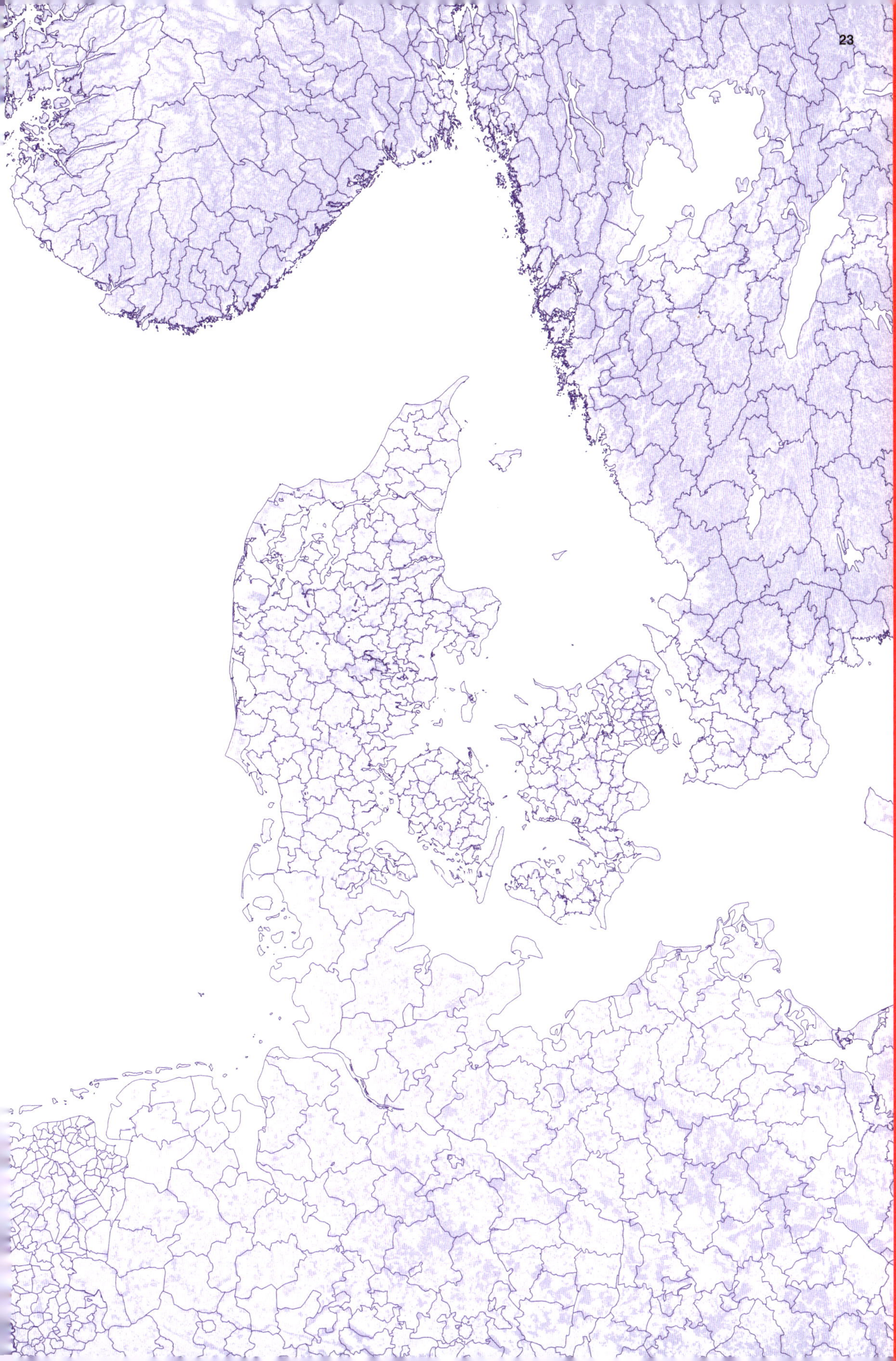

Municipal borders, 2020s

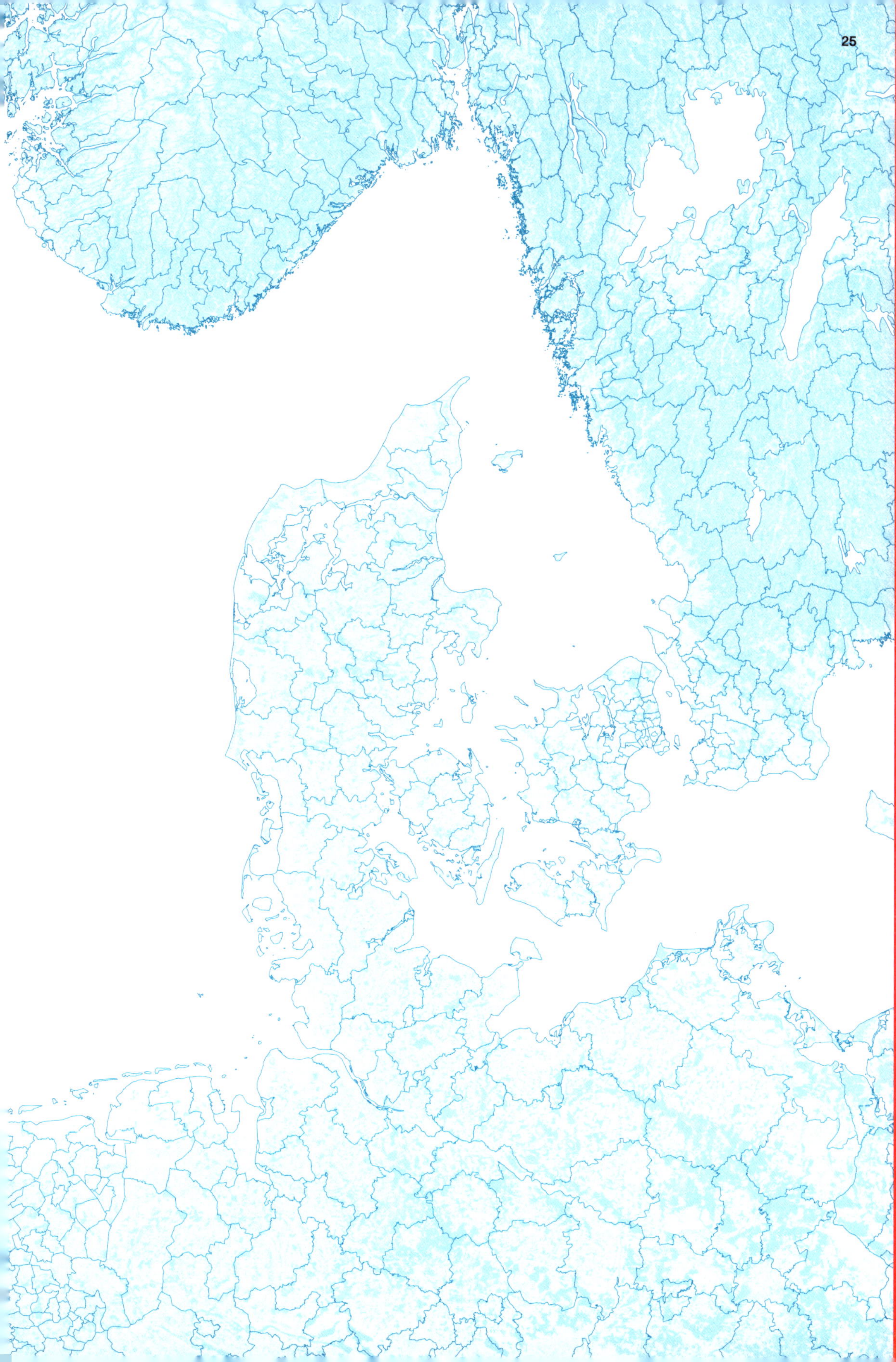

Foreword: Exploring Spaces of Danish Welfare

Kirsten Marie Raahauge

Principal Investigator
of Spaces of Danish Welfare

Spatial amnesia has been ruling within welfare research, while at the same time, spatial studies have not paid much attention to welfare. Yet welfare is indeed spatial.

Welfare spaces are transforming in these years, also in Denmark, impacting society in profound ways that concern balances of center and periphery, institutional and homey interiors, state and market, community and individual. It concerns how we act in society, how we perceive welfare and space, and the impact this has on other aspects of society. The ideas of welfare are contested in these years, since new agendas have become prominent, involving the environment, climate and nature, thus spatializing welfare in new ways. This also impacts the role of architects and designers, who are no longer perceived as societal reformers; rather, there are many complex interrelations to take care of in the métier of a welfare architect. Not only the actual layout, but the ideas and the new political agendas have changed, altering institutions, cities and countryside; the flow of money and of people in and out of these spaces is also transforming. Private funding is becoming more important when building welfare institutions, while the state subsidizes a still more elaborate system of welfare administration to distribute, connect, separate and monitor the vast welfare machine. Meanwhile, balances of urbanites and country dwellers are changing, as well as those of gender, age, education and other such traditional classifications; maybe these groups are not the only valid ones, complicating the efforts to adjust the gaze at the world.

Such changes can be explored in rather telling ways when following the interrelationship between space and welfare. Otherwise hidden shifts and balances become manifest. The changing webs of welfare and space, and the nexus between the spaces of welfare and the surrounding society have been the focus for this book as well as for the research project that is the driver behind it, Spaces of Danish Welfare. We hope to be part of the emergent turn toward focusing on welfare spaces, leaving behind spatial amnesia within welfare research as well as welfare oblivion within spatial studies.

The Process

The starting point of this book is the cross-disciplinary research project Spaces of Danish Welfare, situated at the Royal Danish Academy (2017–22), funded by The Independent Research Fund Denmark. The research project builds on Forming Welfare, a network at the academy (2011–17). Spaces of Danish Welfare has become larger over the years. From the start, the researchers in the project were Kirsten Marie Raahauge (Principal Investigator), Merete Ahnfeldt-Mollerup, Katrine Lotz, Deane Simpson, Runa Johannessen and Max Pedersen. Soon after, Louise Dedenroth Høj came into the group, followed by Niels Grønbæk and Dag Petersson; Jesper Pagh and Martin Søberg later joined the group. Throughout the research project, Aleksander Nowak, Bastian Feltgen and Susanne Eeg have been visualizing the projects; Susanne Eeg has also been coordinating the blog and other activities of the research project, while Sandra Gonon has been production editor of this publication. Regrettably, Merete Ahnfeldt-Mollerup and Dag Petersson had to leave the project earlier than planned. We thank them for their great and valuable input.

Our studies were amputated by the COVID-19 lockdown, which has forced many of us to reinvent our field of study and our approach. Although something is definitely lacking due to this long and unwelcome period of no access to the field and to the archives, it may have brought us insight into yet undiscovered parts of the welfare spaces; as in an X-ray image, you see something new when you have to gaze in different ways. This book is the main publication from our research project. Here, we try to show the disparate methods, perspectives and projects in their context of other researchers. Furthermore, we hope to show some of the synergetic lines in the perspectives and the resonance between the studies.

Spaces of Danish Welfare set out to investigate the intersection of space and welfare through the disciplines of anthropology, architecture/urban planning, and later through art history, and through both academic research and visualizations. The project started with the hypothesis that welfare spaces could be understood through their transformations concerning scale and distribution, and that the nexus between citizens and welfare spaces was of major importance. Furthermore, we set out to explore spaces of welfare with a special concern for what happened after 1970, that is, after the so-called golden age of welfare, 1945 to 1970. We also sought to understand the raison d'être of the Danish welfare system as the concrete ways in which the five pillars traditionally attached to the welfare state (housing, education, social security, employment and health) are met in terms of public services and with regard to social inclusion and justice.[1] The five-pillar-structure, coined by British economist William Beveridge in 1942, has been used far and wide in the discourse on welfare as a project for the state, as well as in research.

During the process, we discovered many other temporal points of reference than 1970; from reforms made in the nineteenth century to restructurings managed in the early twentieth century; a wide range of times is of importance for the welfare spaces of today. Furthermore, we found that the concepts of scale and distribution were too narrow to cover the findings of the subprojects, since rhizomatic, multiple and network-oriented configurations emerged. Also, we found that not only the connections between citizens and welfare systems were of importance, but also nonhuman agents were part of the intermingling of space and welfare, as for example tableaus in hospitals or dementia care homes, photographic representations of architecture and social life, infrastructure cutting off parts of the country, granite or cement blocks acting as security elements, furniture, competing ideas about nature, inclusion, age, communities, health, death, time, the provinces etc. Furthermore, we found that the welfare condition developed into (or has always been) something too complex to be grasped by the pillar metaphor; climate change, infrastructure, tourism, security, pandemic effects, virtualization and other urgent matters have become part of the spaces of welfare, causing new agendas to become prominent and new kinds of spaces of welfare to emerge. These and other pressing questions to welfare spaces have an impact on the balances, perceptions and normativities of welfare and space, and they impact the way welfare spaces are formed, represented, conceived of and used. This also affects the kinds of welfare provided, by whom and in what ways it is carried out. While we have been working with spaces of welfare in Denmark, we have also had an eye to movements taking place in other parts of the world, especially the Nordic countries.[2] As the ways in which welfare is perceived, communicated and linked to spaces are in fluctuation, the research into welfare spaces is also in transformation, concerning the disciplines involved as well as their perspectives on the studies, opening for new ways of exploring these topics.

The Book

With this book, we wish to take part in the emerging research into these areas by exploring the dismantling and restructuring of the spaces of welfare we are studying. Furthermore, we would like to discuss the role of architecture and design, forming welfare spaces, and impacting the societal context. We also wish to bring into the field the entanglement with power relations between state, society and market on a large scale as well as in small-scale everyday life. Apart from the researchers from Spaces of Danish Welfare, other researchers have accepted the invitation to publish articles on their research into related areas; we have received contributions from our advisory board, from participants at the international conference *Spaces of Welfare* (2021) and from our visualization team.

Though leaving the welfare spaces that we have studied for the last five years, we are eager to move toward other parts of this field in the future. We find the material encountered highly relevant as new frictions and passages have been discovered, as well as unexpected transformations of the layering of welfare and space. Here, climate and redistribution of taxes are sometimes two sides of the same coin, while also new kinds of exclusion and inclusions are to be found by focusing on the spatial side of welfare. Furthermore, new ways of funding and of distributing welfare through spaces are emerging. Some of the former ideas and spaces of welfare are now absent, while new modes of creating welfare and space have emerged, among other things prompted by new technology and digital solutions. This gives rise to webs of ideas, activities and imaginaries of welfare spaces that are sometimes present in the same concrete site, always also affecting social relations outside the spaces. We hope this leads to new discussions and investigations into welfare and space involving the urgent matters this nexus touches upon.

Bibliography

Beveridge, William. *Social Insurance and Allied Services Report*. New York: Macmillan Co., 1942.

Notes

1 William Beveridge, *Social Insurance and Allied Services Report* (New York: Macmillan Co., 1942).

2 Among them the Architecture and Welfare Network, accessed February 10, 2022, https://www.architectureandwelfare.net/.

Introduction: The Welfare-Space Nexus

Niels Grønbæk, Runa Johannessen, Katrine Lotz, Kirsten Marie Raahauge, Deane Simpson, Martin Søberg

Architectures of Dismantling and Restructuring: Spaces of Danish Welfare, 1970–Present explores the entanglements of space and welfare through a variety of case studies. From 1970 until today, welfare reforms in Denmark and in most other European countries entail the simultaneous dismantling, diminishing and dissolution of certain kinds of spaces of welfare and the development, expansion and concentration of others. We define *spaces of welfare* as the spatial consolidation – on many scales, including architecture, design and urbanism – of ideas of welfare as well as specific welfare policies and provisions. Such spaces, and whatever kinds of restructurings they are subject to, greatly impacts routines of everyday life and configurations of civic society, only to relay back into the reshaping of welfare ideas, policies and provisions. Hence, spatial perceptions and practices are shaped by transformations of welfare ideas, policies and provisions – and the spatial consolidations and distributions of welfare contribute to shaping the understandings, aspirations and instantiations of welfare for instance through notions of universality, non-commodification and "the good life."

The term *welfare* is closely connected to the formation of different models of European welfare states during the decades immediately following World War II – decades framed in hindsight as the "golden age" of the European welfare state.[1] Increasingly critical perspectives on the welfare state and the social state would emerge during the late 1960s and the '70s. On the left, theoreticians such as Henri Lefebvre and Michel Foucault would challenge the state's concentration of power and the subjugation of the individual subject to its institutions.[2] Marxist critique saw tendencies toward the emergence of an alienated subject compensated for being delivered from the mercy of market forces by universal welfare.[3] On the right, critique of a suboptimal hegemony and constrained freedom of the so-called nanny state was expressed by politicians and theorists promoting a greater role for the market in the development of a reformed welfare state, in which welfare was no longer seen as compensation but as integrated in a modern competitive market economy.

In the 1980s and '90s the concepts of the competitive city region and the competitive state gained discursive and political momentum, and major spatial differentiations developed out of this growing focus.[4] Aligned with these developments would be shifts in the role of the state's relation to the market in the delivery of welfare architecture and urbanism, manifested on the planning level as a shift in the logics of spatial development from managerial "predict and provide" planning to entrepreneurial planning involving state-owned development corporations and public-private partnerships. Strategies of optimization (and digitalization) would be further applied to the provision of welfare, while the original welfare pillar of housing would be eroded at this time by market and governance-supported initiatives.

Particularly since 2000, Denmark, alongside the other Nordic countries (Finland, Iceland, Norway and Sweden), has received much international attention for its flexicurity-based welfare model focusing inquiries on the model's mitigating effects on negative impacts of neoliberalist deregulation.[5] Denmark has been presented as a site of relatively low inequality, high social mobility, high trust in government, a prosperous and uncorrupt society supporting the world's happiest people, paying the world's highest tax rates, living in the world's most livable cities.

It is the intention of this book that this external picture be challenged by an internal and more nuanced understanding of a turbulent period of complex dismantling and restructuring.

Spaces of Danish Welfare

As a political project, the Danish welfare state aligns with what sociologist Gøsta Esping-Andersen has described as the social democratic capitalist welfare state model, a model which was applied in all of the Nordic countries.[6] Such a model entails that public amenities are equally accessible to all citizens and that the state actively interacts with market forces through mitigation and limitation of market influence, for instance via relatively high standards of tax-paid public welfare provisions, but also by sustaining the market. The latter, for instance, through the provision of free education for all as a way of increasing workforce skills and through the extensive expansion of the workforce through institutions such as day care and eldercare, which supported the entry of women into the labor market.

Whereas the formative phase of the Danish welfare state ca. 1945–70 was based on the tax system as a redistribution mechanism, financing services delivered through universal welfare institutions, development in Denmark since 1970 has reinterpreted welfare as a more complex system, where provisions are delivered by an increasingly diverse range of actors, directed toward specific groups. The year 1970 is not a definitive watershed but rather a pivot point. Significant social, political and economic events and shifts occurring around 1970 testified to the exhaustion of the way the Danish welfare state had hitherto been conceived and conducted. This included, for instance, the impact of the international oil crises during the 1970s and tendencies such as increasing inflation, deindustrialization and globalization as well as nation-specific events, in particular the 1970 Danish municipal reform, the 1973 Danish membership in the European Economic Community (EEC) and the same year's landslide national election, which to some degree undermined the political parties traditionally in power. The legalization of audiovisual pornography in 1969 and of abortion in 1973 testify to the changing cultural and biopolitical attitudes of those years.

Spatial planning was an important element of the construction of the welfare system during the post–World War II period; the history of redistributions and of the divisions of responsibilities between governmental bodies, regions and municipalities since 1970 is also a story of planning of institutions and even of housing.[7] Part of this development concerns the changing role of the state in comparison with other actors and organizations, including the unions, which traditionally have played a very significant role in the regulation of the Danish labor market. Also, the roles of civic society and philanthropic actors have changed over time, reflected in spatial transformation. Furthermore, the development of cities and landscape planning are intertwined with welfare policies and ideas.[8]

Since 1970 the social contract between citizen and the Danish state has expanded beyond tax payment and redistribution politics toward a higher degree of integration of individual life choices, interests from the market and overall state interests. The significant increase in citizens' willingness to engage in a still more expanded social contract has proportionally increased the integration of citizens' lives with the life of the state. Main drivers in this integration are arguably the perceived quality, accessibility and relevance of welfare provisions. Danish examples of de-universalization would include the prioritization of Copenhagen and the Øresund region in urban development, including the centralization of investments in connectivity (bridge, metro and airport infrastructure, etc.) and business sectoral specialization. This movement toward centralization was further enhanced with the structural reform of 2007, by which hospitals, places of education and other institutions were abandoned in smaller provincial cities, while super-hospitals were erected in larger cities and other institutions were relocated to larger urban areas.[9]

Well-known structures and associations of the Danish welfare state seem to have dwindled, being replaced to some extent by networks that are not as explicit and as easy to detect since concerned with private and community-oriented aspects of life, leaving the societal welfare associations and the aspirations for universality in access to provisions less obvious. This implies, for instance, changing values supporting the performative logics of the institutions of the welfare state, for example, changes in school pedagogy, changes in hospital care logics and even changes in the handling of the bodies of deceased citizens through cremation. Yet the relationships between architecture, welfare and processes of spatial, material and cultural transformation in Denmark have hitherto received relatively little scholarly attention.[10] Understanding the inner dynamics and friction lines within a contemporary welfare state, its many interrelated systems and related society, however, depends on a thorough understanding of its spatial conditions and consequences. *Where* do the dynamics of the gradual expansion of the social contract occur is an unavoidable question.

Dynamics of Change

The history of welfare and the development of the European welfare state has been inspected, narrated and theorized during the past couple of decades within the fields of economy, political science, humanities and sociology. In his seminal book *The Three Worlds of Welfare Capitalism*, Gøsta Esping-Andersen identified the bifurcations and several models of welfare states, suggesting that the huge influx of women into the labor market was the single most economically advantageous feature of the Nordic models.[11] Several recent political science studies of the Danish welfare state have added further facets to this explanation: Jacob Torfing has argued that in a Danish context a substantial change has occurred in the structure which organizes policymaking, from a top-down, centralist and center-periphery organization of few steps in the post–World War II era to the multidimensional neocorporatist form of today.[12] Ove Kaj Pedersen has uncovered a shift in Denmark from a Keynesian welfare state toward a *competition state* characterized by extensive and ever-increasing mobilization of still-not-marketized human labor resources in order to secure competition advantages on a globalized market as a precondition for continuously securing its citizens' welfare.[13] In the context of understanding the welfare state as a survival unit, as coined by Lars Bo Kaspersen, the change from a focus on social security to physical security becomes visible.[14] The urgent matters in terms of threats to the continued supply of welfare provisions today are well-known: climate change, demographic changes, health-related matters – including pandemics such as COVID-19 – political threats, administrative changes and technological changes including digitalization.

Alongside theorizations of the state's restructuring and redistributions of welfare, geographers and planners have grappled with the territorial restructuring and concomitant redistribution of equality/inequality under the influence of shifting political rationales. As mentioned, in fields such as the humanities and design studies, various narratives and critiques of welfare have been present since the late 1960s. The critique of modernist planning rationales that came in the aftermath of the long period of "predict and provide" planning was developed in many different environments. The critique voiced among others by urbanist Jane Jacobs and architect Jan Gehl addressed architects, city authorities and a wider public in concrete critiques of specific space.[15] The critique of modernist urban planning projects has also influenced humanist, social and traditionalist perspectives, for instance focusing on the ways cities are continually producing differences and inequalities, as theorized by Edward Soja, David Harvey, Doreen Massey, Mustafa Dikeç and others, often in dialogue with philosophies of space such as Michel de Certeau's.[16]

Although these discourses concern entangled phenomena and objects of distributions of societal goods, they rarely identify the spatial implications of state-territorial restructuring and how social amenities and welfare systems are structured in space or how they structure space. This book investigates some of the gaps. Counter to earlier stages of the welfare state, it presents evidence suggesting that some of the most important impacts of change are not to be found at the level of central government, but are experienced at a decentralized and concrete level, where the surrounding society is impacted by changes within the welfare system and where institutions – including civic society and market actors – directly engage in daily struggles to tie together managerial demands of optimization from one side with demands of good service on the other. In fact, local, regional and national governmental bodies rely on these daily institutional struggles to translate welfare discourse into everyday activities. The locus of this struggle is where the welfare state happens.

Spaces of Danish welfare have changed; to a higher degree expressed by way of ambiguity, hybridity and situatedness on the one hand, while on the other hand figures from the middle-class concerning privacy or consumer culture or logics of efficiency have become stronger. Some spaces of welfare have been blended into commercial spaces or into community-led spaces, while at the same time there is a tendency of some spaces of welfare to imitate models of middle-class life, gentrified neighborhoods and consumer society. These figures point toward a higher degree of ambiguity concerning spaces of welfare, blending private and public spheres, consumer society and welfare, and at the same time displaying an explicit trope of logics of efficiency. The emergent tendency of spaces of welfare to have become more homely is to be observed in, for instance, libraries becoming urban living rooms. Hybrids of public, private, common, intimate and semipublic spaces seem to have become more common.

As mentioned at the beginning of this text, the notion that ideologies or grand visions create new worlds seems to be supplemented by a feedback mechanism whereby materializations impact ideologies. Discussions of the avant-garde, the utopias of yesterday, the quests for emancipation through design and equality through architecture seem by now to have faded. There are no typologies that can be commonly agreed on, and instead of emancipation, state-guaranteed communality seems to have become pervasive. Utopian visions have been replaced by the gloomy sensation of uncertainty connected to inhabiting a threatening world of unwanted globalization effects and a severe climate crisis. Furthermore, economic restructuring during recent decades have had spatial implications: Denmark's experience of urban deindustrialization and the spatial impacts on former industrial sites that have now become postindustrial housing areas for well-off citizens is a concrete example of this. Another example is the internal movement of industry and jobs within Denmark, leaving the larger cities as areas of speedy development, while the rest of the country is becoming deprived of economic drivers, political power, cultural life and welfare institutions.

Structure and Approaches

The analytical approaches presented in this book stem from several disciplines, including architecture, planning, anthropology and art history. Collectively, the texts engage the interfaces between various kinds of knowledge production: firstly, a cross-disciplinary interface; and secondly, an interface between tools and methods of text- and graphic-based mediation.

The cross-disciplinary interface is obvious in the many ways we have been working with gathering material. From historical archives, registration of spatial and material organization, interpretation of plans, models and sketches, participant observation, interviews and desktop surveys of literature and images, we have built up our empirical fields through a series of methods and sources that have been in dialogue with each other. This multitude of gathering methods provides the possibility of having several gazes and of being aware of what is invisible from one perspective while visible from another.

The chapters address different scales through a variety of visualizations, often conducting analysis-through-representation in different ways. This emphasis on visualization is part of a larger effort to find synergetic connections between artistic research conducted at the fine arts academies and research as it is dealt with at the universities. Neither of these modes of reflecting is new, but the urge to connect the two, the intertwinement that we seek, is less common. This has led to the construction of text-graphic hybrids with the implication of supplementing text mediation as traditionally privileged in scholarly research.

The methodological accounting of the types of drawing and visualizations employed is diverse. The visualizations have different areas of focus between methodological reflections from within the fields of architecture, urban design and planning, and others from cartography, philosophy and information design/information graphics. In practical terms, the visualization aspect of the project explores an ecosystem of different visualization registers and typologies that collectively contribute to a larger system of information, including: (1) distribution/scales (including maps and drawings); (2) organizations (organizational and actor-network diagrams); (3) dynamics/timelines (the historical time frame and the everyday time frame); (4) dissections; (5) composite drawings; (6) emblems (diagrams); and (7) atmospheres (photographs). The selection of these different forms of visualization is informed by an evolving sensitivity to the selection of the right tool for the job. Axonometric drawing, for example, prompts another level of analytical consciousness compared to the photograph, in terms of what is included and excluded from the drawing. The statistical graph of the total numbers of hospitals and beds communicates differently from the interior comparison of the bed wards. The historical event timeline of institutional development communicates differently from an actor-network diagram.

In this sense, the book explores a role for *showing* as well as *telling*, the visual as well as the textual. It explores the hypothesis that some aspects of research into spatial phenomena could be better shown than written about, in the sense that inscriptive practices such as drawing or diagramming might, as architect and social anthropologist Ray Lucas has suggested, "offer significantly different insights, not easily accessible through textual models of discourse analysis, critical theory, or observation."[17] This raises a series of productive questions concerning the status of the entanglement of text and visualization as a scientific method in knowledge production.

A shifting focus toward space and materiality in the humanities and in the social sciences has informed the work presented here: the spatial turn, the material, the atmospheric turn, the sensuous turn, the turns of actor-network theory and science and technology studies, the perspectivism turn, the post-human turn, the affective turn and still others. Concurrently, the texts are informed by turns of recent prominence within architectural discourse, including a politico-societal turn, as for instance promoted by architectural historian Tom Avermaete and architectural anthropologist Albena Yaneva; an ontological turn, as promoted by philosophers Graham Harman and Manuel DeLanda and architect Keller Easterling; and a performative turn with points of departure in feminist architecture theory, as promoted for example by architectural theorists Jane Rendell and Doina Petrescu and art and media scholar Giuliana Bruno.[18] Here, these developments suggest the possibility for space and materiality to be questioned in alternative ways concerning the empirical material as well as a series of epistemological issues.

Architectures of Dismantling and Restructuring is divided into three parts: Security; Adaptability; and Community. Before turning to the thematic parts, two explorations of the relationships between spaces of welfare and practices of visualization are presented. In their chapter "Visualizing Welfare," Bastian Feltgen and Aleksander Nowak reflect on their own work developing, in close collaboration with the authors, the visualizations which are presented in this book and which form part of its framework, namely the research project Spaces of Danish Welfare. When discussed through visualizations, questions of interpretation tend to be obvious: lines, colors, connections, scales, distributions and techniques all become important as analytical devices. Furthermore, the visuals give way for normative aspects to emerge. This is also evidenced in Martin Søberg's exploration of photographs as an architectural discourse in "Children as Symbolic Figures in Welfare Space Photography."

Søberg points to the huge impact of visualization in the form of photographs in the discourse, desires and imaginaries of welfare. Turning to a historical perspective, he demonstrates how ideas and imaginaries of welfare were expressed in Danish architectural discourse from the 1930s until the early '70s, conveyed through visual means, in pictures, with the staging of children as important symbolic figures.

Security

This part addresses the dynamics between regularity, homogeneity and states of exception and how such states of exception might lead to changes in our perception of "normality." These states of exception may be caused by ideologically based movements and include deterritorializing forces such as the feminist movement, the antiracist movement and the queer movement, or they may be part of re-territorializing forces that strive to stabilize and bring into order the lives and material conditions of society. The latter is demonstrated discursively as well as through actual policymaking, In "From Architecture of the Architect to the Architecture of *Salus Populi* and the Architecture of Security," Lars Bo Kaspersen explores the genealogy of the concept of welfare and discusses the development of Western European discourses on welfare and the welfare state, through which he identifies implications of this development for the spatialization of welfare. In "Spaces and Measures between Welfare State and Security State," Deane Simpson discusses the evolution of physical security measures in the public spaces of Copenhagen in the context of the state's response to actual and perceived threats to the state and its ability to provide ontological security through physical amenities. These dynamics are placed in a longer time frame of the city's development of "livable" public space, which is itself predicated on conceptions of security and safety. When welfare space translates into security spaces, as suggested by Simpson, its visualizations add an extra layer of interpretation and of observations about how to interpret, thus countering a design protocol of hiding security measures at work in public space, for instance by using colors, flowers or soft shapes.

Broadening the topic of so-called ghetto representations in a Scandinavian perspective, Heidi Svenningsen Kajita, Jennifer Mack, Svava Riesto and Meike Schalk in "Between Technologies of Power and Notions of Solidarity: A Response to the Danish *Ghetto Plan* and Swedish *Vulnerable Areas* Documents" show how shifts in the notion of solidarity is discursively articulated through official, government-sponsored documents that support the physical and social reshaping and redefinition of social housing estates in Denmark and municipal housing estates in Sweden. In Mette Mechlenborg and Marie Stender's "Holes in the Spaces of the Welfare State: Media Coverage and Residents' Responses in the So-Called Hardest Ghettos in Denmark," the relationship between the stories of the welfare state and its excluded spaces is analyzed through the media representations of such areas, and in turn, how residents cope with the stigmatization of being "holes" in the welfare state.

Technology of care by spatial means is considered by Louise Dedenroth Høj in "Are We Caring? Dilemmas Between Home and Institution in Architectures for the Elderly." Through case studies of dementia care homes, Dedenroth Høj explores the negotiations and dilemmas that are part of the ambitions for creating homely environments in an institutional setting. The importance of occasionally calibrating the relationship between text and visuals in such a way that their hybrid entanglement forms the medium carrying (certain) research findings is demonstrated by Dedenroth Høj. Her juxtaposition of two perspectival plans of the same 33-square-meter room, one – combining technical drawing and short textual descriptions – emphasizing technical care features built into the room, next to a similar plan showing the personal appropriation of the room by for instance, furniture and curtains belonging to its resident.

Adaptability

The second part of the book considers the shifting distribution of welfare and the effect it has on the spaces of welfare and their surroundings, adapting in various ways to the changes. Furthermore, it discusses in which ways the shifting relationships between ideologies and technologies of care are part of these changes. Additionally, this part addresses how structural matters interrelate with questions of affect, that is, how welfare is practiced and experienced in specific spaces.

Kirsten Marie Raahauge explores the town of Tønder as a case of peripheralization in her chapter "A Welfare Situation in Tønder." The town used to be a "city of institutions" and a center for a large hinterland. Now it has become the periphery of other centers after the relocation of many of its welfare institutions to larger cities. This has left Tønder in a new situation, looking back at its former vitality and gazing toward the plans for UNESCO tourism in the future, remembering the social impact of the former institutions while rhizomatic networks of social life emerge. In the visualization of Raahauge's text, the mere mapping of welfare amenities before and after the major Danish structural reform of 2007 proves to become not so much a way of representing the ethnographic fieldwork or the anthropological perspective of the study, as it – if unintended – became an easily politicized statement about what has happened to the provinces in these years.

How contradictions are at play in the handling of dead bodies on their way to and through the central crematorium in Ringsted is demonstrated by Niels Grønbæk in "From Purgatory to District Heating: Extending the Last Journey within the Danish Welfare State." Grønbæk presents a sociospatial and material analysis of the crematorium and shows what happens if you gaze at the welfare state through the perspective of the death of its citizens. His analysis of four-coffin hearse design entangles with investigations into instructions for their drivers and the geographical location of decentrally positioned temporary coffin-cooling facilities as part of a logistically complex transport infrastructure. Here, the relationship between visual and textual elements becomes important as a process of gathering and representing in which the stream of material and analytical perspectives that runs toward the visualization work is fueled by having a reverse stream running, namely from visualizations, provoking new findings or asking new questions to the material and the analytical perspectives.

In "Are We All Here? Inclusion and Spatial Restructurings in the Danish Primary School 1993–2020," Katrine Lotz addresses how different spaces are enmeshed in the activities taking place in a school, thus having an impact on the exclusion and inclusion of pupils. She shows how school policies and concrete objects and spatial restructurings on all scales are interwoven and act together in the classroom. Lotz explores the complex choreography of the classroom following the interconnectedness of pupils, teachers, furniture and objects as well as spatial divisions as they together obtain a version of inclusion. Here, the interplay between methods of gathering becomes evident, enabling a reflection on how to deal with ways of gazing, methods of analyzing and cross-disciplinarily informed interpretations.

The design of affects through spatial technologies in hospitals is explored by Runa Johannessen in "Healing Architecture and the Crisis of Care." Here, the ideas and ideals that underpin the design method *healing architecture* are understood structurally as a sign of a crisis of care in the welfare system, in which architecture becomes a proxy caregiver. Through the analysis of recent developments in the design of special hospital wards for prospective parents and by cross-pollinating archival studies and visual explorations, Johannessen shows the concurrent presence of a designed homeliness and an engineered instrumentalization of the space, and points to unresolved contradictions between affect and instrumentalization of care.

In the interview "Exploring Health Promotive Spaces of New Welfare: A Transdisciplinary Approach," Sten Gromark points out that architecture should be capable of realizing the dreams of people. This gives rise to layers of private and common spaces, and to the possible intermingling of age groups and of people from different walks of life. It also gives rise to new ways of thinking about the building process and the process of involving people in the building of dwellings; from the smallest door handle to the larger layout of the area, everything is important to improve life within the building. Yet who is designing, where and for whom? And whose dreams of "the good life" are materialized in specific spaces of welfare? Such critical questions of agency are presented by Alison J. Clarke in her chapter "Design and Decolonization in the 1970s: Beyond Spaces of Danish Welfare," in which she provides a historical perspective by exploring the emergence of the idea of a socially responsible Danish industrial design in the 1960s and '70s, a political refashioning of design that was applied with questionable effect as a quasi-anthropological social intervention in the Global South.

Community

The final part of the book explores communities as a resource in three different settings, pointing to the connections between space, welfare and community from each perspective. It addresses how new kinds of creativity arise from citizen-initiated social-spatial constructions. Following Lars Bo Kaspersen, the state, market and civic society play different roles in varying power balances in different societies. Here we follow the civic society angle of this triangle, dealing with communities as a forceful agent.

Maja Hojer Bruun in "Anthropological Perspectives on Housing as Welfare and Everyday Welfare Practices" points to the fact that housing as welfare is far more than the spaces of the state and its institutions. It is also a space of welfare practices and certain "ethical orientations and normative expectations." Thus, Hojer Bruun in several ways shows how blurred the borderlines are between the state, market and civic society, while she also points out the multilayered sociality of housing, welfare and everyday life. In "The Social Omnipotence of Neighborship," Max Pedersen explores the manifestations of neighborship in four senior housing projects. Pedersen points to the importance of meeting and being together with neighbors, as it is manifested daily, through random meetings, through organized gatherings and through the personal relationships developed between neighbors. In all cases, the shape of all the senior housing projects is interrelated with the possibilities for building up neighborship. At the same time, another friction line is crossing the research project, as when senior housing as studied by Pedersen is dealt with visually, displaying not only the shades of private-public collective, but also the blind angle of not being able to represent the ambiguity of the spaces being sometimes neither/nor, at other times both/and, seldomly either/or.

Claus Bech-Danielsen in "Ideology of the Welfare State in Solidified Concrete for Housing" describes the way in which social housing is connected to the time in which it was built: on the one hand the societal conditions at the time of planning and construction, and on the other hand, the physical conditions that were feasible. Furthermore, Bech-Danielsen points to the tension between the good intentions behind many of the residential areas and the problems that they are now facing, bringing up the question of how to deal with the planning of social housing in the future. In "New Housing Economics," Silje Erøy Sollien discusses housing as a financial product and what might be done to enhance the side of housing that has to do with being a place to dwell. She looks for ways to take back power and create dwellings, where use value and dwelling quality is the focus instead of exchange value and housing as storage of monetary value for capital gains, presenting more collective, less money-driven alternatives to today's monoculture on the housing market. Through a series of events, Jesper Pagh in "On the Battle for Amager Common: A Power Play of Housing Politics in Copenhagen" investigates urban policies in Copenhagen and demonstrates how the balance between planning for a green, growing or just city has changed over time. The battles between groups of citizens and the municipalities display different kinds of communities at play, and Pagh uses these events to uncover disputes about housing policies.

Dismantling and Restructuring

The dismantling and restructuring of spaces of Danish welfare, and perhaps in other countries too, implies that emergent figures of a more rhizomatic and network-oriented character become visible. As these chapters demonstrate, shifting and changing spatial figures of welfare means that some spaces of welfare are centralized, leaving others as peripheral, only for them to become new centers of their own periphery. At the same time, these welfare spaces are multilayered. Through all the scales explored here, from that of the body to the scale of urban or regional planning, traversing the widespread geographical distribution of the case studies themselves, the major concern is with the interplay of social and spatial relations of welfare. The chapters address the dilemmas and paradoxes built into this interplay, proposing a critical reflexive approach rather than only an explanation of the topic. Although several of them explore transformations of what may appear as tiny details, describing the operation of welfare services at close distance, these particularities nevertheless mirror or influence larger parts of society.

Time and the dynamics of change are major concerns in this book, be it in the form of *longues durées* or as swift changes. Each chapter makes specific reference to events, transformations, political decisions or novel interpretations of space and welfare that have led to significant changes. At times, these changes induce a nostalgic feeling of loss, while in other settings, they give rise to new aspirations or alternative ways of perceiving the interrelations of welfare and space. Sometimes, the events that had a large impact were small, at other times they were of a structural kind. The future adds another layer to the temporalities of welfare spaces. In many of the chapters, aspirations, hopes, threats or fear of the future lingers in the background. Currently, rapid changes of welfare spaces are evident on a larger scale. Some of these changes might be repetitions of already well known figures. Others perform as transformations toward something entirely new.

Bibliography

Albertsen, Niels, and Bülent Diken. "Welfare and the City." *Nordisk Arkitekturforskning* 17, no. 2 (2004): 7–22.

Bedford, Joseph, ed. *Is There an Object-Oriented Architecture? Engaging Graham Harman*. London: Bloomsbury Academic, 2021.

Rosenberg Bendsen, Jannie, Mette Jerl Jensen, Katrine Lotz, Deane Simpson, Kirsten Marie Raahauge and Kjeld Vindum, eds. *Forming Welfare*. Copenhagen: Danish Architectural Press, 2017.

Bruno, Giuliana. *Atlas of Emotion: Journeys in Art, Architecture, and Film*. London: Verso, 2002.

Cox, Robert Henry. "The Social Construction of an Imperative: Why Welfare Reform Happened in Denmark and the Netherlands but Not in Germany." *World Politics* 53 (April 2001): 463–98.

De Certeau, Michel. *The Practice of Everyday Life*. Translated by Steven Rendall. Berkeley: University of California Press, 1984.

Dansk Velfærdshistorie. Six vols. University of Southern Denmark Studies in History and Social Sciences. Odense: Syddansk Universitetsforlag, 2010–15.

DeLanda, Manuel. *Assemblage Theory*. Edinburgh: Edinburgh University Press, 2016.

Dikeç, Mustafa. *Space, Politics and Aesthetics: Taking on the Political*. Edinburgh: Edinburgh University Press, 2015.

Easterling, Keller. *Extrastatecraft: The Power of Infrastructure Space*. London: Verso, 2016.

Einhorn, Eric S., and John Logue. "Can Welfare States Be Sustained in a Global Economy? Lessons from Scandinavia." *Political Science Quarterly* 125, no. 1 (2010): 1–29.

Esping-Andersen, Gøsta. *The Three Worlds of Welfare Capitalism*. Cambridge: Polity Press, 1990.

Ferrera, Maurizio, and Martin Rhodes. "Recasting European Welfare States: An Introduction." *West European Politics* 23, no. 2 (2000): 1–10.

Fonsmark, Henning B. *Historien om den danske utopi: Et idépolitisk essay om danskernes velfærdsdemokrati*. 3rd ed. Copenhagen: Gyldendal, 1991.

Foucault, Michel. "Of Other Spaces." Translated by Jay Miskowiec. *Diacritics* 16, no. 1 (Spring 1986): 22–27.

——. "Space, Knowledge, and Power: An Interview with Michel Foucault by Paul Rabinow." Translated by Christian Hubert. *Skyline* (March 1982).

Gehl, Jan. *Cities for People*. Translated by Karen Ann Steenhard. Washington, DC: Island Press, 2010.

Harvey, David. *Social Justice and the City*. London: Edward Arnold, 1976.

Hojer Bruun, Maja, Stine Krøier and Mikkel Rytter. "Indledende Perspektiver: Forandringsstaten og selvstændighedssamfundet." "Velfærdsstaten I." Special issue, *Tidsskriftet Antropologi* 72 (2015): 11–37.

Jacobs, Jane. *Cities and the Wealth of Nations: Principles of Economic Life*. New York: Random House, 1984.

Jensen, Carsten. *Velfærdsstaten: En Introduktion*. 2nd ed. Copenhagen: Reitzel, 2014.

Kaspersen, Lars Bo. *Denmark in the World*. Copenhagen: Gyldendal, 2013.

"Kommunalreformen i 2007." Indenrigs- og Boligministeriet. https://im.dk/arbejdsomraader/kommunal-og-regionaloekonomi/kommunale-opgaver-og-struktur/kommunalreformen-i-2007. Accessed December 5, 2021.

Lefebvre, Henri. *Critique of Everyday Life: Foundations for a Sociology of the Everyday*. Translated by John Moore and Michel Trebitsch. London: Verso, 1991.

Lucas, Ray. *Drawing Parallels: Knowledge Production in Axonometric, Isometric and Oblique Drawings*. New York: Routledge, 2019.

Madsen, Hans Helge. *Dansk byplanlægning: 1938–1992, plan over land*. Nykøbing Sjælland: Bogværket, 2009.
Massey, Doreen. *Space, Place and Gender*. Cambridge: Polity, 1994.
Pedersen, Ove Kaj. "Efterord." "Velfærdsstaten II." Special issue, *Tidsskriftet Antropologi* 73 (2016): 137–49.
Pedersen, Ove Kaj. *Konkurrencestaten*. Copenhagen: Reitzel, 2011.
Petersen, Jørn Henrik, Klaus Petersen and Niels Finn Christiansen, eds. *Dansk Velfærdshistorie III: Velfærdsstaten i støbeskeen: 1933–1956*. University of Southern Denmark Studies in History and Social Sciences 434. Odense: Syddansk Universitetsforlag, 2012.
Petrescu, Doina. *Altering Feminine Practices: Feminist Politics and Poetics of Space*. London: Routledge, 2007.
Pierson, Christopher. *Beyond the Welfare State? The New Political Economy of Welfare*. 3rd ed. Cambridge: Polity Press, 2006.
Rendell, Jane, Barbara Penner and Iain Borden, eds. *Gender Space Architecture: An Interdisciplinary Introduction*. London: Routledge, 2007.
Soja, Edward W. *Thirdspace: Journeys to Los Angeles and Other Real-and-Imagined Places*. Cambridge, MA: Blackwell, 1996.
Swenarton, Mark, Tom Avermaete and Dirk van den Heuvel, eds. *Architecture and the Welfare State*. London: Routledge, 2015.
Søberg, Martin, ed. "Forming Welfare." Special issue, *Nordic Journal of Architecture* 5, no. 4 (2015).
Torfing, Jacob. *Det stille sporskifte i velfærdsstaten: En diskursteoretisk beslutningsproces-analyse*. Aarhus: Aarhus University Press, 2004.
Welland – Reconfiguring Welfare Landscapes (2016–2020). https://ign.ku.dk/english/welland/. Accessed December 5, 2021.
Wilthagen, Ton, and Frank Tros. "The Concept of 'Flexicurity': A New Approach to Regulating Employment and Labour Markets." *European Review of Labour and Research* 10, no. 2 (2004): 166–86.
Wolff, Robert Paul, Barrington Moore and Herbert Marcuse. *A Critique of Pure Tolerance*. Boston: Beacon Press, 1965.
Yaneva, Albena. *The Making of a Building: A Pragmatist Approach to Architecture*. Oxford: Peter Lang, 2012.

Notes

1 See Gøsta Esping-Andersen, *The Three Worlds of Welfare Capitalism* (Cambridge: Polity Press, 1990); see also Chapter 4 in Christopher Pierson, *Beyond the Welfare State? The New Political Economy of Welfare*, 3rd ed. (Cambridge: Polity Press, 2006), 121–28; see also Jannie Rosenberg Bendsen, Mette Jerl Jensen, Katrine Lotz, Deane Simpson, Kirsten Marie Raahauge and Kjeld Vindum, eds., *Forming Welfare* (Copenhagen: Danish Architectural Press, 2017); and Martin Søberg, ed., "Forming Welfare," special issue, *Nordic Journal of Architecture* 5, no. 4 (2015).

2 See Henri Lefebvre, *Critique of Everyday Life: Foundations for a Sociology of the Everyday*, trans. John Moore and Michel Trebitsch (London: Verso, 1991); Michel Foucault, "Space, Knowledge, and Power: An Interview with Michel Foucault by Paul Rabinow," *Skyline* (March 1982); Michel Foucault, "Of Other Spaces," trans. Jay Miskowiec, *Diacritics* 16, no. 1 (Spring 1986): 22–27.

3 See Robert Paul Wolff, Barrington Moore and Herbert Marcuse, *A Critique of Pure Tolerance* (Boston: Beacon Press, 1965).

4 See Henning B. Fonsmark, *Historien om den danske utopi: Et idépolitisk essay om danskernes velfærdsdemokrati*, 3rd ed. (Copenhagen: Gyldendal, 1991); and Ove Kaj Pedersen, *Konkurrencestaten* (Copenhagen: Reitzel, 2011).

5 See, for example, Robert Henry Cox, "The Social Construction of an Imperative: Why Welfare Reform Happened in Denmark and the Netherlands but Not in Germany," *World Politics* 53 (April 2001): 463–98; Eric S. Einhorn and John Logue, "Can Welfare States Be Sustained in a Global Economy? Lessons from Scandinavia," *Political Science Quarterly* 125, no. 1 (2010): 1–29; Ton Wilthagen and Frank Tros, "The Concept of 'Flexicurity': A New Approach to Regulating Employment and Labour Markets," *European Review of Labour and Research* 10, no. 2 (2004): 166–86.

6 The Danish welfare state was most intensively developed from 1945 until around 1970, although significant public welfare services had already been introduced prior to this, especially during the 1890s, with the development of old-age amenities and cooperative associations and with the political and social reforms of the 1930s. The universal right to an old-age pension was adopted in 1956. See Esping-Andersen, *The Three Worlds; Carsten Jensen, Velfærdsstaten: En Introduktion*, 2nd ed. (Copenhagen: Reitzel, 2014); and Jørn Henrik Petersen, Klaus Petersen and Niels Finn Christiansen, eds., *Dansk Velfærdshistorie III: Velfærdsstaten i støbeskeen: 1933–1956. University of Southern Denmark Studies in History and Social Sciences* 434 (Odense: Syddansk Universitetsforlag, 2012).

7 The authoritative three-volume history of Danish planning does not systematically cover the relations between the formation of the welfare state and planning. See Hans Helge Madsen, *Dansk byplanlægning: 1938–1992, plan over land* (Nykøbing Sjælland: Bogværket, 2009).

8 The welfare city is explored for example in Niels Albertsen and Bülent Diken, "Welfare and the City," *Nordisk Arkitekturforskning* 17, no. 2 (2004): 7–22. For research into Danish welfare landscapes, see the research project Welland – Reconfiguring Welfare Landscapes (2016–20), https://ign.ku.dk/english/welland/, accessed December 5, 2021.

9 "Kommunalreformen i 2007," Indenrigs- og Boligministeriet, https://im.dk/arbejdsomraader/kommunal-og-regionaloekonomi/kommunale-opgaver-og-struktur/kommunalreformen-i-2007, accessed December 5, 2021.

10 The authoritative six-volume history of Danish welfare, *Dansk Velfærdshistorie*, covers a wide span in its presentation of politics, economics, ideologies and the development of various welfare installments, but it does not provide a systematic take on the spatial implications: *Dansk Velfærdshistorie*, six vols., University of Southern Denmark Studies in History and Social Sciences (Odense: Syddansk Universitetsforlag, 2010–15).

11 See Esping-Andersen, *The Three Worlds*. See also Maurizio Ferrera and Martin Rhodes, "Recasting European Welfare States: An Introduction," *West European Politics* 23, no. 2 (2000): 1–10.

12 See Jacob Torfing, *Det stille sporskifte i velfærdsstaten: En diskursteoretisk beslutningsproces-analyse* (Aarhus: Aarhus University Press, 2004).

13 See Pedersen, *Konkurrencestaten*; Ove Kaj Pedersen, "Efterord," in "Velfærdsstaten II," special issue, *Tidsskriftet Antropologi* 73 (2016): 137–49. Maja Hojer Bruun, Stine Krøier and Mikkel Rytter, "Indledende Perspektiver. Forandringsstaten og selvstændighedssamfundet," in "Velfærdsstaten I," special issue, *Tidsskriftet Antropologi* 72 (2016): 11–37.

14 See Lars Bo Kaspersen, *Denmark in the World* (Copenhagen: Gyldendal, 2013).

15 See Jane Jacobs, *Cities and the Wealth of Nations: Principles of Economic Life* (New York: Random House, 1984); Jan Gehl, *Cities for People*, trans. Karen Ann Steenhard (Washington, DC: Island Press, 2010).

16 See, for example, Edward W. Soja, *Thirdspace: Journeys to Los Angeles and Other Real-and-Imagined*

Places (Cambridge, MA: Blackwell, 1996); David Harvey, *Social Justice and the City* (London: Edward Arnold, 1976); Doreen Massey, *Space, Place and Gender* (Cambridge: Polity, 1994); Mustafa Dikeç, *Space, Politics and Aesthetics: Taking on the Political* (Edinburgh: Edinburgh University Press, 2015); and Michel de Certeau, *The Practice of Everyday Life*, trans. Steven Rendall (Berkeley: University of California Press, 1984).

17 Ray Lucas, *Drawing Parallels: Knowledge Production in Axonometric, Isometric and Oblique Drawings* (New York: Routledge, 2019), 1.

18 See Mark Swenarton, Tom Avermaete and Dirk van den Heuvel, eds., *Architecture and the Welfare State* (London: Routledge, 2015); Albena Yaneva, *The Making of a Building: A Pragmatist Approach to Architecture* (Oxford: Peter Lang, 2012); Joseph Bedford, ed., *Is There an Object-Oriented Architecture? Engaging Graham Harman* (London: Bloomsbury Academic, 2021); Manuel DeLanda, *Assemblage Theory* (Edinburgh: Edinburgh University Press, 2016); Keller Easterling, *Extrastatecraft: The Power of Infrastructure Space* (London: Verso, 2016); Jane Rendell, Barbara Penner and Iain Borden, eds., *Gender Space Architecture: An Interdisciplinary Introduction* (London: Routledge, 2007); Doina Petrescu, *Altering Feminine Practices: Feminist Politics and Poetics of Space* (London: Routledge, 2007); and Giuliana Bruno, *Atlas of Emotion: Journeys in Art, Architecture, and Film* (London: Verso, 2002).

Visualizing Welfare

Bastian Feltgen, Aleksander Nowak

What role can visualization play in analyzing and communicating changing spatial conditions and their feedback effects on society? Can a map or a visualization be not a mere mean of representation but also an integrated tool for research? How do the textual and visual forms of knowledge production align, supplement, form tensions or contradict each other when pursuing research objectives? These are only some of the questions which accompanied us continuously throughout the process of the co-research with the authors of this anthology. The mappings and visualizations created for the publication are a result of a long process of data collection, interpretation and frequent discussions in the research group. The collaboration resulted in numerous visualization experiments of various types and scales, and while not all of them ended up in the final book, they constituted an indispensable analytical foundation for all the final visualizations.

The cross-disciplinary collaboration between anthropology, architecture, art history and the diverse body of research projects required an individual approach to the production of visualizations for each chapter. As each chapter of the book highlights different spatial and societal dynamics, the methodologies behind the data collection, interviews with the authors, fieldwork and site visits as well as the resulting visualizations were highly varied. In some cases, this included qualitative approaches such as field notes, photography, surveys and interviews for the analysis of human behavior, spatialities of everyday life or societal changes; in other cases, the patterns, shapes and materiality of specific physical environments were at state. In our work, we were constantly facing a dilemma of balancing this variety of perspectives.

The identification of coherences and divergences between the highly heterogeneous research projects helped to establish connections – visual echoes – throughout the anthology, forming an unconstrained yet consistent visual material. In close collaboration with the book's graphic designer, Studio Joost Grootens, and through several workshops, tools as varied and sublime as color coding, indexing, gradients, transparencies or symbols eventually developed into an exploratory and more coherent information system representing the spaces of Danish welfare in transition.

In line with urbanist and sociologist William H. Whyte or architect and urbanist Jan Gehl, we were trying not to limit ourselves to the mathematical precision of technological modes of measure-taking and data representation but to take into consideration the poetic, imaginative, intangible and symbolic aspects of human life and map production.[1] The ambition of the visualizations in this book would be to build upon and extend the possibility for mappings to analyze and unfold local everyday life, and considerations of well-being, health and social capital in urban spaces.

Although attempting to visualize the spatial dynamics, architectural typologies, impressions, time frames, numbers and systems behind the transformation of the Danish welfare state as accurately as possible, it has been necessary to acknowledge the subjective nature of every mapping endeavor. Yet despite the scholarly progress, we still can observe the wide acceptance of maps and graphs as pure "mirrors of nature" and the belief in advanced technologies' power to increase the analytical resolution, reinforcing the idea that the mapping methods deliver what philosopher Larry Laudan has described as "true, probable, progressive, or highly confirmed knowledge."[2] Predominantly, maps and visualizations representing numerical data sets carry a special sense of authority, anticipated by their audience to be accurate and objective. However, by disregarding some features and appropriating others, visual forms of knowledge render cultural and societal expressions of the society which drew them as well those of the mapping author herself, characterizing themselves by steady selectivity.[3]

In this context, the diversity of data sources and methodological approaches to dissect the changing sociopolitical spatialities supported a diversification of perspectives on the problems investigated. The visuals helped to enhance the validity and increase the confidence in the studies conducted. Thinking about their role through perspectives of mixed method research, we can see them as tools for convergence, complementarity and divergence.[4] Firstly, some of the visualizations, the data and argumentation behind them, characterize themselves by a strong degree of overlap with the text. Other mappings complement it, building a richer picture of the research problem by allowing the results from different methods to inform each other. Finally, some of the visualizations stand independently, alongside the text, pointing to new research results, directions or problems.

Throughout the mapping and visualization process for this book, several notions about the power of making things visual became evident, predominantly that mapping and visualization allow the structure and highlighting of spatial and social interactions not possible by other means of analysis and communication, such as text.

In our work, we adopted graphical forms of communication to help analyze and reveal trends and patterns within huge numerical tables. For example, the visualization and mapping on changing amounts of beds and hospitals revealed how the administrative favoritism of the centralized healthcare system forms specific spatial tendencies (Runa Johannessen's chapter). We generated maps and plans of spaces which formed a basis for enhanced ethnographic fieldwork. Mappings of the past and present distribution of welfare institutions in Tønder allowed for a critical reflection on their absence and presence in the Danish periphery (Kirsten Marie Raahauge's chapter). 3D scanning of Copenhagen touristic sites and visual analysis of the positioning of recently installed physical security measures at Amagertorv Square showed how preexisting decorative elements such as Storkespringvandet (The Stork Fountain) accidentally or deliberately became part of the counterterrorism infrastructure (Deane Simpson's chapter). Juxtaposition of the historical and current plans and photos of the same public spaces revealed how cultural, societal and political constructs such as striving for economic progress, city competitiveness, terrorism or livability materialize themselves in public space. Furthermore, maps and axonometries comparing the past and present spatial logics of cremation make visible, and bring into question, the efficiency behind the seemingly new, ultraoptimized system (Niels Grønbæk's chapter). Sketching during fieldwork helped to register the observed engagement and necessary work done by one of the Svend Gønge-School's teachers (Katrine Lotz's chapter). The space of the classroom turned into a stage for an elaborate and intentional choreography to orchestrating a meaningful learning experience tailored to all pupils' needs, beyond any differences between them. Retracing the design of dementia care facilities helped to juxtapose and understand the relationships between the architect's original intention, imposed regulations and guidelines and the actual, nonobvious appropriation of space by its users (Louise Dedenroth Høj's chapter). It allowed us to begin to engage more directly with the logics behind the production of space.

Human geographer Gillian Rose, in her book *Visual Methodologies*, identifies the value of visual research methodologies in their capacity to provide other forms of evidence than methods such as the univocal capabilities of numerical and textual representations.[5] Our experience made the analytical power of visual tools obvious. The project therefore treats visual means of knowledge production as research tools, forms of theoretical inquiry and fieldwork as well as a "way of using vision to intellectually and intuitively critique architecture and space" to engage in "critical visuality."[6] This allowed us to address and make the ever-changing relationship between the social and the spatial tangible, leading to a deeper and more fine-grained understanding of the spatial dynamics and implications of the complex transformations of the Danish welfare system.

Furthermore, as any analysis is inherently processual, the produced mappings themselves shall be treated as processes, "fluid objects that are always in the making," in the words of cultural geographer Veronica Della Dora, rather than ready, frozen products of science representing a spatial truth about the world.[7]

This constant re-inscription means that space is constituted through mapping practices, which do not merely represent but recreate the world around us. According to landscape architect James Corner, maps remake "territory over and over again, each time with new and diverse consequences," therefore the focus should shift toward the analysis of what maps do in the world rather than limited to issues of representation.[8] Cartography theorist Emanuela Casti has argued that "Maps are icons in themselves, in the most compelling sense of tools whereby a metamorphosis of the world is carried out."[9] In other words, rather than merely representing a territory, they produce new meanings and replace it. Maps produce space and meaning by selectively choosing or neglecting spatial phenomena and legitimizing them by usage of graphical forms.[10]

This approach developed through writings of postrepresentational theorists brings methodological implications with regards to spatial and anthropological research.[11] Here the focus shifts toward the interactions and coauthorships between the often contested actors and their interests in producing the map and the audience.

Taking up this particular angle in practice allowed us to refocus attention from narrow concerns of accuracy or representation and instead to consider ways in which our mappings *are,* in fact, evolving "immutable mobiles" formed on the one hand by us – the authors – and on the other through larger technical, social and political processes.[12] According to Bruno Latour and Steve Woolgar's ethnographic analysis, scientific facts come about through a relational process of negotiating and stabilizing facts rather than an exploratory process of something ready, which waits to be uncovered.[13] Through this mode of thinking knowledge, production happens via an equal assemblage and contribution of unstable relations between human and nonhuman actors. In our case this meant the multiple and iterative renegotiations with the researchers, interviews, technologies, GIS software, data access, aesthetic choices, color-coding, COVID-19 pandemic influencing the process, etc.

This argumentation reveals how practices of seeing, representing and positioning are linked to systems of knowledge (and power) that shape what can be understood as true. It locates visual practices not only as forms of space and knowledge representation but also production. Following the Latourian idea of power as a "consequence of association,"[14] words and images are knowledge-making and rhetorical devices able to mobilize and "muster allies on the spot-allies, that is, in the struggle over what is to count as a fact."[15] As we view systematized ways of seeing as central to world or cities' politics, in our process we were constantly facing the challenge of the rhetorical spectrum within which every map or visual representation operates.[16]

In this perspective, we hope that the mappings and visualizations in this book do not merely depict the transformations within the space of Danish welfare but also have a chance to leave a positive "inscription" in the world.[17]

Bibliography

Casino, Vincent J. Del, and Stephen P. Hanna. "Beyond the 'Binaries': A Methodological Intervention for Interrogating Maps as Representational Practices." In *The Map Reader: Theories of Mapping Practice and Cartographic Representation*, edited by Martin Dodge, Rob Kitchin and Chris Perkins, 102–7. New York: John Wiley and Sons, 2011. https://doi:10.1002/9780470979587.ch13.

Casti, Emanuela. *Reflexive Cartography: A New Perspective in Mapping.* Amsterdam: Elsevier, 2015.

Corner, James. "The Agency of Mapping: Speculation, Critique and Invention." In *Mappings*, edited by Denis Cosgrove, 89–101. London: Reaktion Books, 1999.

Crampton, Jeremy W. *The Political Mapping of Cyberspace*. Chicago: University of Chicago Press, 2003.

Creswell, John W. *A Concise Introduction to Mixed Methods Research.* Thousand Oaks, CA: Sage, 2015.

Dora, Veronica Della. "Performative Atlases: Memory, Materiality, and (Co-)Authorship." *Cartographica: The International Journal for Geographic Information and Geovisualization* 44, no. 4 (2009): 240–55. https://doi.org/10.3138/carto.44.4.240.

Drucker, Johanna. *Graphesis: Visual Forms of Knowledge Production.* Cambridge, MA: Harvard University Press, 2014.

Gehl, Jan. *Cities for People*. Translated by Karen Ann Steenhard. Washington, DC: Island Press, 2010.

Harley, John Brian. "Deconstructing the Map." *Cartographica: The International Journal for Geographic Information and Geovisualization* 26, no. 2 (1989): 1–20, doi:10.3138/e635-7827-1757-9t53

Grayson, Kyle, and Jocelyn Mawdsley. "Scopic Regimes and the Visual Turn in International Relations: Seeing World Politics through the Drone." *European Journal of International Relations* 25, no. 2 (2018): 431–57, https://doi:10.1177/1354066118781955.

Larry Laudan. *Progress and Its Problems: Towards a Theory of Scientific Growth*. Berkeley: University of California Press, 1978.

Latour, Bruno. "Drawing Things Together." In *Representation in Scientific Practice*, edited by Michael Lynch and Steve Woolgar, 19–68. Cambridge, MA: MIT Press, 1990.

——. "The Powers of Association." *The Sociological Review* 32, no. 1, suppl. (May 1984): 264–80. https://doi.org/10.1111/j.1467-954X.1984.tb00115.x.

Latour, Bruno, and Steve Woolgar. *Laboratory Life: The Construction of Scientific Facts*. Princeton, NJ: Princeton University Press, 1986.

Lucas, Ray. *Drawing Parallels: Knowledge Production in Axonometric, Isometric and Oblique Drawings*. London: Routledge, 2020.

Mirzoeff, Nicholas. *The Right to Look: A Counterhistory of Visuality*. Durham, NC: Duke University Press, 2011.

Pickles, John. *A History of Spaces: Cartographic Reason, Mapping and the Geo-coded World*. London: Routledge, 2006.

Rose, Gillian. *Visual Methodologies: An Introduction to the Interpretation of Visual Materials*. London: Sage Publications, 2016.

Troiani, Igea, and Suzanne Ewing. "Introduction: Visual Research Methods and 'Critical Visuality'." In *Visual Research Methods in Architecture*, edited by Igea Troiani and Suzanne Ewing, 1–32. Bristol: Intellect, 2021.

Turnbull, David. *Maps Are Territories: Science Is an Atlas: A Portfolio of Exhibits*. Chicago: University of Chicago Press, 1997.

Whyte, William Hollingsworth. *The Social Life of Small Urban Spaces*. New York: Project for Public Spaces, 2018.

Wood, Denis. *The Power of Maps*. London: Routledge, 1993.

Notes

1 See William Hollingsworth Whyte, *The Social Life of Small Urban Spaces* (New York: Project for Public Spaces, 2018); Jan Gehl, *Cities for People* (Washington, DC: Island Press, 2010).
2 Larry Laudan, *Progress and Its Problems: Towards a Theory of Scientific Growth* (Berkeley: University of California Press, 1978), 2.
3 See John Brian Harley, "Deconstructing the Map," *Cartographica: The International Journal for Geographic Information and Geovisualization* 26, no. 2 (1989): 1–20, doi:10.3138/e635-7827-1757-9t53; Denis Wood, *The Power of Maps* (London: Routledge, 1993).
4 See John W. Creswell, *A Concise Introduction to Mixed Methods Research* (Thousand Oaks, CA: Sage, 2015).
5 See Gillian Rose, *Visual Methodologies: An Introduction to the Interpretation of Visual Materials* (London: Sage Publications, 2016); Johanna Drucker, *Graphesis: Visual Forms of Knowledge Production* (Cambridge, MA: Harvard University Press, 2014).
6 Igea Troiani and Suzanne Ewing, "Introduction: Visual Research Methods and 'Critical Visuality,'" in *Visual Research Methods in Architecture*, ed. Igea Troiani and Suzanne Ewing (Bristol: Intellect, 2021), 3; see also Ray Lucas, *Drawing Parallels: Knowledge Production in Axonometric, Isometric and Oblique Drawings* (London: Routledge, 2020).
7 Veronica Della Dora, "Performative Atlases: Memory, Materiality, and (Co-)Authorship," *Cartographica: The International Journal for Geographic Information and Geovisualization* 44, no. 4 (2009): 240, doi:10.3138/carto.44.4.240.
8 James Corner, "The Agency of Mapping: Speculation, Critique and Invention," in *Mappings*, ed. Denis Cosgrove (London: Reaktion Books, 1999), 213.
9 Emanuela Casti, *Reflexive Cartography: A New Perspective in Mapping* (Amsterdam: Elsevier, 2015), 29.
10 See Nicholas Mirzoeff, *The Right to Look: A Counterhistory of Visuality* (Durham, NC: Duke University Press, 2011).
11 See Jeremy W. Crampton, *The Political Mapping of Cyberspace* (Chicago: University of Chicago Press, 2003); Vincent J. Del Casino and Stephen P. Hanna, "Beyond the 'Binaries': A Methodological Intervention for Interrogating Maps as Representational Practices," in *The Map Reader: Theories of Mapping Practice and Cartographic Representation*, ed. Martin Dodge, Rob Kitchin and Chris Perkins (New York: John Wiley and Sons, 2011), 102–7, doi:10.1002/9780470979587.ch13.
12 See Bruno Latour, "Drawing Things Together," in *Representation in Scientific Practice*, ed. Michael Lynch and Steve Woolgar (Cambridge, MA: MIT Press, 1990), 19–68.
13 See Bruno Latour and Steve Woolgar, *Laboratory Life: The Construction of Scientific Facts* (Princeton, NJ: Princeton University Press, 1986).
14 Bruno Latour, "The Powers of Association," *The Sociological Review* 32, no. 1, suppl. (May 1984): 264–80, https://doi.org/10.1111/j.1467-954X.1984.tb00115.x.
15 See David Turnbull, *Maps Are Territories: Science Is an Atlas: A Portfolio of Exhibits* (Chicago: University of Chicago Press, 1997).
16 See Kyle Grayson and Jocelyn Mawdsley, "Scopic Regimes and the Visual Turn in International Relations: Seeing World Politics through the Drone," *European Journal of International Relations* 25, no. 2 (2018): 431–57, doi:10.1177/1354066118781955.
17 John Pickles, *A History of Spaces: Cartographic Reason, Mapping and the Geo-coded World* (London: Routledge, 2006), 67.

Children as Symbolic Figures in Welfare Space Photography

Martin Søberg

The formation of the Danish welfare state ca. 1930–70, with its social and cultural programs and the way that it materialized in spatial, architectural form, was intertwined with certain ideas of social equality, collectivism, universality and distributions of services and resources, as well as with certain imaginaries of a brighter future, of the "good" life.[1] As historian Casper Jørgensen and others have pointed out, Danish architectural discourse during this period was characterized by an interest in the rationalization of design through the means of standardization and typological thinking. The concepts of *welfare*, *welfare architecture* and *welfare space* were, however, more or less absent, even if many architects were engaged in the realization of those social and cultural programs, for instance in the form of publicly supported housing and institutions. Yet this absence of the concept of welfare in architectural discourse does not necessarily imply that ideas and imaginaries relating to welfare in both affirmative and critical ways did not exist. As Jørgensen states, "it does not hinder that the aim was welfare [...]. Besides clarifying how and when the buildings have been designed, by whom and for whom, there is a need for clarification of how the ideas of welfare were transformed into architectural notions and forms."[2] Along similar lines, sociologist and architectural historian Nan Dahlkild asks in his introduction to the anthology *Danish Architecture and Society*: "What similarities are there between social welfare–based thinking and modernist architecture vis-à-vis ideas of democratization and the creation of better living conditions through optimum planning?"[3] Further on, he stresses the importance of "the dreams, hopes and intentions of the relevant architects and planners."[4]

In this chapter, I argue that one of the vehicles of transformation from ideas to architectural notions and forms was photographic images used in Danish architectural discourse during the period ca. 1930–70. Such photographs were able to express those dreams, hopes and intentions that Dahlkild refers to – that is, the "ideas and imaginaries" of welfare – even if the concept itself was not yet fully in use.[5] And by doing so, photographs became discursive tools with latent power to cause action, for instance resulting in the materialization of architectural spaces.[6] My empirical base stems from *Arkitekten*, the journal published by the Danish Association of Architects, and to narrow it down even further, but also to add another analytical lens, I will be looking only at photographs that contain representations of children. Why photographs with children? Human figures are usually included as staffage in architectural photography to provide a sense of scale and to indicate how the construction frames and accommodates specific functional programs. They may suggest specific everyday practices and lifestyles. The figure of the child, I will argue, nonetheless also functioned as a trope, a symbolic figure embodying ideas and imaginaries relating to a modern society, to modern architecture and to the welfare state and its spatialization.

New concepts of the child and of childhood developed during the eighteenth century along with the formation of a bourgeois urban culture, including ideas of the nuclear family and the home as society's central institution. The child represented what was to come, unsaturated by the old, liberated from tradition and dogma but also in need of care, guidance, education and enculturation – conceptualized as both an angel and a noble savage who is ripe with potentiality but in dire need of civilizing.[7] Gradually and particularly during the twentieth century – "the century of the child," as it was famously termed by the writer Ellen Key – the education and enculturation of children became something the state was involved in, to some degree as part of nation-building initiatives. From the perspective of the state, children are a resource in the competition between other states, and it is the task of the state to make the most of this resource. Furthermore, as historians Marta Gutman and Ning de Coninck-Smith have argued, the ideals of the "good" society translated during this period as the society which provides the "good" childhood, for instance through material cultures, everyday experiences and architecture.[8] It included improvements of housing conditions as well as the construction of nurseries, schools, playgrounds, sanatoria, orphanages and hospitals targeted at children, their education and health.

Particularly during the post–World War II decades, children and their specific needs, rights and conceptions of the world gained significant attention from various professions, including architects. This interest, as reflected in the Danish architectural discourse, was stimulated by a significant increase in the Danish population caused by high birthrates during the years 1942–48, which affirmed an already existing shortage of urban housing and made the construction of public or publicly supported institutions rather urgent during the postwar years. Yet this interest reflected more than a professional concern with solving present problems; it was saturated by the abovementioned concepts of the child and of childhood. As Juliet Kinchin, curator of the 2012 MoMA exhibition *Century of the Child: Growing by Design, 1900–2000*, argues in the catalogue: "Elastic and powerful, the symbolic figure of the child masked paradoxical aspects of the human predicament in the modern world and enabled irreconcilable sets of beliefs, which are reflected in the material forms of modern design."[9] The child now embodied a new lifeworld, a society to come.

It is in this regard that I will address the photographic representation of children in Danish architectural discourse ca. 1930–70 by asking: what role did the symbolic figure of the child play in the expression of ideas and imaginaries of welfare and welfare space in photography? To find answers to this question, I will analyze the Danish architectural discourse on housing, institutions and public spaces as they relate to children with attention to the relation between photography and architecture.

Housing and Imagination

Hardly a surprise, children often appear in photographs which illustrate the publication of institutional architecture programmed for children. But they also often appear in photographs of housing projects or in reports or essays relating to housing, which will be our focus to begin with before we shift to the architecture of institutions and public space. Children were used to emphasize the dire condition of derelict urban slums in which the deprivation and the lack of sunlight and fresh air were presented as arguments for change and public involvement. And children were included in photographs of new housing projects intended to improve their quality of life, projects which would move them out of the slums and facilitate a "good" childhood.

Slum clearance was of particular concern during the 1930s; it was addressed in *Arkitekten* for instance in 1935 in an inquiry entitled "Har Samfundet Midler til Afhjælpning af daarlige Boligforhold" (Does society have the means to remedy the poor housing conditions).[10] The

1 Photograph of courtyards in Vesterbro, Copenhagen. Published in "Har Samfundet Midler til Afhjælpning af daarlige Boligforhold?" *Arkitekten Ugehæfte* 37, no. 1 (1935): 4.

situation in Copenhagen received specific attention, particularly the working-class areas of Nørrebro and Vesterbro and their densely built housing blocks stemming from the period ca. 1860–90, many of which were in horrendous, unsanitary conditions. In his contribution to the inquiry, municipal doctor Richard Kjer-Petersen stated that "Whatever is written on the modernization of construction, the *first* task, the nearest demand for a society and not least in a metropolis, is the *toddlers.*"[11] Kjer-Petersen argued strongly for more nurseries to be established and argued that "any new orientation in the question of metropolitan housing must *begin* with the consideration of toddlers and the commencement must happen immediately. What does it help that we have up-to-date housing in ten to twenty years if those who move there have been damaged on soul and body?"[12] A photograph illustrating the inquiry shows the rather blurry figures of two girls, dressed in long coats, standing in a "Baggaard paa Vesterbro" (Courtyard in Vesterbro), demonstrating the inhuman circumstances.⟨fig. 1⟩ With white, mask-like faces appearing from the black tunnel-like perspectival depths of several courtyard openings, the girls look like ghosts, as if they were already damaged body and soul by their surroundings.

Improving the quality and quantity of housing was an important aspect of many Western countries' social programs during the early twentieth century. It was targeted at solving problems caused by the rapid urban growth following the industrialization such as the poor living conditions in densely built tenement blocks. For instance, housing conditions received significant political attention in Germany during the 1920s and early '30s as part of the Weimar Republic's Neues Bauen (New Building) program and formed part of contemporary cultural analysis and critique.[13] Cultural theorist Walter Benjamin addressed the question of the metropolis in several radio broadcasts between 1927 and 1933. In his 1930 "Mietkaserne" ("The Rental Barracks") broadcast, he described the infamous Meyer's Hof tenement block in Ackerstrasse, Berlin, a huge system including six courtyards: "If you look from the street down the row of courtyards, it's as if you were looking into a tunnel."[14] Architectural historian Alexander Eisenschmidt has demonstrated that this specific motif was represented in various contexts during the 1920s and '30s, for instance by the artist László Moholy-Nagy in his film *Berliner Stilleben* (1931), which linked the courtyards to childhood play. Eisenschmidt writes:

> For Benjamin, children possessed a heightened receptiveness and unique capacity to imagine alternative worlds. [...] The child's imagination proved to be the most prolific source for a re-thinking of the city. [...] Just as a child is able to collage an imaginary scene

> onto the existing city that productively transforms it into another world, so Benjamin tried to juxtapose images of his childhood with perceptions from the present, while Moholy-Nagy montaged scenes of child play with images of fast-paced urban life.[15]

Eisenschmidt points out that Benjamin was a strong supporter of modern housing and the Neues Bauen, inspired by such writers as Adolf Behne and Sigfried Giedion.[16] Furthermore, Moholy-Nagy's "new optics" played a significant part in Benjamin's acknowledgment of the new urban possibilities, for instance as seen through Moholy-Nagy's abstract views from the Berliner Radio Tower (1928). As Eisenschmidt argues: "The familiar environment of the city is cropped and abstracted, providing a new, unfamiliar topography saturated with unexpected visual productivities."[17] In his speech "The Author as Producer," Benjamin stated:

> But now follow the path of photography further. What do you see? It becomes ever more *nuancé*, ever more modern; and the result is that it can no longer record a tenement block or a refuse heap without transfiguring it. Needless to say, photography is unable to convey anything about a power station or a cable factory other than, "What a beautiful world!"[18]

According to art historian Georges Didi-Huberman, Benjamin did not imply that the photographic image is deprived of agency, that it is merely an aesthetic object. In fact, quite the contrary. If used dialectically, such an image possesses the potential for creating an "image of thought," that is, to invigorate the ability of the imagination to install difference and to propose new constructions.[19] The photographs of children in *Arkitekten* and the way they were used discursively were indeed, as we shall soon see, productive in exactly this sense: exposing the viewer to a new sort of welfare space. In his text "To Make Symptoms or to Make Syntheses?" Didi-Huberman describes how a montage of images allows one to take a position "dialectically, poetically and politically [...] in front of history." They do so by creating: "Forms that, in their poetics, arouse a thinking of history and a practice of politics."[20] He points to how the montage is able to institute either a situation of poetic, imaginary openness, which he terms a "symptomatic" dialectics – or a situation of specific solutions, a "synthetic" dialectics. This makes him wonder: "Is it therefore the *poem* in which all possible multiples might blossom, or the *formula* in which all possible multiples might be dogmatically reduced to something like a definite truth?"[21] What he calls for, is

> a practice devoted to *symptoms*, whose *rhythm* cannot be reduced to a "measure" nor to an "order," not to a "line," and that aims only for something unforeseeable, which we might call suspense of desire [...] because it renounced axioms at once and is situated fully in the open of a heuristics of images.[22]

2 Cover of *Arkitekten Maanedshæfte* 42, no. 1 (1940), special issue on child welfare in the metropolis.

3 Cover of *Arkitekten Ugehæfte* 40, no. 1 (1938).
4 Illustration from "Befolkningsspørgsmaalet og Boligen," *Arkitekten Ugehæfte* 40, no. 1 (1938): 1.

Although photographic images and not montages are the subject of this chapter, similar symptoms can be located within the former, indeed "something unforeseeable." This might not necessarily be the case with each photograph. But in some instances, we may locate something else than the expression of welfare or in fact the desire to create welfare spaces. In the words of Didi-Huberman, this could be described as a suspense of such a desire beyond the "measures," "orders" and "lines" so characteristic of modern spatial configurations.

Facing the Future

A particular motif recurs: A group of children with their backs toward the viewer, looking at a new housing project, as if looking into a bright and rational future. In its first issue of 1938, *Arkitekten* addressed the topic of the population question and housing ("Befolkningsspørgsmaalet og Boligen"). The population question concerned the decreasing reproduction rate of the Danish population during the 1930s, a question which gained significant political attention. In fact, many of the public welfare initiatives during the 1930s were directly related to these dropping numbers and the question of how to encourage people to have more children. Answers included increased public financial support for housing and childcare since it was assumed that the high cost of housing prevented people from having more children. The lack of childcare institutions was also an obstacle, since more women were entering the labor market and not able to have children unless they could be cared for during working hours.

5 Cover of *Arkitekten Maanedshæfte* 48, nos. 1–2 (1946), special issue on new blocks of flats. With photograph of the Ringgaarden housing estate, Aarhus, designed by Edvard Thomsen, C. F. Møller and Gunnar Krohn.

Families with many children were of special concern. As was stated by the editors in *Arkitekten*: "In many countries, the population question is one of the most important social problems. The question is also pertinent in Denmark. The housing conditions of families with many children rightfully stand at the front of the line."[23] The cover of the issue shows a cut-out photograph of three children holding hands, their backs turned toward the spectator and placed on a white background.⟨fig. 3⟩ We don't realize what they're looking at until we reach page one. Here it becomes clear that the children are facing a drawn elevation of a clearly functionalist housing project, which seems to emanate a strong light, casting long shadows on the rugged cobblestone paving, signifying that the children are about to step from the old, crumbling city into a bright, promising future.⟨fig. 4⟩ It is an imaginary scene – the drawing is not a real house – hence suspending rather than explicating desire. This emphasizes exactly the ability of children to transform the existing into something new by means of their imagination, as proposed by Benjamin.

This type of image, although with fewer elements of imagination and suspension, reappears for instance in a striking photograph published in 1946 of the housing complex Ringgaarden in the city of Aarhus; it even graces the cover of the issue.[24] ⟨fig. 5⟩ Similar photographs of children in the presentation of new housing estates recur through the following decades, often showing the children in the foreground moving or gazing toward the buildings in the middle or background, photographed in strong sunlight and perhaps framed by trees or shrubbery.⟨fig. 6⟩ The faces of the children are often not visible or perhaps rather blurry; these human figures appear as universal types rather than individuals, embodying the symbolic figure of "the child" and notions of "youth" and "novelty" rather than displaying specific traits. This resonates with the principles of universality and uniformity bordering on genericness, which also characterizes the design of the buildings. The children are transformed into standardized, model children for standardized, model living in images supporting such ideals of typification, that is, the abstracted ideals of welfare space. Their small bodies, along with natural elements such as trees and clouds, bring the sharps lines and prismatic, geometric forms of modern architecture to life. Literally functioning as media, the children guide our gaze to their built surroundings.

Sometimes they might hold or sit on a bicycle, the emblematic machine for modern individual transportation, like in a photograph of a boy in front of the Bellavista housing estate.⟨fig. 7⟩ The tiny figure of the boy is presented in front of the gleaming white wall of the round corner, exactly as streamlined as his bike. But something else also occurs. Like an empty canvas, a vast open space of imagination,

6 Skoleparken housing estate, Gladsaxe, designed by Knud Hallberg and Jørgen Bo. Published in *Arkitekten Månedshæfte* 58, nos. 8–9 (1956): 130.
7 Bellavista housing estate, Klampenborg, designed by Arne Jacobsen. Published in *Arkitekten Maanedshæfte* 36, nos. 8–9 (1934): 144.
8 Chain house estate in Gentofte, designed by Arne Jacobsen. Published in *Arkitekten Maanedshæfte* 47, no. 4 (1945): 42.

7

6

8

the wall surrounds the boy and his bike, in direct contrast to the rest of the facade, which is adorned with commercial signs and pleated in sharp zigzagging angles, indeed as busy as modern life itself. Hence, through its dialectic means of composition, this photographic image allows the boy and perhaps then also the viewer to remain in the open.

Just as constructed is a photograph of two girls demonstratively placed in front of a line of row houses in Gentofte, published in 1945. It points to the improving housing conditions as an actual case but also on a general level, perhaps referencing such images as the girls in the courtyard or the children facing the phantom of a better future life.⟨fig. 8⟩ The clearly staged children are dressed in summer clothing, barelegged, a strong sunlight falling from the left part of the picture, condensing a general desire for improvement of livelihoods. Behind them the apparently endless row of houses are clearly distinguishable as individual houses with a pitched roof and chimney, as a child would draw a house. This schematism on the one hand makes the image appear somewhat banal. On the other hand, it pronounces the image exactly as image, as a presentation of photographic space rather than as a transparent representation of architectural space, further emphasized by the graphic effects of the empty surfaces of the foreground and sky and the black formless shape and shadow of the large tree to the left.[25] While the houses and background are presented in a two-point perspective, the tree and its shadow form a right angle parallel to the edges of the image, mirrored by the girls, who are facing the picture plane. The result is a tension between background spatial depth and foreground flatness with the girls, placed in the intersection of the background's crossing axes, functioning as elements of transition between the two types of pictorial space. Following Benjamin, the children are disclosed as figures of transformation.

9 Rowhouse estate on Bispebjerg Parkallé, Copenhagen, designed by Kooperative Arkitekter. Published in Kay Fisker, "Rækkehustyper 1," *Arkitekten* 43, no. 2 (1941): 32.

10 Rowhouse estate on Vigerslev Allé, Copenhagen, designed by Ivar Bentsen in collaboration with Ole Buhl and T. Miland Petersen. Published in Kay Fisker, "Rækkehustyper 1," *Arkitekten* 43, no. 2 (1941): 33.

11 Brønsparken, Copenhagen, designed by Kay Fisker, C. F. Møller and Erik Jensen. Published in Hans Erling Langkilde, "De børnerige Familiers Boligproblem," *Arkitekten Ugehæfte* 45, no. 21 (1943): 105.

Other photographs are less dialectically composed and appear more like snapshots, that is, showing the children moving about and engaged in play. A large group of fair-haired children have gathered in front of the row houses on Bispebjerg Parkallé,⟨fig. 9⟩ smiling and enjoying the strong sunlight, which also highlights the facades. Another photograph shows children playing in the private garden of a row house on Vigerslev Allé in Copenhagen, framed by lush flowers, again in strong sunlight.⟨fig. 10⟩ Both photographs were published in *Arkitekten* in 1941 as part of a survey of rowhouses conducted by the architect Kay Fisker.[26] More happy children appear in a photograph of Brønsparken, which was built specifically for large families.⟨fig. 11⟩

This vision of welfare, of sunlight, healthiness and free bodies would turn into quite a different picture only a few decades later.⟨fig. 12⟩ Construction of high-rises as part of the new suburban residential project faced

12 Brøndby Strand housing estate, designed by Svend Høgsbro and Th. Dreyer. Published in *Arkitekten* 73, no. 20 (1971): 431.

13 Exterior of a high-rise housing block. Published in Poul Erik Skriver, "Børnene i de nye byområder," *Arkitekten* 66, no. 22 (1964): 457. Photo by Poul Erik Skriver.

criticism during the early 1960s. Milestedet and its high-rise housing blocks were denounced in 1961 by the architect and editor of *Arkitekten* Poul Erik Skriver, who stated that: "The housing estate must be characterized as being in opposition to the human being and in particular the child."[27] In his 1964 article "Børnene i de nye byområder" (The children in the new urban areas), Skriver referred to an August 1964 international meeting in Stockholm of the World Organization for Early Childhood Education (OMEP), at which critique of the design for children in urban settings, including urban planning and traffic planning, had been uttered: "the presentations from a number of well-known urban planners clearly showed that the child's urban environment is poor and full of dangers."[28] Children's point of view provided a general lens through which to coin the critique of the lack of welfare, either nonexistent welfare measures, as in the case of the girls in the backyard, or failed ones. As Skriver continued: "The environment facing the children outside the front door of the high-rise is harsh and brutal – concrete, tarmac, bikes and cars"[29] ⟨fig. 13⟩ The intended pastoral sentiment of the modern urban landscape had turned into austerity.

A photograph from a suburban area of Copenhagen, published in 1970, shows a leftover space where a highway was later to be installed.⟨fig. 14⟩ What happens in this icy landscape, dominated by white, white snow, a narrow white sky, blank white gables, yet without the potentials of whiteness, its blankness offering itself as an open space for imaginaries and alternative worlds? Instead, there are frozen plantations and diminutive figures, probably children; one of them appears to be sitting on a sled. The image does not advance itself for imaginations of alternative worlds of welfare, of sunshine and the "good" life, but rather suspends desire by proposing a shocking, almost postapocalyptic scenery of no alternatives.

Still, alternatives were desired. Counterculture reactions to centralized, industrialized housing production and the housing programs of the welfare state appeared during the second half of the 1960s and the '70s, especially in response to slum clearance and the lack of affordable

14 Land intended for a highway extension, Valby. Published in Martin Rubow, "Arbejderbyer anno 1970," *Arkitekten* 72, no. 8 (1970): 191. Photo by Erik Gleie/Ritzau Scanpix.

15 Hudegården, Vesterbro, Copenhagen. Published in "På Vesterbro," *Arkitekten* 72, no. 23 (1970): 552.

housing. Famously, this resulted in the formation of an experimental urban area, the so-called freetown of Christiania in Copenhagen in 1971, anticipated by the occupation of Sofiegården during the late 1960s and succeeded by the Hudegården commune on Vesterbro, which included explicit attention to the needs of children in the form of nurseries and an adventure playground. Now children themselves were building amid the ruins of the nineteenth-century tenement houses.[30] ⟨fig. 15⟩

Education and Care

Architecture intended specifically for child-related functional programs have existed in Denmark since the seventeenth century; however, most of such buildings were constructed during the twentieth century in connection to the development of the welfare state.[31] As Ning de Coninck-Smith has demonstrated, the design of spaces for children, including various types of institutions, has been part of welfare policies and programs since the 1930s and particularly after World War II. How nurseries could be integrated into a housing project was demonstrated in an issue of *Arkitekten* in 1935 with the publication of *Kollektivhuset* (The collective house) in Stockholm, designed by the architect Sven Markelius in collaboration with the writer and politician Alva Myrdal.[32] The same issue also contained the article "Indretning af moderne Børnehaver" (Design of modern nurseries) written by nursery managers Margrethe Finsen and Asta Jensen. At the time, most nurseries in Copenhagen were either private or parochial institutions, receiving public financial support from the municipality and the state. Sundhedskommissionens Regulativ af 24. April 1931 (the Health Commission Regulation of 24 April 1931) had provided several regulations for the spatial organization of nurseries, for instance that nurseries were not allowed to be situated in basements, that a minimum of 5 cubic meters was required per child in common rooms and that children should have easy access to an outdoor space.[33]

Photographs of contemporary institutions for children demonstrate the public involvement in nurture; for instance, the three little girls doing the dishes, like little adults, in a photograph of a nursery and after-school care in Frederiksberg.⟨fig. 16⟩ Their miniature kitchen only increases the sense that this could just as well have been three grown women at work. On the one hand the image speaks of a synthesis between bodies and the functions these subjects are able to perform in this particular architectural space. On the other hand, and in particular from the point of view of the children, the image addresses the desire of children to playfully and imaginatively imitate the actions of grownups.

16 Nursery and after-school care at Fuglevangsvej, Frederiksberg, designed by Tage Gerstrøm and Ellen Gjerløv-Knudsen. Published in *Arkitekten Månedshæfte* 53, no. 6 (1951): 87.

17 Cover of *Arkitekten Månedshæfte* 55, no. 9 (1953). Photograph of Rungsted skole, designed by Steen Eiler Rasmussen.

Arkitekten dedicated several issues to new schools and institutions during the postwar decades. For instance, detailed considerations of school design were presented in an issue of *Arkitekten* in 1953 by the architect Steen Eiler Rasmussen as part of the presentation of Rungsted school.⟨fig. 17⟩ The more open, flexible planning of the 1960s is demonstrated in the "Typebørnehaver" (standard nurseries), one of which was constructed in Trørød.⟨fig. 20⟩ When the project was published in 1965, Poul Erik Skriver stated that because of industrialization, the Danish economy was prospering, resulting in a high level of consumption; yet society was still not in balance. Housing, educational, health and care institutions were still lacking, including nurseries.[34] Photographs show the central room, which comprises an open kitchen and facilities for play, including a small water basin, clearly occupying the children watched attentively by the nursery teacher, who is also busy in the kitchen. The design was based on a 120 cm module and allowed for extensive floor plan variations.

Open planning evolved even further during the late 1960s and early '70s, for instance in the experimental school Rugvængets skole in Ballerup-Måløv, based on the pedagogical ideas of deputy headmaster Henrik Hestbech.⟨fig. 21⟩ The school was designed without the involvement of a professional architect. Testifying to the significance of "welfare professionals" such as architects, Skriver lamented: "It would hardly have disabled the use of the building had it been touched by the spirit of architecture."[35] The open-plan school corresponded to new pedagogical principles, which included flexible "home bases:" Furniture and other equipment should be moveable. Open-plan-teaching was integrated into the design of many schools during the 1970s and '80s, with classrooms grouped around open communal areas with the intention of creating an impression of "schools in schools."[36] ⟨fig. 22⟩

A photograph published in *Arkitekten* in 1972 shows such a "home base." A number of children are sitting casually on the floor or on a bookcase, some of them engaging with each other and not all of them facing the teacher, who apparently is the only one sitting on a chair yet seems more like a participant than an authority.⟨fig. 23⟩ Casualness and social interaction are presented as ideals. Noteworthy, the lack of distance to the children is almost unprecedented, several heads being cropped by the frame of the image. What the physical space looks like is less visible. First and foremost, the adjustable shelving and moveable screens attest to the increasing importance of the notions of changeability and flexibility in architecture but also in society in general at the time.

Measurement and Play

As in other Western countries, standardization and typological thinking were important aspects of modernist architecture in Denmark. Measure, order and line – principles of universality – were the means not only to

18

19

20

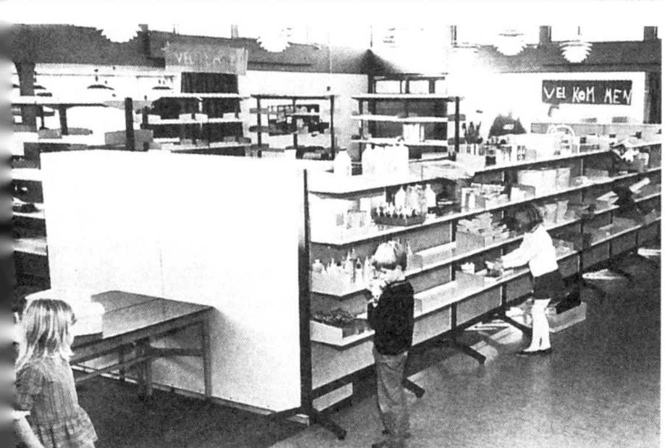

21

18 Buddinge skole, designed by Eva and Nils Koppel. Published in *Arkitekten* 57, no. 45 (1955): 372.
19 Buddinge skole, designed by Eva and Nils Koppel. Published in *Arkitekten* 57, no. 45 (1955): 373.
20 Central space in a standard nursery, Trørød, designed by Tutti Lütken, Asger Barfod and Helmer Remark. Published in *Arkitekten* 67, no. 7 (1965): 126. Photo by Lundhans © Helmer Lund Hansen/VISDA.
21 Central space in the experimental school Rugvængets skole, Ballerup-Måløv. Published in Poul Erik Skriver, "En eksperimentskole ved Rugvængets skole," *Arkitekten* 73, no. 3 (1971): 51. Photo by Palle Hestbech.

22 Cover of *Arkitekten* 75, no. 1 (1973). Photograph of Trørødskolen, Søllerød, designed by Peer Hougaard Nielsen and C. J. Nørgaard Pedersen.
23 "Home base" in Krogårdskolen, Greve. Published in *Arkitekten* 74, no. 13 (1972): 263. Photo by Henrik Fog-Møller. Published with kind permission from © Henrik Fog-Møller.
24 A playground in a backyard in Copenhagen and drawing showing the 2 km distance from the nursery to a proper playground. Published in Max Siegumfeldt, "Hvornaar kommer Børnehaverne?" *Arkitekten Ugehæfte* 40, no. 22 (1938): 109.
25 A nursery in Copenhagen. Published in Max Siegumfeldt, "Hvornaar kommer Børnehaverne?" *Arkitekten Ugehæfte* 40, no. 22 (1938): 110.

22

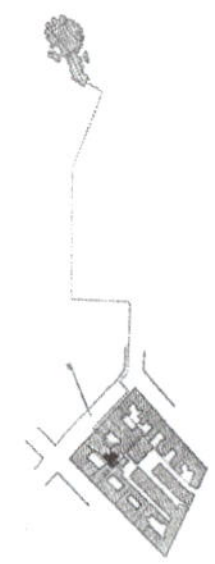

Legeplads i en københavnsk Gaard
En indhegnet Legeplads med Sand for Børnehavens Børn. Tegningen viser Børnehavens Beliggenhed paa den tæt bebyggede Grund og den 2 km lange Strækning, som Børnene maa gaa for at komme til den egentlige Legeplads

24

23

25

26 Photograph with measurements of the children's department, Frederiksberg Main Library, designed by A. S. K. Lauritzen. Published in *Arkitekten Maanedhæfte* 39, nos. 9–10 (1937): 139.

27 Photograph with measurements of the reading room, Frederiksberg Main Library, designed by A. S. K. Lauritzen. Published in *Arkitekten Maanedhæfte* 39, nos. 9–10 (1937): 138.

28 Cover of *Arkitekten Maanedhæfte* 39, nos. 9–10 (1937), special issue on libraries, with photograph of children in the Frederiksberg Main Library.

raise the quality of built space but also to address the ideas of the anonymous citizen of a modern society which after World War II would become synonymous with the concept of the welfare state. It related to actual bodies in various ways, the human body providing measurements to spaces, but it also allowed for an empathetic current of bodily sensation to enter the architectural discourse. Architectural historian Anthony Vidler has described various "fictions of the body" produced in relation to specific types of architecture. While the Renaissance body is stable and unified, a centralized body in space characterized by potential yet controlled movement, the modernist body is psychological, a nonphysical body of psychoanalytical space.[37] Yet rather than confirming Vidler's opposition between the Renaissance body and the modernist body, the photographs examined so far suggest a dialectics between measurable Euclidian space and a psychoanalytical space of imagination and desire. A tension or perhaps a suspending openness between architecture's perspectival framings and the formless potentiality, conceptually instituted since the eighteenth century, of the body as well as the imagination of the child.

Questions of universality were particularly pertinent in connection with the design of institutions and of public space. Measurements were applied to indicate urban distances. A map published in 1938 in connection with a debate on the lack of public nurseries represents the 2 km distance between a nursery located in the densely built tissue of a typical Copenhagen perimeter block and the children's playground. An adjoining photograph provides a bird's-eye view of the spatial situation of the backyard with a sandbox, a poor substitute for the actual, distant yet more spacious playground. A dotted line suggests a journey through unknown territory, suspending the bodies of the children like clothes on the washing line.⟨figs. 24–25⟩

Bodies in framing, measured spaces are presented in photographs published in 1937 of the new main public library in Frederiksberg, completed in 1935.[38] ⟨figs. 26–28⟩ Children are sitting at tables or standing in front of bookshelves. Measurements have been added, drawn on top of the images to indicate distances, lengths and depths. Scale drawings could aid construction of a building, which later would be inhabited. Here the reverse situation unfolds, the inhabited space is measured and is thereby returned to the abstract spaces of drawn and measurable representation, yet in contrast to the faces and bodies of real children who are already present. In fact, such annotated photographs are quite rare. The photographs of the library were part of a special issue on library buildings, in which numerous plan drawings were provided in a discussion of typologies, along with

29 Cover of *Arkitekten Maanedshæfte* 37, no. 4 (1935), special issue on the garden in the block of flats.

diagrams and the annotated photographs. The universality of measurements, ideally transportable to other spaces, meet the specificities of these human bodies in an attempt to create what Didi-Huberman describes as synthesis, that is, a specific solution rather than a situation of poetic openness.

Possible multiplicities would blossom elsewhere. Dense urban housing, its poor conditions for children's play and the possibility of constructing new playgrounds were addressed by the landscape architect C. Th. Sørensen in 1935 in the article "Etagehusets Have" (The garden in the block of flats) in which he quoted at length from Kjer-Petersen's inquiry statement.⟨fig. 29⟩ As Sørensen argued: "Undoubtably, it is extremely important to provide toddlers the possibility of staying outdoors in proximity to the dwellings."[39] He bemoaned the lack of interest for children's well-being, even among architects: "It should be a given that architects as well as developers and tenants would be interested in creating good conditions for the children. But that is not the case at all."[40] Sørensen gave detailed instructions in how playgrounds could be designed and integrated into urban housing projects, illustrating his article with a photograph of children playing in a sandbox.⟨fig. 30⟩ The area is densely packed, indeed not an ideal situation, yet the children seem to display aspects of social engagement and creative enterprise, reshaping the heaps of sand into an imaginary landscape. These gestures are indeed symbolic of a future society, a new sort of open landscape populated by emancipated, creative bodies, freed from the confines of the courtyard and its social restrictions and actively transforming the existing into other worlds.

A special double issue of *Arkitekten* was dedicated to playgrounds in 1952 based on the results of an ideas competition held in 1947, organized by the student magazine *A5* and funded by the late landscape architect G. N. Brandt.⟨fig. 35⟩ The issue contained an "Analyse af legepladsproblemet – med særlig henblik på København" (Analysis of the playground problem – with special attention to Copenhagen) by the second-prize winners, architects Grethe Meyer, Ibi Trier Mørch and Max Siegumfeld with landscape architect Agnete Petersen and psychologist Jens Sigsgaard. It contained the statement:

> Prerequisites
>
> THE FAMILY
> is the cell on which all social planning builds.
> THE CHILDREN
> are the most important part of this cell – they are the future.
> ALL CHILDREN
> have the right to space for expression.
> THE PLAYGROUND
> which together with home, school, nursery and other institutions fulfills the need for a healthy and full life expression, is therefore an important social problem.[41]

30

31

32

33

30–33 Children at play, published in C. Th. Sørensen, "Etagehusets Have," *Arkitekten Maanedshæfte* 37, no. 4 (1935): 49–64.

34 Cover of *Arkitekten Maanedshæfte* 37, no. 10 (1935), special issue on the urban apartment and children.

The team concluded that the playground was a social problem which state and municipalities ought to contribute to solving: "The playground should naturally slide into the row of preventive institutions with the right to subsidies from the state and the municipality and with the subsequent advantages." The goal was to lead the children toward "a healthy social comprehension, to make them familiar with collaboration and consideration for others and thereby to turn them into valuable members of society."[42] Here, the notion of children as a resource and the necessity of their enculturation is expressed unequivocally.[43]

The analysis is abundantly illustrated with primarily photographs of children engaged in various sorts of play in both urban and rural settings, with reference to specific types of spaces which would have been recognized as belonging to national pastoral imaginaries in very general terms. A group of four photographs is accompanied by the caption: "Opportunities for plan in the countryside: the water – the village – the field – the wood."[44] Yet one of the photographs also moves beyond the notion of children's expression as being part of their enculturation toward productive adult life.⟨fig. 36⟩ It shows a child jumping at a beach, suspended in midair, as if an angel flying – or a wild animal. This symbolic figuration taps into the modern concept of the child as angel and noble savage, as mentioned previously, but exactly through the suspense of the child's body in the open, the image also suspends the desire for civilizing: We simply don't know what will happen, hence the image acts on us as symptom rather than as resignation to a state of synthesis.

35 Cover of *Arkitekten* 54, nos. 1–2 (1952), special issue on playgrounds, showing a play sculpture by Egon Møller Nielsen.

Conclusion

While the concept of welfare was largely absent from Danish architectural discourse until the final decades of the twentieth century, ideas and imaginaries of welfare and welfare space were expressed in photographic images published in *Arkitekten* during the period ca. 1930–70. This chapter has provided a diachronic investigation of the relationship between welfare spaces, photographic images and children, the latter appearing as symbolic figures embodying the need for change and the sensation of change from the numb to the vigorous. Such photographs, by including these symbolic figures, expressed the role of physical welfare spaces in processes of enculturation and subjectivation. The analysis has furthermore pointed to a development of the modern concepts of children and of childhood since the eighteenth century and the connection to ideas and imaginaries of welfare and its materialization and spatialization

36 Child jumping at a beach, published in Grethe Meyer, Ibi Trier Mørch, Max Siegumfeldt, Agnete Petersen and Jens Sigsgaard, "Analyse af legepladsproblemet – særlig med henblik på København," *Arkitekten* 54, nos. 1–2 (1952): 3.

during the period in question: From the image of deprived courtyard girls, pointing to the promise of salvation of the young bodies and souls from the bleak backyards and later the harshness of the high-rise – to post-World War II images of children lost in play or jumping into the open air of potentialities, conceptualizing children and childhood as a matter of imagination and openness, in the sense of Walter Benjamin, of flexibility and social interaction. These photographs were not all functioning the same way. Applying the notions of symptom and synthesis, as described by George Didi-Huberman, we have seen that some images were instrumental in their attempted synthesis between ordering measurements and the bodies of children in space, while others were successful at creating expressions of a suspended desire, that is, of a certain semantic openness. Ideas and imaginaries of welfare were, however, situated in both categories. To paraphrase Didi-Huberman, such ideas and imaginaries could be formulaic, but they could just as well be poetic.

Bibliography

"Befolkningsspørgsmaalet og Boligen." *Arkitekten Ugehæfte* 40, no. 1 (1938): 1.

"Biblioteksbygninger." *Arkitekten Maanedshæfte* 39, nos. 9–10 (1937): 125–52.

"Boligbebyggelsen 'Ringgaarden.'" *Arkitekten* 48, nos. 1–2 (1946): 1–5.

"Et Kollektivhus." *Arkitekten Maanedshæfte* 37, no. 10 (1935): 151–59.

"Har Samfundet Midler til Afhjælpning af daarlige Boligforhold?" *Arkitekten Ugehæfte* 37, no. 1 (1935): 9.

"På Vesterbro." *Arkitekten* 72, no. 23 (1970): 548–53.

"Sundhedskommissionens Regulativ af 24. April 1931." Reprinted in Margrethe Finsen and Asta Jensen, "Indretning af moderne Børnehaver." *Arkitekten Maanedshæfte* 37, no. 10 (1935): 159–64.

Benjamin, Walter. "The Author as Producer." In *Selected Writings*, vol. 2, part 2, *1931–1934*, edited by Michael W. Jennings, Howard Eiland and Gary Smith, translated by Rodney Livingstone et al., 768–82. Cambridge, MA: Harvard University Press, 1999.

——. "The Rental Barracks." In *Radio Benjamin*, edited by Lecia Rosenthal, translated by Jonathan Lutes with Lisa Harries Schumann and Diana K. Reese, 56–62. London: Verso, 2014.

Colomina, Beatriz. *Privacy and Publicity: Modern Architecture as Mass Media*. Cambridge MA: MIT Press, 1994.

Dahlkild, Nan. Introduction to *Danish Architecture and Society: From Absolute Monarchy to the Welfare State*, edited by Nan Dahlkild, 11–17. Copenhagen: Museum Tusculanum Press, 2020.

De Coninck-Smith, Ning. *Barndom og arkitektur: Rum til danske børn igennem 300 år*. Aarhus: Klim, 2011.

Didi-Huberman, Georges. *The Eye of History: When Images Take Positions*, translated by Shane B. Lillis. Cambridge, MA: MIT Press, 2018.

——. "To Make Symptoms or to Make Syntheses?" In *What Images Do*, edited by Jan Bäcklund, Henrik Oxvig, Michael Renner and Martin Søberg, 207–25. Aarhus: Aarhus University Press, 2019.

Eisenschmidt, Alexander. *The Good Metropolis: From Urban Formlessness to Metropolitan Architecture*. Basel: Birkhäuser, 2019.

Fisker, Kay. "Rækkehustyper 1." *Arkitekten* 43, no. 2 (1941): 17–40.

Gutman, Marta, and Ning de Coninck-Smith. "Introduction: Good to Think with – History, Space, and Modern Childhood." In *Designing Modern Childhoods: History, Space, and the Material Culture of Children*, edited by Marta Gutman and Ning de Coninck-Smith, 1–19. New Brunswick, NJ: Rutgers University Press, 2008.

Holloway, Sarah L., and Gill Valentine. "Children's Geographies and the New Social Studies of Childhood." In *Children's Geographies: Playing, Living, Learning*, edited by Sarah L. Holloway and Gill Valentine. London: Routledge, 2000.

Hygom, Louis. "Har Samfundet Midler til Afhjælpning af daarlige Boligforhold? En Enquête." *Arkitekten Ugehæfte* 37, no. 1 (1935): 1–3.

Jørgensen, Caspar. "Velfærdssamfundets bygninger – en introduktion." *Architectura* 35 (2013): 7–27.

Kinchin, Juliet. "Hide and Seek: Remapping Modern Design and Childhood." In Juliet Kinchin and Aidan O'Connor, *Century of the Child: Growing by Design 1900–2000*. New York: Museum of Modern Art, 2012.

Kozlovsky, Roy. *The Architectures of Childhood: Children, Modern Architecture and Reconstruction in Postwar England*. London and New York: Routledge, 2013.

Mattsson, Helena, and Sven-Olov Wallenstein. Introduction to *Architecture, Consumption and the Welfare State*, edited by Helena Mattsson and Sven-Olov Wallenstein, 6–33. London: Black Dog Publishing, 2010.

Mayne, Alan. *Slums: The History of a Global Injustice*. London: Reaktion Books, 2017.

Meyer, Grethe, Ibi Trier Mørch, Max Siegumfeld, Agnete Petersen and Jens Sigsgaard. "Analyse af legepladsproblemet – særlig med henblik på København." *Arkitekten Månedshæfte* 54, nos. 1–2 (1952): 3–18.

Nørgaard Pedersen, C. J. "Om de åbne muligheder." *Arkitekten* 75, no. 1 (1973): 2.
Pagh, Jesper. "Myten om velfærdsarkitekten: En undersøgelse af danske arkitekters bidrag til udviklingen af velfærdssamfundet." PhD diss. The Royal Danish Academy of Fine Arts, Schools of Architecture, Design and Conservation, 2019.
Petersson, Dag, with Walter Niedermayr. "Photographic Space." In *Representational Machines: Photography and the Production of Space*, edited by Anna Dahlgren, Dag Petersson and Nina Lager Vestberg, 107–47. Aarhus: Aarhus University Press, 2013.
Sanzani, Carlo. "Experience and Play: Walter Benjamin and the Prelapsian Child." In *Walter Benjamin and the Architecture of Modernity*, edited by Andrew Benjamin and Charles Rice, 175–98. Melbourne, re-press, 2009.
Skriver, Poul Erik. "Arkitekten og sovebyen." *Arkitekten* 63, no. 26 (1961): 476–85.
——. "Børnene er storforbrugere af udemiljø." *Arkitekten* 71, no. 9 (1969): 212–13.
——. "Børnene i de nye byområder." *Arkitekten* 66, no. 22 (1964): 455–57.
——. "De vil ikke bo i højhuse – men de skal." *Arkitekten* 72, no. 6 (1970): 147–49.
——. "En eksperimentskole ved Rugvængets skole." *Arkitekten* 73, no. 3 (1971): 49–51.
——. "En typebørnehave." *Arkitekten* 67, no. 7 (1965): 125–28.
Sørensen, C. Th. "Etagehusets Have." *Arkitekten Maanedshæfte* 37, no. 4 (1935): 49–64.
Vallgårda, Karen, Kristine Alexander and Stephanie Olsen. "Emotions and the Global Politics of Childhood." In *Childhood, Youth and Emotions in Modern History: National, Colonial and Global Perspectives*, edited by Stephanie Olsen, 12–34. Houndsmill: Palgrave Macmillan, 2015.
Vidler, Anthony. "The b-b-b-Body: Block, Blob, Blur." In *The Body in Architecture*, edited by Deborah Hauptmann, 130–37. Rotterdam: 010 Publishers, 2006.
Voigt, Wolfgang, Dorothea Deschermeier and Peter Cachola Schmal, eds. *New Human, New Housing: Architecture of the New Frankfurt 1925–1933*. Berlin: DOM Publishers, 2019.
Whittaker, Edward. "Photography and the Subject of Architecture." In *Camera Constructs: Photography, Architecture and the Modern City*, edited by Andrew Higgott and Timothy Wray, 125–34. Farnham: Ashgate, 2012.

Notes

1 The Kanslergade Agreement in 1933 was a political agreement which included significant social reforms and hence can be seen as a milestone in the establishment of the Danish welfare state. Although the welfare state continued to develop during the 1970s and '80s, the early 1970s nevertheless mark a significant period of change politically, economically and culturally, for instance indicated by the Danish municipal reform in 1970, the Danish membership in the European Community in 1972 and the international oil crisis in 1973. See also Lars Bo Kaspersen's contribution in this volume.
2 According to Caspar Jørgensen, the number of Danish historical studies of this period and topic are quite limited. This is contrasted by the relatively high number of comparable Swedish studies which, argues Jørgensen, have demonstrated how the Swedish welfare society was in formation already during the 1930s. Caspar Jørgensen, "Velfærdssamfundets bygninger – en introduction," *Architectura* 35 (2013): 21. All translations from the Danish by the author. One example of what Jørgensen points to, is Helena Mattsson and Sven-Olov Wallenstein's coinage and discussion of a particular *soft* approach to modernism in Swedish architecture articulated both in terms of design and discourse already around 1930, demonstrated by the publication of the famous *acceptera* book in 1931 in continuation of the 1930 Stockholm Exhibition. Helena Mattsson and Sven-Olov Wallenstein, Introduction to *Architecture, Consumption and the Welfare State*, ed. Helena Mattsson and Sven-Olov Wallenstein (London: Black Dog Publishing, 2010), 6–33. One of the few Danish examples of an investigation into the connections between architecture and welfare is Jesper Pagh's PhD dissertation focusing on the period 1957–2013. See Pagh, "Myten om velfærdsarkitekten: En undersøgelse af danske arkitekters bidrag til udviklingen af velfærdssamfundet" (PhD diss., The Royal Danish Academy of Fine Arts, Schools of Architecture, Design and Conservation, 2019).
3 Nan Dahlkild, Introduction to *Danish Architecture and Society: From Absolute Monarchy to the Welfare State*, ed. Nan Dahlkild (Copenhagen: Museum Tusculanum Press, 2020), 11.
4 Dahlkild, Introduction, 12.
5 The relationship between architectural discourse, photography and print media has been investigated by Beatriz Colomina, for instance in her book *Privacy and Publicity: Modern Architecture as Mass Media* (Cambridge MA: MIT Press, 1994).
6 For more on the relationship between photography, space and architecture, see for instance: Dag Petersson with Walter Niedermayr, "Photographic Space," in *Representational Machines: Photography and the Production of Space*, ed. Anna Dahlgren, Dag Petersson and Nina Lager Vestberg (Aarhus: Aarhus University Press, 2013), 107–47; and Edward Whittaker, "Photography and the Subject of Architecture," in *Camera Constructs: Photography, Architecture and the Modern City*, ed. Andrew Higgott and Timothy Wray (Farnham: Ashgate, 2012), 125–34.
7 This notion of the child and of childhood was developed during the eighteenth century not least in continuation of the work of Jean-Jacques Rousseau. See Sarah L. Holloway and Gill Valentine, "Children's Geographies and the New Social Studies of Childhood," in *Children's Geographies: Playing, Living, Learning*, ed. Sarah L. Holloway and Gill Valentine (London: Routledge, 2000), 2–5. See also Karen Vallgårda, Kristine Alexander and Stephanie Olsen. "Emotions and the Global Politics of Childhood," in *Childhood, Youth and Emotions in Modern History: National, Colonial and Global Perspectives*, ed. Stephanie Olsen (Houndsmill: Palgrave Macmillan, 2015), 12–34.
8 Marta Gutman and Ning de Coninck-Smith, "Introduction: Good to Think with – History, Space, and Modern Childhood," in *Designing Modern Childhoods: History, Space, and the Material Culture of Children*, ed. Marta Gutman and Ning de Coninck-Smith (New Brunswick, NJ: Rutgers University Press, 2008), 2.
9 Juliet Kinchin, "Hide and Seek: Remapping Modern Design and Childhood," in Juliet Kinchin and Aidan O'Connor, *Century of the Child: Growing by Design 1900–2000* (New York: Museum of Modern Art, 2012), 12.
10 Louis Hygom, "Har Samfundet Midler til Afhjælpning af daarlige Boligforhold? En Enquête," *Arkitekten Ugehæfte* 37, no. 1 (1935): 1–3. The first Danish act on slum clearance was adopted in 1939. See also Alan Mayne, *Slums: The History of a Global Injustice* (London: Reaktion Books, 2017).
11 Richard Kjer-Petersen in "Har Samfundet Midler til Afhjælpning af daarlige Boligforhold?" *Arkitekten Ugehæfte* 37, no. 1 (1935): 9. Italics in original.
12 Kjer-Petersen in "Har Samfundet Midler," 9.
13 See for instance: Wolfgang Voigt, Dorothea Deschermeier and Peter Cachola Schmal, eds., *New Human, New Housing: Architecture of the New Frankfurt 1925–1933* (Berlin: DOM Publishers, 2019).

14 Walter Benjamin, "The Rental Barracks," in *Radio Benjamin*, ed. Lecia Rosenthal, trans. Jonathan Lutes with Lisa Harries Schumann and Diana K. Reese (London: Verso, 2014), 59.
15 Alexander Eisenschmidt, *The Good Metropolis: From Urban Formlessness to Metropolitan Architecture* (Basel: Birkhäuser, 2019), 157. For more on Benjamin's ideas on childhood and imagination, see Carlo Sanzani, "Experience and Play: Walter Benjamin and the Prelapsian Child," in *Walter Benjamin and the Architecture of Modernity*, ed. Andrew Benjamin and Charles Rice (Melbourne, re-press, 2009), 175–98.
16 Eisenschmidt, *The Good Metropolis*, 158.
17 Eisenschmidt, *The Good Metropolis*, 161.
18 Walter Benjamin, "The Author as Producer," in *Selected Writings*, vol. 2, part 2. *1931–1934*, ed. Michael W. Jennings, Howard Eiland and Gary Smith, trans. Rodney Livingstone et al. (Cambridge, MA: Harvard University Press, 1999), 775.
19 Georges Didi-Huberman, *The Eye of History: When Images Take Positions*, trans. Shane B. Lillis (Cambridge, MA: MIT Press, 2018) 233.
20 Georges Didi-Huberman, "To Make Symptoms or to Make Syntheses?' in *What Images Do*, ed. Jan Bäcklund, Henrik Oxvig, Michael Renner and Martin Søberg (Aarhus: Aarhus University Press, 2019), 207.
21 Didi-Huberman, "To Make Symptoms," 217.
22 Didi-Huberman, "To Make Symptoms," 222.
23 "Befolkningsspørgsmaalet og Boligen," *Arkitekten Ugehæfte* 40, no. 1 (1938): 1.
24 "Boligbebyggelsen 'Ringgaarden,'" *Arkitekten* 48, no. 1–2 (1946): 1–5.
25 Petersson, "Photographic Space," 107–47.
26 Kay Fisker, "Rækkehustyper 1," *Arkitekten* 43, no. 2 (1941): 32–33.
27 Poul Erik Skriver, "Arkitekten og sovebyen." *Arkitekten* 63, no. 26 (1961): 479.
28 Poul Erik Skriver, "Børnene i de nye byområder," *Arkitekten* 66, no. 22 (1964): 455. See also Poul Erik Skriver, "Børnene er storforbrugere af udemiljø," *Arkitekten* 71, no. 9 (1969): 212–13; Poul Erik Skriver, "De vil ikke bo i højhuse – men de skal," *Arkitekten* 72, no. 6 (1970): 147–49, with illustrations by Jan Gehl.
29 Skriver, "Børnene i de nye byområder," 457.
30 "På Vesterbro," *Arkitekten* 72, no. 23 (1970): 548–53.
31 Ning de Coninck-Smith, *Barndom og arkitektur: Rum til danske børn igennem 300 år* (Aarhus: Klim, 2011), 231.
32 "Et Kollektivhus," *Arkitekten Maanedshæfte* 37, no. 10 (1935): 151–59.
33 "Sundhedskommissionens Regulativ af 24. April 1931," printed in Margrethe Finsen and Asta Jensen, "Indretning af moderne Børnehaver," *Arkitekten Maanedshæfte* 37, no. 10 (1935): 161.
34 Poul Erik Skriver, "En typebørnehave," *Arkitekten* 67, no. 7 (1965): 125.
35 Poul Erik Skriver, "En eksperimentskole ved Rugvængets skole," *Arkitekten* 73, no. 3 (1971): 49.
36 Such plan layouts were inspired by English schools. See C. J. Nørgaard Pedersen, "Om de åbne muligheder," *Arkitekten* 75, no. 1 (1973): 2.
37 Anthony Vidler, "The b-b-b-Body: Block, Blob, Blur," in *The Body in Architecture*, ed. Deborah Hauptmann (Rotterdam: 010 Publishers, 2006), 131–32.
38 "Biblioteksbygninger," *Arkitekten Maaneshæfte* 39, nos. 9–10 (1937): 125–52.
39 C. Th. Sørensen, "Etagehusets Have," *Arkitekten Maanedshæfte* 37, no. 4 (1935): 50.
40 Sørensen, "Etagehusets Have," 51.
41 Grethe Meyer, Ibi Trier Mørch, Max Siegumfeld, Agnete Petersen and Jens Sigsgaard, "Analyse af legepladsproblemet – særlig med henblik på København," *Arkitekten Månedshæfte* 54, nos. 1–2 (1952): 3.
42 Meyer, "Analyse af legepladsproblemet," 18.
43 Roy Kozlovsky has brilliantly analyzed the connection between space, power and the construction of institutions for children during the postwar years in his book *The Architectures of Childhood: Children, Modern Architecture and Reconstruction in Postwar England* (London: Routledge, 2013).
44 Meyer, "Analyse af legepladsproblemet," 13.

Global events, 1970–2022

The AIDS epidemic officially begins in the United States.

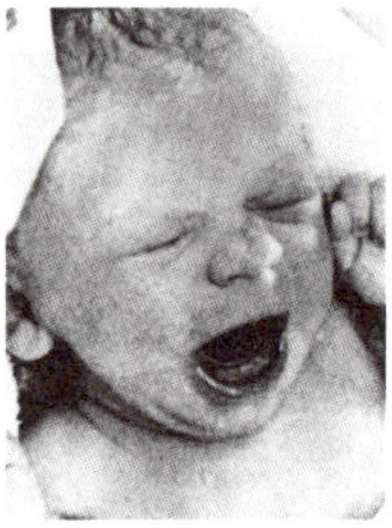

First child successfully born after her mother received in vitro fertilization treatment

Deng Xiaoping commences the Chinese economic reform

Death of Mao Zedong. End of the Cultural Revolution in China

First outbreak of the Ebola virus in Zaire

Release of first commercially successful personal computer

World population reaches four billion

First Oil Crisis/ OPEC oil price shock

Ratification of the Treaty on the Non-Proliferation of Nuclear Weapons

Removal of the gold standard for the US dollar

Ronald Reagan is elected US President

Beginning of the Iran–Iraq War (until 1988)

WHO announces the eradication of smallpox

Margaret Thatcher elected UK Prime Minister

Dissolution of the USSR

First website published

German Reunification

Fall of the Berlin Wall

Tiananmen Square Massacre

World population reaches five billion

Stock market collapse

The antidepressant drug fluoxetine (Prozac) becomes commercially available

The Chernobyl disaster in Ukraine

Schengen Agreement on open borders within Europe

Mikhail Gorbachev becomes General Secretary of the Communist Party of the Soviet Union

Establishment of the World Trade Organisation

End of apartheid in South Africa and election of Nelson Mandela as President

European Union ratified with the Maastricht Treaty

1970 1975 1980 1985 1990 1995

Dot-Com bubble collapses

World population reaches six billion

Google Search developed by Larry Page and Sergey Brin

First successfully cloned mammal from an adult cell: Dolly the sheep

The Kyoto Protocol comes into effect

Launch of Facebook

US-led coalition invades Iraq

Euro currency adopted in participating EU countries

The African Union is founded

September 11 Terror Attacks in New York, Washington DC and Pennsylvania

China becomes a member of the World Trade Organization

Russia annexes Crimea

Facebook acquires Instagram

World population reaches seven billion

Arab Spring begins

Launch of cryptocurrency Bitcoin

Global financial crisis

Russia invades Ukraine

Glasgow Climate Pact

Collapse of the Islamic Republic of Afghanistan following Taliban offensive

First case of COVID-19

#MeToo movement begins

UK votes to leave EU in a referendum (BREXIT)

So-called European Migrant Crisis

Paris Climate Agreement

US-led coalition intervenes against ISIS in Iraq and Syria

2000 2005 2010 2015 2020

Events in Denmark, 1970–2022

Law on equal wages for women and men for work of equal value is passed

Social Assistance Act becomes effective, known as the "Crown on the Welfare State"

Increasing unemployment rates, tax relief

National building activity peaks with 60,000 completed homes. A total of 915,000 new homes were built between 1960 and 1979

Abortion is legalized

Government introduced a halt to immigration

Landslide election, 40 percent of voters change party

Denmark joins the European Economic Community (EEC)

Educational reform: compulsory education is extended from seven to nine years

The former Bådsmandsgades Barracks is squatted and declared as Freetown Christiania

Public health insurance act guarantees free medical treatment for all

Weekly working hours are reduced from 42.5 to 41.75 hours; in 1976 to 40 hours; in 1985 to 39 hours; in 1988 to 38 hours; and in 1990 to 37 hours

New national planning acts, which include increasing involvement of citizens in the planning process

State Educational Grant and Loan Scheme is introduced

Major municipal reform which reduces the number of municipalities from 1098 to 277 and the number of counties from 25 to 14

Universal right to *efterløn*, pension benefits payable between early retirement and normal retirement pension, is introduced

Greenland obtains *hjemmestyre* (home rule), though it remains a part of the Kingdom of Denmark

New Hospital Act and act on free choice of general practitioner and hospitals

Same-sex civil partnership is legitimized

The Act on Equality between Women and Men requires public authorities to promote equality

Bill concerning a stop for the construction of care homes to senior homes. Permanent and free home help is introduced

Tax reform: Earlier arrangements for families with children were abandoned and replaced by a tax-free, income-dependent child family benefit

Kartoffelkuren (The Potato Diet), fiscal initiatives to reduce private spending and borrowing

National referendum on the European Single Market results in acceptance

Act on Equality between Women and Men in the Appointment of Members to Public Committees, Commissions, etc., is adopted

Pension reform gathers different types of pensions into an early retirement benefit

Work reform introduces a more active labor market policy, resulting in a tightening of the unemploy ment benefit rules and the control and activation of th unemployed, the so-called flexicurity model

Educational reform abolish streaming of children into different levels

National referendum on the Edinburgh Agreement results in acceptance with four major reservations: The Euro-opt out, Common Security and Defence Policy, Justice and Home Affairs-concerned laws that are regulated by the EU, citizenship in EU

National referendum on the Treaty on European Union (Maastricht Treaty) results in nonacceptance

National Planning Report marks the first time a focus is laid on making the Capital competitive on a regional/global scale

1970 1975 1980 1985 1990 1995

Øresundsbron (The Sound Bridge), the bridge connecting Copenhagen in Denmark and Malmö in Sweden is opened, enhancing the growth of Copenhagen

National referendum on the European Union's economic and monetary union, including the euro, results in nonacceptance

Denmark participates in attacks on Serbia as part of the Kosovo conflict. This marks the introduction of an "activistic foreign policy"

First act on the integration of immigrants

Reform of the social security system: The Social Assistance Act is replaced by a new Service Act, the Activation Act and Legal Rights act

Reform of the *efterløn*, prolonging the age of retirement and restricting access to the benefit

Tax reform, the so-called Pinsepakken (The Whitsun Package)

Storebæltsbroen (The Great Belt Bridge) is opened, connecting Funen and Zealand with car and train infrastructure

Act on discriminatory practices on the labor market prohibits discrimination on the basis of ethnicity, religion, sexual orientation, social origin and political wiews

Recovery plan includes changes to the unemployment benefit rules

Copenhagen named Europe's Most Sustainable City in the Siemens Index

Copenhagen is named the World's Most Livable City by *Monocle Magazine*

Structural reform reduces the number of municipalities from 271 to 98 and replaces the 13 counties with 5 regions

Welfare reform includes changes to the labor market policy and educational system

So-called Muhammed Crisis following the publication of satirical drawings of the Islamic prophet Muhammed

Denmark enters the Iraq War as part of the United States-led NATO coalition (until 2007)

Introduction of amortization-free real estate loans

Governmental Welfare Commission is appointed, presents report in 2005. Suggests a number of reforms, including phasing out *efterlønnen*, gradual raising the pension age and decreasing the right to unemployment benefits from four to two and a half years

First antiterrorism package is passed by the Danish Parliament

Denmark enters the Afghanistan War as part of the United States-led NATO coalition (until 2014)

Taxation stop is introduced

Agreement to raise Denmark's defence and security spending permanently to 2 percent of GDP by the end of 2033

Government initiative to decentralize higher education

Climate Act, aiming for 70 percent reduction of greenhouse gasses by 2030

Ban of wearing face-masking garments in public, the so-called burka ban

Final approval of the construction of the Femarnbelt tunnel connecting Denmark and Germany

National referendum on the European Union's justice and home affairs agreement, resulting in nonacceptance

Terror attack at the culture house Krudttønden and the Jewish synagogue in Copenhagen are carried out; three persons are killed

2000 2005 2010 2015 2020

1

Security

From Architecture of the Architect to the Architecture of *Salus Populi* and the Architecture of Security

Lars Bo Kaspersen

In 2017 the Royal Danish Academy of Fine Art, Schools of Architecture, Design and Conservation launched a major research project titled Spaces of Danish Welfare. The title itself was intriguing, and it opened for a new field of research. This article concerns the relationship between welfare and space – a relationship that has led to new ways of thinking about welfare and space as concepts as well as social phenomena. Scholars affiliated with the research project have explored different ways in which welfare and space relate to each other.

Some of the questions and claims emanating from the "welfare of spaces, spaces of welfare" relationship make it relevant to investigate whether different discourses of welfare produce different spaces. Are different types of welfare services linked to different types of spaces (social and/or physical) or spatial constructions? For example, do we find some common denominator among school buildings in Denmark built in the postwar period? One could also claim that different forms of welfare produce different forms of social space. Most obviously, specific welfare policies produce special categories of welfare subjects.[1]

Most people will agree that buildings and the physical space are often a function of the particular welfare service offered in that building. For example, schools are designed to reflect the needs of the pedagogy of the time as well as the need to provide educational welfare to children in their particular country and neighborhood. There might be something to this claim but, of course, it is not entirely correct. Over the years, we have witnessed how welfare institutions have been placed in buildings and physical spaces which were originally built for other purposes, such as day nurseries placed in restored and redecorated Georgian houses built for the upper class. Or we find libraries or archives placed in old farmhouses or former factories.

An equal number of scholars and architects will probably argue that a large number of welfare institutions were constructed according to a list of criteria tied into, for example, different discourses of welfare, but also the ideas of architects of the time: the contemporary modes of expression in architecture, the dominant architectural discourses of the time and the financial and material resources available. Others will argue that financial resources allocated to welfare constructions such as offices, schools, hospitals, job centers, medical centers, etc., are the determining factor. The financial situation, at the time of deciding about new spaces for welfare, plays a crucial role when politicians must decide between new buildings or adapting old buildings to new activities. In similar ways, we might experience some visionary welfare architects constructing new buildings and new landscapes during a period with the booming economies.[2] And finally, it is important to remember that a plausible hypothesis could be that there is no systematic pattern in the relation between welfare and space. Thus, many different sorts of buildings are converted into welfare institutions when need be.

Before we jump into some kind of analysis and conclusion about the welfare-space relationship, we need to specify what we mean by *welfare* and *space*. We will take them in order.

Welfare and the Welfare State from the Nineteenth to the Twenty-first Century

The welfare state is often seen as an institutional answer to the most important question following from the rise of capitalism: the increasing division of labor and the rapid internationalization which took place from the late eighteenth century and onward – the so-called Social Question. The implications of the Industrial Revolution and the rise of capitalism were increasing wealth for a minority and more poverty, inequality and insecurity for the large majority of the population. The guilds and the village-based communities that had provided some form of social security even for the very poor during late feudalism and absolutism did not play the same role in the rapidly growing industrial cities.

In the social sciences and in ordinary political discourses we most often use the terms *welfare state* or *welfare society* to describe the postwar period in which proper social rights developed in many Western countries, in particular, in the Nordic countries.[3] The very expression *welfare state* is mainly a concept of World War II.[4] The term was coined to oppose the "warfare state" of Nazi Germany.[5] Prior to the post-1945 period, we find the term *Sozialstaat* used to describe Bismarck's introduction of extended social rights to the working class – a construction based upon insurance systems. Some welfare researchers argue that the welfare state mainly is the outcome of the two world wars in the twentieth century.[6] They see the welfare state as an institution allotting extended social rights to the working class, partly as a compensation for their contribution to the country during the war and partly as a means of providing them with decent living conditions because the war had destroyed housing, schools, healthcare, etc.

These different understandings of *welfare* and *welfare state* are quite common in contemporary political debates and in social sciences as well. We tend to forget, however, that *welfare*, *welfare state* and *welfare society* are ideological concepts and not clearly defined analytical concepts. These and other similar concepts usually escape definition because their content and meaning are constantly being produced, defined and redefined in an ongoing political struggle. The intellectual historian Quentin Skinner has demonstrated that concepts such as *state* and *liberty* can be seen as ideological and therefore without a clear definition. Skinner claims that methodologically, we need to trace the history of these concepts or, put differently, we must work with a "genealogy."[7]

Inspired by the tradition Skinner calls "conceptual history," we will construct a quasi-genealogy of the concept of welfare.[8] After this, we shall proceed with a discussion of how welfare and the welfare state developed in selected discourses in Western Europe and, following from this, we shall look at the implications of this and the development of particular spaces.

Welfare in the Seventeenth Century: *Salus Populi*

The term *welfare state* consists of a prefix, *welfare*, and a suffix, *state*; and these two terms might not come from the same context or discourse. It is beyond the scope of this chapter to trace and determine the precise origin and development of the concept *welfare state*, but a possible line of development starts with the philosopher Thomas Hobbes's book

1 Kronborg Castle, Elsinore, 1574.

Leviathan from 1651. This book is often regarded as one of the first works about the modern state – a particular form of political and social order developing in the aftermath of the European Renaissance. Thus, Hobbes writes the following:

> For by Art is created that great LEVIATHAN called a COMMON-WEALTH, or STATE, (in latine CIVITAS) which is but an Artificiall Man; though of greater stature and strength than the Naturall, for whose protection and defence it was intended; and in which, the *Sovereignty* is an Artificiall *Soul*, as giving life and motion to the whole body; The *Magistrates*, and other *Officers* of Judicature and Execution, artificiall *Joynts*; *Reward* and *Punishment* (by which fastned to the seat of the Sovereignty, every joynt and member is moved to performe his duty) are the *Nerves*, that do the same in the Body Naturall; the *Wealth* and *Riches* of all the particular members, are the *Strength*; *Salus Populi* (the *peoples safety*) its *Businesse*.[9]

Hobbes's *Leviathan* is one of the most significant books about the modern state and its development – a development from the mid-seventeenth to the mid-nineteenth century. The quotation clearly states that the business of the state is the *salus populi*. *Salus* (Latin: "safety," "salvation," "welfare") was a Roman goddess. She was the goddess of safety and well-being (welfare, health and prosperity) for both the individual and the state. In other words, *salus* is more than security in its narrow sense (for example, protection from assault or violent intruders). The state must provide security.⟨fig. 1⟩ This is a top priority, which is understandable in the context of the English civil war. Fear of violence, related to intrusions from foreign enemies or violence applied in civil wars, was a normal feature of those societies. Hobbes was aware that uncertainty undermines the capacity to create a daily life where we can work, go to school, build roads and houses and harvest the fields. The feeling of insecurity goes deeper than just fear of death. Security is crucial, but by referring to *salus populi*, he extends the otherwise narrow notion of security to a broader meaning which includes safety and welfare. Safety, security and welfare fuse into one discourse. When Hobbes claims that the modern state must deliver security to its population, it is not a specific need people have in the modern state. He assumes that the feeling of some form of (ontological) security is a necessity for all people across time and space. It is a human feature: it is not tied to any particular period or place on earth; it is related to a general need in the population. This need is again related to a trust and what is called *ontological security*.

From Continual Fear to Trust and Ontological Security

Hobbes argues that some forms of security are necessary for human society to exist and develop. In *Leviathan*, he argues that:

> Whatsoever therefore is consequent to a time of Warre, where every man is Enemy to every man; the same is consequent to the time, wherein men live without other security, than what their own strength, and their own invention shall furnish them withall. In such condition, there is no place for Industry; because the fruit thereof is uncertain: and consequently no Culture of the Earth; no Navigation, nor use of the commodities that may be imported by Sea; no commodious Building; No Instrument of moving, and removing such things as require much force; no Knowledge of the face of the Earth; no account of Time; no Arts; no Letters; no Society; and which is worst of all, continuall feare, and danger of violent death; And the life of man, solitary, poore, nasty, brutish, and short.[10]

Hobbes emphasizes continual fear and the danger of violent death as the key sources to general fear and uncertainty. This claim seems to correspond to observations done by twentieth-century sociologists and social psychologists.[11]

An important concept to understand is *ontological security*: it is the fundamental form of security needed for a society to be livable. Ontological security, according to the sociologist Anthony Giddens,

> refers to the confidence that most human beings have in the continuity of their self-identity and in the constancy of the surrounding social and material environments of action. A sense of reliability of persons and things, so central to the notion of trust, is basic to feelings of ontological security; hence, the two are psychologically closely related.
>
> Ontological security has to do with "being" or, in the terms of phenomenology, "being-in-the-world." However, it is an emotional, rather than a cognitive, phenomenon, and it is rooted in the unconscious. Philosophers have shown us that on a cognitive level there are few, if any, aspects of our personal existence about which we can be certain.[12]

Elsewhere, Giddens defines ontological security as the "Confidence or trust that the natural and social worlds are as they appear to be, including the basic existential parameters of self and social identity."[13]

The concepts of ontological security and trust are important because they contribute to an understanding of the general need for feeling secure among the people in a particular state. Trust in social relations provides the foundation for a well-functioning society. Mutual trust is vital if we want to collaborate, maintain a social contract and live a life in peace and prosperity. Therefore, trust and ontological security are crucial to state formation and nation-building.

By referring to Thomas Hobbes and the *salus populi*, a new perception of welfare comes about. By linking the state to the *salus populi*, Hobbes both represents a discourse of welfare which pushes the notion of welfare back in history, and also operates with a much broader welfare discourse in which elements (such as security, safety and welfare) fuse together.[14] In each state and society, we find a particular perception of security and insecurity (ontological security) and the ruling perception is linked to the issues of welfare, safety and security. Remedying problems of insecurity can only be done by providing the appropriate form of welfare (security/safety measures) to reduce ontological insecurity. The type of welfare (*salus populi*) needed to reduce the level of ontological insecurity is different from state to state. The insecurity of a particular state or society is linked to a specific form of welfare and these different forms of welfare are linked with different spaces. Put differently, we see how security is perceived differently, and how particular forms of security determine the space and spatial constructions in different national contexts in different periods. We shall investigate three periods in the history of Denmark in order to analyze how particular versions of the relationship between security, welfare and space unfold:

- 1860s to the end of World War II: different actors (private persons, philanthropists, voluntary associations, the church, parishes, municipalities and the state) produce different welfare institutions, welfare solutions and a particular form of welfare state/society. An outcome of bottom-up/top-down processes.
- End of World War II to 2001: toward the peak of the social democratic welfare state and beyond.
- 2001 onward: the new experimental welfare state – new actors and new players.

The Welfare-Security-Space Nexus

The exposition and analysis of the welfare-security-space nexus in various parts of Denmark in three different periods are very tentative. Again, the purpose of this chapter is to point to the different forms of ontological security that different types of states or societies must produce in order to reduce fear, uncertainty, anxiety and maybe even angst in the population. Moreover, the thesis is that the type of security needed by a society requires a spatial entity or construction to reduce insecurity and uncertainty. The notion *spatial entity* is very preliminary because we have no clear understanding of what a spatial entity really is and how it acts. Thus, our entry point to the nexus welfare-security-space is the discourses of welfare and of security. Our point of observation is the state and how the most powerful social groups define the type of security the state must provide to produce a legitimate social order. The spatial dimension might seem to follow from the security discourse. This is, however, far from the case. I am not arguing that the welfare-security discourse is causing a particular conception of space. This chapter is an explorative piece of research with the intention to contribute to the research agenda of the future. Therefore, we just provide examples of these different welfare spaces, and we will try to ask questions about the spatial dimension. Hopefully, we can contribute to an opening of the concept and, eventually, a definition.

The Struggle between the Welfare Society and the Welfare State: Denmark between the 1860s and 1950s

In the decades after a defeat by Prussia in 1864, Denmark was divided into two groups with different strategies to rebuild Denmark as a strong nation. The Right, the conservative forces, controlled the upper House

2 The Svendborg Sickness Fund, a voluntary association dating back to 1855 (here from 1949).
3 Øvelseshuset (The Exercise House), Martin Nyrop, 1884, at Vallekilde Højskole (Vallekilde Folk High School), founded 1855. A unique Nordic educational initiative led to the establishment of many folk high schools, which became an important educational base for peasants, farmers and workers. Photo by Jens Cederskjold.
4 A tuberculosis sanatorium from 1911 in Kolding, built and financed by philanthropic organizations.

2

3

4

5 The Finsen Institute, built in the 1910s and '20s, was financed by a philanthropic association.

6 Odense Technical School, photographed ca. 1925–35, founded in 1899. From early in the nineteenth century technical schools began to appear all over the country, initiated and run by voluntary associations. Later in the nineteenth century these schools began to receive funding from the state.

7 Garderhøjfortet, a part of the last segments built (Fortification of Copenhagen/Vestvolden). This part of the fortification of Copenhagen was financed through public collections.

8 The Fortun fortification, begun in 1891 and completed in 1893. It is one of the smallest parts of the fortification – also a part of the fortification of Copenhagen.

in the Parliament and thus the state budget. The Left, mainly the new class of independent farmers with ownership of their own farms, challenged the balance of power. The social question in Denmark was mainly related to the problem of old and very poor people in the countryside. When Left and Right struck a compromise in 1891–92, both parties accepted the introduction of social rights and the responsibility of the state to provide social security for the poor and old. In addition to this step, Denmark developed many different institutions (health, cooperatives, people's high schools, technical schools) as an outcome of decisions taken by voluntary associations, philanthropists, private people and other organizations.⟨figs. 2–6⟩ This was mainly driven by bottom-up processes, which eventually merged together with top-down processes initiated by the state. Many philanthropists fought to erase illnesses such as tuberculosis, and ordinary people came together to create sick-benefit associations, to which they made contributions into an insurance system to pay for medical help. Many movements built education systems, for instance, technical schools or *Folkehøjskoler* (people's high schools/folk high schools). These many institutions were often initiated by voluntary associations but supported by the state. It was called the "help-to-self-help" principle, a strong social-liberal principle.

The social programs introduced in 1892 were extended in the 1930s, but social security in Denmark remained an amalgam of local and national institutions, often developed by voluntary associations or philanthropists, but gradually seized by the state during the twentieth century. From the 1970s, most welfare institutions were financed and managed by the state. The social democratic welfare state came into being, though many welfare institutions were still managed by voluntary associations. Therefore, the typical institutions in Denmark providing welfare and security from the 1870s to the end of World War II were the privately owned property either of the institutions themselves or of a foundation.

The type of security and welfare offered by this mixture of private and public institutions, voluntary associations and foundations were most importantly social security (poverty, old people, health, housing, employment) but also education. The heavy military defeat by Prussia in 1864 raised a huge debate about the future of physical security – a military defense. There were several opinions and suggestions about this future defense. The outcome of the discussions was the establishment of a large fortification west and north of Copenhagen.⟨figs. 7–8⟩ It was more in agreement with the ideas of the Right and the conservative forces. This fortification was built between the 1880s and World War I. In reality, most politicians did not believe that such a fortification could prevent a Danish defeat. Consequently, Denmark went through a disarmament process and turned neutral almost simultaneously the construction of the fortification, which was finalized in 1914. The key strategic person and the mastermind behind Danish foreign policy, the politician Peter Munch argued:

> We can no more defend the Danish state with culture than with fortifications. Culture, on the other hand, can build a spiritual defense for the Danish people. [...] If conditions were to be shaped so calamitously that the Danish state was conquered, it is fitting to face the fact that this might occur; then a distinctive, highly evolved Danish culture, as far from the militaristic culture of the conquering state as possible, may safeguard the Danish people's ability to preserve their own national life until they also regain their external independence.[15]

These statements demonstrate Munch's understanding of the national and the international as intertwined processes. Thus, to Munch, domestic policy was an important instrument in the struggle for Denmark's survival. Munch also considered social cohesion as an important element in the state's struggle for survival. The goal was to safeguard Danish sovereignty and the means was the development of internal cohesion by establishing national institutions, not least those we would now call welfare institutions. Among other things, this required a strong national healthcare system as well as institutions to ensure a minimum of social security in the form of pensions, poverty relief and housing, etc. The endeavor should be

> to achieve equal rights for all Danes, regardless of what walk of life they were born into, to provide satisfactory economic conditions for all and equal influence on the governance of Danish society. [This will promote] the equity within our society that is the only firm basis for a true feeling of fellowship.[16]

General education and enlightenment, educational institutions and science are key instruments for realizing Munch's vision.

The Welfare-Security-Space Nexus from the 1860s to the End of World War II: Some Preliminary Remarks

Obviously, the nexus was not the same from the beginning to the end of this period (almost a century). We observe a Denmark in which social insecurity became the dominant security problem. Therefore, the struggle for better (material) living conditions became the most important issue in Denmark during this period and an improvement of the ontological security in relation to health, avoiding poverty, housing with good sanitary conditions and education had high priority. In the second part of the nineteenth century and the first part of the twentieth century, the Danish state and society went through radical changes in relation to welfare institutions. Many different actors (voluntary associations, philanthropists, foundations, the state, private investors and others) contributed to the erection of a number of different buildings serving the purpose of supporting people and removing a general ontological insecurity. This led

9 Munkegårdsskolen in Gentofte, north of Copenhagen, Arne Jacobsen, 1952–56. Many public schools were built in the 1940s and the '50s. These new egalitarian public schools were seen as an instrument for increasing social mobility and therefore were the engines of the welfare state.

10 Rødovre Town Hall, Arne Jacobsen, 1955–57.

to a spatial transformation of Denmark in which a large number of houses, buildings, squares, fields and parks emerged as an outcome of a general agreement on building a welfare society. Without a willingness to fight social insecurity, these many buildings would hardly have been built during this period. The buildings are different in style, based upon different architectural ideas and materials, etc. In retrospect, however, we know that the transformation of spaces was driven by the state and other actors in order to generate security – mainly social security.

The Rise and Fall of the Social Democratic Welfare State and Beyond: Denmark from the 1960s to the Millennium

In the postwar period, the Social Democratic Party became stronger both in Parliament and in society as a whole. Ideals, norms and values closely tied together, as a part of Danish identity were also closely knitted to the social democrats. The Social Democrats came out of the 1930s and '40s as a "catchall" party representing all Danes, not only the working class. Consequently, the Party in government (either alone or in a coalition with other parties) during the 1950s and '60s step-by-step developed a social democratic welfare state. An extended set of universal social rights for all citizens financed by taxes was the key characteristic of the welfare state in Denmark.⟨figs. 9–10⟩ In 1970 a big administrative reform took place: the old heterogeneous structure of more than a thousand parish municipalities was replaced with 275 new municipalities, which became the point of departure for providing welfare services to all citizens, who now had the same rights. A set of well-educated professions was at the core of the administration of the welfare services. A big welfare reform with equal rights for men and women was introduced in 1976. The complete social democratic welfare state was in place. Figures 11 and 12 show buildings and spatial constructions that represent the welfare-security-space nexus related to the ideal typical social democratic welfare state (approximately built between 1970 and 2010).

According to Hobbes, the principal business of the state was to provide security (including safety and welfare).[17] The social democratic welfare state was a Cold War project. Military security and physical protection were, of course, major issues, but the Danish state left the hard-military security business to NATO and the United States. Denmark as a NATO member was protected by the US nuclear umbrella, which enabled Denmark to spend less on conventional defenses. This made the redistribution of wealth and social security the overshadowing political question in the twentieth century.

11 Tietgen Dormitory, Copenhagen, Lundgaard & Tranberg, 2004–05 for the Nordea Foundation.

12 Holstebro Town Hall and Library, Dall & Lindhardtsen, 1981–86.

Toward an Experimental Welfare State: Guardian of New Threats and New Uncertainties

The social democratic welfare state peaked in the 1980s, but criticism from the left and particular from the right (the neoliberal turn inspired by the American President Ronald Reagan and the British Prime Minister Margaret Thatcher) led to many reforms, and only a skeleton of the conventional top-down social democratic welfare state based upon universalism was left in the new millennium. Some events disturbed the social security consensus. After the collapse of the Soviet Union and an intensified globalization, the welfare state was exposed to severe competition and a major reform process started. Moreover, the incidents of September 11, 2001, brought back the need for physical security, and therefore many Western states had to allocate more resources to weaponry and surveillance technology. The rise and intensification of so-called terrorism, the rise of neonationalism and the rise of East Asia indicates that we are moving towards a more insecure world in which military threats play a role. The old security issue referring to physical security has returned.

People in modern societies have increasingly become more ontologically insecure, and it leads to identity problems, psychological problems and even personality disorders. More and more people are facing ontological insecurity, and increasingly they expect the state or other actors (for example voluntary associations, private firms, self-help groups, etc.) to provide help. In other words, a new form of insecurity has become important to address; whether or not the state can solve it, people have begun to expect that the state will take on that responsibility the same way it solves social security issues such as housing or poverty.

A fundamental trust in societal and public institutions combined with a basic trust in the people around us is the precondition for a stable life and the possibility of developing a self-identity with sufficient self-esteem to be an independent and competent person and citizen. The more people feel a lack of trust in public institutions, the more low self-esteem and greater difficulties behaving as a competent person in an increasingly complex world arise.

In other words, a key feature of contemporary society is a general, widespread ontological insecurity. We can add that many feel a strong need for protection of the environment. Climate change and environmental degradation are threats causing a lot of fear. Dystopia has certainly become a major dimension in recent film, fiction and poetry.

During the twentieth century, the Danish welfare state could usually deliver the type of security most people needed. During the last twenty to forty years, however, many new threats and uncertainties have appeared, and these could not be solved by the classic social democratic welfare state. In recent years we have been able to observe the emergence of what we could call the "experimental welfare state," in which the Danish state accepts the responsibility for providing security. The security pattern has become more complex. This has led to state experiments with new forms of collaboration with private businesses, philanthropic foundations, voluntary associations and other actors to find security solutions. Today, most citizens in the country expect the state to be responsible for providing security from these threats:

- Physical insecurity (random violence, state violence, terror, war);
- A general ontological uncertainty (low self-esteem, depression, obsession, PTSD);

- Spiritual insecurity (lack of meaning of life, lack of confidence or trust in public or private institutions);
- Environmental insecurity (environmental degradation, pollution);
- Climate change and insecurity (risk of extreme weather and floods, climate anxiety);
- Social insecurity (unemployment, lack of affordable housing, lack of childcare, healthcare, etc.).

The question is, of course, how this new "experimental welfare state" expresses itself in a spatial form. Is it possible to detect a change from the social democratic welfare state in the mid- and late twentieth century compared to the pluralistic welfare state of the twenty-first century? Of course, it is extremely difficult to point to buildings belonging to new discourses and a new paradigm, when we are just beginning to discover that a radical transformation is taking place and new discourses are emerging. Figures 13 to 18 are tentative examples of spatial constructions which contribute to a new conception of security and welfare – the experimental welfare state.

Welfare of Spaces, Spaces of Welfare: Architecture of Security and Architecture of *Salus Populi* – Instead of a Conclusion...

This chapter has questioned the conventional understanding of welfare and security. I have argued that security and welfare are concepts and practices which can hardly be distinguished from the other. They have merged into each other. Therefore, welfare and security are two sides of the same coin. Obviously, we can conclude that each period has a particular welfare-security-space nexus. It is, however, difficult to specify what this "space" is. One way to discuss the spatial character of these different nexuses would be to concentrate on the buildings applied to providing different welfare services. In other words, we define "welfare of space" and "space of welfare" as the buildings used for offering welfare to all citizens. Then we run into the problem of finding criteria with which we can categorize buildings and hereby determine whether two buildings belong to the same category. When we look at buildings from the early part of the twentieth century compared to buildings erected in the second part of the twentieth century, often regarded as the peak of the social democratic welfare state, we need criteria of importance to help us to determine the common denominators of welfare buildings designed in the early part of the twentieth century, in contrast to the common denominators we find among welfare buildings from the 1970s onward. Moreover, the challenge of pointing out common features among buildings from one of these two periods might not have anything to do with the welfare discourse. Differences and similarities might be linked to the dominant ideas

13 Copenhagen, 2018: A sculpture or an anti-terrorism spatial entity – or both?

14 Sønæs Climate-adaptation and Park-strategy. Møller & Grønborg for Viborg Kommune/Energy Viborg Sewage, 2016.

15

16

17

15 *Your Rainbow Panorama* by artist Olafur Eliasson at the ARoS Art Museum in Aarhus, 2010–11. The welfare state subsidies art – it can be seen as a way of providing spiritual security.
16 Livsrum Cancer Care Center, Herlev, Cornelius Vöge, 2017–20 for the Kræftens Bekæmpelse (Danish Cancer Society) with Realdania.
17 Psychiatric Hospital in Slagelse, Karlsson Arkitekter, 2010–15.
18 Job- and citizen service, Vordingborg, Casa Architects, 2019.

18

among architects, their many similar ideas reflecting a particular time or trend which has merged with some specific forms of aesthetics and cultural norms representing our time.

Another way of comparing the spatial aspect of these different nexuses – Denmark from the 1860s to World War II; the postwar period peaking in the best (social democratic) welfare state in the world (1950–2000); and the third nexus 2000–?, the "experimental welfare state" – can be done by observing that the key welfare and security institutions are few and simple in the beginning, but gradually, the number and complexity of welfare buildings increases until in the twenty-first century, all buildings and "accessories" (fences, stairs, stones, etc.) potentially can be turned into welfare/security issues. This might be one way of analyzing the spatial dimension. Space is redefined all the time from nexus to nexus because space is only conceived as buildings in the early period while in the twenty-first century, due to the extension and intensification of welfare/security conceptions, space explodes into many different aspects of the human environment, which become welfare- and security issues.

Despite our endeavor to unfold the concept of space and to look into space as a part of the welfare-security-space nexus, we have not succeeded in creating a more distinctive and precisely defined concept of space that can explain the spatial dimension of different types of welfare. We need more research here.

Yet it can be useful to start looking for concepts, theoretical-analytical frameworks and methodologies which can push us into a conceptualization of the spatial dimensions of welfare development.

A strong potential can be found in some of the work on spatiality done by the geographer Edward W. Soja, who operates with the concept of Thirdspace, which must be seen in relation to the three urban spaces: Firstspace, Secondspace and Thirdspace. The concept of Firstspace covers the physical built environment. In other words, this is the material dimension of the welfare institution emerging as an outcome of decisions, planning laws, etc. Secondspace is space perceived and conceived by the people who live in this space. Some norms determine how people might act or behave in that space. Thirdspace is "real and imagined" space, lived space, the way that people actually live in and experience urban space. Firstspace is tangible; we see and touch it. It is the buildings, the bench in the park, sculptures, the fire station or the lawns where children are playing. It is welfare as physical and "real." However, we perceive it differently and behave differently when we walk into parks, offices, leisure centers or schools. This is Secondspace, and it is a subjective process. In Thirdspace, "everything comes together [...] subjectivity and objectivity, the abstract and the concrete, the real and the imagined, the knowable and the unimaginable, the repetitive and the differential, structure and agency, mind and body, consciousness and the unconscious, the disciplined and the transdisciplinary, everyday life and unending history."[18]

Bibliography

Briggs, Asa. "The Welfare State in Historical Perspective." *European Journal of Sociology* 2, no. 2 (1961): 221–58.

Erikson, Eric. *Childhood and Society.* New York: W. W. Norton, 1963.

Giddens, Anthony. *The Consequences of Modernity*. Stanford: Stanford University Press, 1990.

——. *The Constitution of Society: Outline of the Theory of Structuration*. Cambridge: Polity Press, 1984.

——. *Modernity and Self-Identity: Self and Society in the Late Modern Age*. Cambridge: Polity Press, 1991.

Goffman, Erving. *The Presentation of Self in Everyday Life*. New York: Doubleday, 1959.

Hobbes, Thomas. *Leviathan*. Cambridge: Cambridge University Press, 1991 [1651].

Kaspersen, Lars Bo. *Denmark in the World*. Copenhagen: Hans Reitzels, 2014.

Laing, R. D. *Self and Others*, 2nd rev. ed. London: Penguin Books, 1971.

Lidegaard, Bo. "Systemet Munch – 50 år efter." *Radikal Historie* 1, appendix to *Radikal Politik* 9 (1998).

Marshall, T. H. *Social Policy*. London: Hutchinson & Co, 1965.

Marwick, Arthur. *War and Social Change in the Twentieth Century*. London: Macmillan, 1984.

Munch, Peter. *Det ny Aarhundrede* 2 (1907–08).

Nietzsche, Friedrich Wilhelm. *On the Genealogy of Morals: A Polemic*, translated by Michael A. Scarpitti. London: Penguin Books, 2013 [1887].

Skinner, Quentin. "Freedom and the Historian." In *Liberty Before Liberalism*, 101–20. Cambridge: Cambridge University Press, 1998.

——. "States and the Freedom of Citizens." In *States and Citizens: History, Theory, Prospects*, edited by Quentin Skinner and Bo Stråht, 11–27. Cambridge: Cambridge University Press, 2003.

Soja, Edward W. *Thirdspace*. Malden, MA: Blackwell, 1996.

Notes

1 Thus, the development of social policies in many European countries created a category of "social benefit receivers." Many people tacitly regard the segment of society receiving different forms of public money (social benefits) as existing in the same social space (in which people drink, smoke, use drugs, etc.).

2 Some new buildings have been spectacular in recent years. For example, new schools and new buildings at higher educational institutions such as Kilen at Copenhagen Business School or The Mærsk Tower at the University of Copenhagen.

3 "The welfare state" and "the welfare society" are often used interchangeably. They are often used in political discourses and they are often defined and understood in different ways. They are excellent examples of ideological concepts which "escape definition."

4 Asa Briggs, "The Welfare State in Historical Perspective," *European Journal of Sociology* 2, no. 2 (1961): 221–58.

5 Arthur Marwick, *War and Social Change in the Twentieth Century* (London: Macmillan, 1984).

6 T. H. Marshall, *Social Policy* (London: Hutchinson & Co, 1965).

7 Quentin Skinner, "States and the Freedom of Citizens," in *States and Citizens: History, Theory, Prospects*, ed. Quentin Skinner and Bo Stråht (Cambridge: Cambridge University Press, 2003), 11–27; and Quentin Skinner, "Freedom and the Historian," in Skinner, *Liberty Before Liberalism* (Cambridge: Cambridge University Press, 1998), 101–20. Skinner is inspired by the method applied by the philosopher Friedrich Wilhelm Nietzsche in his *On the Genealogy of Morality: A Polemic*, trans. Michael A. Scarpitti (London: Penguin Books, 2013 [1887]).

8 By quasi-genealogy, we mean a "short version" – it is beyond the scope of this paper to do a more comprehensive conceptual history of the concept of welfare.

9 Thomas Hobbes, *Leviathan* (Cambridge: Cambridge University Press, 1991 [1651]), 9.

10 Hobbes, *Leviathan*, 89.

11 See, for example, Eric Erikson, *Childhood and Society* (New York: W. W. Norton, 1963); R. D. Laing, *Self and Others*, 2nd rev. ed. (London: Penguin Books, 1971); Erving Goffman, *The Presentation of Self in Everyday Life* (New York: Doubleday, 1959); Anthony Giddens, *Modernity and Self-Identity: Self and Society in the Late Modern Age* (Cambridge: Polity Press, 1992).

12 Anthony Giddens, *The Consequences of Modernity* (Stanford: Stanford University Press, 1990), 92.

13 Anthony Giddens, *The Constitution of Society: Outline of the Theory of Structuration* (Cambridge: Polity Press, 1984), 375.

14 The Hobbesian welfare discourse is broader than those we find in the nineteenth and twentieth centuries. Although safety and security might seem almost interchangeable, we find that there are small differences. *Salus* comes from *salvus*, and it becomes *safety* in English. It means the condition of being safe, freedom from danger, harm or risk. In Danish we will translate it into "i behold," *uskadt og rask*. *Security* stems from *securus* which means "the state of being secure," feeling safe and not worried. *Security* seems to cover the notion of ontological security as well as protection against lawbreakers, etc. *Salus/safety* is almost a more visible protection against physical and spiritual dangers.

15 Peter Munch, quoted in Bo Lidegaard, "Systemet Munch – 50 år efter," *Radikal Historie 1*, appendix to *Radikal Politik 9* (1998). Translation from the Danish by the author.

16 Peter Munch, *Det ny Aarhundrede* 2 (1907–08): 549.

17 These concepts cover physical protection (from violent assaults, the encroachment on the domain of sovereignty by foreign enemies); protection against market failures (social security); protection against the tacit and unintelligible fear which appears now and again (ontological security); and protection against mental disturbances (the existence of ideologies which provide meaning of life).

18 Edward W. Soja, *Thirdspace* (Malden, MA: Blackwell, 1996), 56–57.

Spaces and Measures between Welfare State and Security State

Deane Simpson

This article explores transformations in public space in Denmark in the period 1970 to today. It focuses first on the evolving presence of physical security measures in public spaces within the urban core of Copenhagen, in the context of theorizations of the security turn's reorientation of the role of the state and its priorities vis-à-vis welfare.[1] Here, the actors, planning and implementation processes of adopting physical security measures are addressed, along with their spatial impact; to interpret the extent of a hypothetical shift.[2] Second, the article explores these developments in a longer time frame by comparing the contemporary spatial and material conditions of securitized spaces of today with those same spaces around 1970, at the height of the so-called golden age of the Danish welfare state. I will attempt to frame the contrasting conditions of those public spaces within a broader urban development context and reflect on the shifting urban welfare imaginaries evident from the spatial conditions themselves. To what extent do these postmillennium (terror) security-driven transformations of public space represent a rupture from – or continuity with – the wider post-1970 developments in urban public space?

Methodologically, the work draws upon empirical, theoretical and historical material; surveys of theoretical and applied literature, media reporting and public discourse; interviews with key actors and experts; urban fieldwork including drawn documentation and comparative mapping; and analysis incorporating contemporary and archival photography.

Urban Security

The concept of urban security is linked to a long historical conception of cities as the physical manifestation of an ongoing dialogue between defensive and offensive military technologies.[3] This has resulted in generations of perimeter defenses increasingly distanced from urban centers.[4]

1.01
Copenhagen's historical fortification development

This tendency would be disrupted, according to geographer Stephen Graham, with events such as the World Trade Center terror attacks of 2001, and attacks in the years following in the public spaces of European cities such as Madrid, London, Paris, Brussels, Oslo, Stockholm, Nice and Berlin. Following the détente of the Cold War, and the so-called end of history[5] marked by the breakdown of the Soviet Union, these events would define "the first time since the Middle Ages [that] the city becom[es] the main 'battlespace' both at home and abroad."[6] Whereas the historical conception of the secure city was based on a symmetrical threat from the outside (e.g. a competing city- or nation-state), this evolving contemporary conception would be framed as an asymmetrical threat from within – in which "both security and military doctrine within Western states now cent[ers] on the task of identifying [and securing against] insurgents, terrorists or malign threats from the chaotic background of urban life."[7] The evolving nature of this threat and associated forms of attack – from armed attack to suicide bombing, to car or truck bomb, to vehicle-based pedestrian attack – has led to varying degrees of target hardening of cities through the introduction of physical measures, such as walls, barriers, gates, bollards, guard-posts, X-ray stations, sluices, etc. in spaces of airports, ports and increasingly in public spaces of the city itself.[8]

1 Development of physical security measures at Christiansborg Slotsplads, 2009, 2014, 2021.

The focus on securing populations against the threat of terrorism in the post-9/11 period has been identified by commentators as pointing to significant transformations in the role and focus of the state. Stephen Graham, for example, refers to a "securocratic transformation" taking place, particularly in the US and UK, in which "welfare states are simultaneously being re-engineered as risk-management systems [...] geared not towards the social welfare of communities but towards controlling the location, behavior and future of seemingly risky 'anti-citizens.'"[9] This is linked to the implementation of policies such as zero tolerance/quality-of-life policing beginning in the 1990s and the notion of what Phil Scraton has described as "authoritarian renewal."[10] These developments are commonly linked in a European context to intensified public debates on immigration and integration and unfold in a broad range of operations focused on profiled areas of the city and profiled segments of the population – from increased police presence to digital surveillance and deradicalization initiatives.[11]

Between Social Security and Physical Security

Security has been positioned similarly by sociologist Lars Bo Kaspersen as a central notion in framing the development of the Danish welfare state. He describes state formation in terms of Norbert Elias's notion of "the survival unit" – an entity attempting to secure itself against various existential threats at different moments in history, whether physical, spiritual, social or otherwise.[12] The example of the post–World War II welfare state is described by Kaspersen according to its predominant focus on *social* security – addressing the threats of the European industrial city.[13] Post-9/11, the Danish state underwent a shift in focus toward physical security. He argues that this corresponds to a shift from a liberal democratic state toward an authoritarian liberalist one – within the context of Denmark's participation in the war on terror; in light of anti-terrorism legislation limiting civil rights central to democracy; etc. For Kaspersen, this reorientation not only emerges as a response to terror, but to a wider form of "ontological insecurity," including climate change, crime, pandemics, etc. This implies that evolving forms of physically secured space correspond to evolving conceptions of welfare delivery. Such a framing provides a departure point from which to map and analyze whether or not emerging physical security measures might constitute a tendency toward an emerging security (welfare) state in the setting of Denmark's capital, Copenhagen – and they provide a relevant context from which to reflect on the transformations of public space over the last five decades, and their relation to welfare.[14]

2 Introduction of physical security measures at Nyhavn, 2017.

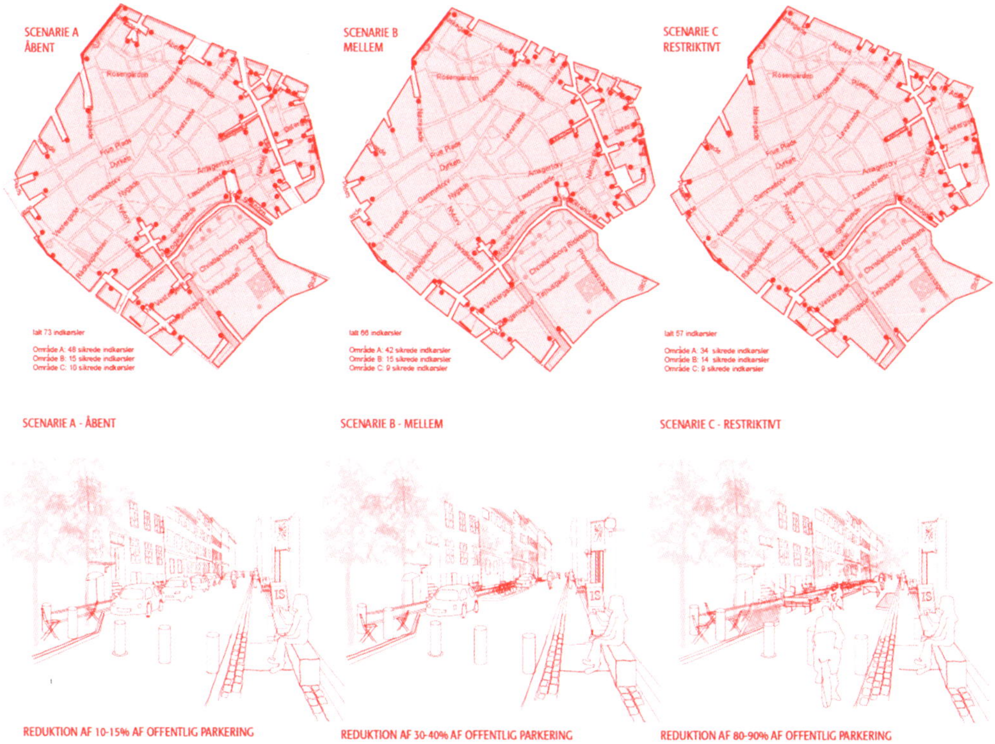

3 Three scenarios for securitization/traffic reduction of medieval urban core commissioned by Copenhagen Municipality, 2017–19.

Short Game: State-of-Exception Planning

Urban planning decisions addressing key public spaces in Copenhagen have, particularly since 2011, been informed by a different hierarchy of drivers, actors and decision-making processes to those of the typical democratic conventions of the Danish planning system.

The July 2011 truck bombing of Oslo's government quarter, for example, would trigger significant debate in Denmark, including the Danish Police Intelligence Service (PET)'s advising that the level of security at the Danish parliament be elevated significantly from December 2011.[15] A perimeter of rough-hewn granite blocks would be installed at Christiansborg Slotsplads as a temporary counter-terrorism measure in April 2013, which would be replaced by a permanent ring of granite balls in January 2019.[16] ⟨fig. 1⟩ The February 2015 terror attack in Copenhagen would be followed by the introduction of physical security measures (PSMs) at sites of the Jewish community along with the introduction of around-the-clock policing presence.[17] The December 19, 2016, Berlin Christmas market truck attack would be followed on December 20 by PET's and Copenhagen Police's advice for extensive PSMs, leading to the same-day installation of concrete barriers by the municipality of Copenhagen.[18] ⟨fig. 2⟩ The Barcelona truck attack on August 17, 2017, would be followed on August 24, 2017, by a controversial proposal by Copenhagen Municipality's Technical and Environmental Administration (TMF) to close off the medieval urban core from car traffic – a proposal previously floated in November 2015.[19] ⟨fig. 3⟩

4 *Ekstra Bladet* newspaper headline, October 13, 2010: "Al Qaeda threatens Denmark: Killing Machine on Strøget."

Within these distant and lightning-fast (in urban development terms) action and reaction dynamics, the complex actor-network of city space production defines increasingly important roles for certain actors: particularly the police and intelligence agencies; and politicians – with the Danish media playing an important role in building up an enhanced psychological sensitivity to the theme of terror through its extensive coverage of related events and its elaboration, particularly in the popularist press of an "Islamic terror threat."[20] ⟨fig. 4⟩

Responsible for monitoring, evaluating and advising on a landscape of threats, PET's more recent central role in influencing public space is articulated through a series of mechanisms, including their published threat advisories; specific advisory maps; and published terror security guidelines.[21] ⟨fig. 5⟩ Perhaps the most influential of these on the physical environment has been the protected areas map drawn up by PET in 2017 identifying nine sites requiring further protection based on a series of parameters including "busy places where many people gather, vehicle availability, possible escape routes for civilians, internationally known sites and obvious tourist destinations as well as special local conditions."[22]

1.05–07
Nine [terror-]protected zones recommended by PET to Copenhagen municipality and Copenhagen Police, 2017

Copenhagen Police play an important role in the local assessments and recommendations with respect to securing specific local spaces in dialogue with TMF. Within this dynamic action-reaction environment, fast political decisions also play a central role.[23] The media prominence and political nature of the theme has intensified the political discourse around it – to the extent that the physical elements themselves have become heavily loaded symbolically. Architect and commentator Holger Dahl, for example, sketches the concept of a political spectrum of interpretation between

> well-intended diversity advocates [who] would of course like to see the futile barriers covered in flowers to avoid "letting the terrorists win," while the anti-immigration wing sees the planters as the quintessential symbol of left-wing hypocrisy. The right wing prefers the raw concrete; like the armed police in front of the Copenhagen synagogue that puts everyone on notice that our freedom is under threat. The raw concrete barrier has become a political recruitment tool; the civil war that the most aggressive members of the anti-immigrant wing anticipate is made visible by the barriers.[24]

These controversies have extended to Far Right politicians such as Pernille Vermund (Nye Borgerlige), who provocatively referred to concrete Jersey barriers (normally referred to as "betonklodser") as "koranklodser" (Koran blocks).[25]

5 PET guideline: "Think terrorist security in outdoor public spaces: A guide to addressing the risk of vehicle attacks in outdoor public spaces," 2019.

The speed and reactiveness of these dynamics has tended to circumvent, reduce or delay the roles of other actors and processes, particularly civil society actors. In a contrasting development, the last decade has seen an intensification of private-sector actors in the Danish context promoting the need for and use of security products (for example, Perimeter Security) and security advisory or design services (for example, Schønherr/SLA/Gehl etc.). Contributing to the latter development has been the Confederation of Danish Industry's focus on this "growth sector" with its Vagt- og SikkerhedsIndustrien (VSI) group – representing income of around 4.4 billion DKK in 2018.[26] Many of its member firms have been actively lobbying entities such as the Municipality of Copenhagen to sell goods or services to be deployed in the city's public spaces.[27]

While difficult to quantify fully in terms of exact values of shifting resources from social security to physical security measures, there has been a significant amount of public resources attributed to terror security projects across a range of contexts since 2001, and more intensively since 2011.[28] In broad terms, categories of expenditures on security across various contexts include: airport and port security, costs of contributing to the war on terror, parliamentary and ministry security, embassy security, media security, security for the Jewish community, PET operations, security advisory and public space security, etc. Copenhagen, for example, with its three-digit millions kroner security budget in the mid-2010s, would be among four of Denmark's largest urban municipalities addressing the national government with concerns over budget trade-offs between physical and social security, in 2017, warning that: "If the municipalities are to continue to pay for terrorist security themselves, it will affect core welfare and slow down the construction of, for example, kindergartens and schools."[29] A number of cases point to not-insignificant expenditures: the perimeter protection of Danish Parliament, for example, cost approximately 50 million DKK,[30] while the proposed scenarios for the protection of Copenhagen's medieval city perimeter range in cost from 143–261 million DKK.[31] And these costs addressing physical security measures should be placed within a wider context of counterterrorism and security expenditures addressing dynamic security (for example, police personnel), public space surveillance (such as CCTV); online/digital surveillance; and also programs directed toward preventing and countering violent extremism and radicalization (CVE), which play an important supplementary role in the Danish context. In its integrated approach across various ministries, social agencies, schools, police, etc, the latter item highlights the blurry line between categories of physical and social security.[32] ⟨fig. 6⟩

Et stærkt værn mod terror

12 nye tiltag mod terror

Februar 2015 Regeringen

Tabel 1. Nye tiltag mod terror

Mio. kr. (2015-pl)	2015	2016	2017	2018	I alt 2015-2018
Udgifter på politiets område i alt	**80**	**125**	**146**	**146**	**497**
Udbygning af politiets og PET's beredskabs- og overvågningsindsats	50	50	50	50	200
Øget it- og analysekapacitet	21	44	44	44	153
Udvidelse af livvagtsstyrken	-	11	22	22	55
Udvidelse af aktionsstyrken	-	11	21	21	53
Forstærket nationalt døgnberedskab	9	9	9	9	36
Udgifter på Forsvarsministeriets område i alt	**55**	**100**	**130**	**130**	**415**
Øget indhentnings- og analysekapacitet	51	93	121	121	386
Styrkelse af det internationale samarbejde og samarbejdet med PET	2	4	6	6	19
Styrket indsats mod cyberterror	1	2	3	3	9
Udgifter på Udenrigsministeriets område i alt	**44**	**7**	**4**	**4**	**59**
Styrkelse af Det Arabiske Initiativ (3-årigt tilsagn afgivet i 2015)	40	-	-	-	40
International dialog om terror, sikkerhed og anti-radikalisering mv.	4	7	4	4	19
Udgifter i alt	**179**	**232**	**280**	**280**	**971**

6 Danish Government's 2015 proposal "A strong defense against terrorism: 12 new measures against terrorism," committing 971 million Danish kroner to terror defense between 2015 and 2018.

Long Game: Circumscribed Securitization

In this network of actors, TMF has played an expanded role in the longer-term negotiation, reduction or transformation of physical security measures after their immediate introduction as a response to PET and the Copenhagen Police's call for concrete Jersey barrier construction measures.[33] This has developed in stages, firstly as a temporary upgrading through "beautification" or "naïve-ification," followed by their replacement with permanent or semipermanent "aesthetically processed" measures resembling urban furniture, such as bollards, large planters, trees, bike stands, benches or sculptures.[34] ⟨fig. 7⟩ Many of these elements were already incorporated in the city's urban design manual – driven by an attempt to minimize their visual and psychological presence in public space.[35]

1.08–09
Copenhagen physical security measures
1.10
Copenhagen physical security measures, detail

In responding to the 2016/17 situations, TMF's emerging stance on physical security measures would evolve into six principles that would actively attempt to limit and minimize their impact: (1) intervene proportionally; (2) accept risk; (3) add value; (4) minimize; (5) cooperate; and (6) consider temporality.[36] This would contribute toward producing a significantly circumscribed form of securitized public space in comparison to that produced in environments such as the US, UK or Israel. Anthropologist Stine Illum argues that this evolving reaction of TMF allowed for "continuity with a long-term urban morality, including values and materiality

7 Naïve-ification and beautification of physical security measures: Gammel Torv, Nyhavn, Rådhuspladsen, Copenhagen.

associated with liberal democracy and the Danish welfare state such as community, inclusiveness, openness, and spaciousness."[37]

Urban Structures of Security/Inaccessibility

Mapping these evolving securitization-effected spaces at an overall city scale reveals different typologies of a partially securitized city.[38] The recently secured public spaces identified in PET's 2017 assessment as potentially at risk of terror attack in the city due to their crowded nature come into focus. The resulting map of the city – distinguishing between those areas secured and those not – corresponds to an overlay of the most heavily populated touristic and commercial/retail/entertainment public spaces with the city center (Tivoli, Strøget, Nyhavn, Kongens Nytorv, Amalienborg Slotsplads, Langelinie); the most important political/representational/democratic spaces in the form of the symbolic spaces of municipal government (Rådhuspladsen) and national government (Christiansborg Slotsplads); and the busiest local collective transport hubs (Central Station and Nørreport Station). The location of and concentration of terror-secured spaces, articulates a centripetally oriented city – heavily directed toward the center of the urban core.

Copenhagen's network of secured or inaccessible spaces at the beginning of the 1970s – which were not designed to perform an anti-terror security role – reveals a quite different structuring of the city. In a period in which the urban core of the city was simultaneously experiencing industrial decline, economic stagnation and growing problems of social exclusion the secured areas around 1970 would be concentrated not along the pedestrian spine of the city, but along the harbor's edge in particular, bounding the areas of more significant (although declining) military, heavy industry and port activity compared to that of today.[39] Many of those formerly restricted harborfront sites have since become accessible as prominent public spaces of the livable city.

1.03
Copenhagen inaccessible and secure spaces, 1970
1.04
Copenhagen inaccessible and secure spaces, 2022

Public Space Transformation 1970–Today

By analytically mapping relevant contemporary securitized public spaces identified in PET's "green map" and a corresponding mapping of those same spaces based on archival photographs from around 1970, it is possible to identify shifts in the use, character, and symbolism of these public

spaces between these periods. In this case, three of Copenhagen's most iconic touristic/retail/entertainment spaces are analyzed:
Kongens Nytorv,
1.12–13
Securitized public space: Kongens Nytorv, ca. 1970/2022
Nyhavn,
1.15–16
Securitized public space: Nyhavn, ca. 1970/2022
and Amagertorv;
1.18–19
Securitized public space: Amagertorv, ca. 1970/2022
along with the politically representative space of Christiansborg Slotsplads
1.21–22
Securitized public space: Christiansborg Slotsplads, ca. 1970/2022
in front of the Danish Parliament. All of them are located at the center of the historical core of Copenhagen and may be framed as emblematic Danish examples of contemporary terror-secured public space. Those same spaces, however, stand at the margins of the public space production of the larger centrifugal urban development dynamics of the early 1970s. The massive expansion of the suburban periphery according to the principles of the 1947 Finger Plan during this period was governed to a large extent by the tenets of modernist urban planning applied broadly as a response to the shortcomings of the industrial city.⟨fig. 8⟩ This involved the buildup of state welfare institutions such as kindergartens, schools, hospitals, care homes and so forth, and an extensive development of nonprofit housing.[40] ⟨fig. 9⟩ Within a modernist, rationalist and functionalist framework of planning, the "ground" of the figure-ground relation would play a significant but often secondary role to the "figure" of housing and welfare institutions. In this sense, a primary function of public space has been that of a spacing device operating at three levels: (1) as a spacing device between buildings (institutions/housing) irrigating for light and air, filled with greenery/nature – and often the default material of lawn; (2) the spacing between functional zones of the city, separating for example, industry functions from housing to limit contamination, such as industrial air pollution; and (3) spacing apart and linking together the larger functional areas of the city schematically conceptualized according to the 8+8+8 hour day – the palm of the Finger Plan as the predominant site of work, commerce and to some extent leisure; the fingers as site of housing; and the wedges, recreation. The four public spaces addressed in more detail here reinforce a conception of public space within the declining urban core at the beginning of the 1970s ⟨fig. 10⟩ functioning as an important infrastructure between the space of residence and the space of work, commerce and leisure – effectively as traffic infrastructure for mobile and parked automobiles, which is so evident in archival photographs.[41]
1.14
Securitized public space: Kongens Nytorv, ca. 1970
1.17
Securitized public space: Nyhavn, ca. 1970
1.20
Securitized public space: Amagertorv, ca. 1970
1.23
Securitized public space: Christiansborg Slotsplads, ca. 1970

8 Building age, Copenhagen.
9 Brøndby Strand, Copenhagen, ca. 1970.

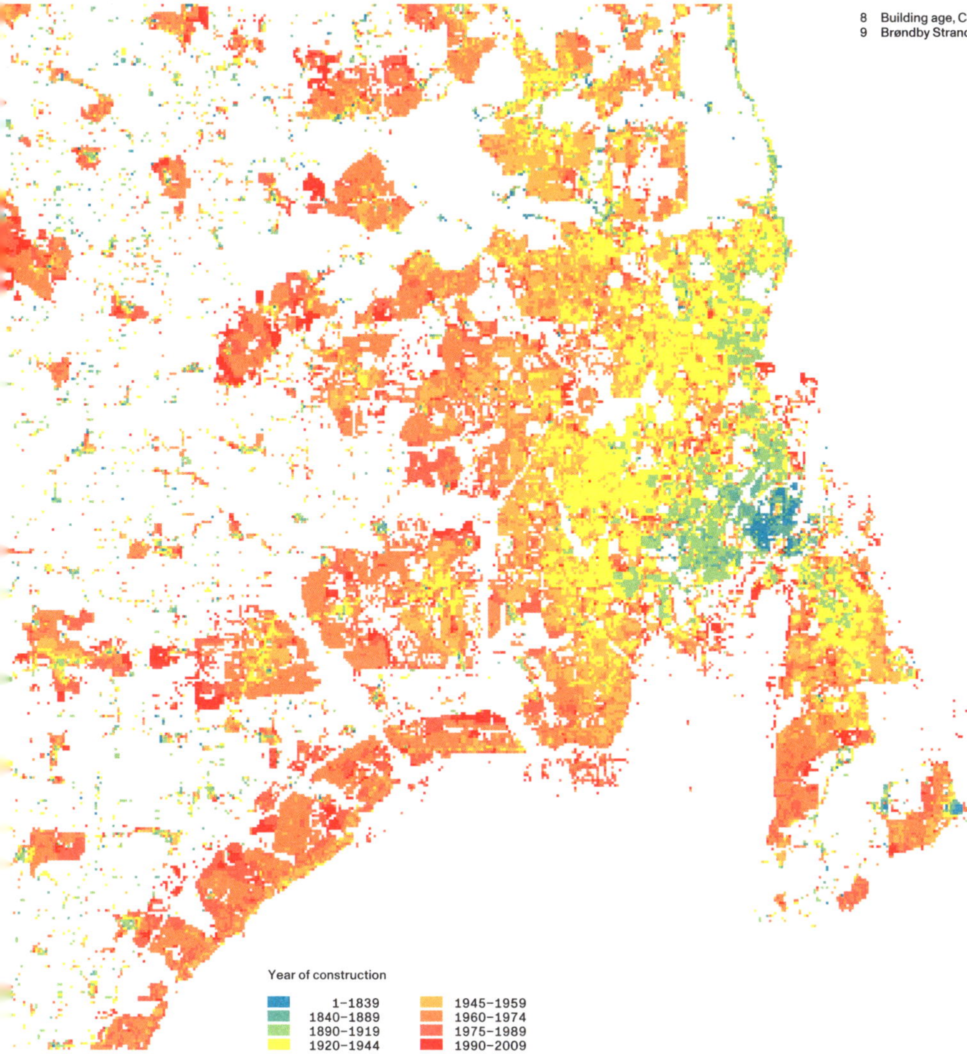

8

9

10 Sankt Annæ Gade, Christianshavn, Copenhagen, 1969. Museum of Copenhagen/Visda.

Significant developments over this period in the physical condition, performance and conceptual framing of public space – and its relation to welfare – should be understood in the context of two parallel developments during the last half century. On the one hand, evolving cultural conceptions of the role of public space in the inclusive, solidaric or "good" city,[42] and on the other, growing considerations of public space's central role in performing according to the political-economic logic of an evolving competitive, attractive or entrepreneurial city paradigm.[43] Over the last two decades, these developments, have been increasingly absorbed under the term *liveability* – a term that itself has been entwined with the theme of security, and one that has been broadly used in place of *welfare*.

Political-Economic Shifts toward Public Spaces of the Competitive City

In economic terms, the radical decentralized development of the postwar welfare city, would see the erosion of the tax base as Copenhagen municipality's population declined considerably from 1950 to 1975,[44] leaving behind what has been characterized by some as a city of welfare recipients. Coinciding with the oil crisis and developing economic crisis of the 1970s, the continued erosion of the municipality's economic position throughout the 1970s and '80s would find the city in deep crisis on the verge of bankruptcy in the early 1990s. This was addressed with initiatives led by the national conservative government to refocus investment and development on the city and the capital region to develop its competitiveness with respect to other European centers in attracting tourists, investment, multinational companies and highly educated international knowledge workers. This would play out in a wider strategy of "entrepreneurial urbanism" with investments in infrastructure.[45] At a municipal level a strategy to counter conventional housing career patterns to retain taxpayers, focused on improving the attractiveness of Copenhagen for keeping young families and the middle class in the city. As Copenhagen's head of planning Holger Bisgaard explained in 2000:

> If we can't change [Copenhagen's] housing stock, we will continue to be the poorest municipality in the capital region. We won't change the type of people living here, and so the municipality won't become sustainable... We have made a study that shows that we get all the trash, pardon the expression, because of the cheap housing. The middle class, who we would want to stay, moves to Sweden.[46]

This period would see changes in the housing policy agreed between the conservative government and the social democratic-led municipality, investments in institutions, but also importantly in a range of developments addressing public space framed as a form of strategic investment.[47]

Cultural Shifts toward Public Spaces of the Good City

Culturally, resistance to modernist functionalist planning of cities was already developing internationally in the 1960s, when protests in the Danish context against larger infrastructural and urban development projects within the historical urban core challenged projects such as City West, and the Søringen project within the inner city, along with local neighborhood uplift projects.⟨figs. 12–13⟩ This shift would be supported by more articulate arguments for the urban fabric and public space of the premodernist planned city, including Jane Jacobs and William H. Whyte, and locally, a number of actors, including Jan Gehl.[48] Gehl's *Life Between Buildings* – influenced by his wife, the psychologist, Ingrid Gehl – provided broad critiques and analyses of the implication of modernist urban planning on public space and public life – particularly the negative impact of the car and the challenges of inhuman scale, monotony and social alienation it contributes to.[49] The Gehls' project would be based around the notion of placing the universal psychosocial and physical needs of the human subject at the center of a conception of public space within the good city. Tom Nielsen describes this development as one distinguishing between a modernist and contemporary logic of the welfare city: "The early idea was centered around the more mechanical demands, such as fresh air, a minimum supply of space and accessibility. The contemporary idea of universal demands promoted by Gehl is related more to the psychological and social needs of the human being."[50]

11 Demonstration against Søringen, Fredensgade, Copenhagen, 1971.

12 Model of City Plan Vest/Søringen proposal, Copenhagen, 1959.

13 Cover of Mette Lis Andersen et al, *Bedre Byrum* [Better Public Space], 2002.

These intentions are expressed in Gehl's notion of a reprioritizing of the componentry of the modernist city considering "public life before public space and public space before buildings in a way that sets the frame for community but also for diversity and individual needs"[51] with an emphasis on the role of public space as central in facilitating society's social coherence – as a kind of glue for the welfare society. The development of this approach toward public space's role in the "good city" has been framed also more generally as "a reflection of wider societal values of liberal democracy and the welfare state, including community, inclusiveness, openness, and spaciousness."[52] Nielsen frames the influence of these cultural shifts in forming the notion of a Danish model of democratic urban public space built upon the ethos of the Danish welfare state: to provide "all citizens with equal rights and chances for a good life [...] through equal access to common public goods."[53] This developing approach to public space would be supported, in broader terms, by other influential actors including foundations such as Realdania, founded in 2000, providing important philanthropic support for research, public debate and the support of realizing projects in the face of scarcer public funds.[54] ⟨fig. 13⟩

Common Ground: Toward the Livable City

The evolving conceptions of the good and competitive city would converge at the beginning of the 2000s around the term *livability*. Livability would gain political support by absorbing, on the one hand, the intention to develop a socially coherent infrastructure of public space for the good life of all citizens; and on the other, an attractive urban landscape capable of competing internationally in the market for tourists, investment, knowledge workers, etc.[55] In relation to the latter, public space would play a central role in the urban experience economy of the livable city as a so-called quality-of-life driver and key to interurban competitiveness. Livability would structure a range of influential political initiatives that would impact the physical composition of the city. These would include the Copenhagen municipality TMF's various published strategies, which place public space in focus.[56] *Liveability* recurs as a ubiquitous term in these publications, while the term *welfare* is conspicuous in its absence. The importance of the concept of livability and the role of livability rankings in policy is underlined by the former mayor's claims that "The philosophy behind all the development in the city [of Copenhagen] comes down to the question of livability."[57]

14 Video stills, *Copenhagen, World's Most Livable City from Quality of Life Cities*, 2014.

Middle-class-ization of Copenhagen and Its Public Space/Middle-class-ization of Welfare

Several commentators have described the impact of Copenhagen's livability-focused urban redevelopment in transforming much of the unruly urban core of the 1970s, '80s and '90s into a more polished series of urban spaces, just as the socioeconomic demographic makeup of the city would undergo radical transformation.[58] While receiving international acclaim as a model of urban livability,⟨fig. 14⟩ critics have accused the city of promoting an overly economically focused urban planning framework, primarily addressing the affluent local and global middle class rather than a universal welfare subject.[59] This condition aligns to political scientist Carsten Jensen's description of the transformation of welfare and its delivery in Denmark over recent decades.[60] He describes how it is still a central concept in Danish society and politics, but one that is eroding in its universality, according to a middle-class agenda – on the platform of commonly demanded healthcare, childcare and education. Critique has focused on increasingly gentrified areas and public spaces within the large urban centers, accessible to those with the resources to operate within an increasingly unaffordable context.[61] This evolving gentrification of the international model of the "livable city" and its natural extension as the "smart city," represents, according to Rem Koolhaas, a radical shift from the ethos of the postwar modernist welfare city in which

> traditional European values of liberty, equality and fraternity have been replaced in the twenty-first century by comfort [livability], security, and sustainability [...] With safety and security as selling points, the city has become vastly less adventurous and more predictable [...] Maybe it is no coincidence that "livable" – flat – cities like Vancouver, Melbourne and even Perth are replacing traditional metropolises in our imaginary.[62]

Jens Kvorning, Carsten Thau and Martin Zerlang articulate a similar de-metropolitization of the predictability and banality of the contemporary "Whopper-ization" of parts of Strøget, along with the dominating commercial logics that have pushed out smaller retailers and more complex urban life to other parts of the city – compared to Strøget's more dynamic role as a public space in the 1960s.[63] An awareness of this process is emphasized in the city's own reaction to these concerns, in the 2015 Co-Create Copenhagen Strategy call for "A City with an Edge."[64]

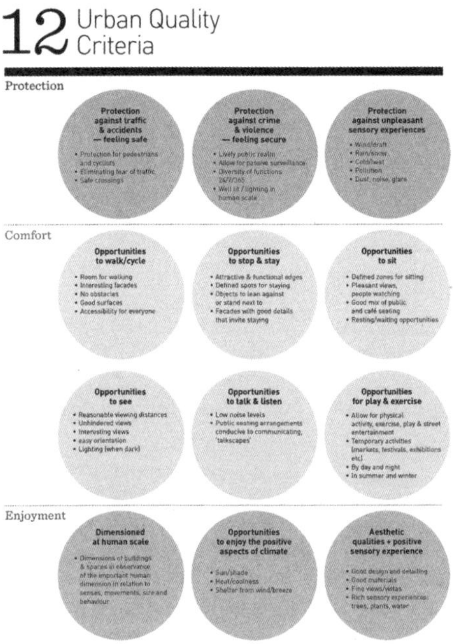

15 Urban Quality Criteria, 2018.

Securitization as Rupture vs Continuity of the Livable (Welfare) City

While recent securitization developments of certain public spaces of Copenhagen have been described as a challenge or rupture to the livable city,[65] it is suggested here that these developments may also be understood in their longer-term transformations as more continuous with the logics of the livable city – as a transformation of the welfare city according to the combined logics of the good city (which Illum focuses on) and the competitive city. Safety and security for example play a central role in Jan Gehl's quality criteria for livable public space – involving three of the twelve categories – and these concepts play an equally central role in the various liveability indexes, from *Monocle* to *Mercer*.[66] ⟨fig. 17⟩ The prioritization of taming and controlling acceptable urban activity, its focus on commercial behavior, the regime of outdoor café seating and its policing and surveillance by police, commercial actors and security guards has a considerable impact on what behavior is encouraged or tolerated within public space. The safety and cleanliness of the livable and attractive tourist city has been the grounds for incidents or defensive measures against, for example, the homeless and Romani in public spaces.[67]

In physical material terms, after the initial short-term shock of the introduction of crude concrete blocks as antivehicle physical urban security measures in 2016 for example, the deliberate downplaying of security theater and aestheticization of measures in the form of planters, and their absorption into other urban furniture components of the livable city such as bike racks or urban sculptures would further articulate their integration with livable city concepts.[68] This longer-term process of circumscribed and negotiated securitization and its conscious absorption into the livability frameworks of the city can be contrasted to the more extensive and less aesthetically considered security theater in the UK or US contexts.

Similar techniques to those developed by Gehl to quantify the success of dense vibrant urban life would be used to identify the sites of greatest threat/vulnerability in the context of exposure to the risk of terror, as described in the UK Government's guidelines "Crowded Spaces: The Planning System and Counter-Terrorism" and PET's own counterterrorism guide, "Tænk terrorsikkerhed i udendørs offentlige rum."[69] ⟨fig. 5⟩ It would therefore be the most trafficked and iconic spaces of the livable city that would also require the greatest physical protection – just as the COVID-19 pandemic would align the threat of contagion with crowded spaces and a lack of social distancing. Just as the state played a key role in imposing physical protection in public space against a perceived terror threat, it has also assumed responsibility for securing the use of and access to public space, through the pandemic – whether in the form of limiting public gathering numbers, closing outdoor

Kritik: Kabell misbruger terror-anbefaling til bilfri bymidte

Et københavnsk, rødt flertal stemte torsdag aften for et forslag om at lukke Københavns bymidte for biltrafik. Et snigangreb, mener Venstre og Konservative.

Lyt til artiklen

16 News headline: "Criticism: Kabell misuses terror advisory for car-free city center," 2017. Source: TV2/Lorry.

17 Early registrations of conflict between pedestrian and automobile: Carl Røgind, Excerpts from "Automobilet kommer" postcard series, Aalborg, Ribe, Assens, ca. 1900–10.

café seating areas, demarcating one-way pedestrian routes, or cordoning off playgrounds etc.

The livable city focus on the role of public space in quality of life and subjective well-being holds both physical and psychological components.[70] These have been emphasized in political documents addressing public space over the last two decades along with the messaging from key actors such as the city architect – in which public space's capacity to support bicycling is presented in terms of improved health conditions, in which the use of and access to outdoor public space is attached to improved physical and mental health outcomes. The dimension of subjective well-being as a measurement of welfare and its measurement in the form of happiness indexes has been identified as being both aligned to discourses on the good city and as an emerging form of neoliberal governmentality aligned to what Eva Illouz has framed as "emotional capitalism."[71] With this intensifying attention to the impacts of physical environment on mental wellbeing, TMF's concerns over the emotional responses of physical security measures have played an important role in their reflections. This would relate to diverse findings addressing the levels of fear or safety or trust that these measures would invoke in citizens.[72] While PET was involved in a survey in 2016 that argued that the majority of those exposed to physical security measures in public space would feel safer rather than fearful,[73] a number of prominent urban researchers have documented the impact of the expanded application of physical security measures in introducing or intensifying spatial and social fragmentation and exclusion in our cities, producing spaces that engender a sense of distrust.[74] Furthermore, this intersection of securitization and urbanization has been defined by a series of thinkers such as Stephen Graham or Peter Marcuse as a threat to what Mona Fawaz et al. describe as "the very core of what urbanization means in terms of encounters with strangers, the freedom of anonymity, or the potential for political action for which the city has long been celebrated."[75]

The livable/secure city nexus is further highlighted in the alignments and interchangabilty of arguments that followed the TMF mayor's 2017 proposal to close car access to the medieval urban core justified according to reducing the risk of a terrorist attack.[76] PET would follow with a later statement that this measure would in fact not necessarily reduce the threat. The TMF mayor would be accused by liberal and conservative politicians of "misusing terrorist securitization to promote personal [anti-car] ideology"[77] and the scheme would later be presented again to the public in terms of its primary potential to increase the livable quality and climate performance of the medieval core of the city.[78] ⟨fig. 16⟩

18 Amagertorv 3D scan.

Central to the intersection of logics of the livable and securitized city has been the consistent positioning of the automobile at the core of urban public space concerns. Firstly, as the vehicle of empowered personal mobility across the spaced functional zones of the modernist welfare city – and then as the radical colonizer and disrupter of urban public space in the critique that would support the introduction of the pedestrian precincts of the livable city.⟨fig. 17⟩ And most recently, as the site of terror threat – whether bearing explosives or as a weapon against pedestrians – and as an unsustainable and climate-incompatible consumer of limited and sought-after public space in the urban core.

Shifting Urban Welfare Imaginaries in Response to Shifting Urban Threats

In this light, the oversized planters stand as an emblem, not for the metropolitan city (with an edge), but for a circumscribed urban securitization driven by a determined but compromised reassertion of the livable city. This is implicit in its carefully calculated relation with two nearby pots and a historical fountain, and the intention for these elements to fall habitually into the background as objects, surfaces and spatialities of the livable city.⟨fig. 18⟩

The significant transformations in public space in this half-century period articulates shifting materializations of public space's role in delivering welfare. This can be interpreted as a response to a complex set of evolving and expanding actual and perceived threats to the state, market or society – the evolving ontological insecurity Lars Bo Kaspersen refers to. Rather than these spaces' exemplifying the classic narrative of European dismantlement of welfare, the welfare system or the welfare state post-1970, the heavy investments in and overall improved qualities of public spaces developed in Copenhagen's urban core over this half-century period embody an expanded conception of key welfare-providing roles of public space in terms of physical (as well as social) security. These public space transformations articulate an expanded set of responsibilities of the state that include the classical provision of security – in addressing threats beyond those of the welfare state's responses to the postwar industrial city (summed up in Beverage's "evils" of disease, ignorance, want, idleness and squalor) – with public space's modernist spacing role within the squalor pillar.

Between the early 1970s and today, strategic development of public space was engaged to respond to an expanded series of threats to the survival unit – the unintended evils of the postwar modernist welfare city. These would range from economically framed threats of a welfare-reliant populace, municipal bankruptcy, urban uncompetitiveness and regional and global peripheralization; to the psychological and social ills of the modernist-planned "unlivable" city, including its claimed contribution to crime, alienation, unhappiness, boredom and monotony in the lives of those inhabiting it; to shortfalls in democratic involvement implicit in predict-and-provide planning; and later to the emerging social fragmentation and sorting of the city; and to the environmental threats of unsustainability, such as extreme rainfall events and the rising sea level. Since 2001, and particularly since 2011, the threat of terror has played a central role in public space considerations in the center of Europe and Denmark's largest cities – and this has been further supplemented and expanded since 2020 with the threat of crowded, livable public space as a potential site of contagion in the time of a global pandemic.

As the welfare pillar of affordable housing provision has withered considerably over the half century period studied, and those of education and health have been strengthened,[79] public space has increasingly cemented itself a strategic site of Danish welfare delivery toward both social and physical forms of security.

Bibliography

Albertsen, Niels, and Tom Nielsen. "Welfare City Theory: Editorial Introduction." *Nordic Journal of Architectural Research* 17, no. 2 (2004).

Andersen, John, and Gestur Hovgaard. "Welfare and Urban Planning in Transition: A Copenhagen Case Study." Research paper no. 8/03. Research Papers from the Department of Social Sciences, Roskilde University, 2003.

Andersen, John, and John Pløger. "The Janus Face of Urban Governance in Denmark." Montreal: Cahiers du Centre de recherche sur les innovations sociales (CRISES), May 2009. http://www.crises.uqam.ca/upload/files/publications/etudes-theoriques/CRISES_ET0906.pdf.

Amin, Ash. "The Good City." *Urban Studies* 43, no. 5/6 (2006): 1009–23. http://www.jstor.org/stable/43197514.

Astrup, Søren. "Frank Jensen: Islamisk Stats tilbagegang gør terrorsikring nødvendig." *Politiken*, August 25, 2017. https://politiken.dk/indland/kobenhavn/art6080897/Islamisk-Stats-tilbagegang-gør-terrorsikring-nødvendig.

Beveridge, William. *Social Insurance and Allied Services Report*. New York: The Macmillan Co., 1942.

Bøgh, Nikolaj. "Christiansborg Slotsplads: Ødelagt kulturatv for 50 mio. kr." *POV*, February 1, 2019. https://pov.international/christiansborg-slotsplads-odelagt/.

Brandt, Kasper Bruun Vindum. "Flertal ønsker bilfri bymidte: "Vi skal beskytte københavnerne." *TV2 Lorry,* August 24, 2017. https://www.tv2lorry.dk/artikel/flertal-oensker-bilfri-bymidte-vi-skal-beskytte-koebenhavnerne.

Brandt, Kasper Bruun Vindum, and Mette Serup. "Kritik: Kabell misbruger terror – anebfaling til bilfri bymidte." *TV2 Lorry,* August 25, 2017. https://www.tv2lorry.dk/artikel/kritik-kabell-misbruger-terror-anbefaling-til-bilfri-bymidte.

Bøgh, Nikolaj. "Christiansborg Slotsplads: Ødelagt kulturarv for 50 mio. kr." *POV. International*, February 1, 2019. https://pov.international/christiansborg-slotsplads-odelagt/.

Carstensen, Ivar. "Kommune bruger millioner på at gøre terrorisikrende betonklodser 'københavnervenlige.'" *Berlingske*, October 12, 2017. https://www.berlingske.dk/kultur/kommunen-bruger-millioner-paa-at-goere-terrorsikrende-betonklodser.

Cathcart-Keays, Athlyn, and Tim Warin. "Story of Cities no. 36: How Copenhagen Rejected 1960s Modernist 'Utopia.'" *The Guardian*, May 5, 2016. https://www.theguardian.com/cities/2016/may/05/story-cities-copenhagen-denmark-modernist-utopia.
Christiaanse, Kees. "The Open City and its Enemies." In *Open City: Designing Coexistence*, edited by Tim Rieniets, Jennifer Sigler and Kees Christiaanse. Rotterdam: Sun Architecture, 2009.
Clarke, Ronald V. "Situational Crime Prevention: Its Theoretical Basis and Practical Scope." *Crime and Justice* 4 (1983): 225–56.
Coaffee, John, "Protecting Vulnerable Cities." In *International Affairs* 86, no. 4 (2010): 939–54.
Coaffee, John, Paul O'Hare and Marian Hawkesworth. "The Visibility of (In) Security: The Aesthetics of Planning Urban Defences Against Terrorism." *Security Dialogue* 40, no. 4/5 (2009): 489–511.
Croix, Horst de la. *Military Considerations in City Planning: Fortifications.* New York: G. Braziller, 1972.
Dahl, Holger. "Conflict, Concrete and Communication." In Weiss, *Critical City*, 319–31.
Dalgaard-Nielsen, Anja, Jesper Laisen and Charlotte Wandorf. "Visible Counterterrorism Measures in Urban Spaces: Fear-Inducing or Not?" *Terrorism and Political Violence* 28, no. 4 (2016): 692–712.
Dansk Industri Vagt- og Sikkerheds-Industrien. "Politiforlig 2019: Et trygt og sikkert Danmark." Copenhagen: DI, 2019. https://www.danskindustri.dk/globalassets/billedarkiv/univers-brancher-og-foreninger/brancher-og-foreninger/di-branchefallesskaber/di-service/viden-og-analyser/politiforlig-2019-vsi-folder-web.pdf?v=210516.
——. "Vagt- og Sikkerheds- Industriens Årsrapport 2019." Copenhagen: DI, 2019. https://www.danskindustri.dk/globalassets/billedarkiv/univers-brancher-og-foreninger/brancher-og-foreninger/di-branchefallesskaber/di-service/viden-og-analyser/vsi-rapport-2019.pdf/Download.
Fallah, Daniel Nøjsen. "Vermund anmeldt for racisme: 'De hedder koranklodser.'" *BT*, February 28, 2019. https://www.bt.dk/politik/vermund-anmeldt-for-racisme-de-hedder-koranklodser.
Fawaz, Mona, Mona Harb and Ahmad Gharbieh. "Living Beirut's Security Zones: An Investigation of the Modalities and Practice of Urban Security." *City & Society* 24, no. 2 (2012): 173–95.
Folketinget. "Ansigtsløft til Christiansborg Slotsplads." *Folketinget*, January 30, 2019. https://www.ft.dk/da/aktuelt/nyheder/2019/01/slotspladsen.
——. "Granitsten skal sikre mod terror." *Folketinget*, April 8, 2013. https://www.ft.dk/aktuelt/nyheder/2013/04/granitsten
Fukuyama, Francis. *The End of History and the Last Man*. New York: The Free Press, 1992.
Gaardmand, Nola Grace, and Lars From. "Mere tungt bevæbnet politi i Danmark." *Jyllands-Posten*, July 19, 2015. https://jyllands-posten.dk/indland/ECE7877128/Mere-tungt-bev%C3%A6bnet-politi-i-Danmark/.
Galison, Peter. "War against the Center." *Grey Room*, no. 4 (2001): 7–33.
Garutti, Francesco. "The Happiness Plan." In *Our Happy Life: Architecture and Well-Being in an Age of Emotional Capitalism,* edited by Garutti, Francesco, 29–60. Berlin: Sternberg Press, 2019.
Gehl Architects. "Twelve Quality Criteria." https://gehlpeople.com/tools/twelve-quality-criteria/. Accessed May 22, 2020.
Gehl, Ingrid. *Bo-Miljø*. Copenhagen: SBi, 1971.
Gehl, Jan. *Cities for People*. Washington DC: Island Press, 2010.
——. *Life Between Buildings*, translated by Jo Koch. Washington, DC: Island Press, 2011.
Gehl, Jan, and Lars Gemzøe. *New City Spaces*. Copenhagen: Danish Architectural Press, 2000.
Gottschalck, Anna, Mathilde Graversen and Kirstine Benedicta Lauritzen. "Efter angreb i Berlin: Politi sætter beton-afspæring op i København." *Berlingske*, December 20, 2016. https://www.berlingske.dk/samfund/efter-angreb-i-berlin-politi-saetter-beton-afspaerring-op-i-koebenhavn.
Graham, Stephen. "Cities as Battlespace: The New Military Urbanism." *City* 13 (2009): 383–402.
——. *Cities Under Siege: The New Military Urbanism.* London: Verso, 2010.
——. "When Life Itself Is War: On the Urbanization of Military and Security Doctrine." *International Journal of Urban and Regional Research* 36, no. 1 (2011): 136–55. https://onlinelibrary.wiley.com/doi/abs/10.1111/j.1468-2427.2011.01026.x.
Greenwald, Glenn. *No Place to Hide: Edward Snowden, the NSA, and the U.S. Surveillance State.* London: Hamish Hamilton, 2014.
Habermas, Jurgen. *The Structural Transformation of the Public Sphere.* Cambridge, MA: MIT Press, 1989.
Hansen, Anders Lund. "Space Wars and Urban Governance: Inhumane Creative Urban Transformations." In *Urban Governance in Europe*, edited by Felix Eckhardt and Ingemar Elander, 111–32. Berlin: BMV, 2009.
Harvey, David. "From Managerialism to Entrepreneurialism: The Transformation in Urban Governance in Late Capitalism." *Geografiska Annaler. Series B, Human Geography* 71, no. 1 (1989): 3–17.
Hemmingsen, Ann-Sophie. *The Danish Approach to Countering and Preventing Extremism and Radicalisation.* Copenhagen: DIIS, 2015. https://www.ft.dk/samling/20151/almdel/reu/bilag/248/1617692.pdf.
Hjortdal, Marie, and Jesper Vangkilde. "PET vil terrorsikre Christiansborg." *Politiken*, December 14, 2011. https://politiken.dk/indland/politik/art5387766/PET-vil-terrorsikre-Christiansborg.
Ifversen, Carsten. "The Long Haul." In Weiss, *Critical City*, 131–39.
Illouz, Eva. *Cold Intimacies: The Making of Emotional Capitalism.* Cambridge, MA: Polity Press, 2007.
Ilum, Stine. "The Good City." *Journal of Extreme Anthropology* 4, no. 1 (2020): 157–76. https://doi.org/10.5617/JEA.7359.
Jacobs, Jane. *The Death and Life of Great American Cities.* New York: Random House, 1961.
Jackson, Richard, Harmonie Toros, Lee Jarvis and Charlotte Heath-Kelly, eds. *Critical Terrorism Studies at Ten: Contributions, Cases and Future Challenges.* London: Routledge, 2019.
Jacobsen, Sara Jul, Tina Gudrun Jensen, Katerine Vitus and Kristina Weibel. *Analysis of Danish Media Setting and Framing of Muslims, Islam and Racism: Working Paper 10:2013.* Copenhagen: The Danish National Centre for Social Research, 2013. https://pure.vive.dk/ws/files/224036/WP_10_2013.pdf.
Jeffrey, C. Ray. *Crime Prevention Through Environmental Design.* Beverly Hills, Sage Publications, 1971.
Jensen, Carsten. *Velfærd.* Aarhus: Aarhus University Press, 2017.
Kabell, Morten. "Her skal København være bilfri." *Politiken*, November 26, 2015. https://politiken.dk/debat/kroniken/art5600682/Her-skal-K%C3%B8benhavn-v%C3%A6re-bilfri.
Kaspersen, Lars Bo. *Denmark in the World.* Copenhagen: Hans Reitzels Forlag, 2013.
Koolhaas, Rem. "My Thoughts on the Smart City." In European Commission, *Digital Minds for a New Europe*, 2014. http://ec.europa.eu/archives/commission_2010-2014/kroes/en/content/my-thoughts-smart-city-rem-koolhaas.html. Accessed March 12, 2017.
Kristensen, Frederik Buhl. "Tre scenarier: København overvejer at lukke middelaladerbyen for biler." *Politiken*, November 28, 2018. https://politiken.dk/indland/kobenhavn/art6873230/København-overvejer-at-lukke-middelalderbyen-for-biler.
Krivý, Maroš, and Leonard Ma. "The Limits of the Livable City: From *Homo Sapiens* to *Homo Cappuccino*." *Avery Review* 30 (2018).

Kvorning, Jens. "Copenhagen Restructured." In *Urban Reports: Urban Strategies and Visions in Mid-Sized Cities in a Local and Global Context*, edited by Nicola Schüller, Petra Wollenberg and Kees Christiaanse, 175–95. Zurich: Gta-Verlag, 2009.

——. "The Social Sorting Machine." In Weiss, *Critical City*, 131–39.

Kvorning, Jens, Carsten Thau and Martin Zerlang. *København på lattergas: Når byen bliver banal.* Copenhagen: Gads Forlag, 2020.

København Kommune. *Architecture Policy for Copenhagen 2017–2025.* Copenhagen: København Kommune, 2017 https://kk.sites.itera.dk/apps/kk_pub2/pdf/1904_4b203fafa9a8.pdf.

——. *Arkitektur for Mennesker*, Copenhagen: København Kommune, 2017. https://kk.sites.itera.dk/apps/kk_pub2/?mode=detalje&id=1646.

——. "Borgerrepraesentationens modemateriale 24082017." http://www.kk.dk/indhold/borgerrepraesentationens-modemateriale/24082017/edoc-agenda/4ed0c77c-a82b-4636-82a4-d7e8ca0aee9e/cd9d6966-6e53-4e20-b3e4-09a6e8341dbb. Accessed March 2, 2018.

——. *Co-Create Copenhagen: A Vision for 2025.* Copenhagen: København Kommune, 2015. https://kk.sites.itera.dk/apps/kk_pub2/pdf/1534_0TdC5G2XZr.pdf.

——. "Træer, cykelstativer og bænke skal erstatte betongrise." Københavns Kommune, August 28, 2017. https://www.kk.dk/nyheder/traeer-cykelstativer-og-baenke-skal-erstatte-betongrise.

——. *Urban Life Account: Trends in Copenhagen's Urban Life.* Copenhagen: København Kommune, 2010–. https%3A%2F%2Fkk.sites.itera.dk%2Fapps%2Fkk_pub2%2Fpdf%2F1258_0B5eEF1cF5.pdf&usg=AOvVaw0MoN9IlFTwbHVXTwsdmDck.

København Kommune. (developed in association with Gehl Architects). *A Metropolis for People: Visions and Goals for Urban Life in Copenhagen 2015.* Copenhagen: København Kommune, 2009. http://kk.sites.itera.dk/apps/kk_pub2/pdf/646_mlr0dQ6Wdu.pdf.

Lambert, Leopold. "Interview: Leopold Lambert." In Simpson, Jensen and Rubing, *The City Between Freedom and Security.*

Low, Setha. "The Erosion of Public Space and the Public Realm: Paranoia, Surveillance and Privatization in New York City." *City and Society* 18, no. 1 (2006): 43–49.

Marcuse, Peter. "Security or Safety in Cities? The Threat of Terrorism after 9/11." *International Journal of Urban and Regional Research* 30, no. 4 (2006): 919–29.

Minton, Anna, *Ground Control: Fear and Happiness in the Twenty-First Century City.* London: Verso, 2009.

Minton, Anna, and Jody Aked. "Fortress Britain: High Security, Insecurity and the Challenge of Preventing Harm." In Simpson, Jensen and Rubing, *The City Between Freedom and Security.*

Nielsen, Tom. "The Making of Democratic Urban Public Space in Denmark." In *Public Space Design and Social Cohesion: An International Comparison*, edited by Patricia Aelbrecht and Quentin Stevens. London: Routledge, 2019.

Newman, Oscar. *Defensible Space: Crime Prevention through Urban Design.* New York: Macmillan, 1972.

Olsen, Troels Vorre (Viatrafik), and Sanne Slot Hansen (Schønherr). "Fredeliggørelse af Middelalderbyen." 2019.

Politiets Efterretningstjeneste (PET). *Tænk terrorsikkerhed i udendørs offentlige rum.* Copenhagen: PET, 2019. https://www.pet.dk/Publikationer/Vejledninger.aspx.

Pinborg, Niels. "Al Qaeda truer Danmark: Dræbermaskine på Strøget." *Ekstra Bladet*, October 13, 2010. https://ekstrabladet.dk/112/article4138334.ece.

Ritzau. "Kommuner vil have flere penge til terrorsikring." *Berlingske*, September 20, 2017. https://www.berlingske.dk/samfund/kommuner-vil-have-flere-penge-til-terrorsikring.

Scraton, Phil. "Streets of Terror: Marginalization, Criminalization and Authoritarian Renewal." *Social Justice* 31, nos. 1–2 (2004).

Schuilenburg, Marc. *The Securitization of Society: Crime, Risk, and Social Order.* New York: New York University Press, 2015.

Simpson, Deane, Kathrin Gimmel, Anders Lonka, Marc Jay and Joost Grootens. *The Atlas of the Copenhagens.* Berlin: Ruby Press, 2018.

Simpson, Deane, Vibeke Jensen and Anders Rubing. *The City Between Freedom and Security: Contested Public Space in the 21st Century.* Basel: Birkhauser, 2017.

Sorkin, Michael, ed. *Indefensible Space: The Architecture of the National Insecurity State.* New York: Routledge, 2008.

Swenarton, Mark, Tom Avermaete and Dirk van den Heuvel, eds. *Architecture and the Welfare State.* New York: Routledge, 2015.

Tagtomat. "Grøn terrorsikring = standard betonklodser beklædt med bænk, cykelstativ og planter." In *TagTomat*, 2017. https://www.tagtomat.dk/2017/06/13/gron-terrorsikring-standard-betonklodser-beklaedt-med-baenk-cykelstativ-og-planter/.

TV2 Lorry. "Hus Forbi laver indsamling til udvist hjemløs." *TV2 Lorry,* November 5, 2018. https://www.tv2lorry.dk/kobenhavn/hus-forbi-laver-indsamling-til-udvist-hjemlos.

UK Government. *Crowded Spaces: The Planning System and Counter-Terrorism.* London: UK Government, 2012.

Weiss, Kristoffer, ed. *Critical* City. Copenhagen: Danish Architecture Press, 2019.

Weizman, Eyal. *Hollow Land.* London: Verso, 2007.

Whyte, William H. *The Social Life of Small Urban Spaces.* New York: Project for Public Spaces, 1980.

Zuboff, Shoshana. *The Age of Surveillance Capitalism: The Fight for a Human Future at the New Frontier of Power.* New York: Public Affairs, 2019.

Notes

1 Stephen Graham, *Cities Under Siege: The New Military Urbanism* (London: Verso, 2010); and Lars Bo Kaspersen, *Denmark in the World* (Copenhagen: Hans Reitzels Forlag, 2013).
2 Physical security measures (PSM) are physical objects designed and placed in space with the intention of heightening the security of a given space. These range from bollards to concrete Jersey barriers; from flower pots to consciously placed bicycle racks, etc.
3 Horst de la Croix, *Military Considerations in City Planning: Fortifications* (New York: G. Braziller, 1972).
4 Peter Galison, "War against the Center," *Grey Room*, no. 4 (2001): 7–33.
5 Francis Fukuyama, *The End of History and the Last Man* (New York: The Free Press, 1992).
6 Stephen Graham, "Cities as Battlespace: The New Military Urbanism," *City* 13 (2009): 389.
7 Graham, "Cities as Battlespace," 389.
8 The physical response to this perception has been less informed by classical military doctrine than by various theories of physical security at the intersection of architecture, risk analysis and criminology. These include notions such as: C. Ray Jeffrey, *Crime Prevention Through Environmental Design* (Beverly Hills, Sage Publications, 1971); Oscar Newman, *Defensible Space: Crime Prevention through Urban Design* (New York: Macmillan, 1972); Ronald V. Clarke, "Situational Crime Prevention: Its Theoretical Basis and Practical Scope," *Crime and Justice* 4 (1983): 225–56; and Police Crime Prevention Initiatives, *Secured by Design*, https://www.securedbydesign.com/.
9 Graham, *Cities Under Siege.*
10 Phil Scraton, "Streets of Terror: Marginalization, Criminalization, and Authoritarian Renewal," *Social Justice* 31, nos. 1–2 (2004). These developments have been challenged by the field of critical terrorism studies (CTS), which has been concerned with "the political manipulation of terrorism fears and increase in draconian anti-terrorism legislation" and the asymmetries between "the actual material threat posed by terrorists and the level of investment and activity devoted to responding to this threat" particularly since 2001. See Richard Jackson, Harmonie Toros, Lee Jarvis and Charlotte Heath-Kelly, eds., *Critical Terrorism Studies at Ten: Contributions, Cases and Future Challenges* (London: Routledge, 2019).
11 This intersection has been notable in a Danish context, particularly in the late 2010s, during the period of the so-called refugee crisis in Europe, a sequence of ongoing terror attacks across Europe, the buildup of anti-Muslim sentiment in the popularist media and the expansion of Far Right political parties trading on these sentiments. This development has contributed to shifting conceptions of the universal nature of welfare in a Danish context and in recent years with an emerging distinction between so-called worthy and unworthy welfare subjects. See Carsten Jensen, *Velfærd.* (Aarhus: Aarhus University Press, 2017), 60.
12 In *Denmark in the World*, Lars Bo Kaspersen describes the role of different spatial formations historically, e.g. the medieval city-state delivers physical security through walled fortifications, while the chapel or cathedral support the provision of spiritual security.
13 William Beveridge, *Social Insurance and Allied Services Report* (New York: The Macmillan Co., 1942). Framed by Beveridge in his internationally influential report, in terms of idleness, want, disease, ignorance and squalor. These would be addressed by five corresponding pillars of (social) welfare: measures to promote (1) full employment; (2) social insurance; (3) health services; (4) education – which would by and large have spatial correlates in institutions such as hospitals, schools and other institutions – and (5) town planning and housing.
14 This article will focus on physical security, but this is not intended to diminish the significant and increasing role of virtual or digital surveillance and securitization, both from the (welfare) state – for example, see Glenn Greenwald, *No Place to Hide: Edward Snowden, the NSA, and the U.S. Surveillance State* (London: Hamish Hamilton, 2014) – and corporations – see Shoshana Zuboff, *The Age of Surveillance Capitalism: The Fight for a Human Future at the New Frontier of Power* (New York: PublicAffairs, 2019).
15 Marie Hjortdal, Jesper Vangkilde, "PET vil terrorsikre Christiansborg." *Politiken*, December 14, 2011. https://politiken.dk/indland/politik/art5387766/PET-vil-terrorsikre-Christiansborg/.
16 See "Granitsten skal sikre mod terror," *Folketinget*, April 8, 2013, https://www.ft.dk/aktuelt/nyheder/2013/04/granitsten; and "A nsigtsløft til Christiansborg Slotsplads," *Folketinget*, January 30, 2019, https://www.ft.dk/da/aktuelt/nyheder/2019/01/slotspladsen.
17 Nola Grace Gaardmand and Lars From, "Mere tungt bevæbnet politi i Danmark", *Jyllands-Posten*, July 19, 2015, https://jyllands-posten.dk/indland/ECE7877128/Mere-tungt-bev%C3%A6bnet-politi-i-Danmark/.
18 Anna Gottschalck, Mathilde Graversen and Kirstine Benedicta Lauritzen, "Efter angreb I Berlin: Politi sætter beton-afspæring op i København," *Berlingske*, December 20, 2016. https://www.berlingske.dk/samfund/efter-angreb-i-berlin-politi-saetter-beton-afspaerring-op-i-koebenhavn.
19 See Kasper Bruun Vindum Brandt, "Flertal ønsker bilfri bymidte: 'Vi skal beskytte københavnerne,'" *TV2 Lorry*, August 24, 2017, https://www.tv2lorry.dk/artikel/flertal-oensker-bilfri-bymidte-vi-skal-beskytte-koebenhavnerne.; and Morten Kabell, "Her skal København være bilfri," *Politiken*, November 26, 2015, https://politiken.dk/debat/kroniken/art5600682/Her-skal-K%C3%B8benhavn-v%C3%A6re-bilfri.
20 See, for example, Sara Jul Jacobsen, Tina Gudrun Jensen, Kathrine Vitus, Kristina Weibel "Analysis of Danish Media Setting and Framing of Muslims, Islam and Racism" The Danish National Centre For Social Research, Copenhagen, Denmark; Working Paper 10:2013: https://pure.vive.dk/ws/files/224036/WP_10_2013.pdf. See, for example, "Al Qaeda truer Danmark: Dræbermaskine på Strøget", EB, accessed 5 March 2019: https://ekstrabladet.dk/112/article4138334.ece
21 Updated threat advisories communicate the anticipated nature of threats in a general way; and a set of Terror Security Guidelines, released in 2019 addressing clients and designers in securing crowded spaces and buildings have been another important influence. While not introducing security standards in terms of physical measure specifications, and intended as a tool to avoid disproportional responses, the guides point to the heightened role of risk-management and securitization logics in urban imaginaries and in production of the physical urban settings.
22 København Kommune, "Borgerrepraesentationens modemateriale 24082017" http://www.kk.dk/indhold/borgerrepraesentationens-modemateriale/24082017/edoc-agenda/4ed-0c77c-a82b-4636-82a4-d7e8ca0aee9e/cd9d6966-6e53-4e20-b3e4-09a6e8341dbb "Specifically, in Copenhagen, PET has at the moment recommended that assessments be made of the zones around the following locations designated in random order; Tivoli, Strøget, City Hall Square, Nyhavn, Kongens Nytorv, Amalienborg Palace Square, Lange- linie, Central Station and Nørreport Station. It is the Copenhagen Police that makes the concrete safety assessments, and the administration contributes in this connection to the technical and environmental expertise, so that the assessments are created in a holistic perspective."
23 Some commentators speculate that advice is typically taken by politicians based on their risk of potential blame in the case of an event taking place. [Conversation with Prof. John Andersen, RUC, 2019]

24 Holger Dahl, “Conflict, Concrete and Communication,” in *Critical City*, ed. Kristoffer Weiss (Copenhagen: Danish Architectural Press, 2019), 321. Translation by the author.
25 Daniel Nøjsen Fallah, “Vermund anmeldt for racisme: ‘De hedder koranklodser,’” *BT*, February 28, 2019. https://www.bt.dk/politik/vermund-anmeldt-for-racisme-de-hedder-koranklodser
26 Dansk Industri Vagt- og Sikkerheds- Industrien, “Politiforlig 2019: Et trygt og sikkert Danmark.” Copenhagen: DI, 2019. https://www.danskindustri.dk/globalassets/billedarkiv/univers-brancher-og-foreninger/brancher-og-foreninger/di-branchefallesskaber/di-service/viden-og-analyser/politiforlig-2019-vsi-folder-web.pdf?v=210516
27 Interview with Lene Bjerg Kristensen, Special Consultant and Leader of Terror Security at TMF, KK, October 2018. The rhetoric tied to these approaches is evident in the framing of the private sector’s contribution to security. For example, an excerpt from Dansk Industri Vagt- og Sikkerheds-Industrien (DI-VSI) reads: “The police contribute to the daily security of the public space, but the police can never be everywhere at the same time. At the same time, surveys (2016) show that 53% of the Danish population see it as likely or very likely that Denmark will be exposed to a terrorist attack. A similar survey also shows that a predominance (53%) of Danes agree or strongly agree that prevention of terrorism outweighs considerations of privacy. There is thus a desire for a safer public space among Danes, which intelligent technology can remedy. Experiences from New York and Paris, among others, show that new technology can create a number of solutions that secure citizens when the accident is out, but with respect for the individual’s freedoms. Modern technology can increase security in public areas: At VSI, we believe that intelligent tools in the form of, among other things, video, senso-smart street lamps, drones and smartphones can help to create security in public areas, where it requires extra effort to make Danes feel safe. Tools like these can help identify speed, smoke, movement, changing circumstances and other activities. With the establishment of ‘Safety Zones’, you as a citizen in busy public areas and at major events can feel safe and move safely, and in case of emergency be alerted via your smart-phone immediately.” https://www.danskindustri.dk/globalassets/billedarkiv/univers-brancher-og-foreninger/brancher-og-foreninger/di-branchefallesskaber/di-service/viden-og-analyser/politiforlig-2019-vsi-folder-web.pdf?v=210516
28 Information on costs aligned to many security projects are difficult to obtain or publicly unavailable, for example, the increased costs, post-2001, of airport security at Copenhagen Airport.
29 Ritzau. “Kommuner vil have flere penge til terrorsikring.” *Berlingske*, September 20, 2017. https://www.berlingske.dk/samfund/kommuner-vil-have-flere-penge-til-terrorsikring. Translation by the author.
30 Nikolaj Bøgh, “Christiansborg Slotsplads: Ødelagt kulturarv for 50 mio. kr.” *POV. International*, February 1, 2019. https://pov.international/christiansborg-slotsplads-odelagt/
31 Troels Vorre Olsen (Viatrafik), Sanne Slot Hansen (Schønherr), “Fredeliggørelse af Middelalderbyen.” 2019.
32 Ann-Sophie Hemmingsen, *The Danish Approach To Countering And Preventing Extremism And Radicalisation* (Copenhagen: DIIS, 2015). https://www.ft.dk/samling/20151/almdel/reu/bilag/248/1617692.pdf
33 København Kommune. “Træer, cykelstativer og bænke skal erstatte betongrise”, Københavns Kommune, August 28, 2017. https://www.kk.dk/nyheder/traeer-cykelstativer-og-baenke-skal-erstatte-betongrise
34 Tagtomat, “Grøn terrorsikring = standard betonklodser beklædt med bænk, cykelstativ og planter,” *TagTomat*, 2017. https://www.tagtomat.dk/2017/06/13/gron-terrorsikring-standard-betonklodser-beklaedt-med-baenk-cykelstativ-og-planter/. See also: Ivar Carstensen, “Kommune bruger millioner på at gøre terrorisikrende betonklodser ‘københavnervenlige,’” *Berlingske*, October 12, 2017. Accessed 5 March 2019: https://www.berlingske.dk/kultur/kommunen-bruger-millioner-paa-at-goere-terrorsikrende-betonklodser. See also: København Kommune. “Træer, cykelstativer og bænke skal erstatte betongrise”, Københavns Kommune, August 28, 2017. https://www.kk.dk/nyheder/traeer-cykelstativer-og-baenke-skal-erstatte-betongrise
35 Stine Ilum, “The Good City,” *Journal of Extreme Anthropology* 4, no. 1 (n.d.): 157–75. doi:10.5617/JEA.7359.
36 Interview with Lene Bjerg Kristensen, Special Consultant and Leader of Terror Security at TMF, KK, October 2018.
37 Illum, “The Good City,” 172.
38 These include, for example: a) remaining military spaces such as barracks or command posts; b) spaces of critical infrastructure such as airports, port facilities for cruise or cargo shipping responding to international security standards heightened since 2001; c) international representational spaces of embassies, with varying degrees of security informed by their own risk-assessments in dialogue with local police; d) specific sites of risk related to religious, ethnic or political tension, e.g. local sites of the Jewish community, or newspaper offices involved in publishing the Mohamed cartoons; and lastly, e) recently secured public space.
39 John Andersen, Gestur Hovgaard, “Welfare and urban planning in transition: a Copenhagen case study.” Research Papers/Department of Social Sciences. No. 8. 2003: 9. It is in this time frame that a considerable number of industrial concerns and their related port activities moved activities to other locations such as Jutland and offshore as the military was in the process of restructuring its presence in the center of the city.
40 Iconic examples being areas such as Bellahøj, Brøndby Strand, Høje Gladsaxe.
41 Although obviously to a lesser extent on the already pedestrianized sections of Strøget.
42 Andersen et al, “Welfare and urban planning in transition” 2003; Ash Amin, “The Good City” *Urban Studies* 43, no. 5/6 (2006): 1009–23. http://www.jstor.org/stable/43197514.
43 David Harvey, “From Managerialism to Entrepreneurialism: The Transformation in Urban Governance in Late Capitalism,” *Geografiska Annaler. Series B, Human Geography* 71, no. 1 (1989): 3–17; Andersen et al., “Welfare and urban planning in transition” 2003.
44 974,901 inhabitants in 1950; 729, 357 in 1975
45 John Andersen and John Pløger, “The Janus Face of Urban Governance in Denmark.” Montreal: Cahiers du Centre de recherche sur les innovations sociales (CRISES), 2009. http://www.crises.uqam.ca/upload/files/publications/etudes-theoriques/CRISES_ET0906.pdf. For example: the expansion of Copenhagen Airport, the building of the Øresund Bridge connecting Copenhagen to Malmö in Sweden, and the development of new urban districts in post-industrial port and brownfield sites, which would in turn finance the construction of a new metro.
46 Anders Lund Hansen, “Space Wars and Urban Governance: Inhumane Creative Urban Transformations,” in *Urban Governance in Europe*, ed. Felix Eckhardt and Ingemar Elander (Berlin: BMV, 2009), 111–32.
47 Jens Kvorning, “Copenhagen restructured,” in *Urban Reports: Urban strategies and visions In mid-sized cities in a local and global context*, ed. Nicola Schüller et al. (Zurich: Gta-Verlag, 2009), 175–95.
48 Jacobs, Jane, *The Death and Life of Great American Cities* (New York: Random House, 1961); and William H. Whyte, *The Social Life of Small Urban Spaces* (New York: Project for Public Spaces, 1980).

49 Jan Gehl, *Life Between Buildings* (Copenhagen: Danish Architectural Press, 2001 [1971]); Ingrid Gehl, *Bo-Miljø* (Copenhagen: SBi, 1971).
50 Tom Nielsen, "The Making of Democratic Urban Public Space in Denmark," in *Public Space Design and Social Cohesion: An International Comparison*, ed. Patricia Aelbrecht and Quentin Stevens (London: Routledge, 2019): 41.
51 Gehl's position paraphrased in København Kommune, *Architecture Policy for Copenhagen 2017–2025.* (Copenhagen: København Kommune, 2017): 6 (a document Gehl architects contributed to.) https://kk.sites.itera.dk/apps/kk_pub2/pdf/1904_4b203fafa9a8.pdf
52 Illum, "The Good City," 165. This has become increasingly important in light of the breakdown of housing affordability – the breaking down of housing as a welfare pillar. Here, public space investments in neighbourhood uplift projects in vulnerable areas are an essential aspect of this.
53 Nielsen "The Making of Democratic Urban Public Space," 43. Using another series of Copenhagen public spaces – mostly in the first row of the bridge neighborhoods (Superkilen, Dronning Louises Bridge, Israels Plads, Havneparken Islands Brygge) – Nielsen describes five principles framing this form of public space production: (1) public space as a common point of identification; (2) free and equal access for all; (3) extended user inclusion; (4) Gehlian principle of the universal invitation; and (5) accommodating the "everyday" and "a world of strangers."
54 2000 was also the same year that Jan Gehl founded his own consultancy "Gehl Architects." An important early initiative of Realdania's was the 2002 competition "Better Public Space".
55 Nielsen "The Making of Democratic Urban Public Space," 42.
56 See, for example, København Kommune. (developed in association with Gehl Architects), *A Metropolis for People: Visions and Goals for Urban Life in Copenhagen 2015.* Copenhagen: København Kommune, 2009. http://kk.sites.itera.dk/apps/kk_pub2/pdf/646_mlr0dQ6Wdu.pdf, which begins: "Copenhagen has a Vision: We will become the world's most livable city" (2009: 2). Other important documents include København Kommune. *Architecture Policy for Copenhagen 2017–2025.* Copenhagen: København Kommune, 2017 https://kk.sites.itera.dk/apps/kk_pub2/pdf/1904_4b203fafa9a8.pdf; København Kommune, *Co-Create Copenhagen: A Vision for 2025.* Copenhagen: København Kommune, 2015. https://kk.sites.itera.dk/apps/kk_pub2/pdf/1534_0TdC5G2XZr.pdf; to the metric system of public life measurement started in 2010: København Kommune, *Urban Life Account: Trends in Copenhagen's Urban Life* Copenhagen: København Kommune, 2010. https%3A%2F%2Fkk.sites.itera.dk%2Fapps%2Fkk_pub2%2Fpdf%2F1258_0B5eEF1cF5.pdf&usg=AOvVaw0MoN9IlFTwbHVXTwsdmDck
57 Athlyn Cathcart-Keays and Tim Warin, "Story of Cities no. 36: How Copenhagen Rejected 1960s Modernist 'Utopia.'" *The Guardian*, May 5, 2016. https://www.theguardian.com/cities/2016/may/05/story-cities-copenhagen-denmark-modernist-utopia. Central to the conceptualization of urban liveability is an assumed relation between the urban setting and individual subjective well-being or quality of life, and secondly, the notion that this is quantifiable and therefore possible to competitively rank the liveability of cities (see Deane Simpson, Kathrin Gimmel, Anders Lonka, Marc Jay and Joost Grootens, *The Atlas of the Copenhagens* (Berlin: Ruby Press, 2018)) (also see Maroš Krivýand and Leonard Ma, "The Limits of the Livable City: From Homo Sapiens to Homo Cappuccino," *Avery Review* 30 (2018)) – articulating what has been described as the metrics for a form of neo-liberal urban governmentality. Urban liveability rankings would expand in the 2000s to include The Mercer Quality of Living ranking, The *Economist*'s EIU Global Liveability Ranking and *Monocle* magazine's World's Most Livable City Index, amongst others. Copenhagen would be frequently positioned near the top of these indexes – with public spaces being most visible in the photographic and video documentation of the city. Indexes such as these raise questions concerning what metrics are taken into account in accessing "liveability," and according to whom. *Monocle*'s index, for example, is described as partially subjective – touching upon metrics such as retail mix, the quality of cocktails, and the interior design of the airport, while issues such as social segregation or spatial inequalities are not (see Simpson et al, *The Atlas of the Copenhagens,* 2018).
58 Simpson et al, *The Atlas of the Copenhagens*; Kristoffer Weiss (ed.), *Critical City* (Copenhagen: Danish Architecture Press, 2019); Jens Kvorning, Carsten Thau and Martin Zerlang, *København på lattergas: Når byen bliver banal* (Copenhagen: Gads Forlag, 2020).
59 Kvorning et al., *København på lattergas.*
60 Carsten Jensen, *Velfærd* (Aarhus: Aarhus University Press, 2017).
61 Andersen et al, "Welfare and urban planning in transition"; Simpson et al., *Atlas of the Copenhagens*; Weiss, *Critical City*; Kvorning, "The Social Sorting Machine"; Ifversen, "The Long Haul"; Kvorning et al., *København på lattergas.*
62 Rem Koolhaas, "My Thoughts on the Smart City – by Rem Koolhaas," *European Commission: Digital Minds for a New Europe,* 2014. Accessed March 12, 2017. http://ec.europa.eu/archives/commission_2010-2014/kroes/en/content/my-thoughts-smart-city-rem-koolhaas.html
63 Kvorning et al, *København på lattergas.*
64 København Kommune, *Co-Create Copenhagen: A Vision for 2025.* Copenhagen: København Kommune, 2015. https://kk.sites.itera.dk/apps/kk_pub2/pdf/1534_0TdC5G2XZr.pdf. A City with an Edge would be one that "pave[s] the way for the city's diversity to play an even more prominent role. it would be good if Copenhagen were even bolder and had more of an edge. We need room for wild, creative initiatives and architecture that evokes strong emotions..."
65 Illum, "The Good City."
66 The twelve criteria are organized according to three sub-themes: protection, comfort, enjoyment. The protection theme involves three criteria: (1) protection against traffic and accidents – feeling safe; (2) protection against crime and violence – feeling secure; and (3) protection against unpleasant sensory experiences. Gehl Architects. "Twelve Quality Criteria." Accessed May 22, 2020. https://gehlpeople.com/tools/twelve-quality-criteria/.
67 Such developments of anti-terror architecture may be placed within broader discussions of what Judith Butler has described as an ongoing shrinking, commodification, monitoring and control of public space – with the central role that broader forms of defensive architecture play in this – from gated communities, to anti-biker, anti-skater, or anti-rough-sleeping measures. Such tendencies toward risk perception and securitization not only impact the physical composition of urban public space, or the signals it communicates, but also extend to the public's access to it, and the activities and uses legally or practically tolerated within it – as seen in the militarization of police measures in the context of large events, or the increasing intolerance of protest. For a Copenhagen example see TV2 Lorry, "Hus Forbi laver indsamling til udvist hjemløs," *LV2 Lorry*, November 5, 2018. https://www.tv2lorry.dk/kobenhavn/hus-forbi-laver-indsamling-til-udvist-hjemlos
68 Illum, "The Good City."
69 UK Government. *Crowded Spaces: The Planning System and Counter-Terrorism.* London: UK Government, 2012; and Politiets Efterretningstjeneste (PET). *Tænk terrorsikkerhed i udendørs*

offentlige rum (Copenhagen: PET, 2019). https://www.pet.dk/Publikationer/Vejledninger.aspx.
70 Nielsen, "The Making of Democratic Urban Public Space."
71 See Francesco Garutti, "The Happiness Plan," in *Our Happy Life: Architecture and Well-Being in an Age of Emotional Capitalism*, ed. Garutti, Francesco (Berlin: Sternberg Press, 2019), 29–60. See also Eva Illouz, *Cold Intimacies: The Making of Emotional Capitalism* (Cambridge: Polity Press, 2007).
72 See Anna Minton and Jody Aked, "Fortress Britain: High Security, Insecurity and the Challenge of Preventing Harm," in *The City Between Freedom and Security*, ed. Deane Simpson, Vibeke Jensen and Anders Rubing (Basel: Birkhäuser, 2017); also see John Coaffee, Paul O'Hare and Marian Hawkesworth, "The Visibility of (In)Security: The Aesthetics of Planning Urban Defences Against Terrorism," *Security Dialogue* 40, no. 4/5 (2009): 489–511.
73 Anja Dalgaard-Nielsen, Jesper Laisen and Charlotte Wandorf, "Visible Counterterrorism Measures in Urban Spaces – Fear-Inducing or Not?" *Terrorism and Political Violence*, 28:4 (2016): 692–712
74 See Kees Christiaanse, "The Open City and its Enemies," in *Open City: Designing Coexistence*, ed. Tim Rieniets, Jennifer Sigler and Kees Christiaanse (Rotterdam: Sun Architecture, 2009); Stephen Graham, *Cities Under Siege: The New Military Urbanism* (London: Verso, 2010); Anna Minton, *Ground Control: Fear and Happiness in the Twenty-First Century City* (London: Verso, 2009); Michael Sorkin (ed.), *Indefensible Space: The Architecture of the National Insecurity State* (New York: Routledge, 2008); Eyal Weizman, *Hollow Land* (London: Verso, 2007).
75 Stephen Graham, "When Life Itself is War: On the Urbanization of Military and Security Doctrine," *International Journal of Urban and Regional Research* 36:1 (2011): 136–55. https://onlinelibrary.wiley.com/doi/abs/10.1111/j.1468-2427.2011.01026.x; Peter Marcuse, "Security or Safety in Cities? The Threat of Terrorism after 9/11" *International Journal of Urban and Regional Research* 30(4) 2006: 919–929; Fawaz Mona, Mona Harb and Ahmad Gharbieh, "Living Beirut's Security Zones: An Investigation of the Modalities and Practice of Urban Security," *City & Society* 24, no. 2 (2012): 175.
76 Kasper Bruun Vindum Brandt, "Flertal ønsker bilfri bymidte: Vi skal beskytte københavnerne." *TV2 Lorry,* August 24, 2017. https://www.tv2lorry.dk/artikel/flertal-oensker-bilfri-bymidte-vi-skal-beskytte-koebenhavnerne
77 Kasper Bruun Vindum Brandt and Mette Serup, "Kritik: Kabell misbruger terror – anebfaling til bilfri bymidte," *TV2 Lorry,* August 25, 2017. https://www.tv2lorry.dk/artikel/kritik-kabell-misbruger-terror-anbefaling-til-bilfri-bymidte
78 Frederik Buhl Kristensen, "Tre scenarier: København overvejer at lukke middelaladerbyen for biler," *Politiken*, November 28, 2018. https://politiken.dk/indland/kobenhavn/art6873230/København-overvejer-at-lukke-middelalderbyen-for-biler
79 Jensen, *Velfærd.*

1.01 Copenhagen's historical fortification development

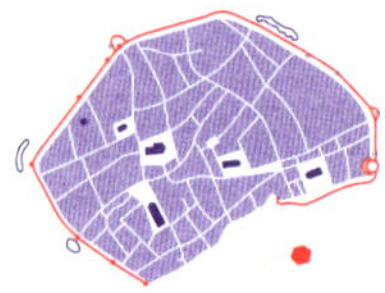

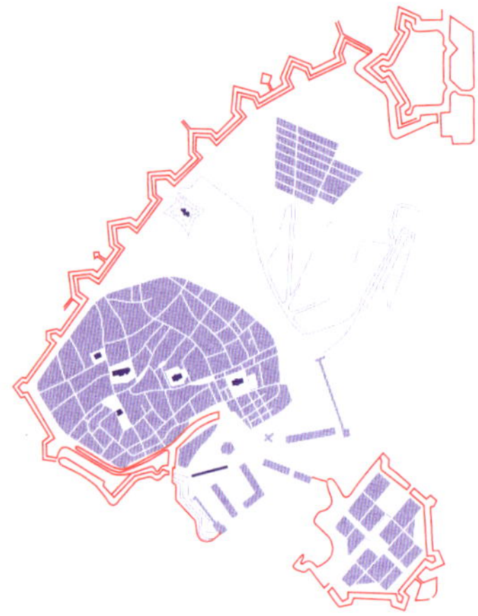

Copenhagen 1337
Similar to many European settlements, Copenhagen's early development followed an expanded series of rampart defense systems.

Copenhagen 1659
By the seventeenth century, the ramparts surrounding the city had expanded to measure ca. 2.5 km across.

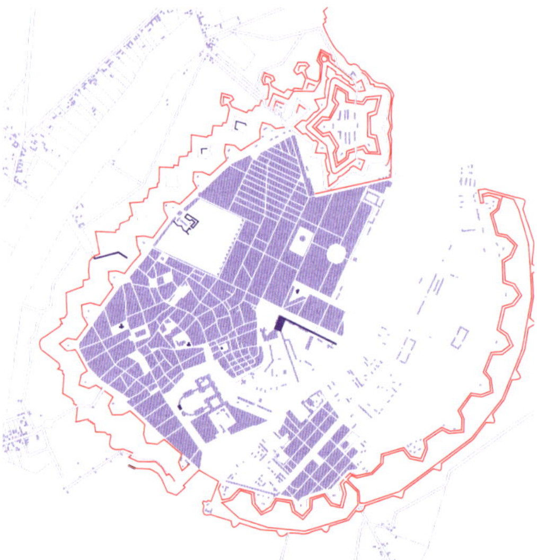

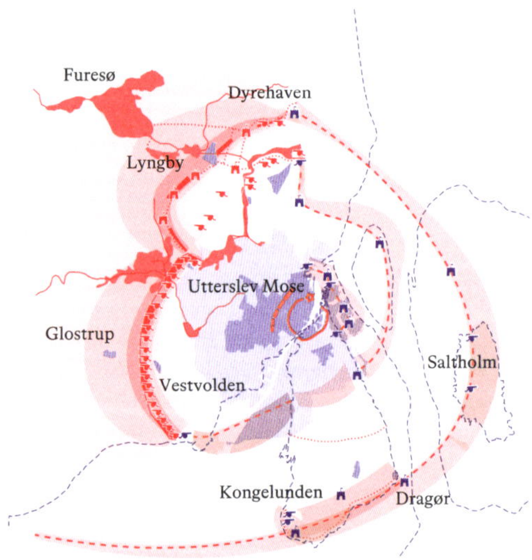

Copenhagen 1850
In the middle of the nineteenth century the military function of the ramparts would be made obsolete due to the extended range of rifled artillery, along with the crises of overcrowding and the Cholera epidemic.

Copenhagen 1914
The late nineteenth and early twentieth century would see the development of the next ring of military defense, including Vestvolden, which defines a perimeter varying between ca. 8–11 km from Copenhagen's center, which would itself be made obsolete with advancements in artillery and later aircraft technology in the early twentieth century.

Urban area
Landscape/forest
Flood area

Historical land border
Fortified field position
Medieval ramparts

Kastellet
Coastal/sea battery
Land battery

Coastal/sea fort
Land fort

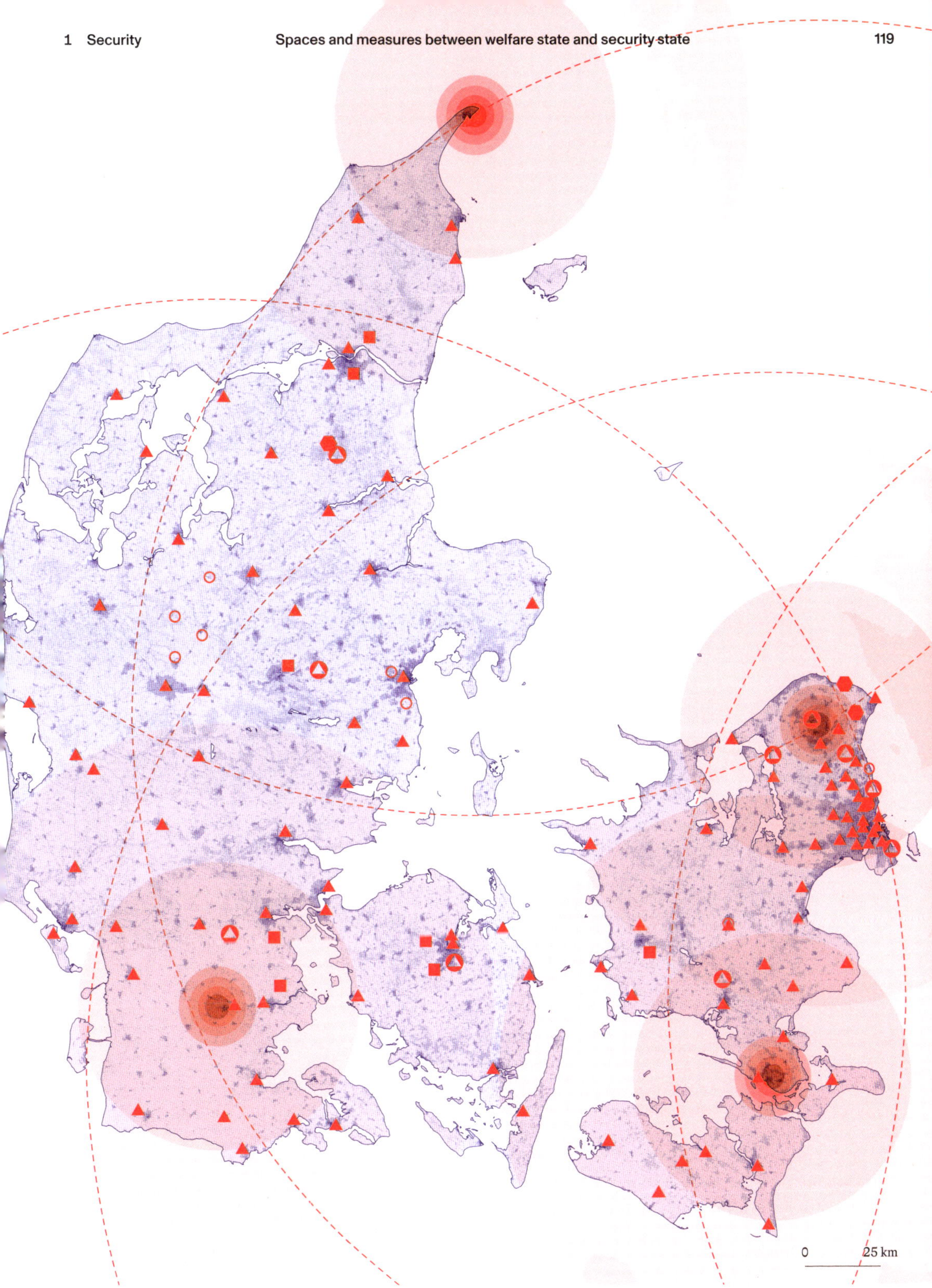

Copenhagen/Denmark 1970
The NATO-coordinated nuclear defenses of the post–World War II Cold War would be further distanced from the city center, forming a network of early detection bases, missile batteries and airfields in locations such as Gunderød, Skalstrup and Stevns, ca. 27 km, 32 km and 48 km from Copenhagen's core.

- Air Force radar stations
- National command center
- Regional command center
- Municipal command center
- Military headquarters
- Civil defense mobilization station

1.02 Copenhagen/international securitization, 2001–22

11 Sep 2001
World Trade Center and Pentagon terror attacks, USA

20 Sep 2001
Term "War on Terror" introduced by US President George W. Bush

2 Oct 2001
Danish Parliament Executive Committee explores increased level of parliament security

Jan 2002
Visitors to Danish Parliament required to use new entrance with security check-in

6 Jun 2002
Danish Anti-Terror Package signed into law, expanding definition of terrorism and Danish Security and Intelligence Service's rights to secret investigation

16 Dec 2002
EU Regulation (EC) No 2320/2002 establishes common rules and requirements for passenger aviation security

20 Mar 2003
Iraq War begins

19 Nov 2003
United Nations' International Maritime Organization (IMO) outlines international ports must be secured against terror

6 Feb 2004
Moscow Metro bombing

11 Mar 2004
Madrid train bombings

1 Jul 2004
Danish ports require anti-terror security measures to receive international shipping

9 May 2005
Danish Parliamentary member Svend Auken concerned over "too much security at the Parliament"

7 Jul 2005
London transport bombings

30 Sep 2005
Danish Newspaper *Jyllands-Posten* publishes cartoons depicting the Islamic prophet Muhammad

Jan 2006 – Feb 2006
Muhammad Cartoons Crisis includes bomb threats against *Jyllands-Posten* in Copenhagen and Aarhus; international demonstrations; attacks on Danish Embassies in Indonesia, Syria, Lebanon and Iran; and boycotts of Danish products.

8 Jun 2006
Danish Anti-Terror Package II signed into law, intended to improve the Danish Security and Intelligence Service (PET's) potential to fight and investigate terrorism

10 Dec 2007
Danish Parliament Executive Committee agrees to develop new more secure visitors' entrance to Parilament

Oct 2008
Danish Parliament's new visitors' entrance completed

2009
Danish Parliament Executive Committee Chairman Thor Pedersen suggests closing adjacent street Rigsdagsgården to vehicular traffic

1 Jan 2010
Muhammad cartoonist Kurt Westergaard subject to assassination attempt at his home

13 Oct 2010
Al Qaeda's "Inspire Magazine" promotes terrorist attacks with vehicles on pedestrian streets in western countries, including Denmark.

11 Dec 2010
Stockholm bombings

22 Jul 2011
Oslo bombing and Utøya shooting

31 Jul 2011
Visitor's entrance to Danish Parliament to be renewed and enlarged for security purposes

13 Dec 2011
Liège attack

14 Dec 2011
Danish Security and Intelligence Service (PET) argue for increased security at Danish Parliament

14 Dec 2012
Head of Venstre party and former Prime Minister Lars Løkke Rasmusse questions extent of parliamentary security, warning "we give in to the terrorist threat"

14 Dec 2012
At request of Danish Security and Intelligence Service (PET), Danish Parliament Executive Committee agrees to close Rigsdagsgården to vehicular traffic

7 Jan 2013
Danish Parliament engages Copenhagen's former chief police inspector Kai Vittrup parliamentary security advis

1 Apr 2013
Boston Marathon bombi

Apr 2013
Granite blocks installed a Christiansborg Slotsplads (Parliament Square) as temporary anti-terrorism security measure

23 May 2013
US President Barack Obama announces "end Global War on Terror"

16 Oct 2013
Danish Government proposes lifting stan of anti-terrorist secu at minor Danish port

2001 2002 2003 2004 2005 2006 2007 2008 2009 2010 2011 2012 2013 2014

25 Nov 2014
Temporary anti-security measures at Christiansborg Slotsplads (Parliament Square) criticized by Copenhagen City Councillor Jakob Næsager for looking like a meteor impact”

7 Jan 2015
Paris Charlie Hebdo shootings

14 Feb 2015
Copenhagen attack

19 Feb 2015
Danish Government anti-terrorism passes DKK 971 million initiative: “A strong defense against terrorism: 12 new measures against terrorism”

19 Jul 2015
Debate over increased public space presence of police with machine guns and bulletproof vests in Copenhagen

Sep–Nov 2015
Peak of 2015 European Migrant Crisis

13 Nov 2015
Paris attacks

26 Nov 2015
Technical and Environmental Mayor of Copenhagen Morten Kabell suggests closing Copenhagen Medieval City to vehicular traffic for security reasons

2 Dec 2015
San Bernadino attack

5 Feb 2016
Danish Parliament passes so-called “Jewellery Law” allowing for the search and seizure of certain assets of asylum seekers

22 Mar 2016
Brussels bombing

22 Mar 2016
Information Newspaper debates question of societal loss due to the increased security level in Denmark

13 Jun 2016
Danish Parliament completes plan for permanent anti-terrorist security at Christiansborg Slotsplads (Parliament Square)

14 Jul 2016
Nice truck attack

19 Dec 2016
Berlin Christmas Market truck attack

20 Dec 2016
Copenhagen police require Municipality of Copenhagen to place concrete jersey barriers as anti-terror measures in key public spaces in response to Berlin Christmas Market truck attack

22 Mar 2017
London Westminster vehicle attack

28 Mar 2017
“Berlingske” newspaper reflects on increasing visibility of anti-terror security

3 Apr 2017
St Petersburg Metro bombing

7 Apr 2017
Stockholm truck attack

8 Apr 2017
Mayor of Copenhagen reflects on consideration of permanent anti-terror security measures for Copenhagen

12 Apr 2017
Copenhagen City Council member Cecilia Lonning-Skovgaard suggests need for improved anti-terrorist security on Copenhagen's Strøget

13 Apr 2017
Jyllands-Posten newspaper publishes that crash tests reveal “concrete blocks cannot stop a truck”

1 May 2017
Copenhagen Police warns garbage truck drivers to not leave vehicles unlocked

9 May 2017
Copenhagen Police require concrete blocks to be installed at Copenhagen's Nyhavn

22 May 2017
Manchester Arena bombing

23 May 2017
Former head of PET Jakob Scharf suggests the Manchester Arena bombing “must lead to an increased focus on security on places where many people are gathered”

23 May 2017
Roskilde Festival and Copenhagen street festival Distortion plan to increase levels of anti-terrorist security

3 Jun 2017
London Bridge attack

13 Jun 2017
Some Copenhagen concrete jersey blocks decorated and camouflaged by artists and designers

17 Aug 2017
Barcelona truck attack

24 Aug 2017
Copenhagen City Council decides to close off Medieval City for car traffic, to reduce risk of terrorist attack

25 Aug 2017
Copenhagen Technical and Environmental Mayor Morten Kabell (EL) is criticized for misusing anti-terrorist security as an excuse to promote personal anti-car ideology

28 Aug 2017
Copenhagen City Council agree to replace concrete jersey blocks with planters, trees, bike stands, benches and other urban elements at a cost of 5.2 million Kroner

12 Oct 2017
School children invited by Copenhagen Technical and Environmental Administration to decorate anti-terrorist concrete jersey blocks

31 Oct 2017
New York vehicle attack

30 Nov 2017
Copenhagen Technical and Environmental Administration to spend DKK 2 million to study the possibilities of closing off the Medieval City for vehicular traffic

23 Apr 2018
Toronto vehicle attack

3 Dec 2018
Copenhagen Technical and Environmental Administration agree to continue development on three proposals to close off the Medieval City for vehicular traffic

11 Dec 2018
Strasbourg attack

30 Jan 2019
Inauguration of renewed anti-terror secured Christiansborg Slotsplads (Parliament Square).

28 Feb 2019
Right-wing Nye Borgerlige party leader Pernille Vermund reported to police for calling concrete jersey barriers “koranklodser”

15 Mar 2019
Christchurch Mosque shootings

20 Aug 2019
Copenhagen Municipality decide to pause [road closure] “mega-projects to avoid traffic chaos” until further overall studies are made

10 Sep 2019
Amalienborg Palace to be anti-terror secured with anti-vehicle bollards

29 Nov 2019
London Bridge attack

11 Dec 2019
Danish Security and Intelligence Service (PET) make twenty arrests across Denmark, of whom eight are charged with attempted terrorism

9 Feb 2020
Hanau shootings

2 Nov 2020
Vienna attack

9 Feb 2021
Danish Security and Intelligence Service (PET) make thirteen arrests in Holbæk related to supposed attempted bomb and shooting plot

2015 2016 2017 2018 2019 2020 2021 2022

1.03 Copenhagen inaccessible and secure spaces, 1970

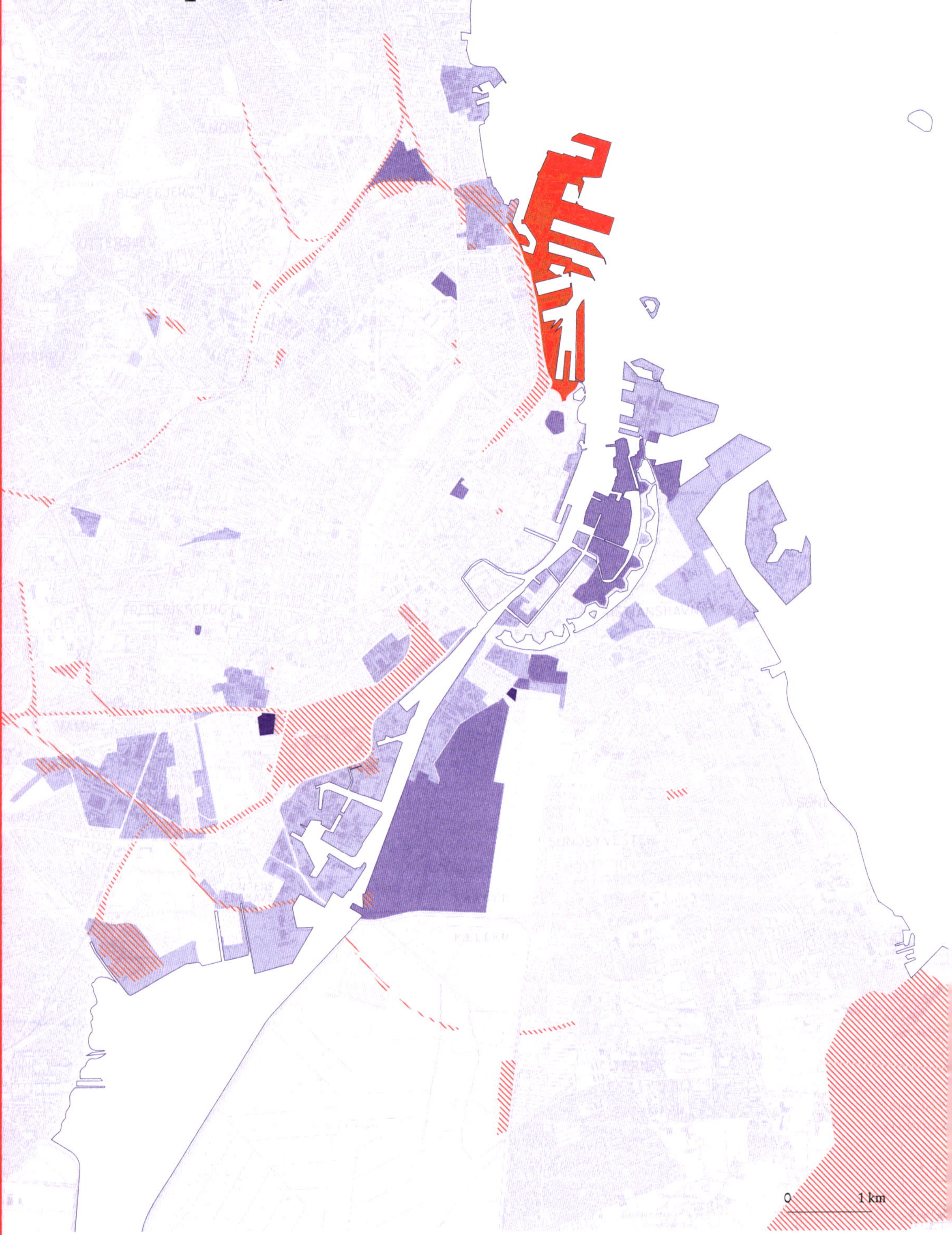

Industry
Military
Police/Corrections
Port
Transport/technical infrastructure

1.04 Copenhagen inaccessible and secure spaces, 2022

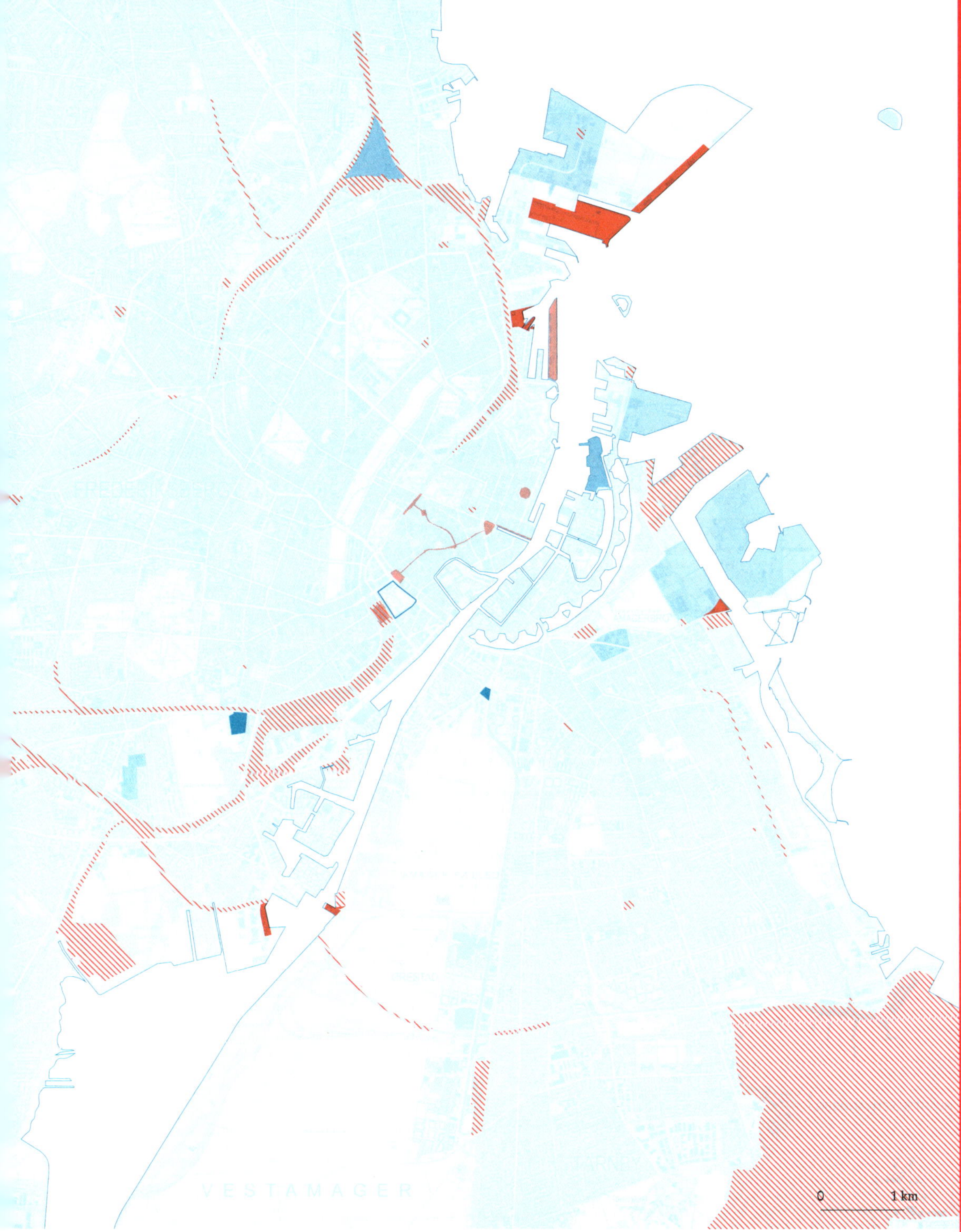

Industry
Military
Police/Corrections
Parliament
Port
Protection zone (PET)
Transport/technical infrastructure

1.05 Nine [terror-]protected zones recommended by PET to Copenhagen municipality and Copenhagen Police, 2017

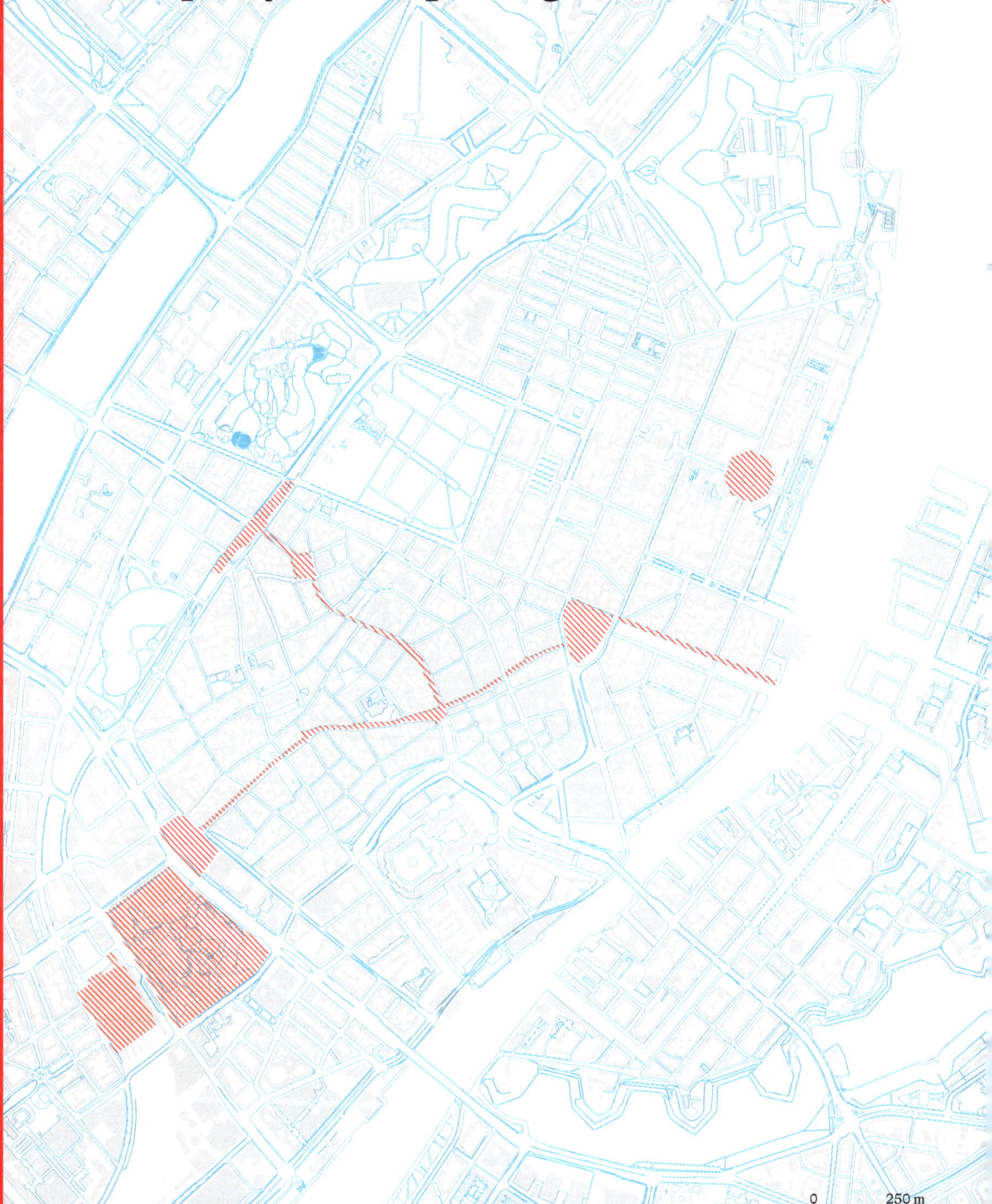

Indication of nine protected zones recommended by PET

1.06

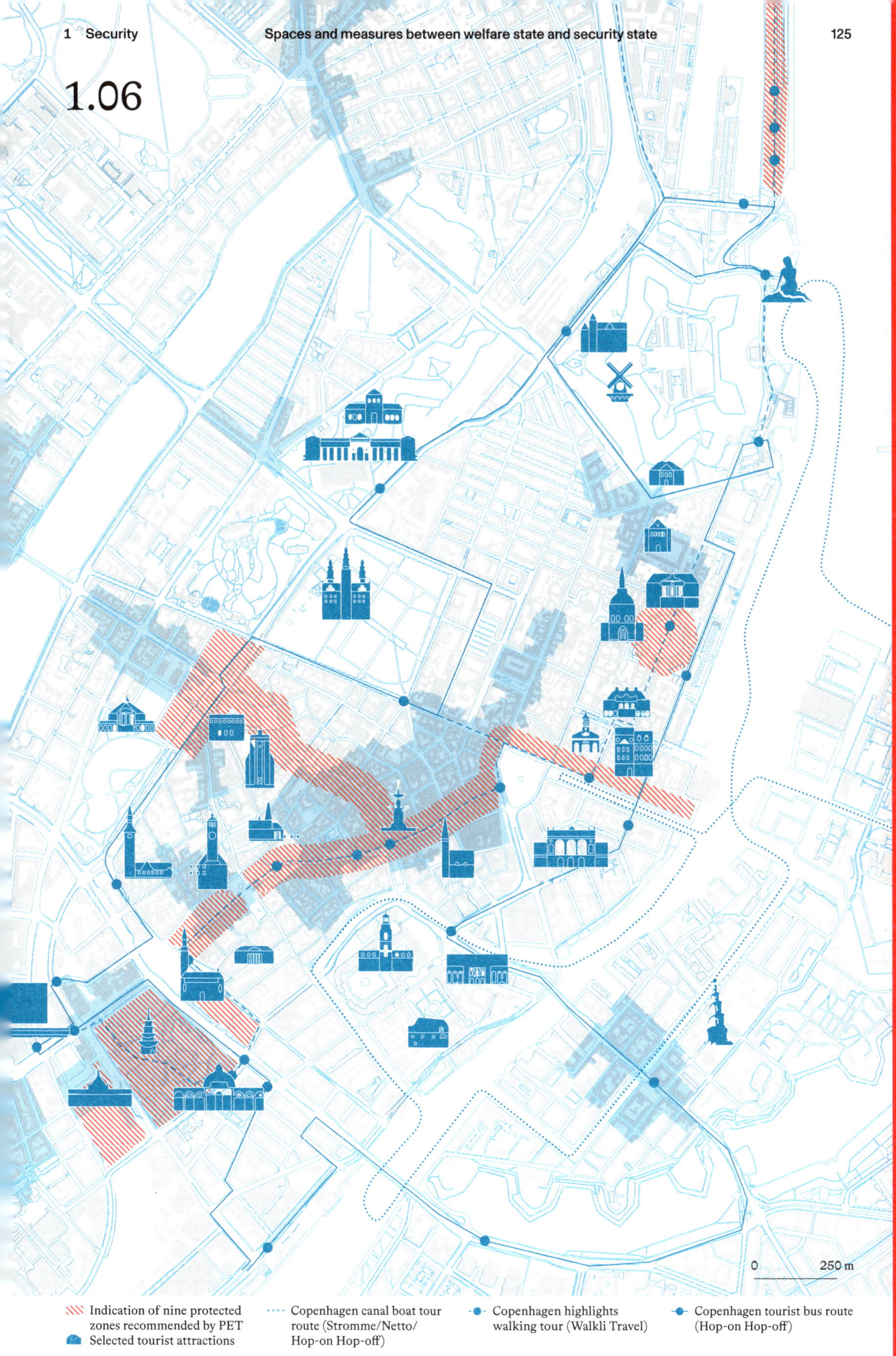
0 250 m
Indication of nine protected zones recommended by PET
Selected tourist attractions
Copenhagen canal boat tour route (Stromme/Netto/Hop-on Hop-off)
Copenhagen highlights walking tour (Walkli Travel)
Copenhagen tourist bus route (Hop-on Hop-off)

1.07

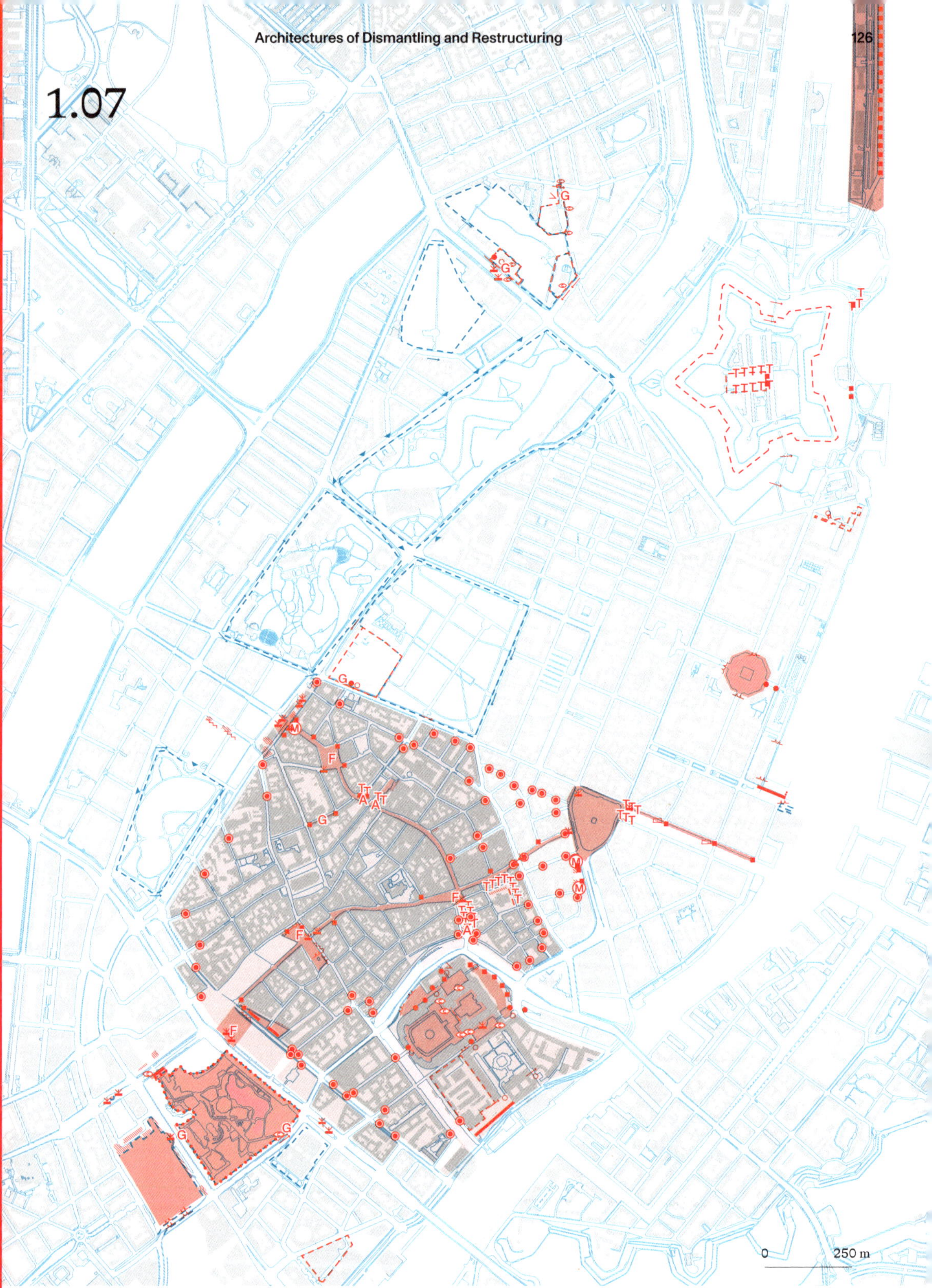

PET-recommended [terror-]protected zones
Proposed medieval city protection (scenario B)
Bike racks (as PSM)
Military/diplomatic/national protected areas
Private sector security areas
Fenced or Partially fenced public space
Entrance
Protection Nodes (Medieval City Scenario B)
Boulders
Fixed benches (in any materials)
Vehicle barrier (low)
Vehicle barrier (high)
Vehicles barrier (retractable)
Reinforced planters
Gate
Bollards (permanent)
Bollards (retractable)
Level difference
CCTV
G Guard presence
A Public art (as PSM)
T Tree (as PSM)
F Fountains (as PSM)

1.08 Copenhagen physical security measures

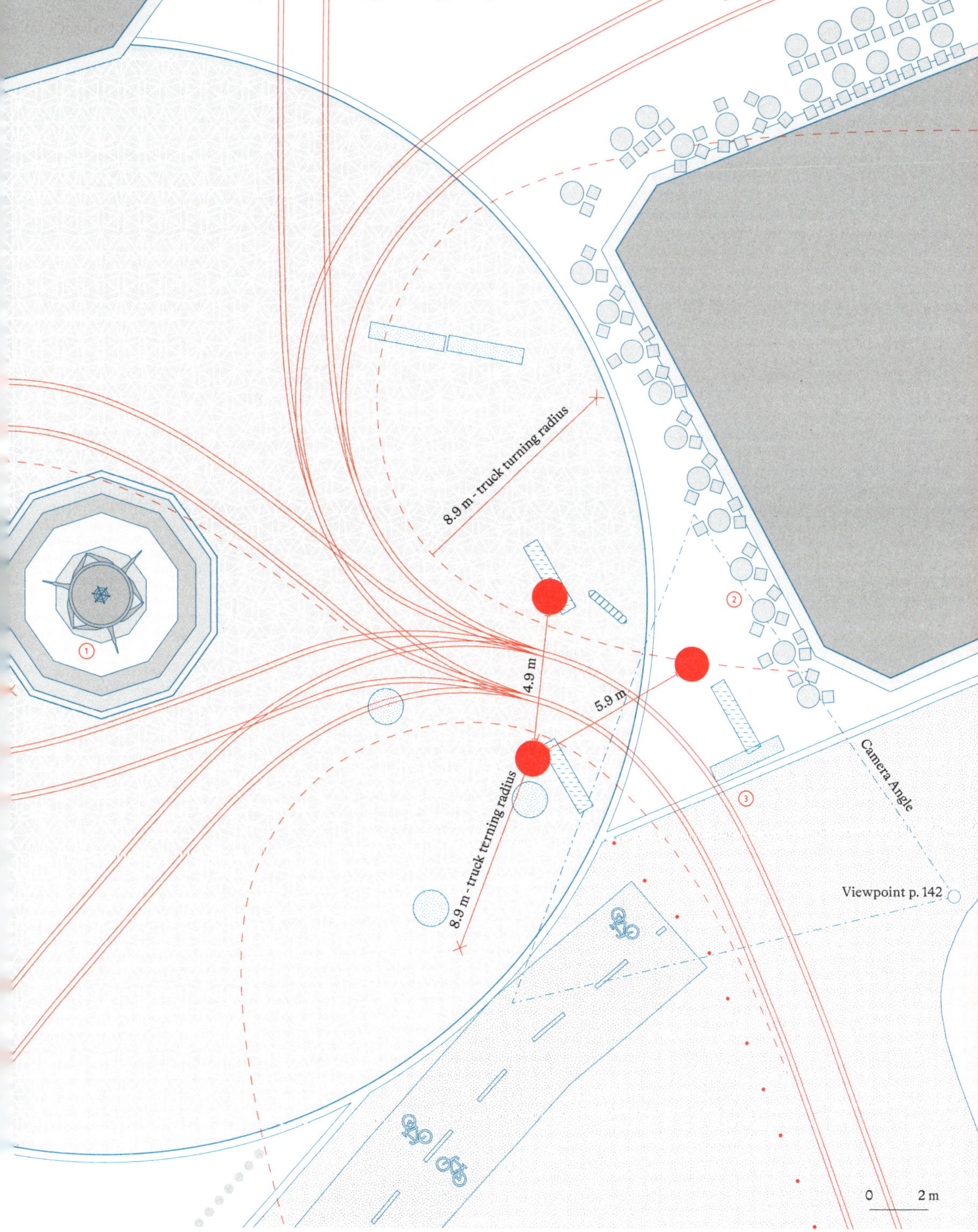

Jersey Barrier
Concrete Barrier
Reinforced Planter
PSM layout 2009
PSM layout 2017
PSM layout 2018
PSM layout 2021

(1) Stork Fountain, 1894 Silver wedding anniversary present to Crown Prince Frederik and Crown Princess Louise (listed monument).

(2) Reinforced Planter Role: speed reducer and deterrent against vehicle-based attack. Material: cast concrete, soil, planting.

(3) PSM placement Forced vehicle direction deviations: ca. 20–30 degrees. Associated speed reduction: ca. 30–60%. Weight: ca. 500 kg Cost: ca. DKK 20,000 per unit.

1.09 Copenhagen physical security measures

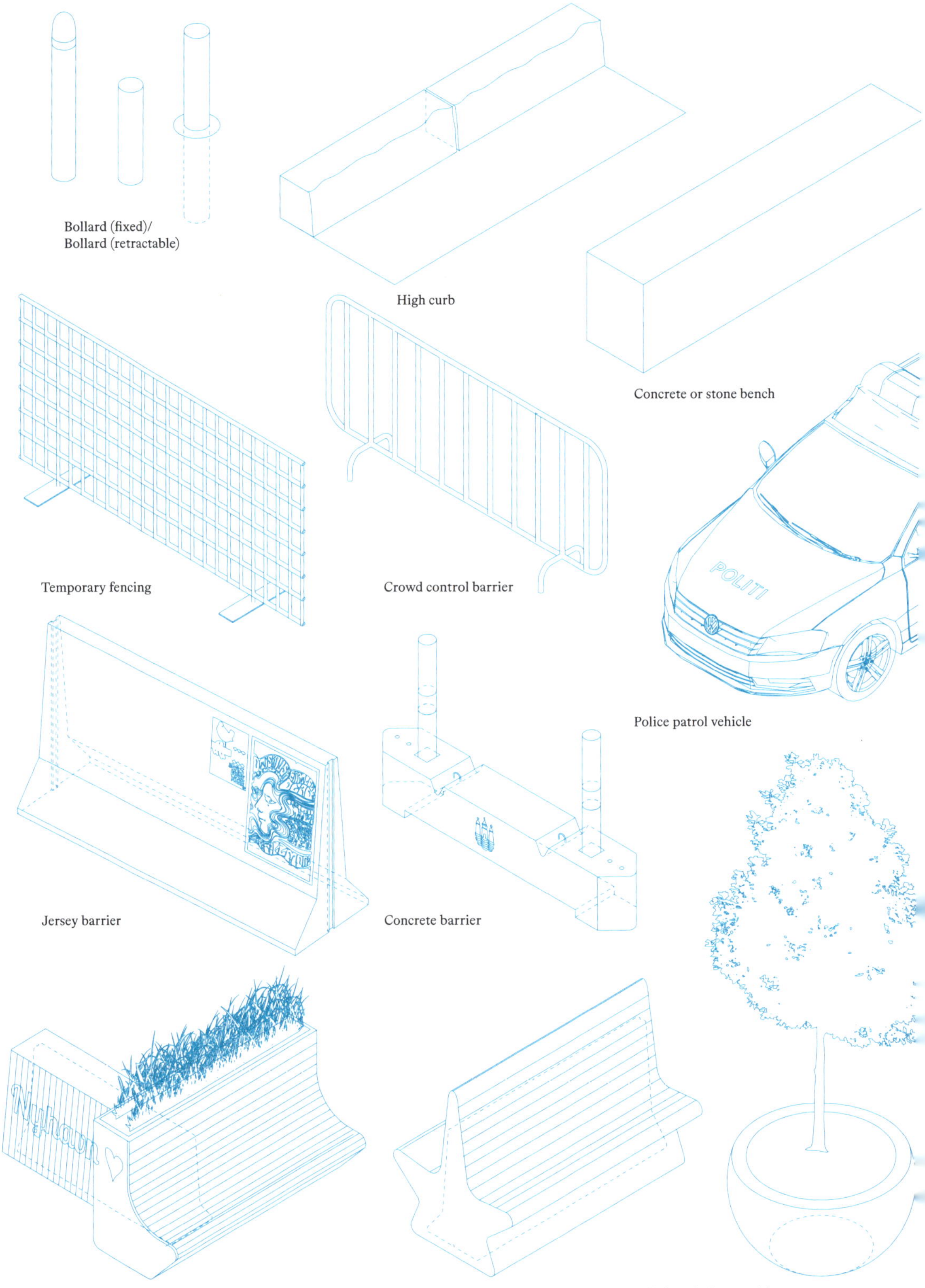

Bollard (fixed)/
Bollard (retractable)

High curb

Concrete or stone bench

Temporary fencing

Crowd control barrier

Police patrol vehicle

Jersey barrier

Concrete barrier

Jersey barrier clad as signage, planter or seating

Jersey barrier clad as seating

Reinforced planter with tree

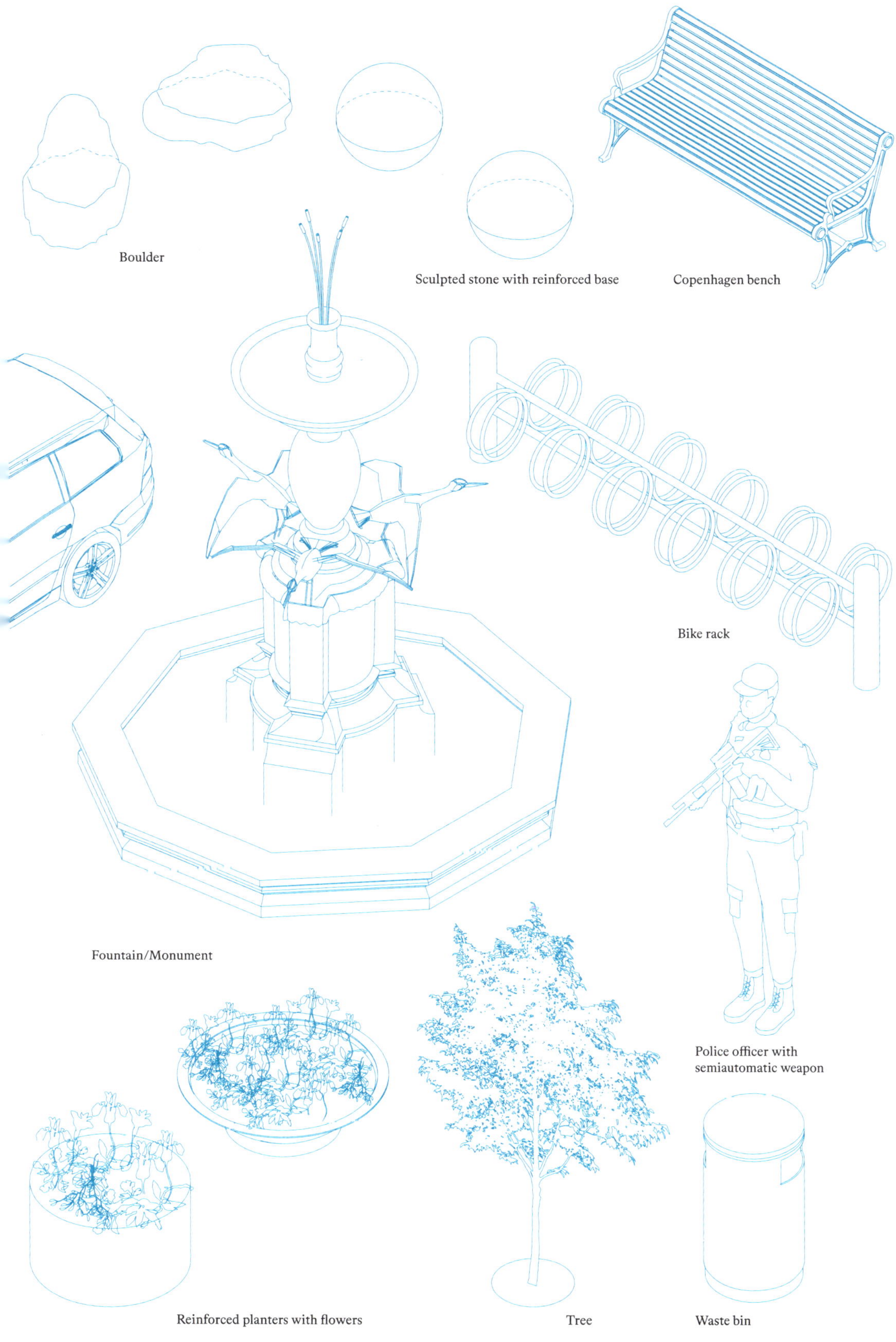
Boulder
Sculpted stone with reinforced base
Copenhagen bench
Bike rack
Fountain/Monument
Police officer with semiautomatic weapon
Reinforced planters with flowers
Tree
Waste bin

1.10 Copenhagen physical security measures, detail

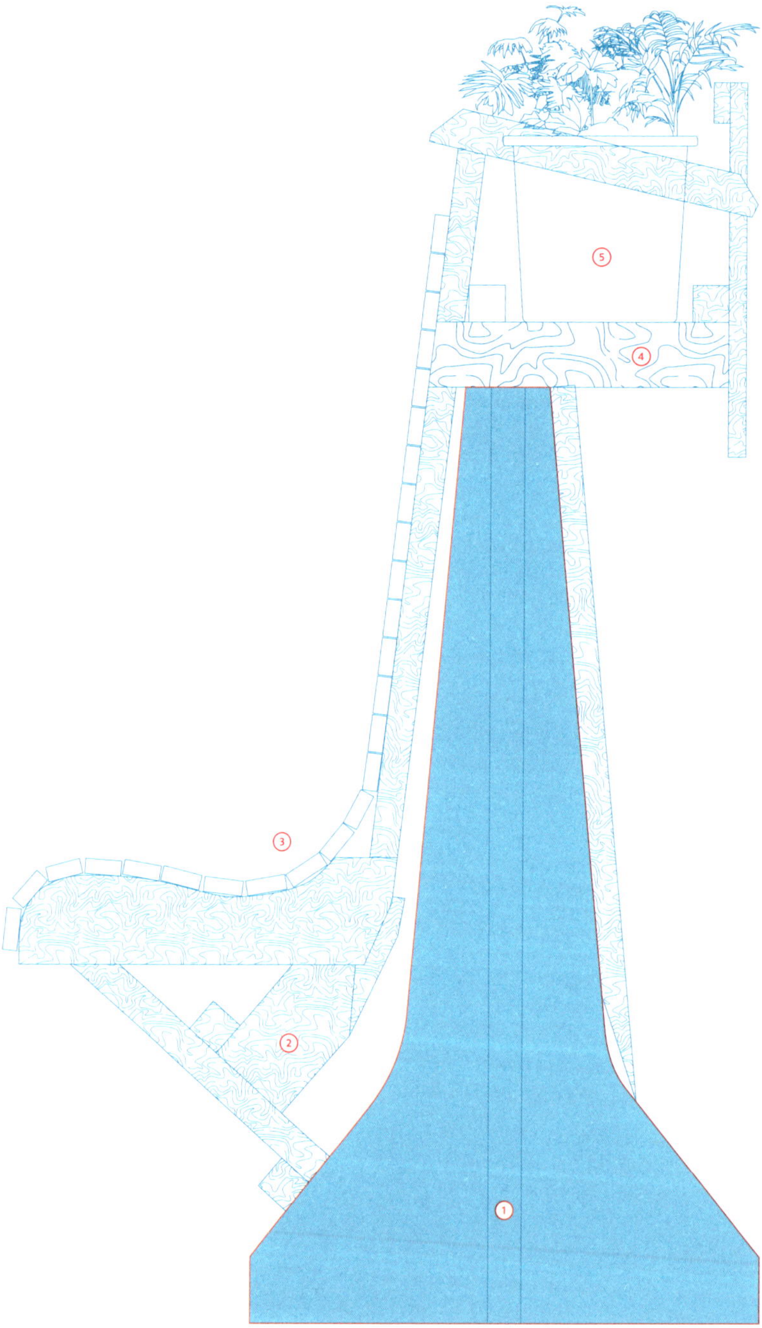

Cross-section of 2017 "Tag Tomat" Jersey barrier transformation

1. Reinforced concrete Jersey barrier
2. Wood support armature
3. Wood seating planking
4. Wood support for potted plant
5. Potted plant

1.11 Securitized public space case studies

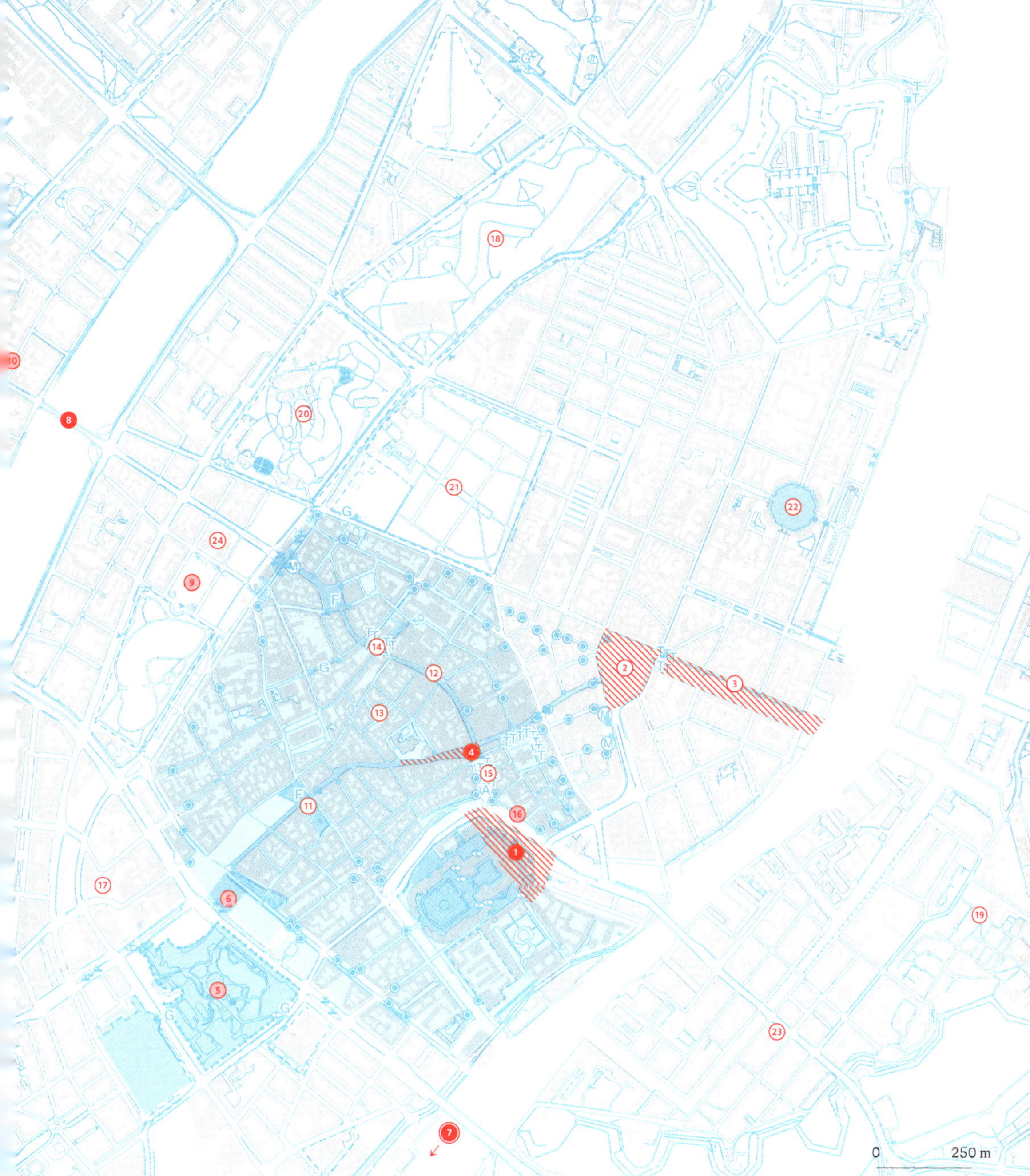

Securitized case study areas

Numbers of books in which the public space is mentioned

1 2 3 4

a) J. Gehl, L. Gemzøe, *Urban Spaces Urban Life*, 1996
b) Monocle Magazine, *Annual Quality of Life Survey*, 2013
c) D. Simpson, K. Gimmel, A. Lonka, M. Jay, J. Grootens, *Atlas of the Copenhagens*, 2018
d) T. Nielsen, *The Making of Democratic Urban Public Space in Denmark*, 2019
e) D. Simpson, *Spaces and Measures between Welfare State and Security State*, 2022

1. Christiansborg Slotsplads [a, b, e]
2. Kongens Nytorv [a, b, c, e]
3. Nyhavn [a, b, c, e]
4. Amagertorv/Strøget [a, c, e]
5. Tivoli [a, c]
6. Rådhuspladsen [a, c]
7. Islands Brygge Havnepark [a, b, c, d]
8. Dronning Louises Bro [b, c, d]
9. Israels Plads [a, d]
10. Superkilen [c, d]
11. Gammeltorv – Nytorv [a]
12. Købmagergade [a]
13. Gråbrødretorv [a]
14. Kultorvet [a]
15. Højbro Plads [a]
16. Ved Stranden [a]
17. Axeltorv [a]
18. Ørstedsparken [a]
19. Christiania [c]
20. Botanisk Have [a]
21. Kongens Have [a]
22. Amalienborg Slotsplads & Haven [a]
23. Christianshavns Torv [a]
24. Torvehallerne [b]

1.12 Securitized public space: Kongens Nytorv, ca. 1970/2022

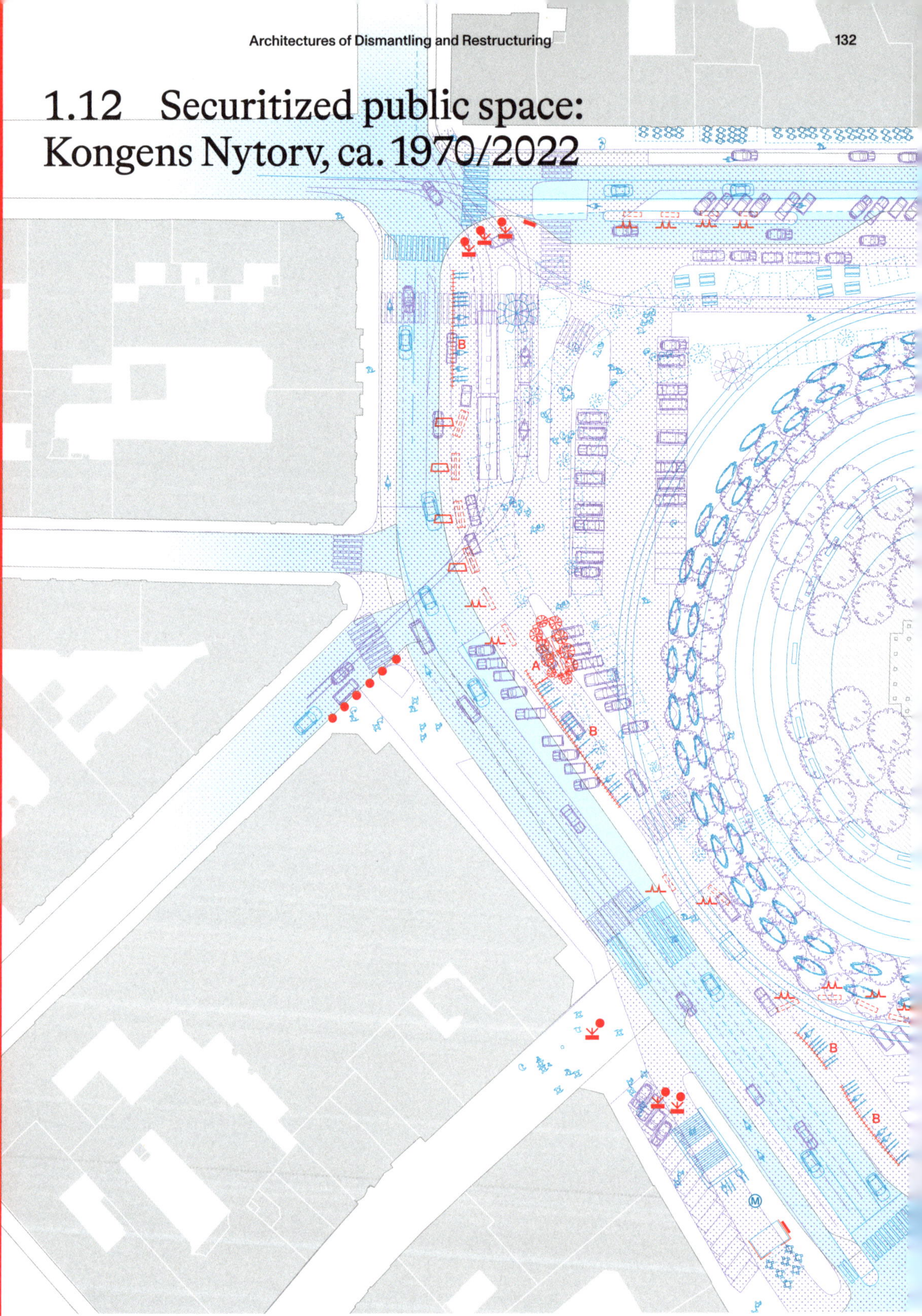

1970 plan
1970 vehicular access
2020 plan
2020 vehicular access

Permanent physical security measures (today)
Temporary physical security measures (Christmas Market)

Reinforced planters
Vehicle barrier (low)
Bollards
Fixed benches
Vehicle barrier (high)

A Art
M Monument (as PSM)
G Guard presence
B Bike racks (as PSM)

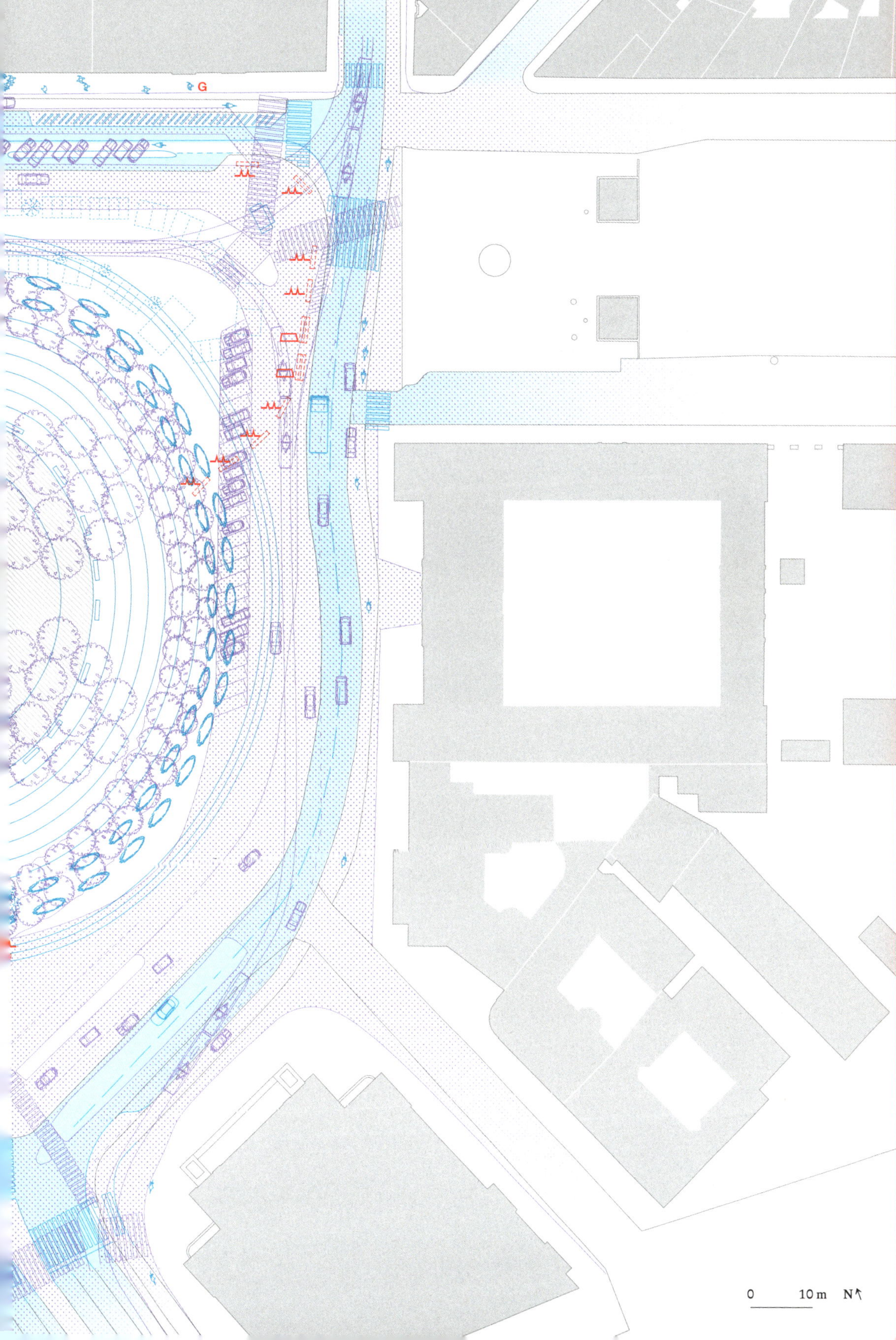
G
0 10 m N

1.13 Securitized public space: Kongens Nytorv, ca. 1970/2022

Reinforced planters with trees

1970 archival photo 2022 3D scan Physical security measures (today)

1.14 Securitized public space: Kongens Nytorv, ca. 1970

1975

1971

1.15 Securitized public space: Nyhavn, ca. 1970/2022

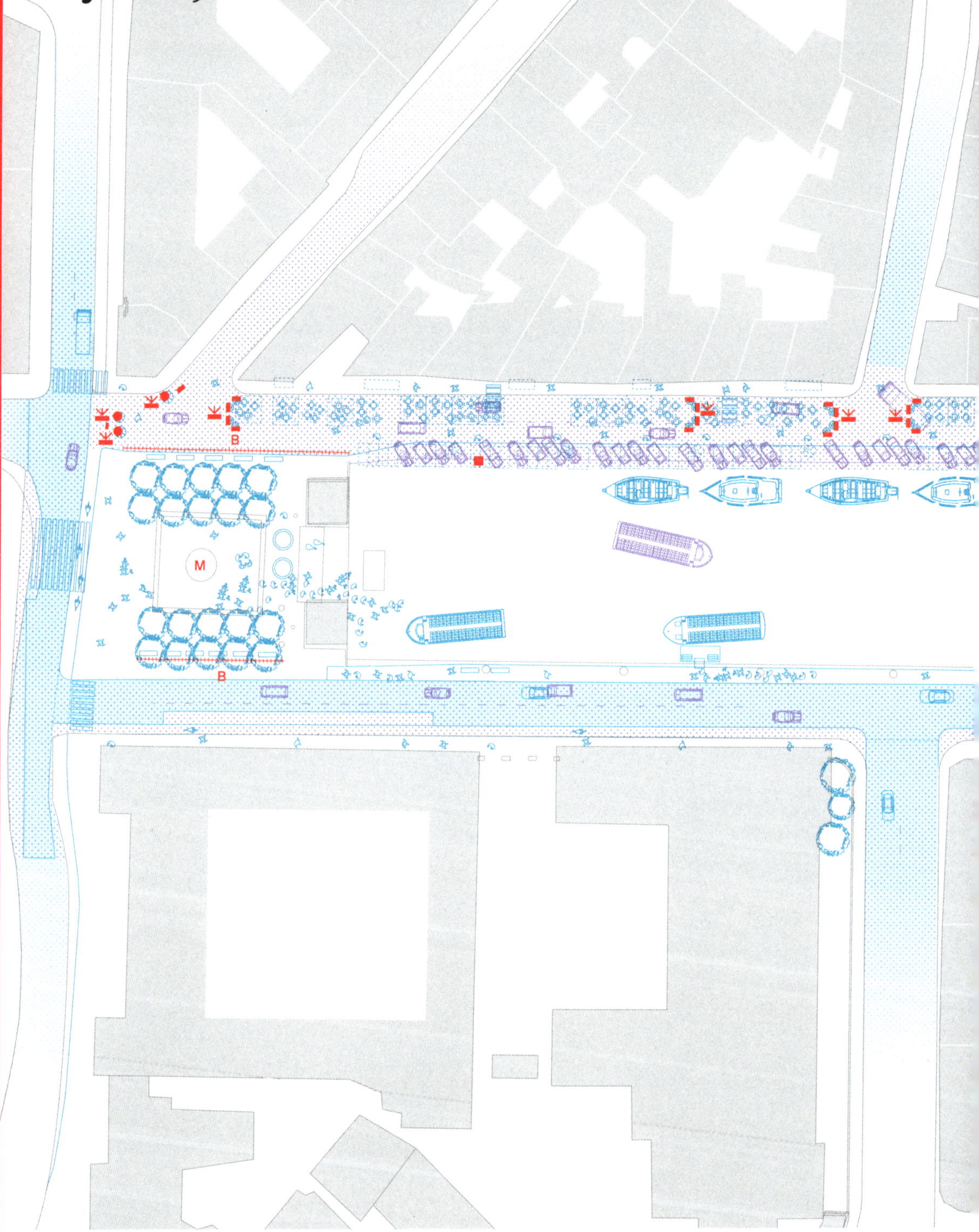

1970 plan
1970 vehicular access
2020 plan
2020 vehicular access

Permanent physical security measures (today)
Reinforced planters
Bollards

Fixed benches
M Monument (as PSM)
B Bike racks (as PSM)

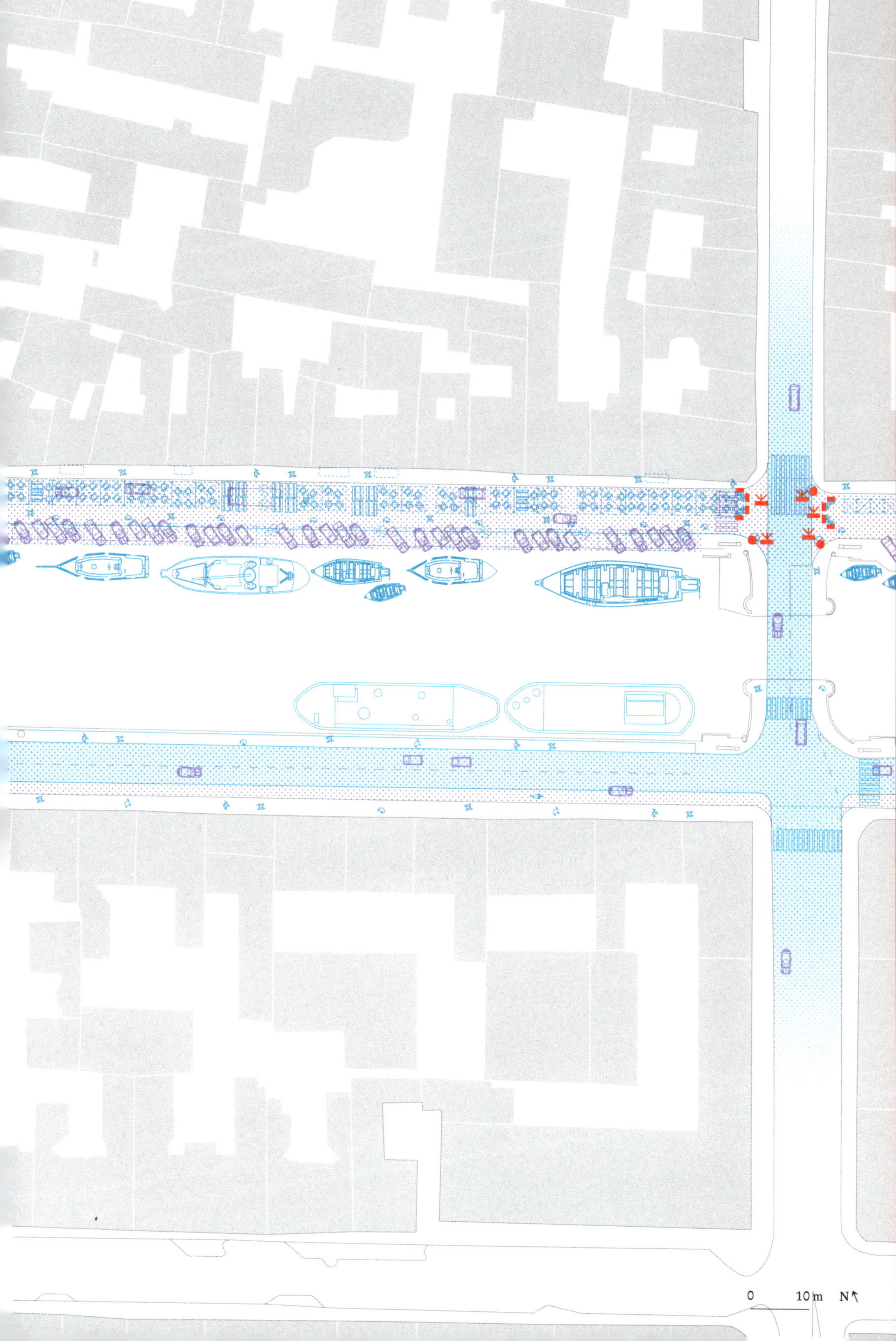
0
10 m
N

1.16 Securitized public space: Nyhavn, ca. 1970/2022

Reinforced planters with flowers

Reinforced planters: with tree and camouflaged jersey barrier

■ 1970 archival photo ■ 2022 3D scan ■ Physical security measures (today)

1.17 Securitized public space: Nyhavn, ca. 1970

ca. 1980

1970

1.18 Securitized public space: Amagertorv, ca. 1970/2022

- 1970 plan
- 1970 vehicular access
- 2020 plan
- 2020 vehicular access
- Permanent physical security measures (today)
- Reinforced planters
- Bollards
- F Fountains (as PSM)
- B Bike racks (as PSM)
- T Sunken toilet railing

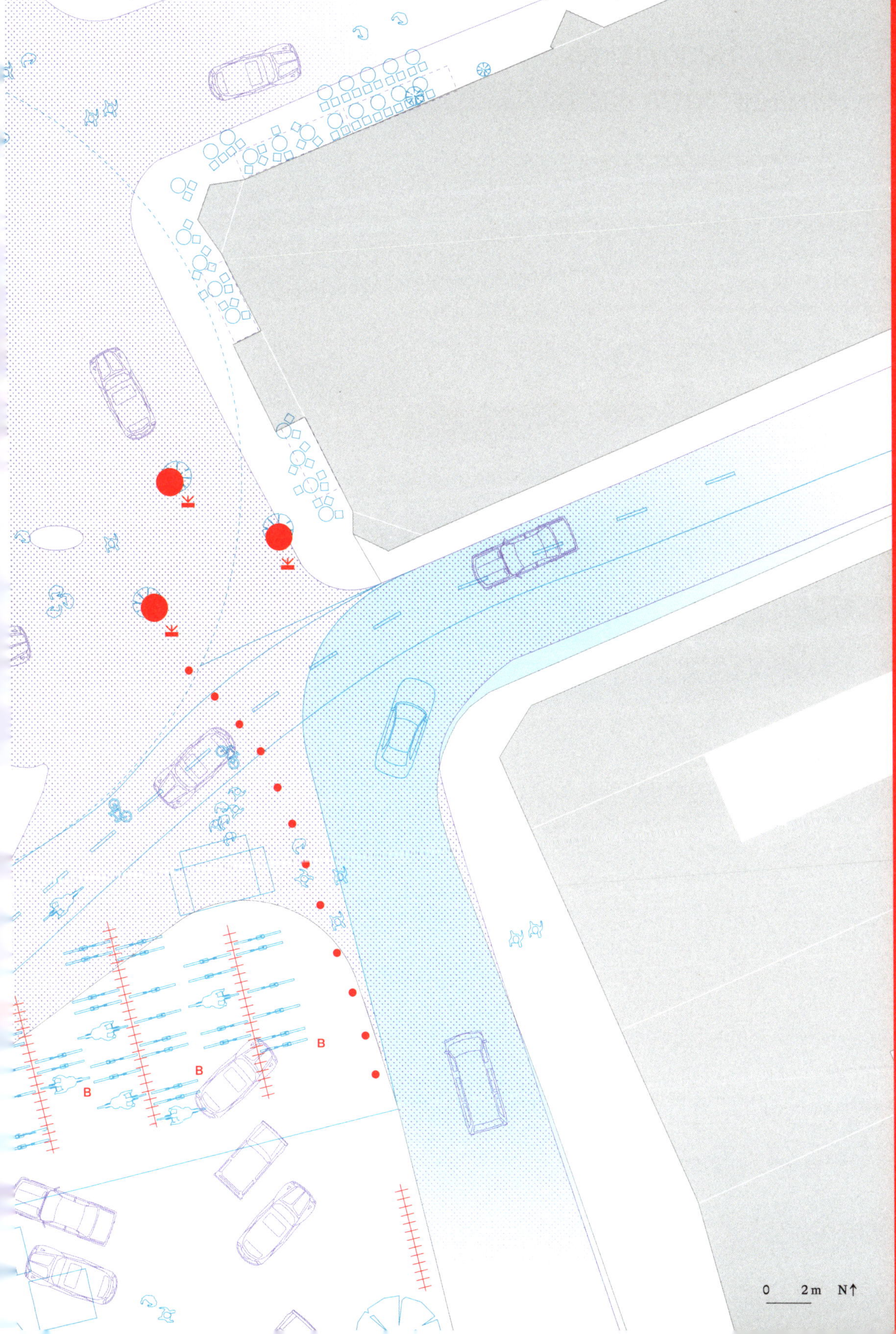
B
B
B
0 2 m N↑

1.19 Securitized public space: Amagertorv, ca. 1970/2022

Reinforced planters with trees

■ 1970 archival photo ■ 2022 3D scan ■ Physical security measures (today)

1.20 Securitized public space: Amagertorv, ca. 1970

1962

1975

1.21 Securitized public space: Christiansborg Slotsplads, ca. 1970/2022

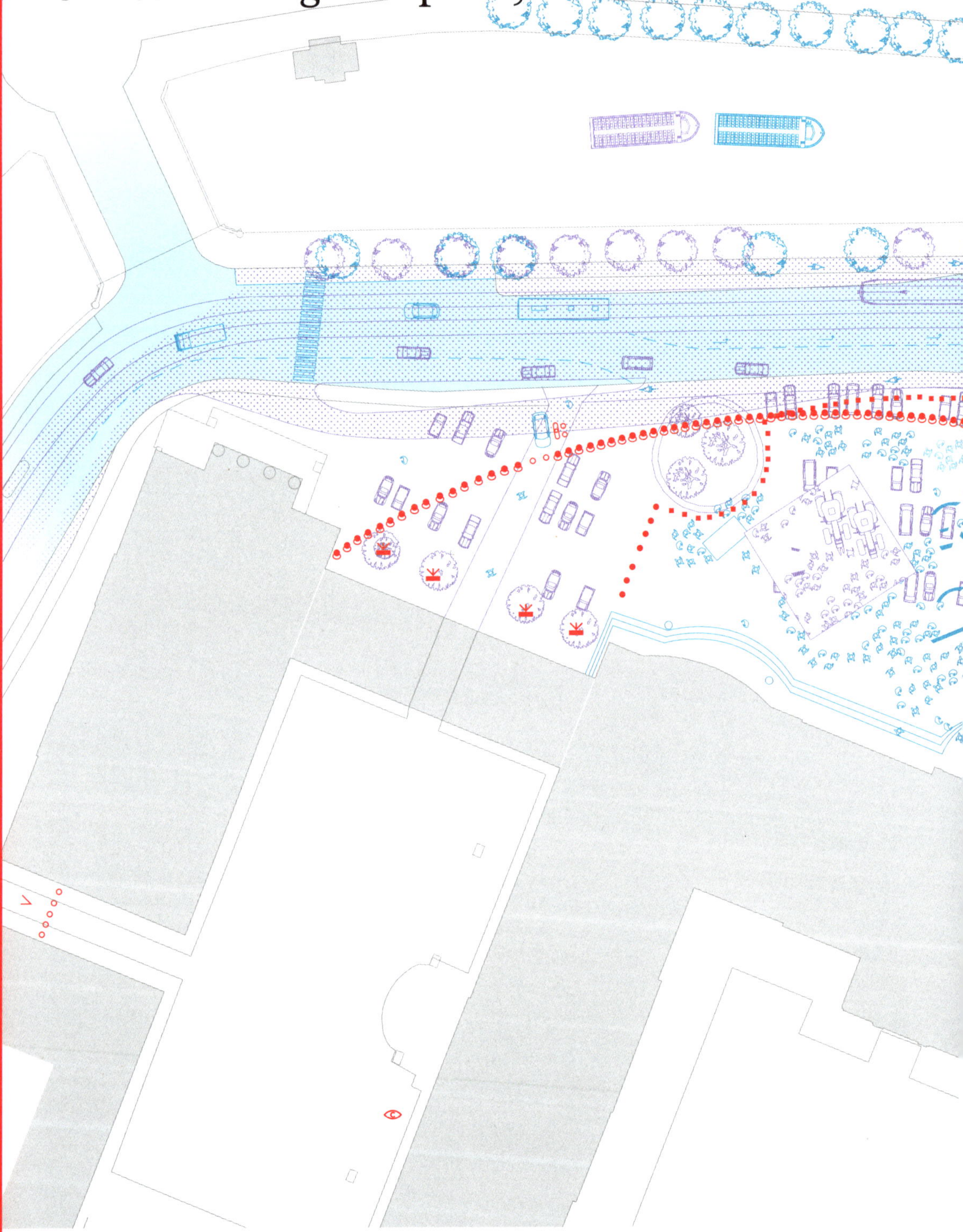

1970 plan
1970 vehicular access
2020 plan
2020 vehicular access

Permanent physical security measures (today)
Reinforced planters
Boulders 2013–18

Permanent bollards
Retractable bollards
Sculpted stone with reinforced base

Fixed benches
CCTV
Vehicle barrier (retractable)

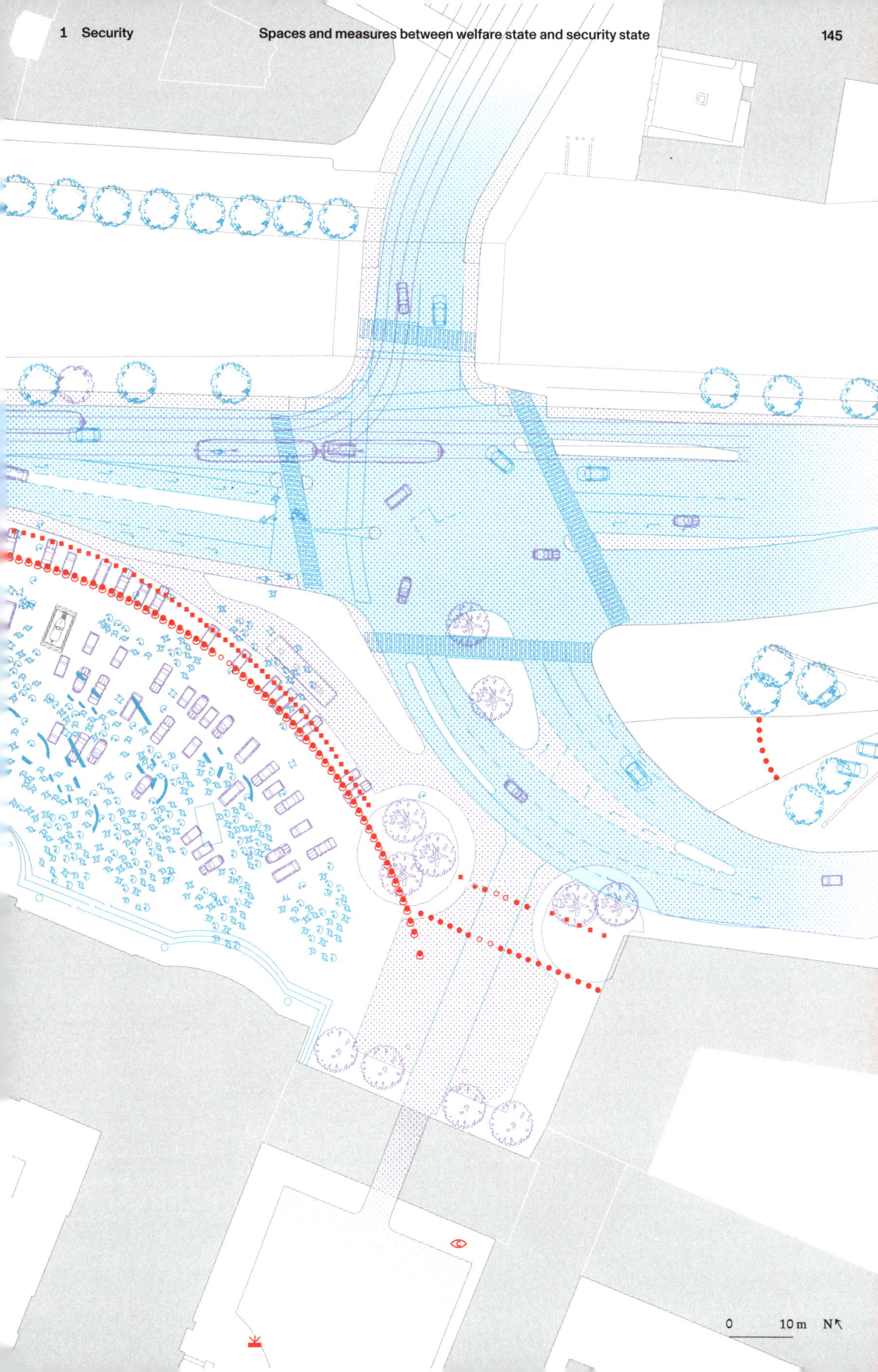
0 10 m N

1.22 Securitized public space: Christiansborg Slotsplads, ca. 1970/2022

Granite bollards with reinforced base

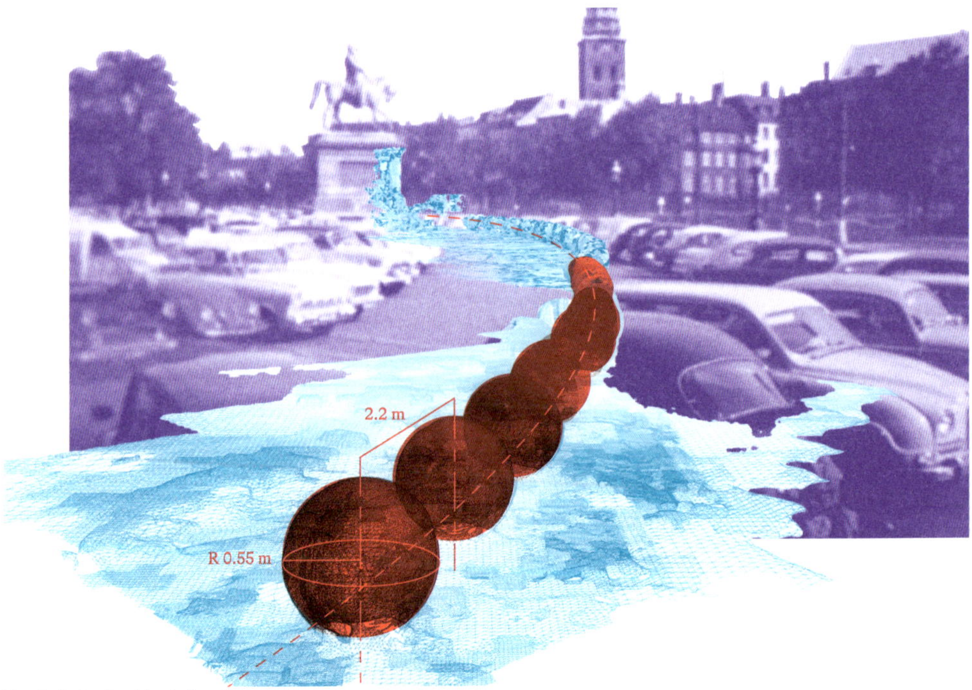

Granite bollards with reinforced base

1970 archival photo | 2022 3D scan | Physical security measures (today)

1.23 Securitized public space: Christiansborg Slotsplads, ca. 1970

1969

1965

Between Technologies of Power and Notions of Solidarity
A Response to the Danish *Ghetto Plan* and Swedish *Vulnerable Areas* Documents

Heidi Svenningsen Kajita, Jennifer Mack,
Svava Riesto, Meike Schalk

1 Front cover, *Ét Danmark uden parallelsamfund: Ingen ghettoer i 2030.* One Denmark without Parallel Societies: No Ghettos in 2030.

2 Front cover, *Rätt insats på rätt plats: Polisens arbete i utsatta område.* The Right Action in the Right Place: Police Work in Vulnerable Areas. Photo by Joachim Nywall.

Recently, a dramatic paradigm shift in notions of solidarity has occurred within Nordic welfare states.[1] With this transformation, the universal notion of welfare for all, which has guided numerous welfare policies in the Nordic countries since World War II, is losing ground.[2] We study the expression of this shift in official, government-sponsored documents that support and recommend the reshaping and redefinition of social housing estates in Denmark and municipal housing estates in Sweden.

Key political measures appear in both what is known as the *Ghetto Plan*, authored by the Danish government and in the equivalent classification of *vulnerable areas* established by the Swedish police.[3] These policies are instrumentalized via planning, architecture and design and have direct spatial, material and social consequences, affecting people's neighborhoods, everyday lives, rights and opportunities. In connection, we argue, these measures alter residents' access to welfare-state practices of solidarity. Both the *ghetto* and *vulnerable area* categories support radical interventions that understand mixed tenure and demographics as ideal and intend to do away with so-called parallel societies. Communities are presented as voluntarily outside the otherwise solidaric community of the welfare state, or even as a plague on the nation. In this sense, solidarity signifies agreements between and support for other members of a community. While other researchers have studied these plans from various perspectives, we analyze how these recent stigmatizing policies redefine solidarity and what boundaries of inclusion and exclusion are established through labels, images and documents.[4]

In particular, we investigate how three specific policy documents build an argument for radical physical and social interventions by combining photos, diagrams and words.[5] ⟨figs. 1–3⟩ These policy documents, we contend, can be understood as a technology of power closely related to Michel Foucault's famous analysis of the penal system and its requisite collection of knowledge.[6] When government agencies use these documents to identify neighborhoods said to require disciplinary interventions, these agencies intend to seize power over the built environment and, explicitly or implicitly, to discipline the body (typically the migrant or minority body) at the same time. Thus, we scrutinize them as devices supporting political arguments with controversial consequences: material, social and even personal. To provide a background for understanding what we see as a shift in notions of solidarity, we will first briefly introduce the initial paradigm of the Nordic welfare state, under which unprecedented quantities of social and nonprofit housing estates were built: these are the neighborhoods that contemporary policy documents target.

3 Screen shot of webpage *Områden som kan påverka rätten till ersättning för asylsökande.* Areas that May Affect the Right to Compensation for Asylum Seekers.

Housing as Solidarity in the Post–World War II Welfare States in Denmark and Sweden

Several key historical trajectories shaped the lines along which social and municipal housing was constructed during the mid-twentieth century in Denmark and Sweden. Although the two countries built different administrative and economic models for housing, both produced multifamily housing programs implemented as part of a larger scheme of distributing wealth to create socioeconomic equality.[7] These nonprofit housing programs were imagined as vehicles to offer housing for all, as their official names reflect: Allmännyttan/Almennyttige.

The focus on the neighborhood scale centered on an idealized nuclear family and the mixture of people of different socioeconomic classes. But during the years following World War II, Scandinavian borders opened to a large influx of labor migrants and refugees. Many migrants have since settled largely in the social and municipal housing areas, thereby contributing to major changes in the demographics over time.[8] Meanwhile, the systemic economic redistribution behind the twentieth-century industrial city of the Nordic welfare state changed from egalitarian to a support of private home ownership that disfavored people in social housing, supporting a newly financialized and speculative planning ethos during the twenty-first century. Despite these changes, we observe that the idea of mixed communities as a path to promote solidarity remains at the core of contemporary urban planning, though this approach is now justified by other arguments, as we will explain.

Connecting all members of the state through the image of the state as a home or family – called Folkhemmet (the People's Home) in the Swedish context – architects, planners, landscape architects and others aimed to find a spatial category that could bridge the microscale of the individual and family and the macroscale of the state as a community for solidarity. This quest was exemplified in the shared topic and research object of the neighborhood unit, originally developed by American planner Clarence Perry in the 1920s and exported broadly.[9] The widespread preoccupation with linking social phenomena to design in research and planning practice could be described as order-thinking or social engineering. Swedish and Danish experts concluded that the spatial ordering of housing into less dense areas, with limited units at an "appropriate" scale in relation to the number, age, sex, type and marital status of residents, would improve society at large.[10] Social engineering reflected the belief that planning and design could stimulate certain social activities, like communal gatherings, certain types of play and even ethical behavior. Deterministic and universalizing ideas about how residents would live in modern housing were, however, soon to be criticized. However, already during the 1970s, a shift from top-down governmental standardization to participatory planning initiatives appeared. Today, the statistical approaches developed in relation to the neighborhood unit have resurfaced in another form.

Images and Words in the Danish *Ghetto Plan* and Swedish *Vulnerable Area* Documents

The political action plan *Ét Danmark uden parallelsamfund: Ingen ghettoer i 2030* (One Denmark without Parallel Societies: No Ghettos in 2030; hereon *Ghetto Plan*), is a thirty-seven-page document produced by the Danish Government in 2018 including no named authors and thus suggesting a position of neutrality.[11] The austere illustration on its front page does not give much of a clue as to where one is heading, beyond, well, austerity.⟨fig. 1⟩ Even so, this document prodigiously uses illustrations and infographics, including housing icons and bar charts, along with photographs of everything from deteriorating housing to children playing, all in connection to certain titillating words such as *parallel societies*.

The front cover of the Swedish National Audit Office's investigative report *The Right Action in the Right Place: Police Work in Vulnerable Areas* shows several burning cars in a scene lit by a tall floodlight.[12] ⟨fig. 2⟩ This eighty-four-page audit names the individuals and authorities responsible for the publication and its dystopian narrative. The methodology of the investigation is clarified in detail, emphasizing the rational objectivity of the report, even though subjective assessments of the areas are included as facts. Except for the dramatic photograph on its front cover, the report uses no images and almost no other visual material. The lack of appealing graphic design applied to the dry report seems to underscore its production according to strictly scientific rules.

The map shown in figure 3 is a tool developed by the Swedish Migration Agency to guide asylum seekers away from socioeconomically challenged areas. Since 2019 any asylum seekers who move to these areas lose their housing benefit and daily allowances as a consequence.

Importantly, these documents exemplify how a government of paper – to use Matthew S. Hull's term – arises via the use of maps, action plans, audits, surveys and more.[13] Rather than mere accounts of bureaucratic processes, they come to act as a technology of power in fields where "power produces knowledge."[14] In introducing solutions to crime, socioeconomic inequality and what is presented as migration-related concerns by means of policies controlling access to housing and social benefits in specific geographic areas, the documents also resituate solidarity as achievable by force. The reports show how visualization of the facts supports a fait accompli.

To support their claims and proposals, these policy documents link architecture and planning to social problems in three specific ways: (1) "proving" connections between social problems and built environments by presenting numbers and images as unassailable evidence of decline; (2) using testimony from police and other officials as facts – without questioning the possible biases of these accounts – in reports and maps that "demonstrate" the intractability of social problems; and (3) making the family and family units the focus of reform. We will now illustrate and expand upon these three categories of our analysis, which sometimes appear in just one country but raise questions about both countries' approaches.

4 Page 10 from *Ghetto Plan*. Ét Danmark uden parallelsamfund: Ingen ghettoer i 2030.

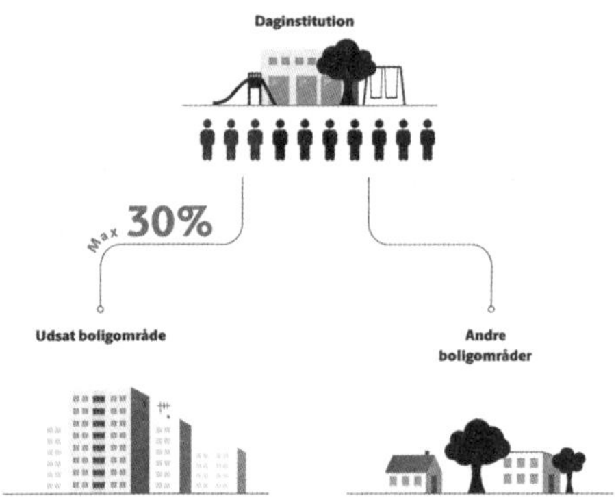

5 Infographic from *Ghetto Plan*. Ét Danmark uden parallelsamfund: Ingen ghettoer i 2030.

"Proving" Connections: Numbers and Images as Evidence of Decline

Denmark presents truly drastic measures in its *Ghetto Plan*, most of which are founded on the stigmatized understandings of the neighborhoods in question. It designates "ghettos" and "hard ghettos."[15] Following these categories, the plan targets a small selection of social housing for demolition, recategorization and/or privatization and bases these changes mostly on statistics. For instance, the report positions the residents of non-Western origin or their descendants as a problem and then links the percentage of these residents to other numerical data, such as incidence of crime, unemployment, education levels and income levels.[16] It then says that a key solution to the problems – both social and physical – will be to reduce the percentage of family units in the social housing stock.[17] It also presents other requirements for reforming the areas, such as enforcing mandatory childcare for families on social benefits and requiring doubled sentences for crimes committed within specific geographical zones.[18]

Illustrations are instrumental to the *Ghetto Plan*'s arguments. The first action presented is subheaded "Physical demolition and conversion/transformation of vulnerable areas," where a full-page illustration shows a close-up of balconies constructed with large concrete components.[19] ⟨fig. 4⟩ Despite Landsbyggefonden's (National Building Foundation) billion-DKK investment in renovation of the social housing stock between 2003 and 2012, a photograph of moldy concrete is chosen to illustrate problems.[20] Another illustration outlining the logic of day care distribution suggests that vulnerable social housing areas are synonymous with bleak high-rise blocks and thus are the opposite of nonvulnerable housing areas, here illustrated as detached houses with a couple of trees.⟨fig. 5⟩ The document encourages municipal monitoring of children by cross-referencing data that will identify children "at risk of experiencing violence and failure to thrive at home."[21] Finally, the existing environment of the day care is described as a threat, because "a high concentration of children [in day care] who live in vulnerable areas result in worse precondition for familiarity with Danish norms and values and the institution itself can be a mini-parallel society."[22] A photograph suggests instead a new playful environment charged with promises of a mix of children of different ethnicities amusing themselves on a merry-go-round. ⟨fig. 6⟩ In short, these visualizations imprint certain forms and characters of the built environment to support a logical chain of reasoning – where the logic is defined by an end goal already determined.

6 Photograph from *Ghetto Plan*. Ét Danmark uden parallelsamfund: Ingen ghettoer i 2030.

The circular logic of the plan to "[break] up concrete and [pull] down buildings" is quite new, in fact, and quite different from Denmark's approach than in 2010.[23] Then, in the report *Ghettoen tilbage til samfundet*, the agenda for social housing was to make "more attractive dwellings that disrupts isolation."[24] Housing was seen to have an active role in mending social relationships and its improvement (not erasure) was the focus. In short, the logic of that equation, we note, was as follows:

Broken buildings → Broken society
Attractive buildings → Cohesive society

Today, however, stigmatization has created a new agenda and approach. The introductory words for the *Ghetto Plan* read as follows: "There will be no ghettos in Denmark in 2030. We hope to break down parallel societies once and for all."[25] It is notable that the "we" here is the Danish national government, expressed as one voice, implying solidarity among those comprising a collective. The correlative logic – as supported in the numbers and the images – is radically different than the one of just a decade before. It is as follows:

Broken buildings → Broken society
Demolish buildings → Cohesive society

Testimony as Facts: Presenting Subjective Claims as Evidence

Defining categories of Danish ghettos or parallel societies and Swedish vulnerable areas also adheres to new logics of redistribution of the competitive state, by which economically resourceful residents will buy apartments rather than rent them, while – at the same time – ethnic mixing is prioritized as a strategy of migrant integration. This is also a form of renoviction, as unwanted families are pushed out of social and municipal housing – and into somewhere else.[26] This, the reports suggest, will produce desirable new gentrification, suggesting that banal notions of social mixing will mix resident demographics and forms of tenure.[27]

Likewise, in Sweden, the categories of "vulnerable areas" and "particularly vulnerable areas" (*särskilt utsatta områden*) were invented by the national police as a method to identify what they demmed socially vulnerable areas. *The Right Action in the Right Place* defines these as areas in relation to their need for extra police resources and personnel, within geographically defined zones with high levels of crime, and where residents have low socioeconomic status and supposedly subscribe to "a culture of silence" (*tystnadskultur*) that makes fighting crime difficult.[28]

The report explains that a list of such areas was developed according to the following process:

> Every police department in Sweden was given the opportunity to contribute to this list through the suggestion of areas they saw as "vulnerable" and the compilation of an area document that provided a comprehensive impression of the area in question. These area documents were then completed with statistics by the Security Police, Statistics Sweden [Statistiska Centralbyrån, SCB] and law enforcement [*kriminalvården*]. All the proposed areas were then assessed according to three main criteria: (1) the residents' reluctance to participate in the legal process; (2) the police's ability to fulfill their duties; and (3) the possible development of parallel social structures. Beyond this, every area was evaluated in relation to whether there was recurring violent religious extremism in the area and, if so, to what degree.[29]

In Sweden, as in Denmark, the universal welfare system meant that social benefits and compensation follow individuals, rather than being assigned to specific dwelling units.[30] In Sweden this principle was lost recently, when the Swedish Migration Agency introduced a measure by which allowances for asylum seekers can be refused, depending on the address of the person in relation to the police's classification list.⟨fig. 7⟩ The agency offers a search engine where an applicant can enter a potential address and be given one of two results: "Red cross = You can lose your right to benefits if you move to the address," or "Green check = The right to benefits is not affected if you

RÄTT INSATS PÅ RÄTT PLATS – POLISENS ARBETE I UTSATTA OMRÅDEN

Översynen bör ske ihop med en diskussion om hur det subjektiva bedömningsinslaget kan kombineras med en kvantitativ ansats för att ytterligare effektivisera och utveckla tillvägagångssättet.[91]

3.4 Listan över utsatta områden har bidragit till att synliggöra problemen

Det faktum att den nationella lägesbilden över utsatta områden utgörs av en offentlig lista har enligt Polismyndigheten bidragit till att synliggöra de problem som finns i områdena. Den allmänna uppfattningen var tidigare att problemen i dessa områden främst var ett polisiärt problem men uppfattas nu som ett samhällsproblem, vilket har underlättat för polisen i deras arbete.

Resultatet av Polismyndighetens bedömning av vilka områden som identifieras som utsatta presenteras i en offentlig lista. Det faktum att listan över alla utsatta områden är offentlig är en omdebatterad och kontroversiell fråga. Det är väl känt att utpekandet av utsatta områden kan vara stigmatiserande för området. Det förekommer en debatt där värdet av hela processen ifrågasätts. Exempel på aktörer som lyfter fram det negativa med att identifiera utsatta områden är kommuner och fastighetsägare. Vi tar inte ställning i frågan om huruvida listan över utsatta områden bör vara offentlig eller inte, men vi har frågat polisen om deras uppfattning eftersom den uppmärksamhet som finns kring utsatta områden kan tänkas påverka polisens arbete.

Fallstudierna visar att majoriteten av tillfrågade poliser är positiva till att listan över utsatta områden är offentlig, eftersom det har bidragit till att synliggöra de problem som finns där. Enligt en lokalpolisområdeschef har detta lett till en väl utbyggd kamerabevakning i området och till att kommunen tillfört resurser till området. Ett annat lokalpolisområde uppger att offentliggörandet av listan har medfört en prioritering av området, från att det tidigare har varit svårt att få gehör för ett utökat behov av resurser.[92] Enligt företrädare för Noa är det viktigt att listan över utsatta områden fortsätter att vara offentlig, eftersom det finns en risk att någon annan tar över om polisen börjar hemlighålla underlaget. Innan listan blev offentlig var den allmänna uppfattningen enligt Polismyndigheten att problemen i utsatta områden främst var ett polisiärt problem. Numera anses det vara ett samhällsproblem, vilket har underlättat för polisen i deras arbete.[93]

7 *Rätt insats*, 32.

8 Screen shot of webpage *Vissa bostadsområden kan påverka din rätt till ersättning* (Some Residential Areas May Affect Your Right to Compensation).
9 Screen shot of webpage *Områden som kan påverka rätten till ersättning för asylsökande* (Areas That May Affect the Right to Compensation for Asylum Seekers).

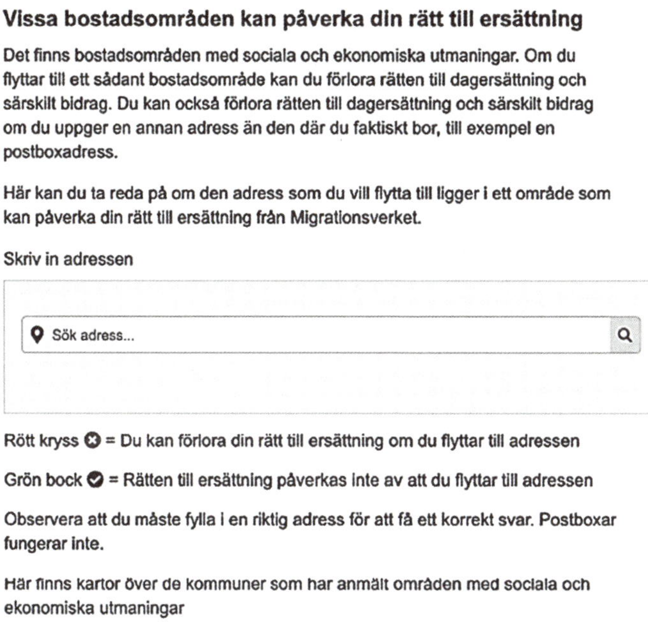

Vissa bostadsområden kan påverka din rätt till ersättning

Det finns bostadsområden med sociala och ekonomiska utmaningar. Om du flyttar till ett sådant bostadsområde kan du förlora rätten till dagersättning och särskilt bidrag. Du kan också förlora rätten till dagersättning och särskilt bidrag om du uppger en annan adress än den där du faktiskt bor, till exempel en postboxadress.

Här kan du ta reda på om den adress som du vill flytta till ligger i ett område som kan påverka din rätt till ersättning från Migrationsverket.

Skriv in adressen

Sök adress...

Rött kryss = Du kan förlora din rätt till ersättning om du flyttar till adressen

Grön bock = Rätten till ersättning påverkas inte av att du flyttar till adressen

Observera att du måste fylla i en riktig adress för att få ett korrekt svar. Postboxar fungerar inte.

Här finns kartor över de kommuner som har anmält områden med sociala och ekonomiska utmaningar

8

9

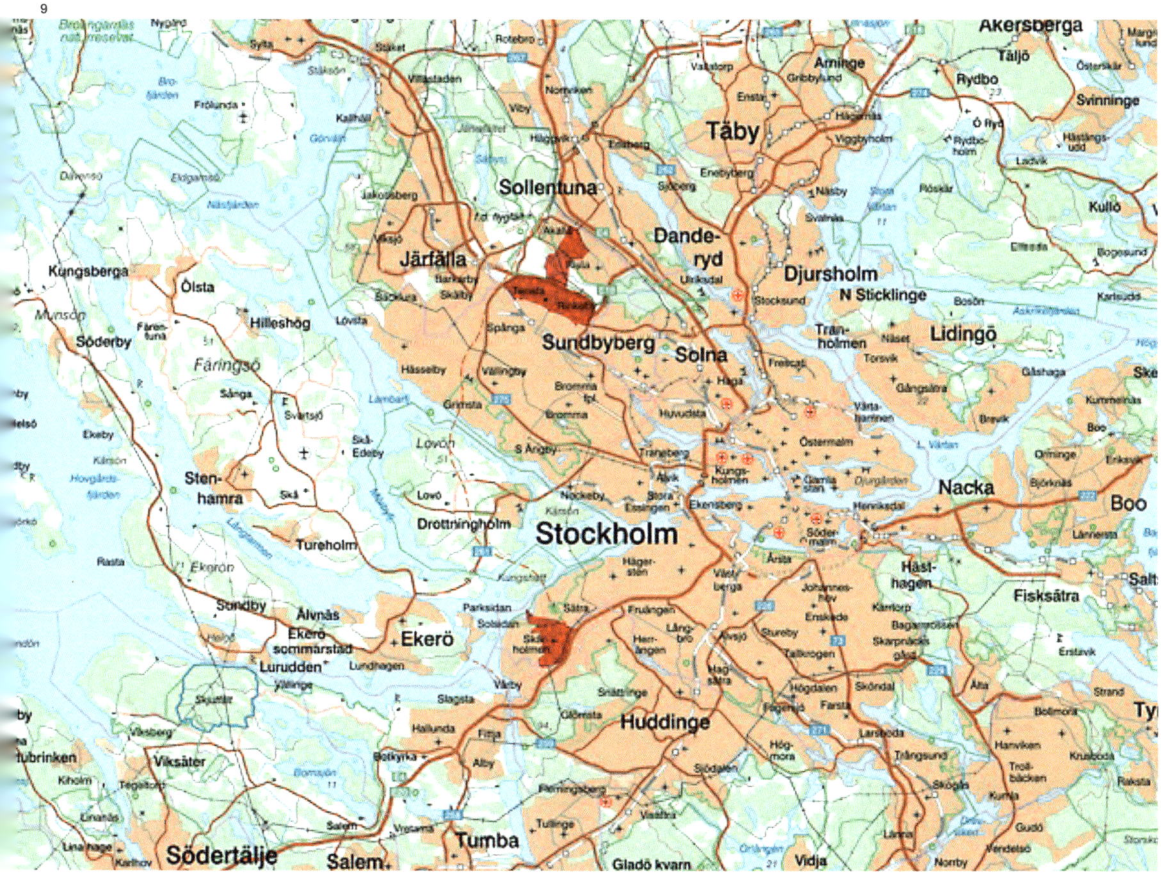

move to the address."[31] ⟨fig. 8⟩ For those able to find it (after a series of complicated links), a map of red zones across different regions in Sweden shows these areas – without respect to housing categories.⟨figs. 3 and 9⟩ For example, large areas around the Stockholm regional zone of Järva Field (Tensta, Rinkeby and Kista) are marked in red.[32] The red zone is not homogenous in its urban character: here are mixed types of housing and urban forms and housing with varying forms of tenure, both rental and cooperative ownership (*hyresrätt* and *bostadsrätt*). These decisions, to associate certain addresses with social problems and to threaten migrants with economic loss if they move there, are based on municipal reports of their social and economic challenges.

The Family as the Problem

As we have already insinuated, the most notable intervention that Swedish and Danish authorities present as the solutions to the causal links they develop through numbers, images and subjective accounts of the neighborhoods are new interventionist housing policies. The Danish analysis of parallel societies stresses families as a whole.[33] The analysis published in *Parallelsamfund i Danmark*, which preceded the *Ghetto Plan*, states that it is difficult to draw conclusions when measures of integration into Danish society are evaluated at the level of the non-Western individual.[34] This analysis therefore focuses on non-Western families, arguing that the family serves "as the baseline of most people's lives" and that "one's values are based on upbringing and the family that one comes from."[35] For these reasons, the report suggests that the accumulation of indicators within a family may add up to show that the family as a unit is not integrated. Small families are likely to tick fewer indicator boxes than big families.

From this analysis, we understand that links drawn between architecture and social problems in the Danish context are typically based on creating discursive connections between family structures and cultural values. With that in mind, it is not surprising that the *Ghetto Plan* specifically eliminates family dwellings: to do away with the "wrong" families, the document does away (sells off, changes use or demolishes) collectively organized family living.[36] No longer is this housing – as it was in the peak of the Danish welfare state – positioned as an essential building block for the larger society and a means of promoting solidarity for all. Instead, the *Ghetto Plan* treats the family unit as evidence of the emergence of parallel societies, as though family living and antipolice attitudes are connected and, following this logic, actually disrupt what are positioned as more desirable forms of solidarity.

Curiously, the solution to the problem of the family is not solved by developing family units for a nonparallel society. Instead, families are casually displaced, with the action plan giving no indication about where they will go.⟨figs. 5 and 8⟩ If the family as a social unit is, along these lines, only successfully integrated outside the tenure of social housing, there remains no discussion of what any alternatives for these families would look like. And if the family dwelling is no longer the dominant unit in social housing – traditionally configured as multifamily housing – what are we to make of social housing in relation to larger notions of solidarity within Sweden and Denmark?

In fact, both the *Ghetto Plan* and *The Right Action in the Right Place* assert ideas of state power and normative notions of who the rightful members of the Danish and Swedish nations actually are. For instance, the requirement to conduct an expert assessment of a child's personal and social conditions before giving parenting orders (*forældrepålæg)* has been removed for families living in so-called hard ghettos, "to simplify the demand in action – so as to avoid excuses" (from municipalities).[37]

The Right Action in the Right Place addresses similar issues of norms and membership, stating that it is: "Criminal structures, rather than the state, that define the norms in these areas. There is also the risk that the state cannot maintain important key values in the areas. Thus, trust in the state and, further, its legitimacy, can suffer as consequence."[38] In their focus on instilling new norms, both the *Ghetto Plan* and *The Right Action in the Right Place* use imperative and punitive language, implying that social structures that are somehow beyond the reach of the state – the family in particular – produce unwanted norms. Their efforts to intervene thus command change and measures in the most intimate sphere of domestic life, suggesting a belief that solidarity with the Nordic welfare state cannot coexist with solidarity in the forms practiced by migrant families.

Conclusion

In recent years, the categories of ghettos and vulnerable areas have been highly effective political tools to support major changes to the existing urban fabric in Denmark and Sweden. To develop these labels in an effective way, official government reports, action plans, audits, maps and brochures have used graphic design, statistics and subjective accounts to develop associated concepts like parallel society and social mix. Images and words are meant to support a solution-driven political argument, with plans often simplifying understandings of complex conditions that causally link the built environment, migration, the family and other social concerns. Graphic design is linked to stigmatizing texts to create a sense of inevitability that underscores the solidarity agenda of the Ghetto Plan and its Swedish counterparts. Extreme practices of coercion, violence and demolition become normalized when translated into visually appealing action plans and when the police desperately exclaim that they are unable to perform their duties. In all of these actions and approaches, the very notions of solidarity upon which the Swedish and Danish welfare states were constructed – both socially and in built form – are not just questioned but upended.

In short, this chapter is a call for a very different kind of action than those supported in recent Danish and Swedish reports, or in the market solutions that appear by their side. Instead, by identifying these reports as technologies of power used to create a spatial imaginary (and reality) of demolition, punishment and renoviction, we call for further examination of what an architectural and urban policy of twenty-first-century solidarity might become (perhaps focused on housing) and suggest inquiries into the authorship of these reports. Further investigation into how graphic artifacts are made available as neutral information supporting governmental policies could offer new modes of analysis, as could their resonance for architects and planners who are using and reusing this material. Additional knowledge about the housing areas in question – beyond the statistics and beyond the subjective, negative views of them – is desperately needed. Ghettos and vulnerable areas are in fact the lifeworlds of people who live here. From perspectives of architecture and planning, we call for responses to these housing policies through insider approaches, including recent work in anthropology, ethnology, architecture and planning, and ways to reintegrate them so that the bases for future action can acknowledge diversity of opinions and visions of the future while crafting an environment that privileges the care of both people and the built environment.

These situated approaches, we contend, can offer alternatives to deterministic understandings. Rather than one-sided failures, we call for alternative histories and practice-oriented responses so that we can begin to understand this legacy and how to make futures of city building based upon solidarity.

Bibliography

Andersen, Hans Skifter. *Ethnic Spatial Segregation in European Cities*. Abingdon: Routledge, 2019.

Baeten, Guy, Sara Westin, Emil Pull and Irene Molina. “Pressure and Violence: Housing Renovation and Displacement in Sweden.” *Environment and Planning A: Economy and Space* 49, no. 3 (2017): 631–51.

Cupers, Kenny. “Mapping and Making Community in the Postwar European City.” *Journal of Urban History* 42, no. 6 (2016): 1009–28.

Esping-Andersen, Gøsta. *The Three Worlds of Welfare Capitalism*. Cambridge: Polity Press, 1990.

Foucault, Michel. *Discipline and Punish: The Birth of the Prison*. Translated by Alan Sheridan. New York: Vintage Books, 1977.

Frandsen, Martin Severin, and Jesper Visti Hansen. “Parallelsamfundspakkens Genealogi.” *Dansk Sociologi* 31, no. 1 (2020): 10–29.

Freiesleben, Anna Mikaela. “Et Danmark af parallelsamfund: Segregering, ghettoisering og social sammenhængskraft: Parallelsamfundet i dansk diskurs 1968–2013 – fra utopi til dystopi.” PhD diss. University of Copenhagen, 2016. https://forskning.ku.dk/soeg/result/?pure=da%2Fpublications%2Fet-danmark-af-parallelsamfund(d385d3c8-a326-4fce-a9fa-508558368af5).html.

Hull, Matthew S. *Government of Paper*. Berkeley: University of California Press, 2012.

Jensen, Carsten. *Velfærd*. Aarhus: Aarhus Universitetsforlag, 2017.

Kristensen, Hans. “Social Housing Policy and the Welfare State: A Danish Perspective.” *Urban Studies* 39, no. 2 (2002): 255–63.

Kuchenbuch, David. *Geordnete Gemeinschaften: Architekten als Sozialingenieure: Deutschland und Schweden im 20. Jahrhundert*. Bielefeld: transcript Verlag, 2010.

Migrationsverket (Swedish Migration Agency). *Områden som kan påverka rätten till ersättning för asylsökande*. Accessed 2020. https://www.migrationsverket.se/Privatpersoner/Skydd-och-asyl-i-Sverige/Medan-du-vantar/Boende/Eget-boende/Omraden-som-kan-paverka-ratten-till-ersattning-for-asylsokande.html.

Molina, Irene, and Sara Westin. “Renoviction: Even in Sweden: An Effect of Common Benefit Companies Acting ‘Business-like’?” Presentation, Association of American Geographers Annual Conference Meeting, New York, February 24–28, 2012.

Rasmussen, Lars Løkke. *Prime Minister's New Year Address*. January 1, 2018. https://www.regeringen.dk/aktuelt/statsministerens-nytaarstale/lars-loekke-rasmussens-nytaarstale-1-januar-2018/.

Regeringen (The Danish Government). *Ét Danmark uden parallelsamfund: Ingen ghettoer i 2030*. Copenhagen: Økonomi- og indenrigsministeriet/Ministry of Economic Affairs and the Interior, 2018. https://www.regeringen.dk/media/4937/publikation_%C3%A9t-danmark-uden-parallelsamfund.pdf.

——. *Ghettoen tilbage til samfundet: Et opgør med parallelsamfund i Danmark*. Copenhagen: Socialministeriet/The Ministry of Social Affairs, 2010.

——. *Parallelsamfund i Danmark*. Økonomisk Analyse, February 30, 2018. https://www.regeringen.dk/media/4836/analyse-om-parallelsamfund-090218-final.pdf.

Riksrevisionen. *Rätt insats på rätt plats: Polisens arbete i utsatta områden*. Stockholm: Riksdagens interntryckeri, 2020.

Rogaczewska, Anna, Rikke Lønne and Kristoffer Friis Sørensen, eds. *At Huse Alle/How to House*. Copenhagen: BL Social Housing, 2017.

Staver, Anne Balke, Jean-Paul Brekke and Susanne Søholt. *Scandinavia's Segregated Cities: Policies, Strategies and Ideals*. Oslo: Norwegian Institute for Urban and Regional Research, Oslo Metropolitan University, 2019.

Trädghårdh, Lars. “Scaling up Solidarity from the National to the Global: Sweden as Welfare State and Moral Superpower.” In *Sustainable Modernity: The Nordic Model and Beyond*, edited by Nina Witoszek and Atle Midttun, 79–101. London: Routledge, 2018.

Notes

1 See, for example, Guy Baeten, Sara Westin, Emil Pull and Irene Molina, “Pressure and Violence: Housing Renovation and Displacement in Sweden,” *Environment and Planning A: Economy and Space* 49, no. 3 (2017): 631–51; Anne Balke Staver, Jan-Paul Brekke and Susanne Søholt, *Scandinavia's Segregated Cities: Policies, Strategies and Ideals* (Oslo: Norwegian Institute for Urban and Regional Research, Oslo Metropolitan University, 2019); Carsten Jensen, *Velfærd* (Aarhus: Aarhus Universitetsforlag, 2017); and Lars Trädghårdh, “Scaling up Solidarity from the National to the Global: Sweden as Welfare State and Moral Superpower,” in *Sustainable Modernity: The Nordic Model and Beyond*, ed. Nina Witoszek and Atle Midttun (London: Routledge, 2018), 79–101.
2 Gøsta Esping-Andersen, *The Three Worlds of Welfare Capitalism* (Cambridge: Polity Press, 1990), 27ff.
3 See Regeringen (The Danish Government), *Ét Danmark uden parallelsamfund: Ingen ghettoer i 2030* (Copenhagen: Økonomi- og indenrigsministeriet/Ministry of Economic Affairs and the Interior, 2018), https://www.regeringen.dk/media/4937/publikation_%C3%A9t-danmark-uden-parallelsamfund.pdf; and Riksrevisionen, *Rätt insats på rätt plats: Polisens arbete i utsatta områden* (Stockholm: Riksdagens interntryckeri, 2020).
4 See Hans Skifter Andersen, *Ethnic Spatial Segregation in European Cities* (Abingdon: Routledge, 2019); Martin Severin Frandsen and Jesper Visti Hansen, “Parallelsamfundspakkens Genealogi,” *Dansk Sociologi* 31, no, 1 (2020): 10–29; Anna Mikaela Freiesleben, *Et Danmark af parallelsamfund: Segregering, ghettoisering og social sammenhængskraft: Parallelsamfundet i dansk diskurs 1968–2013 – fra utopi til dystopi* (PhD diss., University of Copenhagen, 2016), https://forskning.ku.dk/soeg/result/?pure=da%2Fpublications%2Fet-danmark-af-parallelsamfund(d385d3c8-a326-4fce-a9fa-508558368af5).html; and Staver, Brekke and Søholt, *Scandinavia's Segregated Cities.*
5 See Regeringen, *Et Danmark af parallelsamfund*; Riksrevisionen, *Rätt insats på rätt plats;* and Migrationsverket (Swedish Migration Agency), *Kartor över områden som kan påverka rätten till ersättning för asylsökande*, https://www.migrationsverket.se/Privatpersoner/Skydd-och-asyl-i-Sverige/Medan-du-vantar/Boende/Eget-boende/Omraden-som-kan-paverka-ratten-till-ersattning-for-asylsokande.html.
6 Michel Foucault, *Discipline and Punish: The Birth of the Prison*, trans. Alan Sheridan (New York: Vintage Books, 1977), 23–31.
7 Hans Kristensen, “Social Housing Policy and the Welfare State: A Danish Perspective,” *Urban Studies* 39, no. 2, (2002): 255–63; and Anna Rogaczewska, Rikke Lønne and Kristoffer Friis Sørensen eds, *At Huse Alle/How to House* (Copenhagen: BL Social Housing, 2017).
8 Kristensen, “Social Housing Policy,” 259.
9 Kenny Cupers, “Mapping and Making Community in the Postwar European City,” *Journal of Urban History* 42, no. 6 (2016): 1009–28.
10 David Kuchenbuch, *Geordnete Gemeinschaften: Architekten als Sozialingenieure: Deutschland und Schweden im 20. Jahrhundert* (Bielefeld: transcript Verlag, 2010).
11 Regeringen, *Ét Danmark.*
12 Riksrevisionen, *Rätt insats på rätt plats.*
13 Matthew Hull, *Government of Paper* (Berkeley: University of California Press, 2012).
14 Foucault, *Discipline and Punish*, 27.
15 Regeringen, *Ét Danmark parallelsamfund.* All translations from the Danish by the authors.
16 Regeringen, *Ét Danmark*, 4–9.
17 Regeringen, *Ét Danmark*, 13.
18 Regeringen, *Ét Danmark*, 25.
19 Regeringen, *Ét Danmark*, 10.
20 Regeringen, *Ghettoen tilbage til samfundet: Et opgør med parallelsamfund i Danmark* (Copenhagen: Socialministeriet/The Ministry of Social Affairs, 2010), 41.
21 Regeringen, *Ét Danmark*, 30.
22 Regeringen, *Ét Danmark*, 25.
23 Prime Minister Lars Løkke Rasmussen, *New Year Address*, January 1, 2018, https://www.regeringen.dk/aktuelt/statsministerens-nytaarstale/lars-loekke-rasmussens-nytaarstale-1-januar-2018/.
24 Regeringen, *Ghettoen tilbage til samfundet*, 40.
25 Regeringen, *Ét Danmark*, 6.
26 Irene Molina and Sara Westin, “Renoviction: Even in Sweden: An Effect of Common Benefit Companies' Acting ‘Business-like’?” presentation, Association of American Geographers Annual Conference Meeting, New York, February 24–28, 2012.
27 Regeringen, *Ét Danmark*, 11 and 14.
28 Riksrevisionen, *Rätt insats*, 16.
29 Riksrevisionen, *Rätt insats*, 19–20.
30 Rogaczewska, Lønne and Sørensen, eds., *At Huse Alle/How to House.*
31 Migrationsverket, *Vissa bostadsområden kan påverka din rätt till ersättning*, accessed 2020, https://www.migrationsverket.se/Privatpersoner/Skydd-och-asyl-i-Sverige/Medan-du-vantar/Boende/Eget-boende.html.
32 Migrationsverket, *Områden som kan påverka rätten till ersättning för asylsökande*, accessed 2020, https://www.migrationsverket.se/Privatpersoner/Skydd-och-asyl-i-Sverige/Medan-du-vantar/Boende/Eget-boende/Omraden-som-kan-paverka-ratten-till-ersattning-for-asylsokande.html.
33 Regeringen, *Parallelsamfund i Danmark* (Økonomisk Analyse February 30, 2018), 2, https://www.regeringen.dk/media/4836/analyse-om-parallelsamfund-090218-final.pdf.
34 Regeringen, *Parallelsamfund i Danmark*, 10–11.
35 Regeringen, *Parallelsamfund i Danmark*, 2.
36 Regeringen, *Ét Danmark*, 13.
37 Regeringen, *Ét Danmark*, 27.
38 Riksrevisionen, *Rätt insats*, 9.

Holes in the Spaces of the Welfare State

Media Coverage and Residents' Responses in the So-Called Hardest Ghettos in Denmark

Mette Mechlenborg, Marie Stender

"Across the country we find parallel societies. People with the same kind of problems situate themselves in enclaves. [They] do not participate; do not use the opportunities we offer. They place themselves outside. Holes have been made in the map of Denmark." These were some of the words Prime Minister Lars Løkke Rasmussen used in his New Year speech to the nation on January 1, 2018, to address the disadvantaged neighborhoods on the annual updated ghetto list a few months prior to launching new legislation on disadvantaged housing areas.[1] By doing so, the Prime Minister not only strengthened the political ambition to eliminate well-known public challenges on the housing market, he also added new layers to the public rhetoric on Danish social housing and fueled the public debate on how to address its problems.

The Danish social housing sector plays a crucial role in the Danish welfare state; today 20 percent of all housing units in the country is social housing.[2] Since 1922, when the state established the national fund for social housing, the sector has been a front-runner in the development of new, modern housing schemes, especially after World War II, when the need for housing was huge.[3] In the following decades social housing was an important national project that combined planning for infrastructure and sanitation in the biggest cities. This also means that several well-established architects and landscape planners took on the prestigious task of developing large-scale housing projects, like Tingbjerg outside Copenhagen, by architect Steen Eiler Rasmussen in collaboration with landscape architect C. Th. Sørensen from 1950 with more than 2,000 housing units, green areas, school, church and shopping area.[4] Offering average families modern, comfortable housing at affordable prices in green areas outside the urban centers was closely linked to a political social democratic transformation of the housing market. In comparison with the private sector, it was believed that the social housing sector was better at producing homes on a large scalo, which were at the same time of good housing quality and with a strong residential democracy that would transform residents into becoming active citizens in the welfare state.[5]

1 Vollsmose, outside Odense, is one of the most well known disadvantaged neighborhoods on the national list of the "hardest ghettos" with more than 1,500 articles in the local, regional and national newspapers over a twelve-month period.

However, during the late 1960s and '70s the private-owned single-family house took over as the ideal dwelling and many Danish housing areas slowly lost their attractiveness. At the same time mass production and industrialized building techniques and materials were introduced, and during the nineties the social housing sector slowly started being associated with disadvantaged neighborhoods with low socioeconomic residential profiles and a high number of vacancies. Also due to new political housing initiatives, which allowed municipalities the right to allocate up to 25 percent of all housing vacancies in an area to particular – often deprived – citizens.[6]

2 Tingbjerg outside Copenhagen was a prestigious social housing project built in the 1950s by the well-respected Danish architect Steen Eiler Rasmussen and world-famous landscape architect C. Th. Sørensen. The area is now on the national list of hardest ghettos and is undergoing radical transformations.

In 2004, after several riots in the social housing area Rosenhøj outside Aarhus, the Danish government launched the first of several so-called ghetto strategies, in which physical and social initiatives were presented.[7] In 2010 came a fully coherent strategy and the first ghetto list, both slightly revisited in 2013. The Danish ghetto strategies of 2010 and 2013 were based on an ambition to "dissolve parallel communities" and to "(re)integrate them into Danish society," while the new national ghetto list identified the specific deprived housing areas that were then named ghettos based on socioeconomic and ethnical criteria and with more than 1,000 housing units.[8] With the Prime Minister's New Year's speech and the 2018 ghetto strategy *Ét Danmark uden parallelsamfund: Ingen ghettoer i 2030* (One Denmark without Parallel Societies: No Ghettos in 2030), the ghetto list was divided into three categories, with fifteen areas identified as the "hardest ghettos" and therefore subject to new, radical interventions, such as partial demolition.[9]

As some researchers have stated, the parallel society legislation and ghetto list are explicit elements in a normative socioethnic profiling, which stigmatizes residents of non-Western origins in this context.[10] Others have argued that the rhetoric of the parallel society legislation is part of a dystopian discourse representing deprived areas as dystopian places and emphasizing a dichotomy between "them" and "us."[11] With the definition of "holes in the map of Denmark," the former Prime Minister suggests – in a spatial interpretation – that these areas are not just deviant or different, but decidedly unconnected, cut off from the rest, nonrelatable to the general society. Due to political debate, and a new government, the recent Minister of Housing, Kaare Dybvad Bek (2019–), has decided to cancel the official use of the term *ghetto* and instead use the softer term *parallel society*.[12]

However, political discourse does not fly and spread over the country by itself; it is communicated through various platforms and communications channels, in which national and local media play a huge role. Thus, media coverage is an important focus in investigating how negative place reputation and public stories are linked and how media coverage is understood by residents in eight deprived housing areas on the hardest ghetto list in Denmark in 2018. In summary, how does media coverage contribute to the political discourse on "holes" in the Danish welfare state and how does the media affect residents' perceptions of their domestic spaces of welfare?

Place Reputation and the Role of Media

In this chapter, we connect media analysis with residents' responses to media representations. We build on Matthieu Permentier's understanding of place reputation as referring to "the meaning and esteem that residents and other involved parties attribute to a neighborhood. Reputation also refers to the relatively stable image a neighborhood has among city residents and to its place in the urban neighborhood hierarchy."[13] Their relationship to other places and positions in the housing hierarchy are essential parts of a place's reputation.[14]

Only limited research on place reputation and media coverage – in this case newspaper stories – on disadvantaged neighborhoods has been conducted in the Danish context, although this is recognized as a

3 This study is based on eight case studies of disadvantaged neighborhoods, the so-called hardest ghettos according to the national ghetto list.

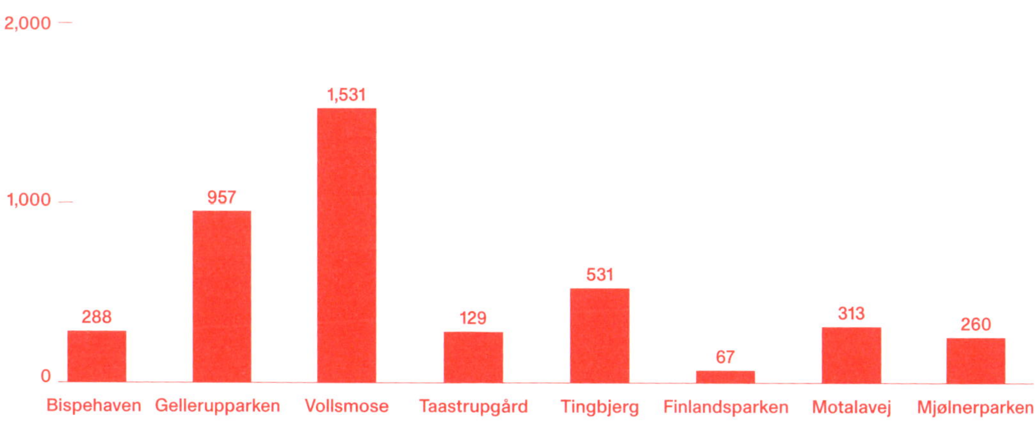

4 Number of total newspaper articles in each case over a twelve-month period. The media analysis shows a substantial variation from 67 at the lowest (Finlandsparken) to 1,531 at the highest (Vollsmose).

particularly relevant focus.[15] Stories in media present specific images that means mental pictures or imageries about how a specific area is.[16] Images that relate to the more abstract place reputation rather than to embedded lived experiences.[17] Studies on disadvantaged neighborhoods stress that in conventional media such areas are stereotypically portrayed as scenes of crimes, drugs and social problems.[18] Other studies state that media is the key platform through which different positions of class and territorial stigma are shaped, enlarged, and reproduced.[19] Some even state that media representations may have the same effect on a place's reputation as socioeconomic factors and political legislation.[20] Others find an emerging critical awareness among residents trying to contest media representations.[21] Yet several studies indicate that the external image affects the internal one, as residents tend to internalize negative representations of their neighborhood and question their own spatial experiences.[22] Relating to "holes" in the Danish welfare state, media coverage and resident's responses are therefore highly relevant to investigate.

Mixed Methods: Qualitative Interviews and Media Analysis

Based on empirical material from the research project Regeneration of Danish Disadvantaged Neighbourhoods: Long-term Evaluation (2019–28), this chapter builds on more than eighty qualitative interviews and a media analysis of eight case studies from disadvantaged neighborhoods on the national ghetto list: Vollsmose, Gellerupparken, Mjølnerparken, Tingbjerg, Taastrupgård, Motalavej, Bispehaven and Finlandsparken. Four reports have already been published.[23]

In each housing area, we conducted ten to fifteen qualitative interviews with residents. The interviewees were recruited through an on-site outdoor survey among 200 to 300 people staying in or passing through the area. The last question was whether we could contact them again for an in-depth interview, and among those who agreed, we included interviewees of various ages, genders, ethnic backgrounds and so on. They were asked about daily life in the area, the relationship to the surrounding city, their own use and perception of the place and its reputation. Though media representations were not an explicit focus, most interviewees addressed this on their own initiative.

Our eight media analyses are based on a database search of newspapers articles for a period of one year in the database Infomedia (infomedia.dk) in three categories: national, regional and local newspapers. All articles were skimmed before sorting relevant clips into categories and subcategories according to the scope of article.⟨fig. 5⟩ As in similar studies, we categorized all articles according to the image they convey of the neighborhood in question to a reader with little or no prior knowledge of the neighborhood, using three categories: unconditionally positive, unconditionally negative and ambivalent media clips.[24] The ambivalent articles represent the remnant category from the other two categories or stories that can be perceived as ambivalent, such as a positive story on a negative background.[25]

	Negative stories	Ambivalent stories	Positive stories
All cases	Episodes of violence, drugs and crimes Arson/vandalism Ghetto listing	Regeneration Political/social/physical initaitives and results	Specific events or social/cultural initiatives (e.g. school projects) Regeneration
Many cases	Unsafe environment/ tresspassing Gang-related issues Police initiatives Named convictions	Ghetto listing Integration, education and (un)employment Demolition plans Portraits of residents	Portraits of residents Sport events Art projects Private investment
Few cases	Terror and radicalization Demolition plans	Divestment of apartments	New architecture/ buildings/functions

5 Main subjects registered in media coverage in all eight disadvantaged neighborhoods divided into three categories: unconditionally negative stories, ambivalent stories and unconditionally positive stories.

Analysis: Media Contribute to a Bad Place Reputation

The total number of articles fluctuates from 67 newspaper articles on Finlandsparken to up to 1,561 articles on Vollsmose over a year, which suggests that some neighborhoods are more negatively perceived than others.⟨fig. 4⟩ If we examine the image that media outlets convey of the neighborhood to a reader with little or no prior knowledge, the average proportion of negative articles in our eight cases is 43 percent.⟨fig. 5⟩ Thus, two out of five articles have an unconditionally negative attitude toward the specific neighborhood. However, the actual differences of negative articles between the neighborhoods are remarkable. In Mjølnerparken and Motalavej, more than 70 percent of all articles are unconditionally negative, whereas Tingbjerg and Taastrupgård have a negative share of only 27 percent.⟨fig. 5⟩ The significantly higher amount of negative content in media coverage across the country and across media categories (local, regional and national newspapers) indicates that the often stated thesis that media in general contribute to a negative place reputation is also the case in Danish national newspapers.

As in international studies, a large proportion of negative articles in the Danish media coverage are specific stories on drugs and gang-related activities, violent attacks, bonfires, vandalism and riots.[26] In many cases, this is 20–30 percent of all coverage and more than half of all negative stories in total. In contrast, ambivalent and positive stories tend to be about more complex, nonspectacular events or stories.⟨fig. 6⟩ In all eight cases, examples exist of single incidents resulting in multiple articles in the same newspaper. Sometimes, the same incident is published in multiple regional media outlets across the country, turning a local story into a national story covered through various regional newspapers.

Negative stories are often factually orientated toward the incident with little information about the neighborhood. Often articles use short phrases, such as “from Vollsmose,” “raised in Mjølnerparken” or “a group from Gellerupparken,” while those involved are rarely identified by name, but by a few general characteristics, such as “youngster,” “gang members,” “young men of non-Western origin” or “vandals.” Despite their

Indirect Stories
Detached archetype
Definition: When an area becomes an archetype that other areas measure up against.

	Example	Example	Example
All cases	"We find that the residents are happy to live there. [...] So we do not think it is appropriate to compare our housing area with ghettos like Vollsmose or Gellerupparken."	"Some people still think it's a dangerous area of crime, but it's not. This is neither Mjølner-parken nor Vollsmose."	"Yet, I do not think you should compare Resedavej and Lupinvej with ghettos like Gellerupparken in Århus. It is not as bad here. And the area does not look like a ghetto."
	Fredericia Dagblad, November 2018	*Fredericia Dagblad*, December 2018	*Midtjyllands Avis*, December 2018

6 Examples of a specific type of implied generalization. In these examples, areas become the archetype of a ghetto to which others measure themselves against.

factual descriptions, articles like these have a major influence on a place reputation. First, they overlook the lived realities of most residents in the area, and link a few selected characteristics, such as criminal behavior and certain ethnicity, age, gender, or behavioral profiles to the neighborhood in question. This method of conveying incidents can be conceptualized as a pathological description, interpreting bad behavior as a result of a lack of morals and norms of a group, rather than the consequence of structural conditions in society.[27] Second, this representation of incidents as taking place in a spatially closed entity demonstrates how media tend to take on the role of "providing a window into this place from which the audience themselves are socially distant," and by doing so, add to the opposition between "them" and "us."[28]

Turning to residents' responses, our interviews indicate that media coverage is intricately linked to the residents' self-reflected image, that is, the image that residents believe is held by people not living in their neighborhood.[29] Place reputation in residents' view is extremely sensitive to specific stories in the media. In our interviews, residents often referred to recent articles and media stories about their neighborhood, which obviously affected their responses to our questions regarding place reputation. Even in cases with a relatively low proportion of negative media coverage (such as Tingbjerg and Taastrupgård, with only 27 percent negative articles), residents blamed the media for the gap between how they esteem their neighborhood in comparison to how they think outsiders perceive the area. As a resident puts it: "These stories are out of proportion. Of course, we have problems out here, but the media only pay attention to the bad things and makes it a lot worse than it is."

However, media narratives not only communicate spatial images to outsiders, they also turn inward and play an active role in residents' own perceptions.[30] In our interviews, residents often provided examples of incidents that they did not experience themselves but that were communicated to them from outside via newspapers, radio, television or family members and friends who had read the news. In fact, in many interviews, media served as the most important generator of collective spatial experiences, or as Amanda Haynes, Eoin Devereux and Martin J. Power put it, the media outlets "inform their knowledge of the neighborhood."[31]

In general, the negative news often overshadows residents' own spatial experiences and makes them question their own internal place reputation.[32] As others have suggested, residents' ability to cope with a bad place reputation depends on how residents identity and the materiality of their surroundings intersect with the native narratives.[33] Some residents, especially those who had only recently moved to or who did not feel at home in the neighborhood, viewed these stories as important confirmation of a negative place reputation. They tended to regard media stories as objective and revealing what was occurring in their neighborhoods. A woman from Tingbjerg repeated stories she had read in the news to validate to us why she wanted to move, even though neither she and her family nor anyone she knew in the neighborhood had ever experienced anything negative themselves.

Most residents, however, try to distance themselves from negative stories in the media by stressing that what happened was "in the other end of the area," "did not have anything to do with our life," or did not made them uncomfortable because "these kinds of incidents happen everywhere," just to mention some examples. Nevertheless, residents recognized how media contribute to a negative place reputation and to territorial stigmatization.[34] A resident stated that she was very frustrated about a specific story that she had just heard and that stories like these make her feel that she is deprived of the opportunity to form her own spatial experience.

However, media coverage of negative incidents also serves as a platform for negotiating a rather abstract negative place reputation. In fact, most residents revealed a sophisticated understanding of how bad place reputation operates through public stories.[35] Most residents agreed that the media tend to focus on the negative stories, while the more positive or ambivalent stories are rarer and less important for place reputation. "You never hear about the good stories. You only hear the bad ones," as one resident put it. Another stated, "People see our neighborhood as a criminal area, mostly known for its violent incidents. But much of this [bad reputation] has to do with the media." Residents also claimed that media exaggerate bad stories or even link incidents elsewhere to their neighborhood by claiming it happened there, or that residents were involved in bad incidents even though they were not. Some even have an explanation for why the media outlets tend to focus on a certain behavior. "My impression is quite clear that media twist everything. Stories are a little exaggerated. Scandals sell better, and it sells better to keep writing about a troubled area [although] most of the time I have lived here, which is a year, everything has been completely quiet," a resident tells us.

This illustrates that residents do not passively take on the negative place reputation placed on them by the media. They (also) negotiate or object to the stories by comparing them with their personal experiences. Hence, a negative place reputation is not a constant, static concept assigned to a neighborhood but deeply embedded in residents' everyday actions and reflections.[36] Furthermore, for residents, contesting media stories is a way of making a negative place reputation subject to resistance, although it may still have a direct influence on their spatial experiences.

Detached Stories Are Hard to Object To

While many negative stories are based on specific incidents, several articles also reinforce a negative place reputation via contextual descriptions. The most typical contextual description is often short and typically embedded in dominating narratives, such as "Vollsmose and Gellerupparken are known as Denmark's biggest ghettos"; "it is a real ghetto"; "an area of concrete building stocks"; "the well-known deprived neighborhood"; or "troubled residential area."[37] In many cases, these descriptions serve as rhetorical ploys to make it easy for the reader to understand the cultural context in which the story takes place. They set the scene, so to speak. Thus, stories are often presented on a stereotypical background on which the specific, nuanced characteristics of the neighborhood are reduced. In contrast, spatial generalizations link to implied and often negative understandings. This explains why seemingly positive stories still turn ambivalent because they are presented on the background of the implied generalization of disadvantaged neighborhoods.[38] ⟨fig. 5⟩

In our interviews, several residents expressed awareness of these spatially implied generalizations used to describe their neighborhood. An example is from a resident who reflected on an article covering the Prime Minister's visit to her neighborhood. He describes a picture in the newspaper of a block of flats on a dark and gray December day, with no green grass to be seen and resonates: "It is pictures like these, I mean, media use in a propaganda scare campaign showing how awful it is. To show that it is a ghetto. You could have taken the picture today, where there are families with children out, because that's how I see it." This implied negative background in media stories may also explain the conservatism in place reputation and contribute to a better understanding why regeneration and social and architectural initiatives in deprived housing areas have difficulties transforming a negative place reputation: A strong negative place reputation tends to transform positive stories into to ambivalent stories by the connotation to its negative background.

However, our media analysis also identified a more fundamental, but subtle, implied understanding of some neighborhoods, namely, the indirect stories that would probably have been categorized as irrelevant to the analysis in some studies.[39] Often these articles were about another disadvantaged neighborhood, for example, a post in a debate on the parallel society legislation or an article that did not even relate to social housing at all. An example was a portrait in a newspaper about a Danish politician, Henrik Sass-Larsen, in which the place name Taastrupgård, one of our cases, appears: "Henrik Sass Larsen is known for being a 'tough dog' – one who would rather go into a fight than bypass it. Maybe because he grew up on the Copenhagen West bank in Taastrupgård."[40] In some of these articles disadvantaged neighborhoods, such as Vollsmose, Mjølnerparken, Gellerupparken and sometimes Tingbjerg, were represented not as specific geographically located neighborhoods but as archetypical ghettos, though often even without actually using the term *ghetto*. The point is that the place reputation presented in these indirect stories does not express its position in the housing hierarchy based on other related housing areas in the local context, which is otherwise considered an essential part of place reputation.[41] Instead, these indirect stories demonstrate that a national hierarchy is established through the relationship to other disadvantaged neighborhoods across the country centered on an implied but easy recognized definition of a ghetto. Thus, some neighborhoods are so notorious in public life and so integrated into the public discourse on disadvantaged neighborhoods that, purely by their name, they become dystopian symbols of the problems addressed by the legislation of the Parallel Society and ghetto list.

Some residents saw the political discourse as a kind of "political bullying," as one resident put it. Others argued that the term *ghetto* contributes to newspapers' interest in negative spectacular incidents and to spatial generalizations. It "sells the story," as the saying goes among residents. In general, residents perceive the term *ghetto* as severely damaging the place's reputation and outsiders' images of their neighborhood. Though the indirect stories of detached spatial generalization are not explicitly recognized as harmful by residents, they may be even more effective in reinforcing a devastating and long-lasting negative place reputation of their neighborhood.⟨fig. 6⟩ Their nonspecific descriptions are key in the process of territorial stigmatization, rendering disadvantaged neighborhoods as holes in the space of the welfare state.[42] In addition, detached spatial generalizations in media stories prevent residents from objecting to and negotiating a bad place reputation because of its abstract, nonspecific connotations of their lived neighborhood. This is also contributing to the impact of spatial stigmatization and to the conservatism of negative place reputation of Danish deprived neighborhoods on the national list, though at the same time addressing how a national hierarchy among these neighborhoods are distributed in public discourse.

Concluding Remarks

The neighborhoods that were originally designed as ideal residential welfare spaces for the generations of citizens have come to occupy the reverse role today, namely, as dystopian places representing the spatial limits of the welfare state epitomized in the expression "holes in the map of Denmark." Our study demonstrates that media coverage, one newspaper article after another, has a direct and fundamental influence on residents' self-reflected image of their neighborhoods. Our interviews with residents reveal that media is an important knowledge platform examining what is occurring in their neighborhoods outside of their own social circle. Media allows the residents to become witnesses to incidents which they might not have even discovered themselves or only experienced as remotely relevant. Moreover, residents often confuse media coverage with outsiders' perception of their neighborhood. This demonstrates that stories are important elements in a constant, dynamic negotiation of place reputation between residents' own perceptions of their neighborhood and their perceptions of how other people view the neighborhood, according to the concept of self-reflecting image.[43] In contrast to an abstract, nonspecific negative place reputation, specific – often negative – stories are subject to scrutiny in terms of right and wrong, exaggeration or truthful information. Media coverage has been criticized for producing a negative place reputation but is also a specific platform where a negative place reputation can be disproved, disputed, and discredited. While this study only focuses on written articles, this insight into the dynamics of negotiations calls for research into social media and related democratic communications platforms to fully understand how place reputation and spatial images are produced and reproduced.

We conclude that media representations, in this case, newspaper articles, of disadvantaged neighborhoods on the ghetto list shake up and reinforce a common negative place reputation. By focusing on incidents, such as crime, violence, drug activities and vandalism, these singular negative stories become the dominant narrative of a neighborhood characterized by a certain ethnicity, age cohort and gender profile, young men of non-Western origin, a certain social conduct, nonnormative behavior, often criminal, and concrete housing blocks labelled ghettos. Our study also demonstrates, in some cases, that media detach local areas from their spatial, specific context and turn them into dystopian symbols of a publicly recognized perception of a ghetto, contributing new implied generalizations of disadvantaged neighborhoods. Therefore, we conclude that media coverage of disadvantaged neighborhoods is closely related to or even a direct by-product of the political discourse on Danish ghettos since the government started listing the areas in 2010. On the other hand, this is also open to the suggestion that media also influences the political understanding and that political and media discourses are coproducing actors in building up negative place reputations.

What do these insights tell us about Danish social housing in the welfare state? Though we have not focused here on the actual social, physical, and demographic challenges that these disadvantaged neighborhoods are subject to, we emphasize that such challenges should not be neglected. Yet representation in public life and media is also part of the problem. Some of the stories that are circulated contribute to a downward negative spiral of place reputation that detach these areas not only from their local geographical context but also from the very idea of being an integrated part of a spatially coherent welfare state. Living in a "hole in the map of Denmark" casts a significant dark shadow on residents' spatial experiences and on the welfare state's ability to integrate these areas into the common story of residential development of modern dwellings to which they were born.

Acknowledgments

The empirical data are part of Regeneration of Danish Disadvantaged Neighbourhoods: Long-term Evaluation (2019–28), funded by Landsbyggefonden (The National Building Fund). We express gratitude to our colleagues for commenting on the preliminary findings.

Bibliography

Andersen, Hans Skifter. "Etnisk segregation: Årsager og betydning for udsatte boligområder." *Samfundsøkonomen* 3 (2020): 55–64.

——. "Why Do Residents Want to Leave Deprived Neighbourhoods? The Importance of Residents' Subjective Evaluations of Their Neighbourhood and Its Reputation." *Journal of Housing and the Built Environment* 23, no. 2 (2008): 79–101. https://doi.org/10.1007/s10901-008-9109-x.

Arthurson, Kathy. "Mixed Tenure Communities and the Effects on Neighbourhood Reputation and Stigma: Residents' Experiences from Within." *Cities* 35 (December 2013): 432–38. https://doi.org/10.1016/j.cities.2013.03.007.

Arthurson, Kathy, Michael Darcy, and Dallas Rogers. "Televised Territorial Stigma: How Social Housing Tenants Experience the Fictional Media Representation of Estates in Australia." *Environment and Planning.A* 46, no. 6 (2014): 1334–50. https://doi.org/10.1068/a46136.

BARK and Mogens Morgen, eds. *Bygningskultur og bevaringsværdier: 1940'ernes og 1950'ernes murede boligbebyggelser*. Copenhagen: Realdania, 2015.

Bech-Danielsen, Claus, Marie Stender and Mette Mechlenborg. *Bispehaven: Arbejdsrapport – Baselineundersøgelse 2019.* SBi no. 2020:2. Copenhagen: Statens Byggeforskningsinstitut, 2020.

——. *Gellerupparken: Arbejdsrapport – Baselineundersøgelse 2019.* SBi no. 2020:1. Copenhagen: Statens Byggeforskningsinstitut, 2020.

——. *Taastrupgård: Arbejdsrapport – Baselineundersøgelse 2019.* SBi no. 2020:3. Copenhagen: Statens Byggeforskningsinstitut, 2020.
——. *Vollsmose: Arbejdsrapport – Baselineundersøgelse 2019.* SBi no. 2020:7. Copenhagen: Statens Byggeforskningsinstitut, 2020.
Blokland, Talja. "'You Got to Remember You Live in Public Housing': Place-Making in an American Housing Project." *Housing, Theory and Society* 25, no. 1 (2008): 31–46. https://doi.org/10.1080/14036090601151095.
Dean, Jo, and Annette Hastings. *Challenging Images: Housing Estates, Stigma and Regeneration.* Bristol: The Policy Press, 2000. https://www.jrf.org.uk/report/challenging-images-housing-estates-stigma-and-regeneration.
Devereux, Eoin, Amanda Haynes and Martin J. Power. "At the Edge: Media Constructions of a Stigmatised Irish Housing Estate." *Journal of Housing and the Built Environment* 26, no. 2 (2011): 123–42. https://doi.org/10.1007/s10901-011-9210-4.
Freiesleben, Mikala von. *Et Danmark af parallelsamfund: Segregering, ghettoisering og social sammenhængskraft: Parallelsamfundet i Dansk diskurs 1968–2013: Fra utopi til dystopi.* Copenhagen: Københavns Universitetsforlag, 2016.
Hastings, Annette. "Stigma and Social Housing Estates: Beyond Pathological Explanations." *Journal of Housing and the Built Environment* 19, no. 3 (2004): 233–54. https://www.jstor.org/stable/41107263.
Hastings, Annette, and Jo Dean. "Challenging Images: Tackling Stigma through Estate Regeneration." *Policy & Politics* 31, no. 2 (April 1, 2003): 171–84. https://doi.org/10.1332/030557303765371663.
Haynes, Amanda, Eoin Devereux and Martin J. Power. "Media Representations, Stigma and Neighbourhood Identity." In *Social Housing, Disadvantage and Neighbourhood Liveability: Ten Years of Change in Social Housing Neighbourhoods*, edited by Michelle Norris, 192–218. London: Routledge, 2014.
Houlind, Birthe. *Håndbog om almene boliger KAB.* Copenhagen: KAB, 2016.
Indenrigs- og Boligministeriet. *Blandede boligområder: Næste skridt i kampen mod parallelsamfund.* Copenhagen: Indenrigs- og Boligministeriet, 2021.
Jensen, Sune Qvotrup, and Ann-Dorte Christensen. "Territorial Stigmatization and Local Belonging." *City* 16, nos. 1–2 (April 1, 2012): 74–92. https://doi.org/10.1080/13604813.2012.663556.
Jørgensen, Mette, and Svante Bram Sørensen. *Informationsstrømme: Erfaringer fra tre udsatte boligområder i Aarhus.* Copenhagen: Ministeriet for Børn, Ligestilling, Integration og Sociale Forhold, 2011.
Karkov, Rasmus, and Anders Ladefoged. "Drengene fra gården." *Berlingske*, December 2, 2018.
Kearns, Ade, Oliver Kearns and Louise Lawson. "Notorious Places: Image, Reputation, Stigma: The Role of Newspapers in Area Reputations for Social Housing Estates." *Housing Studies* 28, no. 4 (June 1, 2013): 579–98. https://doi.org/10.1080/02673037.2013.759546.
Kullberg, Agneta, Toomas Timpka, Tommy Svensson, Nadine Karlsson and Kent Lindqvist. "Does the Perceived Neighborhood Reputation Contribute to Neighborhood Differences in Social Trust and Residential Wellbeing?" *Journal of Community Psychology* 38, no. 5 (2010): 591–606. https://doi.org/10.1002/jcop.20383.
McLaren, Lindsay, Rosemary Perry, Lesley Carruthers and Penelope Hawe. "Introducing a Means of Quantifying Community Reputation: The Print Media as a Data Source." *Health Place* 11, no. 2 (2005): 187–94. https://doi.org/10.1016/j.healthplace.2004.06.002.
Mechlenborg, Mette. "Reintegrating Ghettos into Society: Lessons Learnt from the Danish Ghetto Strategy." *Nordic Journal of Architectural Research* 31, no. 1 (2019): 59–87. http://arkitekturforskning.net/na/article/download/1170/654945.
Palmer, Catherine, Anna Ziersch, Kathy Arthurson and Fran Baum. "Challenging the Stigma of Public Housing: Preliminary Findings from a Qualitative Study in South Australia." *Urban Policy and Research* 22, no. 4 (2004): 411–26. https://doi.org/10.1080/0811114042000296326.
Permentier, Matthieu. "Neighbourhood Reputation." In *International Encyclopedia of Housing and Home*, edited by Susan J. Smith, 5:85–89. San Diego: Elsevier, 2012. https://search.credoreference.com/content/entry/esthouse/neighbourhood_reputation/0
Permentier, Matthieu, Gideon Bolt and Maarten van Ham. "Determinants of Neighbourhood Satisfaction and Perception of Neighbourhood Reputation." *Urban Studies* 48, no. 5 (2010): 977–96. http://www.jstor.org/stable/43084283.
Pinkster, Fenne M., Marijn S. Ferier and Myrte S. Hoekstra. "On the Stickiness of Territorial Stigma: Diverging Experiences in Amsterdam's most Notorious Neighbourhood." *Antipode* 52, no. 2 (2020): 522–41. https://doi.org/10.1111/anti.12608.
Regeringen. *Ét Danmark uden parallelsamfund: Ingen ghettoer i 2030.* Copenhagen: Økonomi- og indenrigsministeriet/Ministry of Economic Affairs and the Interior, 2018. https://www.regeringen.dk/media/4937/publikation_%C3%A9t-danmark-uden-parallelsamfund.pdf.
——. *Ghettoen tilbage til samfundet: Et opgør med parallelsamfund i Danmark.* Copenhagen: Socialministeriet/The Ministry of Social Affairs, 2010.
——. *Regeringens strategi mod ghettoisering.* Copenhagen: Ministeriet for Flygtninge, Indvandrere og Integration, 2004.
Rogers, Dallas, Michael Darcy and Kathy Arthurson. "Researching Territorial Stigma with Social Housing Tenants: Tenant-Led Digital Media Production about People and Place." In *Negative Neighbourhood Reputation and Place Attachment: The Production and Contestation of Territorial Stigma*, edited by Paul Kirkness and Andreas Tijé-Dra, 178–93. London: Routledge, 2017.
Wacquant, Loïc. "Territorial Stigmatization in the Age of Advanced Marginality." *Thesis Eleven* 91, no. 1 (2007): 66–77. https://doi.org/10.1177/0725513607082003.
Warr, Deborah. "Social Networks in a 'Discredited' Neighbourhood." *Journal of Sociology* (Melbourne) 41, no. 3 (2005): 285–308. https://doi.org/10.1177/1440783305057081.
Wassenberg, Frank. "Renewing Stigmatised Estates in the Netherlands: A Framework for Image Renewal Strategies." *Journal of Housing and the Built Environment* 19, no. 3 (2004): 271–92. https://www.jstor.org/stable/41107265.

Notes

1 Regeringen, *Ét Danmark uden parallelsamfund: Ingen ghettoer i 2030* (Copenhagen: Økonomi- og indenrigsministeriet/Ministry of Economic Affairs and the Interior, 2018). https://www.regeringen.dk/media/4937/publikation_%C3%A9t-danmark-uden-parallelsamfund.pdf.
2 The Danish social housing sector, called *den almene boligsektor*, bears similarities to both the nonprofit housing sector and the public sector, leaving the translation slightly incorrect.
3 Birthe Houlind, *Håndbog om almene boliger* (Copenhagen: KAB, 2016).
4 BARK and Mogens Morgen, eds., *Bygningskultur og bevaringsværdier: 1940'ernes og 1950'ernes murede boligbebyggelser* (Copenhagen: Realdania, 2015), 1–176.
5 See Houlind, *Håndbog om almene boliger*; and Frank Wassenberg, "Renewing Stigmatised Estates in the Netherlands: A Framework for Image Renewal Strategies," *Journal of Housing and the Built Environment* 19, no. 3 (2004): 275.
6 See Houlind, *Håndbog om almene boliger*.
7 See Mette Mechlenborg, "Reintegrating Ghettos into Society: Lessons Learnt from the Danish Ghetto Strategy," *Nordic Journal of Architectural Research* 31, no. 1 (2019): 59–87; and Regeringen, *Regeringens strategi mod ghettoisering* (Copenhagen: Ministeriet for Flygtninge, Indvandrere og Integration, 2004).
8 See Regeringen, *Ghettoen tilbage til samfundet: Et opgør med parallelsamfund i Danmark* (Copenhagen: Socialministeriet/The Ministry of Social Affairs, 2010).
9 Regeringen, *Ét Danmark uden parallelsamfund*.
10 Hans Skifter Andersen, "Etnisk segregation: Årsager og betydning for udsatte boligområder," *Samfundsøkonomen* 3 (2020): 55–64.
11 Mikala von Freiesleben, *Et Danmark af parallelsamfund: Segregering, ghettoisering og social sammenhængskraft: Parallelsamfundet i Dansk diskurs 1968–2013: Fra utopi til dystopi* (Copenhagen: Københavns Universitetsforlag, 2016).
12 Indenrigs- og Boligministeriet, *Blandede boligområder: Næste skridt i kampen mod parallelsamfund* (Copenhagen: Indenrigs- og Boligministeriet, 2021).
13 Matthieu Permentier, "Neighbourhood Reputation," in *International Encyclopedia of Housing and Home*, ed. Susan J. Smith (San Diego: Elsevier, 2012), 5:86.
14 Wassenberg, "Renewing Stigmatised Estates in the Netherlands," 275.
15 Mette Jørgensen and Svante Bram Sørensen, *Informationsstrømme: Erfaringer fra tre udsatte boligområder i Aarhus* (Copenhagen: Ministeriet for Børn, Ligestilling, Integration og Sociale Forhold, 2011); Sune Qvotrup Jensen and Ann-Dorte Christensen, "Territorial Stigmatization and Local Belonging," *City* 16, nos. 1–2 (April 1, 2012): 74–92.
16 The study is aware that today's social media, like Twitter, Facebook etc., plays an important role in people's understanding everyday media practices.
17 Ade Kearns, Oliver Kearns and Louise Lawson, "Notorious Places: Image, Reputation, Stigma: The Role of Newspapers in Area Reputations for Social Housing Estates," *Housing Studies* 28, no. 4 (June 1, 2013): 579–98, https://doi.org/10.1080/02673037.2013.759546.
18 Kearns, Kearns and Lawson, "Notorious Places," 579–98; Jensen, "Territorial Stigmatization and Local Belonging," 74–92; Annette Hastings, "Stigma and Social Housing Estates: Beyond Pathological Explanations," *Journal of Housing and the Built Environment* 19, no. 3 (2004): 233–54; Amanda Haynes, Eoin Devereux and Martin J. Power, "Media Representations, Stigma and Neighbourhood Identity," in *Social Housing, Disadvantage and Neighbourhood Liveability: Ten Years of Change in Social Housing Neighbourhoods*, ed. Michelle Norris (London: Routledge, 2014).
19 Catharine Palmer et al., "Challenging the Stigma of Public Housing: Preliminary Findings from a Qualitative Study in South Australia," *Urban Policy and Research* 22, no. 4 (2004): 411–26, https://doi.org/10.1080/0811114042000296326; Talja Blokland, "'You Got to Remember You Live in Public Housing': Place-Making in an American Housing Project," *Housing, Theory and Society* 25, no. 1 (2008): 31–46; Eoin Devereux, Amanda Haynes and Martin J. Power, "At the Edge: Media Constructions of a Stigmatised Irish Housing Estate," *Journal of Housing and the Built Environment* 26, no. 2 (June 1, 2011): 123–42, https://doi.org/10.1007/s10901-011-9210-4.
20 Deborah Warr, "Social Networks in a 'Discredited' Neighbourhood," *Journal of Sociology* (Melbourne) 41, no. 3 (2005): 285–308, https://doi.org/10.1177/1440783305057081.
21 Jensen, "Territorial Stigmatization and Local Belonging," 74–92; Dallas Rogers, Michael Darcy and Kathy Arthurson, "Researching Territorial Stigma with Social Housing Tenants: Tenant-Led Digital Media Production about People and Place," in *Negative Neighbourhood Reputation and Place Attachment: The Production and Contestation of Territorial Stigma*, ed. Paul Kirkness and Andreas Tijé-Dra (London: Routledge, 2017), 178–93.
22 Blokland, "You Got to Remember You Live in Public Housing"; Kathy Arthurson, "Mixed Tenure Communities and the Effects on Neighbourhood Reputation and Stigma: Residents' Experiences from Within," *Cities* 35 (December 2013), 432–38, https://doi.org/10.1016/j.cities.2013.03.007; Rogers, Darcy and Arthurson, "Researching Territorial Stigma with Social Housing Tenants"; Lindsay McLaren, Rosemary Perry, Lesley Carruthers and Penelope Hawe, "Introducing a Means of Quantifying Community Reputation: The Print Media as a Data Source," *Health Place* 11, no. 2 (2005): 187–94, https://doi.org/10.1016/j.healthplace.2004.06.002.; Agneta Kullberg et al., "Does the Perceived Neighborhood Reputation Contribute to Neighborhood Differences in Social Trust and Residential Wellbeing?" *Journal of Community Psychology* 38, no. 5 (2010): 591–606, https://doi.org/10.1002/jcop.20383; and Fenne M. Pinkster, Marijn S. Ferier and Myrte S. Hoekstra, "On the Stickiness of Territorial Stigma: Diverging Experiences in Amsterdam's Most Notorious Neighbourhood," *Antipode* 52, no. 2 (2020): 522–41, https://doi.org/10.1111/anti.12608.
23 Claus Bech-Danielsen, Marie Stender and Mette Mechlenborg, *Bispehaven: Arbejdsrapport – Baselineundersøgelse 2019*. SBi no. 2020:2 (Copenhagen: Statens Byggeforskningsinstitut, 2020); Claus Bech-Danielsen, Marie Stender and Mette Mechlenborg, *Gellerupparken: Arbejdsrapport – Baselineundersøgelse 2019*. SBi no. 2020:1 (Copenhagen: Statens Byggeforskningsinstitut, 2020); Claus Bech-Danielsen, Mette Mechlenborg and Marie Stender, *Taastrupgård: Arbejdsrapport – Baselineundersøgelse 2019*. SBi no. 2020:3 (Copenhagen: Statens Byggeforskningsinstitut, 2020); Claus Bech-Danielsen, Mette Mechlenborg and Marie Stender, *Vollsmose: Arbejdsrapport – Baselineundersøgelse 2019.* SBi no. 2020:7 (Copenhagen: Statens Byggeforskningsinstitut, 2020).
24 Kearns, Kearns and Lawson, "Notorious Places."
25 Devereux, Haynes and Power, "At the Edge"; and Haynes, Devereux and Power, "Media Representations, Stigma and Neighbourhood Identity."
26 Kearns, Kearns and Lawson, "Notorious Places"; Kullberg, "Does the Perceived Neighborhood Reputation Contribute to Neighborhood Differences in Social Trust and Residential Wellbeing?" 591–606.
27 Haynes, Devereux and Power, "Media Representations, Stigma and Neighbourhood Identity."
28 Quote from Devereux, Haynes and Power, "At the Edge"; and from Freiesleben, *Et Danmark af parallelsamfund*.

29 Hans Skifter Andersen, "Why Do Residents Want to Leave Deprived Neighbourhoods? The Importance of Residents' Subjective Evaluations of Their Neighbourhood and Its Reputation," *Journal of Housing and the Built Environment* 23, no. 2 (2008): 79–101, https://doi.org/10.1007/s10901-008-9109-x.
30 Andersen, "Why Do Residents Want to Leave Deprived Neighbourhoods?"; and Devereux, Haynes and Power, "At the Edge."
31 Haynes, Devereux and Power, "Media Representations, Stigma and Neighbourhood Identity," 219.
32 See Jo Dean and Annette Hastings, *Challenging Images: Housing Estates, Stigma and Regeneration* (Bristol: The Policy Press, 2000); Annette Hastings and Jo Dean, "Challenging Images: Tackling Stigma through Estate Regeneration," *Policy & Politics* 31, no. 2 (April 1, 2003): 171–84, https://doi.org/10.1332/030557303765371663; McLaren, Perry, Carruthers and Hawe, "Introducing a Means of Quantifying Community Reputation"; and Kullberg, "Does the Perceived Neighborhood Reputation Contribute to Neighborhood Differences in Social Trust and Residential Wellbeing?" 591–606.
33 Pinkster, Ferier and Hoekstra, "On the Stickiness of Territorial Stigma."
34 See Warr, "Social Networks in a 'Discredited' Neighbourhood," 285–308; and Jensen, "Territorial Stigmatization and Local Belonging," 74–92.
35 Kathy Arthurson, Michael Darcy and Dallas Rogers, "Televised Territorial Stigma: How Social Housing Tenants Experience the Fictional Media Representation of Estates in Australia," *Environment and Planning.A* 46, no. 6 (2014): 1334–50, https://doi.org/10.1068/a46136.
36 Hastings, "Stigma and Social Housing Estates."
37 The term *dominating narratives* is from Kearns, Kearns and Lawson, "Notorious Places," 579–98.
38 As Haynes et al. wrote: "It can be argued that the newsworthiness of these stories [...] was derived not from the event reported but from the juxtaposition of a positive event with the stigmatised image of the neighbourhood." See Haynes, Devereux and Power, "Media Representations, Stigma and Neighbourhood Identity," 222.
39 *Indirect stories* is a term developed in Kearns, Kearns and Lawson, "Notorious Places."
40 Rasmus Karkov and Anders Ladefoged, "Drengene fra gården," *Berlingske*, December 2, 2018.
41 Wassenberg, "Renewing Stigmatised Estates in the Netherlands"; Matthieu Permentier, Gideon Bolt and Maarten van Ham, "Determinants of Neighbourhood Satisfaction and Perception of Neighbourhood Reputation," *Urban Studies* 48, no. 5 (2010): 977–96.
42 Loïc Wacquant, "Territorial Stigmatization in the Age of Advanced Marginality," *Thesis Eleven* 91, no. 1 (2007): 66–77; Hastings, "Challenging Images"; Devereux, Haynes and Power, "At the Edge."
43 Andersen, "Why Do Residents Want to Leave Deprived Neighbourhoods?"

Are We Caring?
Dilemmas Between Home and Institution in Architectures for the Elderly

Louise Dedenroth Høj

1 Salem Old People's Home, garden space, 1923.

The Danish model of care homes for elderly people is a special housing option with care staff around the clock, comparable to similar models in other countries.[1] It typically contains small apartments connected to common spaces for a group of residents and spaces for staff, as well as common spaces for communal activities for the entire care home. In 2021 around 40,000 Danes over the age of sixty-five are living in a care home, which corresponds to 3.4 percent of the total elderly population.[2] With a rapidly growing elderly population due to demographic changes, the need for care is increasing, and over the next ten years a minimum of 13,500 new care home residencies will be needed.[3]

The current Danish model has developed from earlier models of housing specially intended for this group of people. There is, in these architectures for the elderly, a very close entanglement between spatial conditions and an understanding of who these people are and how to treat them in the best possible way, reflecting different understandings of what welfare is. In this chapter these architectures are explored, specifically related to the Danish context, focusing on how the design of these spaces relates to ideas of institutionalization, care and home.

The first part explores current trends in the provision of care and how the distribution and size of care homes has developed in different municipal settings over the past fifty years, related to different demographic and economic conditions. This part is developed in relation to maps drawn from different statistical data. The second part is based on archival studies and explores the development of architectures for the elderly, studying the specificities of exemplars related to certain societal, political, cultural, clinical and economic shifts. In the third part, a study of a new care home is presented, highlighting the challenges and negotiations in a current setting in relation to its use and daily routines. This part builds on field studies as well as drawn and written material from the architectural competition and the design process.[4] At the end of the chapter the different parts are joined in a discussion of how the idea of welfare has changed and the current dilemmas between home and institution in these architectures.

Provision of Care

Overall, there is in the provision of care a tendency toward increased diversity as well as more individualized care. This is linked to more specialized care related to the increase in people with dementia.[5] Today, three out of four residents in care homes are suffering from dementia, and many new care homes are built as specialized dementia care facilities.[6] This adds new challenges to the architecture related to negotiations between aspects of home and institution, which are further complicated by the safety and protection needs of people with dementia.[7] Furthermore, there is a growing private care market, following *Friplejeboligordningen* (The Free Care Housing Act), in which private actors are entering the care market and competing with the municipal offers to attract residents.[8] These private companies can make a profit by selling extra services to the residents, such as extra cleaning and wellness treatments.

Although the general development is toward a greater variety in the care choices, there are huge national differences in this development related to different demographic and economic conditions between the municipalities. This is manifesting spatially, showing varying developments in the size and distribution of care home facilities and painting an increasingly unequal map of care, with great differences between urban, suburban and rural settings.[9]

1.27
Percentage of inhabitants older than 65 years, 1972–2017

1.28
Number of care dwellings per 1,000 inhabitants older than 65 years, 1972–2017

1.29
Percentage of inhabitants older than 65 years, 1972

1.30
Percentage of inhabitants older than 65 years, 2017

1.31
Number of care dwellings per 1,000 inhabitants older than 65 years, 1972

1.32
Number of care dwellings per 1,000 inhabitants older than 65 years, 2017

As an example of an urban setting, development in the municipality of Copenhagen is showing a downscaling of huge facilities over the past fifty years, as well as a greater spread in the distribution of care homes across the urban area.

1.33
Distribution and size of care homes in the municipality of Copenhagen, 1972

1.34
Distribution and size of care homes in the municipality of Copenhagen, 2020

Where there was earlier a great concentration of elderly people, especially around the area known as De Gamles By (The Old People's City), the current youthification of the city has resulted in a decrease in the care need and an upgrade of the care facilities.[10] Further, the high population density in the urban setting of Copenhagen makes it possible to offer a wide variety of care choices, with specialized dementia care facilities as well as profile care homes aimed at individualized care for specific lifestyle groups.[11] Another development is seen in Høje Taastrup, representing a suburban municipal setting, where there has been a huge expansion of the urban area.

1.35
Distribution and size of care homes in the municipality of Høje Taastrup, 1972

1.36
Distribution and size of care homes in the municipality of Høje Taastrup, 2020

This has resulted in an increasing care need, due to the population growth and rise in the number of elderly people. In this case, new care homes have been built in the new urban areas in the municipality to meet the growing care need and to keep the provision of care close to the citizens. In Tønder, a so-called rural or outskirts municipality, the overall population is slightly declining, while the share of elderly people is increasing at a fast pace.

1.37
Distribution and size of care homes in the municipality of Tønder, 1972

1.38
Distribution and size of care homes in the municipality of Tønder, 2020

Here, existing care homes have expanded to meet the increasing care need, gaining importance within the local environment in an aging community, where other welfare amenities are diminishing or disappearing (see Kirsten Marie Raahauge's chapter in the present volume). However,

2

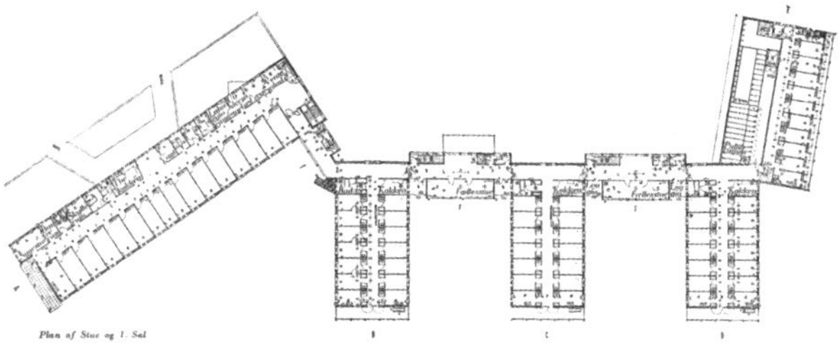

3

4

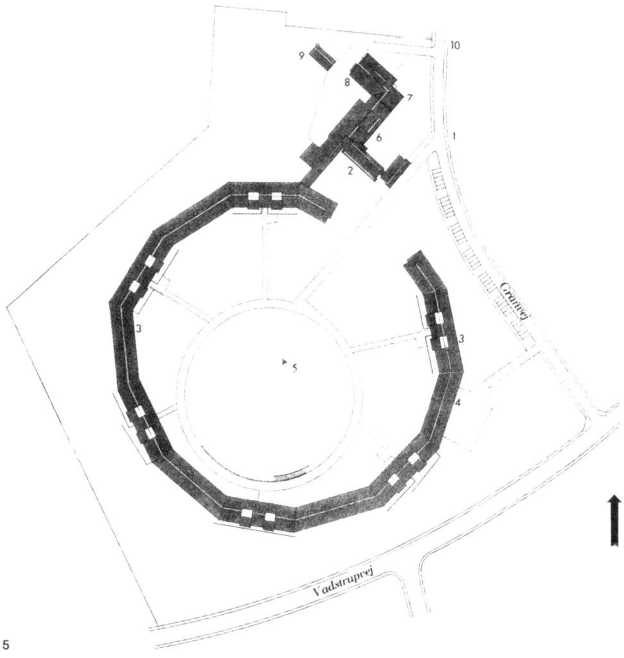

5

2 Salem Old People's Home, resident dormitory. Photography, around 1901.
3 Solhjem Old People's Home, 1940, plan drawing. Published in *Arkitekten Maanedshæfte* 5 (1941): 82.
4 Solhjem Old People's Home, 1940. Published in *Arkitekten Maanedshæfte* 5 (1941): 83.
5 Ringbo Nursing Home, 1961–63, plan drawing. F. O. Lund and Hans Chr. Hansen, *Arkitektur* 6 (1964): 225.

6 Ringbo Nursing Home, 1961–63, occupational therapy room. *Arkitektur* 6 (1964): 236.

in Tønder, specialized care offers are often far away, as only one care home provides specialized dementia care, located in the southern part of the municipality. This means that citizens are potentially forced to move quite far away from their network and relatives to get the right type of care, thus isolating them further.

Development of an Institutional Model of Care for Elderly

The first steps toward an institutional model of care in Denmark came after the Lov om Alderdomsunderstøttelse (Law of Old Age Support) from 1891, which directed municipalities to create "asylums or similar institutions" for recipients of the new old age support.[12] This led to what is known as old people's homes, first emerging in the bigger cities in the beginning of the 1900s. An exemplar of this is Salem Old People's Home in Copenhagen from 1901,⟨fig. 1⟩ an enormous institution for 470 residents.[13] The main purpose of the old people's home was to provide housing for the elderly who could no longer support themselves and who would have earlier been placed in a poorhouse, with the loss of all their societal rights.[14] Care was here limited to a section for residents who needed extensive care. Residents were referred to as *husfæller* (roommates), living together in dormitories with up to eight people in one room. Their private space was limited to the bed where they slept and a chair placed next to it, where they could sit during the day. In front of the bed was a small cupboard that functioned as a sort of threshold between the private and the shared space, where residents could display personal objects and items important to them, such as a knitted tablecloth or photographs.⟨fig. 2⟩

In the following period, elderly care expanded, with an increase in the number of old people's homes, toward the idea of universal welfare.[15] Sick wards also became a mandatory part of the housing model.[16] An exemplar of this development is Solhjem Old People's Home in Gentofte, from 1940,⟨fig. 3–4⟩ where the aim was to give residents "the feeling of having preserved a little home of their own."[17] Solhjem was built with private rooms for seventy residents and communal rooms placed in the connecting hallway, thus increasing the residents' privacy and offering the possibility of both separation and togetherness.

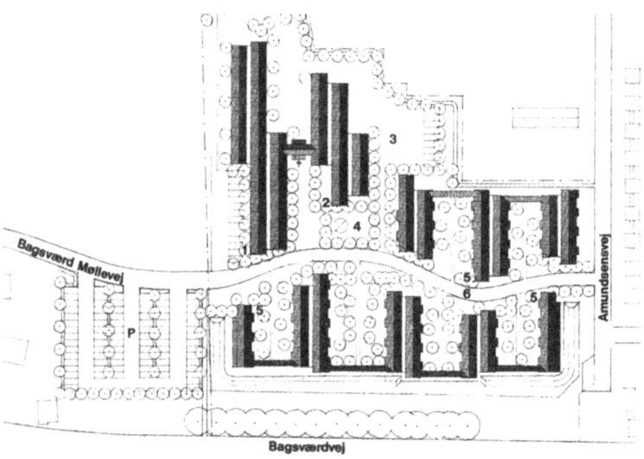

7 Møllegården Care Centre, 1978, plan drawing. *Arkitektur DK* 6 (1978): 228.

There was a shift in elderly care in the middle of the twentieth century. To meet the increasing care need caused by the rising elderly population, the nursing home emerged as a new model between the hospital and the old people's home.[18] Residents were now referred to as patients and sorted into different disease

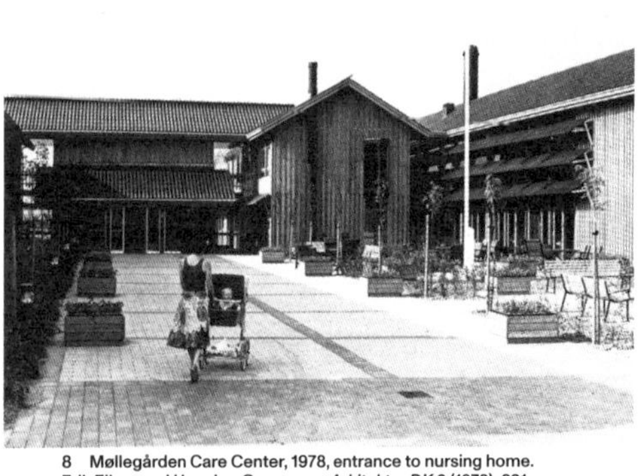

8 Møllegården Care Center, 1978, entrance to nursing home. Erik Ejlers and Henning Graversen, *Arkitektur DK* 6 (1978): 231.

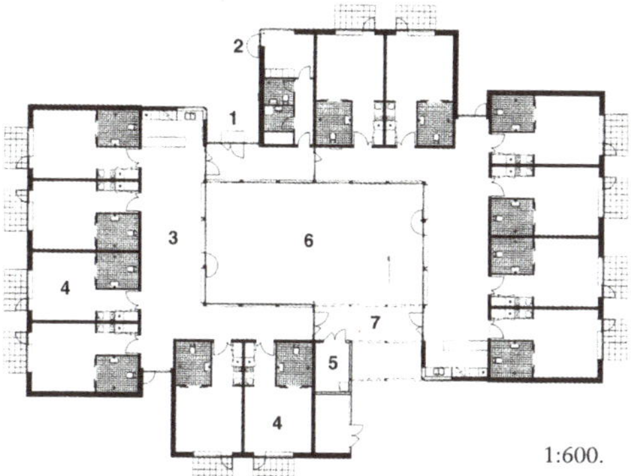

9 Torndalshave Care Home, 1998, designed by Frederiksen & Knudsen A/S Arkitekter. Plan drawing.

10 Torndalshave Care Home, 1998, designed by Frederiksen & Knudsen A/S Arkitekter. Common room.

groups, placed in different nursing homes – for example, the chronically ill, psychiatric diseases, and what was at the time called senile dementia.[19] Ringbo Nursing Home in Bagsværd from 1961–63⟨fig. 5–6⟩ is an exemplar of this new model, with 280 residents, or elderly psychiatric patients.[20] Ringbo is divided into patient wards, and residents live in double rooms. The wards are connected to treatment rooms for physiotherapy and occupational therapy, reflecting the dominant care thinking of the time, where the focus was on treatment and rehabilitation activities rather than other (personal) activities.[21] In this medical model illness and disability were viewed as deviations from the norm, and the focus is on curing or managing the symptoms.[22]

The following period marked the beginning of the deinstitutionalization of care, with a move away from a top-down universal model of equal distribution, where the old person is viewed as a passive client and isolated in an institution.[23] An exemplar of this development is Møllegården Care Center in Gladsaxe from 1978,[24] ⟨fig. 7–8⟩ which is a mixed facility woven into the existing urban fabric. Møllegården contains a nursing home, a day center for the elderly, and protected senior dwellings, and the focus is on supporting a continuity of elderly life and reintegrating the elderly into the surrounding society. This development is linked both to a wider institutional critique – such as the sociologist Erving Goffman's descriptions of the dehumanization of the individual in "total institutions,"[25] and the philosopher Michel Foucault's critique of the power of the state over the individual – as well as to broader societal changes with increased individualization.[26]

As a continuation of this development, welfare delivery completely changed in the 1980s with a dismantling of the institutions separating care and housing forms,[27] and a new model emerged: the care home. In this model, the residents were made tenants under the Public Housing Act, renting their own apartment and referred to as residents or citizens rather than as patients. There was as well a shift in entire care thinking. This is seen, in dementia care, as a shift from the medical model to a person-centered model, where the focus changed from the disease or disabilities to the person as a whole.[28] Linked to this was a growing focus on the sociomaterial environment in relation to care, with an expansion of studies in the field of environmental gerontology, on the therapeutic qualities of the physical environment for elderly and people with dementia.[29] An exemplar showing this development is the Torndalshave Care Home in Hvidovre from 1998,⟨fig. 9–10⟩ a small-scale care home with only twelve residents, as a sort of collective living for people with dementia.[30] Here residents have their own small apartment with one room, a bathroom, and a kitchenette. The private living area of the apartment continues directly into the communal space with a "home-like" kitchen facing the inner protected courtyard. This spatial layout reflects the importance of this as a home as well as a space for social activities linked to daily life in the person-centered care model.

11 Tornhøjhaven, town square.

12 Tornhøjhaven, main street.

Tornhøjhaven: A Current Exemplar Care Home

There is today a great focus on creating a homely environment in care home facilities, especially related to people with dementia.[31] Most residents with dementia spend all their time within the care home facility, which becomes their total universe. A focus on the inclusion of other aspects of everyday life is part of a current trend referred to as "dementia villages," as a way of offering more freedom to the residents.[32] Tornhøjhaven in Aalborg from 2018 is an exemplar of these ambitions to create a homely environment and a "village" community for people with dementia. At the same time, it highlights current challenges and negotiations in these architectures between conflicting demands of the home and institution.

Unfulfilled Visions and Subsequent Changes

Tornhøjhaven is a dementia care home for seventy-two residents and a day center for people with dementia living at home. The facility is organized as a sort of village structure, with housing units placed along the edge of the site, creating an inner protected outdoor area. Responding to the ambitions from the competition brief of "homeliness" and "village,"[33] the facility was envisioned as a lively environment with small shops along a "main street," with market days and concerts at the town square, as well as a variation of experiences connected to the outdoor spaces.[34]

However, when the care home opened in 2018, it did not meet the vision of a lively environment that was imagined, which disappointed both its users and politicians. The "village life" was difficult to see. There was only one shop – a kiosk operated by volunteers and open two to three mornings a week. The outdoor space felt bare and, as an employee explained, it is all "yellow and gray and gray."⟨fig. 11⟩ A reason for this is that the project was altered during the design process, with much of the outdoor aspects cut away due to budgetary constraints. Further it was overlooked in the planning process, how the shops should be run and how the visions for the vibrant village life should be carried through.

Because of these unfulfilled visions, the municipality, after half a year, decided to fix the outdoor area and implement many of the elements that were cut away in the design process. The municipality and the housing association found some money in the budget and began a process, named Project Homeliness, which ran from August 2019 until February 2021.[35] Many changes were made to the outdoor environment: more trees and greenery were planted, and shops such as a bar, a café and a hair salon were added; signs were put up to enhance wayfinding in the facility.⟨fig. 12⟩ These alterations have improved the atmosphere of the environment; as a manager of the care home says afterwards, "it is bright and nice to walk around." However, many of the village functions are not being used and therefore just lie empty. The hairdresser, for example, still goes around to residents' apartments instead of residents' going

13 Tornhøjhaven, common room.

14 Tornhøjhaven, common room.

15 Tornhøjhaven, original main entrance.

16 Tornhøjhaven, new entrance foyer.

to the hair salon, which could imply that a change in the use and the care culture is needed to fit the new surroundings.

The common spaces in the housing units have also been changed. When the care home opened, the only interior colors used were white and gray, and the same furniture was used throughout, giving the home an institutional feeling.⟨fig. 13⟩ The rooms felt very bare, with only a few decorative elements, such as some posters, a clock, a calendar, and a small bookcase. "There is a lack of atmosphere in the common spaces," a relative said; a caregiver stated "The furniture is very modern. [...] They do not fit our residents." The changes made in the common spaces offer a more homely atmosphere, with colors, hanging lamps over the tables, and different types of furniture, both new and secondhand, supplementing the existing furniture.⟨fig. 14⟩

Issues of Safety

The entrance is placed in the north corner of the facility in connection to the main square. On the one hand there is an ambition to signal openness and transparency to the outside; and on the other, a need to protect and guarantee the safety of the residents, as highlighted in the competition brief.[36] In the project development, the entrance changed from being a staffed reception to a single door leading directly to the inner outdoor area. Because of this, several residents had walked out and left the facility, as they were attracted by the activity and the glass door was a luminous spot in a dark corner.⟨fig. 15⟩

The entrance was rebuilt a year after the opening of the care home, moving it to the corner of the facility, through a small foyer.⟨fig. 16⟩ A small loop was created where the old entrance was, so residents approaching the exit are led back into the facility through a small garden space; it also functions as a delay, so care staff have time to come and assist the resident back.[37]

Circulation Outdoors

All circulation is placed outdoors, meaning both residents and care staff must go outside to move between the housing units and different functions of the care home. On one level, this creates a closer connection between indoors and outdoors and a greater sense of home, without the long corridors normally associated with an institution. As one relative described it, it gives more freedom to the residents. On another level, however, this has created discontent among the staff, as they feel disconnected from their colleagues in the other housing units. This is especially an issue when there are caregivers working between several of the housing units, or for those working the night shifts, who are isolated in their housing unit. The design vision is thus not implemented in daily use, which could point to a need for a different way of working that will fit this type of "village" structure.

1.41
Layout of outdoor spaces, Tornhøjhaven

Empty Common Spaces

The housing units are organized with six apartments placed around a common space at the center. This space is divided into several rooms, derived from the ambition to support "the everyday life of the residents" and "avoid an institutional feeling," as well as to secure a "recognizable and homely environment."[38] However, the common spaces are often empty. When residents spend time in the common room, they are most often sitting in the dining area, which is the largest and most central of the spaces.

1.42
Layout of common areas in the housing units, Tornhøjhaven

The staff cannot see how to use all the spaces. "We cannot sit together with all the residents and watch a movie together," one caregiver told me. Another caregiver, talking about the activity corner, said: "There is no reason to sit here; you just sit and look at the wall." What they are pointing to is a lack of spatial qualities in these spaces; they are too small or without any daylight or purpose. This might imply that the number of rooms are too many for the small number of residents in a housing unit.

Another reason for the empty common spaces is a lack of activities; as a relative says, "There is nothing to attract the residents." This is linked to the fact that the caregivers are often not present in the common spaces. They spend a lot of time away from the residents in the closed kitchen placed between two housing units.[39] That the staff is often not present also makes it difficult for relatives to find them when visiting. "The doors to the kitchen [...] are hermetically sealed," a relative says. "You have no idea if they [the caregivers] are there or not." It also causes frustration for the staff, as they feel disconnected from the residents when they are in the kitchen. "The residents are sitting alone," one caregiver says, "because of the closed doors."

> Fieldnote, June 25, 2018
>
> A resident knocks on the door to the kitchen to get something to drink – "If they will open," she says to herself. The door is opened, and she is told that dinner will be ready in a moment. The door closes again, and she sits down at the dining table together with two of the other residents. They are alone in the common space.

The staff works in teams connected to two housing units. On the one hand, this gives some flexibility, making it possible for staff to decide how to organize the workflow and the community in relation to who the residents are in the specific housing units. However, it also means that the staff is often gathering in one housing unit. They are then bringing the residents over from the other housing unit, and the residents are themselves seeking this community, as this is where the activity is, leaving the common spaces in the other housing unit empty. This again points to the small housing units' being very fragile, with "a vulnerable community," as one relative says. It can be difficult for residents to find any activity or social life.

Intrusion of the Institution

The function of the care home as an institution is evident in the common spaces, conflicting with the function as a home for the residents. Here are many intruding noises, from the garbage suction in the utility room, the constant mechanical ventilation and the beeping of staff alarms disturbing the daily life. Another disturbing element is the many slamming doors from people going in and out. The main entrance door opens automatically. This door also leads into the wintergarden to the side. The glass door in front is used often, as it goes directly into the central dining area. Every time somebody approaches, the main door opens, which is of clear annoyance to many residents.

> Fieldnote, October 16, 2018
> In the wintergarden, a resident is playing cards with a caregiver. The door keeps opening and closing, as people are passing through the other door. "How rude they are. Just opening and closing the door, without coming in," the resident says.

Standard Requirements and Individual Needs

The private apartments are 33 square meters with one room and a bathroom. They are all equipped with a small kitchenette, built-in cupboards, a hospital bed, a height-adjustable toilet and sink and a hygiene station in the bathroom.[40] The bathroom has an extra door, as a possible escape passage for staff, and for safety reasons – to prevent residents from crawling out – the windows cannot open fully, but only tilt a bit from the top.[41] This means that it is not possible to ventilate the apartment with fresh air – a huge problem in a care home setting, where there are often unpleasant smells.[42] The layout of the apartments is very much dictated by standard requirements for accessibility and maneuverability, for example, so caregivers can operate a hoist or residents can maneuver a wheelchair.[43]

1.43
Layout of resident apartment, Tornhøjhaven

The ceiling is an institutional surface, operating as a suspended infrastructure. It contains installations for smoke detectors, power outlets, lighting and rails for a ceiling-mounted hoist, cutting through the surface, covering the bathroom and bed area.[44] These rails are a constant reminder for residents who do not (yet) need a hoist of a possible worse condition in the future.

1.44
Apartment ceiling plan, Tornhøjhaven

The standardized layout of the apartment is the backdrop for the very different furnishings of the residents according to their individual needs. One relative of a resident who needs a lot of care finds the room very practical. But she also refers to it as "sick-room-like" and would have preferred it more "living-room-like," reflecting a time when her father was healthier, which suggests that the requirements for apartments change as the health of the resident worsens.[45]

1.45
Apartment floor plan, Tornhøjhaven
1.46–47
Appropriation of the apartment by residents, Tornhøjhaven

Discussion and Conclusion

What is seen in these architectures for the elderly is an expanding complexity. On the one hand, what is shown here is a development of increased individualization, differentiation and humanization related to a shift at the structural level, from the marginalized position of the old person to the emergence of rights, where they are now tenants of their own apartment and referred to as residents or citizens. The spatial conditions have similarly changed, from the first huge institutions, in which the old person was placed in a dormitory with very limited privacy, to the current conditions, with smaller units as the frame for a community and a very mediated relationship between private and shared space.

Overall there has been a process of deinstitutionalization, moving from a one-size-fits-all welfare thinking toward a greater variety of care provisions. This is connected to a shift in the paradigm of care from the medical model, viewing the old person as a patient and a passive client of the institution, to a more humanized model of care. Today individuality and well-being play a larger role, as reflected in the expanding role of private care providers as part of a growing wellness industry.[46] However, this development also highlights an increased inequality between different municipal settings, where the care need is growing in the aging outskirts areas, but the possibilities of providing differentiated and individualized care offers are not as great as in the dense urban areas.

Related to the process of deinstitutionalization, where old people are staying longer in their own home, the health level of residents in care homes has continuously worsened. At the same time as the focus on "homeliness" has increased in these architectures, care is similarly playing a larger role together with the standardized requirements linked to aspects of hygiene, safety and the work environment of the staff. This is adding complexity with increased dilemmas between "home" and "institution," as seen in the constant negotiation of these architectures and the conflicting uses in everyday life among different users. While the notion of homeliness is on the one hand spreading to the design of the whole facility, institutional demands are simultaneously permeating the space through the choice of materials, care equipment and technological devices in the residents' most private spheres.

Bibliography

Aalborg Kommune. *Demenscenter Tornhøjhaven 2019–2021: Projekt Hjemlighed og forandring af omgivelser – en fortælling om datidens øjebliksbillede,* 2021.

Aalborg Kommune – Ældre- og Handicapforvaltningen. *Vejledning til boliger.* 2014. http://referater.aalborgkommune.dk/usercontrols/Referater/Pdf.aspx?pdfnavn=18049831.PDF&type=bilag&pdfid=26083

Andersson, Morgan. "Assisted Living for the Elderly: Features of a Swedish Model." In *Architecture for Residential Care and Ageing Communities – Spaces for Dwelling and Healthcare,* edited by Sten Gromark and Björn Andersson, 131–41. London: Routledge, 2021.

Anderzhon, Jeffrey W., David Hughes, Stephen Judd, Emi Kiyota and Monique Wijnties. *Design for Aging: International Case Studies of Building and Program.* Hoboken: John Wiley & Sons, 2012.

ArchiMed and Kuben Management. *Konkurrenceprogram – Demensplejehjemmet Aalborg Øst.* Aalborg Kommune, 2015. https://www.aalborg.dk/media/7406563/demensplejehjemmet-aalborg-%C3%B8st.pdf.

Balle Hansen, Morten, and Jens Ringsmose. *Fælles sprog og ældreplejens organisering i et historisk perspektiv.* Odense: Department of Political Science and Public Managements, Faculty of Social Sciences, University of Southern Denmark, 2005.

Beck, Ulrich, and Elisabeth Beck-Gernsheim. *Individualization: Institutionalized Individualism and Its Social and Political Consequences.* London: SAGE Publications Ltd, 2014.

Brawley, Elizabeth C. *Designing for Alzheimer's Disease: Strategies for Creating Better Care Environments.* New York: John Wiley & Sons, 1997.

Bygge- og Boligstyrelsen. *Indretning af ældreboliger for fysisk plejekrævende m.fl. En vejledning.* Forlaget Kommuneinformation, 1997. https://www.yumpu.com/da/document/read/18395164/indretning-af-aeldreboliger-for-fysisk-plejekraevende-mfl.

Cohen, Uriel, and Kristen Day. *Contemporary Environments for People with Dementia.* Baltimore: Johns Hopkins University Press, 1997.

Cohen, Uriel, and Gerald D. Weisman. *Holding on to Home: Designing Environments for People with Dementia.* Baltimore: Johns Hopkins University Press, 1991.

Day, Kristen, Daisy Carreon and Cheryl Stump. "The Therapeutic Design of Environments for People with Dementia: A Review of the Empirical Research." *The Gerontologist* 40, no. 4 (2000): 397–416.

Dempsey, Laura, Kathy Murphy, Adeline Cooney, Dympna Casey, Eamon O'Shea, Declan Devane, Fionnuala Jordan and Andrew Hunter. "Reminiscence in Dementia: A Concept Analysis." *Dementia* (London) 13, no. 2 (2014): 176–92.

Ejlers, Erik, and Henning Graversen. "Omsorgscentret Møllegården, Gladsaxe." *Arkitektur DK* 22, no. 6 (1978): 226–33.

Forsorgsloven: Lov om offentlig Forsorg vedrørende Særhjælp, Kommunehjælp og Fattighjælp. 1933.

Foucault, Michel. *Discipline and Punish.* Translated by Alan Sheridan. London: Allen Lane, 1977.

——. *Madness and Civilization: A History of Insanity in the Age of Reason.* Translated by Richard Howard. New York: Pantheon Books, 1965.

Friis & Moltke. *Konkurrenceforslag – Demensplejehjem I Aalborg Øst.* 2015.

Tornhøjhaven Dispositionsforslag. 2016.

Garutti, Francesco. "The Happiness Plan." In *Our Happy Life: Architecture and Well-Being in the Age of Emotional Capitalism,* edited by Francesco Garutti, 29–60. Berlin: Sternberg Press, 2019.

Goffman, Erving. *Asylums: Essays on the Social Situation of Mental Patients and Other Inmates.* Chicago: Aldine, 1961.

Jørgensen, Lisbeth Balslev. "Alderdom og demokrati." *Arkitektur DK* 25, nos. 3–4 (1981): 85–89.

Kähler, Margrethe. "Fakta og synspunkter om ældre/plejeboliger." *Arkitektur DK* 43, no. 7 (1999): 453–54.

Kitwood, Tom. *Dementia Reconsidered: The Person Comes First.* Buckingham: Open University Press, 1997.

Langkilde, Hans Erling, and Ib Martin Jensen. "Gentofte Kommunes Alderdomshjem." *Arkitekten Maanedshæfte,* 43, no. 5 (1941): 81–84.

Lov om Alderdomsunderstøttelse til værdige trængende udenfor Fattigvæsenet. Copenhagen: Pio, 1891.

Lund, Frederik Christian, and Hans Chr. Hansen. "Plejehjemmet Ringbo, Bagsværd." *Arkitektur DK* 8, no. 6 (1964): 225–37.

Marquardt, Gesine, Kathrin Bueter and Tom Motzek. "Impact of the Design of the Built Environment on People with Dementia: An Evidence-Based Review." *HERD: Health Environments Research & Design Journal* 8, no. 1 (2014): 127–57.

Møller, Anders. "Hvor har alderdommen hjemme?" In Nete Balslev Wingender, Anders Møller, Aske Juul Lassen, Kamilla Nørtoft and Tenna Jensen, *Gammel i København: liv og livsvilkår 1891–2018.* Frederiksberg: Frydenlund Academic, 2019.

National Collaborating Centre for Mental Health (UK). *Dementia: A NICE-SCIE Guideline on Supporting People with Dementia and Their Carers in Health and Social Care.* British Psychological Society, 2007. https://www.ncbi.nlm.nih.gov/books/NBK55480/?report=printable.

Nationalt Videnscenter for Demens. *Demens og depression hyppig blandt plejehjemsbeboere.* 2021. https://videnscenterfordemens.dk/da/pdf/node/866.

Regnier, Victor. *Housing Design for an Increasingly Older Population: Redefining Assisted Living for the Mentally and Physically Frail.* Hoboken: John Wiley & Sons, 2018.

Roesen, Janne. "Ny lov for friplejeboliger." *Nyhedsmagasinet Danske Kommuner* 14 (2015). http://www.danskekommuner.dk/Artikelarkiv/2015/Magasin-14/Ny-lov-for-friplejeboliger.

Sigbrand, Lone. *SBi-anvisning 263: Plejeboliger for personer med demens: detaljer og eksempler.* Copenhagen: Statens Byggeforskningsinstitut, 2016.

Socialministeriet. *Betænkning vedrørende alderdomshjem og plejehjem.* 1962.

Toft, Lasse Vej, and Søren Sønderby. "Hvor mange plejeboliger skal der bruges i fremtiden." *Nyhedsmagasinet Danske Kommuner* 33 (2016). http://www.danskekommuner.dk/Artikelarkiv/2016/Magasin-33/Hvor-mange-plejeboliger-skal-der-bruges-i-fremtiden/.

Van Steenwinkel, Iris. "Offering Architects Insights into Experiences of Living with Dementia: Three Case Studies on Orientation in Space, Time, and Identity." PhD diss. University of Leuven, 2015.

Vinge, Sidsel, Karen Kramhøft and Andreas Bøgh. *Hjemmesygeplejen i Danmark.* Copenhagen: DSI Institut for Sundhedsvæsen, 2006.

Zahle, Karen, and Margrethe Kähler. "Torndalshave." *Arkitektur DK* 43, no. 7 (1999): 401–7.

Notes

1 See Jeffrey W. Anderzhon, David Hughes, Stephen Judd, Emi Kiyota and Monique Wijnties. *Design for Aging: International Case Studies of Building and Program* (Hoboken: John Wiley & Sons, 2012); and Victor Regnier, *Housing Design for an Increasingly Older Population: Redefining Assisted Living for the Mentally and Physically Frail* (Hoboken: John Wiley & Sons, 2018).
2 Danmarks Statistik, Statistikbanken: https://www.statistikbanken.dk/10048, accessed June 6, 2021; Danmarks Statistik, Statistikbanken: https://www.dst.dk/da/Statistik/emner/befolkning-og-valg/befolkning-og-befolkningsfremskrivning/folketal, accessed June 6, 2021.
3 Lasse Vej Toft and Søren Sønderby, "Hvor mange plejeboliger skal der bruges i fremtiden," *Nyhedsmagasinet Danske Kommuner* 33 (2016), http://www.danskekommuner.dk/Artikelarkiv/2016/Magasin-33/Hvor-mange-plejeboliger-skal-der-bruges-i-fremtiden/.
4 The field studies were carried out from 2018 to 2021. The main studies were made in 2018, shortly after the opening of the care home, with two long stays of a week each in June/July and October. Further field studies were carried out in October 2020 and June 2021, after the care home had been running for some years and alterations had been made to the architecture. The case study includes participant observation and qualitative interviews with staff and relatives, as well as conversations with caregivers, care home managers, and residents, adjusted to the capabilities of the participants.
5 Dementia has become a huge societal focus in the past years, both nationally and globally because of the aging of the population and the rising number of people with dementia. In 2017 the first WHO Global Dementia Observatory was held, and in Denmark a National Dementia Action Plan was completed.
6 Nationalt Videnscenter for Demens, *Demens og depression hyppig blandt plejehjemsbeboere* (2021). https://videnscenterfordemens.dk/da/pdf/node/866.
7 Lone Sigbrand, *SBi-anvisning 263: Plejeboliger for personer med demens: detaljer og eksempler* (2016).
8 Friplejeboligordningen (The Free Care Housing Act) from 2007 establishes a new care housing form for private actors, and with a change of the law in 2015, the construction limit of private care homes without public support is removed, making it easier for private actors to access the market. See, for example, Janne Roesen, "Ny lov for friplejeboliger," *Nyhedsmagasinet Danske Kommuner* 14 (2015), http://www.danskekommuner.dk/Artikelarkiv/2015/Magasin-14/Ny-lov-for-friplejeboliger/.
9 Presented here are three exemplar municipal cases, representing an urban (Copenhagen), a suburban (Høje Taastrup), and a rural (Tønder) municipality. The drawn maps, showing size and location of care home facilities, are based on data from 1972 and 2020.
10 De Gamles By (The Old People's City) got its name in 1919, when the first old people's home in Copenhagen merged with a former hospital. Later, many nursing homes, care homes, and elderly homes were built here, and it developed as its own part of the city. But today is has been opened to the rest of the city with new developments creating a mixed urban area.
11 In Copenhagen there are eight profile care homes aimed at specific lifestyles: diversity, sport and games, outdoors and animals, food, music, LGBT, art and culture, and craftmanship. See "Profilplejehjem," *Boliger til ældre*, https://boligertilaeldre.kk.dk/profilplejehjem, accessed January 1, 2022.
12 Lov om Alderdomsunderstøttelse til værdige trængende udenfor fattigvæsenet (1891), § 5. All translations from the Danish by the author.
13 Anders Møller, "Hvor har alderdommen hjemme?" in Nete Balslev Wingender, Anders Møller, Aske Juul Lassen, Kamilla Nørtoft and Tenna Jensen, *Gammel i København: liv og livsvilkår 1891–2018* (Frederiksberg: Frydenlund Academic, 2019).
14 Lisbeth Balslev Jørgensen, "Alderdom og demokrati," *Arkitektur DK* 25, nos. 3–4 (1981): 85–89.
15 Morten Balle Hansen and Jens Ringmose, *Fælles sprog og ældreplejens organisering i et historisk perspektiv* (Odense: Department of Political Science and Public Managements, Faculty of Social Sciences, University of Southern Denmark, 2005), 18. In the Law of Old Age Interest (1922) and the Great Social Reform (1933), the new solutions for more equal rights of the elderly are the demands of uniform criteria, transparency and legal requirements.
16 Forsorgsloven (1933), § 34, paragraph 2: "A sick ward or sick room must be attached to the old people's home, intended for those of the home's residents who need actual medical treatment, but who are not suitable for hospitalization at a hospital or the county care foundation for the chronically ill."
17 Hans Erling Langkilde and Ib Martin Jensen, "Gentofte Kommunes Alderdomshjem," *Arkitekten Maanedshæfte* 43, no. 5 (1941): 81–84.
18 See Socialministeriet, *Betænkning vedrørende alderdomshjem og plejehjem* (1962): 41–42; and Frederik Christian Lund and Hans Chr. Hansen, "Plejehjemmet Ringbo, Bagsværd," *Arkitektur DK* 8, no. 6 (1964): 225–37.
19 Socialministeriet, *Betænkning*, 20.
20 See Frederik Christian Lund and Hans Chr. Hansen, "Plejehjemmet Ringbo, Bagsværd."
21 See Iris Van Steenwinkel, "Offering Architects Insights into Experiences of Living with Dementia: Three Case Studies on Orientation in Space, Time, and Identity" (PhD diss., University of Leuven, 2015).
22 See National Collaborating Centre for Mental Health (UK), *Dementia: A NICE-SCIE Guideline on Supporting People with Dementia and Their Carers in Health and Social Care* (British Psychological Society, 2007), https://www.ncbi.nlm.nih.gov/books/NBK55480/?report=printable; and Van Steenwinkel, "Offering Architects Insights into Experiences of Living with Dementia."
23 Morten Balle Hansen and Jens Ringmose, *Fælles sprog og ældreplejens organisering i et historisk perspektiv*, 20. The slogan "as long as possible in their own home" dominated the elderly care debate in the 1970s. To meet the rapidly growing care need, home care services were expanded, both as a financially viable solution but also to meet the wishes of the elderly to stay in their own homes. Sidsel Vinge, Karen Kramhøft and Andreas Bøgh, *Hjemmesygeplejen i Danmark* (Copenhagen: DSI Institut for Sundhedsvæsen, 2006), 17–18.
24 Erik Ejlers and Henning Graversen, "Omsorgscentret Møllegården, Gladsaxe," *Arkitektur DK* 22, no. 6 (1978): 226–33.
25 Erving Goffman, *Asylums: Essays on the Social Situation of Mental Patients and Other Inmates* (Chicago: Aldine, 1961).
26 See, for example, Michel Foucault, *Madness and Civilization: A History of Insanity in the Age of Reason*, trans. Richard Howard (New York: Pantheon, 1965) and *Discipline and Punish*, trans. Alan Sheridan (London: Allen Lane, 1977), in which Foucault critiques how invisible, structural power and modern institutions intrude into the private lives of citizens. See Ulrich Beck and Elisabeth Beck-Gernsheim, *Individualization: Institutionalized Individualism and Its Social and Political Consequences* (London: SAGE Publications Ltd, 2014).
27 See Morten Balle Hansen and Jens Ringmose, *Fælles sprog og ældreplejens organisering i et historisk perspektiv*, 21–23; and Margrethe Kähler, "Fakta og synspunkter om ældre/plejeboliger," *Arkitektur DK* 43, no. 7 (1999): 453–54. In 1987 the construction of nursing homes was halted with the Elderly Housing Act; instead, municipalities could build a new type of elderly housing, to postpone the move to a

nursing home. With the Care Home Reform in 1996, care homes were introduced as a new, modern type of nursing home, containing private apartments with connected common spaces for social interaction, and service spaces for 24-hour care staff.

28 See Tom Kitwood, *Dementia Reconsidered: The Person Comes First* (Buckingham: Open University Press, 1997); National Collaborating Centre for Mental Health (UK), *Dementia*; and Van Steenwinkel, "Offering Architects Insights into Experiences of Living with Dementia."

29 See, for example, Uriel Cohen and Gerald D. Weisman, *Holding on to Home: Designing Environments for People with Dementia* (Baltimore: Johns Hopkins University Press, 1991); Uriel Cohen and Kristen Day, *Contemporary Environments for People with Dementia* (Baltimore: Johns Hopkins University Press, 1997); and Elizabeth C. Brawley, *Designing for Alzheimer's Disease: Strategies for Creating Better Care Environments* (New York: John Wiley & Sons, 1997).

30 Karen Zahle and Margrethe Kähler, "Torndalshave," *Arkitektur DK* 43, no. 7 (1999): 404–7.

31 Research is pointing to the significance of a homely environment and a noninstitutional character for the well-being and behavior of residents with dementia. See, for example, Kristen Day, Daisy Carreon and Cheryl Stump, "The Therapeutic Design of Environments for People with Dementia: A Review of the Empirical Research," *The Gerontologist* 40, no. 4 (2000): 397–416; and Gesine Marquardt, Kathrin Bueter and Tom Motzek, "Impact of the Design of the Built Environment on People with Dementia: An Evidence-Based Review," *HERD: Health Environments Research & Design Journal* 8, no. 1 (2014): 127–57.

32 Morgan Andersson, "Assisted Living for the Elderly: Features of a Swedish Model," in *Architecture for Residential Care and Ageing Communities – Spaces for Dwelling and Healthcare*, ed. Sten Gromark and Björn Andersson (London: Routledge, 2021), 131–41.

33 See the competition brief for Demensplejehjemmet Aalborg Øst – ArchiMed and Kuben Management (2015): The notion of "home" and "homeliness" are repeated several times throughout the brief, for example, "The environment should be associated with homeliness"; "remind them [the residents] of home"; and it should be "a place to feel at home."

34 The winning competition proposal from Friis & Moltke (2015) and conceptual design, Friis & Moltke (2016).

35 See Aalborg Kommune, *Demenscenter Tornhøjhaven 2019–2021: Projekt Hjemlighed og forandring af omgivelser – en fortælling om datidens øjebliksbillede* (2021). This project addressed twenty-three issues in the overall design, from the outdoor areas to the main entrance as well as staff facilities and the common rooms in the housing units.

36 ArchiMed and Kuben Management, *Konkurrenceprogram – Demensplejehjemmet Aalborg Øst* (2015).

37 Aalborg Kommune, *Demenscenter Tornhøjhaven 2019–2021: Projekt Hjemlighed og forandring af omgivelser – en fortælling om datidens øjebliksbillede* (2021): 16.

38 Friis & Moltke, *Konkurrenceforslag – Demensplejehjem I Aalborg Øst* (2015); and Friis & Moltke, *Tornhøjhaven Dispositionsforslag* (2016).

39 In the competition proposal, the kitchens were designed as part of the communal spaces, which however changed in the process with the user groups. It was assessed that it was important to separate the kitchen, due to safety reasons and in consideration of the residents at Tornhøjhaven with special geronto-psychiatric diagnoses, who cannot cope with too many stimuli and noises. As a consequence, the kitchen was placed instead between two housing units.

40 Aalborg Kommune – Ældre- og Handicapforvaltningen, *Vejledning til boliger* (2014): 16–21.

41 ArchiMed and Kuben Management, *Konkurrenceprogram – Demensplejehjemmet Aalborg Øst* (2015): 56.

42 Conversation with caregiver, October 2020.

43 Aalborg Kommune – Ældre- og Handicapforvaltningen, *Vejledning til boliger* (2014): 15, 17, 18; and Bygge- og Boligstyrelsen, *Indretning af ældreboliger for fysisk plejekrævende m.fl. En vejledning* (1997: 35–38.

44 ArchiMed and Kuben Management, *Konkurrenceprogram – Demensplejehjemmet Aalborg Øst* (2015): 56; and Aalborg Kommune – Ældre- og Handicapforvaltningen, *Vejledning til boliger* (2014): 14.

45 Interview with relative, October 3, 2020.

46 This is linked to a change in the whole idea of care, where happiness is a new political agenda, driven by an increasing amount of well-being indicators, happiness indexes, and quality-of-life rankings as described by Francesco Garutti in "The Happiness Plan," in *Our Happy Life: Architecture and Well-Being in the Age of Emotional Capitalism*, ed. Francesco Garutti (Berlin: Sternberg Press, 2019), 29–60.

1.24 Distribution and size of care homes, 2020

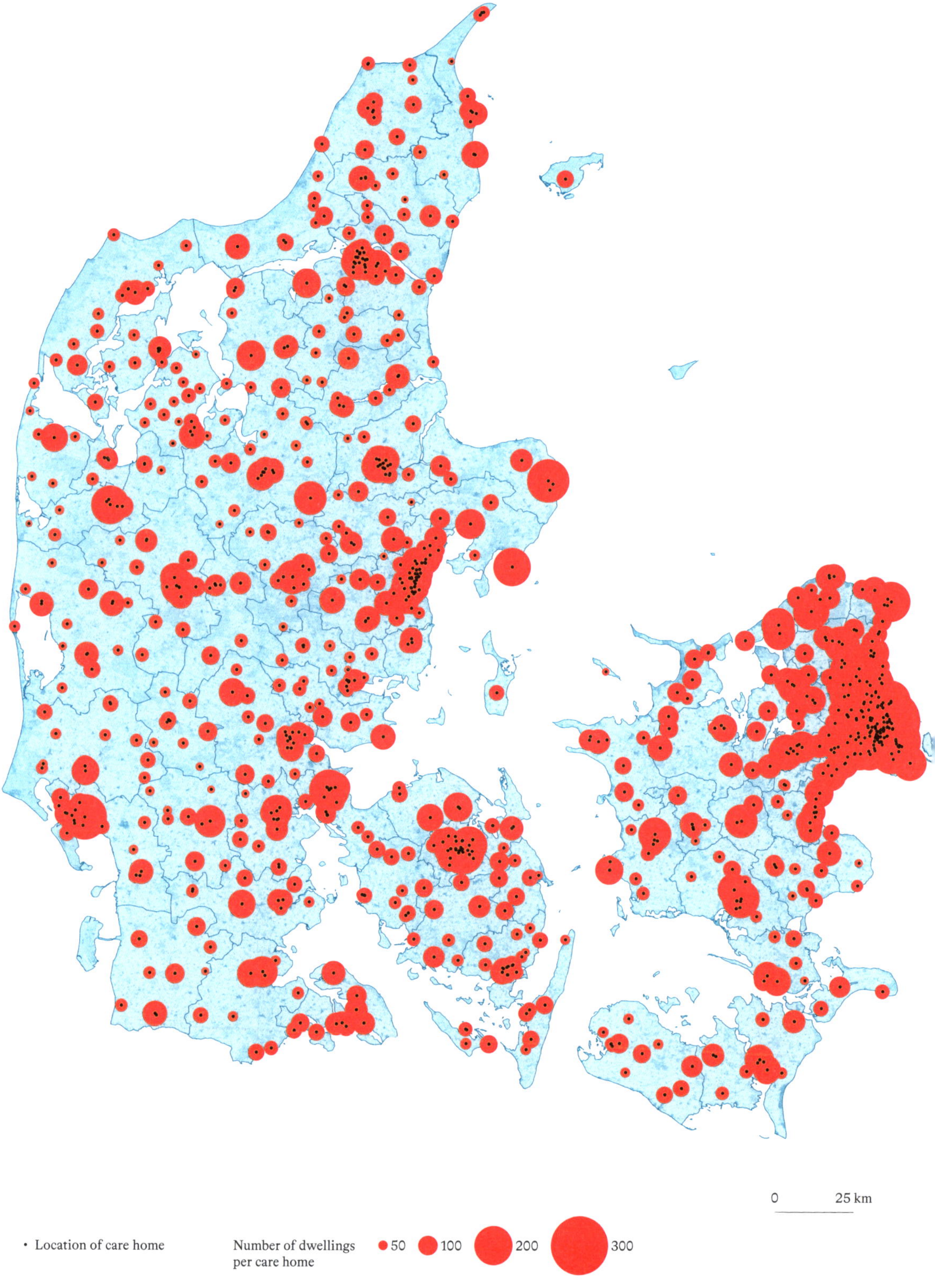

1.25 Distribution of somatic care and specialized dementia care, 2020

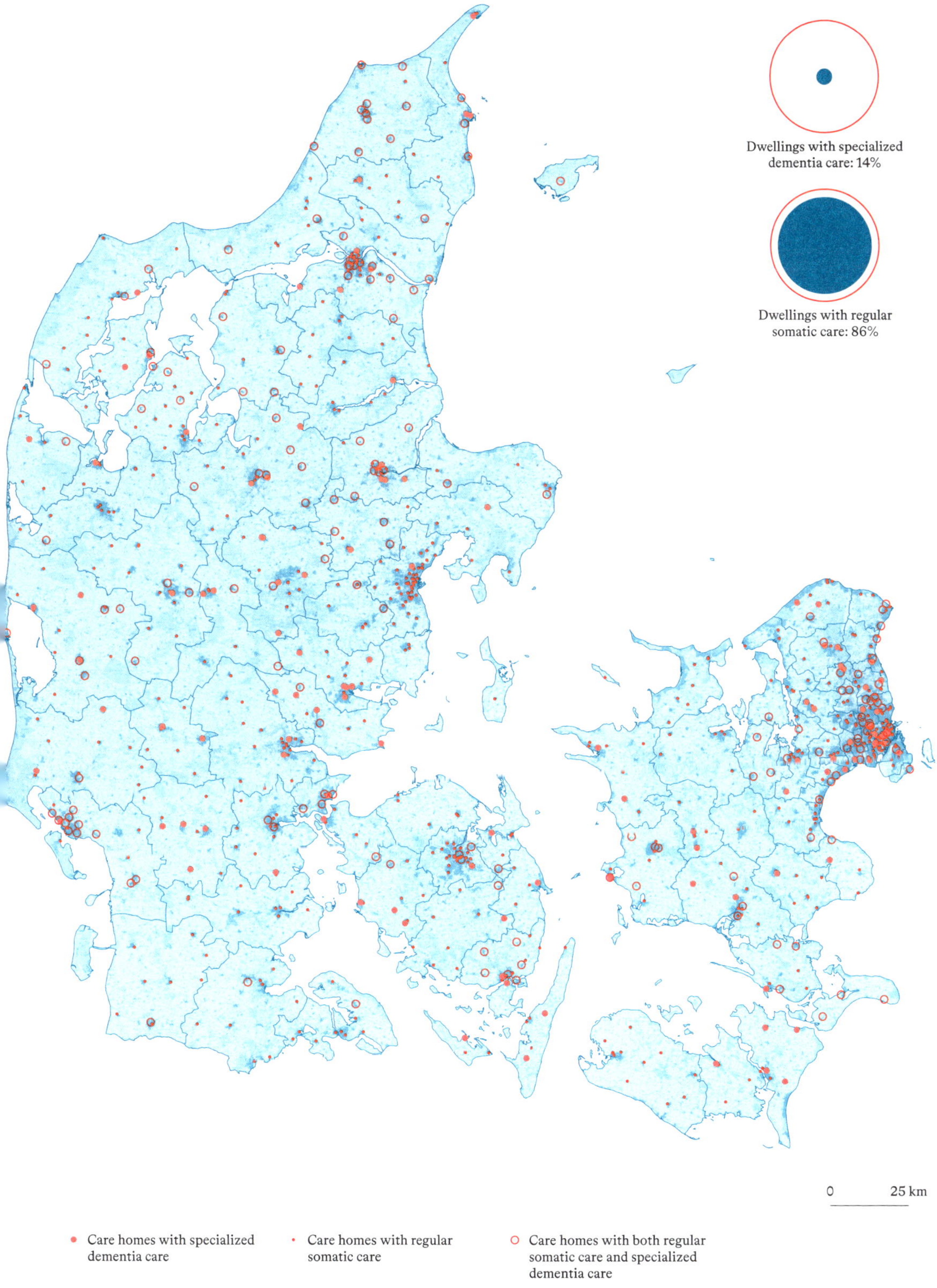

1.26 Distribution of public and private care homes, 2020

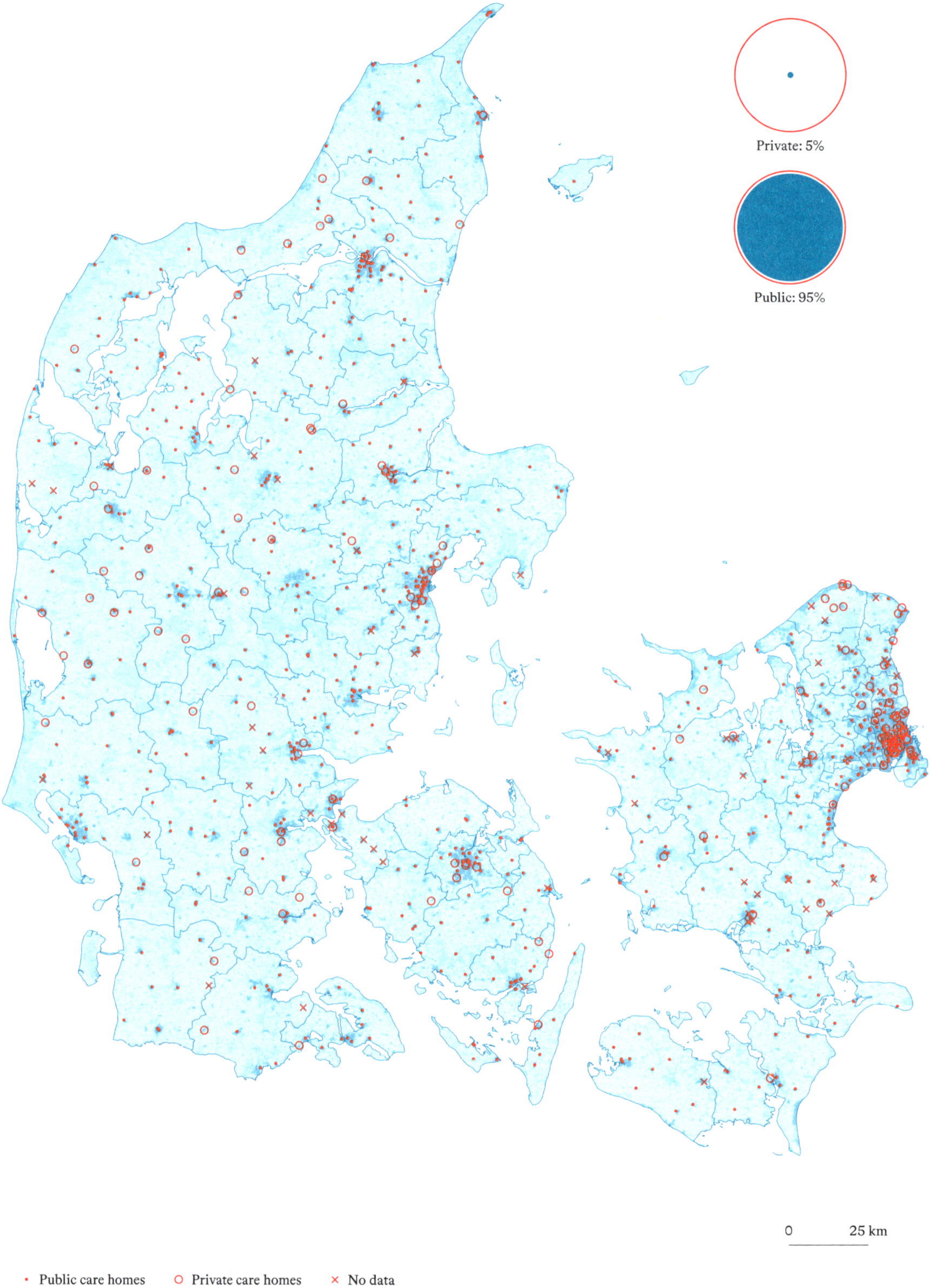

1.27 Percentage of inhabitants older than 65 years, 1972–2017

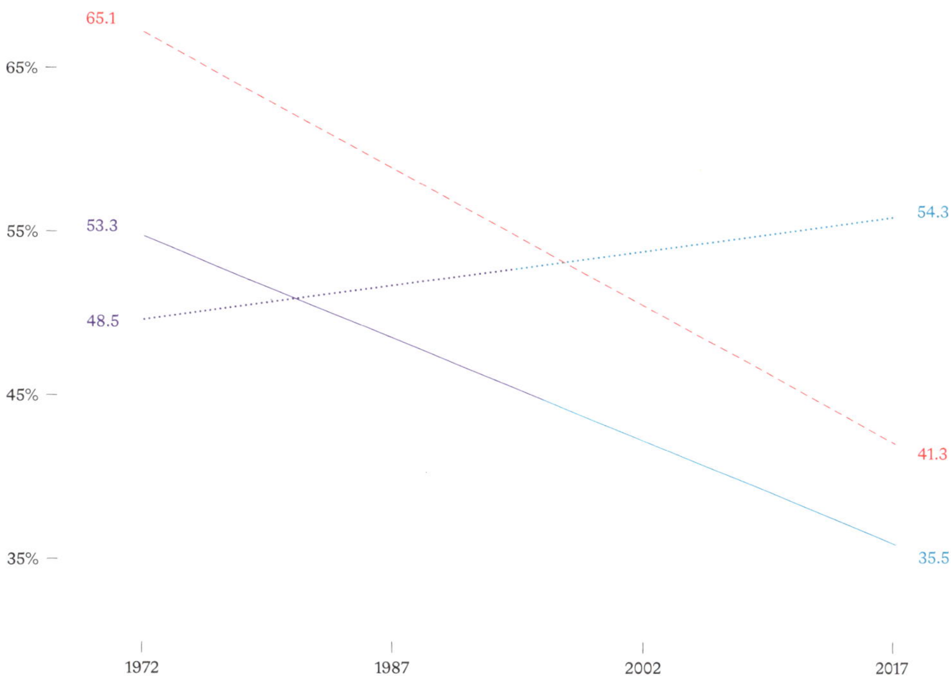

1.28 Number of care dwellings per 1,000 inhabitants older than 65 years, 1972–2017

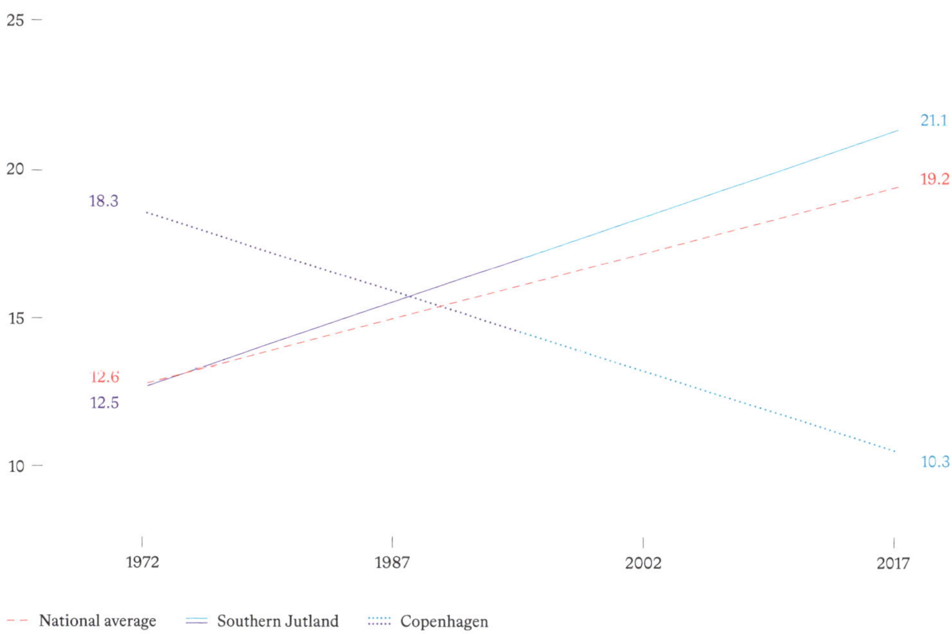

1.29 Percentage of inhabitants older than 65 years, 1972

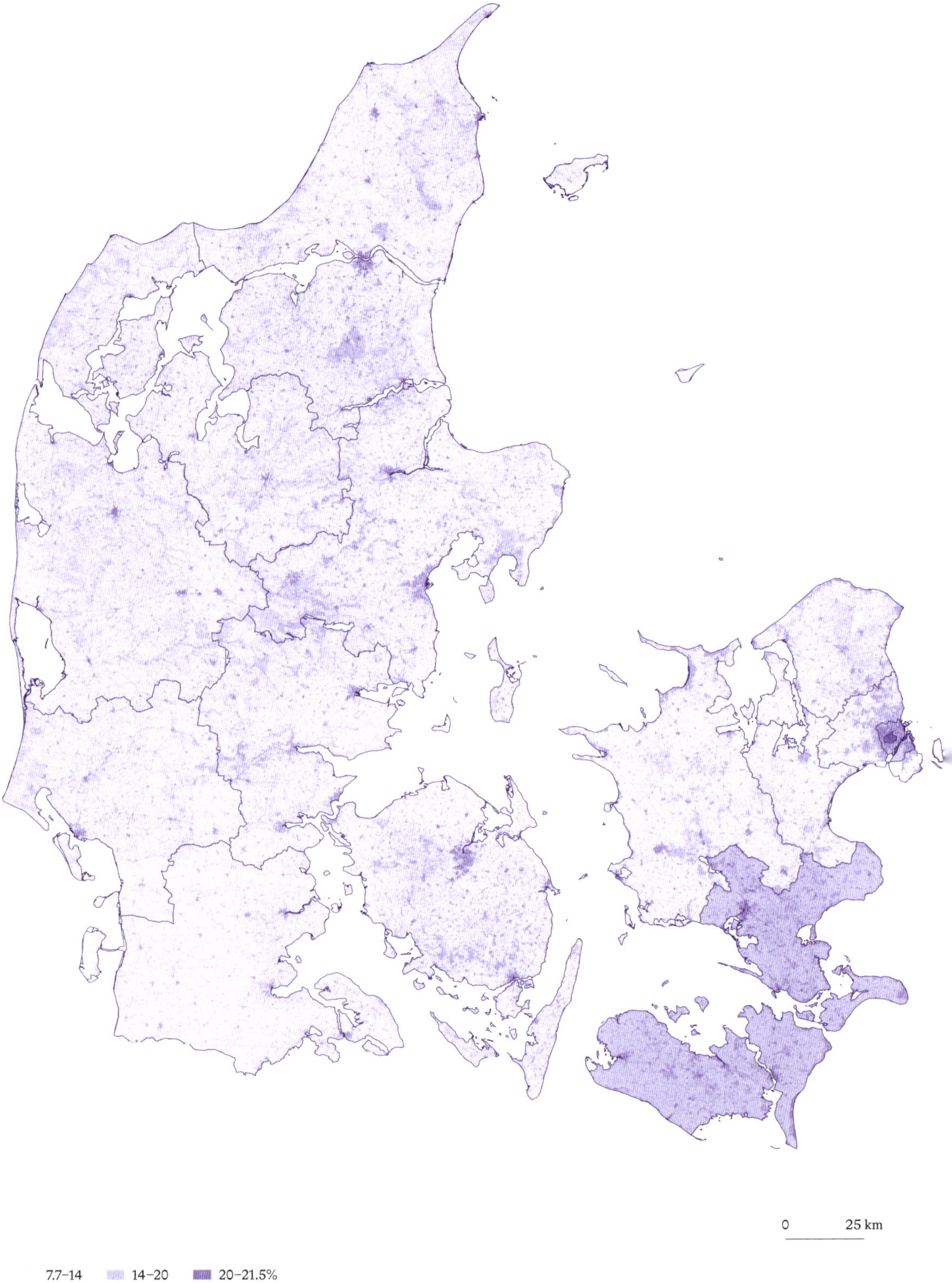

1.30 Percentage of inhabitants older than 65 years, 2017

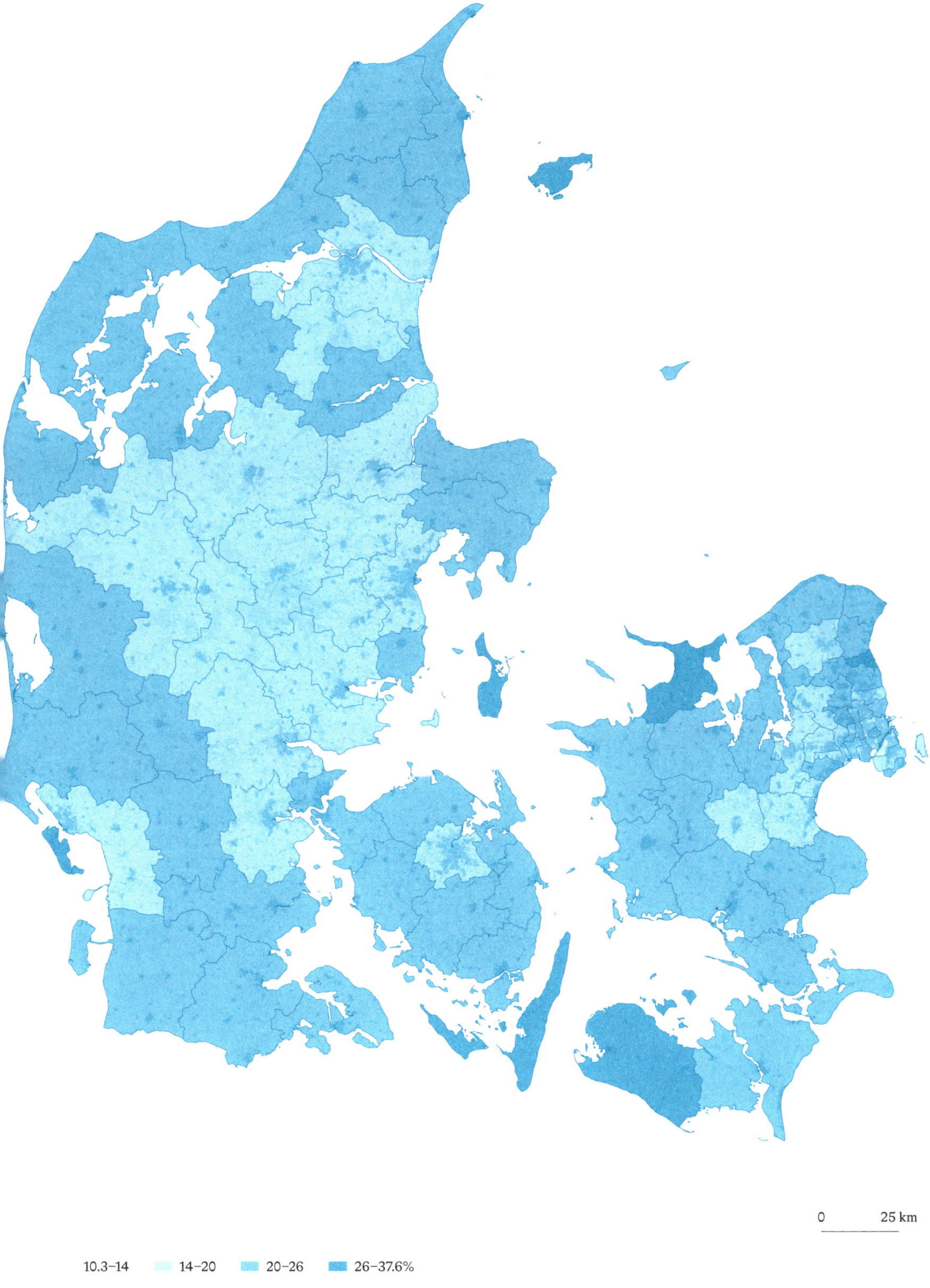

1.31 Number of care dwellings per 1,000 inhabitants older than 65 years, 1972

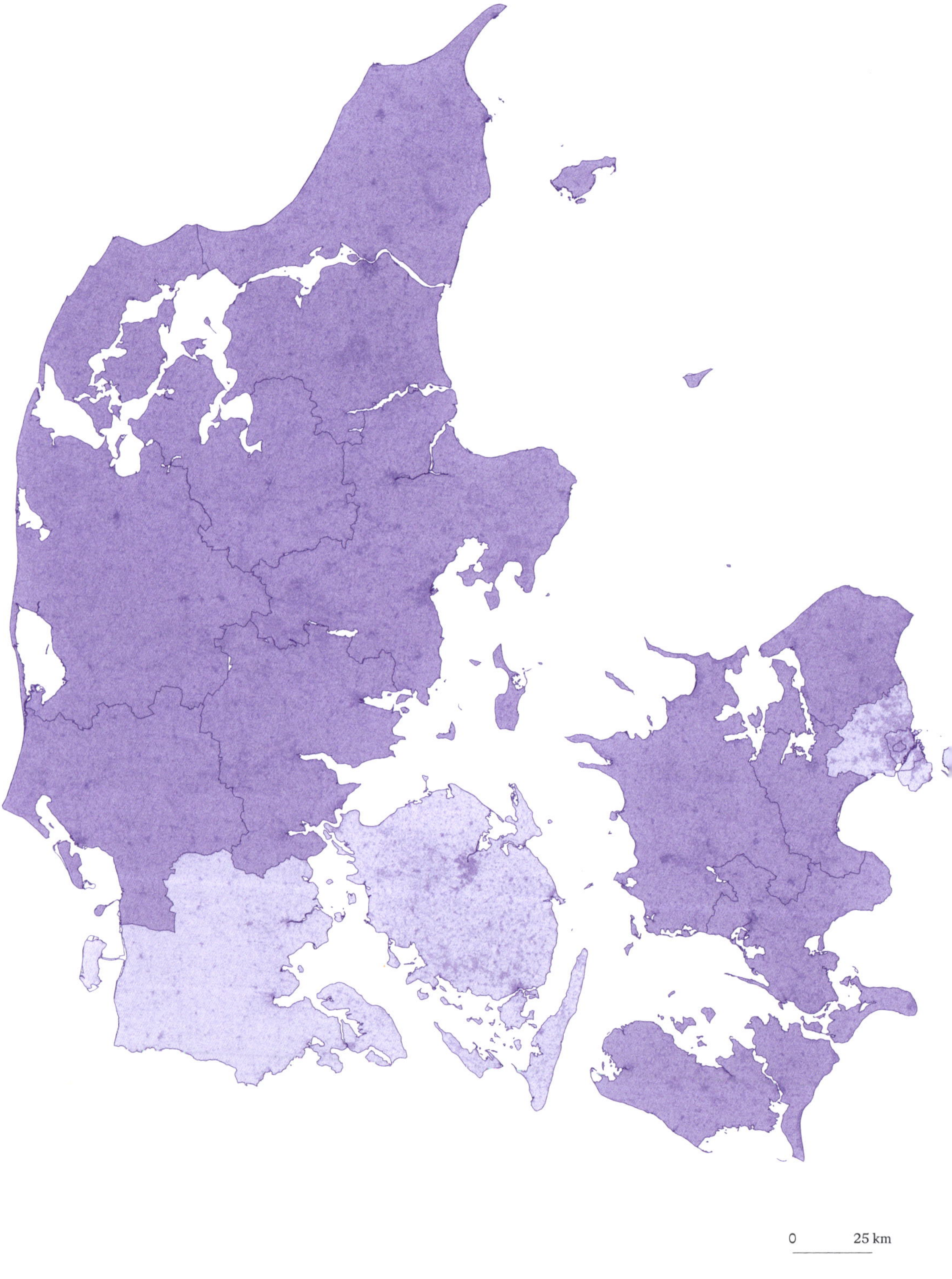

1.32 Number of care dwellings per 1,000 inhabitants older than 65 years, 2017

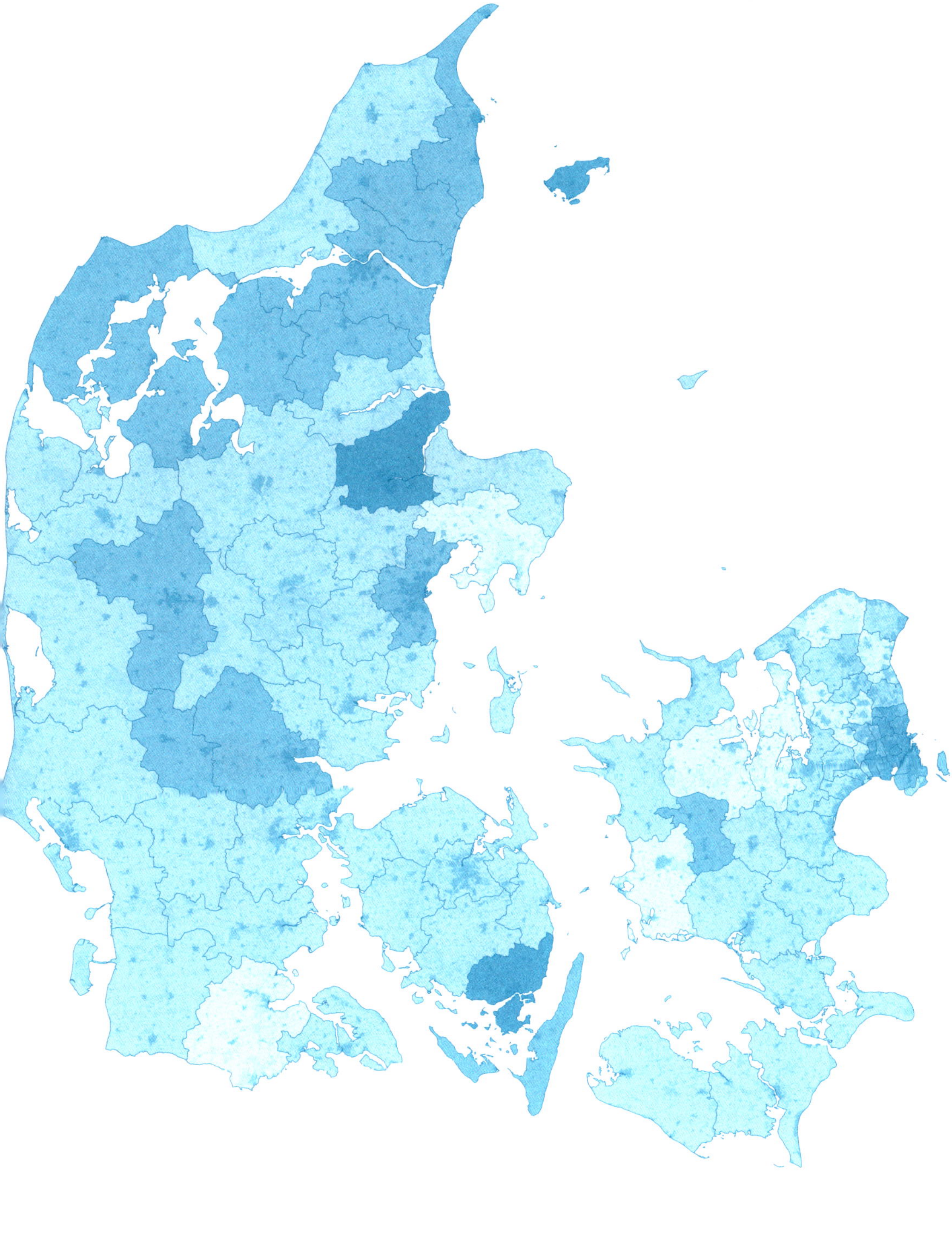

1.33 Distribution and size of care homes in the municipality of Copenhagen, 1972

Inhabitants in the municipality	610,685
Inhabitants 65+	111,525 (18.3%)
Number of care homes	45
Number of care home residents	3,529
Number of care home residents per inhabitants 65+	32

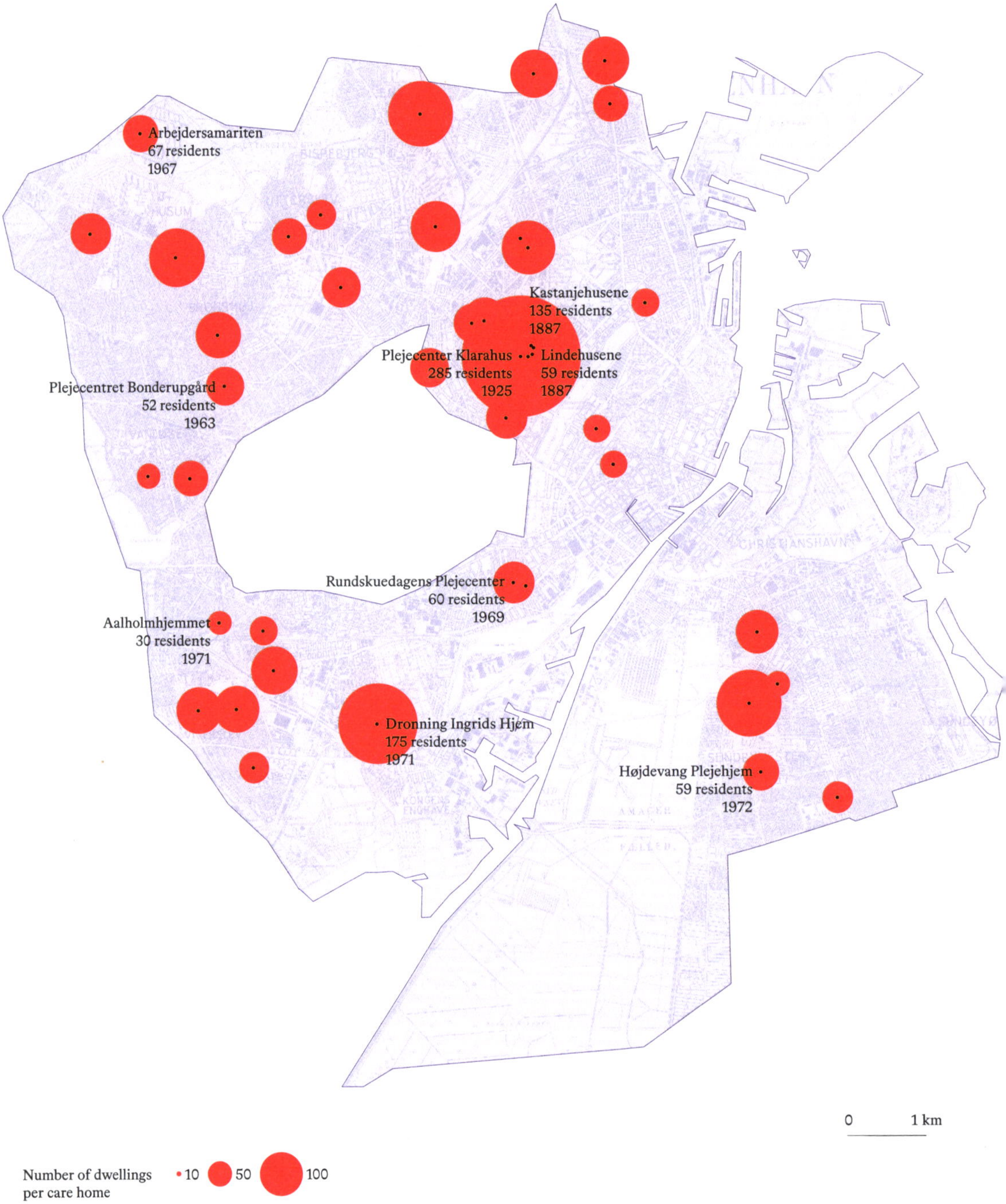

1.34 Distribution and size of care homes in the municipality of Copenhagen, 2020

Inhabitants in the municipality	605,366
Inhabitants 65+	62,522 (10.3%)
Inhabitants with dementia	5.059[1]

1 "Videnscenter for demens" to Danish Dementia Research Centre

Number of care homes	43
Number of care home residents	3,483
Number of care home residents per inhabitants 65+	56
Number of dwellings with specialized dementia care	424 (12%)

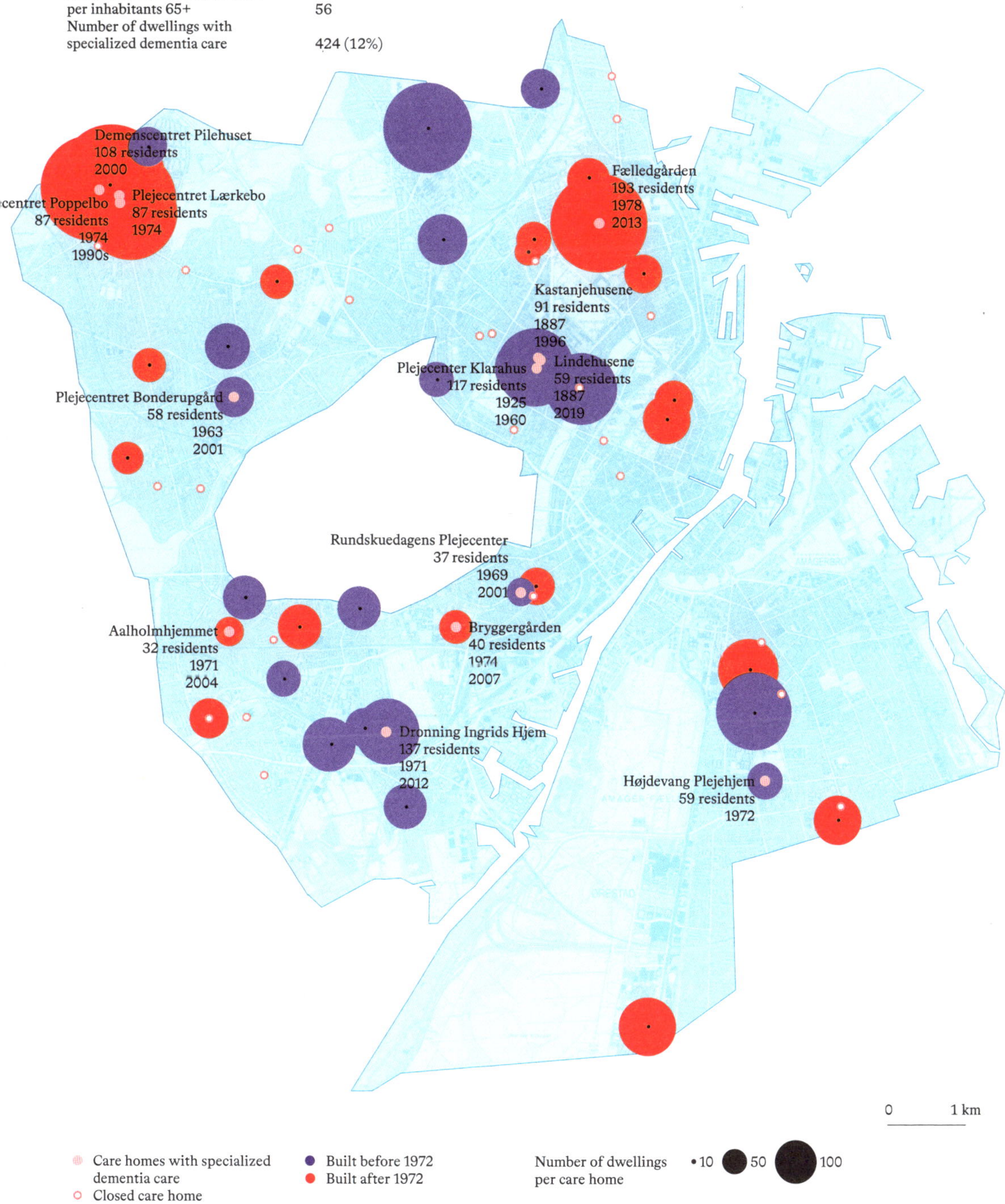

1.35 Distribution and size of care homes in the municipality of Høje Taastrup, 1972

Inhabitants in the municipality	33,858
Inhabitants 65+	1,803 (5.3%)
Number of care homes	2
Number of care home residents per inhabitants 65+	51

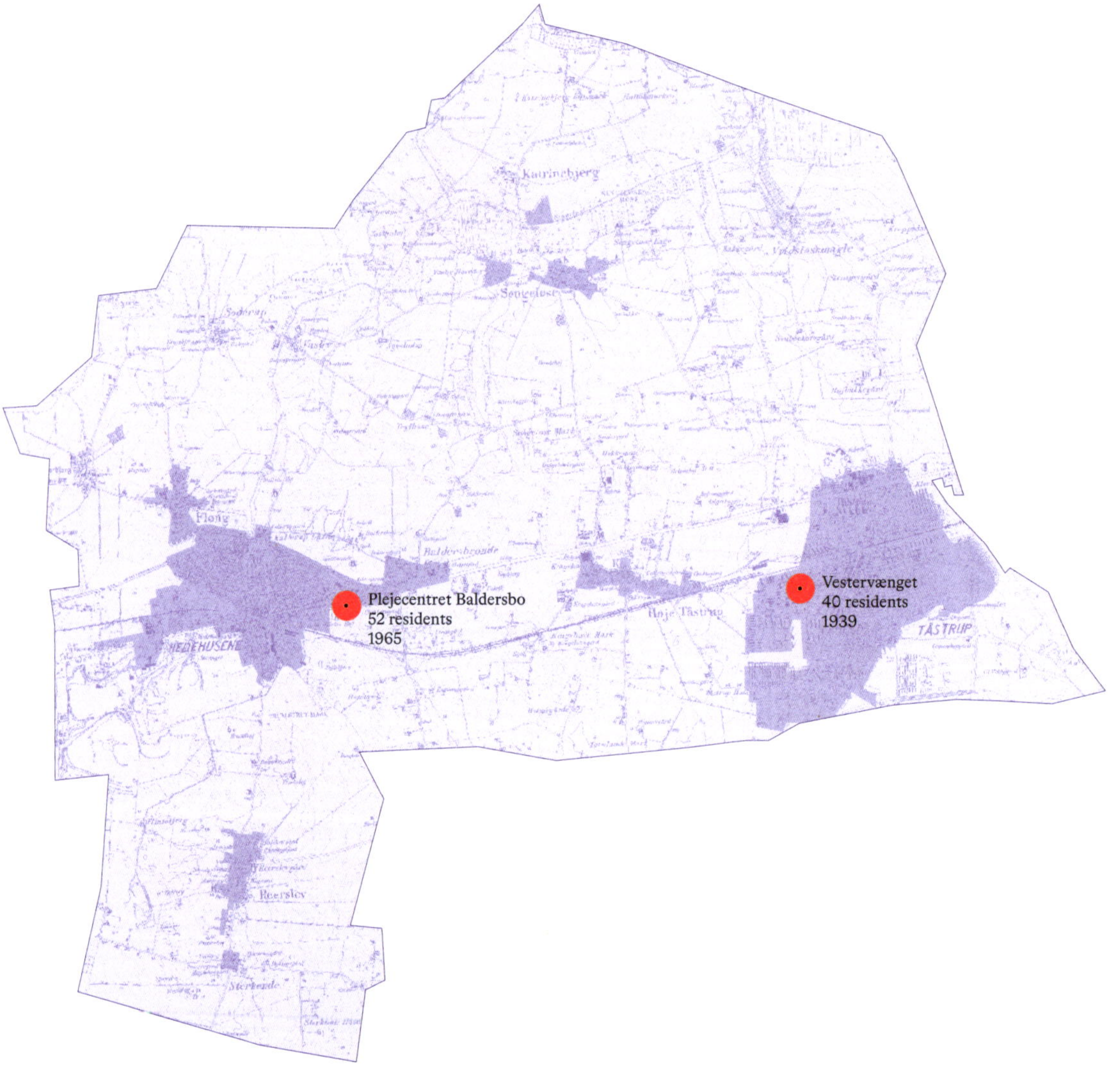

0 1 km

Number of dwellings per care home • 10 • 50 • 100

1.36 Distribution and size of care homes in the municipality of Høje Taastrup, 2020

Inhabitants in the municipality	50,401
Inhabitants 65+	8,634 (17.1%)
Inhabitants with dementia	631[1]

1 "Videnscenter for demens" to Danish Dementia Research Centre

Number of care homes	5
Number of care home residents	260
Number of care home residents per inhabitants 65+	30
Number of dwellings with specialized dementia care	27 (10%)

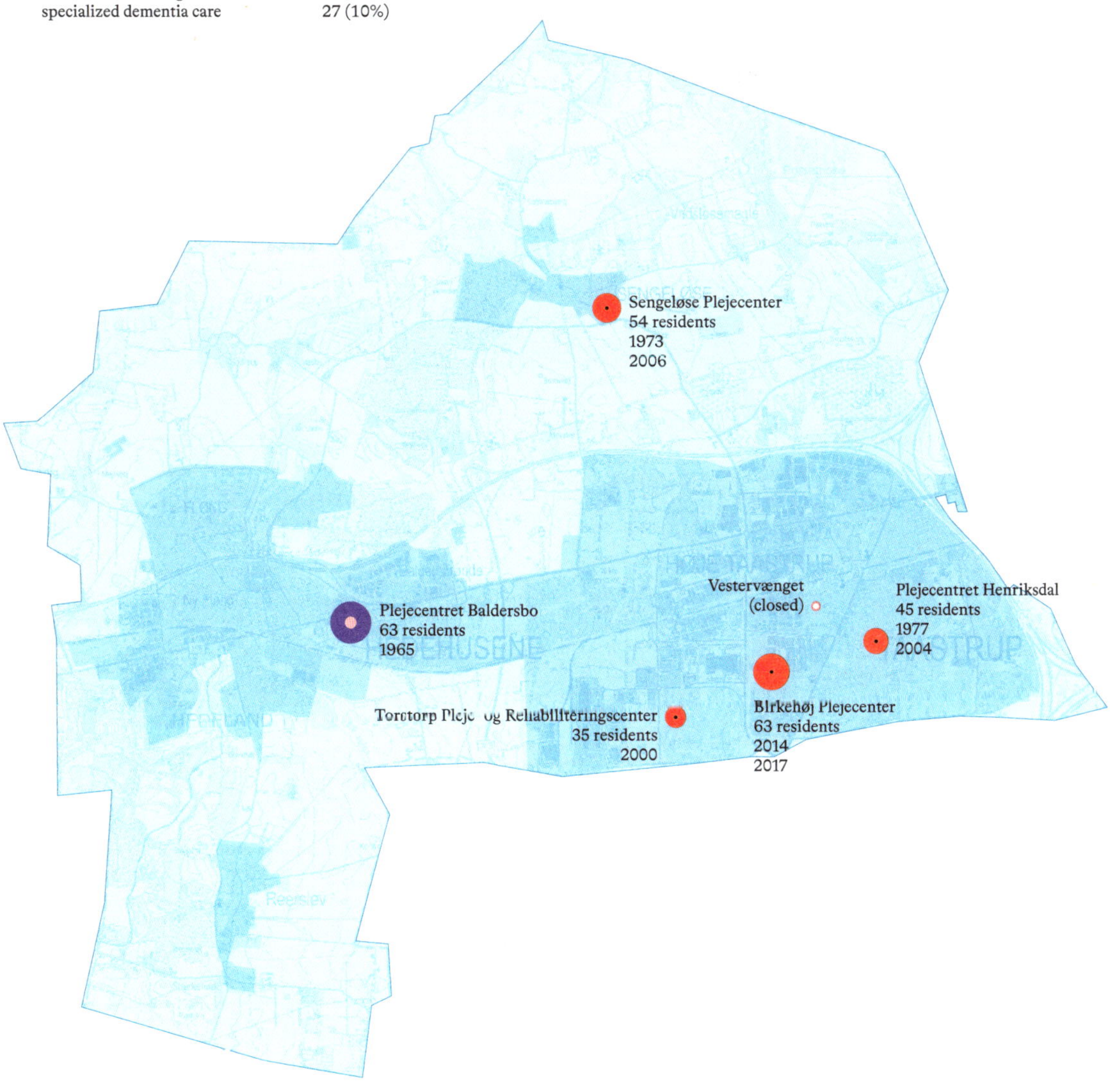

0 1 km

Care homes with specialized dementia care
Closed care home

Built before 1972
Built after 1972

Number of dwellings per care home • 10 50 100

1.37 Distribution and size of care homes in the municipality of Tønder,[1] 1972

1 Earlier the municipalities of Bredebro, Højer, Løgumkloster, Nørre-Rangstrup, Skærbæk

Inhabitants in the municipality	41,302
Inhabitants 65+	5,690 (13.8%)
Number of care homes	9
Number of care home residents	212
Number of care home residents per inhabitants 65+	37

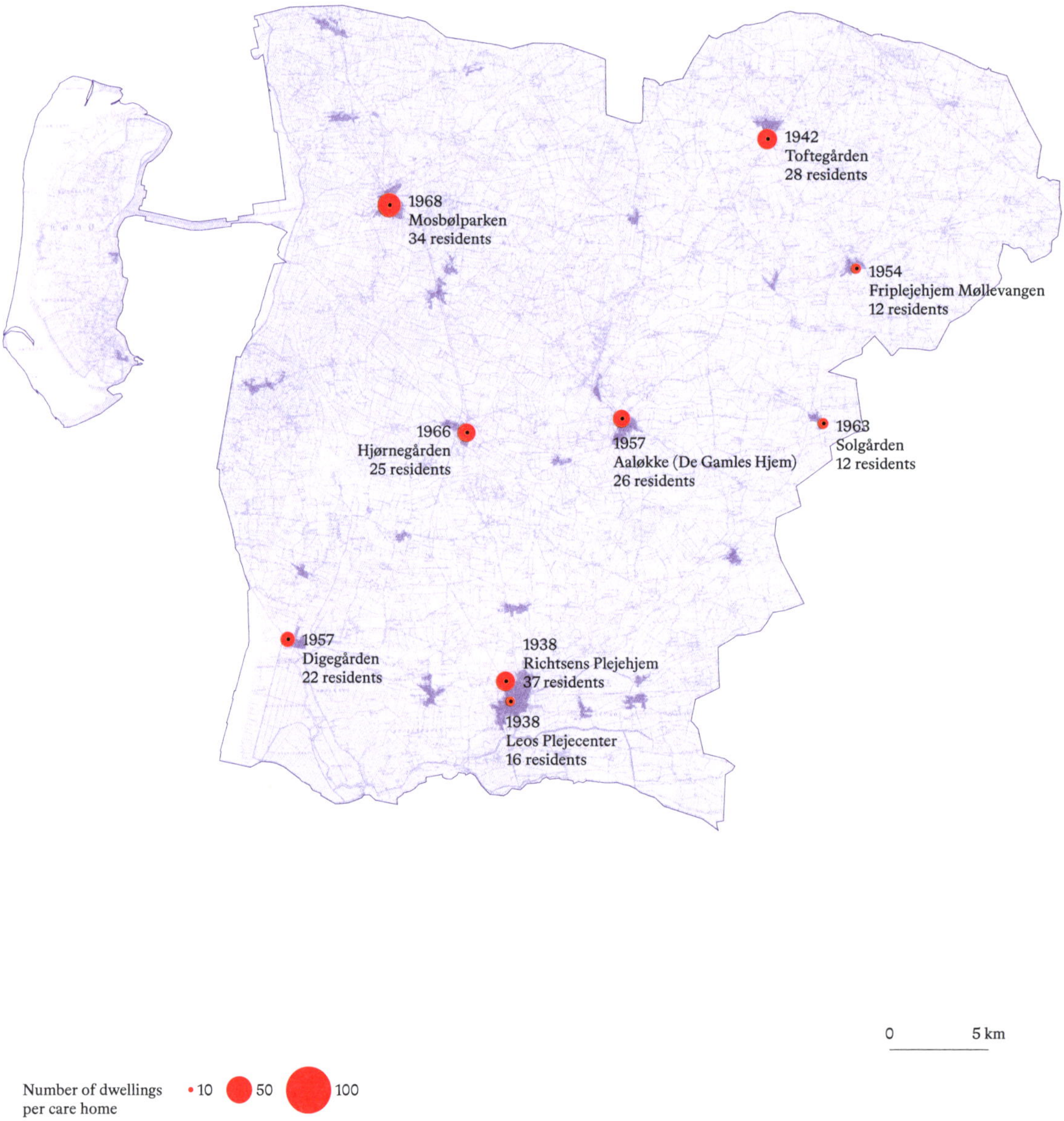

1.38 Distribution and size of care homes in the municipality of Tønder, 2020

Inhabitants in the municipality	37,928
Inhabitants 65+	8,766 (23.1%)
Inhabitants with dementia	772[1]

1 "Videnscenter for demens" to Danish Dementia Research Centre

Number of care homes	9
Number of care home residents	332
Number of care home residents per inhabitants 65+	38
Number of dwellings with specialized dementia care	29 (9%)

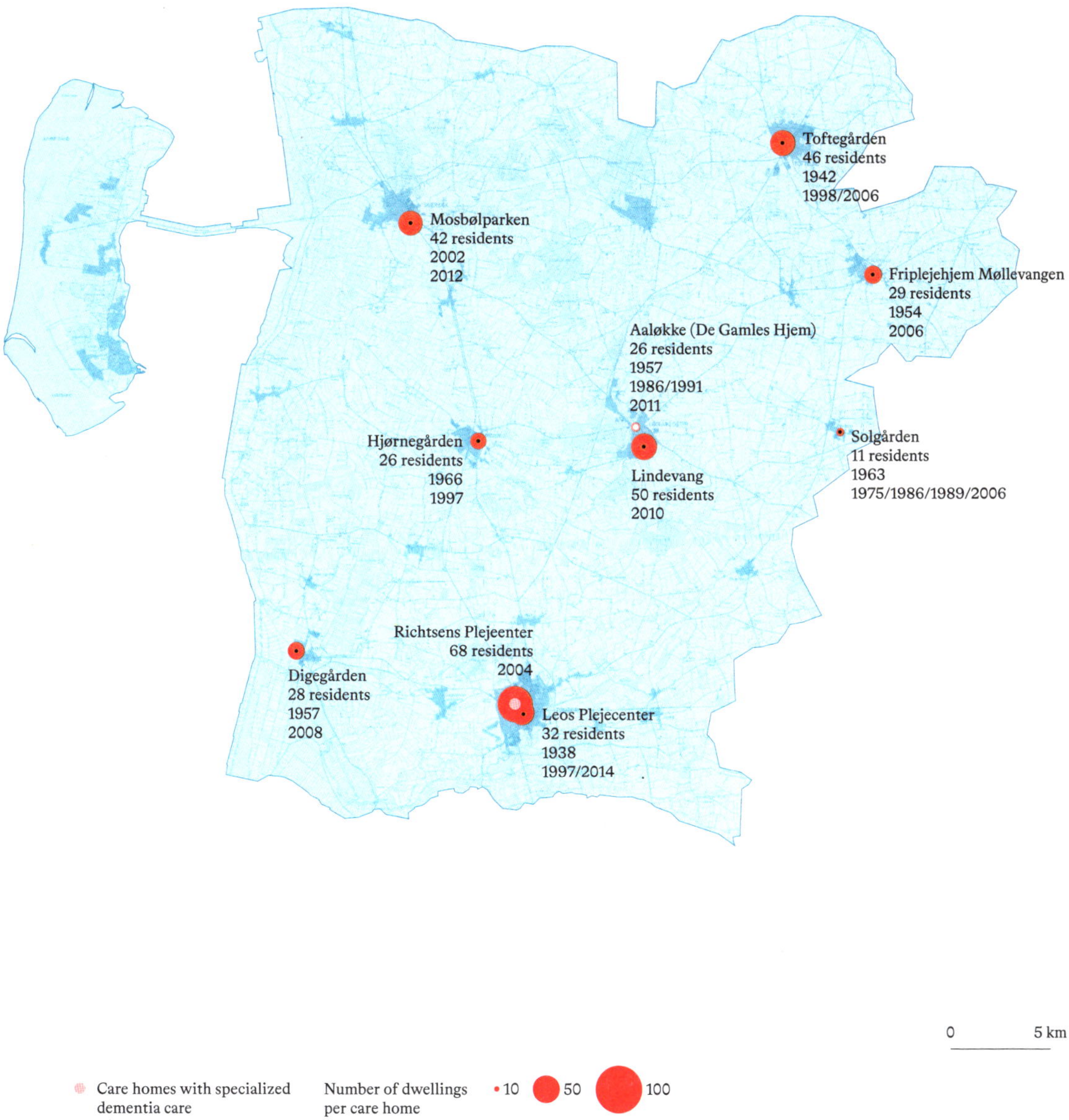

1.39 Development of architectures for the elderly

Building typologies

1915 Old People's Home, Holstebro

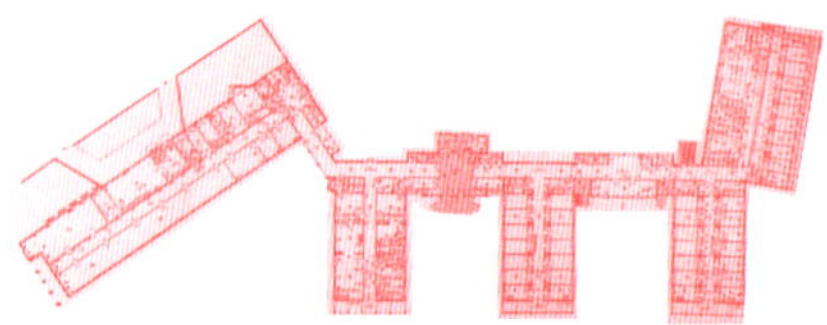

1940 Solhjem Old People's Home, Gentofte

Old people's homes

Retirement homes

Care

Alzheimer's Disease discovered

Medical care model

Technology in care

Electric scooter

Folding wheelchair

Electric wheelchair

Mobile ho

Society and legislation

1922 Law of Old Age Interest

Number of elderly people in Denmark 60+

1891 Law of Old Age Support

1933 The Great Social Reform

1957 The first Home Nursing Ac
1958 Establishment of Home Ca

Technology

Television

Cable TV

1900

1920

1940

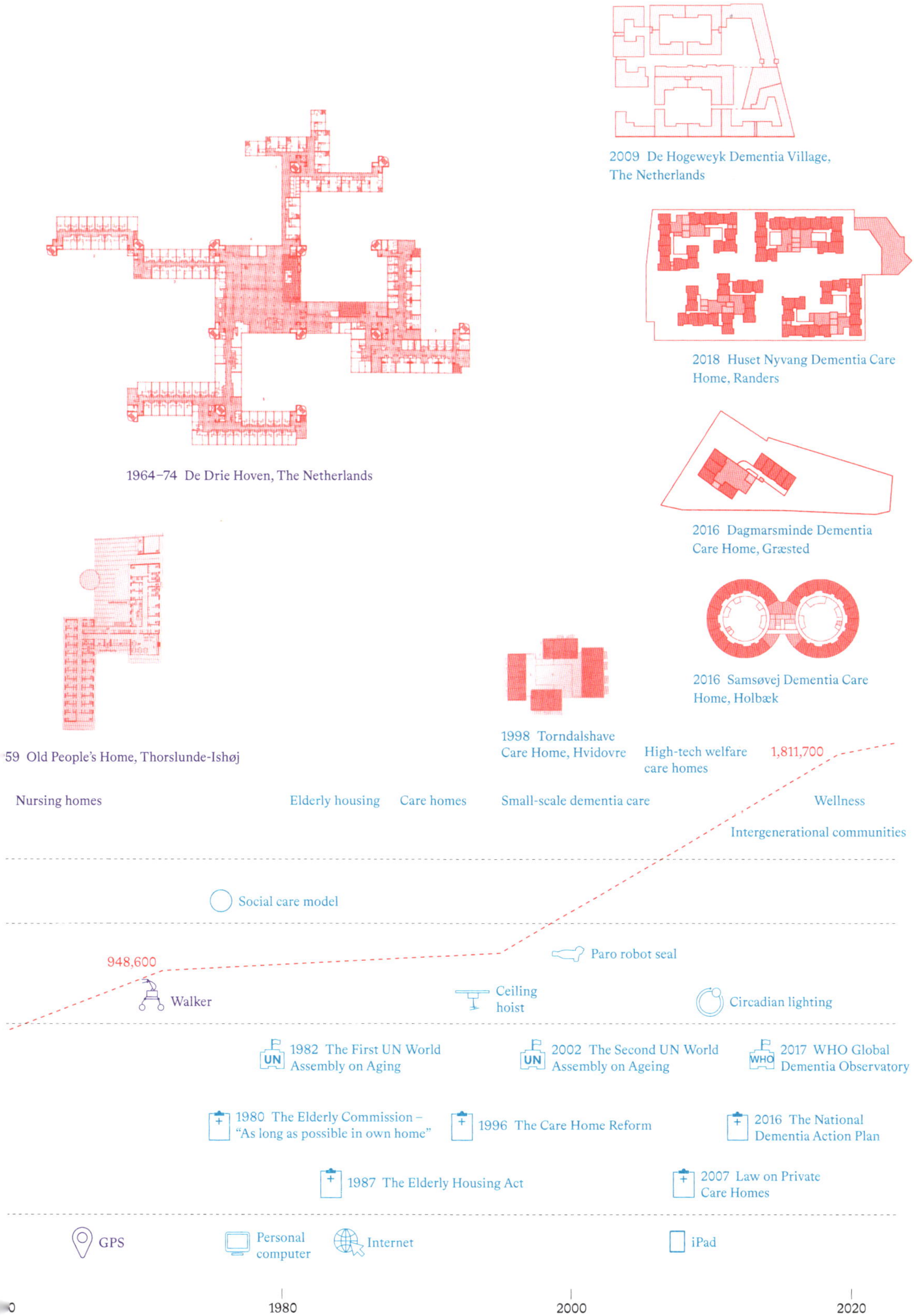
2009 De Hogeweyk Dementia Village, The Netherlands
1964–74 De Drie Hoven, The Netherlands
2018 Huset Nyvang Dementia Care Home, Randers
2016 Dagmarsminde Dementia Care Home, Græsted
2016 Samsøvej Dementia Care Home, Holbæk
59 Old People's Home, Thorslunde-Ishøj
1998 Torndalshave Care Home, Hvidovre
High-tech welfare care homes
1,811,700
Nursing homes
Elderly housing
Care homes
Small-scale dementia care
Wellness
Intergenerational communities
Social care model
948,600
Paro robot seal
Walker
Ceiling hoist
Circadian lighting
UN
1982 The First UN World Assembly on Aging
UN
2002 The Second UN World Assembly on Ageing
WHO
2017 WHO Global Dementia Observatory
1980 The Elderly Commission – "As long as possible in own home"
1996 The Care Home Reform
2016 The National Dementia Action Plan
1987 The Elderly Housing Act
2007 Law on Private Care Homes
GPS
Personal computer
Internet
iPad
0
1980
2000
2020

1.40 Development in the number of care home dwellings for the elderly

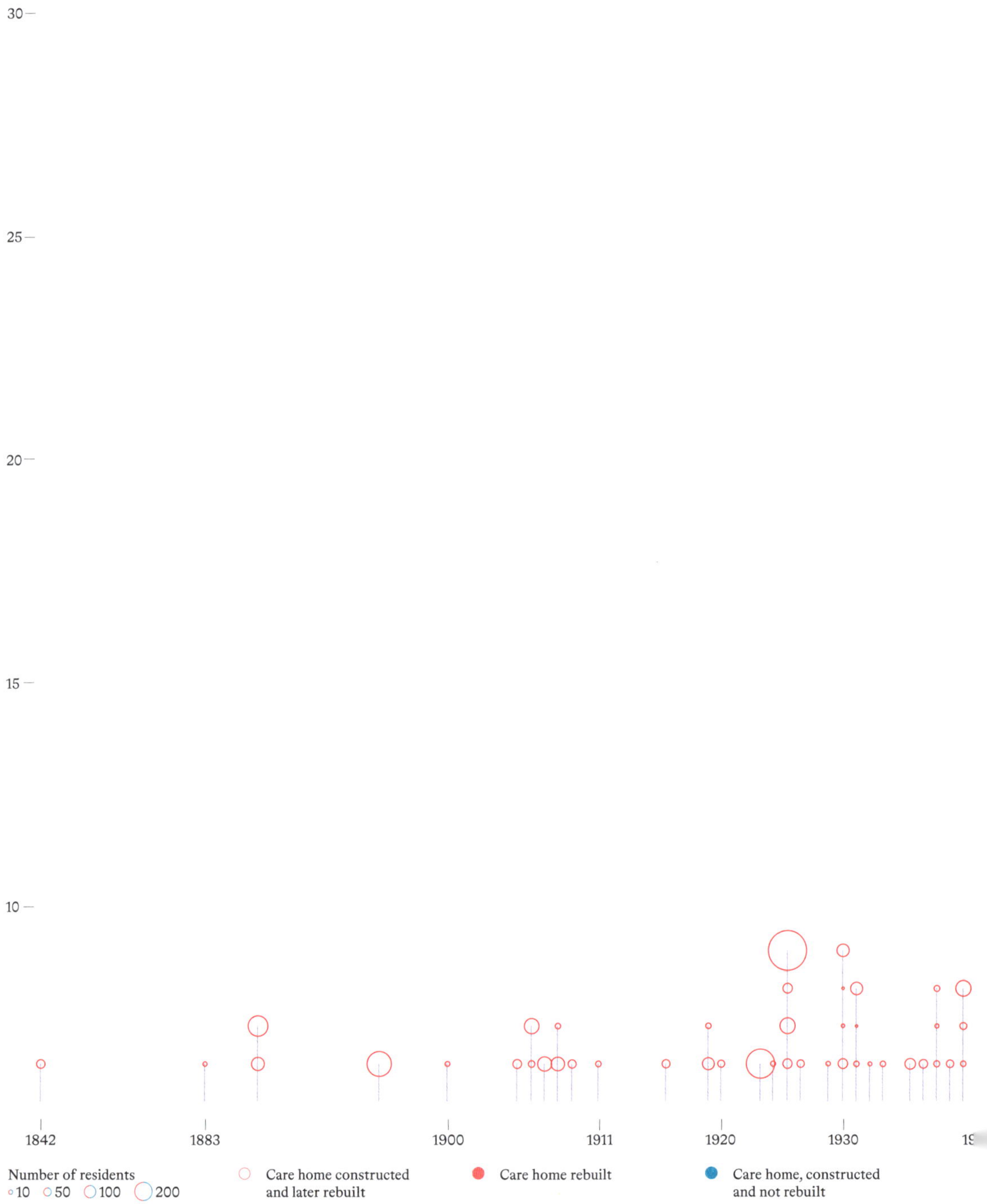

Number of care homes built this year

Number of care homes rebuilt this year

Data is based on 542 care homes out of the total of 940 current care homes

1.41 Layout of outdoor spaces, Tornhøjhaven

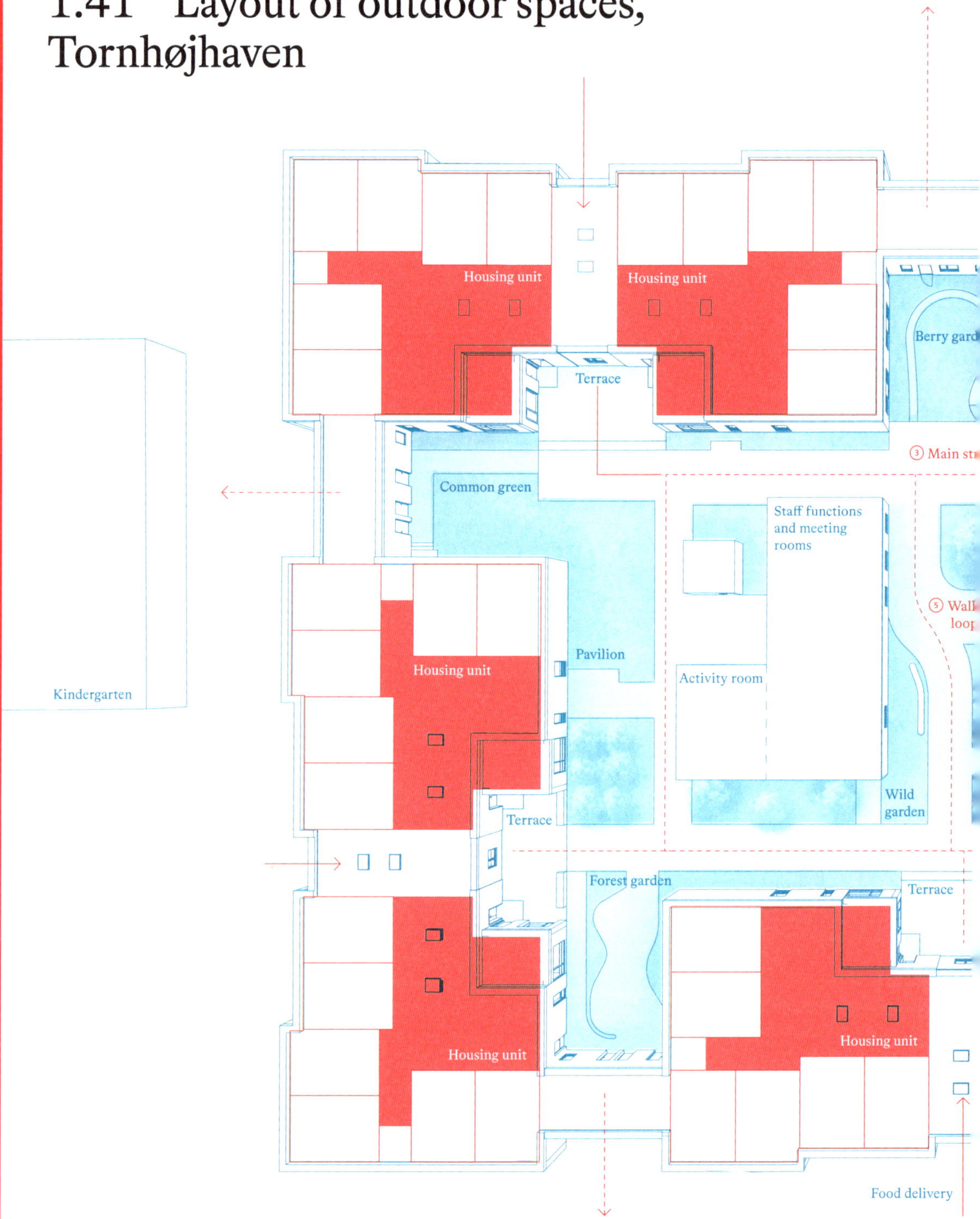

Common areas   Apartments   Walking paths

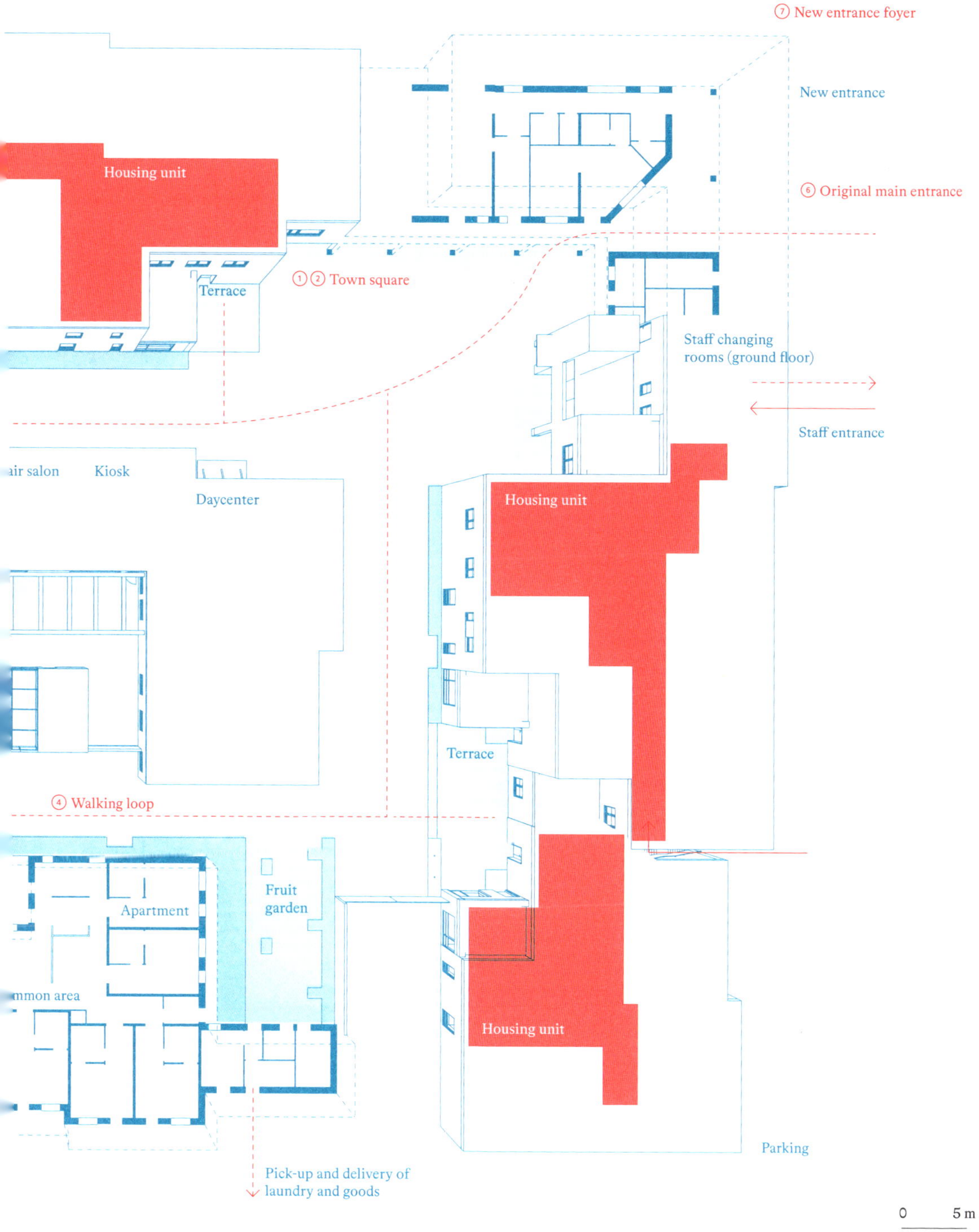
⑦ New entrance foyer
New entrance
⑥ Original main entrance
Housing unit
①② Town square
Terrace
Staff changing rooms (ground floor)
Staff entrance
air salon
Kiosk
Daycenter
Housing unit
Terrace
④ Walking loop
Fruit garden
Apartment
mmon area
Housing unit
Parking
Pick-up and delivery of laundry and goods
0 5 m

③
④
⑤
⑥
⑦

1.42 Layout of common areas in the housing units, Tornhøjhaven

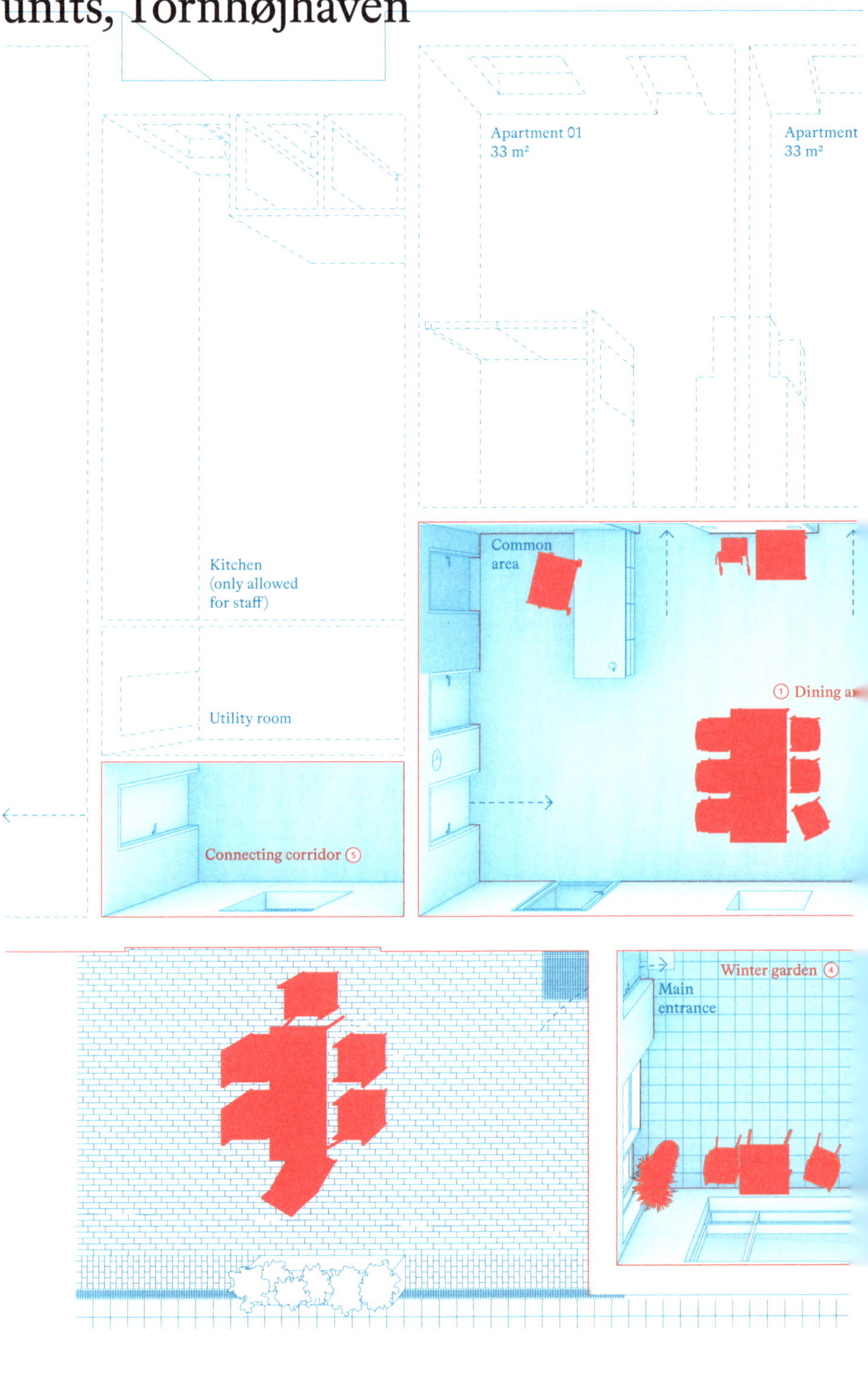

Objects and furniture   Common areas   Apartments and staff rooms

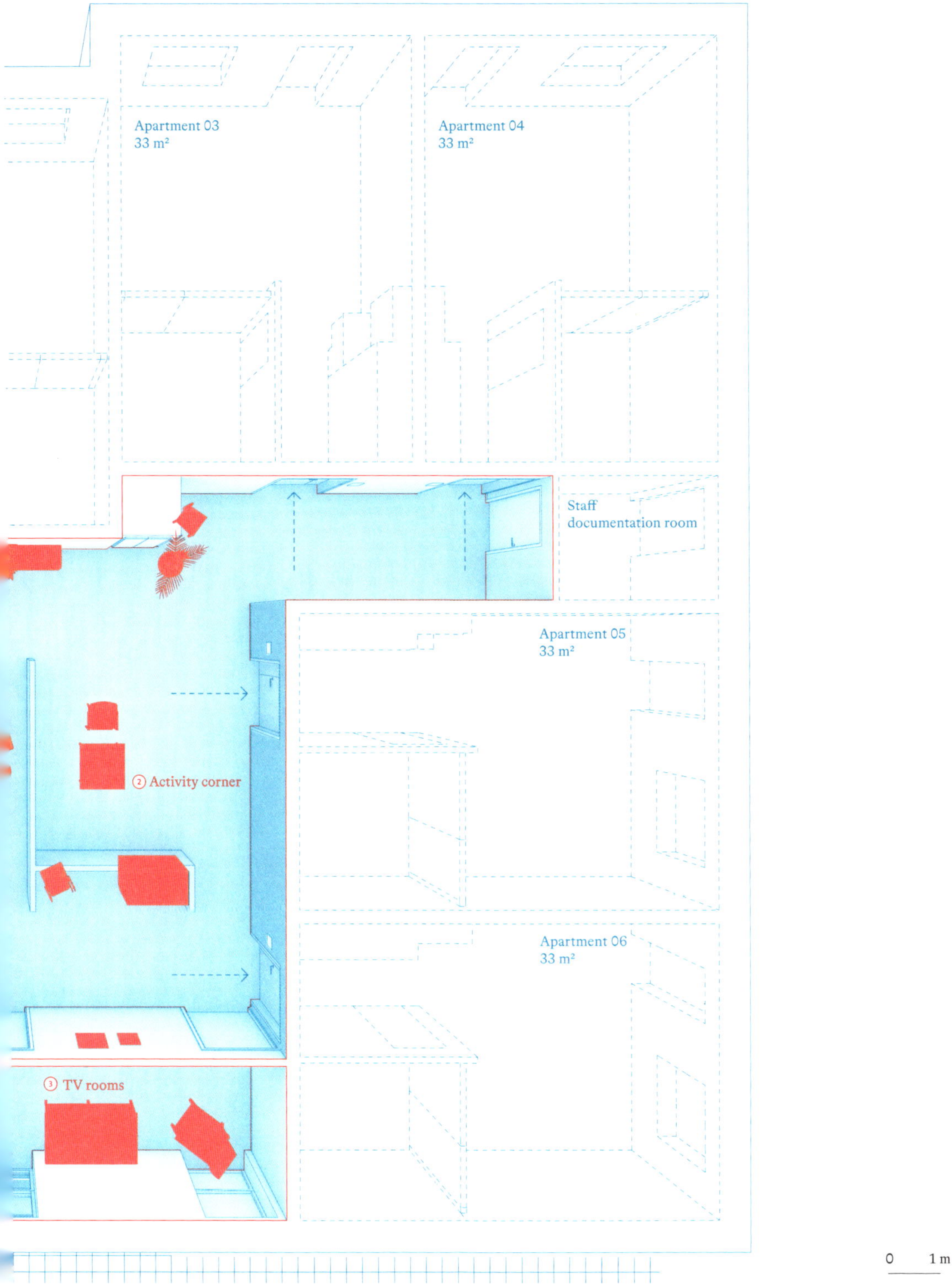
Apartment 03
33 m²
Apartment 04
33 m²
Staff
documentation room
Apartment 05
33 m²
② Activity corner
Apartment 06
33 m²
③ TV rooms
0 1 m

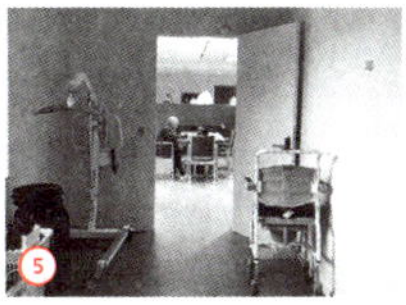

1.43 Layout of resident apartment, Tornhøjhaven

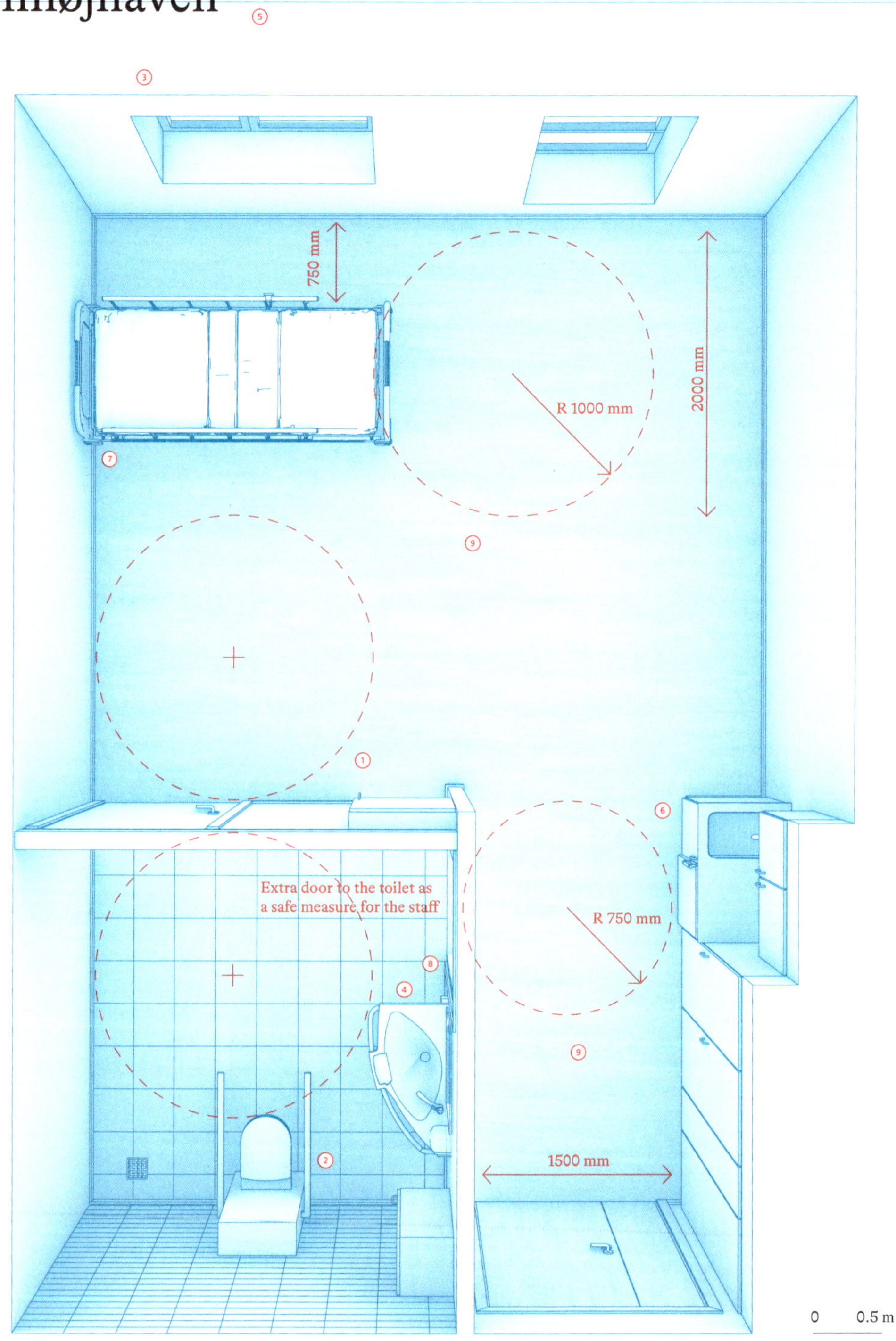

1. Ceiling hoist covering bed area and bathroom
2. Height-adjustable toilet
3. The windows can only tilt a little bit, as a precaution against the residents rawling out
4. Height-adjustable sink
5. Windows shielded with film or blinds, to avoid gazes from the outside
6. Kitchenette and cupboards in entrance
7. All apartments are equipped with a hospital bed
8. Hygiene station in the bathroom with hand sanitizer and paper dispenser placed next to the sink
9. Turning radius on 2 meters required in bedroom and bathroom, to maneuver lift or bath chair for two care givers

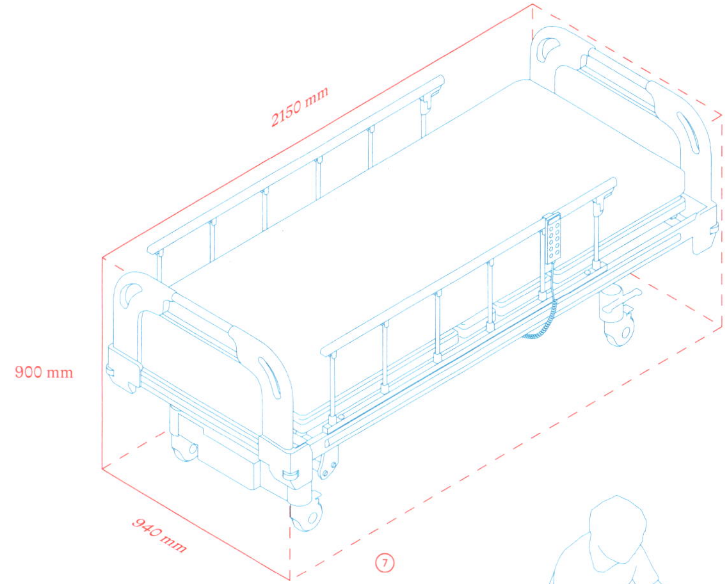

7

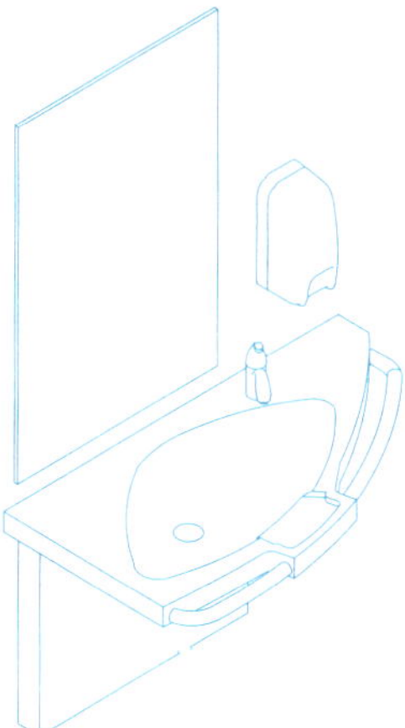
8

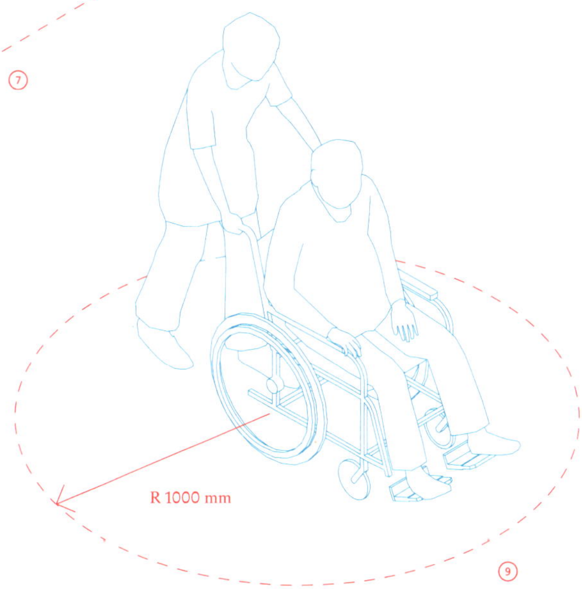

9

1

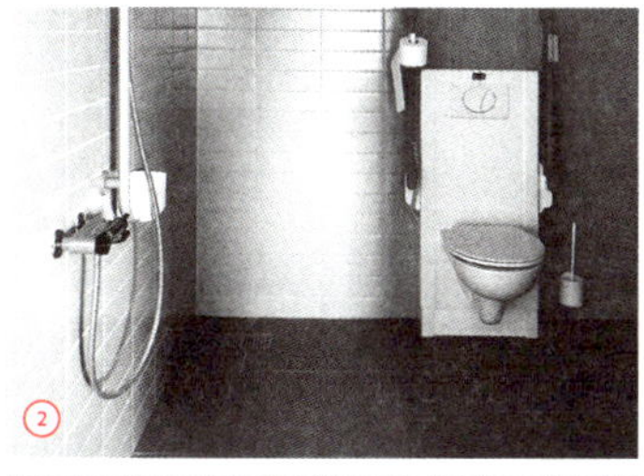
2

3

4

5

6

1.44 Apartment ceiling plan, Tornhøjhaven

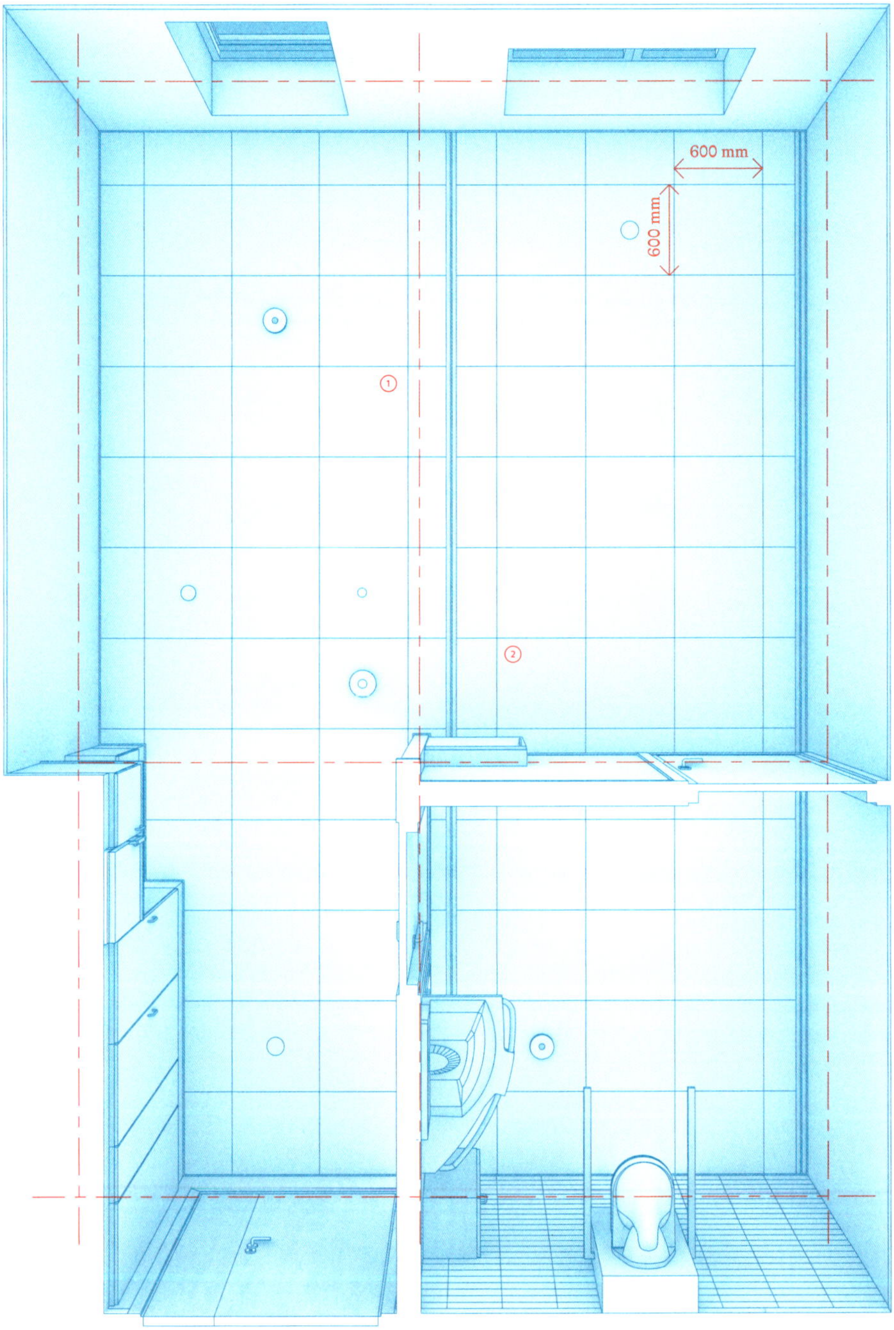

① In the ceiling are different devices, such as light spots, fire sprinklers, smoke detectors, and the rails for the ceiling lift

② There are installed ceiling lifts in all apartments covering the main room and bathroom, out of the potential future use

0 0.5 m

1.45 Apartment floor plan, Tornhøjhaven

0 0.5 m

1.46 Appropriation of the apartment by residents, Tornhøjhaven

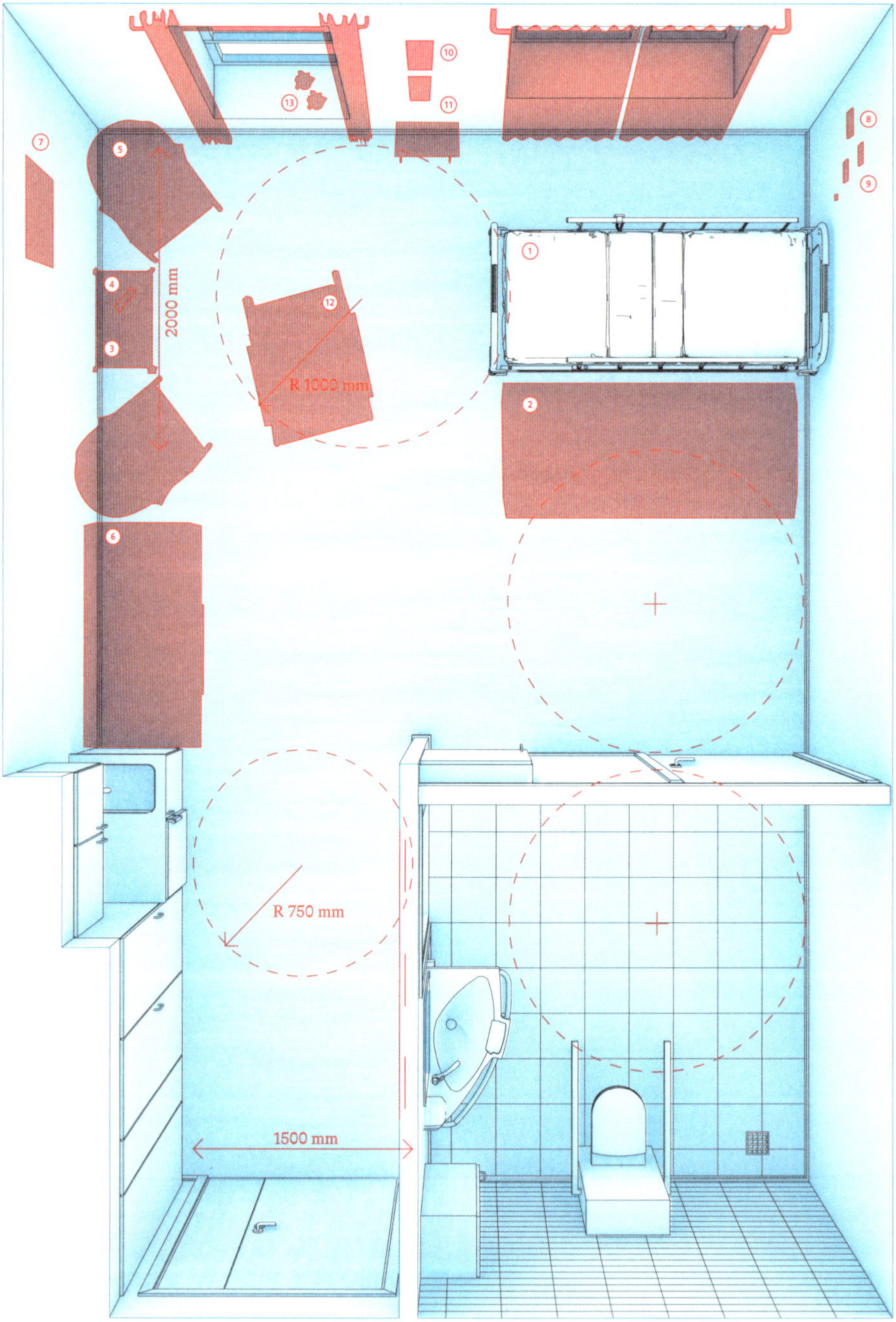

1. Hospital bed
2. Mattress
3. Table
4. Radio
5. Chairs
6. Storage chest
7. Photo collage
8. Photos
9. Electric plug
10. Drawings
11. Table
12. Wheelchair
13. Plants

0 0.5 m

1.47

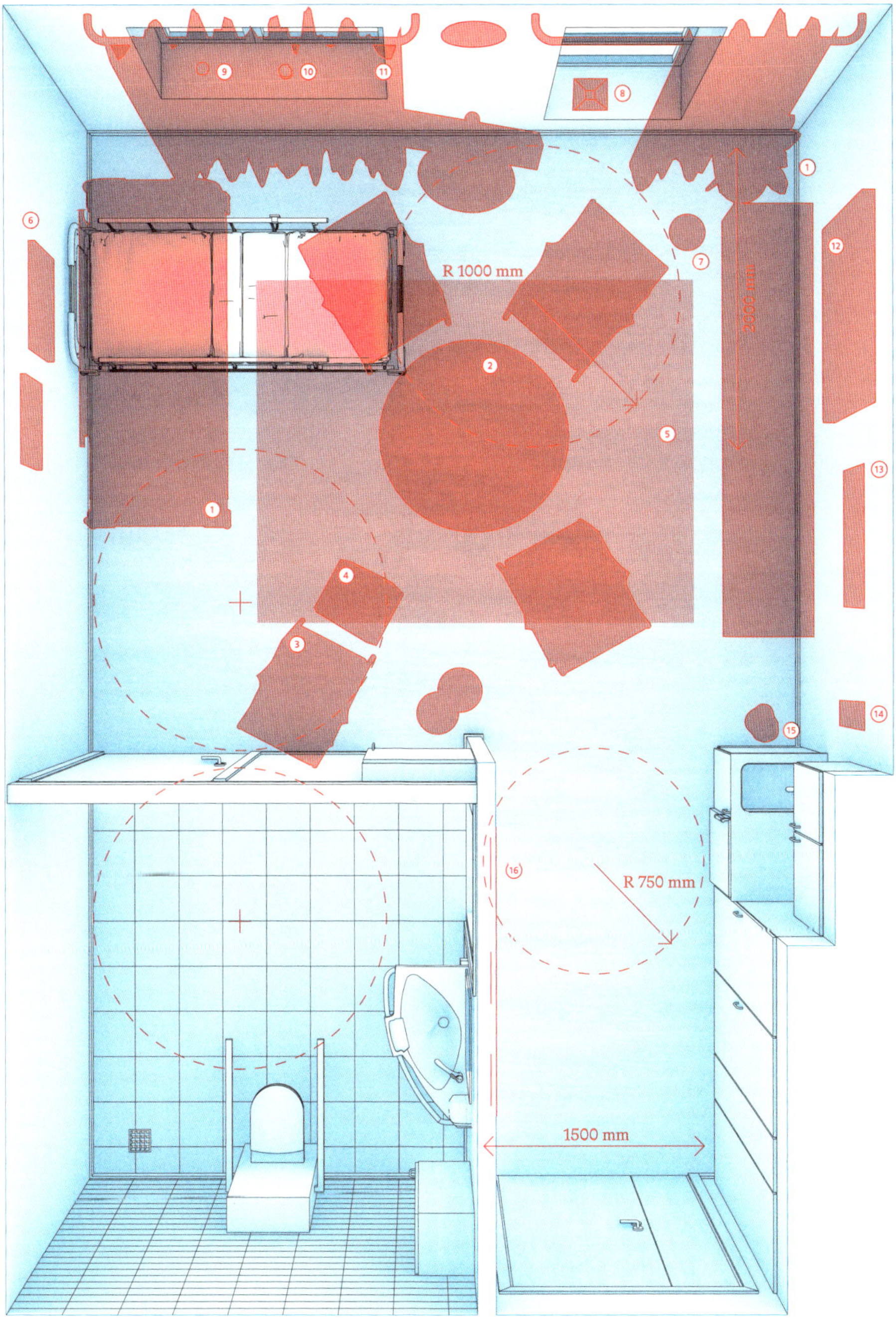

1. Hospital bed
2. Armchairs and table
3. Armchair
4. Footrest
5. Carpet
6. Pictures
7. Floor lamp
8. Lamp
9. Vase
10. Cactus
11. Curtain
12. TV
13. Hi-fi set
14. CD rack
15. Witch sculpture
16. Hangers for jackets over the door

2

Adaptability

A Welfare Situation in Tønder

Kirsten Marie Raahauge

1 Marshlands just outside Tønder (Vidåen).

"The absent position is present by implication."[1]
Donald Judd

In a vintage clothing shop downtown Tønder, I met a doctor with her own practice. Before that, she had worked at the hospital:

> We used to have so much fun back then, when the hospital was still functioning. Everybody knew each other, and when you had just moved to Tønder, it was easy to get to know somebody in the town. Now it has become a more silent town. I don't know how newcomers manage to get new acquaintances without having a workplace like the hospital.[2]

Major relocations of Danish welfare institutions have had a pervading impact on Tønder as well as on large parts of the provinces of Denmark and abroad. The change is echoed in the Danish media. Sites outside the urban web are no longer referred to as "provinces"; typically, they are described as being in the "outskirts" or "periphery" – this is especially true when viewed from the larger urban centers.[3]

Into Tønder

Based on ethnographic fieldwork conducted in Tønder, this chapter explores the impact on everyday life of the relocation of welfare institutions to larger cities.[4] These welfare institutions have an impact both as buildings and as generators of social life and imaginaries that seep out into the rest of the town. My focus will be on the ways in which the interplay of spatial and social configurations changes after the relocation, thus affecting the surrounding town. I am concerned with something that used to be there, namely the welfare institutions and the vividness of the town, and something that still lingers, namely the presence of the concrete buildings and the transformations that they have been undergoing, sometimes leading to an absence of activity while at other times resulting in more diffuse ways of using the buildings, a more fragmented organization of welfare and a less vivid town. These transformations also include countermovements, namely institutions that grow larger, or welfare amenities that are relocated to cities that are closer to the area, thus relocating not only welfare amenities, but also the distribution of center and periphery. This perspective on welfare spaces means that this chapter will focus not only on the distinct welfare institutions but also on the other spaces that they fold in and out of, thus becoming part of a welfare-space web. This has implications for the analysis, and for *welfare* and *space* as notions; the welfare concept refers not only to the overall interplay of state, civil society, market and private communities suggested by the political scientist Lars Bo Kaspersen, it is also extended to deal with the welfare of social life in the town.[5] Thus, the spaces of welfare are substituted with spaces *through* welfare, meaning that they are conceived of as a social space, impacted by concrete institutions and their enmeshment with other social spaces and imaginaries. While keeping a focus on the social and spatial implications of welfare transformation, the time of waiting is also part of my field, as well as the imaginaries of a future to come.[6]

2.01
National center-periphery dynamics, 2020

Tønder, Tynne, Tondern

Tønder is situated in the marshes of southern Jutland, near the German border to the south and the tidal flats to the west. It became a Danish market town in 1243, maybe even before that, and was strategically important for centuries, a center for its hinterland, as the only market town in the region, famed for making and selling lace, for silversmithing, for producing woodcarvings such as sepulchral tablets and for its affluent merchants and markets, where oxen and horses were bought and sold.[7] Up until the sixteenth century, Tønder had a port, and in the course of its history, the town has served as an infrastructural center for roads, and later for railroads. The old part of the town is clearly separated from the marsh. The structure of the new part of the town is somewhat fuzzy. Situated in a border region, Tønder has been a contested site. Its turbulent geopolitical history from the Middle Ages to the present day is evident in the town's architecture, a mixture of Frisian, Danish and German building styles.[8] Many of the buildings of the welfare institutions are older than the Danish welfare state; some were built when Tønder was under German rule: for example, the present-day library is situated in a building that used to be a German school. The marshes are man-made; since medieval times, dikes have been built, creating new land and protecting the marshes from storm surges. In a storm flood known as "Der grote Mandrænke" (the great man-drowning) in 1362, huge areas of land disappeared into the sea, and thousands of people died; a storm surge in 1634 inundated the Tønder marshes. A forward dike was proposed after a devastating storm surge in 1976; completed in 1981, it has since protected the Tønder marshes against flooding from the North Sea.

Several languages have been part of everyday life in Tønder: Danish, German, the local dialect (sønderjysk), Frisian and Low German; the same goes for the citizens' feeling of belonging. Today, most citizens speak Danish and consider themselves Danish by heart.[9] After Denmark's defeat by Prussia in 1864, the Danish duchy Schleswig Holstein became Prussian. At the election in 1920, the northern part of Schleswig, including Tønder, became part of Denmark again.[10] In the years after World War II, an abundance of welfare institutions was placed in Tønder, which became a model of the Danish welfare society.[11] This gave rise to growth in the number of shops, in industry, education, and many cultural events, as well as the prosperous farmland. Inhabitants came from all walks of life concerning both jobs and education; many young people lived in the town, attracted by the teacher-training college, the barracks and other education opportunities situated there. But in the early twenty-first century several institutions were relocated to larger cities as a part of the centralization of the distribution of welfare amenities that happened in this period in Denmark, most importantly through the 2007 Structural Reform. These transformations have had a huge impact on Tønder, leaving its citizens with a feeling of becoming peripheral, dependent on other cities. For many years, the number of inhabitants was constant, somewhere between 7,000 and 8,000.[12] In recent years, Tønder has become more homogenized, since fewer young people get their education there and fewer inhabitants are employed at the institutions and the other workplaces that were dependent on the institutions.[13] According to a real estate agent, a new development might be emerging: "Something new is that it is also the old people who are moving away; they want to be near their children."[14]

Tønder from Afar

Globally, as infrastructure becomes more efficient, the speed of travel has become more important than the distance of travel, leading to so-called timespace compression.[15] The intertwining of virtual and concrete spaces and their mediation of each other further adds to the growing intensity of timespace compression and to the acceleration of speed. All of this has an influence on the outskirts of the provinces globally as well as in Tønder.[16]

This general development merges with everyday life in all sorts of ways. To a large degree, welfare amenities can be accessed online, draining physical space of sociality. Concerning physical space, the location of larger institutions are crucial parameters for the development of cities. Another important space is the H-shaped motorway system that connects the larger Danish cities to form what is known as the H-city;[17] it becomes even more important whether you are part of the H-city or not.

2.04
Routes to welfare institutions, 1970/2020

Tønder is not part of the H-city. Furthermore, Tønder is detached from what has been called Den Østjyske Millionby or simply DØM (The East Jutland Million-City, which includes Aarhus, covering larger part of the east coast of Jutland stretching from Haderslev in the south to Randers in the north), where residents can move swiftly between cities in their daily lives. Tønder's infrastructural connections mainly consists of a couple of trunk roads and primary roads and a train going north–south. The effect of the relocation of welfare institutions to other cities has been enhanced by this detachment from the motorway system. Whereas the town used to be a self-contained entity, it has become dependent on other cities for welfare and to some degree for workplaces, shops and cultural events. This is an obstacle for the rising number of aging citizens who must travel rather far to go to the hospital; other citizens are also troubled by this. A shopkeeper in his fifties with a slipped disc in his back had to attend a doctor at the hospital in Odense, approximately 150 km away by bus, two trains and another bus. The appointment was set around noon; due to the many transfers in public transportation, he did not manage to get there on time. Some residents must work far from town because the institution they work for has been relocated, be it the hospital, the museum, whose management recently was relocated to Haderslev, or the police station that used to be open 24/7 but is now reduced to being open Monday to Wednesday, 1–3 pm and on Thursdays, 3–5 pm. A police officer I met on the street was worried about this development but assured me that police would come rushing by car from all the other parts of Tønder municipality if something bad happened. "They would even come from the border, where they are placed in order to check the corona[virus] regulations!"

Pupils from the high school were about to enter an essay competition with other high schools in Denmark and had decided on the theme *Make Tønder Great Again!* when I approached them. They were assigned to write small essays to me based on some questions, the most popular being about the impact of infrastructure and commuting on their everyday lives. Living in the hinterland of Tønder, they had to travel to Tønder and back again to meet with friends, go to the high school, to parties, to sport facilities, to work with the refugees to whom they teach Danish, etc.[18] Furthermore, they had to travel to other cities to practice sports or meet with friends. Some of them were from divorced families, so they also traveled between two villages. They are up early to catch the bus, and they are used to waiting, since the bus schedule is not always coordinated with the school. As one of them wrote, after a long description about her daily commute: "Transportation takes much time in Tønder." Another also explained her long daily bus tours, and then wrote:

> Many who do not use buses themselves always use the argument that you can use the time in the bus for doing your homework. But since the bus is filled with noisy children and you don't have Internet, it is limited what you are able to get done. For me, the fact that I must sit in a bus is not the problem. The problem is the waiting time and the consequences of it.

A third pupil wrote about life in the hinterland of Tønder:

> To live in the municipality of Tønder is for me on the one hand lovely, because you are always situated in quiet surroundings. Still, in these quiet surroundings it is easy to feel lonely in your home in the middle of the countryside, far away from everything and everybody. I look at myself as a city girl who needs to travel and experience stuff all the time. That is why the municipality of Tønder sometimes drains me of energy.

Some of the pupils that were fortunate enough to have the option had dropped the exhausting bus rides; they were driving to school by car.

Tønder has become peripheral to other centers, such as Aabenraa or Odense, where the larger hospitals are situated, or Esbjerg, where the main police station is placed. As mentioned, Tønder is on the periphery of the H-city and DØM, where the main economic development is concentrated. At the same time, Tønder is the center of its hinterland; furthermore, it attracts German pupils for the high school and tourists from Denmark and Germany, thus serving as a center. This intertwinement of being both center and periphery at the same time is present in many regards; the feeling of becoming periphery is new.

As a center of its hinterland, the range of experiences and amenities offered in Tønder are fewer and less diverse than they used to be. Furthermore, as the centralization of welfare amenities have prioritized the H-city, Tønder has centralized the welfare amenities of the area, leaving the hinterland with the same kind of challenges that Tønder has.[19] In these years, a countermovement of relocation of government institutions in the provinces is taking place, the success of this movement is contested, as many of the employees stay in the H-city, since most of these relocations are placed in larger cities; the same goes for the university campuses in the Southern part of Jutland; they are placed in Sønderborg, Kolding and Esbjerg.[20]

Connected to its transformation from the town of institutions to a town that is not so easily defined, everyday life is changing, silently and without much ado. Tønder is in a waiting position. Many shops have become empty; in the pedestrian street posters advertising for parties or good bargains, or objects for sale from other shops are displayed in the windows of the empty shops. The shopkeepers stress that they do all right. The trade association has invited H&M and other larger franchised shops to come to keep the pedestrian street and its shops alive.

Buildings and Institutions

The buildings that used to contain the welfare institutions are also assigned to the transformations of Tønder, undergoing at least four different types of transformation: Some are still welfare institutions and growing, such as the high school that merged with the high school in Niebüll in Germany; the care homes;[21] or the municipality that has recently extended its main building while also being present in quite a few buildings in Tønder and other towns. Others are still welfare institutions but are diminishing, such as the hospital, which is now a day hospital with the possibility of receiving ambulant treatment concerning diabetes, gastrointestinal-medicine and osteoporosis, combined with a medical day hospital that you should be referred to in order to show up (the homepage hasn't been updated since 2013); the railway station also serves its function in a diminished scale, namely as a waiting room, while staff and ticket sales have been replaced by a slot machine. Yet other buildings have become transient, with changing kinds of activities, such as the teacher-training college: in the last few years it has changed from after-school care to a culture center, a language school, a meeting place for youngsters and back to a culture center, while the headmaster's residence accommodates a center for the rehabilitation of alcoholics. Finally, other buildings remain empty, as is the case with the post office; the statue of the little horn blower on the building now refers to nothing, after this service moved to a supermarket on the outskirts of town.

Close-up on Tønder

As the doctor narrated, the former hospital was a catalyst of vibrant life both inside the building and outside of it, for example, after working hours, when employees met for parties or dinners or tea or whatever. Groups of the staff went on holidays or on biking tours together, and many of them exchanged goods at the hospital, as a retired doctor that I interviewed explained. Some of the cleaning ladies were wives of farmers from the marsh who liked to work a little and meet people in the town, so they took cabbage, eggs, steaks and potatoes to the exchange-circles at the hospital. In these ways, the hospital served as an important location for a network of exchange systems, and thereby became a generator for social life.[22] The staff was enmeshed in a web of relations that circled around the exchanges at the hospital. The parties and holidays as well as the cabbage and the eggs were all elements in this system of exchange. These relations were dependent on a common place to be together, and a certain amount of people from all strands of life being together. The social effect of the hospital spread to the town and the marshes. This social generator vanished after the hospital turned into a day hospital with only a few employees.

The buildings erected as a teacher-training college cause bewilderment among most of the people I have talked to. At an event in the study circle of the church, I met two women who live half a minute's walk from the buildings. When I asked them what the buildings were used for, they were in doubt and had to discuss it with each other without reaching any definite conclusion. "It shifts too often for me to be able to remember what is there and what is not," one of them remarked. Many are confused about this, not being sure what is inside these buildings for the time being. This affects the town at large; it becomes difficult to read the codes of the town. It is a question of navigation in the town, knowing what is placed where, and of navigation through time, having a sense of what is stable and what is fluid. The problem is not that elements of the town are floating,[23] rather, the trouble is connected to elements hithero perceived as stable becoming floating.[24] The signification of the buildings becomes floating, as the building points to a content that is shifting.[25] Confusion grows concerning specific buildings such as the former teacher-training college, going from 200 years of stability to flotation. Everyday life in the town, the routes you take, the activities you engage in, the imaginaries you connect to the town might not change much through this deplacement, still it destabilizes something: the sensation of the town is slightly dislocated toward transformation rather than stability, and as you are not quite aware what the point of the transformation is, you might become confused.

The courthouse is one of the buildings that used to refer to a stable content, while now it has become transient. It was built in the period of German rule (1864–1920) as a courthouse, with a pompous entrance and a location that gives a significant and authoritative impression. Now it contains a travel agency, a rehab for drug addicts and other facilities; other companies and municipal centers have been housed here over the years. The barracks, built for housing soldiers and accommodating their military training, now contains tax offices; a government institution that was relocated to Tønder, it is situated in a small part of the vast, empty building complex.

Many of these buildings were erected under German rule, typically for accommodating other kinds of welfare.[26] The building of the library, for example, was erected for the purpose of accommodating a German school.[27] Since the former welfare buildings are rather significant, and since the town is rather small, the transformation of these buildings has an impact on the town, as many of my interviewees point out; they get confused by the transience of some of the buildings, are saddened by the emptiness of others; more generally, many of them have a sense of nostalgia because of the absence of what used to be present.

2.05
Welfare institutions in Tønder, 1970s
2.06
Tønder, urban context, 2020

Quiet Days in Tønder

These transformations also have their positive side, as a retired teacher from the high school said:

> The town has become very silent. It has its own quality to live in a quiet town. if you would like to experience something, you can travel for it; two hours to the concert hall in Hamburg, three hours to Copenhagen. And we have traveled a lot with our colleagues over the years, trips to Krakow, Prague or Budapest.

Her husband, another retired teacher at the same school consented, but before that, he said to me: “I am sad that you prosper from our misery!”

The town used to have a feeling of being a microcosmos, Nils Gunder Hansen, a professor at the University of Southern Denmark, states in his memoirs:

> Perhaps the historical consciousness was indirectly present: there was a certain laid-back self-awareness about Tønder – there was no ambience of the provinces or the periphery, and there were no inferiority complexes or self-loathing, even though we, all things considered, constituted one of the most remote one-horse towns in the kingdom. I have subsequently been to many places in Denmark that elicited a far greater effect of being province and periphery. Was it history's weight that was the buoyant factor here? Was it because Tønder was situated "centrally," with only an hour's drive to Flensburg, and two to Hamburg?[28]

This was in the 1960s to the '80s; in those decades, the feeling of being a microcosmos was pervasive, a retired librarian married to a dentist recalls. After having ended their education, she and her husband decided to move to Tønder. It used to be normal to settle in the provinces after ending your education, while now, most people want to stay in the larger cities, she notes. When they moved to Tønder, to their surprise, they found an abundance of experiences and places to go. An important reason for this was that the welfare institutions served as attractors for people from many walks of life, thus forming the basis for cultural events to happen. Students from the teacher-training college were especially active: one student was running a basketball team that her son could attend; others gave rise to a variety of music events and study circles for herself and her husband. Another reason for the vibrant city life was that everything came in double, in German and in Danish, from the schools to the butchers, from the doctors to some of the cultural events. Therefore, the town was more vivid than the larger city of Horsens, where she was raised. Now the town has become more silent than it used to be, she says.

"The worst part was to lose the teacher-training college!" "It was a disaster to lose the teacher-training college!" Statements like these are frequent, since this institution attracted young people to the town; Tønder was massively influenced by the students, in the streets, in the bars, in the many music clubs and concerts, in a lot of activities and places, everywhere. Today, the town still offers education, though on a smaller scale. The high school is an example. The growth and the collaboration with the high school in Niebüll, 15 km away has been possible, since the Danish-German relationship in many regards has developed from parallel societies to becoming a more joint community.

New-Old Welfare Spaces

In the vintage clothing shop where I met the doctor, I had an interview with the shopkeeper, a Copenhagener who has had his shop in Tønder for almost ten years. He gave me the example of the back room of his shop as a welfare space. Here, informally, many of his costumers would come by and chat, also about serious matters. Eventually, I have become one of them, hanging out for a little too long in his back room. Furthermore, the shopkeeper arranges ladies' nights, or events where he performs as

Queen Margrethe, to have a social network going on in and around his shop; this, he states, is welfare space to him.

This interpretation of the term *welfare space* is challenging, gliding from a well-defined analytical notion to an empirical notion concerned with social relations on a broader scale.[29] As noted at the start, in addition to the distinct welfare institutions, the focus is on the other spaces that they fold in and out of, thus becoming part of a welfare-space web. Still, the idea of the shop as a welfare space entangles one into the other in a disturbing way. The shopkeeper's hybrid space, mixing privacy, community and market on a small scale in a little shop behind curtains is hard to place into a traditional sociological scheme; rather it might be seen as a substitution for welfare spaces. Furthermore, it points to the layers of sociality that blend into "welfare," as a notion that might be used in disparate ways, mediated by space in multiple ways.[30] Something parallel is at work concerning welfare institutions; these spaces deal with the distribution of welfare amenities while at the same time implying multiple layers of sociality that might not have much to do with "welfare," turning these spaces into hybrid spaces, fraught with other activities and imaginaries, be they private, communal, representative, public or other kinds; the hospital had this character, working as a social generator of exchange.[31]

The shopkeeper talks about an empirical locale in his shop, but at the same time, he might be on to a kind of welfare space that is not part of the amenities of the state or of civic society. The shop as a generator of social life is something else. Maybe it is not welfare space, maybe it is social space, maybe such places have replaced the sociality which came out of the welfare institutions. It is part of the webs that have always been there, and after the welfare institutions have diminished, these alternatives have grown and become more evident: the new-old welfare spaces.

Public transportation might be another ambiguous place for social gathering. It is part of the web of welfare amenities, it connects welfare institutions, yet it is also private space in the sense that it is a place where you create your own zone of privacy among the others present, and at the same time, it is a common space where people meet. Or so I thought, after having talked to the shopkeeper, now keen on finding alternative or disruptive welfare spaces that I had not thought of before. This hypothesis was challenged. As we have seen, the buses are not appreciated as social new-old welfare spaces. They are welfare spaces as locations for a welfare amenity distributed by the municipality to its citizens; in addition they are part of the large, unevenly distributed infrastructural web, thus adding to the topic of timespace compression and being cut off from the H-city. Meanwhile, alternative welfare spaces flourish at other places and in other ways. Maybe the buses are the opposite of the shop: buses offer welfare amenities, they do not offer sociality, while the shop offers sociality but has no amenities to distribute.

As welfare institutions are concentrated in centers, adding to their center status, it seems that a new-yet-old peripheral thinking and acting is emerging in former welfare centers. Social spaces are taking over. Where the welfare institutions are transformed, absent or diminished, social life is also transformed, with new hubs that are not closely connected to the welfare institutions. The landscape of new-old welfare spaces is becoming more rhizomatic and less transparent, and the possible hubs are becoming oriented toward private, transient and floating spaces, such as the shop. In today's waiting position of Tønder, its inhabitants find other ways to meet, more subtle ways, in less obvious spaces. Apart from the backroom of the shop, people meet in the marshes, where they go for a walk or arrange tours; they meet in associations for reading or for bird-watching, or swimming in the public swimming pool in the early morning, or in certain spots in the cityscape. "The bar!," a historian exclaimed when I asked her about the whereabouts of welfare spaces. Neighborhoods also have a role to play; as neighbors grow older, they also grow closer and help one another, driving to the hairdresser or the doctor, going to Germany for cheap goods, exchanging newspapers. So the social generators of welfare institutions have to some degree been substituted by social networks. They were always there, now they got a more vital role. As the anthropologists Eva Gulløv and John Gulløv remark:

> [S]ome mention the possibilities of starting up things, or as one of the young boys [interviewee as part of their fieldwork] says: "that no one interferes." And this industriousness is definitely visible. Now and again, we notice the many activities taking place in small community houses, in churches and at libraries. There is an abundance of initiatives and an engagement in the cultural life that succeeds in attracting esteemed writers, musicians and lecturers and gathering more than 2,000 volunteers for collaborating around the large Tønder Festival that each year makes around 10,000 people travel to Tønder from Denmark as well as from abroad.[32]

It seems that a dwindling spatial order of recognizable welfare institutions is supplemented by a web of gathering sites without a recognizable code or structure. It might not be a matter of absence-presence only going on in Tønder. The transformations are happening in many ways. While the former welfare institutions are replaced with other kinds of amenities and uses, the town is transformed by the entanglement of new-yet-old webs and sites of social life.

Tønder Tomorrow

Tønder, once "a microcosmos" and "a town of institutions," is under transformation to something else.[33] In this chapter, I have tried to understand the transformations of the welfare spaces and their social implications from the citizens' point of view. I have explored the ways space and sociality are intertwined, and how these entanglements are connected to welfare and disconnected from it. The many-folded relationships between social and spatial spheres are as evident as they are uncontrollable; you cannot foresee the impact in all its details of a change in one register on another register.[34] When the events and phenomena happen in condensed or restrained ways, as in Tønder, this might seem peripheral, but although only small details seem to be affected, these details might be the ones that have a large impact.

Tønder's waiting time might be over before too long. Two large private funds and the municipality have joined to lift Tønder and the marsh. There are two major reasons for these private actors to intervene. Firstly, climate change has once again turned the marshes into endangered areas, due to the heavy rain and storms that produce storm surges from the North Sea and flooding from the rivers, streams and lakes in the marshes. Secondly, the peripheralization has turned the region into an area in danger of becoming unattractive to live in. In 2014 the Wadden Sea National Park, a part of the marsh, was added to UNESCO's list of World Heritage Sites. The marsh has accordingly become an enormous museum piece and a landscape of experience, in addition to a landscape of farming.[35] With the rare landscape, the unique birdlife and the old, well-preserved town center, Tønder and the marsh have possibilities for revitalization by way of funding from private sources that have now become decisive. The transformation of Tønder and its landscape means that Tønder awaits a new era, where it might become "Tønder," a town that points to itself to become a hub for tourists who would like to experience bay windows, lace production or black sun.[36] As the province has turned into periphery on a global scale, this new movement into an era of simulation through authenticity is also rather usual on a global scale, maybe it reflects a peripheralization not only of the empirical sites, but also of the idea of a site.

2.07
Presence of welfare institutions in Tønder, 1970s
2.08
Absence of welfare institutions in Tønder, 2020
2.11–12
Tønderstierne, a landscape of experience in addition to a landscape of farming, 2020

2 Marshlands just outside Tønder (wetlands for birds).

Acknowledgments

This chapter is built over a paper presented in Dundee in November 2019 at the AHRA-conference. For further information, please follow this link: https://kglakademi.dk/blog-spaces-danish-welfare/welfare-spaces-tourist-areas-and-peripheral-sites-kirsten-marie-raahauge. Thank you to Alison Clarke and Sten Gromark, Louise Dedenroth Høj and Martin Søberg, Deane Simpson and Katrine Lotz and the external reviewer for their important comments. And thank you to The Independent Research Fund Denmark for funding this project.

Bibliography

Albertsen, Niels, and Bülent Diken. "Welfare and the City." *Nordisk Arkitekturforskning* 17, no. 2 (2004): 7–22. http://arkitekturforskning.net/na/article/view/235/197.

Appadurai, Arjun. "Disjuncture and Difference in the Modern Global Economy." In *Modernity at Large: Cultural Dimensions of Globalization*, 27–43. Minneapolis: University of Minnesota Press, 1996.

Askholm, Anne Sofie, and Kathrine Dalsgaard. "Vandkantsvinkler: Antropologiske blikke på fortællinger fra og om 'udkanten.'" In "Debat: Antropologiske Medier," edited by Christian Suhr and Carolina Sanchez Boe. Special issue, *Jordens Folk: Etnografisk Tidsskrift* 54, no. 1 (2019): 25–39.

Baxstrom, Richard. "Knowing Primitives, Witches, and the Spirits: Anthropology and the Mastery of Nonsense." *Republics of Letters: A Journal for the Study of Knowledge, Politics, and the Arts* 3, no. 2 (2014): 1–22. http://arcade.stanford.edu/rofl/knowing-primitives-witches-and-spirits-anthropology-and-mastery-nonsense. Accessed May 4, 2016.

Becker-Christensen, Henrik. *Byen ved grænsen: Tønder 1920–1970*. Aabenraa: Institut for Grænseregionsforskning, 1993.

Bruun, Maja Hojer, Dorthe Brogaard Kristensen, Stine Krøijer, Julie Rahbæk Møller and Mikkel Rytter, eds. *Velfærdsstaten* 1. Special issue *Tidsskriftet Antropologi* 72 (2016).

——. *Velfærdsstaten* 2. Special issue *Tidsskriftet Antropologi* 73 (2016).

Carbone, Claudia, and Claus Peder Pedersen. "H-BY." *Tidsskriftet Antropologi* 47, *Byer I: Abomey–Mumbai* (2005): 43–57.

Dahl, Henrik. *Den Usynlige Verden*. Copenhagen: Gyldendal, 2010.

de Certeau, Michel. "Walking in the City." In *The Practice of Everyday Life*, 91–110. Berkeley: University of California Press, 1986.

Eskildsen, Claus. *Tønder 1243–1943*. Tønder: Guldhorn, 1943.

Freeman, Carla. "Review of Modernity, an Ethnographic Approach: Dualism and Mass Consumption in Trinidad, by Daniel Miller." *NWIF: New West Indian Guide* 70, nos. 1–2 (1996): 152–56. https://www.jstor.org/stable/41849753?seq=1#metadata_info_tab_contents. Accessed November 18, 2021.

Gottdiener, Mark. *Life in the Air: Surviving the New Culture of Air Travel*. Lanham: Rowman & Littlefield Publishers, 2001.

Gulløv, Eva, and John Gulløv. *Opvækst i provinsen: Om dem, der bliver, og dem, der rejser*. Antropologiske studier 6. Aarhus: Aarhus Universitetsforlag, 2020.

Hansen, Nils Gunder. *Lille dreng med rejseskrivemaskine: Erindringer*. Copenhagen: Kristeligt Dagblads Forlag, 2011.

Harvey, David. *The Condition of Postmodernity: An Enquiry into the Origins of Cultural Change*. Cambridge, MA: Blackwell, 1990.

Judd, Donald. "Symmetry, 1985." In *Donald Judd: Complete Writings 1975–1986*, 18–24. Van Abbemuseum, Eindhoven, 1987.

Kaspersen, Lars Bo. *Denmark in the World*. Copenhagen: Hans Reitzels Forlag, 2013.

Koolhaas, Rem. *Countryside: A Report*. Cologne: Taschen, 2020.

Larsen, Birgitte Romme. "At tage plads i andres kulturhistoriske helligdom: udflytningen af en statslig arbejdsplads fra København til Nakskov." *Kulturstudier*, in review.

Lévi-Strauss, Claude. *Introduction to the Work of Marcel Mauss*. London: Routledge, 2001.

Lægring, Kasper, and Badeloch Vera Noldus, eds. *Skjulte skatte i grænselandet: Dansk bygningsarv i Slesvig og Holsten*. Frederiksberg: Bianco Luno, 2010.

Martínez, Francisco, Lili Di Puppo and Martin Demant Frederiksen, eds. *Peripheral Wisdom: Unlearning, Not-knowing and Ethnographic Limits*. London: Routledge, 2021.

Mauss, Marcel. *A General Theory of Magic*. London: Routledge, 2001.

——. *The Gift: Forms and Functions of Exchange in Archaic Societies*. London: Routledge and Kegan Paul, 1954.

Miller, Daniel. *Modernity, an Ethnographic Approach: Dualism and Mass Consumption in Trinidad*. Exploration in Anthropology Series. Oxford: Berg Publishers, 1994.

Navaro-Yashin, Yael. *The Make-Believe Space: Affective Geography in a Postwar Polity*. Durham, NC: Duke University Press, 2012.

Nielsen, Tom, and Boris Brorman Jensen, eds. *East Jutland Million-City*. Aarhus: Arkitektskolen Aarhus, 2019.

Raahauge, Kirsten Marie. *En Århusantropologi*. PhD diss. Statens Byggeforskningsinstitut, 2007.

——. "Here, There and Nowhere in Provincial Outskirts and Haunted Houses." In Martínez, Puppo and Frederiksen, *Peripheral Wisdom*, 131–46.

——. "Towards the Outskirts." In *Forming Welfare*, edited by Jannie Rosenberg Bendsen, Katrine Lotz, Kjeld Vindum, Mette Jerl Jensen, Deane Simpson and Kirsten Marie Raahauge, 172–89. Copenhagen: Arkitektens Forlag, 2017.

Simmel, Georg, "The Metropolis and Mental Life" (1903). In *The Urban Sociology Reader*, edited by Jan Lin and Christopher Mele, 23–31. 2nd ed. New York: Routledge, 2013.

Svalastoga, Kaare, and Preben Wolf. *En by ved grænsen*. Copenhagen: Gyldendal, 1963.
Swenarton, Mark, Tom Avermaete and Dirk van den Heuvel, eds. *Architecture and the Welfare State*. London: Routledge, 2015.
Thrift, Nigel. "Intensities of Feeling: Towards a Spatial Politics of Affect." *Geografiska Annaler: Series B, Human Geography* 86, no. 1 (2004): 57–78.
Virilio, Paul. "Véhiculaire." In *L'insécurité du territoire*, 243–73. Paris: Éditions Galilée, 1993.

Notes

1 Donald Judd, "Symmetry, 1985," in *Donald Judd: Complete Writings 1975–1986*, 18–24. Van Abbemuseum, Eindhoven, 1987.

2 All translations from the Danish by the author.

3 See Anne Sofie Askholm and Katrine Dalsgaard, "Vandkantsvinkler: Antropologiske blikke på fortællinger fra og om 'udkanten,'" in "Debat: Antropologiske Medier," ed. Christian Suhr and Carolina Sanchez Boe, special issue, *Jordens Folk: Etnografisk Tidsskrift* 54, no. 1 (2019): 25–39; and Kirsten Marie Raahauge, "Towards the Outskirts," in *Forming Welfare*, ed. Jannie Rosenberg Bendsen et al. (Copenhagen: Arkitektens Forlag, 2017), 172–89.

4 My opportunity to conduct fieldwork has been delimited by the restrictions following COVID-19. The remaining part of my fieldwork will focus on the day hospital and other less permanent and small welfare institutions that have moved into the buildings of former welfare institutions, exploring the daily life here and in the surrounding town. Furthermore, some of the associations that play a role in the town will be explored (thank you to Alison Clarke, who gave me this advice), especially bird-watching associations, since the marshes are famously full of birdlife.

5 See Lars Bo Kaspersen, *Denmark in the World* (Copenhagen: Hans Reitzels Forlag, 2013).

6 Since the field material evolves around phenomena and notions of transformation and imaginaries, absence, and periphery, all of them being vague notions, there is a risk that some of the field material remains unseen, simply because it is not looked for. This challenge is part of the premise (see Richard Baxstrom, "Knowing Primitives, Witches, and the Spirits: Anthropology and the Mastery of Nonsense," *Republics of Letters: A Journal for the Study of Knowledge, Politics, and the Arts* 3, no. 2 (2014): 1–22), still, in this context it is even more relevant, due to the vagueness. This brings attention to notions of the peripheral not only as a label for a place that is in this way put into an asymmetrical relationship with the so-called centers; this also touches upon the peripheral as a way of analyzing the field; see Francisco Martínez, Lili Di Puppo and Martin Demant Frederiksen, eds., *Peripheral Wisdom: Unlearning, Not-knowing and Ethnographic Limits* (London: Routledge, 2021), esp. Kirsten Marie Raahauge, "Here, There and Nowhere in Provincial Outskirts and Haunted Houses," 131–46.

7 See Claus Eskildsen, *Tønder 1243–1943* (Tønder: Guldhorn, 1943); and Henrik Becker-Christensen, *Byen ved grænsen: Tønder 1920–1970* (Aabenraa: Institut for Grænseregionsforskning, 1993).

8 See Kasper Lægring and Badeloch Vera Noldus, eds., *Skjulte skatte i grænselandet: Dansk bygningsarv i Slesvig og Holsten* (Frederiksberg: Bianco Luno, 2010).

9 Yet the new mayor elected for Tønder Municipality in the fall of 2021 came from the Schleswig Party, the party representing the German minority.

10 At the time, 77 percent of the citizens of Tønder voted to remain part of Germany, while most of the inhabitants of the countryside voted for Denmark. In 1963 Kaare Svalastoga and Preben Wolf published *En by ved grænsen* (A Town at the Border), a sociological investigation conducted in Tønder with a focus on the relationship between the shifting majorities and minorities there. According to Svalastoga and Wolf, the percentage of German voters in Tønder developed like this: 1867 (three years after the Danish defeat to Prussia): 83 percent; 1920 (the year of the election in Schleswig Holstein, when the northern part of Schleswig, Sønderjylland, became Danish): 77 percent; and 1957: 23 percent. Svalastoga and Wolf, En by ved grænsen (Copenhagen: Gyldendal, 1963), 32.

11 See Becker-Christensen, *Byen ved grænsen*.

12 In 1963 the population was approximately 7,000 inhabitants, according to Svalastoga and Wolf, *En by ved grænsen*; in 2021 it is approximately 7,500.

13 Eva Gulløv and John Gulløv mention that migrant workers in the farms of the hinterlands of Tønder is a rather new development, adding new facets to the question of having groups of mixed background in the area. See Gulløv and Gulløv, *Opvækst i provinsen: Om dem, der bliver, og dem, der rejser*, Antropologiske studier 6 (Aarhus: Aarhus Universitetsforlag, 2020), 15.

14 The consequences and size of this remain to be seen.

15 To explain the effects of this development, the geographer David Harvey forwarded the concept timespace compression; see Harvey, *The Condition of Postmodernity: An Enquiry into the Origins of Cultural Change* (Cambridge, MA: Blackwell, 1990). Later, the sociologist Mark Gottdiener used it to explain the uncomfortable effects it has on people when they travel at high speeds in airplanes over large distances; see Gottdiener, *Life in the Air: Surviving the New Culture of Air Travel* (Lanham: Rowman & Littlefield Publishers, 2001). The urbanist Paul Virilio's notion of dromology has, for several decades, been a key to understanding such

movements, since it calls attention to speed's influence on development in all registers. See, for example, Virilio, "Véhiculaire," in *L'insécurité du territoire* (Paris: Éditions Galilée, 1993), 243–73.

16 See Raahauge, "Towards the Outskirts."

17 Claudia Carbone and Claus Peder Pedersen, "H-BY," *Tidsskriftet Antropologi*, no. 47, *Byer I: Abomey–Mumbai* (2005); Tom Nielsen and Boris Brorman Jensen, eds., *East Jutland Million-City* (Aarhus: Arkitektskolen Aarhus, 2019); and Henrik Dahl, *Den Usynlige Verden* (Copenhagen: Gyldendal, 2010).

18 The refugees are in transition: they live in Tønder for some months and then are relocated, a retired doctor told me.

19 Gulløv and Gulløv, *Opvækst i provinsen*, an ethnographic monograph about why young people leave their hometown in the provinces, quotes a father to a child in a village outside Tønder: "They complain about the government only thinking about Copenhagen, but they do exactly the same here: they gather everything in Tønder city, so that there is nothing left in the small towns." Eva Gulløv and John Gulløv, *Opvækst i provinsen: Om dem, der bliver, og dem, der rejser*. Antropologiske studier 6 (Aarhus: Aarhus Universitetsforlag, 2020), 43.

20 For example, parts of educational institutions and parts of government agencies have been relocated to the provincial cities. Parts of the Tax Administration, the department of debts, was placed in Tønder, thereby adding 83 jobs to the town.

21 See also Louise Dedenroth Høj's chapter in the present volume.

22 Marcel Mauss analyzes exchange systems; see Mauss, *The Gift: Forms and Functions of Exchange in Archaic Societies* (London: Routledge and Kegan Paul, 1954). He claimed that when objects, people, dances, song, and other precious gifts are exchanged, it is the exchange, not the gift that is important, because people become related to each other through exchanging. If you have received a gift, you are in debt, and you must give a gift to the giver, for him to become a receiver and for you to become a giver. This establishes a web of relations, the core of social life. The point here is not that the staff at the hospital followed a set of strict rules of exchange; the point is that the social relations established through exchange also worked in the hospital and influenced the surrounding town.

23 As pointed out by Michel de Certeau in his seminal text "Walking in the City," the city is per se undecodable; see de Certeau, "Walking in the City," in *The Practice of Everyday Life* (Berkeley: University of California Press, 1986), 91–110. Georg Simmel writes about the Geistesleben or "mental life" that is typical of small towns as opposed to metropolises; see Simmel, "The Metropolis of Mental Life," *The Urban Sociology Reader*, ed. Jan Lin and Christopher Mele, 2nd ed. (New York: Routledge, 2013), 23–31. Maybe, despite its small size, Tønder used to be a metropolis kind of town, that has now become a village type of town, affecting social life as well as the mental life in the town. During my fieldwork in Aarhus, I found the understanding of Aarhus as a "city-to-be-managed" or a "metropolis-like-Copenhagen" to be a major point of disagreement, even argument, among my informants, dealing with the right balance of decodable and undecodable elements; see Kirsten Marie Raahauge, *En Århusantropologi* (PhD diss., Statens Byggeforskningsinstitut, 2007).

24 It might be stretching the argument too far to say that the former welfare buildings have become floating signifiers, but still, there seems to be a connection; the floating signifier lingers in the shifting content of the building and the bewilderment it causes. The anthropologist Claude Lévi-Strauss coined the term *floating signifier*, building upon Roman Jacobsen's semiotic theories; see Lévi-Strauss, "Introduction à l'oevre Marcel Mauss" (1950), in Marcel Mauss, *Sociologie et anthropologie* (Paris: Presses Universitaires de France, 2001). He pointed to the need for shifters or empty signs in language, notions that have a floating meaning and point in many directions, for the language to be flexible. Lévi-Strauss developed his theory in connection with an analysis of the meaning of the kind of magic called mana. In language, floating signifiers are necessary, since no language covers the empirical world; however, this seems not to be the case concerning the buildings in Tønder. This interaction between stable and floating elements might be seen from another perspective through the dualism of transcendent and transient elements, following Daniel Miller in *Modernity, an Ethnographic Approach: Dualism and Mass Consumption in Trinidad*, Exploration in Anthropology Series (Oxford: Berg Publishers, 1994). Here, Miller observes the dualism of transience and transcendence. In her book review of Miller's work, Carla Freeman explains Miller's use of these terms: "*transience* emphazised values concerned with 'an ephemeral present ... an exhilarating sense of freedom' while *transcendence* emphasizes 'a sense of roots and tradition ... planning for the future and family descent.'" Carla Freeman, "Review of Modernity, an Ethnographic Approach: Dualism and Mass Consumption in Trinidad, by Daniel Miller," *NWIG: New West Indian Guide* 70, nos. 1–2 [1996]: 153. Miller claims that these values pervade the consumption practice and many other strands of life in Trinidad.

25 This navigation in time and the fact of becoming periphery is also treated in Larsen's ethnographical analysis of what happened when the former town hall in Nakskov (another provincial town in Denmark) was sold and overtaken by a state company as a part of the relocation of government institutions. The idea was to bring new jobs to Nakskov, but the reception of the inhabitants was about the loss of the town hall, having handed over its major symbol of being a living town to outsiders; see Birgitte Romme Larsen, "At tage plads i andres kulturhistoriske helligdom," *Kulturstudier*, in review.

26 See also the chapter by Lars Bo Kaspersen in the present volume.

27 The German architecture in Tønder is yet another layer of codes in the town. In Lægring and Noldus, *Skjulte skatte i grænselandet*, the differences in German and Danish building style in Tønder (among other places) is discussed. The architecture was used to show one's affiliation and it produced a fruitful competition in Tønder. On the one hand these codes were built into the architecture to point to nationality; on the other, as time passed and German buildings became Danish, the codes were confusing. These entanglements of stable and floating sides of the town have always been there and they have been very visible in Tønder. Today's transformation is not different, as regards the floating-stable interchange. The different setting of today is the landscape of peripheralization and uncertainty that the new empty and transient buildings point to.

28 Nils Gunder Hansen, *Lille dreng med rejseskrivemaskine: Erindringer* (Copenhagen: Kristeligt Dagblads Forlag, 2011), 72.

29 In political sociological theories, the notion of welfare is connected either to the welfare state that distributes welfare to its citizens through welfare institutions such as schools or hospitals, or to welfare society, where civil society establishes common welfare in the form of associations such as football clubs, reading circles, bird-watching associations etc. The market also plays a part in this, since the balance between market, state and civil society is crucial. In other words, the overarching approach to welfare includes the idea that a negotiation between state, civil society and market shapes the welfare state; see Mark Swenarton, Tom Avermaete and Dirk van den Heuvel, eds., *Architecture and the Welfare State* (London: Routledge, 2015); Kaspersen, *Denmark in the World*; Maja Hojer Bruun, Dorthe Brogaard Kristensen, Stine

Krøijer, Julie Rahbæk Møller and Mikkel Rytter, eds., *Velfærdsstaten* 1 and *Velfærdsstaten* 2, special issue *Tidsskriftet Antropologi* 72 and 73 (2016); and Niels Albertsen and Bülent Diken, "Welfare and the City," *Nordisk Arkitekturforskning* 17, no.2 (2004): 7–22. Swenarton, Avermaete and van den Heuvel point to the fact that welfare has been a prime area for both architectural historians and political sociologists: "Strangely, these twin developments have taken place virtually in complete ignorance of each other," in *Architecture and the Welfare State*, 1. In the research project Spaces of Danish Welfare we follow this perspective of working interdisciplinarily, with the slightly different focus of space, not only architecture, as the topic, and with art historical and anthropological perspectives supplementing a political sociological perspective, thus focusing on everyday life. This brings the interesting challenge of taking seriously what the people you talk to during fieldwork have to say about key notions such as welfare.

30 See Arjun Appadurai, "Disjuncture and Difference in the Modern Global Economy," in *Modernity at Large: Cultural Dimensions of Globalization* (Minneapolis: University of Minnesota Press, 1996), 27–43.

31 This layering of spaces, welfare spaces, haunted houses, interiors of all kinds, is the focus of a new center at the Royal Danish Academy, Center of Interior Studies. See https://kglakademi.dk/center-interior-studies.

32 Gulløv and Gulløv, *Opvækst i provinsen*, 15–16.

33 Niels Albertsen and Bülent Diken write: "Castells here defines the urban in such a way that the development of the welfare state eo ipso is urban development. The development of the state as a welfare state, insofar as it is focused on goods and services for labor power, is the development of the city as a welfare city, insofar as we look to the spatial form." Albertsen and Diken, "Welfare and the City," 14. And, one might add, the parallel development of smaller cities' losing their status as welfare cities.

34 Nigel Thrift and Yael Navaro-Yashin have discussed this aspect in different contexts, pointing to the fact that micro movements and materiality are directly connected to political levels and global issues. See Thrift, "Intensities of Feeling: Towards a Spatial Politics of Affect," *Geografiska Annaler: Series B, Human Geography* 86, no. 1 (2004): 57–78; and Navaro-Yashin, *The Make-Believe Space: Affective Geography in a Postwar Polity* (Durham, NC: Duke University Press, 2012).

35 Rem Koolhaas suggests that the countryside has the potential for new developments after decennias "characterized by a complacent expectation that one kind of civilization – metropolitan, capital-oriented, agnostic, Western – would remain the template for global development, possibly forever." Koolhaas, *Countryside: A Report* (Cologne: Taschen, 2020), 2.

36 Black sun occurs when tens of thousands of starlings fly together in grand formations known as murmurations, in order to protect one another from attacks by birds of prey as they land or take off. They can be seen during the birds' migrations from February to April and also October through November, attracting tourists from afar.

2.01 National center-periphery dynamics, 2020

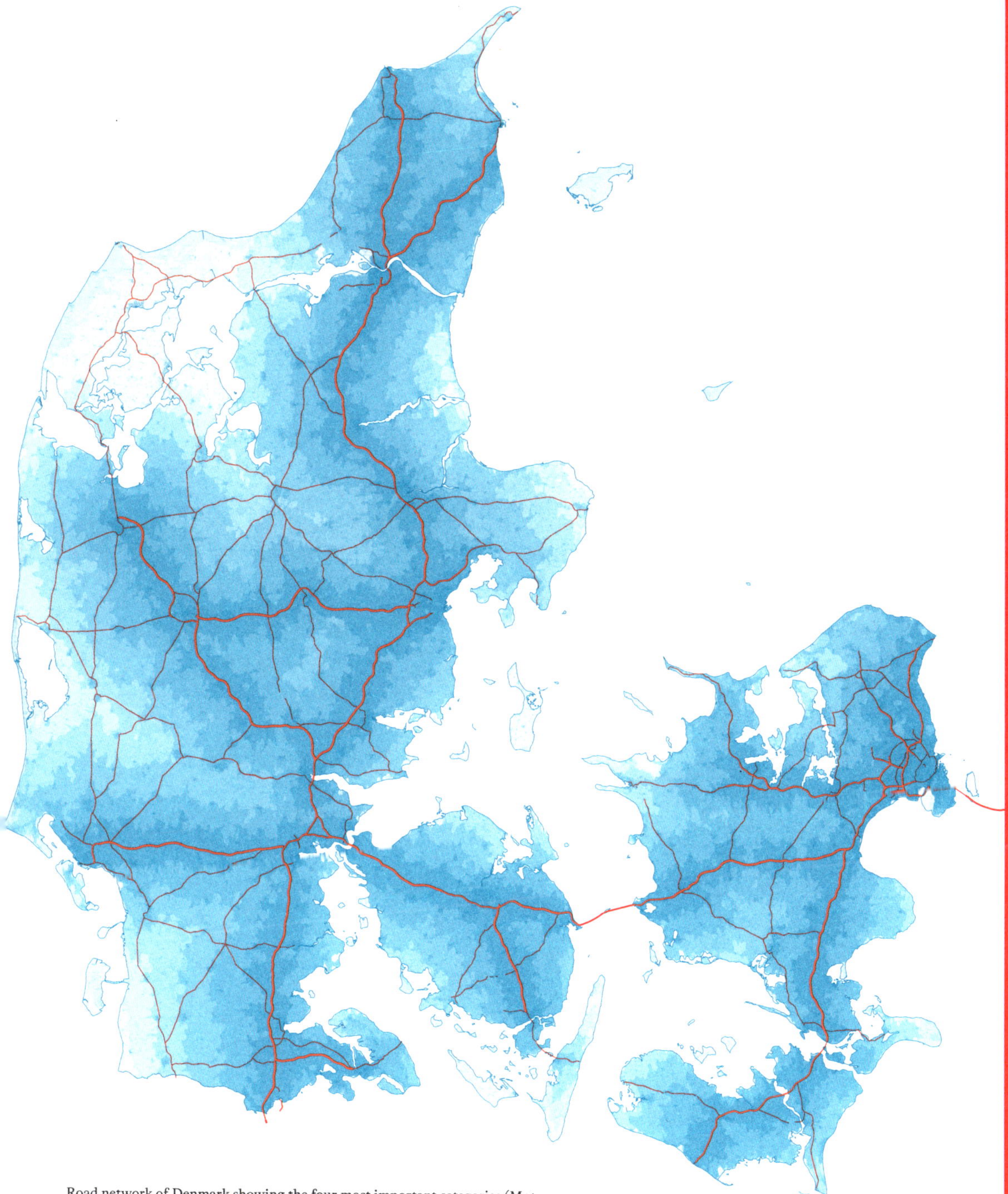

Road network of Denmark showing the four most important categories (Motorways, Trunk roads, Primary and Secondary roads). A gradient in line thickness refers to the speed that one can travel on these roads. Isochrones from blue to light blue to grey represent the distance to the closest highway exit/entrance.

0 25 km

Distance to closest highway exit/entrance
10 >50 min

Travel speed
30 130 km/h

2.02 Distribution of welfare institutions, 1970s

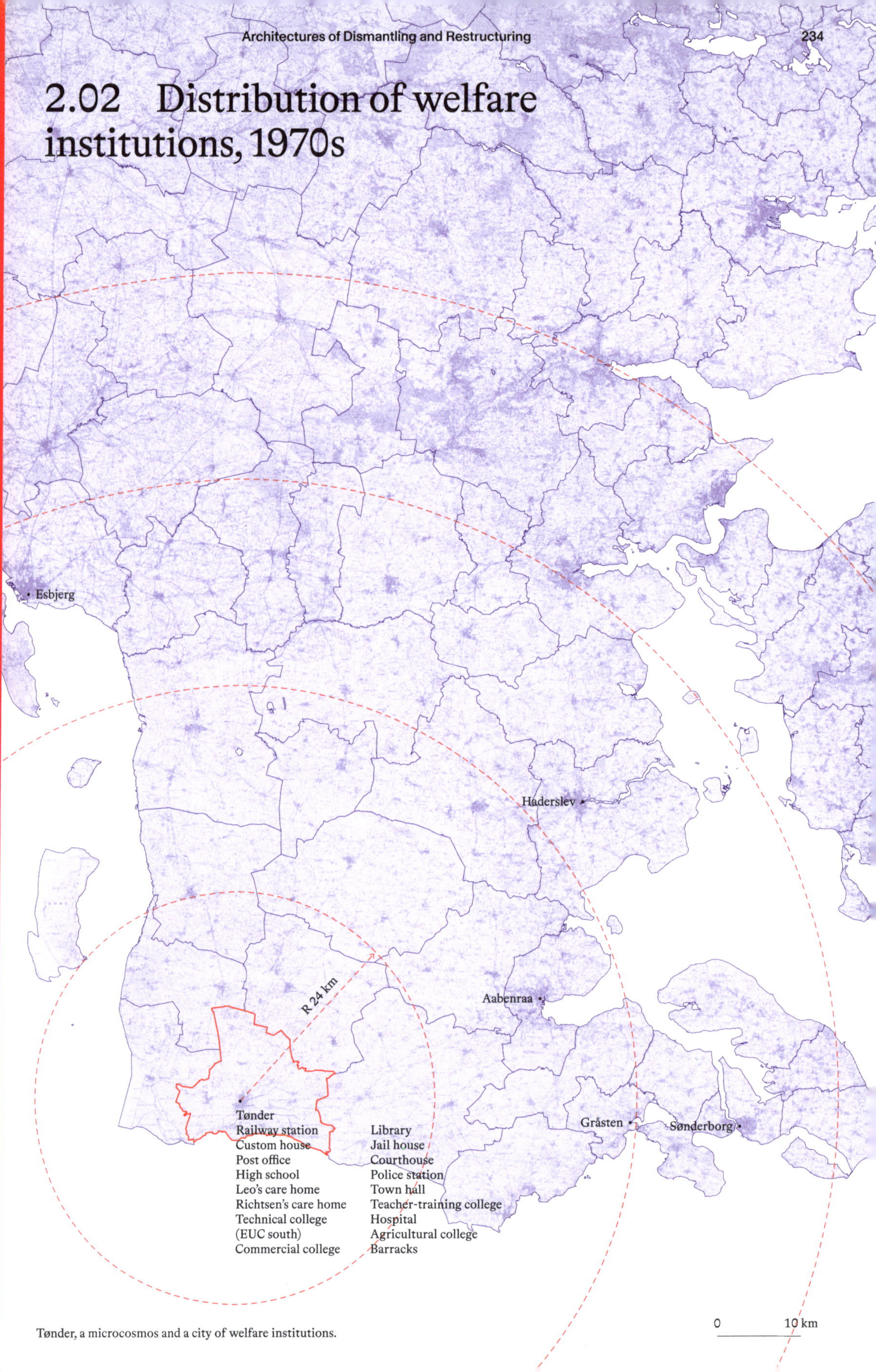

Tønder, a microcosmos and a city of welfare institutions.

2.03 Redistribution of welfare institutions due to centralization and structural reforms, 2020

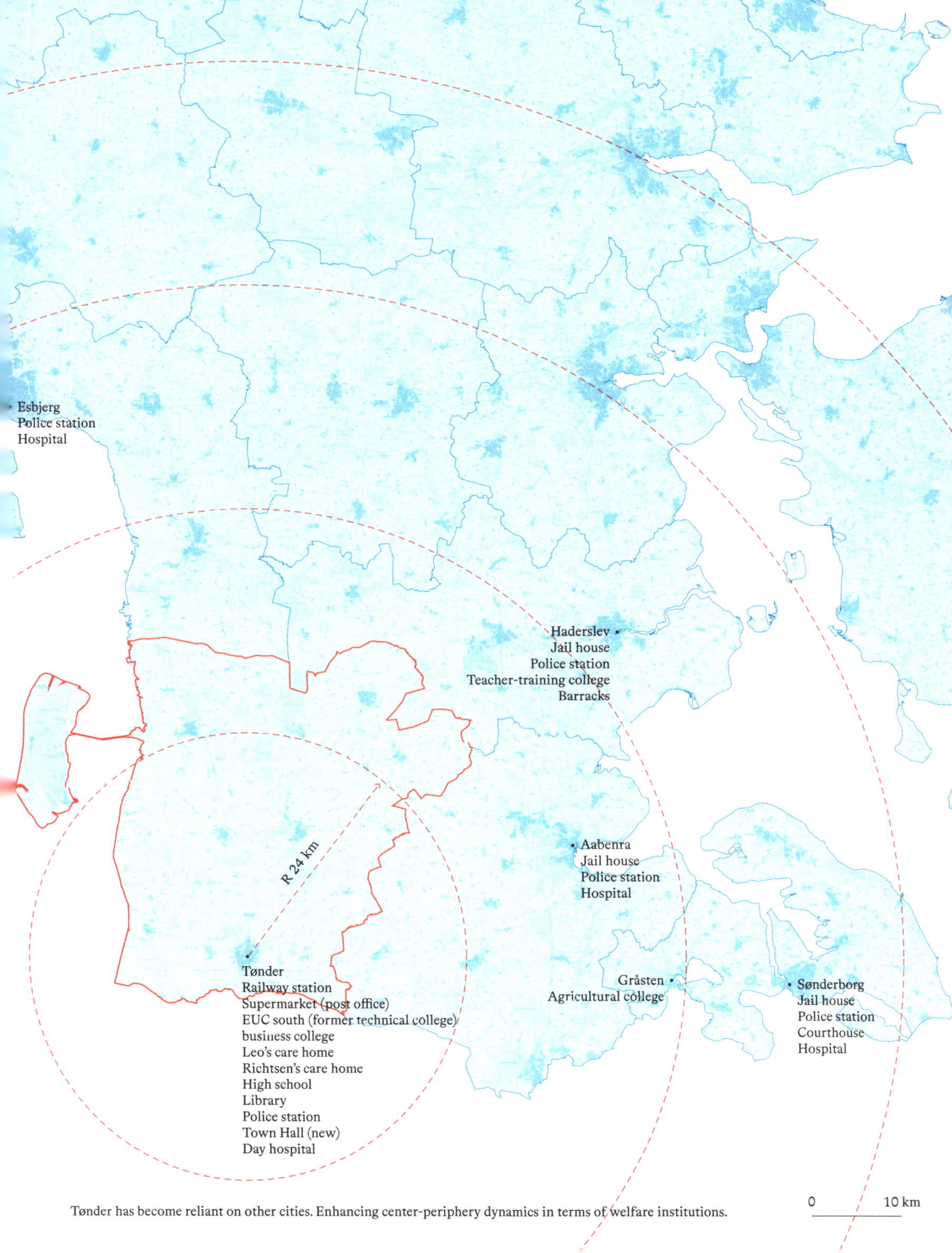

Tønder has become reliant on other cities. Enhancing center-periphery dynamics in terms of welfare institutions.

2.04 Routes to welfare institutions, 1970/2020

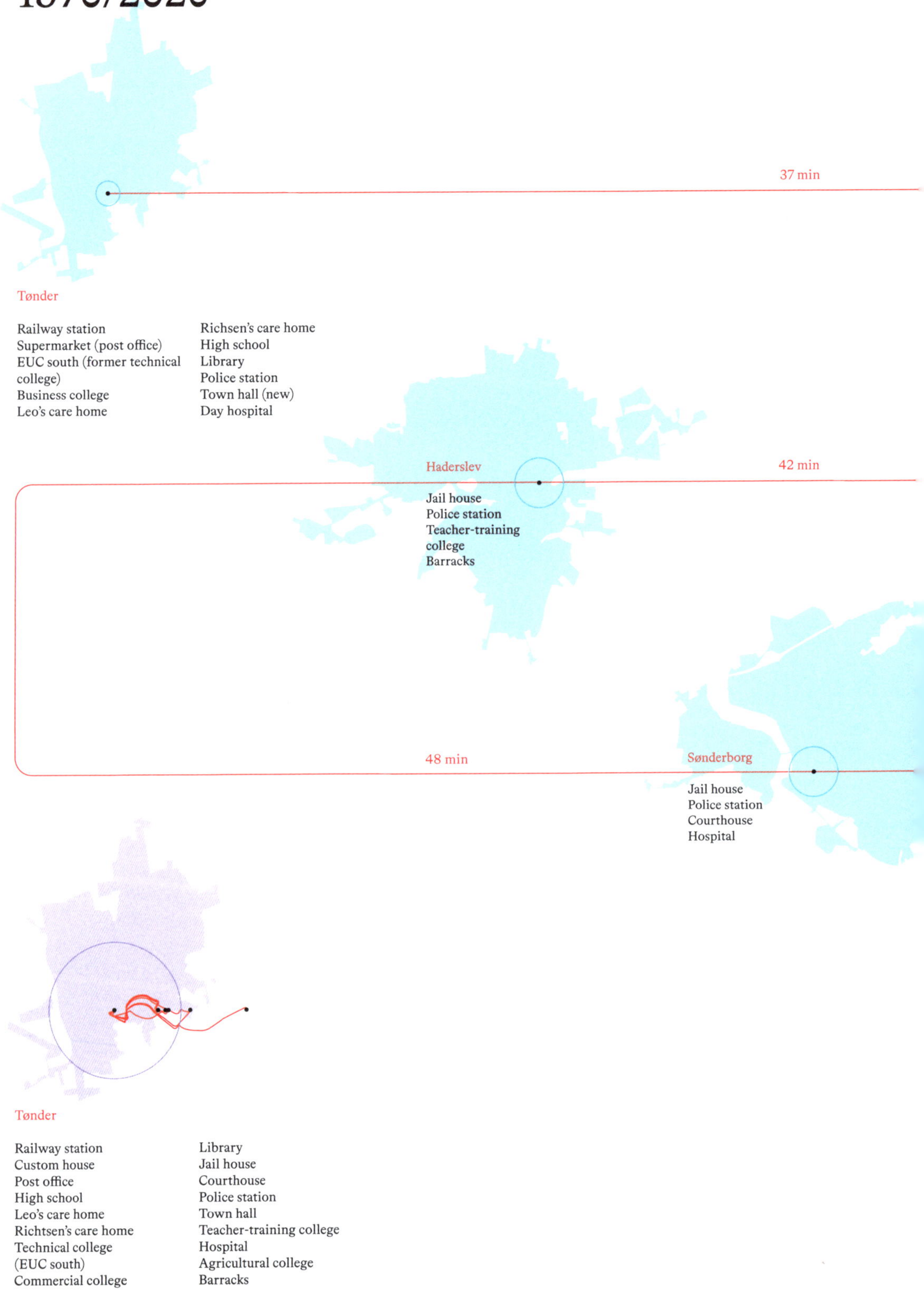

Aabenraa
Jail house
Police station
Hospital
Gråsten
Agricultural college
25 min
1 h 38 min
Esbjerg
Police station
Hospital
0 2 km

2.05 Welfare institutions in Tønder, 1970s

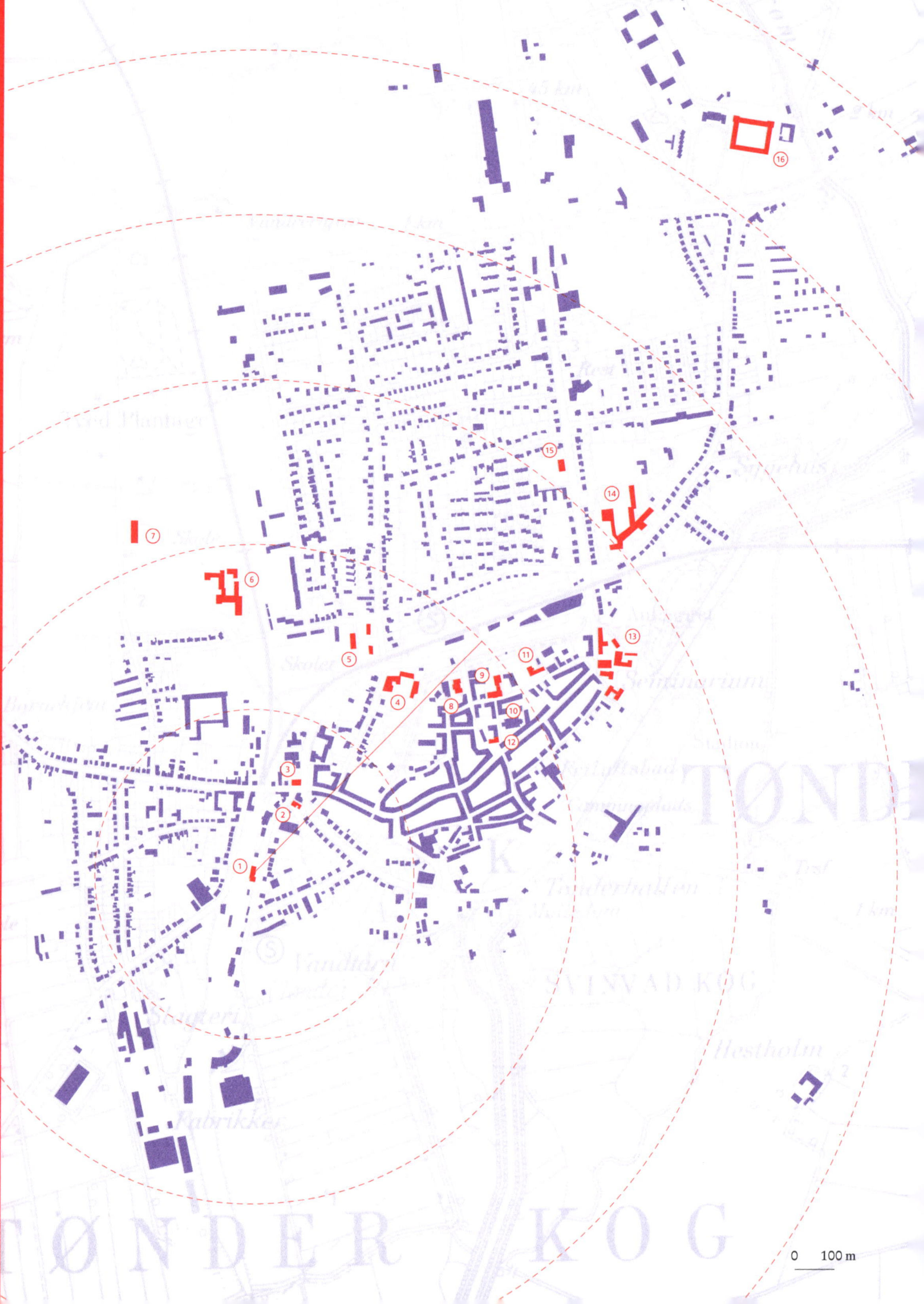

① Railway station (1899), built in 1890

② Custom house (1925), built in 1920

③ Post office (1899–1905), built in 1899

④ High school (1918), built in 1910

⑤ Leo's care home (1989), built in 1938

⑥ Established in 1920, formerly Teknisk Skole, now EUC South's department in Tønder

⑦ Business college (1966), built in 1966

⑧ German School, later Library (1950), built in 1643

⑨ Courthouse and jailhouse (1918), built in 1916

⑩ Girls' school, later Police station (1920), built in 1915

⑪ Town hall (old) (1860), built in 1643

⑫ Teacher-training college (1885), built in 1788

⑬ Hospital (1930), built in 1898

⑭ Agricultural college (1926), built in 1913

⑮ Barracks (1936), built in 1936

2.06 Tønder, urban context, 2020

1 Burger King, Nordre Landevej

2 McDonald's, Nordre Landevej

3 Schouws univers, shop, Østergade

4 Harvest in Ballum, countryside north of Tønder

5 "The Bronze Foot," just outside Tønder

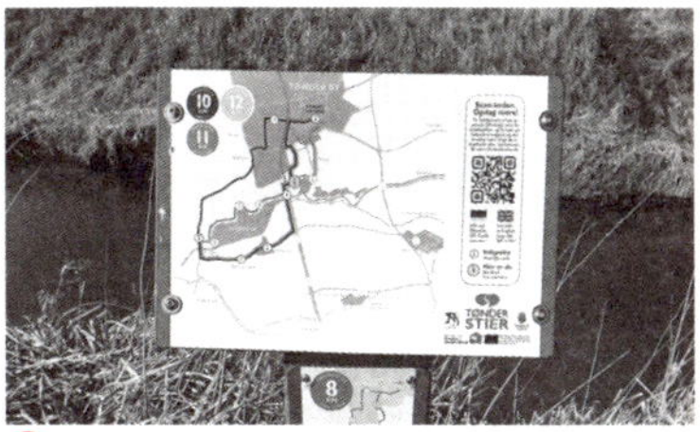

6 Sign south of Tønder, showing some of the pathways for walking tours in the marshlands

7 Traveling Tivoli at Rømø, north of Tønder

8 The marshlands and river Vidåen, south of Tønder

9 Replica of the sculpture "kagmanden"

10 Railway line in the marshlands south of Tønder

11 Renovation of Vidågade

12 Renovation of a park surrounding the city center

13 Sign showing panorama route no. 10 for bicycles, Østergade

14 Liebestempel

15 The police station

16 H&M in their recently opened store, Storegade

17 Shoe shop (recently closed), Storegade

18 Wooden pathway toward Søndergade

2.07 Presence of welfare institutions in Tønder, 1970s

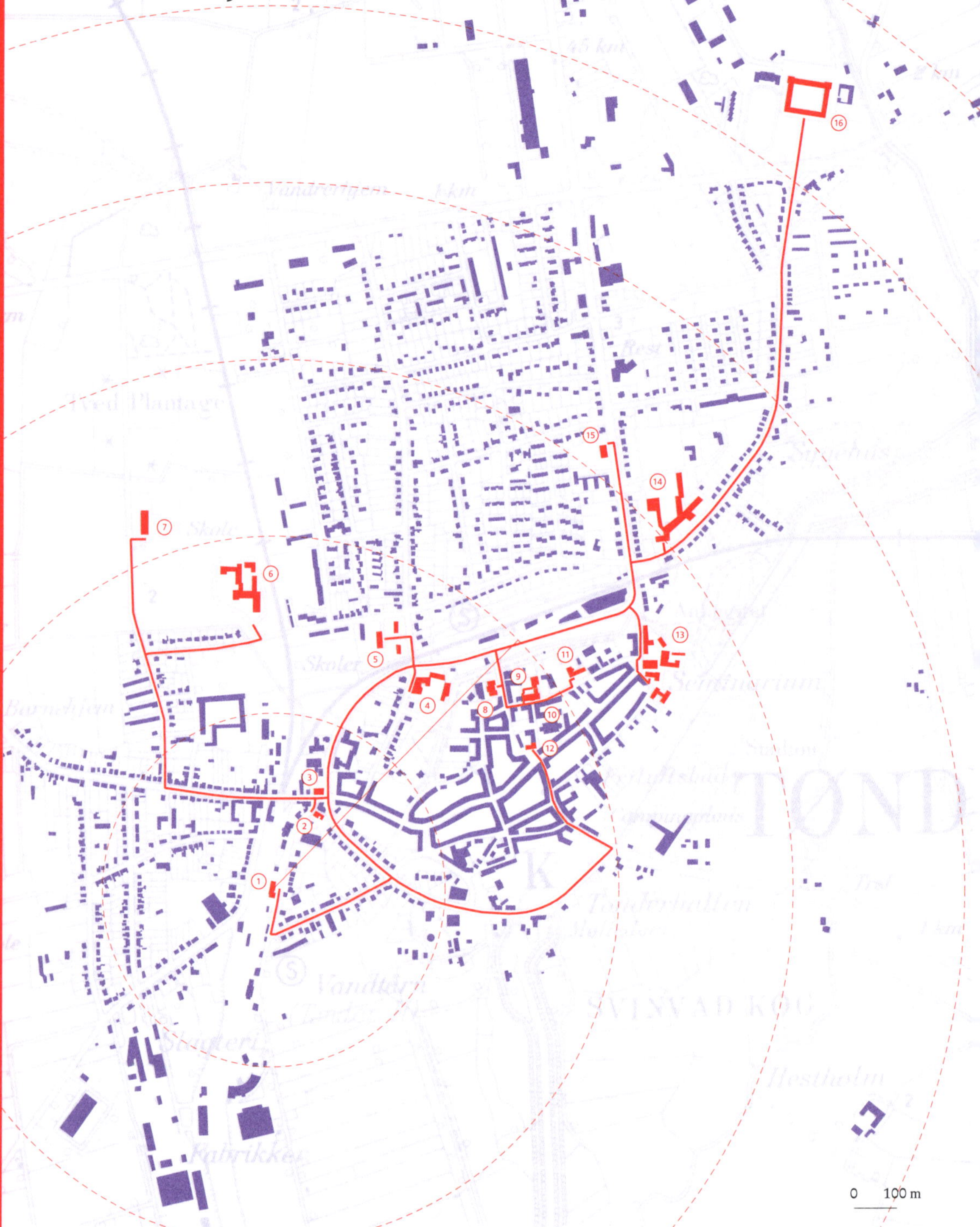

■ Welfare institutions

No.	Institution	Time
1	Railway station	
2	Custom house	0:02 h
3	Post office	0:02 h
4	High school	0:03 h
5	Leo's care home	0:03 h
6	Technical college	0:04 h
7	Business college	0:04 h
8	Library	0:03 h
9	Jail house	0:03 h
10	Courthouse	0:03 h
11	Police station	0:04 h
12	Town hall (old)	0:04 h
13	Teacher-training college	0:04 h
14	Hospital	0:05 h
15	Agricultural college	0:04 h
16	Barracks	0:06 h

2.08 Absence of welfare institutions in Tønder, 2020

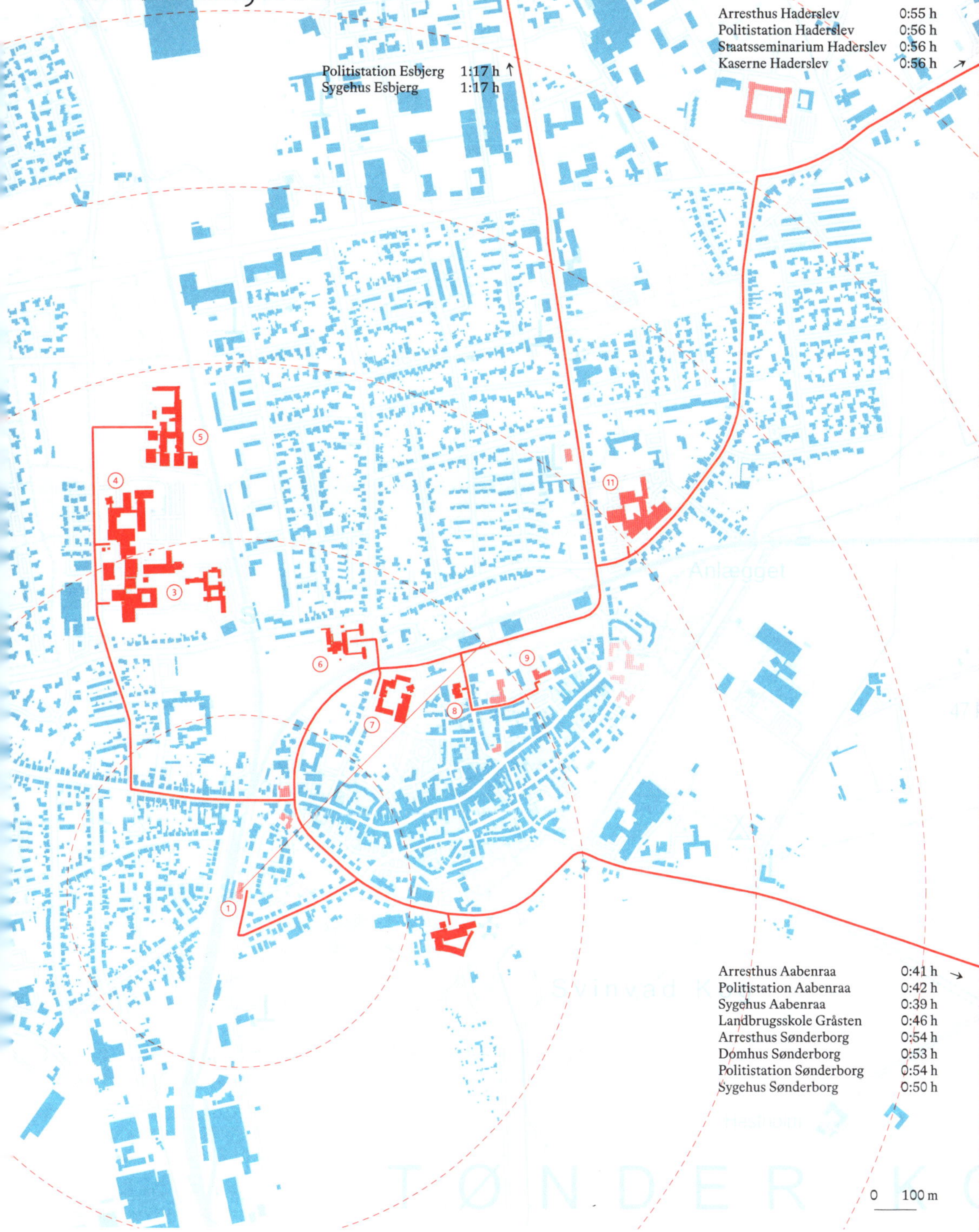

Welfare institutions
Diminished
Transformed
Abandoned

1. Railway station
2. Supermarket (post office) 0:04 h
3. EUC south (former technical college) 0:04 h
4. Business school 0:04 h
5. Richtsen's care home 0:05 h
6. Leo's care home 0:03 h
7. High school 0:03 h
8. Library 0:03 h
9. Police station 0:04 h
10. Town hall (new) 0:01 h
11. Day hospital 0:05 h

2.09 Construction dates of buildings that housed selected welfare institutions in Tønder in relation to the territorial changes

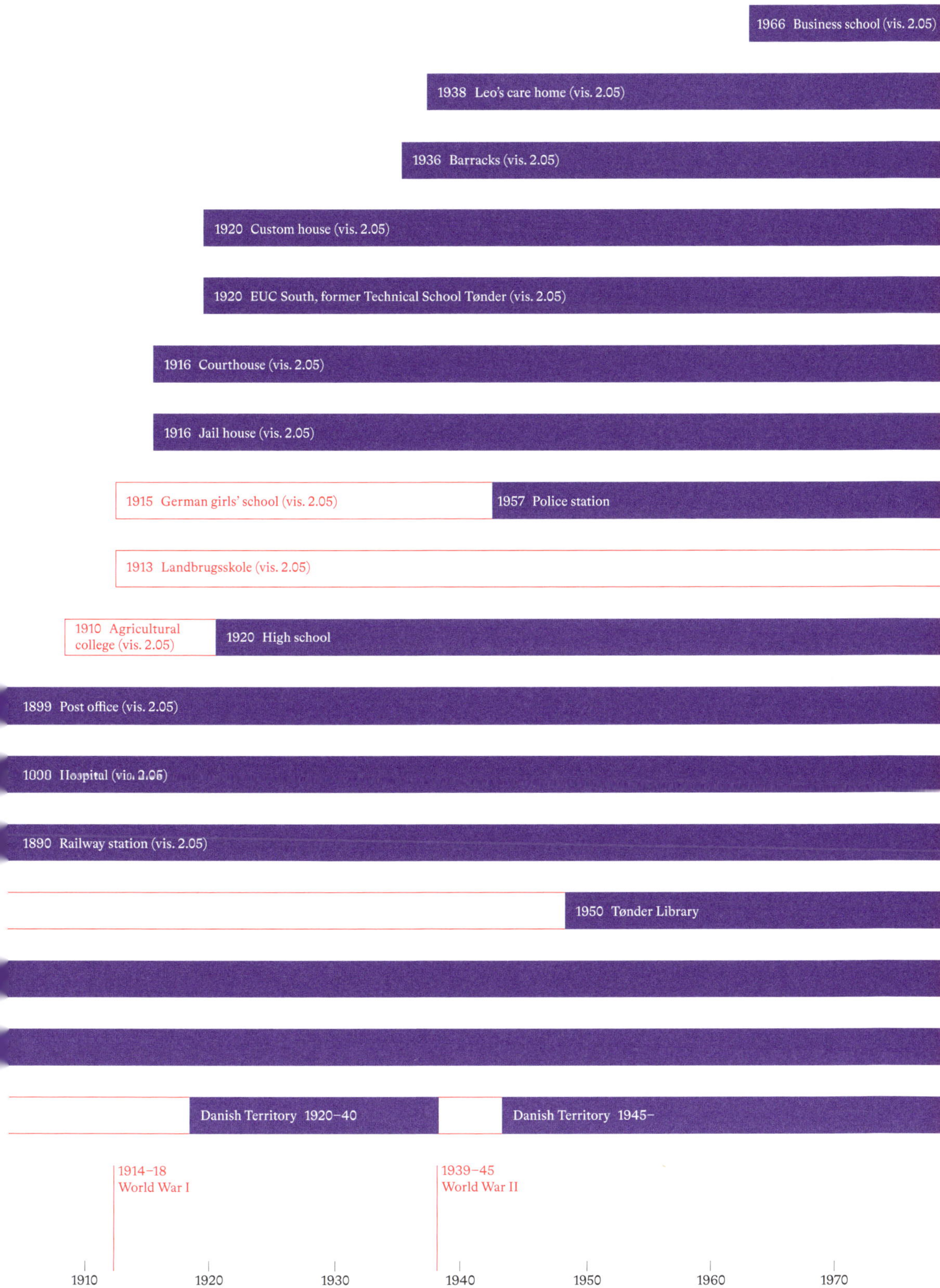
1966 Business school (vis. 2.05)
1938 Leo's care home (vis. 2.05)
1936 Barracks (vis. 2.05)
1920 Custom house (vis. 2.05)
1920 EUC South, former Technical School Tønder (vis. 2.05)
1916 Courthouse (vis. 2.05)
1916 Jail house (vis. 2.05)
1915 German girls' school (vis. 2.05)
1957 Police station
1913 Landbrugsskole (vis. 2.05)
1910 Agricultural college (vis. 2.05)
1920 High school
1899 Post office (vis. 2.05)
Hospital
1890 Railway station (vis. 2.05)
1950 Tønder Library
Danish Territory 1920–40
Danish Territory 1945–
1914–18 World War I
1939–45 World War II
1910
1920
1930
1940
1950
1960
1970

2.10 Presence and absence of selected welfare institutions in Tønder

Stayed the same/enlarged Diminished Abandoned Transformed

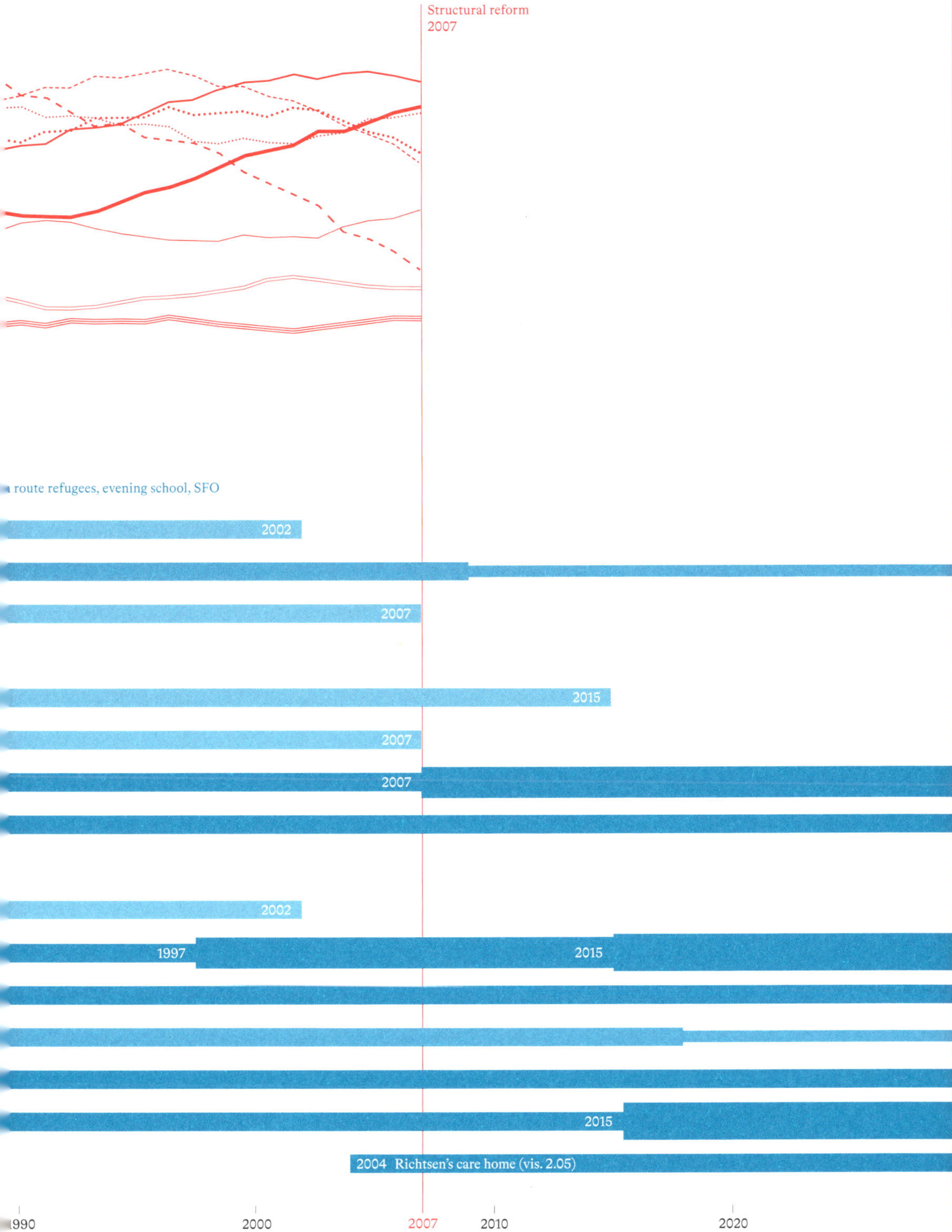
Structural reform
2007
a route refugees, evening school, SFO
2002
2007
2015
2007
2007
2002
1997
2015
2015
2004 Richtsen's care home (vis. 2.05)
1990
2000
2007
2010
2020

2.11 Tønderstierne, a landscape of experience in addition to a landscape of farming, 2020

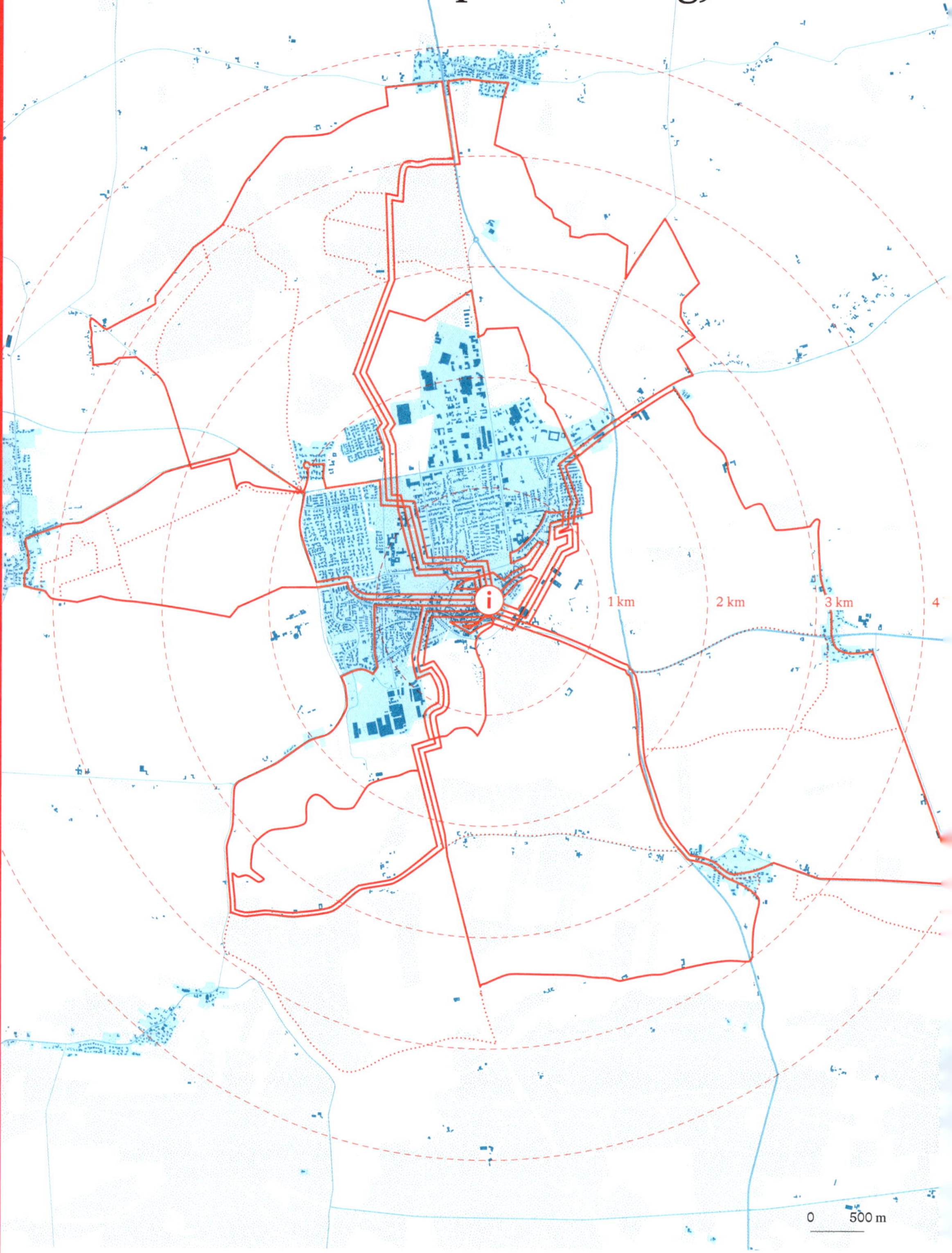

2.12

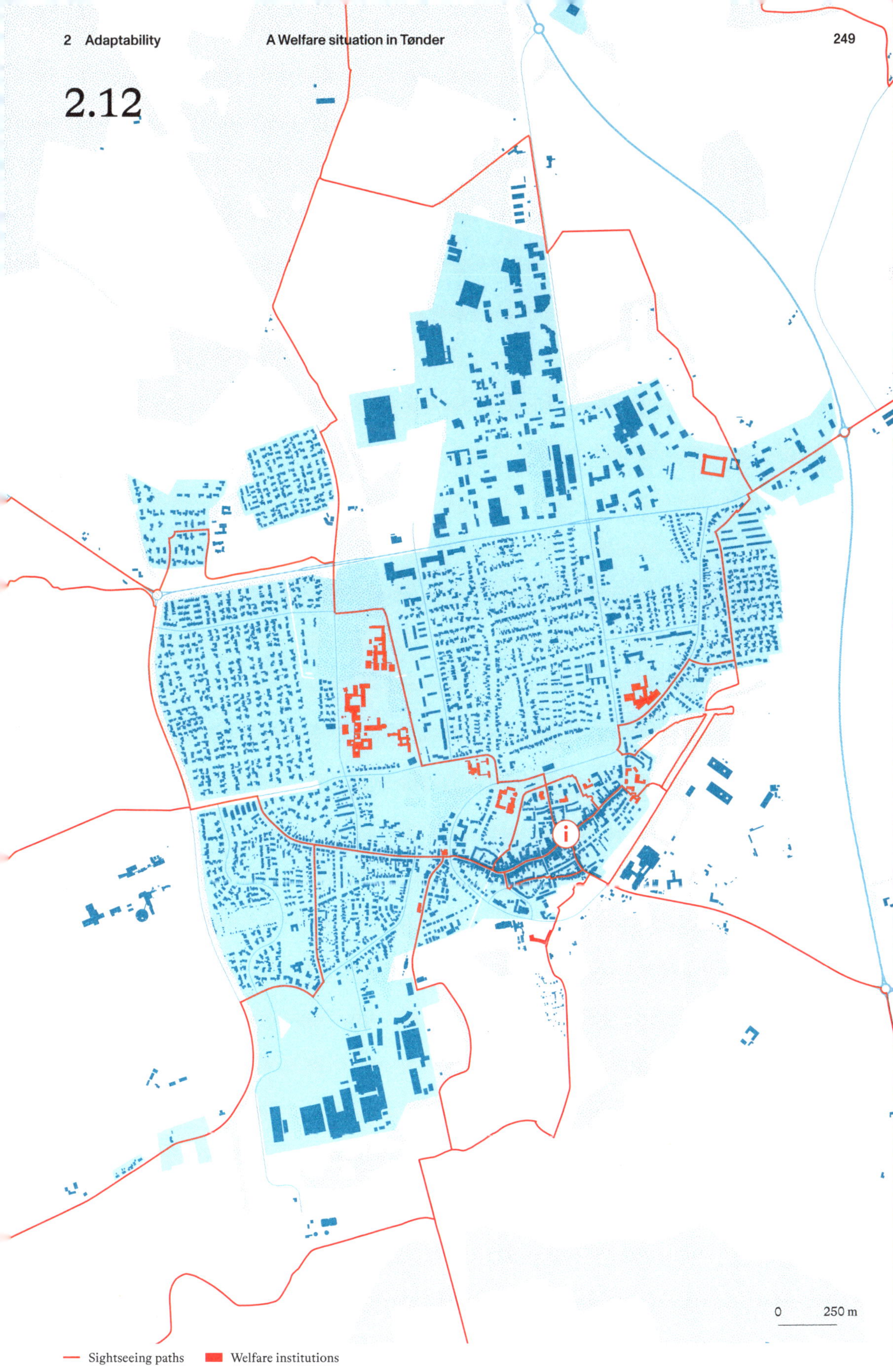

From Purgatory to District Heating

Extending the Last Journey within the Danish Welfare State

Niels Grønbæk

How is death dealt with in the Danish welfare state? What characterizes attitudes toward and thinking about death within the welfare state? Far from offering comprehensive answers to these questions, this chapter looks for patterns in how the handling of death and the human corpse is reflected within and through the architectural expression of a significant new Danish crematorium, *Fælleskrematoriet* (The Common Crematorium) completed in 2013 in the town of Ringsted.

Fælleskrematoriet is chosen as a specific architectural actualization of the typology and function of the crematorium, offering a prism for uncovering an otherwise obscure heterogeneous set of aspects of the various ways death and the human corpse are integrated in contemporary Danish society. Concomitantly, I consider the specific renegotiation of the raison d'être of the crematorium to provide a rich composite research object. The object of investigation will not be space as an exclusively architectural concern, but architecture's implication in the specific complex multilayered "crematorium artifact," materializing a contemporary reflection of human death. Nevertheless, the architectural is considered to offer not only a unique contour providing a relatively clear entry point into a problematic which is not clear in itself; architecture as potentially offering a nontechnical engagement with an otherwise seemingly technically oriented design of the cremation process weighs in.

Exterior Relations of Welfare

In Denmark crematoria are either municipally run or indirectly managed by the Folkekirken (The Evangelical-Lutheran Church in Denmark). They are not directly financed via tax but forced by law to operate as nonprofit, nonsubsidized enterprises[1] with an obligation to provide cost-efficient production on a balanced budget and to offer relatively inexpensive cremation.[2] Hence, the services provided by modern crematoria such as *Fælleskrematoriet* are normally not included among the standard services and welfare amenities offered by the Danish State. However, the various institutions tied to cremation can certainly be said to be integrated into the Danish state in that the services provided by crematoria are indeed strictly state-monitored – as is only to be expected. Currently eight out of ten Danish citizens will eventually pass through a crematorium oven. What happens here demands thorough institutionalization, and this institutionalization is fully inscribed in the regulatory complex of the Danish state. Additionally, the technical aspects of cremation are carefully monitored: for example, fumes stemming from the cremation process are filtered according to new standards from Miljøstyrelsen (The Danish Environmental Protection Agency).[3]

Before engaging in an analysis of the case, certain methodological considerations are called for. One way of researching death in the welfare state would be to focus on how the current institutionalization of death contributes to and is integrated into the Danish universal welfare state[4] – for example, asking questions such as How does the institutionalization of human death contribute to the degree of universality of the Danish welfare state?[5] However, the very category of the universal welfare state will in this context be dismissed as an instance of what the philosopher Manuel DeLanda calls a "reified generality" based on deductive "taxonomic essentialism."[6] In the words of DeLanda:

> Avoiding the use of concepts like "the state" is important not only because such reified generalities are not legitimate ontological entities but also because such notions are too monolithic, that is, they fail to capture the relations of exteriority that exist among the heterogeneous organizations forming a government hierarchy. Without an adequate notion of this heterogeneity, for example, we could make the mistake of thinking that there is no gap between the formulation of public policy and its actual implementation.[7]

As the point of departure will here be an aspect of the spatialization of human death in contemporary Denmark, *welfare*, *welfare state* and *welfare society* as ideas will be considered as merely discursive scholarly and political objects with little concrete spatial and material reality.[8] The content of this chapter thus relates to spaces of Danish welfare indirectly, as the concept *welfare* is here considered a discursive formation – avoiding the label "reified generality" only through each of its actualizations as an actant[9] within academia and political discourse.[10] This heresy finds further support in the fact that *welfare* as word and concept has only limited presence in the wordings of the law corpus *de jure* regulating Denmark – lost as it is in the heterogeneous gaps of translation between policymaking, applicable law and spatial material manifestation.[11] In a Danish context *velfærd* (welfare) is a scholarly and political concept much more than a legal one.[12]

Thus, the approach adopted here turns the motivation for spaces of Danish welfare as a research object on its head by claiming that the main reason why this subject seems somewhat underresearched might not be due to its hitherto finding itself in an academic blind spot. Rather, spatial manifestation operates at a different level than reified generalities such as those based on the concept of welfare – *spatial manifestation* and *concept* being ontologically distinguishable in a flat ontology – another philosophical concept coined by DeLanda. As pointed out by the educational theorist Felicity Armstrong, policy "is not something made by government and handed down through government agencies ready-made. Policy is paradoxical, the product of struggles and contradictions. It is made at many levels in society."[13]

The state is no well-defined Big Brother. Instead of considering the welfare state as something that can be meaningfully defined conceptually, it would maybe make sense to trace a welfare dispositive in struggles and contradictions made at many levels of society.[14] The more modest methodological approach I adopt here is to not leave out "the messiness, variety and unpredictability of policies as they are enacted through social practice" but rather to make expressive a heterogeneity of aspects stemming from an analysis of *Fælleskrematoriet*.[15] Some of these aspects will relate directly to *Fælleskrematoriet* as an architecture, some will relate to the uncovering of some of the conditions for its existence, and others again to how it reflects public sustainability concerns. Later, aspects in this heterogeneous set will be reassembled conceptually – in order to conceptualize from historically materialized aspects rather than merely guiding the exploration via conceptual lenses. This also implies looking for "relations of exteriority" in the heterogeneity of aspects produced through the analysis.

Based on the assemblage theoretical approach adopted here it is less important to collect evidence of how people experience the spatialization of human death as actualized through *Fælleskrematoriet*, and more important to uncover how ways of thinking about – and attitudes toward – death are reflected in the spatial expressions of the various institutions meeting citizens.[16] However, the theoretical engagement with assemblage theory is initially motivated less by the possibility of analyzing the case in question as an assemblage in DeLanda's understanding, yet neither as a seamless whole. Rather, it seeks opportunity in an approach to analysis that takes a step in the direction of preparing a flat ontology of individuals based on the crematorium entity under scrutiny; or even a heterogeneous "mere collection of things" – in assemblage theory understood as a set of discrete elements with no relations of exteriority between them.[17] Thus, it is attempted, through analysis, to arrive at a "flatter" understanding of the specific artifact of cremation in focus than the architectural contour of the actual crematorium building suggests. However, the analysis will also distinguish a number of spatial perspectives such as cremation as seen from rituals of death, the spatialization of cremation as "production," smoke filtering, catchment area, hearse design, and the crematorium in view of relatives. The analysis of these spatializations are mainly captured in the visuals and accompanying descriptions of this chapter.

Flattening *Fælleskrematoriet*

Judging from the arguments for the new crematorium, it was never the intention that it should foremost be a contemporary architectural expression of human death. Here, the expression of the crematorium as a building is considered a side aspect – a visible object form or end form arrived at through the computation of the sum of programmatic[18] concerns negotiated on the way toward the built synthesis.[19] In fact, the crudeness of an early design, based on a set of merely pragmatic concerns – for example, technical, economic and logistical – lead to a shift in design direction.[20] *Fælleskrematoriet* owes its existence to the launch of a more restrictive law on environment protection. Before its realization, a change in the legal framework regulating crematorium operation in terms of investor collaboration was needed. Paving the way through the adoption of two new laws by the Danish parliament, the collaboration between eight dioceses eventually became a reality and soon after resulted in the patching together of eight local catchment areas into one regional catchment area for the new super crematorium.

A spatial and architectural analysis of *Fælleskrematoriet* soon brings to light a certain tension between its geographic position in this new and much expanded catchment area, expressing the spatial implications of a technical or "scale-up" logic of industrial centralization, and then the architectural celebration of the possible presence of relatives and other visitors in the crematorium. Adding to its architectural preparedness for visitors, the house rules prescribe full on-demand accessibility and transparency for all visitors at all times during regular opening hours.[21] This suggests an inverse proportionality relative to the very expanse of the catchment area of the new crematorium, hence discouraging hour-long itineraries for most relatives. The result is fewer visitors to the premises than in the days of multiple small, decentralized crematoria. Yet the few insistent long-distance visitors of today are – different from what was the case in the days of small local crematoria – embraced all the more in terms of process transparency and the architecturally designed atmosphere of *Fælleskrematoriet* receiving them.

Seen in conjunction, the logic of centralizing and scaling-up of production and, further, the decision to position the crematorium in an industrial area and the integration of the crematorium into the local district heating infrastructure, point toward grounding the crematorium in the technical and pragmatic. Against this, the architectural crafting of the atmosphere of the building actually seems to have been guided by a wish to maintain an echo of death as connected to a sacral realm. Yet rather than architecturally building up a tension between an expression of the serene, dignified, modestly sacral, and the technically determined design richly present in *Fælleskrematoriet*, it is as if the architecture merely adds a flavor of the sacral to cover the technical. With a veil of dignity and modest solemnity, the architecture covers the bluntly prosaic expression of commonsensical technical thinking actualized through the careful technical logistical design of this artifact.[22] Rather than engaging with what happens in these ovens – engaging in the sense of recasting it, reactualizing a relation to it – this architecture seems to disguise it.

Already from its introduction in the late nineteenth century, the crematorium has held an uneasy position between death and rational thinking – a tension between pathos, purpose and pragmatics. In Denmark as elsewhere the motivation for cremation was initially related to hygienic issues relative to increased burial pressure on limited cemetery space located in urban centers – also being an issue of hygiene pertaining to the decomposition of substantial numbers of buried corpses.[23] The positioning of *Fælleskrematoriet* in an industrial area at the urban periphery of Ringsted further expands the spatial horizontalization of the handling of the human corpse initiated by the strategic positioning and construction of the first crematoria servicing cemeteries in the main urban centers. Relating *Fælleskrematoriet* to the local district heating grid also seems to contribute to this lasting spatial tendency.

Whereas new demands for filtering smoke produced during cremation, in effect making it invisible, can be said to somehow enter into resonance with the sacral, this is less the case for the ministerial approval of connecting *Fælleskrematoriet* to the local district heating grid. As pointed out by Etisk Råd (The Danish Council on Ethics) consulted by the Ministry of Ecclesiastic Affairs on this matter prior to the decision to build, the way this works technically does not suggest a direct exploiting of corpses for heating. As the council bluntly states, "the bodies are not used as fuel."[24] It is the technical fact that the natural gas, without which cremation would not be possible, is an added resource that makes the difference for Etisk Råd. As often pointed out, the real contribution to heating by crematoria is in fact very limited – to the point where the primary concern seems to be a rhetorical green gesture of not wasting energy.

A number of official answers to inquiries from Danish citizens to the relevant ministerial authority mostly seeking permission to dispose of the ashes of near relatives on private property testifies to some discrepancy between people's wishes and what the authorities are willing to accept within the shallow margins of interpretation of the law.[25] It is in this respect worth noticing that Danish law on the one hand is spatially restrictive regarding ash disposal by private citizens, but on the other hand permits and supports rationalizations of the transport of corpses in multicoffin hearses and that crematoria in a number of places have been connected to local district heating grids.

The architecture of *Fælleskrematoriet* is structured by the compositional interaction of a line and a point. The line carries a logic of production, of process and of transition relating to the corpses passing through. However, it is functionally and ritually somewhat awkward and less pleasing that the urns containing ashes most often will leave the building the same way the dead bodies arrive. The logo combining the name *Fælleskrematoriet* with the contour of the building seems to capture this tension: While reading of the name ends to the right, the cremation process as inscribed in the building contour included in the logo ends with the characteristic chimney to the left. Because the smoke emanating from the actual chimney is in fact invisible, as all particles with visible qualities have been filtered out, it might seem as if this chimney is a mere simulacrum, which in fact it is not. Architecturally, it nevertheless performs a simulacrum – a built, only vaguely iconic image of the primary characteristic of a crematorium. Intentionally or not, this allows a reading of the design of this complex artifact as performing the integration of death into the welfare society as unresolvedly caught between the technical dematerialization of the human corpse and a symbolic rather than architectural expression of this process.

The space of the oven hall architecturally presents an atmosphere of the modestly sacral, whereas the basement presents an expression of technical design – dominated by the machinery for the treatment of the smoke produced during cremations. Most striking from an architectural point of view is that these two immediately adjacent spaces, above and below, expressing concern for the proper treatment of dead bodies through the deployment of the process called cremation in such radically different ways, has not been the question to engage with architecturally. The way this difference is treated architecturally suggests that the architect has not found a compositional opportunity in the tensions between technical design relative to a millennia-long series of architectural expressions devoted to human death since the early pyramidal era.

Radically different from a well-established reading of these pyramidal building excesses as huge, most likely slavery-based enterprises, transforming the relative horizontality of the Nile culture into verticalizing infrastructures of Pharaonic immortality, an enterprise such as *Fælleskrematoriet* seems to exemplify a shift toward integrating death into the commonsensical and technical realms of the contemporary Danish welfare state. The effect of its architecture seems to be to mitigate much more than engage in the creation of conditions for reflections on attitude toward the human corpse and death.

Undertaking a Service to Cover over a Taboo

In "Bodies and Ceremonies: Is the UK funeral industry still fit for purpose?" the sociologist Tony Walter speculates on the role of the undertaker. For Walter, undertaking the handling of almost everything concerning the direct confrontation with death and with a relative as dead makes the undertaker the keeper of a space of avoidance at the core of the service, and indeed the very business model of undertaking.[26] Also cremation

1

2

3

4

5

6

7

1 *Fælleskrematoriet* seen from north-east
Chimney – The main chimney of the crematorium features architecturally prominently in its profile. The smoke emanating from it is in fact invisible as all particles with visible qualities have been filtered out. Only invisible CO and CO_2 passes through.
2 Fire hydrant directly in front of the crematorium.
3 Presentation of *Fælleskrematoriet*.
4 Presentation of *Fælleskrematoriet*.
5 The crematorium "coffin lobby." Undertakers are not allowed beyond this space.
6 Presentation of *Fælleskrematoriet*.
7 Relatives – Presence of relatives in the crematorium – although fully welcomed – is quite rare. The crematorium has a modest chapel room with a catafalque offering relatives the opportunity to perform a ceremony.

8

8 The now closed crematorium in Holbæk. Due to economic concerns vis-a-vis forced investments in environmental protection, representatives from two Zealand bishoprics decided to close seven small local crematoria.
9 The dark metal covered blocks of the five ovens – stripped of most features of "oven" – placed under a roof structure catching the natural light on its undulating whitish underbelly. Five ovens perform six cremations a day.
10 Handling of the coffins are highly automated. At *Fælleskrematoriet* a cremation is executed at 1,100° C. and lasts approx. 75 minutes. The combustion process happens through the addition of natural gas. On average, each of the five ovens perform six cremations a day.

9

10

11

12

13

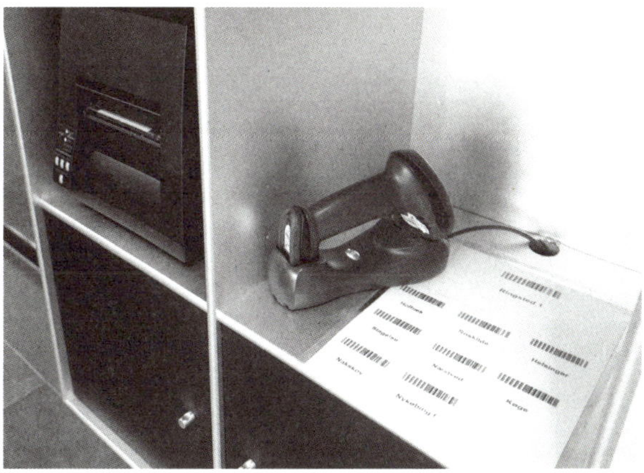

14

11 The basement holds all the technical equipment – dominated by the machinery for the treatment of the smoke produced during cremations.
12 Ash cooling shelves. Unlike, for example, Finland or the UK, Denmark has a restrictive law relative to the disposal of cremains. In general, disposal is only allowed at designated places such as churchyards and cemeteries.
13 Rerecycling of surgical implants made of high-quality metals is a sub-sector in which a Dutch company has taken the lead – collecting from 700 crematoria. Lately, the first pet crematorium has also joined the ranks. *Fælleskrematoriet* is also a subscriber.
14 Upon arrival and before short-term storage, each coffin is labeled with a unique bar code.

plays an important role in the transition that happens during the conveniently hidden activities of the undertaker. Relatives will leave the handling of the corpse to an undertaker, who will return an urn with the ashes of the cremated body. The job of the undertaker has to some extent become similar to that of the police, garbage collecting and infrastructure maintenance. It is commonly appreciated that these services are provided; however, the less present they are in our everyday lives, the better. It is as if even a sense of at least enacting the taboo has been covered over by the impression of the undertaker's providing a service.[27]

In the case of *Fælleskrematoriet* this is further complicated due to the centralization of transportation.[28] Still, the coffin will be collected locally by an undertaker after, for example, a religious ritual but then taken to a local "in transit" cooling room, from where a special hearse, of an inconspicuous gray, metallic color with room for four coffins, will take the dead person together with (up to) three other dead persons to the central crematorium. Cooling relates to the time it takes to collect four bodies. Transport follows certain routes, and hearse drivers are instructed to avoid rush hours and not to take breaks during transport. This all happens in reverse order upon return, now with the urns, so that, again, it will most likely be the local undertaker whom relatives will meet – thus avoiding a scenario in which relatives could have an "urn bus" experience.

Not only is a screen of local undertaking covering over the experiential impact of a rationalized cremation industry. What is further covered over is the very irrationality added by the rationale of spatial centralization when it comes to transport – as exactly all the transport carried out by the new hearses is to be added to the amount of transport from before centralization. Today, relatives from the periphery of the catchment area wishing to witness the cremation of the deceased might face travel times with public transport of three hours each way. In terms of environment protection, the material resources going into the production of the new hearses should be added as well as additional wear and tear on the road system. Derived from this comes the question of the material resources that went into the new crematorium building itself. In terms of the argumentation behind the new crematorium, everything seems to follow rational thinking, but how rational is it in fact? Does it rather present an image of rationalization that the decision makers just happened to believe in? If that is the case, then the questions become: where did this mere image of rationalization with sufficient power to make all of this happen come from, and from where does it operate? Has there been a disposition at work in the decision chains, which in the guise of rationalization – in this case based on environmental concerns – in fact materializes images of a mere rhetoric of rationalization and very real environmental problems?[29]

Emerging Changes

The historian Philippe Ariès has uncovered a plasticity in attitudes in Western societies relative to human death. Also in a Danish context, it makes sense to historicize human attitudes toward death.[30] Thus, statistical evidence suggests a significant change in attitudes toward cremation in Denmark around 1910.[31] From being illegal and considered barbaric and heretical around 1890, cremation is today popular to the extent that even in the least densely populated areas of the country, more than 70 percent of the deceased are cremated – increasing to more than 90 percent in densely populated urban centers. For Ariès one of the most dramatic changes in attitude toward death in Western societies took place at the beginning of the twentieth century. A death-embracing attitude nurtured during the Romantic era was replaced by the downright eradication of death from common experience, being incompatible with modern preferences for rationalization and youth-celebrating lifestyles.[32] Ariès argues that an era otherwise characterized by general processes of demystification and disenchantment and in favor of rationalization and transparency seems to have inflicted a taboo on the experience of death among the living: "Death, so omnipresent in the past that it was familiar, would be effaced, would disappear. It would become shameful and forbidden."[33] As has been pointed out, the new trend probably also found indirect support in massive improvements in public health to the effect that death would further disappear from everyday life.[34]

If not fully an assemblage, then spatial relations of exteriority between various component parts seems to be at work in the case of *Fælleskrematoriet*. Among the components are cremation as technique; the role of the undertaker; challenges to the ritualistic inclusion of longer and more complicated routes of the "last journey" due to centralized cremation and a relatively restrictive law regulating what relatives are allowed to do with the ashes of their loved ones. A process of estrangement or neutralization of the human corpse, following a slow transformation of a taboo into a smoothly operating service provided by authorities and undertakers might indicate an emergent property – referring to a key feature in DeLanda's assemblage theoretical understanding – and thus an assemblage at work,[35] slowly mainstreaming new attitudes toward death and the human corpse.

Another assemblage also seems to be at work – more pragmatic than spatial. From the early modern days of cremation in Europe, the main arguments supporting this new technique were rational and technical. These seem to prevail more than a century after the first crematorium in the country was built. It includes pragmatic components such as productivity, hygiene, enlarging a catchment area, the design of four-coffin hearses, smoke-cleansing standards, low price for cremation, cremation contributing to district heating and, finally, systematic recycling of high-quality metal implants[36] – occasionally finding new purpose in critical parts of jet engines.[37] A certain pragmatics of death seems to emerge. Less an emergent property of a discursive assemblage of cremation, this development seems to stem from a dispositional tendency in processes of institutionalization within the Danish state, including the Danish Council on Ethics.[38]

To conclude this chapter, I tentatively suggest bringing two different aspects of cremation together as component parts in a relation of exteriority: one pertaining to the perspective of relatives, and the other to the perspective of the crematorium as an enterprise. This might allow an attitude to death which happily embraces relations between cremation and jet engines, to meet the attitude behind the restrictive laws that confront relatives when making applications to authorities in the hope of being allowed to place an urn under a tree in their garden. Danish laws pertaining to citizens' private handling of ashes after cremation seems to maintain a state-guaranteed echo of respect for the dead not reflected in new laws facilitating the rationalization of cremation. Within the sphere of death, state level legislation reinforces an increasingly sharp distinction between what is more and more openly inscribed in a logic of production, which, however, does not allow a resulting rhetoric of product. By guarding and amplifying its right to rule by double standard, the Danish state reinforces its authority relative to human death within the state territory. It is the doubleness of this double standard that could be transformed into a relation of exteriority.

A more decentralizing legislative attitude to wishes from the deceased as well as relatives might initiate new spatially creative ash rituals. Thus, decentralizing the spatial aspect of various answers to the question of what to do with the ashes could stimulate more personal questions pertaining to ritual, cremation and death by relatives. An emergent property of the suggested relation of exteriority could be an increase in the number of visitors to *Fælleskrematoriet*. These numbers are not likely to change for as long as shifting Danish governing bodies grant much more space for rationalizing the handling of the corpses of dead citizens than living citizens are allowed in their emotional handling of the ashes of loved ones. *Fælleskrematoriet* contributes to this asymmetry.

Bibliography

Abrahamson, Peter. "The Welfare Modelling Business." *Social Policy & Administration* 33, no. 4 (1999): 394–415.

Andersen, Axel. *Kremationer i Danmark 1893–1993*. Copenhagen: Stadsingeniørens Direktorat København, Kirkegårdsafdelingen, 1994.

Ariès, Philippe. *Western Attitudes toward Death: From the Middle Ages to the Present.* Translated by Patricia M. Ranum. London: Boyars, 1976.

Armstrong, Felicity. *Spaced Out: Policy, Difference, and the Challenge of Inclusive Education.* Dordrecht: Kluwer Academic Publishers, 2003.

Borger.dk. "Guide: Når livet slutter." https://www.borger.dk/sundhed-og-sygdom/Doedsfald-og-begravelse/guide-naar-livet-slutter. Accessed October 30, 2020.

"Cirkulære om beregning af krematorietakster, 12.02.2013." https://www.retsinformation.dk/api/pdf/145299. Accessed November 22, 2021.

Clarke, John. "Reconstructing Nation, State and Welfare: The Transformation of Welfare States." In *Welfare State Transformations: Comparative Perspectives*, edited by Martin Seeleib-Kaiser, 197–209. Houndmills: Palgrave Macmillan, 2008.

Danish State Executive Order. "LBK nr. 948 af 06/07/2017." https://www.retsinformation.dk/eli/lta/2017/948. Accessed October 30, 2020.

Davies, Douglas James, and Lewis H. Mates. *Encyclopedia of Cremation.* Aldershot: Ashgate, 2005.

DeLanda, Manuel. *Assemblage Theory.* Edinburgh: Edinburgh University Press, 2016.

——. *A New Philosophy of Society: Assemblage Theory and Social Complexity.* London: Continuum, 2006.

——. *Intensive Science and Virtual Philosophy*. London: Continuum 2002.

Easterling, Keller. *Extrastatecraft: The Power of Infrastructure Space.* London: Verso, 2014.

Esping-Andersen, Gøsta. *The Three Worlds of Welfare Capitalism.* Cambridge: Polity Press, 1990.

Fahlander, Fredrik. "Becoming Dead: Burial Assemblages as Vitalist Devices." *Cambridge Archaeological Journal* 30, no. 4 (2020): 555–69.

Finansministeriet. *Velfærd først – tryghed, tillid og en grøn fremtid: Finanslovforslaget 2020* (October 2019), Danish Ministry of Finance. https://fm.dk/media/17226/velfaerd-foerst-tryghed-tillid-og-en-groen-fremtid-finanslovforslaget-2020_weba.pdf. Accessed October 30, 2020.

Foucault, Michel. *Security, Territory, Population: Lectures at the Collège de France, 1977–78*. Edited by Michel Senellart, translated by Graham Burchell. Basingstoke: Palgrave Macmillan, 2014.

Greimas, Algirdas Julien. *Structural Semantics: An Attempt at a Method.* Translated by Daniele McDowell, Ronald Schleifer, and Alan Velie. Lincoln: University of Nebraska Press, 1983.

Greve, Bent. "Denmark: Universal or Not So Universal Welfare State." *Social Policy & Administration* 38, no. 2 (2004): 156–69. https://doi.org/10.1111/j.1467-9515.2004.00383.x.

Jacobsen, Michael H. "'Spectacular Death': Proposing a New Fifth Phase to Philippe Ariès's Admirable History of Death." *Humanities* 5, no. 2 (2016): 1–20. https://doi.org/10.3390/h5020019

Kirkeministeriet (Danish Ministry of Ecclesiastical Affairs). *Rapport fra arbejdsgruppen vedrørende krematorievirksomhed i Danmark.* Kirkeministeriet, 2006. https://www.km.dk/fileadmin/share/publikationer/Krematorier/Rapport_om_krematorier.pdf.

Køster, Allan. "Longing for Concreteness: How Body Memory Matters to Continuing Bonds." *Mortality* 25, no. 4 (2020): 389–401. https://doi.org/10.1080/13576275.2019.1632277.

Kriegbaum, Mogens, and Ernst Jensen. "Input til branchebilag for krematorieanlæg: Komentarer og begrundelser, September 23, 2005." Odense: Miljøministeriet, 2005. https://mst.dk/media/94933/indlaeg-fra-branchen-om-krematorieanlaeg-j202.pdf, accessed October 31, 2020.

Laqueur, Thomas Walter. *The Work of the Dead: A Cultural History of Mortal Remains.* Princeton: Princeton University Press, 2015.

Mathijssen, Brenda. "The Ambiguity of Human Ashes: Exploring Encounters with Cremated Remains in the Netherlands." *Death Studies* 41, no. 1 (2017): 34–41. https://doi.org/10.1080/07481187.2016.1257882.

Pedersen, Ove K. *Konkurrencestaten.* Copenhagen: Hans Reitzel, 2014.

Prendergast, David, Jennifer Lorna Hockey and Leonie Kellaher. "Blowing in the Wind? Identity, Materiality, and the Destinations of Human Ashes." *Journal of the Royal Anthropological Institute* 12, no. 4 (2006): 881–98.
Sørensen, Tim Flohr. "The Presence of the Dead: Cemeteries, Cremation and the Staging of Non-Place." *Journal of Social Archaeology* 9, no. 1 (2009): 110–35. https://journals.sagepub.com/doi/abs/10.1177/1469605308099373.
Varnelis, Kazys. "Programming after Program: Archizoom's No-Stop City." *Praxis Journal of Writing + Building* 8 (2006): 82–91.
Vidler, Anthony. "Toward a Theory of the Architectural Program." *October* 106 (2003): 59–74.
Walter, Tony. "Bodies and Ceremonies: Is the UK Funeral Industry Still Fit for Purpose?" *Mortality* 22, no. 3 (2017): 194–208, https://doi.org/10.1080/13576275.2016.1205574.

Notes

1 The operation of crematoria is not subsidized in Denmark – however, cremation expenses can be mitigated for individual persons/estates. See "Cirkulære om beregning af krematorietakster 12.02.2013," https://www.retsinformation.dk/api/pdf/145299, accessed November 22, 2021.
2 The current list price for *Fælleskrematoriet* is approx. DKK 3,000 (€ 400) for a cremation. *Fælleskrematoriet*, accessed October 31, 2020. https://www.fælleskrematoriet.dk/takster/.
3 Mogens Kriegbaum and Ernst Jensen, "Input til branchebilag for krematorieanlæg: Kommentarer og begrundelser, September 23, 2005" (Odense: Miljøministeriet, 2005), https://mst.dk/media/94933/indlaeg-fra-branchen-om-krematorieanlaeg-j202.pdf, accessed October 31, 2020.
4 The universal welfare state is a well-established category within welfare theory, a core feature of it being equal access of all citizens to benefits financed by the state. See Gøsta Esping-Andersen, *The Three Worlds of Welfare Capitalism* (Cambridge: Polity Press, 1990).
5 The degree of universality of a given welfare state depends on the level of free access to state-financed benefits. Today's institutionalization of cremation weighs in toward the subtypology "Partly Universal" – see Bent Greve, "Denmark: Universal or Not So Universal Welfare State," *Social Policy & Administration* 38, no. 2 (April 2004): 158.
6 Manuel DeLanda, *A New Philosophy of Society: Assemblage Theory and Social Complexity* (London: Continuum, 2006), 28.
7 DeLanda, *A New Philosophy of Society*, 85.
8 See, for example, Peter Abrahamson, "The Welfare Modelling Business," *SPOL Social Policy & Administration* 33, no. 4 (1999).
9 A. J. Greimas, *Structural Semantics: An Attempt at a Method* (Lincoln: University of Nebraska Press, 1983).
10 John Clarke, "Reconstructing Nation, State and Welfare: The Transformation of Welfare States," in *Welfare State Transformations: Comparative Perspectives*, ed. Martin Seeleib-Kaiser (Houndmills: Palgrave Macmillan, 2008), 198.
11 The concept of welfare is not directly inscribed in the names of the institutions and institutional actions finally reaching the citizens or "users." The Danish state is not constitutionally a welfare state – it is not a welfare state by constitution or otherwise by law. For instance, in the wordings of *Finanslov for finansåret 2020* (the DKK 750 billion Law of Financing, the Danish national household budget) *welfare* is mostly related to animal welfare, the funding of welfare research, digitalization of welfare services and financing of welfare support functions by national agencies, councils and centers. Thus, returning twenty-seven hits in the wording of the current *Finanslov*, most explicit formal reference to the concept of welfare relates to a relatively new research institution. From an assemblage theory perspective, the weak connections across the gap of translation also indicates the sphere that allows the concept of welfare to be trapped in countless attempts at definition. Such definitions through decontextualization testify to the status of welfare as a reified generality, a discursive attractor that accumulates endless intellectual engagement but does not have any stopping rule – a free-floating signifier subject to countless attempts at definition and political annexation.
12 The 3,604 pages of the recent "Finanslov for finansåret 2020" (the national Danish household budget for 2020) mentions welfare explicitly 102 times. Of these, twenty-five hits refer to animal welfare, twenty-three to funding of welfare research, fourteen to digitalization of welfare services and the remaining – with few exceptions – referring to financing of welfare support functions by national agencies, councils and centers. The big posts in the budget, that is, expenses for social security measures, healthcare, education and pensions, are not explicitly described in terms of welfare or as welfare benefits. Against this already the name of the Danish government's political proposition for the guiding principles behind the 2020 national household budget is "Welfare First," returning fifty hits on the word *velfærd* (welfare) over thirty-seven pages. The first short paragraph of Chapter 1 states that the government intends "a new and more just direction focusing on welfare, education, green transformation and safety [*tryghed*] for Danes." See Finansministeriet, *Velfærd først – tryghed, tillid og en grøn fremtid: Finanslovforslaget 2020* (October 2019), https://fm.dk/media/17226/velfaerd-foerst-tryghed-tillid-og-en-groen-fremtid-finanslovforslaget-2020_weba.pdf, accessed October 30, 2020.
13 Felicity Armstrong, *Spaced Out: Policy, Difference, and the Challenge of Inclusive Education* (Dordrecht: Kluwer Academic Publishers, 2003), 5.
14 For the concept *dispositive* (dispositif) see, for example, Michel Foucault, *Security, Territory, Population: Lectures at the College De France, 1977–78*, ed. Michel Senellart, trans. Graham Burchell (Basingstoke: Palgrave Macmillan, 2014), 25–26.

15 Armstrong, *Spaced Out*, 58.
16 Manuel DeLanda, *Assemblage Theory* (Edinburgh: Edinburgh University Press, 2016), 14.
17 Manuel DeLanda, *Intensive Science and Virtual Philosophy* (London: Continuum, 2004), 117.
18 "Programmatic" in reference to the architectural idiom *program*. For a theoretical elaboration on the heavily used yet somewhat undertheorized concept of program in architecture, see, for example, Antony Vidler, "Toward a Theory of the Architectural Program," *October* 106 (2003): 59–74; or Kazys Varnelis, "Programming after Program: Archizoom's No-Stop City," *Praxis Journal of Writing + Building* 8 (2006): 82–91.
19 *End form* is a concept coined by Keller Easterling; see Easterling, *Extrastatecraft: The Power of Infrastructure Space* (London: Verso, 2014), 65–66.
20 During the planning process, Tom Olsen recommended more "architecture" and less "production logic" as a guiding principle for the expression of the building; interview with Tom Olsen, operational leader of *Fælleskrematoriet*, January 19, 2018.
21 See document on house rules called "Etik" (Ethics) of *Fælleskrematoriet*, https://www.fælleskrematoriet.dk/fileadmin/group/87/Dokumenter/F%C3%A6lleskrematoriet_Etiske_forhold_-_opdateret_012020.pdf, accessed November 23, 2021.
22 *Prosaic*, as understood in resonance with its etymological origin in Latin *prosa* and in *prose*.
23 Thomas W. Laqueur, *The Work of the Dead: A Cultural History of Mortal Remains* (Princeton: Princeton University Press, 2015), 495. Relative to a Danish context, see, for example, Tim F. Sørensen, "The Presence of the Dead: Cemeteries, Cremation and the Staging of Non-Place," *Journal of Social Archaeology* 9, no. 1 (2009): 110–35.
24 Kirkeministeriet (Danish Ministry of Ecclesiastical Affairs), *Rapport fra arbejdsgruppen vedrørende krematorievirksomhed i Danmark* (Kirkeministeriet, 2006), 48–50, https://www.km.dk/fileadmin/share/publikationer/Krematorier/Rapport_om_krematorier.pdf.
25 *Vejledning om urnenedsættelse på privat ejendom m.v.*, VEJ nr 51 af 28/08/2008, https://www.retsinformation.dk/eli/mt/2008/51, accessed October 30, 2020.
26 See Tony Walter, "Bodies and Ceremonies: Is the UK Funeral Industry Still Fit for Purpose?" *Mortality* 22, no. 3 (2017): 194–208, https://doi.org/10.1080/13576275.2016.1205574
27 In support of this, Tim Sørensen argues that – also in a Danish context – the materiality and agency of the dead human body has been neutralized over the past fifty years, as a common trend as well as in academia. See Sørensen, "The Presence of the Dead."
28 See *Fælleskrematoriet*, "Etik."
29 On disposition in an architectural context see Easterling, *Extrastatecraft*; see also Foucault, *Security, Territory, Population*, 25–26.
30 Sørensen, "The Presence of the Dead," 114.
31 Axel Andersen, *Kremationer i Danmark 1893–1993* (Copenhagen: Stadsingeniørens Direktorat København, Kirkegårdsafdelingen, 1994).
32 Especially Philippe Ariès, "Forbidden Death," in *Western Attitudes toward Death: From the Middle Ages to the Present* (London: Boyars, 1976), 85–108.
33 Ariès, *Western Attitudes toward Death*, 85.
34 Lars Iversen, *Kampen for liv: Fem danske forebyggelsessuccceser* (Copenhagen: SIFs Forlag, 2017) provides evidence for the impact of improved health care in the early twentieth century in Denmark but has no reference to cremation anywhere.
35 This claim finds some support in Michael Hviid Jacobsen, "'Spectacular Death': Proposing a New Fifth Phase to Philippe Ariès' Admirable History of Death," *Humanities* 5, no. 2 (2016): 19, https://doi.org/10.3390/h5020019.
36 In the subsector of recycling surgical metal implants, the Dutch company OrthoMetals has taken the lead, operating in twenty countries, systematically collecting high-quality metals from approximately 700 crematoria, saving the metal implants they uncovered after cremation for the company. Lately, even the first pet crematorium has also joined the ranks; see https://www.dignitypetcrem.co.uk/about-dignity-pet-crematorium/environmental-info-at-dignity-pet-crematorium/, accessed December 3, 2021. *Fælleskrematoriet* is also a subscriber.
37 In 2016 the headline of one Danish newspaper article read "Når kroppen får nyt liv som jetmotor" ("When the Body Gets a New Life as a Jet Engine"), *Berlingske Tidende*, February 20, 2016, https://www.berlingske.dk/virksomheder/naar-kroppen-faar-nyt-liv-som-jetmotor, accessed December 3, 2021.
38 Interview with Tom Olsen, operational leader of *Fælleskrematoriet*, January 19, 2018.

2.13 Fælleskrematoriet, floor plan

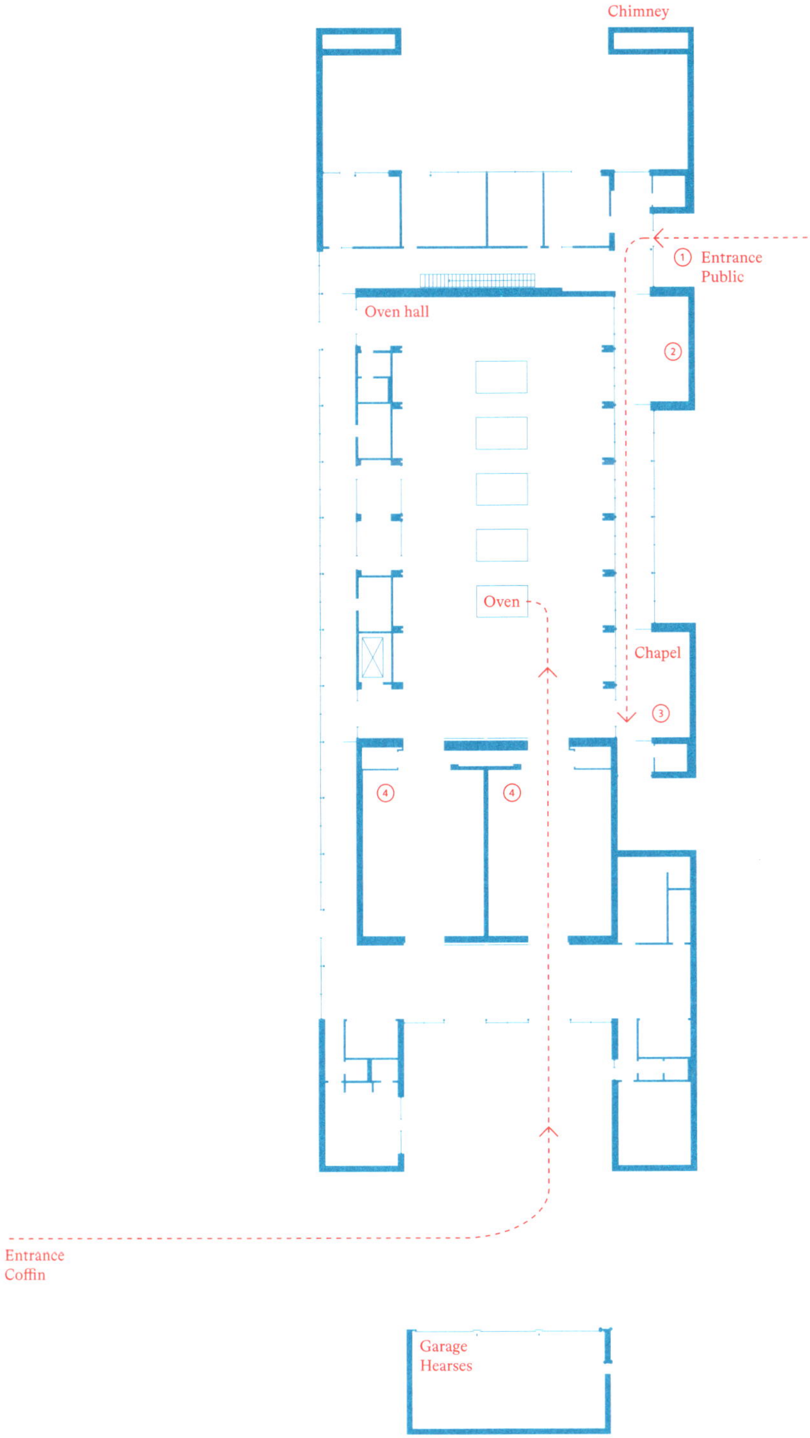

① Public entrance (collecting an urn, general inquiries).
② Space for attending or watching the cremation.
③ Entrance for the mourners, who then gather in the chapel/catafalque toom.
④ Coffin storage.

2.14 Distribution and catchment area of crematoria in Roskilde Stift, 1970s

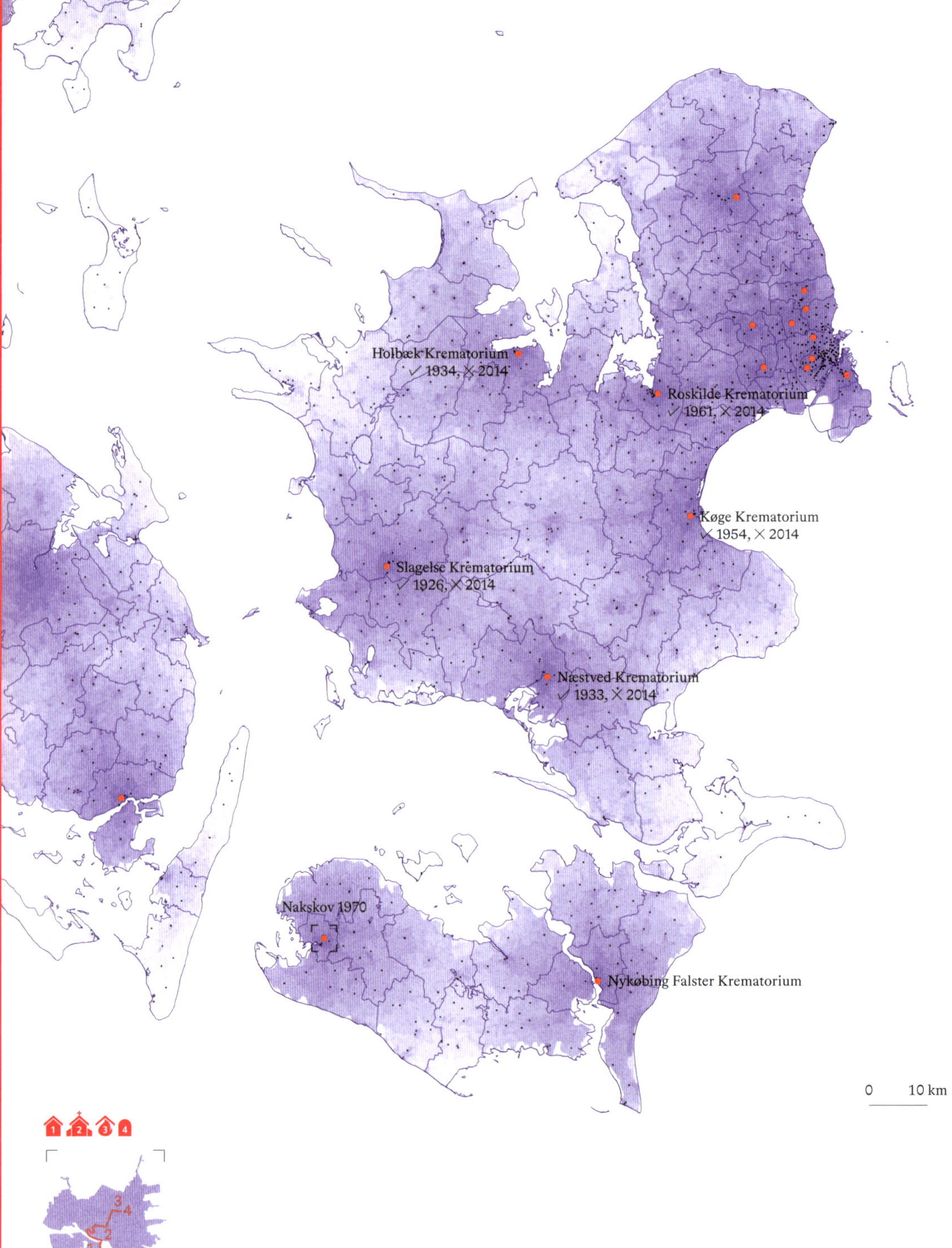

Distance to closest highway exit/entrance 5 >50 min

• Places of worship
• Crematoria

✓ Inauguration
× Closure

2.15 Distribution and catchment area of the new Fælledkrematorium in Roskilde Stift, 2022

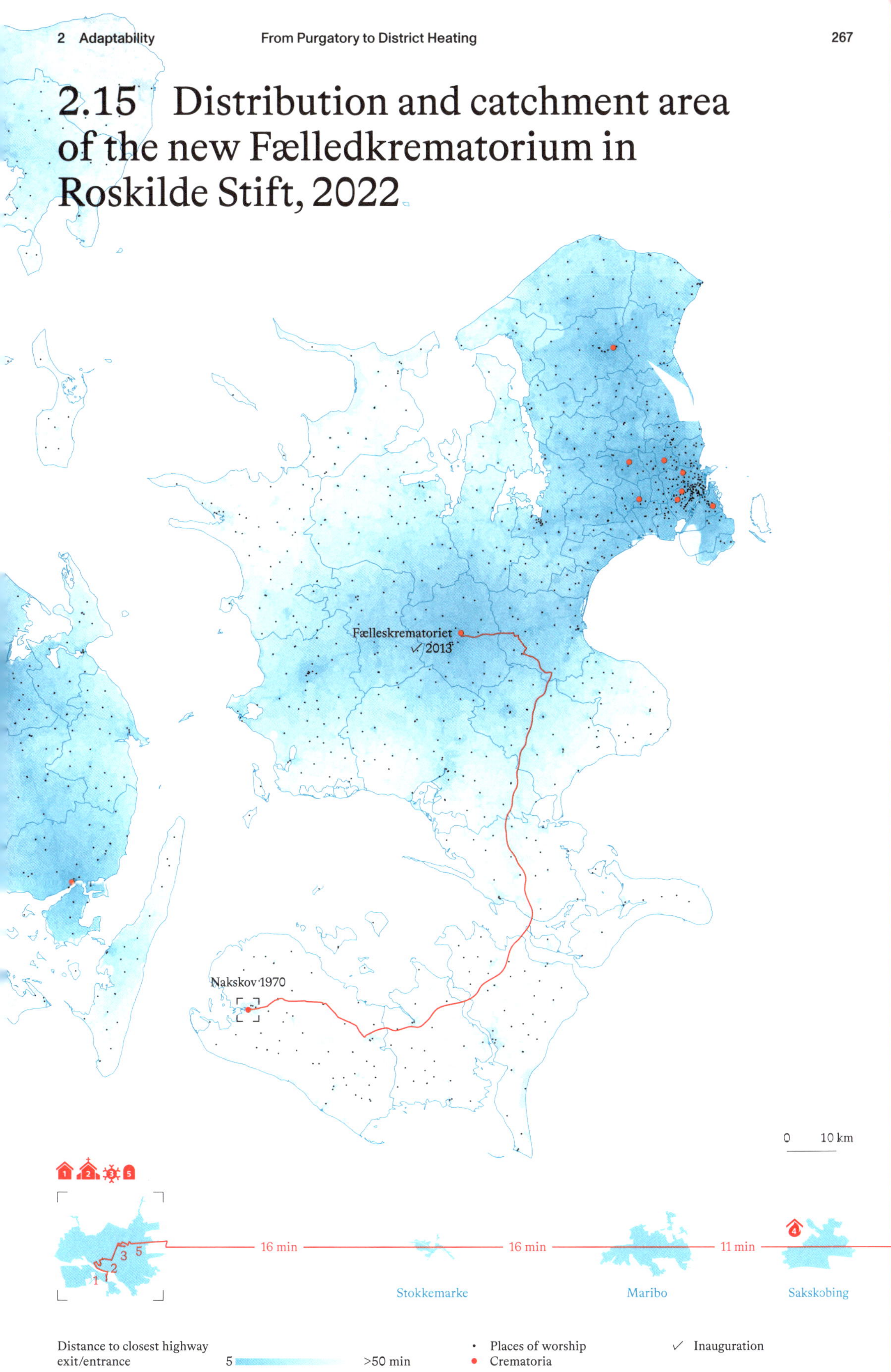

2.16 Route of a dead body in Nakskov, 1970s

Cemetery

2.17 Route of a dead body in Nakskov and beyond, 2022

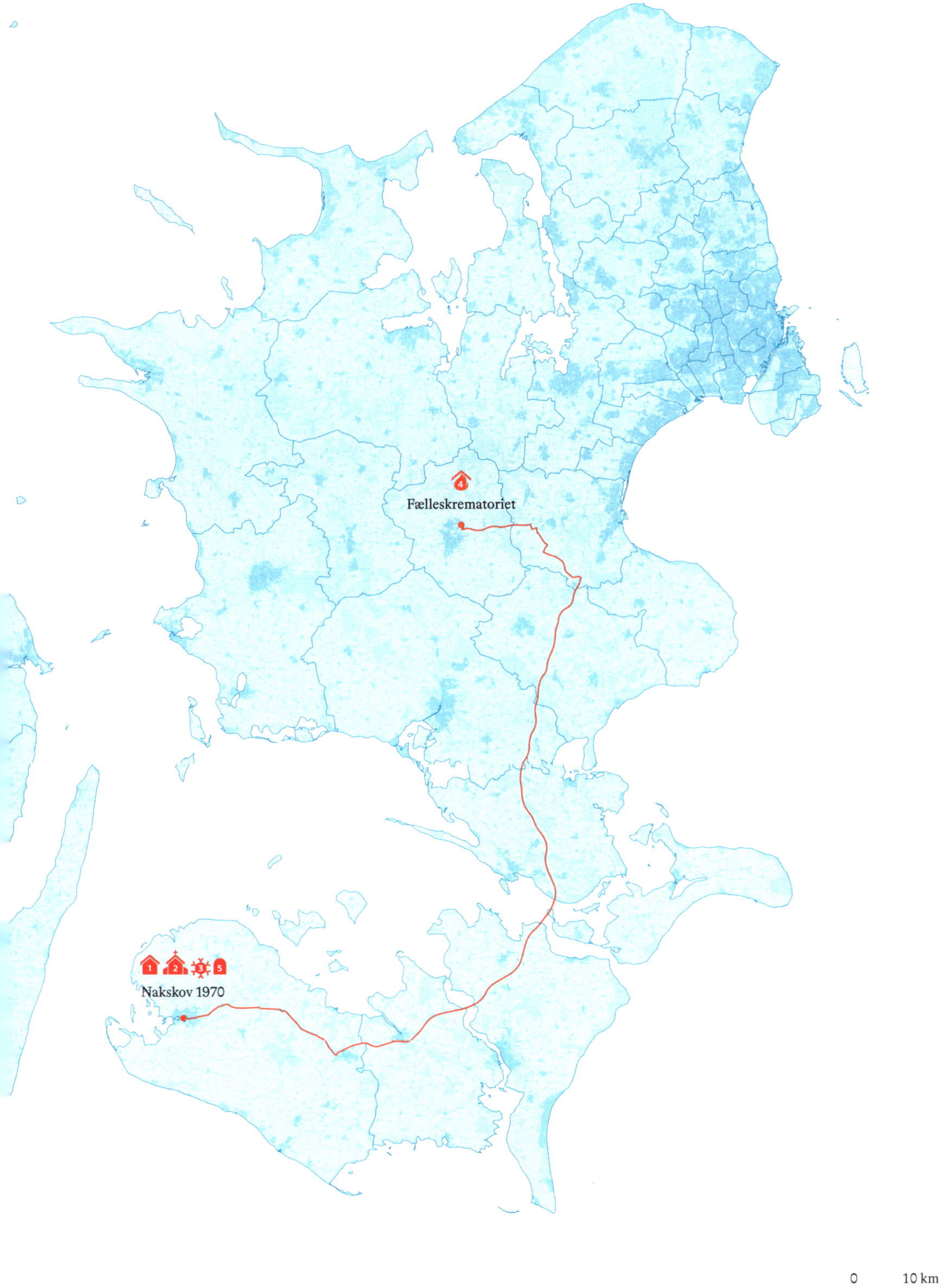

2.18 Traditional versus centralized cremation process

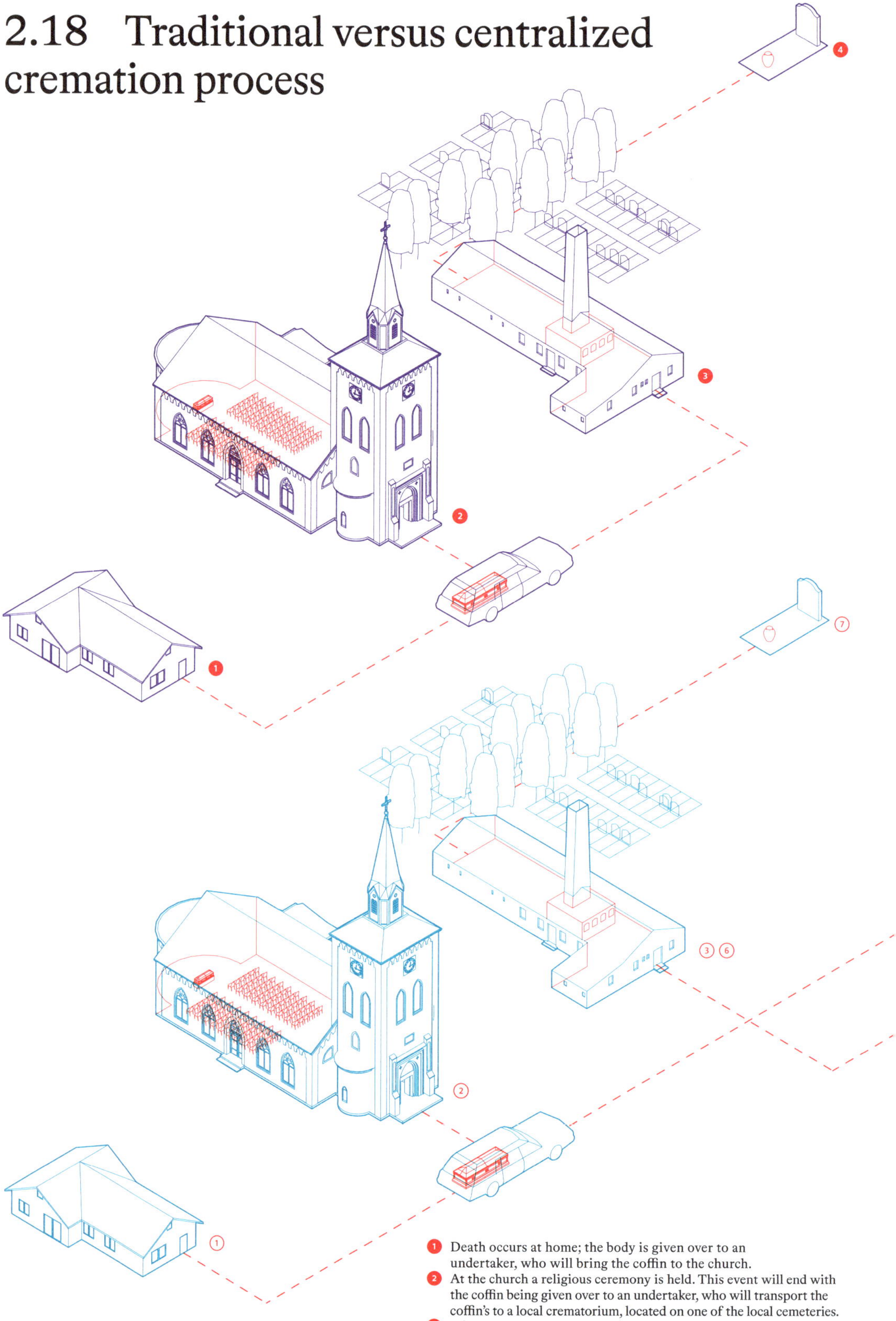

1. Death occurs at home; the body is given over to an undertaker, who will bring the coffin to the church.
2. At the church a religious ceremony is held. This event will end with the coffin being given over to an undertaker, who will transport the coffin's to a local crematorium, located on one of the local cemeteries.
3. After cremation, the undertaker will transport the urn to the burial ground, which will be its final destination.
4. Ceremony, celebrating the arrival of the urn at its final destination.

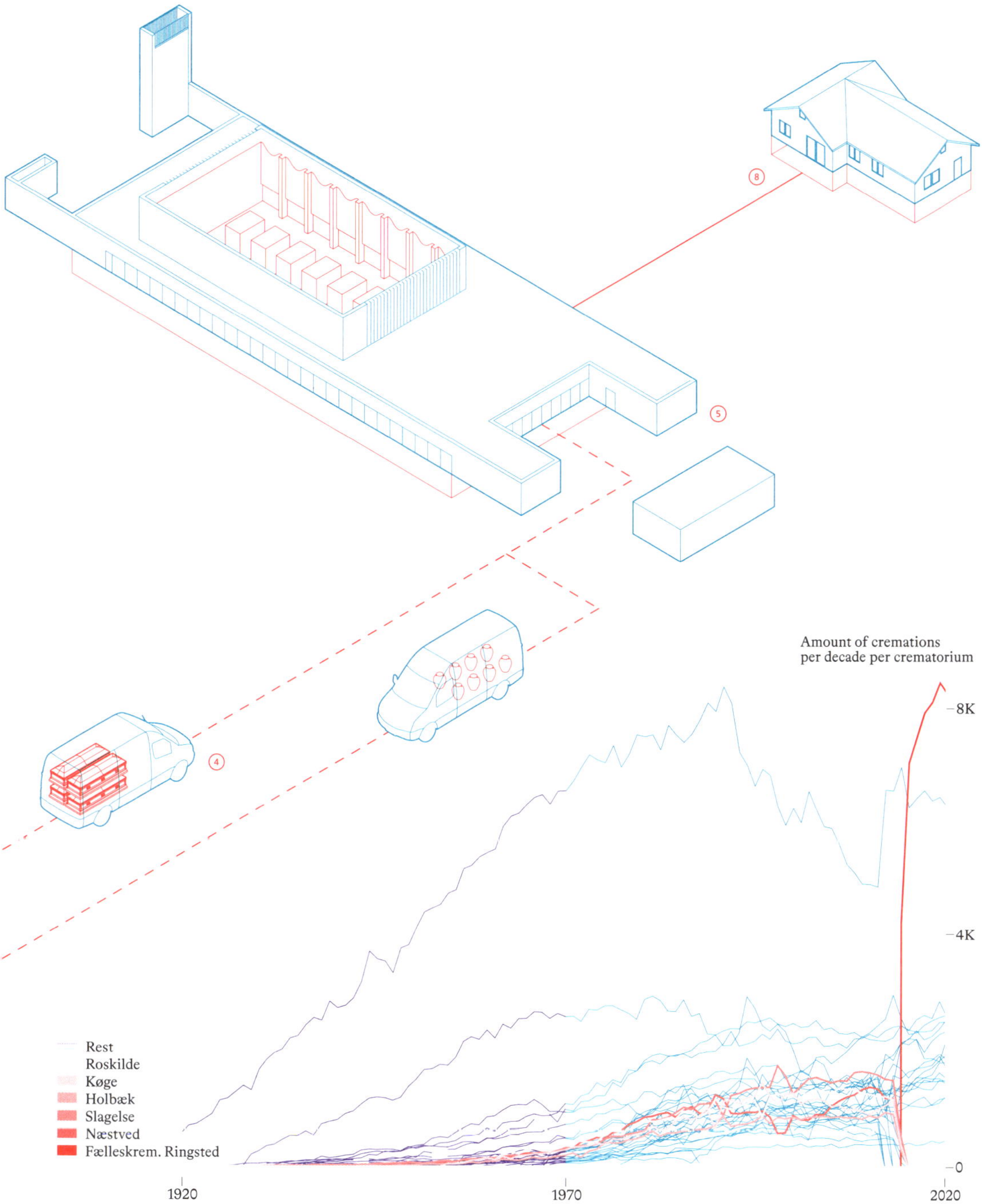

1. Death occurs at home; the body is given over to an undertaker, who will bring the coffin to the church.
2. At the church a religious ceremony is held. The coffin will be collected locally by the undertaker after the religious ritual.
3. The undertaker takes the coffin to a local "in transit" cooling room (old crematorium).
4. A special hearse with room for four coffins will take the dead person together with (up to) three other dead persons to the crematorium.
5. Fælledkrematoriet is well connected to highway infrastructure. That the new crematorium is not situated within an existing cemetery or churchyard is unusual.
6. Transportation of urns back to the cooling facility, where the undertaker will transport the urn to its final burial ground.
7. Final ceremony, celebrating the arrival of the urn to its final destination.
8. The rationalization of productivity behind the new transport system is further developed by linking the ovens of the crematorium to the local district-heating grid in the city of Ringsted.

2.19 Cremations per year and per crematorium, 1890–2020

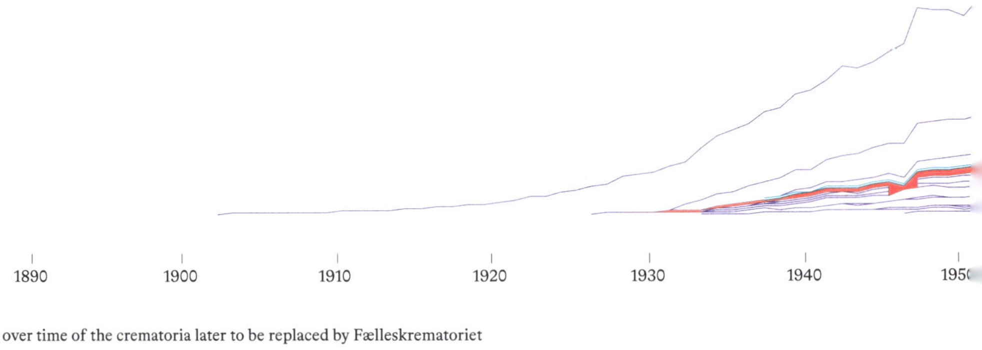

Production over time of the crematoria later to be replaced by Fælleskrematoriet

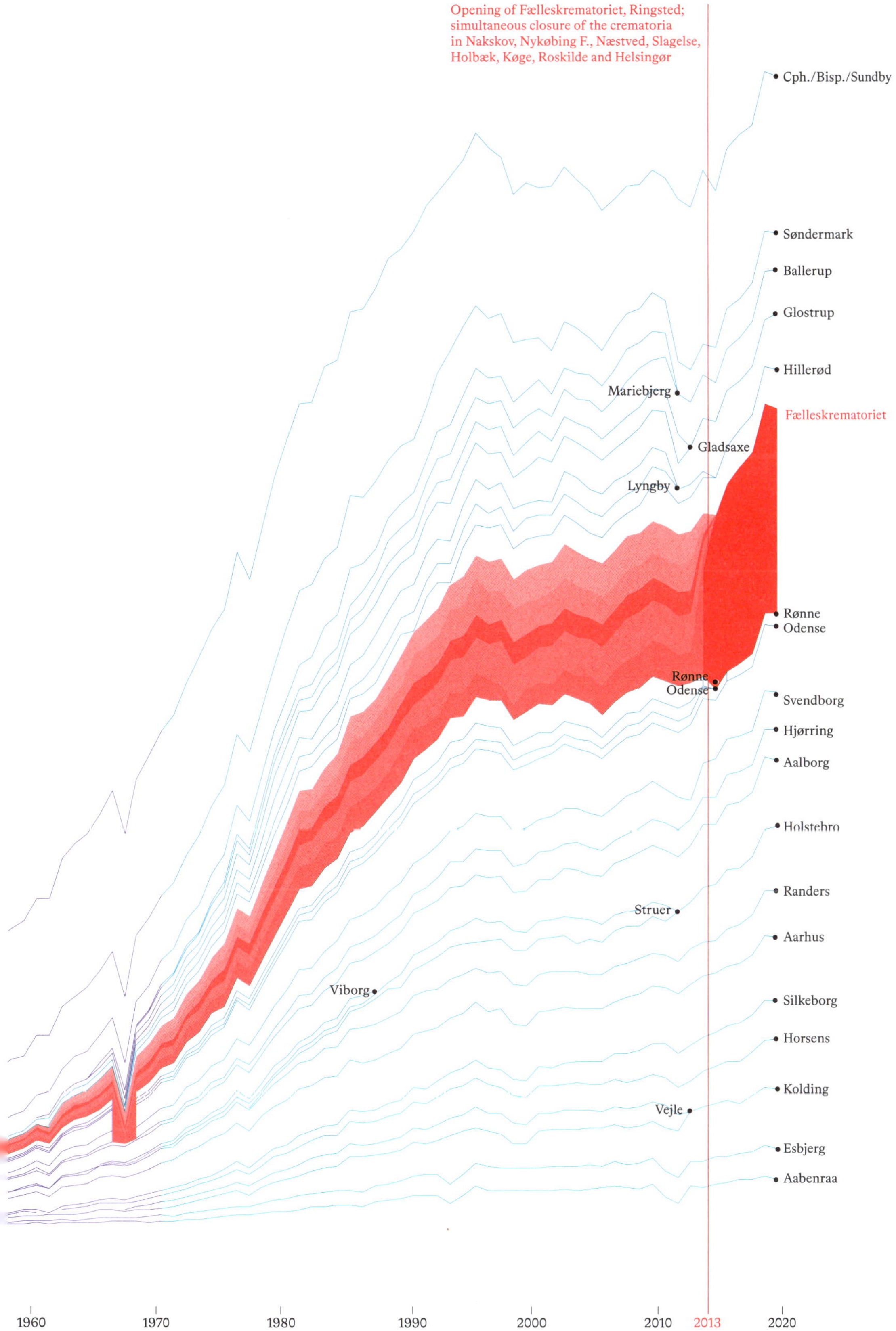
Opening of Fælleskrematoriet, Ringsted; simultaneous closure of the crematoria in Nakskov, Nykøbing F., Næstved, Slagelse, Holbæk, Køge, Roskilde and Helsingør
Cph./Bisp./Sundby
Søndermark
Ballerup
Glostrup
Hillerød
Mariebjerg
Fælleskrematoriet
Gladsaxe
Lyngby
Rønne
Odense
Rønne
Odense
Svendborg
Hjørring
Aalborg
Holstebro
Randers
Struer
Aarhus
Viborg
Silkeborg
Horsens
Kolding
Vejle
Esbjerg
Aabenraa
1960
1970
1980
1990
2000
2010
2013
2020

2.20 Location of the new crematorium Fælleskrematoriet

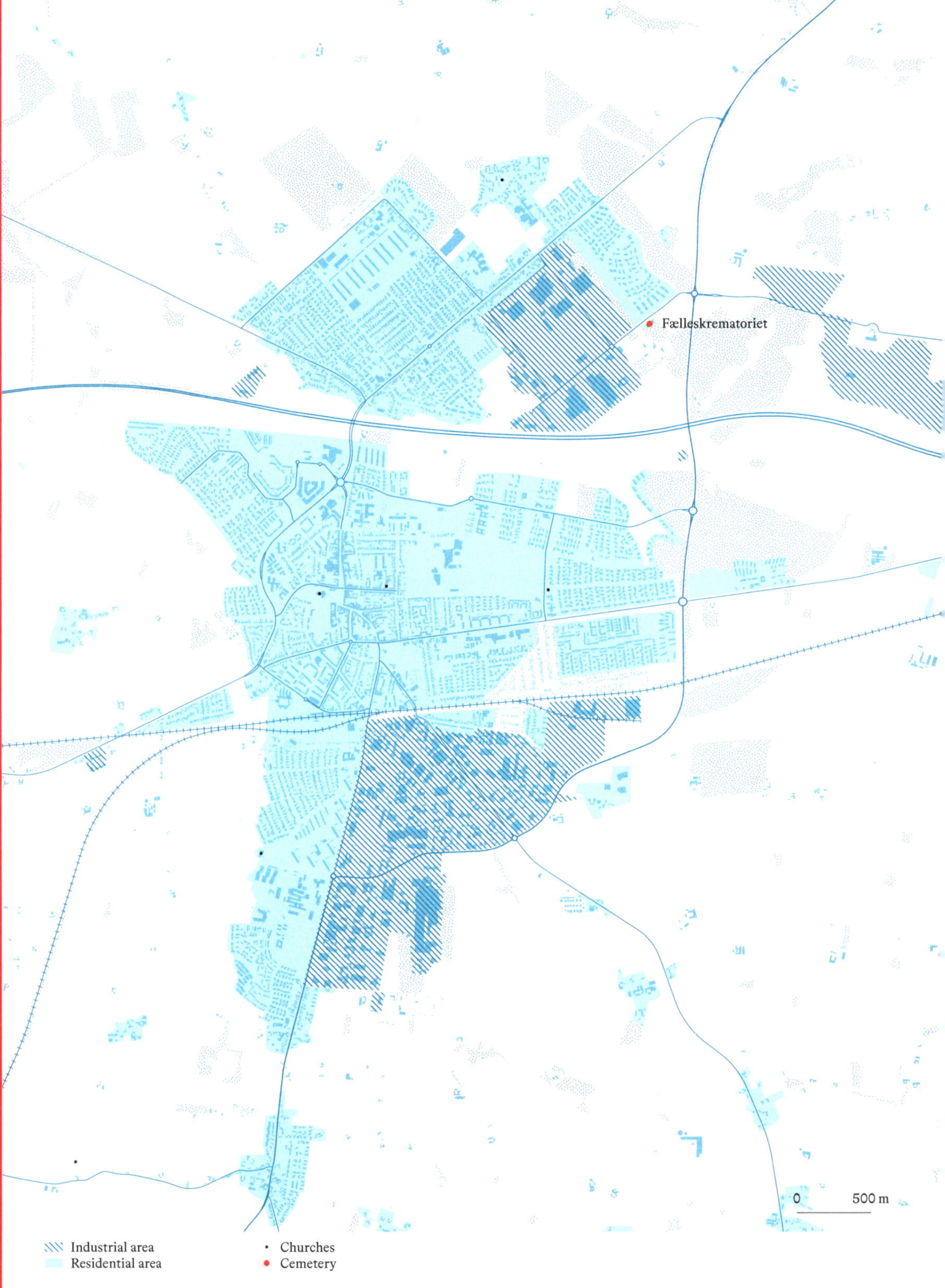

2.21 Context of the new crematorium Fælleskrematoriet

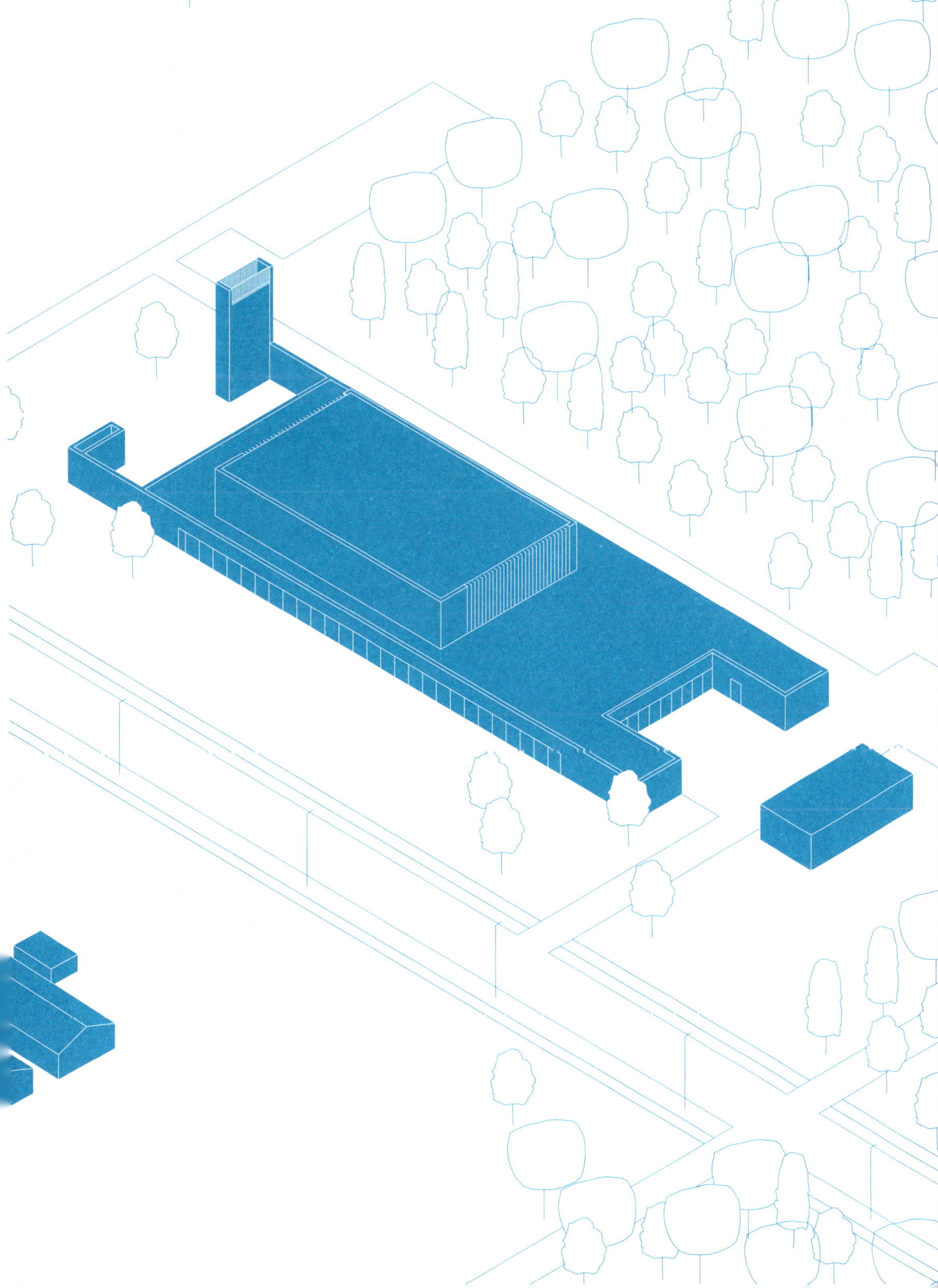

2.22 Traditional hearse versus modern multicoffin hearse

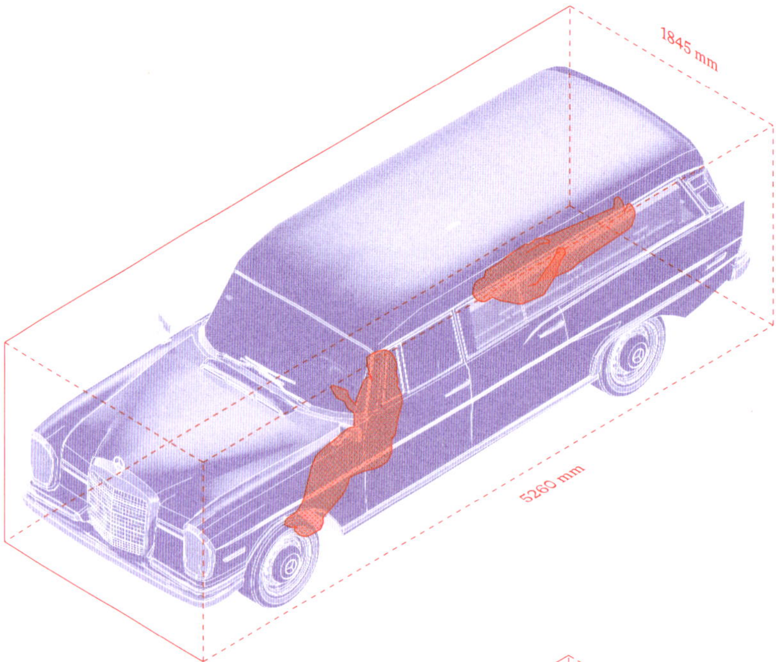

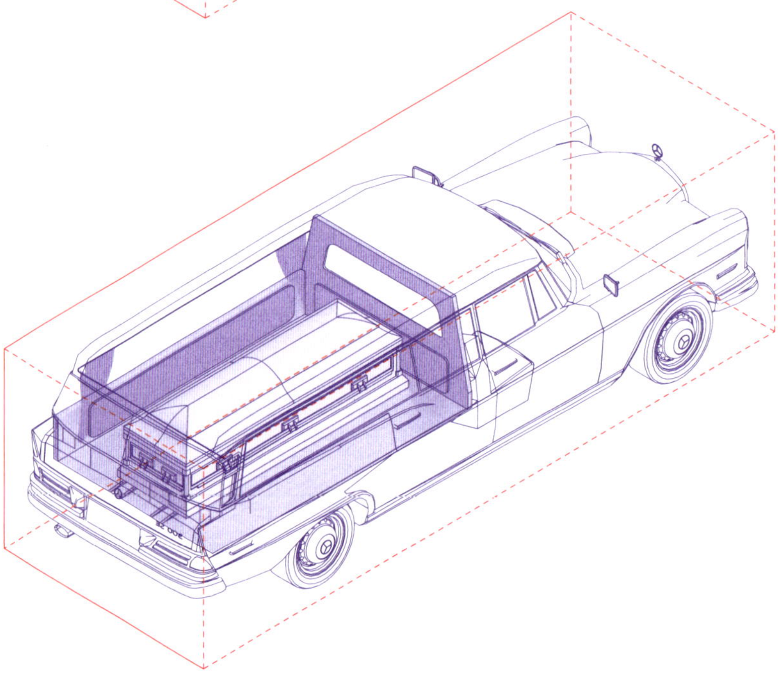

Fuel consumption	14.4 l/100 km
CO_2 emissions	380 g/km
Max. capacity (coffin)	1
Max. capacity (urns)	–
Production year	1965

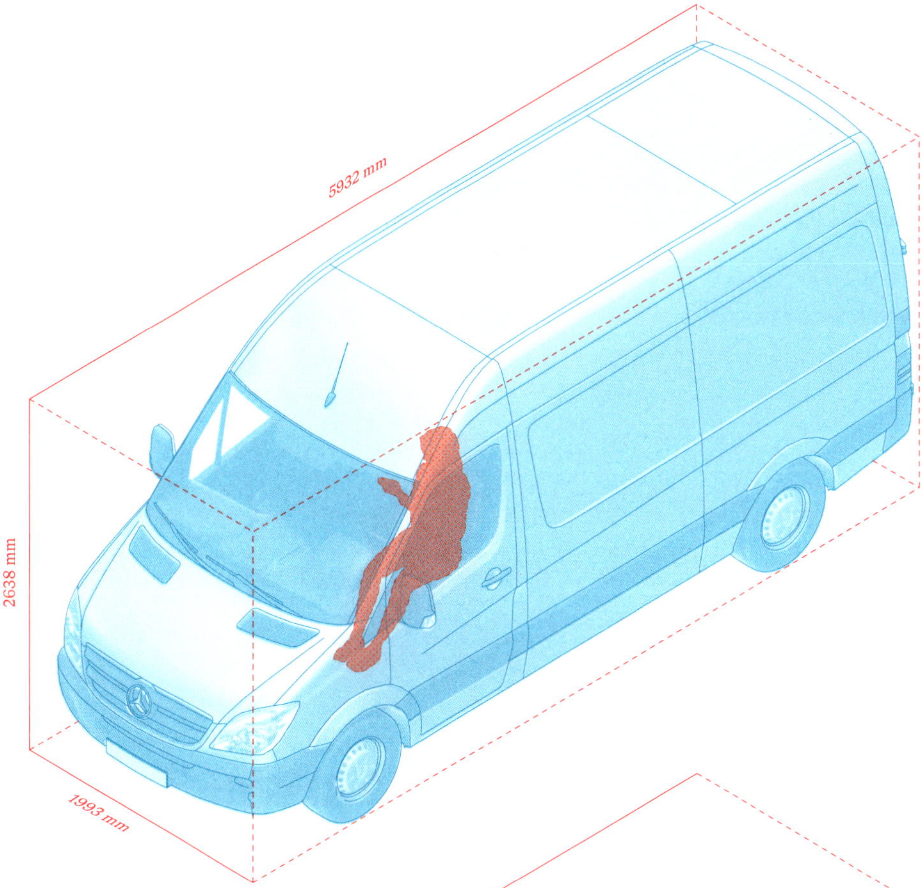

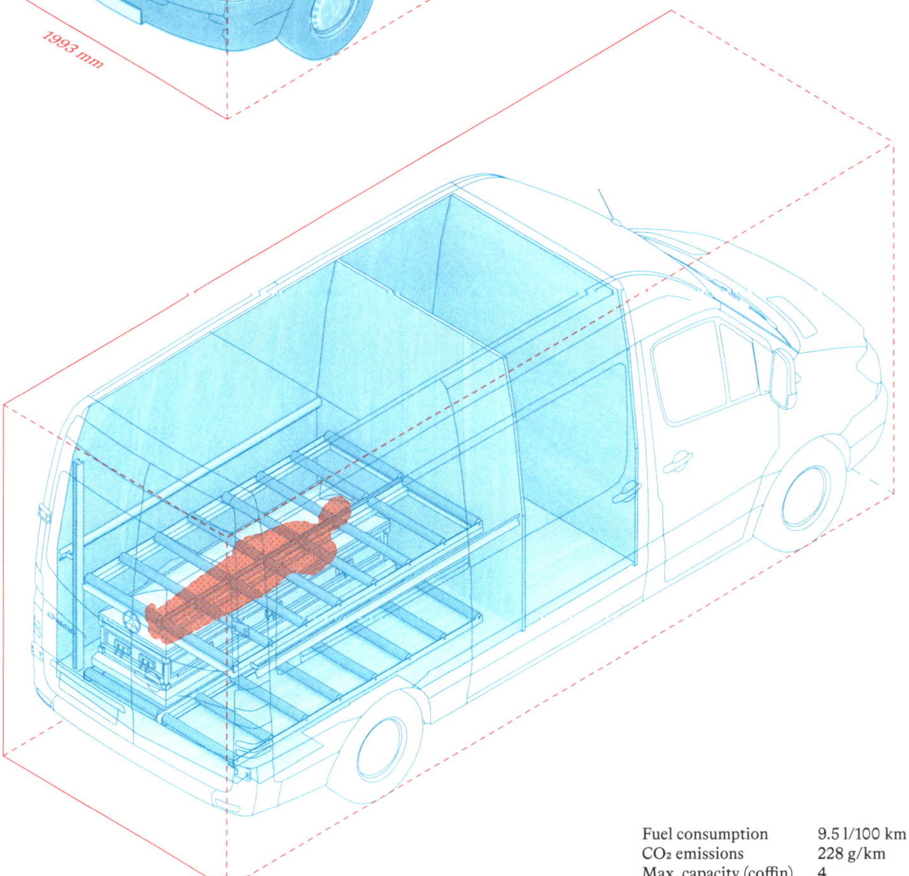

Fuel consumption	9.5 l/100 km
CO_2 emissions	228 g/km
Max. capacity (coffin)	4
Max. capacity (urns)	12
Production year	2020

0 0.5 m

2.23 Fælleskrematoriet, section perspective

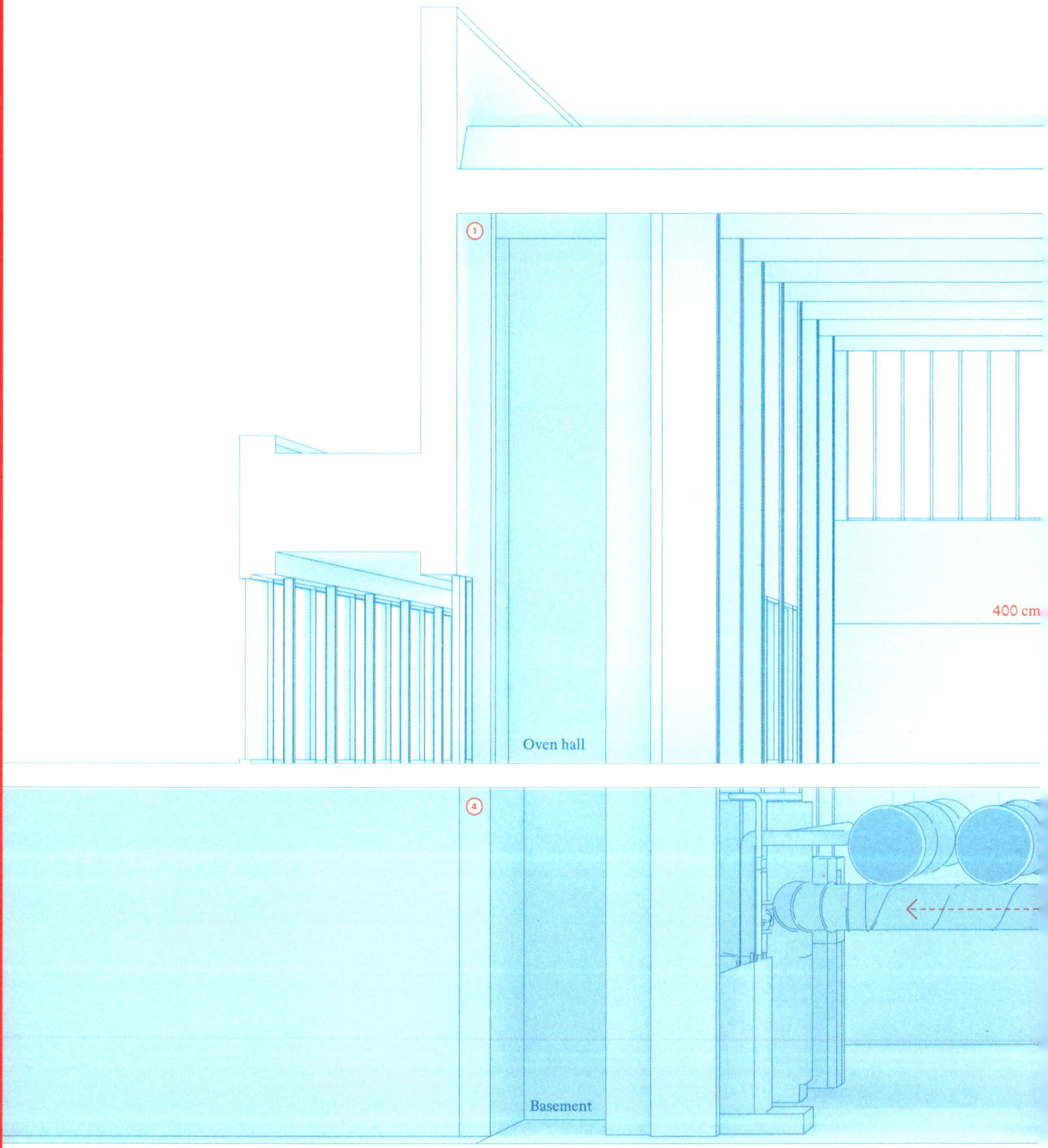

1. The oven hall conveys a sense of pathos and of the modestly sacral. The roof structure catches the natural light on its whitish colored undulating underbelly, creating a diffusion of light, softening the sense of regimented orderliness expressed by the ovens.
2. Simple dark metal-covered blocks of the five ovens, stripped of most features of "oven."
3. The modest chapel room with a catafalque offers relatives the opportunity to perform a ceremony in the crematorium in relation to the actual event of cremation.
4. The basement encompasses most of the technical equipment, dominated by the machinery for the treatment of the smoke produced during cremations.

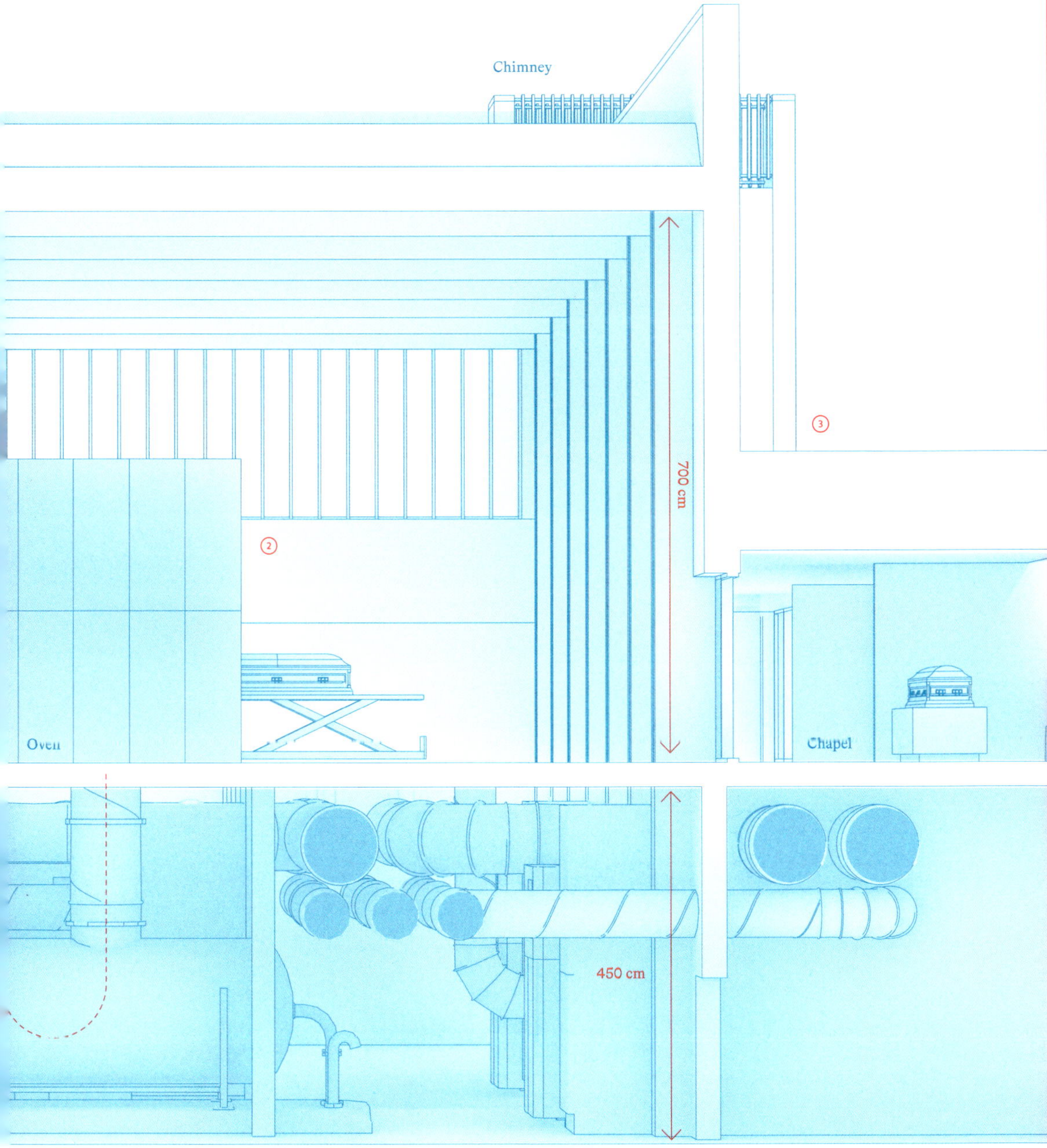
Chimney
③
700 cm
②
Oven
Chapel
450 cm

2.24 Catalogue of all Danish crematoria, by construction date

Crematoria which activity got replaced by the new Fælleskrematoriet in Ringsted

Crematoria which activity got replaced by the Ringsted Crematorium

1893
Frederiksberg Krematorium

1908
Bispebjerg Krematorium

1923
Aarhus Krematorium

1926
Slagelse Krematorium

1931
Sundby Krematorium

1932
Svendborg Krematorium

1933
Kolding Krematorium

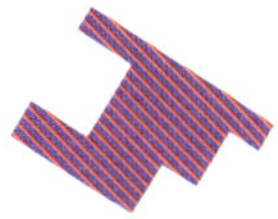

1933
Næstved Krematorium

1936
Mariebjerg/Gentofte Krematorium

1939
Esbjerg Krematorium

1939
Horsens Krematorium

1941
Naskov Krematorium

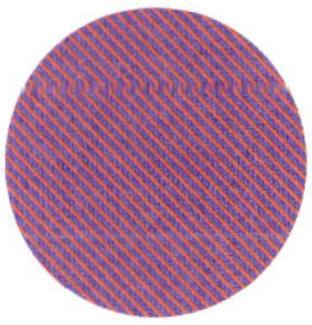

1954
Køge Krematorium

1960
Glostrup Krematorium

1961
Roskilde Krematorium

1964
Gladsaxe Krematorium

1968
Ballerup Krematorium

1977
Holstebro Krematorium

2013
Fælleskrematoriet in Ringsted

Are We All Here?

Inclusion and Spatial Restructurings in the Danish Primary School 1993–2020

Katrine Lotz

1 Photo from Halskovskolen aula.

The term *inclusion* within the realm of Den Danske Folkeskole (The Danish Common School, municipal primary and lower secondary school) is currently understood as a practice where children with special needs are taught in the same place as their peers, unsegregated. The inclusive school is understood as a school where all children are included, regardless of their capacities. Both terms are in many ways tightly interwoven with the ideas of an egalitarian society and with the various understandings of universal welfare that have sustained the development of some of the core elements and amenities of the Danish welfare state.[1] ⟨fig. 1⟩

The main suggestion in this chapter is that if we look at the practices of inclusion and universality both in concrete places but also the extensions of these practices across scale and registers, then we can perhaps start to understand how intricately also spatial relations contribute to these enactments. Perhaps we can get a grasp of how inclusion and universality are or are not coordinated spatially, and how these spatially embedded practices react when related ideas, legislation and economy change locally and nationally.

With a point of departure in a case study at a school in the provincial municipality of Vordingborg in Southern Zealand, different arenas for universality, inclusion and the inclusive school is rendered by drawing in a range of spatial scales; of the state, of the municipality, the school, the class and of the individual child and teacher, and a range of etymological, geographical, historical and economical registers.[2] During my initial research I noticed that a particular set of changes in the regulation of the field in the years 2011–12 on the national level, which I will come back to later, had implications for a major restructuring of all schools in the municipality of Vordingborg in 2012.[3]

Here, the rate of children in ordinary classes – as opposed to those in the segregated special needs schools or special classes – changed from 92.7 percent in 2010, well below the national average, to 98.5 percent in 2013, now among the highest. During a number of years, the municipality had experienced a quite significant decline in the number of children due to depopulation. The political decision on restructuring entailed, among other changes, the reduction of school districts from eight to five, where one district now counted between two and five minor local schools under one head and one central administration. Also, all school leaders were reassigned to these "new" schools regardless of their former affiliation.

2.28
Distribution of schools in Vordingborg, before 2013
2.29
Distribution of schools in Vordingborg, after 2013

A teacher at the Svend Gønge-School, the largest of the two schools in the new district, tells me:

> We used to have a whole separate house for "our" children. We had a lot of expensive special materials, and we had a lot of knowledge together over there for our children. When it was

> suddenly closed I sneaked in and rescued the most valuable things. Now we have the activity center instead. It is not at all manned the same way.[4]

At the same time it was decided to shut down all the local special needs classes and the related special needs centers at every school in the municipality, as all children were to be placed in ordinary classes. The municipality maintained one municipally owned special needs school with the capacity for fifty children with severe disabilities, located in the village of Kalvehave.

Arenas for Inclusion-Exclusion Nexuses

Etymologically, *inclusion* implies a difference; something or someone included is at the outset different from the others. Also, the term implies a spatial position; something or somebody included is *here* at this particular place at this particular time. Somebody excluded or segregated is *not* here; they are elsewhere, at another place, in another space. I will let the philosopher Giorgio Agamben formulate the dynamic of anthropological or human inclusion and exclusion here, because he stresses how the spatial element of what I suggest calling "arenas of inclusion-exclusion" presupposes an *outside* and and *inside* that are inextricably entangled:

> Insofar as the production of man through the opposition man/animal, human/inhuman, is at stake here, the [anthropological] machine necessarily functions by means of an exclusion (which is also always already a capturing) and an inclusion (which is also always already an exclusion). Indeed, precisely because the human is already presupposed every time, the machine actually produces a kind of state of exception, a zone of indeterminacy in which the outside is nothing but the exclusion of an inside and the inside is in turn only the inclusion of an outside.[5]

A main challenge to the ideal of universality in education understood as one kind of school, one curiculum applied, in one place for all – the inclusive school – is thus already embedded when we speak of inclusion, namely the question of who gets to be present – and who does not – in specific settings like the class.[6] The teacher explained to me that the reallocation has given rise not only to a sense of loss of competency, but also to a loss of spatial belonging for "her" children. The arena of inclusion-exclusion that she knew has changed in its character, and her practices have had to change in response to this.

So, the interesting possibility on this occasion of crossbreeding of architectural and anthropological perspectives is the possibility to look into the dynamics of current practices of differentiating and separating schoolchildren, and in particular to investigate them with a spatial perspective that includes but does not limit itself to the situated place of the specific occasions in Vordingborg in order to get a grasp of the wider relations. With anthropologist Niels Bubandt, we might say that "The situated very quickly becomes the place where we do the fieldwork. So, the question quickly becomes how we can draw in the relations of the situatedness."[7]

In order to understand the relations of the situatedness in Vordingborg, the empirics need to also reach further than the situated. Inclusion is obviously not one thing or one kind of practice. The sociologist and philosopher John Law suggests that the ways in which phenomena are brought to cohere can also be understood as rhizomes, as kinds of tissues – both spatial metaphors – alongside the known accounts in singular, branched arborescenses that form beginnings, middles and ends, thus opening ways to grasp how things are fractional and heterogeneous but at the same time also how they are made to cohere.[8] The different versions of inclusion-exclusion arenas related to Vordingborg can, with the vocabulary of ethnographer Albena Yaneva, be studied as a controversy in which many interacting and conflicting interests and agents contribute; or, when we also include a notion of spatiality, as topological network effects.[9] In a dialogue also with the ethnographer Annemarie Mol's extensive work in the medical clinic, we might suggest that this expansion of the situated also include wider spatialities potentially could form a "spaciography" – to supplement Mol's own suggestion of the stories of practices as a "praxiography" – as a way to include the concrete spaces and the relations of the arenas of inclusion-exclusion in different scales in the accounts.[10]

Methodologically, the chapter is based on and in dialogue with these and related authors who have contributed to what is known as *post-actor network theory* which, unlike a theory, forms an ontology that encourages interrogation into the heterogeneousness of objects and favors descriptions over explanations.[11] In short, the trick in the following is to allow for the possibility of taking into account the concrete spatialities and their related and different scales in their 3D Cartesian sense as an integral part of the multiple arenas of inclusion-exclusion nexuses that take place, and to affiliate them in their wider topography. Seen in this perspective, universality, inclusion and the inclusive school are more or less precariously obtained or rather held in place across practices, spaces, scales and registers. And it is these precarious, also spatially embedded arenas that interests us.[12]

Present/Not-Present – History

Schooling has been mandatory for all children in Denmark since 1739.[13] Since the first law of the Folkeskole in 1814, the law has evolved around the idea of Skolen for Livet (The School for Life) formulated by pastor, philosopher and politician N. F. S. Grundtvig as an ideal for education for high as well as low taught together, with a focus on the thriving of children as whole human beings and the education of all to become democratically responsible, participating and even happy citizens.[14]

However, since 1908 most reforms of and amendments to the law have dealt with various versions of the division of children of the same age into different levels and spatial settings. During the 1930s arguments for the different needs of "book-oriented children" and "children more apt for working with their hands," supplemented by arguments for a need for craftsmen in industry, were used to place all children into separate tracks. These trackings often separated one-third of the children, who were considered to be less academically capable than the rest. Concepts like *hjælpeklasser* (assistance classes) and *værneklasser* (protective classes) were meant for children considered too fragile to be taught in ordinary school classes, and later *OBS-klasser* (observation classes), meant for a smaller part of children with specific challenges in one or more fields, emerged within the ordinary school.[15]

From the mid-eighteenth century until the latter half of the twentieth century, private philanthropic institutions for "the weak of mind" and children and adults with severe disabilities had evolved in order to "shield and protect." These institutions were gradually taken over by the state, and from the major 1958 revision of the Law on the Folkeskole, special needs education conducted at the special schools and institutions was understood to be an integral part of the Folkeskole, and all major responsibilities in terms of curriculum and economy were held by the state.[16] In 1975 the responsibility for the institutions was reallocated to the then thirteen counties, who expanded capacities and established new *specialskoler* (special schools) for *vidtrækkende specialundervisning* (far-reaching special education), still under the Law on the Folkeskole. Municipalities could refer children to far-reaching special education, which in practice meant the placement of the child in a county-led special school, but counties had the final say on eligibility and held all responsibilities, including finances and management, development of competencies and the overseeing of the institutions. These referred children were known as *20.2-children* or *amtsbørn* (county children), after the paragraph in the law.[17] Children were often – and for those attending special schools like the one in Kalvehave, Vordingborg, still are – driven by taxi or municipal buses long distances from their home to school and back again every day.

2.26
National distribution of special schools, 2017

2.27
National distribution of schools, 2017

In short, between 1958 and 1993 the legislation expressed a version of the inclusion-exclusion nexus in which universality is seemingly obtained through the universal right to the same education, but not with the right to be present in the same spatial setting with peers.

Observation from a class in a fifth grade at the Svend Gønge-School, Vordingborg 2020

The classroom is square, and the tables are set up so that all children are facing the teacher. At the tables right in front of the teacher's table at the blackboard are three children who to varying degrees display difficulties in maintaining focus on the teacher and on the task at hand. During the lesson, the teacher frequently uses gestures like pointing at a child with one finger and then moving two fingers toward her eyes or quick little snapping with fingers at the children. Other times she makes small, quick sounds like whistles and clicks with her tongue or calls their names to recall their focus, often in the middle of sentences that are addressed to the whole class. Most times, the three children respond by returning their attention to her instructions. After introducing the subject, she poses an assignment that entails all the children to move around in the classroom – up to the board to place a token in different colors and back again, several times. Then she asks the class to break into groups, walking between the tables to tutor individually while still being in contact with the children up front. The noise from voices and the rattling of materials rises significantly while the children work

> on the assignment. Responses from the three children become less frequent; their attention drifts to the activities of the other children in the room. The teacher is in constant physical motion from the start of class to the end.

2.30–31
A fifth-grade classroom at the Svend Gønge-School

The changes toward more inclusion were received in various ways. A class teacher in tenth grade tells me at the lunch break:

> I can understand the idea behind the change. We are two teachers in a class with eighteen pupils. It gives us the possibility to teach quite intensively. But we also have "ugly classes" with young people where one can't help wondering if they really benefit at all from being here.

In this arena of the inclusion-exclusion nexus, the work it takes to make the everyday cohere at a midsize school in Vordingborg becomes visible and is tied to the concrete space. Obviously, the pedagogical tasks involved here are multiple. The teacher employs a number of methods, such as rearranging furniture, physical activity and group work in order to maintain focus from all of the children. They are all there – or almost all of them; but for some it is not possible to maintain presence in terms of focus. They are there, but they are not there. Issues of the "benefit" of their presence becomes part of the nexus.

During the 1980s and '90s, the division of children within the ordinary school in streams did not rhyme with neither the Grundtvigian ideals of a *rummeligt* (not directly translatable, but *spacious* and *inclusive* comes close) society as the foundation for national and societal coherence as well as democracy nor with the ideas of universality.[18] In addition, pressure from international fora was building up; in 1994 the UN Salamanca declaration on special needs education confirmed the universal right to inclusion understood as the right to be taught together with peers.[19]

After attempts at reform in 1958 and 1975 a major reform in 1993, a social-democratic government did away with almost all forms of separation in the ordinary school, introducing *helhedsskolen* (the unity school). The 1993 law stressed that all children at the same grade were to be taught undivided, and that all teaching subsequently had to be carried out within the class.[20] It was, however, still possible to establish *specialklasserækker* (special-education classes) at the schools, and the special schools continued as before. Concepts like differentiation of teaching, *rummelighed* (same meaning as *rummeligt*) and also the term *inclusion* entered or reentered the discourses in both pedagogics, politics and the public debate. The public and professional debate on pedagogics and psychology counted different positions in the period; some advocating for the advantages of inclusion for both the individual child, the class and for the school and society at large, others warning of the risks of placing children with special needs in settings without sufficient economic resources or professional capacities to support them.[21]

The issue of effects of inclusion on the performance of children was also a significant part of the general debate in the wake of the OECD-initiative to PISA (Programme for International Students Assessment) around the year 2000 and was the subject of research in terms of the effects on learning outcomes.[22]

In this inclusion-exclusion nexus, the right to be included both in terms of the curriculum and in terms of place is stated in documents from several authorities. Issues of what "benefit" entails enters the discourse.

Economy, Responsibility, Quality, Proximity

The Svend Gønge-School, Vordingborg, 2020

A child has an agreement to leave the classroom at particular hours during the day. This agreement has been made between him, his teacher, the inclusion consultant at the school and his parents. Each time, he walks from the classroom along corridors and the large common, indoor square, through the office of the administration to two smaller adjacent rooms. In this environment, a smaller number of children sits with one teacher. The child tells me that it helps him to focus, and that it gives him the peace and quiet that he needs.

2.32
The activity center at the Svend Gønge-School

2.33
The Svend Gønge-School and its immediate environment

A child moving between locations; through his walk across the school to be in another place than his peers some of the time, he self-administers his own absence and presence.

2.34
Inclusion-exclusion nexus, 1990–2022

Both before and after 1993, referrals to far-reaching special education were increasing.[23] The major 2007 Danish Structural Reform again reallocated all the responsibilities of far-reaching special needs education, this time from the counties to the municipalities, who independently decide both where referrals to far-reaching special education should be authorized and who should pay the bill: the municipal administration through PPR (The pedagogical-psychological advisory team) or the local school, or various combinations.

In a report carried out in collaboration between the Ministry of Finance, the Ministry of Education and Kommunernes Landsforening (KL, The National Association of Municipalities) from 2010, it is again stated that expenses were not decreasing in spite of the 2007 Structural Reform. The report states that 14.3 percent of children receive some form of special education, including far-reaching special education, equalling 30 percent of all expenses.[24] In 2011 the annual agreement between the Government and KL on inclusion expressed an ambition to "increase inclusion and the teachers' competencies" in the area.[25] The imagined release of resources from the special needs area was supposed to be redirected to strengthen the quality in the expected more inclusive ordinary education. In the public and political debate, this made the issues of inclusion, the quality of special needs education and the total economy of the Folkeskole inseparable from one another, and since then the governmental efforts to control budgets by decreasing the number of children receiving far-reaching special-needs education is pervasive.

In a revision of the law in 2012, the number of support hours needed by a child in order to be granted extra help in class was raised from six to nine. At the same time, access to appeal municipal decisions was limited.[26] In 2013 the annual agreement held a more precise ambition: to increase the percentage of children in the ordinary schools from 95 percent to 96 percent "without any consequences for the well-being of any children."[27] This ratio was coined as "the rate of inclusion."[28] Put the other way around, it meant a decrease by 20 percent of children referred to special schools – from 5 percent to 4 percent.[29]

The expected decrease in referrals was to be measured as an average of all municipalities, but the differences in the change in inclusion rate between municipalities after 2012 are quite significant. Some municipalities remained quite unaffected by the agreement, whereas others took more radical measures to reduce the number of referrals, Vordingborg among them.

2.25
Inclusion rate per municipality, 2017
2.35
Change in inclusion rates across Danish municipalities, 2008–20

Seemingly, there are no obvious socioeconomic or geographic correlations in the pattern; affluent municipalities do not systematically have less segregation for a start than those with lower average income and vice-versa, rural municipalities don't have more or less inclusion than cities, and the changes in rates after 2013 do not follow any identifiable pattern either.

The municipal restructuring in Vordingborg sparked a major controversy among parents and teachers during 2013 that reached the national media.[30] The extent of the problems in the wake of the restructuring prompted a governmental report showing a high degree of dissatisfaction with the situation, and the Minister of Education at the time – an outspoken advocate of school inclusion – as a result granted extraordinary resources to the municipality.[31]

In 2014 an investigation was set up on initiative from the Ministry of Education to look into the quality of inclusion as it was perceived by municipalities, schools, children and parents. The research was led by researchers from the Danish Pedagogical University, and the report concluded that the quality of inclusion was satisfying.[32]

In these political agreements, the understanding of what constitutes successful inclusion is tied to both the number of children placed in concrete settings and to the economy in terms of the amount of hours needed to keep the child in the class; public finances are inextricably related to the inclusion-exclusion nexus. Inclusion is at the same time understood as an expense and a means to cut expenses.[33] The longstanding efforts of decentralization of the financial responsibilities for inclusion have come to the last links in the chain: The municipality, the individual school, the individual teacher has here reached the individual child, who through his movement across the school bears a substantial part of the responsibility for how "the inclusive school" is being obtained in Vordingborg.

Neither the law nor the agreement that focused on lowering the number of children referred to a high volume of special needs teaching, nor did they directly imply that the individual child should be reevaluated, since referrals were now under the authority of the municipalities. However, it had the potential that up to 10,000 children would be placed in another setting than they would have been before, and under different circumstances in terms of support.[34]

In 2014 the inclusion rate briefly touched 96 percent, but already in 2015, the percentage had bounced back to its pre-2012 level. A study of the effects was carried out by the Ministry of Education in 2016, concluding that there were both negative and positive effects after the campaign for more inclusion, and that the efforts to raise the inclusion rate had had almost no effect on a national scale.[35] A 2020 study of the economy of the Folkeskole showed that it was almost impossible to calculate the expenses of the now decentralized special needs education, but that the level of spending most likely was at the same level as before 2012.[36] The policy was officially called off in 2016, but the rate of inclusion in Vordingborg remained at the same level.[37]

Outlines of a Spaceography

We can argue that the inclusion that all documents and observations bear witness of is never isolated. It does not stand by itself in a space- and place-less continuum; it depends on everything and everyone that is active while it is being practiced and thus also performed, even if these entities are not present. Inclusion-exclusion nexuses take place in many different arenas; they are situated in many spatial settings and scales at the same time. So this is not only about rendering the contested and accidental history of all Danish inclusion-exclusion nexuses visible, or only to study situated practices in-depth in one given place like Vordingborg, but to grant them a complex and spatial presence. Not stable and not homogeneous but not entirely unstable or undetectable either; enacted in different ways in different and always spatial settings. Decisions on redistributions and reallocations are also real actions that create differences for practices in concrete spaces. And what is interesting is the arenas in which it is enacted. Arena; not as metaphor for some non-place where we imagine that very different things meet and relate and play out, but as concrete and tangible spaces and places. What becomes visible and tangible in the different arenas are variations of inclusion-exclusion nexuses on many scales: Special schools are established and closed again. Smaller schools are merged into larger school districts or closed. Schools and classrooms and various centers are continuously and simultaneously rearranged as a direct result of changes in policy. The universal right to the same education is but one more or less elusive agency in processes that quite obviously differentiate children spatially in a range of ways.

With very direct reference to Annemarie Mol we might also argue that neither inclusion nor universality is nowhere to be found in all these inscriptions and observations. There are shifting policies, different versions of the history, shifting locations, shifting management and very different understandings in the public debate on what constitutes inclusion or “successful” inclusion. Is it a human right? Is it a certain level of satisfaction among actors? Does it need a special setting in a house? Or is a small activity center enough? How much will we let it cost? Is there a defined and measured level of improvement in learning? Obviously, ethics and ideas of what is right and wrong are also involved. Is it the right way to do things? For whom? Inclusion and the inclusive school – again with Mol – recedes behind all these different understandings and in these different spaces and scales, and exclusion in an equal amount of versions seems to always follow along in the shadows.

The remote Kalvehave special school, the Ministry of Education, the Association of Municipalities, the Municipal Council of Vordingborg, the school boards at both ordinary schools and special schools, the teachers and staff, the school management, children, and parents together with buildings, classrooms, special classes outdoor areas and corridors, tables, screens – they all contribute to making the decentralization of responsibilities for inclusion work. They are, with the words of the philosopher Bruno Latour, continuously mustered and aligned in an arena where a particular version of the inclusion-exclusion nexus is enacted both in terms of concrete, spatial allocations and in the understanding of what the inclusive school should entail and how it could be done.[38]

As hinted at earlier, I suggest that this kind of analytical take on practices, where they are also seen as spatially distributed and spatially dependent in different scales, could form the outline of a spaceography; a way to thicken the descriptions of the concrete situatedness of practices as they are played out both in specific places and in the network-space-topology they are embedded in. A child in a corridor at a school and the distribution of special needs schools in Denmark; an agreement between the government and the Association of Municipalities and a classroom in a school in Southern Zealand; a municipality and a dismantled special center. Perhaps we can get closer to the spatial performances of the welfare state, and vice versa: performances of space tied to the distributions and redistributions of the welfare state.

Acknowledgments

Thank you to Grethe Top and Kamilla Hyldebo Toft in the municipality of Vordingborg, to everyone at the Svend Gønge-School, to Lauge Floris and Aleksander Nowak for seminal co-thinking, and to Martin Søberg, Deane Simpson, Claus Bech-Danielsen and Kirsten Marie Raahauge for their important comments.

Bibliography

Agamben, Giorgio. *The Open: Man and Animal*. Translated by Kevin Attell. Stanford: Stanford University Press, 2003.

Alenkær, Rasmus. *Den inkluderende skole i praksis*. Copenhagen: Frydenlund, 2008.

Alenkær, Rasmus, and Mel Ainscow. *Den inkluderende skole: En grundbog*. Copenhagen: Frydenlund, 2008.

Andersen, Jens F. *Den rummelige skole: Et fælles ansvar*. Vejle: Kroghs Forlag, 2004.

Bubandt, Niels. "Rubber Boots Methods for the Anthropocene: Curiosity, Collaboration, and Critical Description in the Study of Co-Species Worlds." Video of roundtable debate, Aarhus University Research on the Anthropocene (AURA), November 26, 2018. https://vimeo.com/304699420.

Deloitte. *Specialundervisning i folkeskolen – Veje til en bedre organisering og styring*. Finansministeriet and Kontor for videnskab og uddannelse, 2010. https://www.ft.dk/samling/20091/almdel/udu/bilag/244/859480.pdf.

Duedahl, Poul. *Billeder fra en anden verden: De Kellerske anstalters historie*. 2nd ed. Copenhagen: Gad, 2019.

Engsig, Thomas T., and Christopher J. Johnstone. "Is There Something Rotten in the State of Denmark? The Paradoxical Policies of Inclusive Education – Lessons from Denmark." *International Journal of Inclusive Education* 19, no. 5 (2015): 469–86.

Epinion. *Status på arbejdet med inklusion i Vordingborg kommune*. Copenhagen: Børne- og Ungeudvalget, Undervisningsministeriet, 2013. https://www.ft.dk/samling/20131/almdel/buu/bilag/118/1341075/index.htm.

EVA, Danmarks Evalueringsinstitut. *Visitationsprocessen til vidtgående specialundervisning: Kommunernes ansvar for opgaven efter kommunalreformen*. Copenhagen: Danmarks Evalueringsinstitut, 2009.

Gad, Christopher, and Casper Bruun Jensen. "On the Consequences of Post-Ant." *Science, Technology, & Human Values* 35, no. 1 (2010): 55–80.

Gjerløff, Anne Katrine. *Da skolen blev sin egen: 1920–1970*. Dansk skolehistorie: Hverdag, vilkår og visioner gennem 500 år. Vol. 4. Aarhus: Aarhus Universitetsforlag, 2014.

Gullestad, Marianne. *The Art of Social Relations: Essays on Culture, Social Action and Everyday Life in Modern Norway*. Oslo: Scandinavian University Press, 1992.

Hansen, Mogens F. *Skolens rummelighed: Intelligenser, undervisning og læring*. Mesterstykker. 2nd ed. Værløse: Billesø & Baltzer, 2005.
Hansen, Ole. "Et kort historisk blik på vejen fra segregation, integration og rummelighed til inklusion i folkeskolens fællesskaber." In "Er du med? Om inklusion i dagtilbud og skole." Special issue, *UCN Seriehæfte* 5 (2012): 68.
Heeager, Anne, and Jakob Majlund Holm. "Hvordan modtager folkeskoler økonomiske ressourcer, og hvilken betydning har det?" *Politica online* 51, no. 2. (2019): 211–30. http://politica.dk/fileadmin/politica/Dokumenter/politica_51_2/heeager_og_holm.pdf
Heynen, Hilde. "Space as Receptor, Instrument or Stage: Notes on the Interaction between Spatial and Social Constellations." *International Planning Studies* 18 (2013): 342–57.
Index100. *Kommunernes styring af specialundervisningsområdet: Økonomimodeller, visititation og udgifter*. Copenhagen: Indenrigs- og Boligministeriets, February 18, 2020. https://simb.dk/media/37840/kommunernes-styring-af-specialundervisningsomraadet.pdf.
Latour, Bruno. "Drawing Things Together." In *Representation in Scientific Practice*, edited by Michael Lynch and Steve Woolgar, 19–68. Cambridge, MA: MIT Press, 1986.
Law, John. *Aircraft Stories: Decentering the Object in Technoscience*. Science and Cultural Theory. Durham, NC: Duke University Press, 2002.
——. "Objects and Spaces." *Theory, Culture & Society* 19, nos. 5–6 (2002): 91–105.
——. "Objects, Space and Others." Published by the Centre for Science Studies, Lancaster University, 2003. https://www.lancaster.ac.uk/fass/resources/sociology-online-papers/papers/law-objects-spaces-others.pdf.
Mol, Annemarie. *The Body Multiple: Ontology in Medical Practice*. Science and Cultural Theory. Durham, NC: Duke University Press, 2002.
Næsby, Torben, Thomas Thyrring Engsig and Lars Qvortrup. *Tegn på god inclusion: Evaluering og indikatorer på effektfuld inklusion i Vordingborg kommune*. Fulm: Forskningsinformeret Udvikling Af Læringsmiljøer. Aalborg Universitetsforlag, 2016. https://www.ucviden.dk/portal/en/publications/tegn-paa-god-inklusion(da8ce28d-a92e-443e-8c67-6b8c4635ec0f).html.
Rapport fra arbejdsgruppen om specialundervisning. Kommunernes Landsforening Undervisningsministeriet, Amtsrådsforeningen, Finansministeriet, Socialministeriet, Københavns Kommune, Frederiksberg Kommune 2003. http://static.uvm.dk/Publikationer/2003/specialundervisning/rapport_fra_arbejdsgruppen_om_specialundervisning.pdf.
Ratner, Helene. "Settlements in Special Needs Education: Segregated Versus Inclusive Education." *Science as Culture* 25, no. 2 (2016): 193–213.
Regeringen. "Lov 379 om ændring af lov om folkeskolen." Folketinget, 2012. https://www.retsinformation.dk/eli/lta/2012/379.
——. Lov om Folkeskolen (Folkeskoleloven), nr 509, June 30, 1993.
——. Lov om Folkeskolen (Folkeskoleloven), nr 485, May 31, 2000.
Regeringen, and KL. "Aftale om kommunernes økonomi for 2011." 27. Danmark: Kommunernes Landsforening, 2011. https://www.kl.dk/media/7532/oekonomiaftale-2011.pdf.
——. "Aftale om kommunernes økonomi 2013." Regeringen, 2013. https://fm.dk/media/16696/aftale_kommunernesoekonomifor2013.pdf.
Ritchie, Tom, ed. *De mange veje mod inklusion: Metoder og tilgange i pædagogers praksis*. Værløse: Billesø & Baltzer, 2014.
Søgaard Larsen, Michael, Camilla Brørup Dyssegaard and Neriman Tiftikçi. *Effekt og pædagogisk indsats ved inklusion af børn med særlige behov i grundskolen: Forskningskortlægning*. Dansk Clearinghouse for Uddannelsesforskning, 2012. http://edu.au.dk/fileadmin/www.dpu.dk/danskclearinghouseforuddannelsesforskning/SR12mapfinal0409_01.pdf.
Tetler, Susan. *Den inkluderende skole: Fra vision til virkelighed*. Socialpædagogisk Bibliotek. Copenhagen: Gyldendal Uddannelse, 2000.
Undervisningsministeriet. *Folkeskolens vidtgående specialundervisning 1985–2001*. Copenhagen: Børne- og Undervisningsministeriet, 2002.
UNESCO. "The Salamanca Statement and Framework for Action on Special Needs Education." Paper presented at the World Conference on Special Needs Education: Acces and Quality, Salamanca, Spain, June 7–10, 1994.
Vidtgående specialundervisning: Den ændrede opgavefordeling og Kvis-Programmet. Danmarks Evalueringsinstitut, 2003. https://www.eva.dk/sites/eva/files/2017-11/Vidtgende_specialundervisning_KVIS.pdf.
Vordingborg Kommune. *Fokus på folkeskolen: Samlet beskrivelse af hovedindsatsområder i Vordingborg kommunes skoler*. Vordingborg, 2012.
Weigaard Jørgensen, Anna Sofie, Maj Blankenberg, Ulla Skall and Rune Hejlskov Schjerbeck. *Afrapportering af inklusionseftersynet: Et overblik over den samlede afrapportering*. Copenhagen: Ministeriet for Børn, Undervisning og Ligestilling, 2016.
Yaneva, Albena. *Mapping Controversies in Architecture*. Burlington: Ashgate, 2012.

Notes

1 Rasmus Alenkær and Mel Ainscow, *Den inkluderende skole: En grundbog* (Copenhagen: Frydenlund, 2008).

2 The term *arena* is inspired by the architectural theoretician Hilde Heynen, who on the background of a survey of a number of theories on space suggests that space can be understood as receptor, instrument or stage. See Heynen, "Space as Receptor, Instrument or Stage: Notes on the Interaction Between Spatial and Social Constellations," *International Planning Studies* 18 (2013): 342–57.

3 See Vordingborg Kommune, *Fokus på folkeskolen: Samlet beskrivelse af hovedindsatsområder i Vordingborg Kommunes skoler* (Vordingborg, 2012).

4 All translations from the Danish are by the author.

5 Giorgio Agamben, *The Open: Man and Animal*, trans. Kevin Attell (Stanford: Stanford University Press, 2003). See also the Norwegian ethnographer Marianne Gullestad, who has researched into the Norwegian/Scandinavian welfare state touching upon the contemporary dynamics of inclusion-exclusion in Scandinavia: Marianne Gullestad, *The Art of Social Relations: Essays on Culture, Social Action and Everyday Life in Modern Norway* (Oslo: Scandinavian University Press, 1992).

6 An in-depth study with a focus on the negotiations on inclusion, especially in terms of intelligence testing and the challenges to the concept of "the inclusive school": Helene Ratner, "Modern Settlements in Special Needs Education: Segregated Versus Inclusive Education," *Science as Culture* 25, no. 2 (2016): 193–213.

7 Niels Bubandt, "Rubber Boots Methods for the Anthropocene: Curiosity, Collaboration, and Critical Description in the Study of Co-species Worlds," video of a roundtable discussion, Aarhus University Research on the Anthropocene (AURA), November 26, 2018, https://vimeo.com/304699420.

8 See John Law, *Aircraft Stories: Decentering the Object in Technoscience*, Science and Cultural Theory (Durham, NC: Duke University Press, 2002), 4. See also Law, "Objects and Spaces," *Theory, Culture & Society* 19, nos. 5–6 (2002): 91–105; and Law, "Objects, Space and Others," published by the Centre for Science Studies, Lancaster University, 2003, https://www.lancaster.ac.uk/fass/resources/sociology-online-papers/papers/law-objects-spaces-others.pdf.

9 Albena Yaneva, *Mapping Controversies in Architecture* (Burlington: Ashgate, 2012).

10 Annemarie Mol, *The Body Multiple: Ontology in Medical Practice*, Science and Cultural Theory (Durham, NC: Duke University Press, 2002), 31.

11 Christopher Gad and Casper Bruun Jensen, "On the Consequences of Post-ANT," *Science, Technology, & Human Values* 35, no. 1 (2010): 55–80.

12 The inscriptions of governmental and regional bodies that enact inclusion are studied through desktop and archival studies into reports, circulars and laws. The spatial distributions at the scale of the nation and the municipality are studied through statistics, maps and geodata. The public debate is primarily studied through web-based news media. The discourses of professionals and the history of the Folkeskole and related topics are studied through literature and web sources. On the scale of the municipality, of the building and spatial organization of schools and of the concrete space at hand, empirics are derived from observations, walks'n'talks with children, interviews with teachers, heads of schools and the inclusion consultant at the Svend Gønge School as well as interviews and correspondence with municipal staff in the municipality of Vordingborg and desktop research into municipal websites and archives of building drawings. In the pursuit of rendering the concrete spaces in various scales at hand to be understandable and tangible, maps, drawings of buildings and various forms of photo registrations of the settings is also part of the empirics. Fieldwork and interviews were primarily conducted during spring and early fall of 2020.

13 The Folkeskole is well recorded in the fields of history, statistics, economics, political and social sciences and of course in pedagogical discourse. In particular the almost all-encompassing five-volume history of the Danish School, *Dansk Skolehistorie* 1–5, edited by Ning de Coninck-Smith and Charlotte Appel. Especially volume five, edited by Ning de Coninck-Smith, Lisa Rosén Rasmussen and Iben Vyff, *Da Skolen blev alles. Tiden efter 1970. Dansk skolehistorie: Hverdag, vilkår og visioner gennem 500 år. Vol. 1* (Aarhus: Aarhus Universitetsforlag, 2013).

14 In *Den Blå Betænkning* (The Blue Report) from 1960, and in the 1962 law, the happiness of children is a primary objective of the Folkeskole. See "Den Blå Betænkning: Undervisningsvejledning for Folkeskolen, 1960," *DanmarksHistorien.dk*, https://danmarkshistorien.dk/vis/materiale/undervisningsvejledning-for-folkeskolen-1960-den-blaa-betaenkning/ (accessed January 2, 2022). In addition, Nicolai Frederik Severin Grundtvig should be mentioned here as an important figure in the history of the Folkeskole and particularly because much of his thinking later entered into the social-democratic discouse on the development of the welfare state. However, he was not at the outset a universalist himself. See "Grundtvig og velfærdsstaten," *DanmarksHistorien.dk*, https://danmarkshistorien.dk/vis/materiale/grundtvig-og-velfaerdsstaten/ (accessed January 2, 2022).

15 Birgit Kirkebæk, Poul Skov, "Specialundervisning," *Den Store Danske*, last modified May 12, 2016, https://denstoredanske.lex.dk/specialundervisning (accessed January 2, 2022). See also "Skole og undervisning efter 1814," *DanmarksHistorien.dk*, https://danmarkshistorien.dk/leksikon-og-kilder/vis/materiale/skole-og-undervisning-1814-2014/ (accessed January 2, 2022) and Anne Katrine Gjerløff, *Da skolen blev sin egen: 1920–1970*, Dansk skolehistorie: Hverdag, vilkår og visioner gennem 500 år. Vol. 4 (Aarhus: Aarhus Universitetsforlag, 2014).

16 Poul Duedahl, *Billeder fra en anden verden: De Kellerske anstalters historie*, 2nd ed. (Copenhagen: Gad, 2019).

17 The term *far-reaching special needs education* (*vidtgående specialundervisning*) is defined in the beginning of this report: EVA, Danmarks Evalueringsinstitut, *Visitationsprocessen til vidtgående specialundervisning: Kommunernes ansvar for opgaven efter kommunalreformen* (Copenhagen: Danmarks Evalueringsinstitut, 2009).

18 The Danish *rummelighed* or *rummeligt* is not direct translatable, though *rum* means "space." "All-embracing" and "inclusivity" both come quite close, though. It denotes the ability of societies, communities and individuals to be able to embrace and have space for differences. It is tied closely to Grundtvig and his advocacy for religious freedom within the State Church/"Folkekirken," see "Nicolai Frederik Severin Grundtvig, 1783–1872," *DanmarksHistorien.dk*, https://danmarkshistorien.dk/leksikon-og-kilder/vis/materiale/nicolai-frederik-severin-grundtvig-1783-1872/ (accessed January 2, 2022).

19 UNESCO, "The Salamanca Statement and Framework for Action on Special Needs Education," paper presented at the World Conference on Special Needs Education: Access and Quality, Salamanca, Spain, June 7–10, 1994.

20 Lov om Folkeskolen (Folkeskoleloven), nr. 509, June 30, 1993. A principle of proximity was stressed in the changes to the law made in 2000, and municipalities were encouraged to arrange for children to be taught as close to home as possible. Lov om Folkeskolen (Folkeskoleloven), nr 485, May 31, 2000. For a short historical account see Ole Hansen, "Et kort historisk blik på vejen fra segregation, integration og rummelighed til inklusion i folkeskolens fællesskaber," "Er du med? Om inklusion i dagtilbud og skole," special issue, *UCN Seriehæfte* 5 (2012): 68.

21 See, among others: Susan Tetler, *Den inkluderende skole: Fra vision til virkelighed*, Socialpædagogisk bibliotek (Copenhagen: Gyldendal Uddannelse, 2000); Jens F. Andersen, *Den rummelige skole: Et fælles ansvar* (Vejle: Kroghs Forlag, 2004); Mogens F. Hansen, *Skolens rummelighed: Intelligenser, undervisning og læring*, 2nd ed. Mesterstykker (Værløse: Billesø & Baltzer, 2005); Rasmus Alenkær, *Den inkluderende skole i praksis* (Copenhagen: Frydenlund, 2008); and Tom Ritchie, ed., *De mange veje mod inklusion: metoder og tilgange i pædagogers praksis* (Værløse: Billesø & Baltzer, 2014).

22 See, for example, Michael Søgaard Larsen, Camilla Brørup Dyssegaard and Neriman Tiftikçi, *Effekt og pædagogisk indsats ved inklusion af børn med særlige behov i grundskolen: Forskningskortlægning*, Dansk Clearinghouse for Uddannelsesforskning, http://edu.au.dk/fileadmin/www.dpu.dk/danskclearinghouseforuddannelsesforskning/SR12mapfinal0409_01.pdf; Thomas T. Engsig and Christopher J. Johnstone, "Is There Something Rotten in the State of Denmark? The Paradoxical Policies of Inclusive Education – Lessons from Denmark," *International Journal of Inclusive Education* 19, no. 5 (2015): 469–86; and Henrik Stanek, "Skolereformen har heller ikke løftet eleverne i specialundervisning," *Folkeskolen.dk*, January 22, 2020, https://www.folkeskolen.dk/1547844/skolereformen-har-heller-ikke-loeftet-eleverne-i-specialundervisning (accessed December 29, 2021).

23 A number of reports and surveys after 1993 monitor the number of referrals; among others, see Undervisningsministeriet, *Folkeskolens vidtgående specialundervisning 1985–2001, Rapport fra arbejdsgruppen om specialundervisning* (Undervisningsministeriet, Kommunernes Landsforening, Amtsrådsforeningen, Finansministeriet, Socialministeriet, Københavns Kommune, Frederiksberg Kommune), http://static.uvm.dk/Publikationer/2003/specialundervisning/rapport_fra_arbejdsgruppen_om_specialundervisning.pdf; and *Vidtgående specialundervisning: Den ændrede opgavefordeling og KVIS-programmet*, Danmarks Evalueringsinstitut (Evalueringsinstitut, Danmarks), https://www.eva.dk/sites/eva/files/2017-11/Vidtgende_specialundervisning_KVIS.pdf.

24 Deloitte, *Specialundervisning i folkeskolen: Veje til en bedre organisering og styring* (Finansministeriet and Kontor for videnskab og uddannelse),

https://www.ft.dk/samling/20091/almdel/udu/bilag/244/859480.pdf.
25 Regeringen and KL, "Aftale om kommunernes økonomi for 2011" (Danmark: Kommunernes Landsforening), https://www.kl.dk/media/7532/oekonomiaftale-2011.pdf.
26 Regeringen, "Lov 379 om ændring af lov om folkeskolen" (Folketinget), https://www.retsinformation.dk/eli/lta/2012/379.
27 Regeringen and KL, "Aftale om Kommunernes Økonomi 2013" (Regeringen), https://fm.dk/media/16696/aftale_kommunernesoekonomifor2013.pdf.
28 "Bag om inklusion," *Børne- og Undervisningsministeriet*, https://www.uvm.dk/folkeskolen/laering-og-laeringsmiljoe/inklusion/bag-om-inklusion, last modified August 6, 2021 (accessed December 29, 2021).
29 "Regler om inklusion," *Børne- og Undervisningsministeriet*, https://www.uvm.dk/folkeskolen/laering-og-laeringsmiljoe/inklusion/regler-om-inklusion, last modified June 25, 2021 (accessed December 29, 2021).
30 Marie Rask Glerup and Laurits Nansen, "Minister om inklusion: En kæmpe stor omvæltning," *DR*, February 23, 2014, https://www.dr.dk/nyheder/politik/minister-om-inklusion-en-kaempe-stor-omvaeltning (accessed December 29, 2021); Laura Marie Sørensen, Maiken Steen Frederiksen and Laurits Nansen, "Foregangskommune har massive problemer med inklusion i skolerne," *DR*, February 23, 2014, https://www.dr.dk/nyheder/indland/foregangskommune-har-massive-problemer-med-inklusion-i-skolerne (accessed December 29, 2021); Sara Røjkjær Knudsen and Katja Sønder Tuxen, "For mange lærere er ikke klar til inklusion," *DR*, May 22, 2014, https://www.dr.dk/nyheder/indland/mange-laerere-er-ikke-klar-til-inklusion (accessed December 29, 2021); Hans Redder. "Er inklusion i folkeskolen gået for vidt?" TV2, March 18, 2014, https://nyheder.tv2.dk/politik/2014-03-18-er-inklusion-i-folkeskolen-gaaet-for-vidt (accessed December 29, 2021); Dorthe Olsgaard, "Mor: Vi føler os som prøveklude for inklusionen," TV2 ØST, May 27, 2014, https://www.tv2east.dk/vordingborg/mor-vi-foler-os-som-proveklude-inklusionen (accessed December 29, 2021); Pernille Aisinger and Jenniver Jensen, "I Vordingborg er inklusion og heldagsskole nu hverdag," *Folkeskolen.dk*, June 5, 2013, https://www.folkeskolen.dk/530678/i-vordingborg-er-inklusion-og-heldagsskole-nu-hverdag (accessed December 29, 2021); Pernille Aisinger and Jennifer Jensen, "Sådan ændrede politikerne skoleøkonomien," *Folkeskolen.dk*, June 5, 2013, https://www.folkeskolen.dk/530679/saadan-aendrede-politikerne-skoleoekonomien (accessed December 29, 2021); Michael Ørtz Christiansen, "Borgerlige vil have belyst 'brutal' inklusion," *Berlingske*, March 18, 2014, https://www.berlingske.dk/politik/borgerlige-vil-have-belyst-brutal-inklusion (accessed December 29, 2021); Morten Mikkelsen, "Mismod bremser inklusion i skolen," *Kristeligt Dagblad*, March 19, 2014, https://www.kristeligt-dagblad.dk/danmark/mismod-bremser-inklusion-i-skolen (accessed December 29, 2021); "Inklusion: Ny undersøgelse overrasker Christine Antorini," TV2, April 28, 2015, https://tv.tv2.dk/video/MDgyOTg5NEE (accessed December 29, 2021); Steffen Andersen and Hans Jørgen Nielsen, "Hvad man ikke ved om inklusion," *Information*, July 6, 2015, https://www.information.dk/indland/2015/07/ved-inklusion (accessed December 29, 2021); Tine Rock, "Inklusionen halter: Klagerne hagler ned over Vordingborg Kommune," TV2 ØST, November 10, 2017, https://www.tv2east.dk/kommunalvalg-2017/inklusionen-halter-klagerne-hagler-ned-over-vordingborg-kommune (accessed December 29, 2021); Henrik Stanek, "Kommuner må til lommerne: Behovet for specialundervisning vokser på ny," *Folkeskolen.dk*, https://www.folkeskolen.dk/618954/kommuner-maa-til-lommerne-behovet-for-specialundervisning-vokser-paa-ny (accessed December 29, 2021); Anne Bonnevie Lundbye, "Skoleområdet i Vordingborg Kommune får assistance," TV2 ØST, May 24, 2018, https://www.tv2east.dk/vordingborg/skoleomradet-i-vordingborg-kommune-far-assistance (accessed December 29, 2021); and Katja Kafling and Christina Jul Nielsen, "Rod i økonomi og sager om inklusion: Nu skal Vordingborgs skoler løftes," TV2 ØST, May 26, 2018, https://www.tv2east.dk/vordingborg/rod-i-okonomi-og-sager-om-inklusion-nu-skal-vordingborgs-skoler-loftes (accessed December 29, 2021).
31 Epinion, *Status på arbejdet med inklusion i Vordingborg Kommune* (Copenhagen: Børne- og, Undervisningsministeriet, 2013), https://www.ft.dk/samling/20131/almdel/buu/bilag/118/1341075/index.htm; see also the Minister of Education, Christine Antorini on the challenges in Vordingborg, in Pernille Aisinger, "Antorini: Der har været hårdt pres på lærerne i Vordingborg," *Folkeskolen.dk*, August 15, 2013, https://www.folkeskolen.dk/532381/antorini-der-har-vaeret-haardt-pres-paa-laererne-i-vordingborg (accessed January 2, 2022).
32 Epinion, *Status på arbejdet med inklusion i Vordingborg Kommune*, Næsby, Torben, Thomas Thyrring Engsig, and Lars Qvortrup, *Tegn på god inklusion: Evaluering og indikatorer på effektfuld inklusion i Vordingborg kommune*, FULM: Forskningsinformeret udvikling af læringsmiljøer (Aalborg Universitetsforlag, 2016). https://www.ucviden.dk/portal/en/publications/tegn-paa-god-inklusion(da8ce28d-a92e-443e-8c67-6b8c4635ec0f).html.
33 See, for example, Undervisningsministeriet, *Folkeskolens vidtgående specialundervisning 1985–2001* (Copenhagen: Børne- og Undervisningsministeriet, 2002) or Anne Heeager and Jakob Majlund Holm, "Hvordan modtager folkeskoler økonomiske ressourcer, og hvilken betydning har det?" *Politica online* 51, no. 2 (2019): 211–30, http://politica.dk/fileadmin/politica/Dokumenter/politica_51_2/heeager_og_holm.pdf.
34 Laura Marie Sørensen and Mads Rafte Hein, "BAGGRUND Sådan blev inklusion et krav i danske skoler," *DR*, February 23, 2014, https://www.dr.dk/nyheder/indland/baggrund-saadan-blev-inklusion-et-krav-i-danske-skoler (accessed January 9, 2022).
35 Anna Sofie Weigaard Jørgensen, Maj Blankenberg, Ulla Skall and Rune Hejlskov Schjerbeck, *Afrapportering af inklusionseftersynet: Et overblik over den samlede afrapportering* (Copenhagen: Ministeriet for Børn, Undervisning og Ligestilling, 2016).
36 Index100, *Kommunernes styring af specialundervisningsområdet: Økonomimodeller, visititation og udgifter* (Copenhagen: Indenrigs- og Boligmininisteriet, February 18, 2020), https://simb.dk/media/37840/kommunernes-styring-af-specialundervisningsomraadet.pdf.
37 Emma Qvirin Holst, "Regeringen dropper inklusions-målsætning," *Altinget*, May 11, 2016, https://www.altinget.dk/artikel/regeringen-dropper-inklusions-maalsaetning (accessed January 18, 2022).
38 Bruno Latour, "Drawing Things Together," in *Representation in Scientific Practice*, ed. Michael Lynch and Steve Woolgar (Cambridge, MA: MIT Press, 1986), 19–68.

2.25 Inclusion rate per municipality, 2017

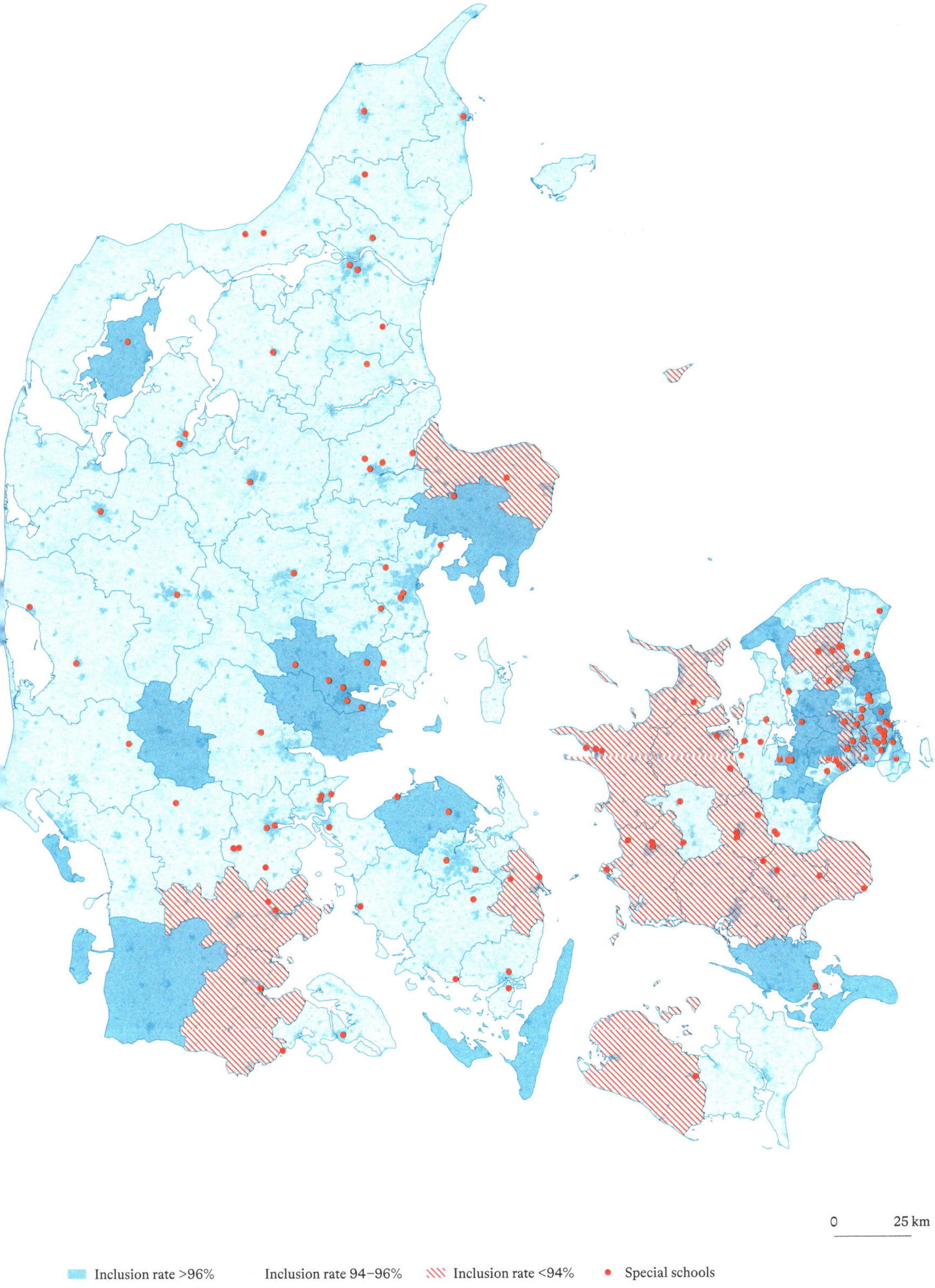

2.26 National distribution of special schools, 2017

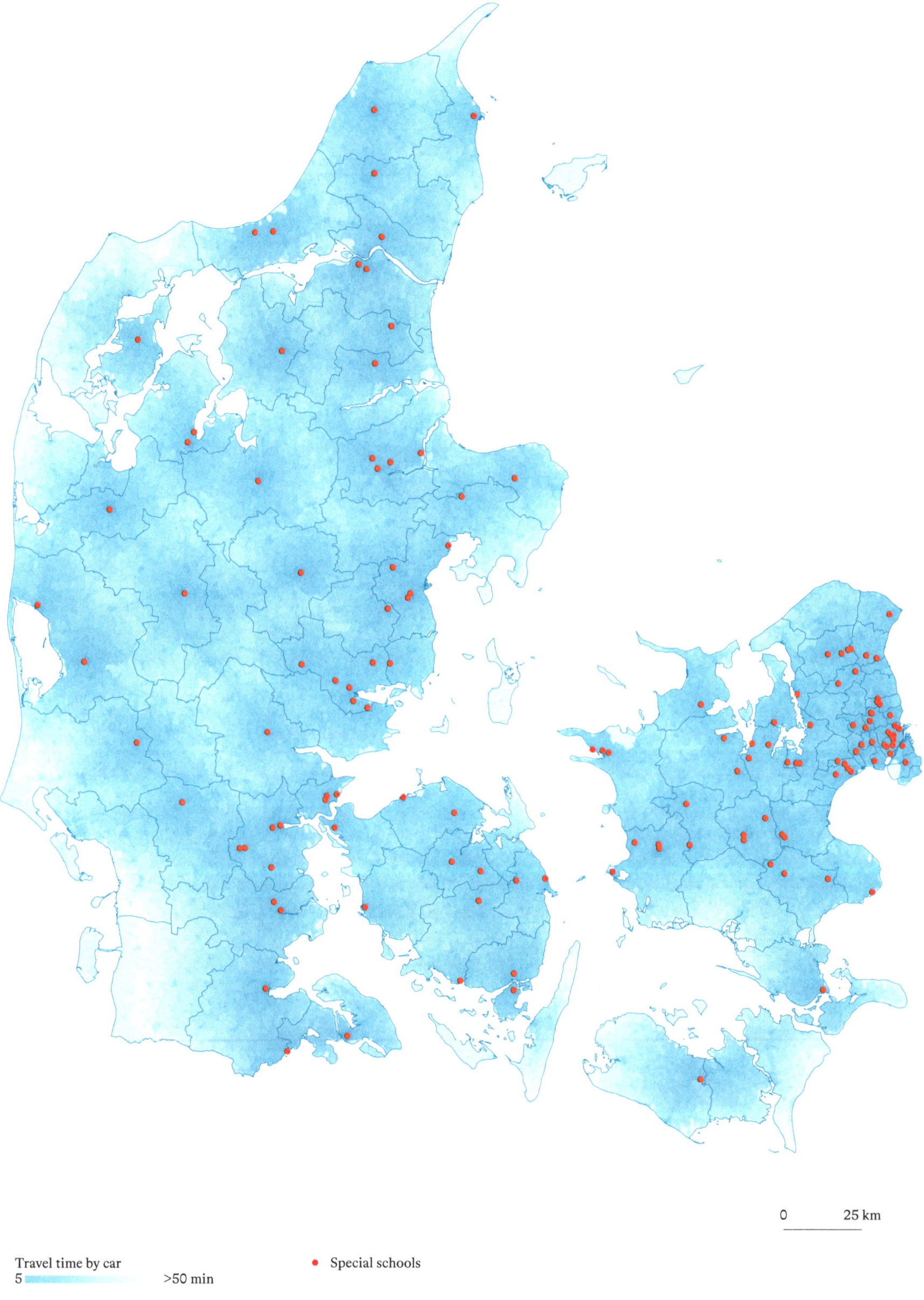

2.27 National distribution of schools, 2017

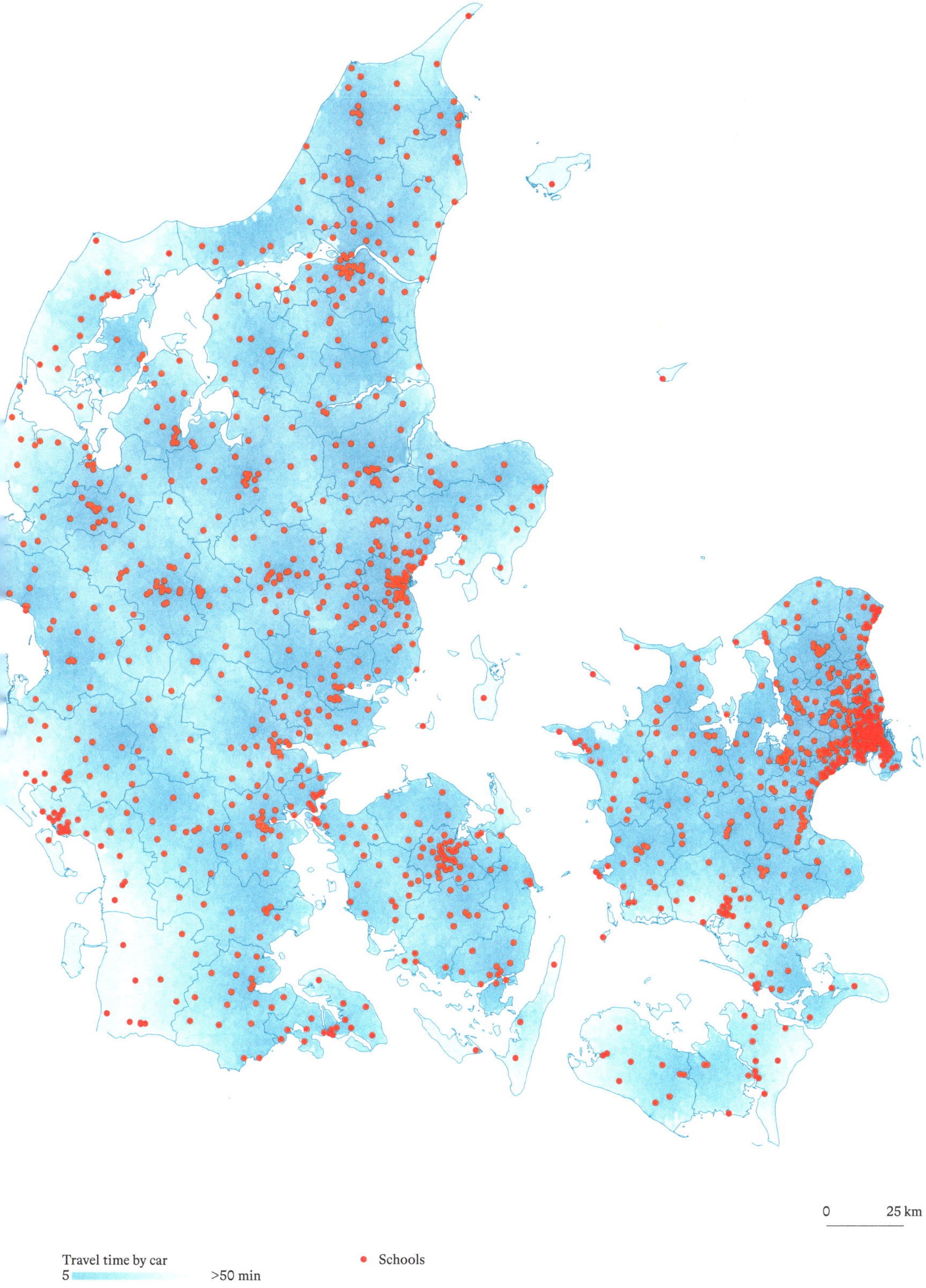

2.28 Distribution of schools in Vordingborg, before 2013

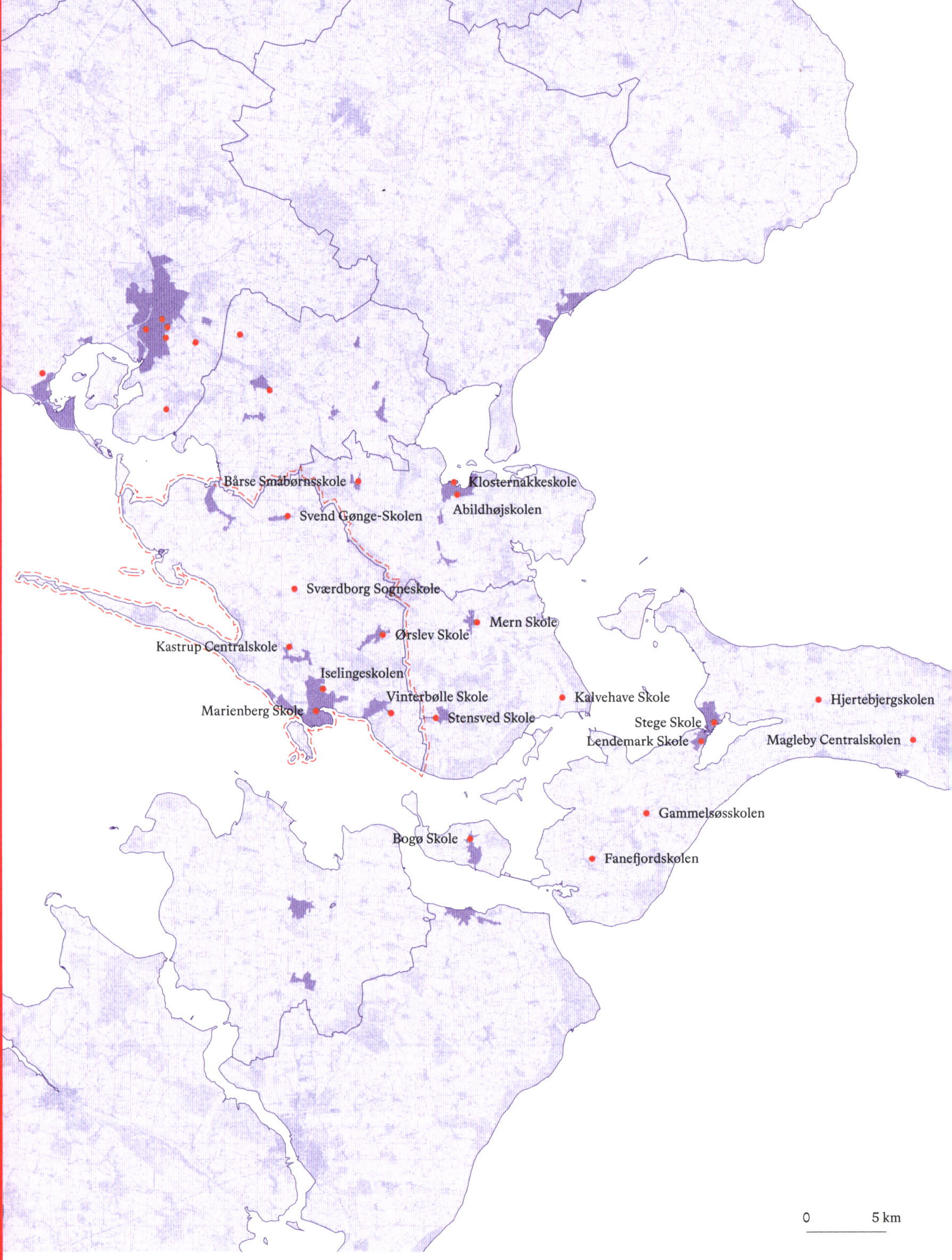

Municipal border of Vordingborg (before Structural Reform in 2007)

Municipal schools before 2013

2.29 Distribution of schools in Vordingborg, after 2013

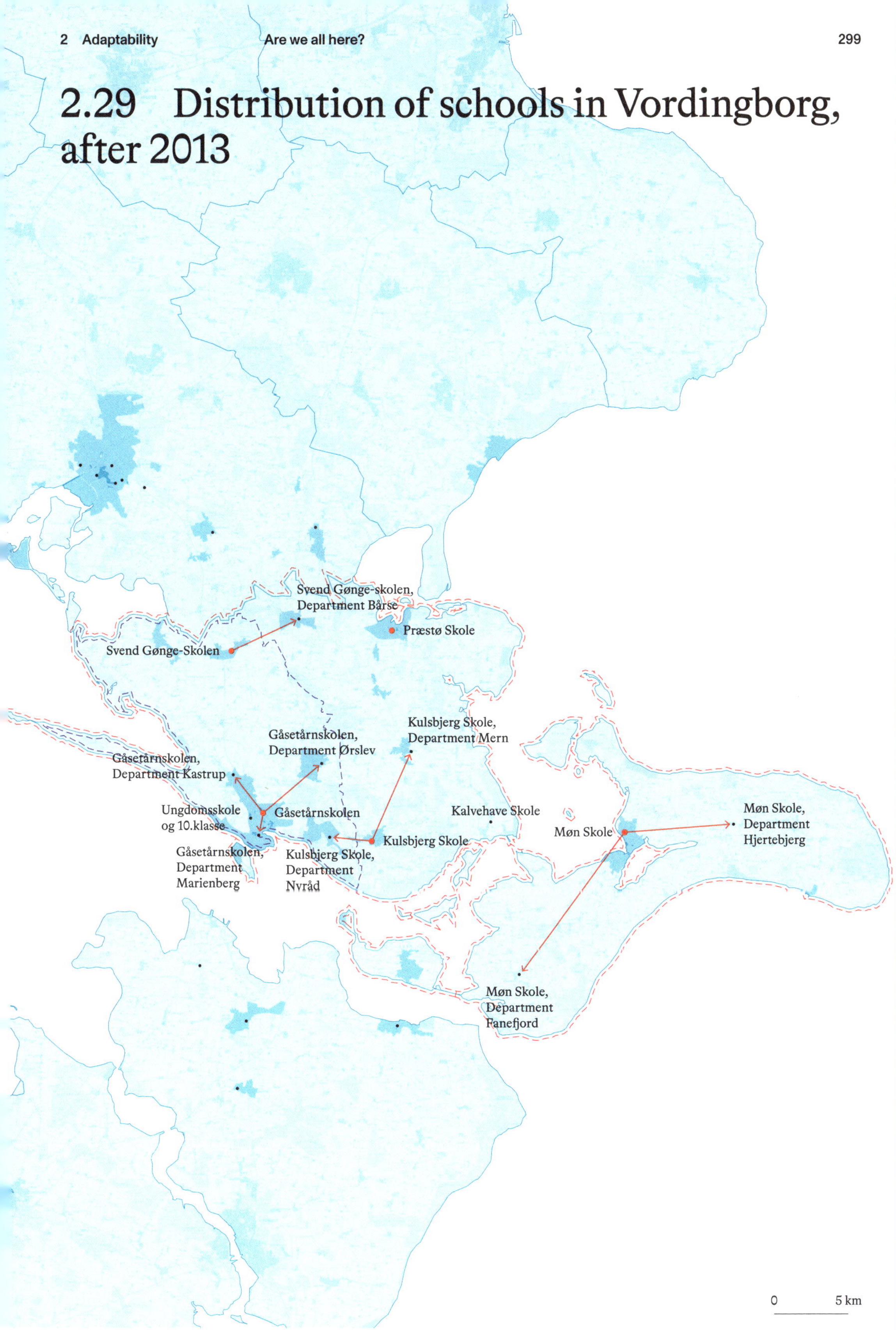

--- Municipal border of Vordingborg (after Structural Reform in 2007)

--- Municipal border of Vordingborg (before Structural Reform in 2007)

• Municipal schools' departments after 2013 (subsumed)

• Municipal schools before 2013

2.30 A fifth-grade classroom at the Svend Gønge-School

2.31

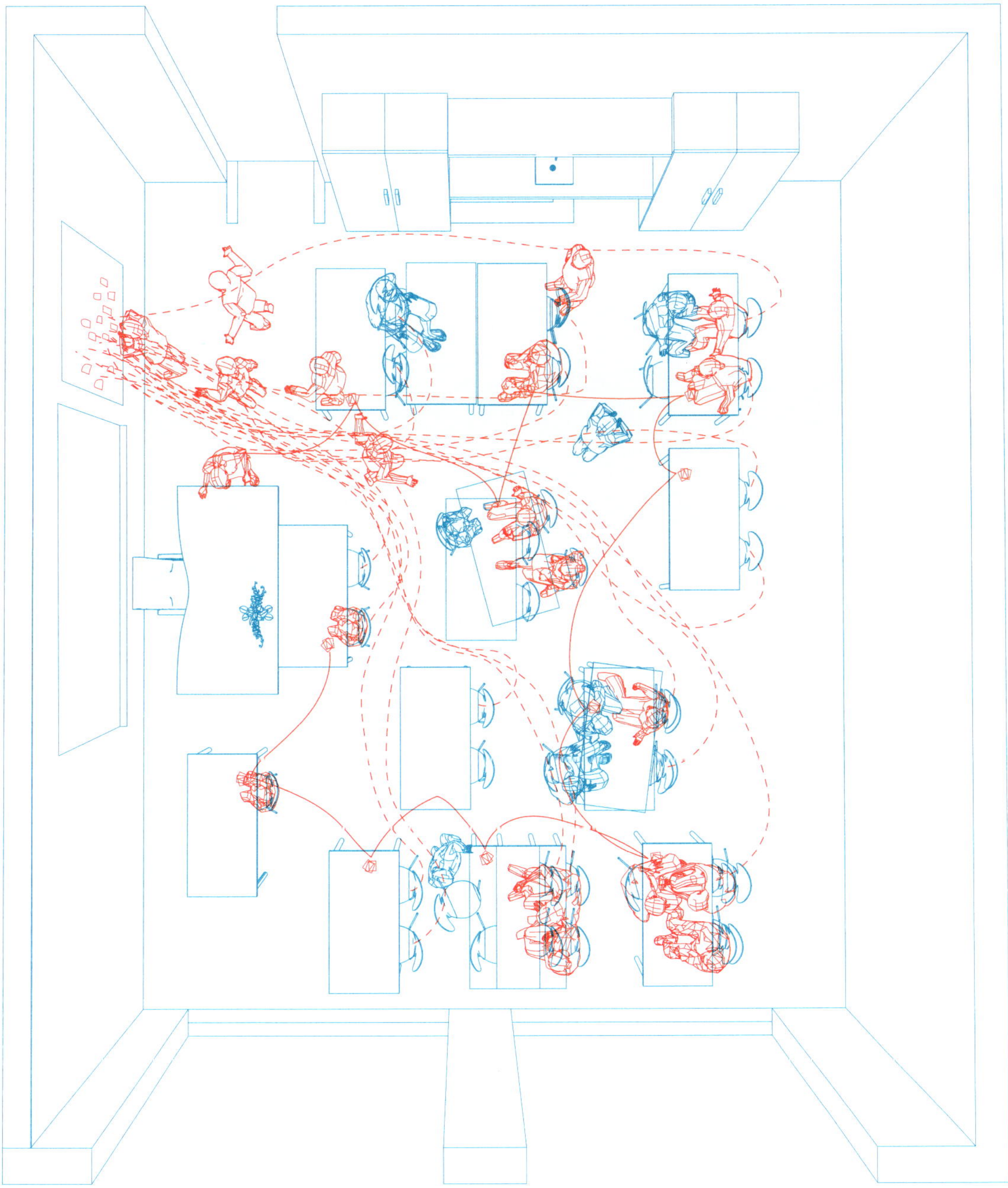

— Stage 1 – Teacher gives instructions and distributes material to pupil

- - - Stage 2 – All children rise from their seats to go to the board where they put their answer to the exercise and return to their seats.

— Stage 3 – Group work: The class breaks up into small groups with about half the pupils changing places; and the teacher moves between tables.

2.32 The activity center at the Svend Gønge-School

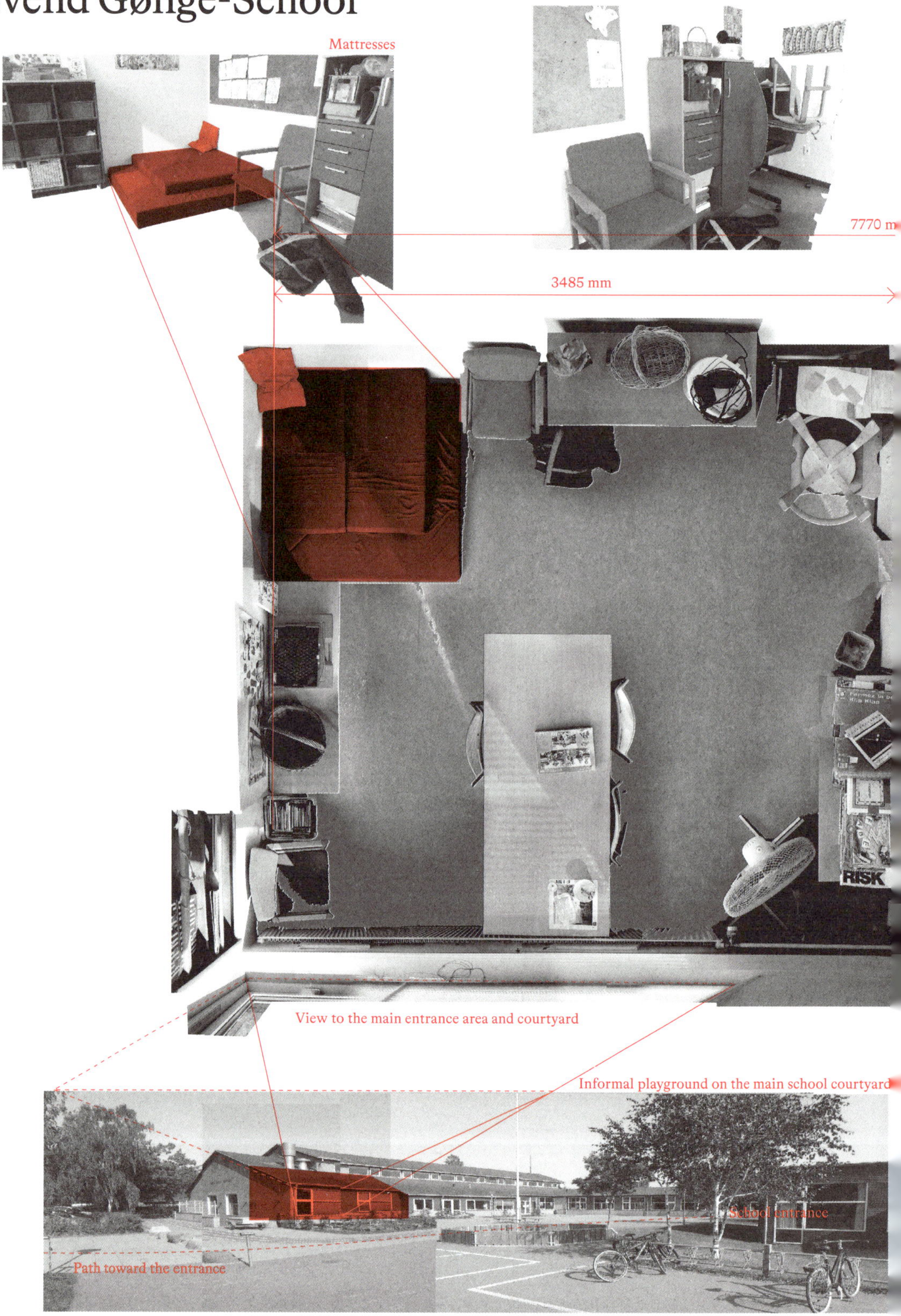

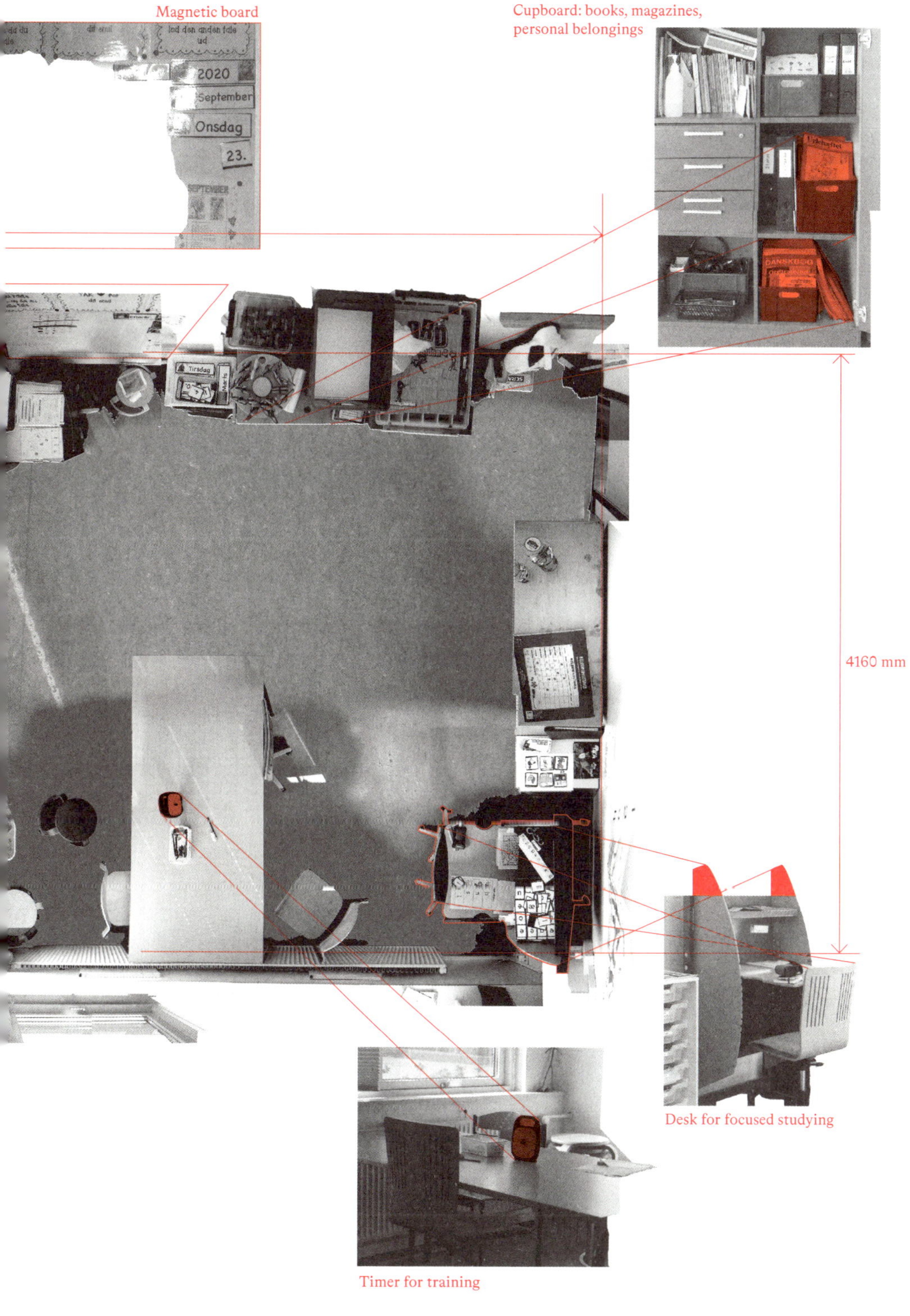
Magnetic board
2020
September
Onsdag
23.
Cupboard: books, magazines, personal belongings
4160 mm
Desk for focused studying
Timer for training

2.33 The Svend Gønge-School and its immediate environment

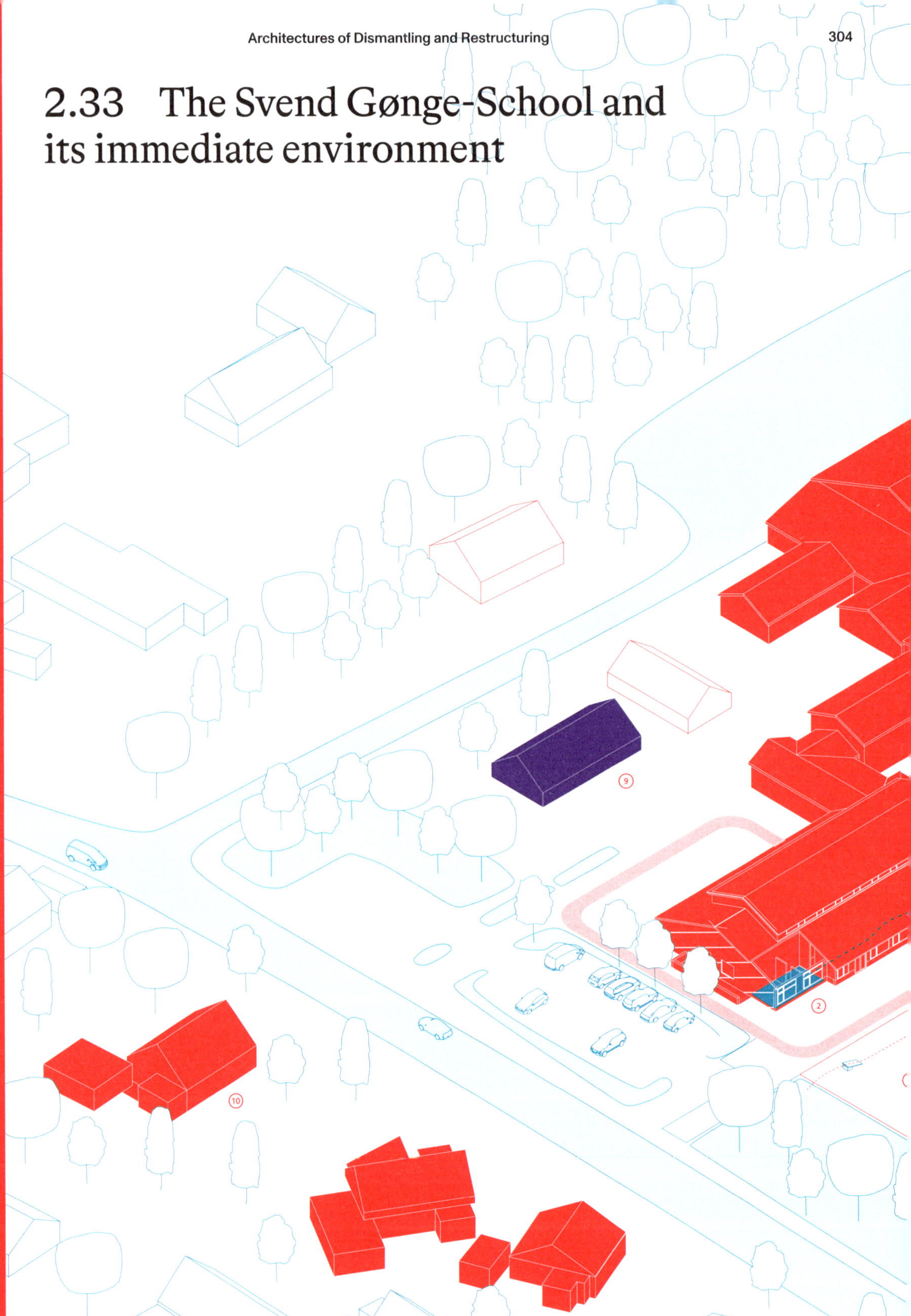

1 Main courtyard
2 Activity Center (vis. 2.31)
3 Path from classroom to activity center
4 Classroom, fifth grade (vis. 2.30)
5 Open field: breaks in open air
6 Sports hall
7 Club: after-school
8 Forest: playing war in the forest
9 Former special classes building
10 Local community takes part in daily activities of the school.

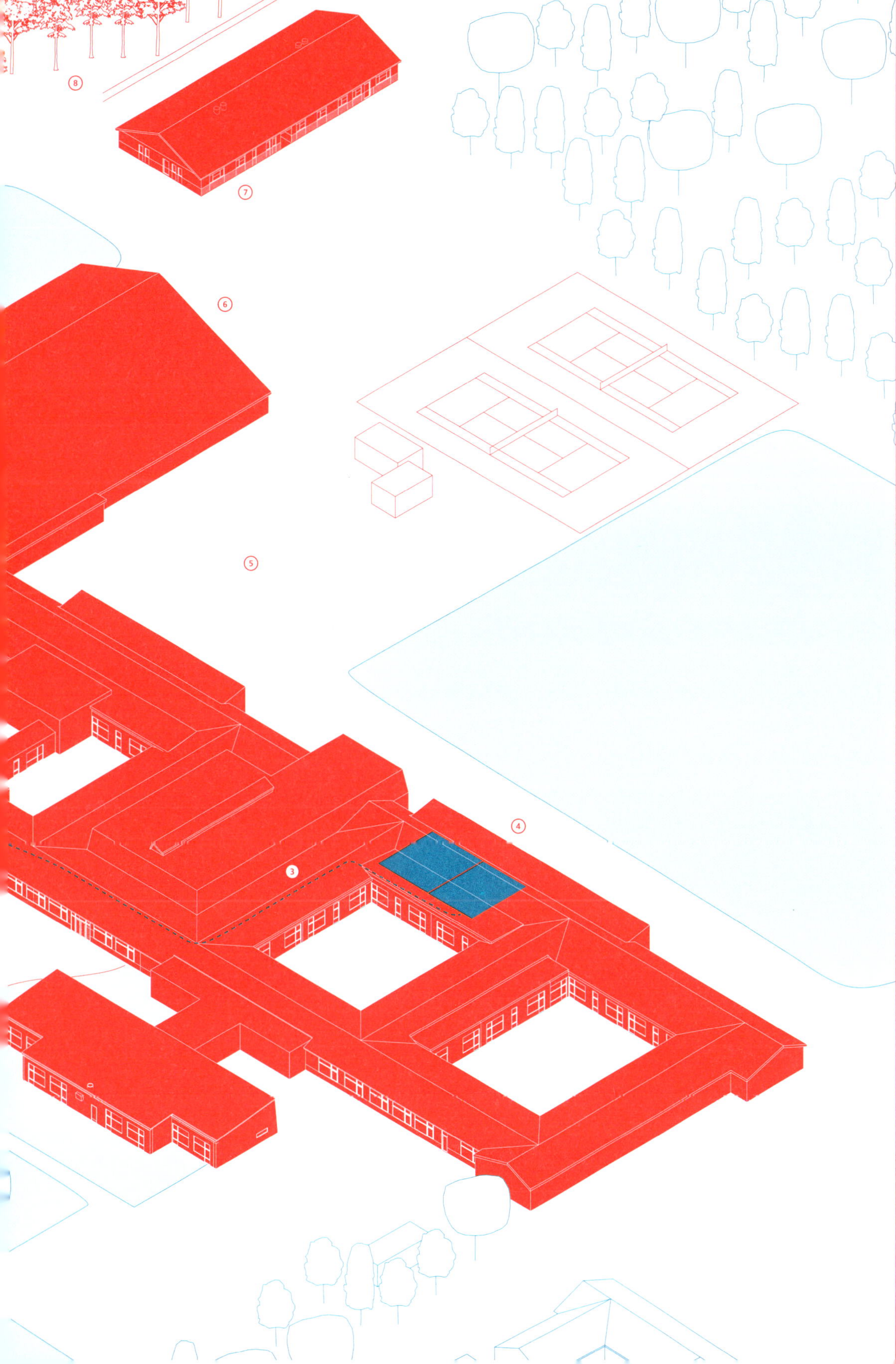
8
7
6
5
4
3

2.34 Inclusion-exclusion nexus, 1990–2022

(!) 2001 KVIS, "quality in special needs education' (Kvalitet i specialundervisningen), a governmental initiative following the changes made to the law in 2000 to sustain more quality in special needs educ *Rummelighed* is a key concept of the initiative, and enters the public debate. Runs until 2004.

(!) May 2003 An evaluation of the cha in legislation from 2000 shows that th number of referrals has bounced back a short period of decline. It's recomme that schools themselves get jurisdictio decide which children should get the c special needs support.
The argument is both one of proximity – that the child should be taught close home and among peers – as well as eco ical: the changes to the law in 2000 di result in a cut in expenses in this area.

(!) 1993 The term *teaching differentiation* enters the public discourse; it means that the teacher should teach each individual child according to their abilities.

(!) 1994 Salamanca UNESCO statement on children's right to inclusion

(!) 2003 Report from a cross-governm workgroup that advocates better mana ment of costs to the special area throu more *rummelighed* in the schools and a reduction in referrals to special school

(§) 2000 The right of the child to be part of its community is further strengthened in the law. Municipalities are asked to build up capacity to teach more children with special needs closer to their own environment instead of sending them to special needs schools far away from home.

(§) 1993 Major changes to the Law on Folkeskolen. Streaming of classes in "higher" and "lower" is abandoned. All children should be taught within the class.

(§) 2005 Minor adjustm the law and the introduc of mandatory national t

(!) 2001 The Ministry of Education issues a rep that concludes that the number of children refe to far-reaching special education/a special scho increased significantly after 1993.

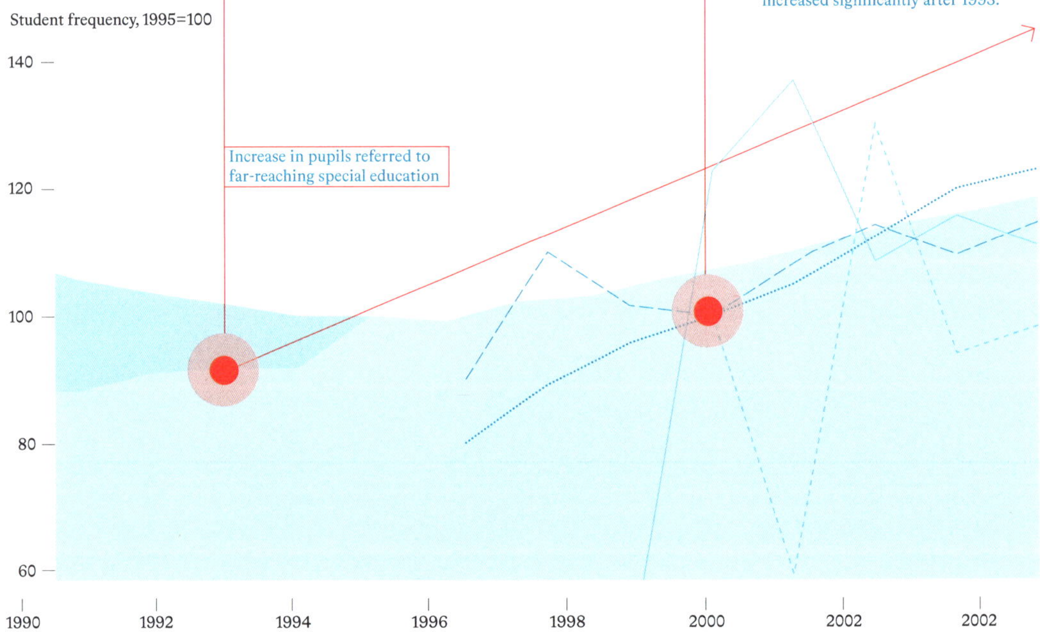

Development in the number of pupils in the primary and lower secondary school's far-reaching special education first–tenth grade
Number of 6- to 16-year-olds

Special schools, incl. regional and national
Special and center classes
Regular classes
Teaching at a place of residence/day care institution

Number of referrals to special education schools
Number of referrals to special education classes in public schools
(!) Relevant events
(§) Related laws, regulations, policies

2014 Governmental report inclusion in Vordingborg: 4 percent of teachers find inclusion to be successful, 55 percent find it not successful. *DR* (Danish National Broadcast) runs articles on the problems in the wake of the increased inclusion, also in Vordingborg Kommune. Public debate on inclusion in national and local media.

2007 A report shows that expenses to ır-reaching special education have risen ·om index 100 in 1995 to 254 in 2005.

2019 Report states a decrease in inclusion in the Folkeskole from 2016 to 2019 after the end of the 2012 policy.

2010 Report on the economy of the special education area states that expenses are still rising and suggests that new ways to manage, think and organize special needs education be developed, especially further decentralization of the financial responsibility to the schools, more inclusion and more cost-efficiency.

2016 Report on inclusion in Vordingborg states that experience with inclusion is satisfactory.

2020 Report on expenses and incentives in relation to inclusion shows that special needs education has an estimated cost ca. 18.1–23.3 percent of all expenses for the Folkeskole.

2011 Aftale om kommunernes økonomi for 2011. Yearly agreement on the economy of municipalities between the government and the organization of municipalities. Expresses agreements on obtaining more inclusion.

2016 The Government officially abandons the 96 percent objective from 2013.

2012 Change in the law: The minimum of hours granted for special needs education is set from 6 to 9h/w.

2007 Major structural reform. Further ·centralizing of economic responsibil- es and increased municipal autonomy: '3 municipalities are reduced to 98, and counties are reduced to 5 new regions. ·e-2007 most special needs schools ·re owned by the counties. The reform ·ocated all responsibility for special ·eds education to the municipalities, d almost all special needs schools got ·unicipal owners.

2013 Yearly agreement on the economy of municipalities between the government and the organization of municipalities. Expresses clear objectives: The percentage of children in the ordinary settings should increase to 96 percent in 2015. Children's well-being should be maintained during the increase of inclusion.

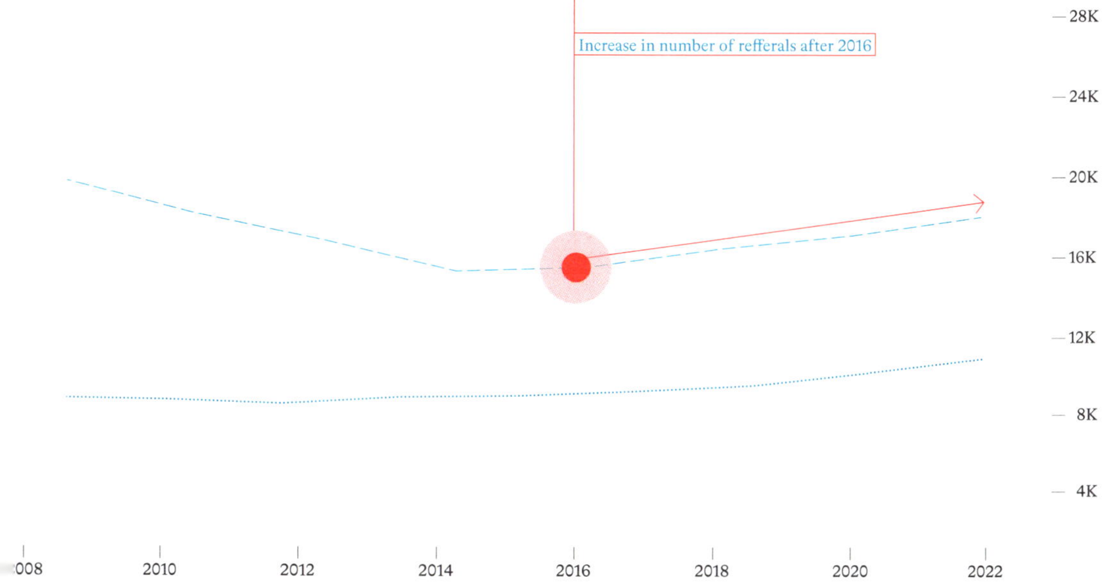

2.35 Change in inclusion rates across Danish municipalities, 2008–20

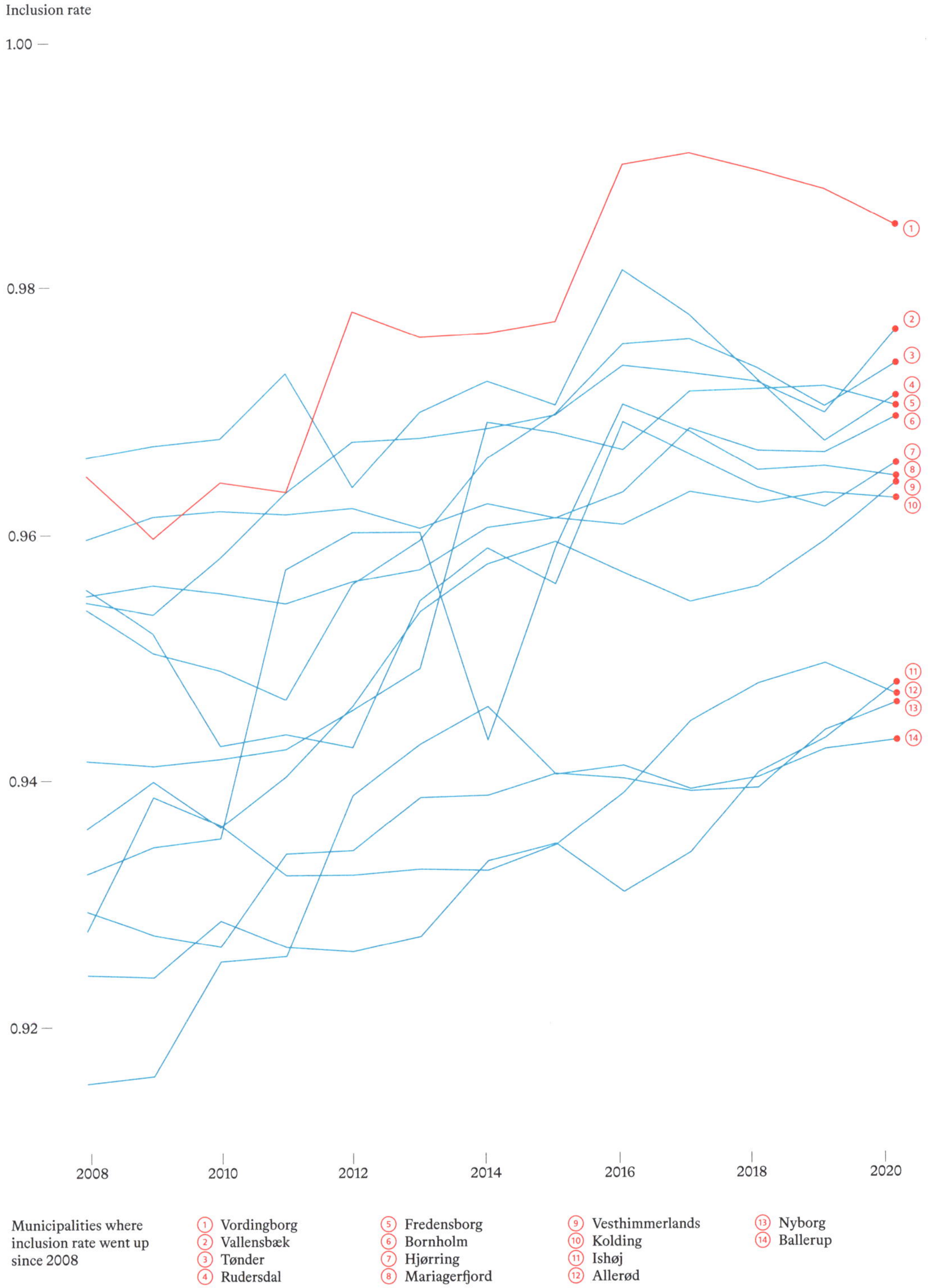

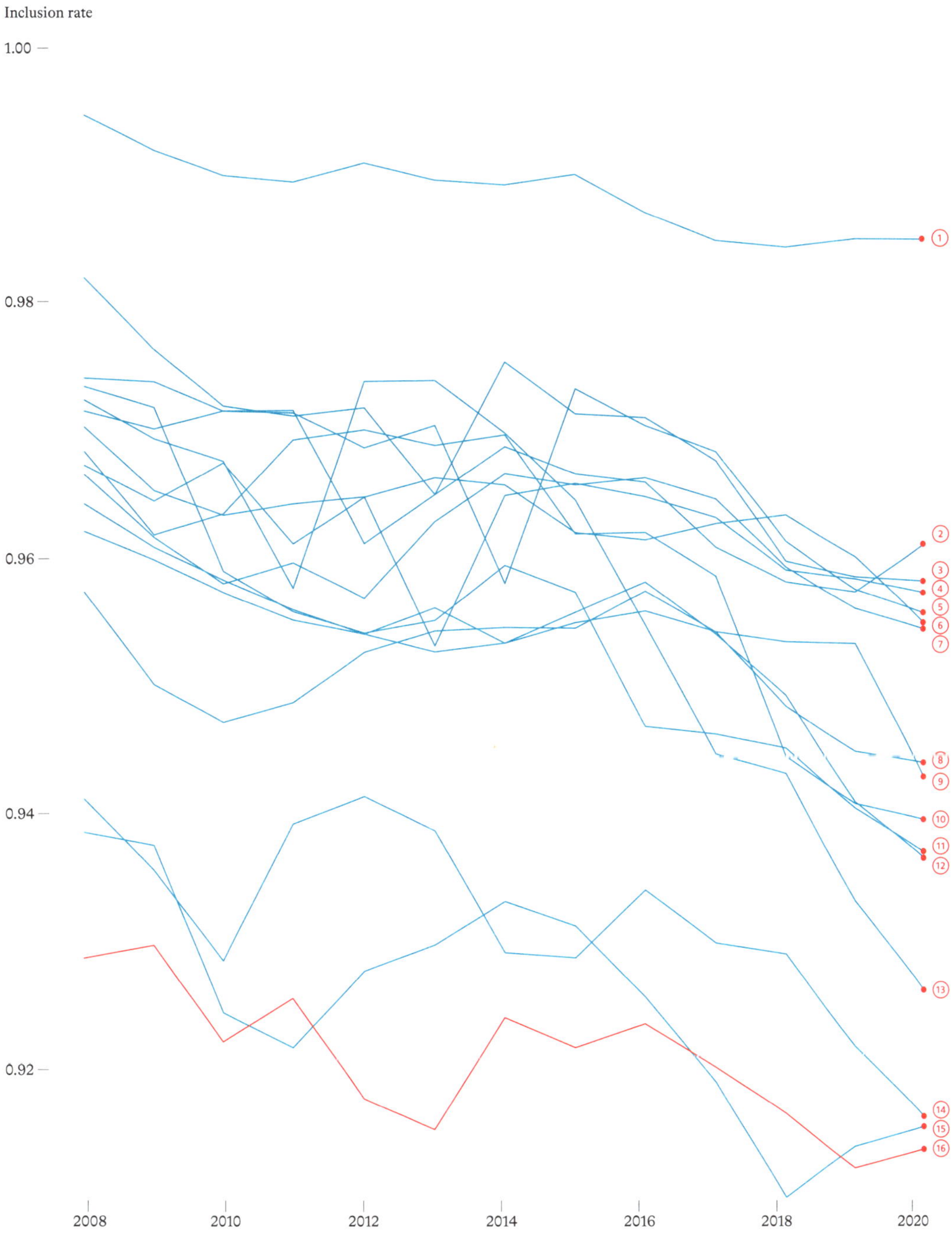

Municipalities where inclusion rate went down since 2008

1 Gentofte
2 Skanderborg
3 Ikast-Brande
4 Viborg
5 Favrskov
6 Sorø
7 Hvidove
8 Greve
9 Helsingør
10 Gribskov
11 Lejre
12 Holstebro
13 Struer
14 Slagelse
15 Næstved
16 Holbæk

Healing Architecture and the Crisis of Care

Runa Johannessen

This chapter explores the prevalent idea of healing architecture in contemporary Danish hospital architecture. *Healing architecture* is a term for the design of spaces that are intended to therapeutically support the healing of patients and promote stress-reducing environments for all users. Both as a slogan and a label for evidence-based design methods, the term is typically used affirmatively across the landscape of academic literature, policy papers, architectural popular journals and mainstream media.

In a Danish context, the interest in healing architecture became a concrete enterprise with the advent of the 2007 Structural Reform. Then, the state's massive capital investment in transforming and future-proofing the hospital system and building stock presented an historic opportunity to recalibrate the relationship between architecture, medicine and welfare on a large scale. Beyond the reform's political demands for optimization of hospital capacity, productivity and operating budgets, the expectation for the "hospitals of the future" was to take part in the curing of patients by caring for their well-being.[1]

With healing architecture, the hospital building itself is medicalized: By *medicalized architecture*, then, I mean the hospital buildings and environments are designed to act as a medical remedy – as a therapeutic, prophylactic or recuperative instrument which has the capacity to cure or care. Much attention has been given to scientifically prove the health impact of particular elements of design.[2] Accordingly, the formula of basing design decisions on evidence is by now a standard practice (and business model) within healthcare architecture. In short, healing architecture has been embraced and celebrated by policymakers and architects alike as a key to improve the quality of Danish hospitals. Moreover, the praise for healing architecture often goes hand in hand with the critique of the cold and clinical "hospital machines" of the 1950s to '70s to which it is put in opposition.

Yet the hospital is still considered a machine for the production of health.[3] The future-proofing of the hospital system is based on an economic calculus of efficiency and frictionless infrastructures where the systematization of health production takes its cues from shipping and supermarket logistics.[4] A recurrent critique from the public as well as healthcare professionals is that the system is foundering under the pressure of optimization. Such critique concerns a wide range of issues – for example, increased distances to the hospital because of centralization, the fragmentation of treatment because of specialization, long waiting lists for treatment and the strain put on healthcare personnel due to understaffing. What role does healing architecture play in this scenario?

Instead of scrutinizing how or whether the architecture of the new Danish hospital is actually capable of curing or caring, I will make an attempt to capture the historical development of a welfare hospital system that eventually embraced healing architecture as its guiding ideal.

2.36
Key events in Danish hospital development, 1990–2022

On that basis, I suggest shifting the focus from celebrating healing architecture as a slogan to diagnosing it as a symptom, that is, to understand it structurally as a sign of a crisis of care in the welfare system under the impact of financialized capitalism. By invoking the current situation as a crisis of care, I lean on the political philosopher Nancy Fraser's analysis of the social-reproductive contradictions of financialized capitalism as a crisis tendency.[5] My contention is that contemporary medicalization

1 Fremtidens Fødestue, Herning.

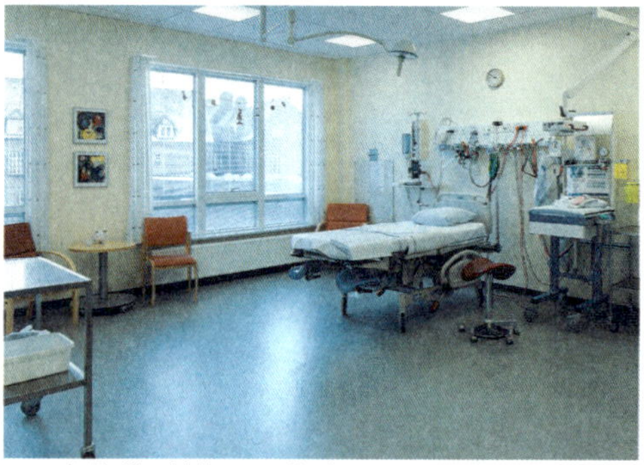

2 Traditional delivery room, Herning.

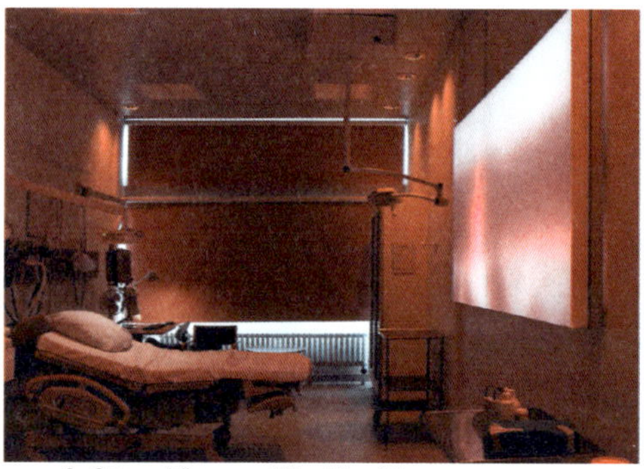

3 Sensory delivery room, Hillerød Hospital.

of architecture assigns care work to architecture through affective engineering. Healing architecture becomes a proxy caregiver at the intersection of medicalized architecture and the welfare system of hospitals in a crisis of care.

In order to explore healing architecture as an ideal as well as a symptom of a crisis, I will make three steps: First, I present the contemporary case of a multisensorial delivery room in Herning, where the architectural environment is designed to care for the woman in labor.[6] Next, I provide a historical account of spatial and medical reconfigurations in the hospital system in order to contextualize present-day healing architecture. Finally, I make the shift in perspective from slogan to symptom and expand on Fraser's idea of a structural crisis of care in which I claim architecture is a proxy caregiver.

The year 2020 presented the world with a global health crisis, namely the COVID-19 pandemic. The consequences for healthcare, hospitals and social reproduction have been acute. Hospitals have had to turn to so-called crisis standards of care, while severe lockdowns of societies have been calculated on the basis of hospital capacity. Epidemiology is likely to impact the next generation of hospitals (and architecture in general) in ways that differ from the healing architecture explored in this chapter. However, in the following, as I subject the affirmative streak of healing architecture to a critical analysis, my aim is neither to disregard the radical impact pandemics might have on our future hospitals nor to denounce any positive aspects of healing architecture and the architectural qualities it might breed. Rather, my task is to understand how our ideas of architecture's very instrumentality reflects political, economic and ideological conceptions of care and welfare.

Multisensorial Induction of Labor

Fremtidens Fødestue (The Delivery Room of the Future) is an experimental project set up at the Regionshospitalet (regional hospital) in Herning.⟨fig. 1⟩ In 2014 a group of midwives initiated a project to rethink the maternity ward's physical space with the ambition of creating a safe and homely atmosphere. According to the midwives, the traditional hospital delivery room is clinical, reminiscent of an operating room, and counterproductive for a "good labor process."[7] ⟨fig. 2⟩

2.38
Conventional delivery room, Thisted, 2020

Therefore, they consulted experts from a broad range of professional disciplines – including *feng shui*, design psychology and animal care – and included knowledge from existing research in healing architecture in order to redesign the delivery room as a multisensorial and interactive installation. The sensorial stimulation is generated by video projections on the walls, adjustable color temperature of the light, a sound system and carefully selected furniture. The laboring woman/couple are invited to modify their surroundings by choosing their preferred images and sounds on an iPad. In this way, the sensory experience is adapted to the individual/couple.

2.37
Multisensorial delivery room, DNV-Gødstrup, 2020

The purpose of the installation is to make the laboring woman feel safe in order to stimulate a natural increase of the hormone oxytocin, which triggers contractions. The midwives' expectation was that the new delivery room would have a positive effect on the woman/couple's well-being and in turn that it would reduce the time spent in labor.[8]

This expectation is currently being documented in a randomized clinical trial.[9] The published study protocol holds as a premise that the production of oxytocin can be disrupted by environments dominated by technology and medical interventions, while bringing nature into the room reduces stress.[10] At Hillerød Hospital, where similar principles have been tested in their so-called sensory delivery rooms since 2014, clinical studies also show that the need for a caesarean section can be reduced if a woman gives birth in a room with soothing light, blurred and calm image projections and pleasant sounds.[11] ⟨fig. 3⟩ Moreover, Fremtidens Fødestue has served as a precursor and testbed for the future maternity ward at the new hospital in Gødstrup, North Zealand.

According to a case description of the delivery room at Danske Regioner's (Danish Regions) website *Godt Sygehusbyggeri* (Good Hospital Building), the room appears as "anything but an operating room."[12] The text repeats no fewer than ten times that the delivery room must create a homely environment. The slightly diffuse idea of homeliness is associated with a sense of security, while visible technology and medical instruments are said to be counterproductive to the labor process. Additionally, the presence of nature is highlighted as a positive affective agent. The productive atmosphere in the delivery room is thus designed as a hybrid mix of home and nature: as a holistic environment of nature images, favorite music and living room furniture. The anonymous author of the text suggests that the healing architecture of the delivery room provides "a qualified bid for patient 'empowerment' that could give flesh and blood to all the nice words about patients' participation and responsibility for their own healing."[13] Empowerment and responsibility for healing is directed at the sensory experience of the laboring woman, and the aim is to optimize the human affective interface with the environment. In other words, the multisensorial and interactive delivery room is an affective technology: a sensory induction of labor that replaces the injection of the synthetic oxytocin that is otherwise normally given to women whose contractions are weak.

Here, the environment is a fully controlled interior space. In contrast to medicalized architecture that positions the patient in, or with a view to, nature to provide sunlight, fresh air or beauty, Fremtidens Fødestue rather evokes a visual and auditory representation of nature; a synthetic nature conveyed through advanced technology.

2.40
Nature as a healing element: hospital garden (exterior), Bispebjerg Hospital, 1913

2.41
Nature as a healing element: visual projections (interior), DNV-Gødstrup, 2020

4 Illustration of Fremtidens Fødestue as planned for Regionshospital Nordjylland, Hjørring.

The main designer of Fremtidens Fødestue, the architect Esben Bala Skouboe, describes the room as a technological composition that embodies the affective atmosphere: When architecture and interactive art work together, "space becomes very dynamic and one can begin to compose experiences."⟨fig. 4⟩ To Skouboe, the experiences they design as a "frame for almost 4,000 childbirths every year" are a kind of applied art – in opposition to fine art – that makes art relevant for the individual and for society.[14]

In Fremtidens Fødestue, features from nature, artistic approaches and various forms of technology are deployed to unite in a sensory composition. For the laboring woman/couple, then, the atmospheric compositions perform a kind of affective engineering on the experience of giving birth. For the purpose of healthcare, architecture assumes the role as an affective provider of care in an institutional setting. In the following, I will turn to the historical conditions for architecture as an instrument for healthcare.

Architecture as Somatic, Social and Affective Engineering

The 2007 Structural Reform and concurrent reorganization of the hospital system created an opportunity to literally recast Danish hospital architecture.[15]

2.42
Geographical distribution of hospitals and number of beds, 1970
2.43
Geographical distribution of hospitals and number of beds, 2020
2.45
Number of hospitals and beds, 1930–2020

In economic terms, the reform stipulated a decrease in the number of hospitals while scaling up their capacity for production of health.[16] In architectural terms, the moment offered an opportunity to create a new ideational foundation for healthcare spaces: discarding the cold functionalism of the so-called golden years of the welfare state (1945–70) and introducing a humanistic, healing architecture.[17] This ideational shift has to be understood against the background of the development of the hospital system and how architecture historically has served as an instrument for medicine.

First of all, the idea that the physical environment has an effect on human health is not new. The medicalization of architecture began in the late eighteenth century as a biopolitical project of ensuring the general state of health of the population.[18] Architecture became a biopolitical "curing machine."[19] The architectural pharmacons were primarily emphasizing improved sanitation and hygiene. A lasting impact on hospital design, for instance, was made by the British nurse Florence Nightingale's mid-nineteenth-century suggestion to build hospitals as pavilions where fresh air, light and cleanliness could increase a patient's chances of survival. In a Danish context, Bispebjerg Hospital in Copenhagen is a celebrated example of a hospital drafted over Nightingale's pavilion scheme.⟨fig. 5⟩

5 Aerial photo, Bispebjerg Hospital, 1933.

2.39
Bed ward in pavilion, Bispebjerg Hospital, 1913

In the absence of medical treatment for bacterial diseases – antibiotics for clinical use were developed in 1943, thirty years later than the construction of Bispebjerg Hospital – architecture was in the service of conducting medical engineering on the biological body, that is, a somatic engineering. Medical discourse and technology came to permeate design and turned into general stylistic ideals for ventilation, sunlight, hygiene, white walls and physical exercise.[20]

In 1930 the state-supported national Danish hospital system was established, a moment which also marks the beginning of medical specialization and the spatial centralization of hospitals.[21] Throughout the height of the welfare state period, a biomedical paradigm dominated in medicine. Illness was predominantly viewed as something biological, and the medical focus gravitated toward diagnostics and medical treatment.[22] The main virtue of architecture in relation to medicine was to be a supportive framework for diagnostics and therapy, while, as a public institution, it conducted a sort of social engineering through the body of the welfare system.[23] The hospitals were growing, and the results of the architectural competitions that were announced in the 1950s and '60s (for example, Glostrup, Odense, Rigshospitalet, Hvidovre, Herlev)[24] introduced new, up-to-date hospital typologies like the characteristic "matchbox on a muffin" (a bed tower on a flat base for general functions) and the low-rise comb structure (bed wings attached to a spine of general functions).[25] Efficiency, functionality, standardization and repetition dominated "hospital machines" well into the 1980s.

The 1970 Municipal Reform reorganized the hospital system by further centralization and rationalization of administration.[26] However, reactions to the biomedical paradigm and increased medicalization of society as a whole was growing in the 1960s and '70s,[27] and the utilitarian and functionalist approach to architecture was beginning to be criticized for being cold, clinical and dehumanizing.[28] Ideologically, the critique of the biomedical view on illness reoriented attention from diagnosis and treatment of the patient as a passive recipient to values of holistic care for the "patient in center" – who was now considered both a market consumer of a service and an active participant in the treatment.[29] The political management of the hospital system was also changing: neoliberal ideas, first introduced in the 1970s, were gradually implemented through the 1990s, with increased focus on performance, productivity, professionalization of administration, the introduction of competing private hospitals and an emphasis on patients' rights. Marketization was presented as the means to increase efficiency and quality in hospital services.[30] In other words, the current recasting of hospital ideals has its immediate roots in the 1970s critique of the clinical institution in combination with a marketization of the patient/hospital relation.

As we have seen, architecture as a cure for illness receded from view with biomedical development from the 1930s to the '70s. Yet at a confluence of the growing institutional critique and increased marketization, a rising preoccupation with neuroscience (the study of our nervous system) added a new direction for hospital architecture: *evidence-based design* (EBD). EBD was born from an emerging interest in human beings' sensory relation to the environment.[31] A seminal study of the potential impact of beauty for the process of healing was carried out by the healthcare design researcher Roger Ulrich in 1984 and published in the article "View through a Window May Influence Recovery from Surgery."[32] As the title indicates, we can see that the attention given to the healing potential of architecture now turns from body to sensation; from soma to affect.[33] In other words: curing and caring for the body is obtained through the patient's neurological response to the environment. This shift from soma to affect goes hand in hand with an ambition to provide scientific evidence for the therapeutic and healthy – the salutogenic – effects of architecture.[34] Beyond the 1980s inaugural studies of beautiful surroundings and the concurrent rise of discourses on holism and critiques of cold and dehumanizing hospitals, EBD is a fundamentally result-oriented approach to sensory experience; the goal is to optimize the human subject's affective encounter with the environment.

6 Illustration of Nyt Bispebjerg's "Healing Gardens" by Erik Brandt Dam Arkitekter and Charlotte Skibsted Landskabsarkitekter.

The concept of healing architecture popularized and manifested in recent Danish hospital construction rests on principles from EBD, although it is occasionally expressed as a rediscovery of knowledge from the past.[35] For instance, with the current renovation and expansion of Bispebjerg Hospital, the old gardens will, according to the hospital director, be "reborn" as "healing gardens."[36] ⟨fig. 6⟩ But architecture's curative role has undoubtedly changed over time. Rather than serving as a remedy to boost the immune system, its current development is incentivized by advances in behavioral and neuroscientific models of understanding human affective responses.[37]

7 One of the new hospitals, Nyt Hospital Nordsjælland, by Herzog & de Meuron and Vilhelm Lauritzen Arkitekter.

Healing architecture is apparently supposed to stand in opposition to the "machines" of the golden era of welfare, because healing architecture cares for the senses. The publication *Sansernes Hospital*[38] and the report *Helende arkitektur*[39] have been particularly influential for the discourse on, and adoption of, healing architecture principles in a Danish context. Both publications focus on the human sensory – or affective – encounter with the surroundings. Since then, guides and recommendations have been distributed widely by public and private actors involved in the hospital building enterprise, from the branding of the "Danish solutions" to the marketing of building materials, to the countless presentations of projects by architecture studios themselves.[40]

In the individual hospital projects designed in the wake of the hospital reform, the purpose of creating healing architecture is translated into concrete form in different ways and to varying degrees.⟨fig. 7⟩ Often, it appears as a curation of particular elements of design, for example, by using wooden details in the interior or anchoring the view to a tree, based on results given by randomized EBD trials. Some of the design solutions are not related to the design of affective environments but have more practical medical purposes: one of the most radical and striking changes to hospitals built after the reform is the termination of multibed wards.⟨figs. 8–10⟩ It was, in fact, a requirement given by the Government's advisors on hospital investments and is based on EBD findings that one-bed wards reduce the spread of infections. Yet equally important is the view that it accommodates the "new patient" as a consumer.[41] At the same time, hospitals are reducing the number of beds, as the goal of the future is to treat people in their own homes rather than at the hospital.[42]

Fremtidens Fødestue is an accomplishment of ideas about medicalized architecture that has developed throughout the modern period, from the salubrious effect of nature to the importance of empowerment. To be immersed in the multisensorial environment of visual and auditory stimulation is no doubt a gratifying experience for the woman/couple, baby and staff alike and is a realization of the slogans of healing architecture. Yet what happens when we turn to consider it as a historically situated phenomena instead? In the following, I will unfold the thesis of healing architecture as a structural symptom of a crisis of care.

Crisis of Care

Cure and care are often presented as the two faces of medicine – a doctor-centered and a patient-centered approach, respectively. In the words of the health psychologist Chris de Valck et al., "cure-oriented attitudes reflect the instrumental, task-oriented dimension of the medical profession while care-oriented attitudes relate to the affective dimension of the medical encounter."[43] As we have seen, cure and care approaches in medicine have changed through history, influenced both by advances in technology and medicine as well as ideological changes.

In healthcare discourses of the twentieth century, a call to move "from cure to care" is often heard. The reason for this is typically explained by the change in population health: chronic diseases and so-called lifestyle diseases, as a well as an aging population, require continuous care. At the same time, in a neoliberal economy, hospital healthcare is, as a market object, measured in productivity and stimulated

8

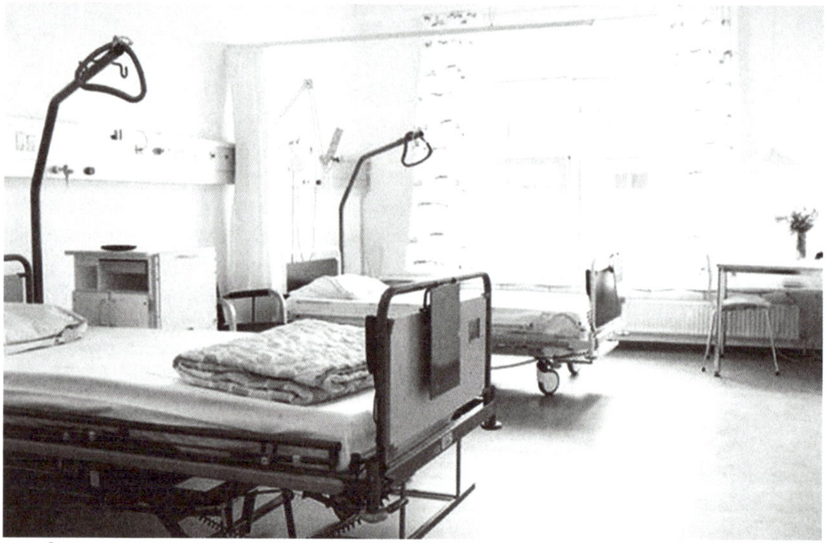

9

10

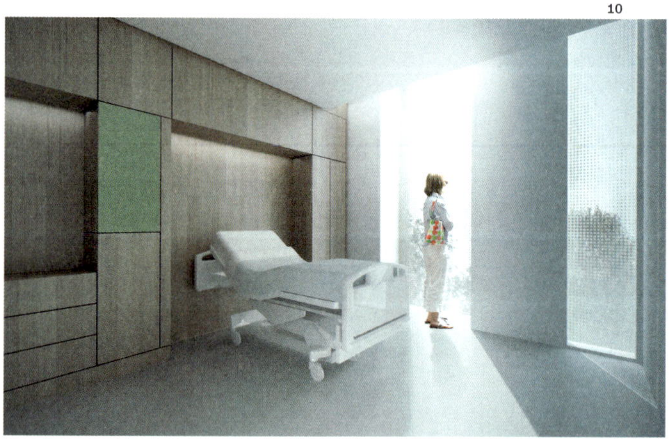

8 Ward for multiple patients at Rigshospitalet, 1930s. Source: Dansk Sygeplejehistorisk Museum.
9 Ward for two patients at Aalborg Hospital, 1970s. Source: Aalborg Hospital, image taken ca. 2020.
10 Single-patient ward at the new Rigshospitalet (opening 2022).

through competition and economic incentives. Why has the question of care become so important? Who is responsible for asserting that care is provided?

For Nancy Fraser, care is understood as a background condition, not only for healthcare, but for society as a whole. Care, or *social reproduction*, is the affective and material labor of maintaining and reproducing life like, for instance, childcare and maintaining households and communities, often performed by women.[44] It is indispensable for society but at present under great pressure. Fraser suggests that the current crisis of care is an "expression of *the social-reproductive contradictions of financialized capitalism*" and argues that the strain on care has systemic and structural roots.[45]

In capitalist societies, social reproduction is a condition of possibility for capital accumulation, yet economic production is simultaneously destabilizing processes of social reproduction, which creates a crisis tendency. The care deficits that result from these contradictions are historically contingent and differ, from the liberal competitive capitalism of the nineteenth century to the state-managed capitalism of the postwar era to the financialized neoliberal capitalism of our time. Fraser suggests that we have to understand the struggles over social reproduction as *boundary struggles* between economic and noneconomic background conditions. The social contradictions in the structure of capitalist society are neither inside nor outside it, but rather at the border, and in periods of crisis, there are struggles over these boundaries.[46]

Under state-managed capitalism of the mid-twentieth century, this boundary struggle was diffused by ascribing public responsibility for social welfare.[47] Under financialized capitalism, we are, however, currently experiencing a re-externalization of care, where care work is a marketized commodity.[48] In Fraser's words:

> Financialized capitalism [...] is stretching our "caring" energies to the breaking point. This "crisis of care" should be understood structurally. By no means contingent or accidental, it is the expression, under current conditions, of a tendency to social-reproductive crisis that is inherent in capitalist society, but that takes an especially acute form in the present regime of financialized capitalism.[49]

Financialization permeates society, in other words, and has made the crisis of care acute. To use Fraser's terms, then, my claim is that the move from cure to care should be understood structurally. With Fraser, I suggest diagnosing healing architecture as an expression, in our time, of a tendency to a crisis of care that is acute. Differently put, healing architecture should not only be read as a slogan for a design approach to affirmatively praise, but also, I contend, as a symptom of a structural deficit of care work when care becomes a marketized commodity. Architecture – itself a commodity – is thus an instrument assigned the task of performing affective and material labor of care. Hereby I do not mean to doubt that healing architecture has an impact on our well-being, and that it is actually capable of supporting processes of recovery. But it is also, I claim, a proxy caretaker in the boundary struggle of care work responsibility.

Conclusion

Architecture can act as a remedy. In Fremtidens Fødestue, a cautious crafting of sensory impressions is designed to stimulate the production of oxytocin in the laboring woman: contractions are affectively engineered through the atmosphere in the room. A feeling of homeliness is one of the key qualities, we are told, through which the institution clearly expresses a concern for the affective dimension of the medical encounter. At the same time, the conditions for care to take place beyond this audiovisual scenery is in crisis, resulting in a boundary struggle between economic and social reproduction, between commodity and care. This is a structural problem that healing architecture cannot solve. Formulated with the architectural theorist Douglas Spencer, the preoccupation with designing affective and immersive environments is even a tool for neoliberal rationality and marketization, which risks turning architecture into a fetish.[50] In a similar manner, an uncritical affirmation of the slogan of healing architecture risks assigning care, by proxy, to architecture itself, blind to the symptoms of a structural crisis and struggles over redistributions of care in the welfare system.

Bibliography

Bates, Victoria. "'Humanizing' Healthcare Environments: Architecture, Art and Design in Modern Hospitals." *Design for Health* 2, no. 1 (2018): 5–19.

Borasi, Giovanna, and Mirko Zardini, eds. *Imperfect Health: The Medicalization of Architecture*. Zurich: Lars Müller Publishers, 2012.

Choudhury, Suparna, and Jan Slaby, eds. *Critical Neuroscience: A Handbook of the Social and Cultural Contexts of Neuroscience*. Chichester: Wiley-Blackwell, 2012.

Colomina, Beatriz. *X-Ray Architecture*. Zurich: Lars Müller Publishers, 2019.

Conrad, Peter. *The Medicalization of Society: On the Transformation of Human Conditions into Treatable Disorders*. Baltimore: Johns Hopkins University Press, 2007.

Danish Architecture Center. *Our Future Hospitals – Healing Architecture*, exhibition web site, 2018. https://dac.dk/en/exhibitions/our-future-hospitals-healing-architecture/. Accessed November 1, 2020.

Dirckinck-Holmfeld, Kim. *Dansk arkitektur – Konkurrencer 1907–1968*. Nykøbing Sjælland: Bogværket, 2016.

Duus, Lisbeth. "Kan man yde omsorg for patienten i centrum." *Sygeplejersken* 10 (1999): 22–25.

Frandsen, Anne Kathrine, Michael Mullins, Camilla Ryhl, Mette Blicher Folmer, Lars Brorson Fich, Turid Borgestrand Øien, and Nils Lykke Sørensen. *Helende arkitektur*. Institut for Arkitektur og Design skriftserie 29. Aalborg: Aalborg Universitetsforlag, 2009.

Frantzen, Jason. "416 New North Zealand Hospital." Herzog & de Meuron presentation at Business of Design Week, Hong Kong, 2018. https://www.herzogdemeuron.com/index/projects/complete-works/401-425/416-new-north-zealand-hospital/video.html. Accessed April 1, 2021.

Fraser, Nancy. "Crisis of Care? On the Social-Reproductive Contradictions of Contemporary Capitalism." In *Social Reproduction Theory: Remapping Class, Recentering Oppression*, edited by Tithi Bhattacharya, 21–36. London: Pluto Press, 2017.

Godt Sygehusbyggeri. "Case: Et helt anderledes hospital." https://godtsygehusbyggeri.dk/inspiration/cases/et-helt-anderledes-hospital. Accessed April 1, 2021.

———. "Erfaringscase: Fremtidens sengestuer fødes i Herning." Godtsygehusbyggeri.dk. https://godtsygehusbyggeri.dk/inspiration/cases/fremtidens-sengestuer-foedes-i-herning. Accessed January 3, 2021.

Hamilton, Kirk D. "Evidence-Based Practice: Four Levels Revisited." *HERD* 13, no. 3 (July 2020): 26–29. https://doi.org/10.1177/1937586720931064.

Hauptmann, Deborah, and Warren Neidich, eds. *Cognitive Architecture: From Biopolitics to Noopolitics*. Rotterdam: 010 Publishers, 2010.

Healthcare DENMARK. *Sustainable Hospitals: New Hospital Construction – Future Hospitals in Denmark*. White paper, version 1, August 2000. https://www.healthcaredenmark.dk/media/trchcof1/hcd-whitepaper-future-hospitals-v1-2020.pdf. Accessed December 29, 2021.

Heslet, Lars, and Kim Dirckinck-Holmfeld, eds. *Sansernes Hospital*. Copenhagen: Arkitektens Forlag, 2007.

Illich, Ivan. *Limits to Medicine: Medical Nemesis – The Expropriation of Health*. London: Marion Boyars, 1976.

Jacobsen, Kurt, and Klaus Larsen. *Ve og Velfærd: Læger, sundhed og samfund gennem 200 år*. Copenhagen: FADL's Forlag, 2017.

Jencks, Charles. "Maggie's Architecture: The Deep Affinities Between Architecture and Health." *Architectural Design* 87, no. 2 (2017): 66–75.

Johannessen, Runa, and Isak Winkel Holm. "Vi bygger for livet: Medikalisering af den danske hospitalsarkitektur." *K&K – Kultur og Klasse* 49, no. 131 (2021): 155–74.

Jørgensen, Caspar. "Velfærdssamfundets bygninger – en introduktion." *Architectura* 35 (2013): 7–27.

Leonard, Sarah, and Nancy Fraser. "Capitalism's Crisis of Care." *Dissent Magazine* (Fall 2016). https://www.dissentmagazine.org/article/nancy-fraser-interview-capitalism-crisis-of-care. Accessed December 29, 2021.

Lorentzen, Iben, Charlotte Sander Andersen, Henriette Svenstrup Jensen, Ann Fogsgaard, Maralyn Foureur, Finn Friis Lauszus and Ellen Aaagaard Nohr. "Study Protocol for a Randomised Trial Evaluating the Effect of a 'Birth Environment Room' Versus a Standard Labour Room on Birth Outcomes and the Birth Experience." In *Contemporary Clinical Trials Communications* 14

(February 15, 2019): 1–7. https://doi.org/10.1016/j.conctc.2019.100336.
Lundin, Stefan. “Healing Architecture: Evidence, Intuition, Dialogue.” Licentiate of Architecture, Chalmers University of Technology, 2015.
Mallgrave, Harry Francis. *Architecture and Embodiment: The Implications of the New Sciences and Humanities for Design*. London: Taylor & Francis Group, 2013.
Meuser, Philipp, ed. *Construction and Design Manual: Hospitals and Medical Facilities*. Berlin: DOM Publishers, 2019.
Nickl-Weller, Christine, and Hans Nickl. *Healing Architecture*. Salenstein: Braun, 2013.
Nyt Hospital Bispebjerg. “Milliondonation skal give nyt liv til de fredede haver på Bispebjerg Hospital.” 2018. https://www.bispebjerghospital.dk/nythospital/nyt-og-presse/nyheder/2018/Sider/Milliondonation-skal-give-nyt-liv-til-de-fredede-haver-på-Bispebjerg-Hospital.aspx. Accessed September 8, 2020.
Olesen, Peter, dir. “Ser på Hospitaler,” *Åbne øjne* (1994), on TV2.
Otto, Lene. *Rask eller lykkelig? Sundhed som diskurs i Danmark i det 20. århundrede*. Copenhagen: Komiteen for sundhedsoplysning, 1998.
Pedersen, Kjeld Møller. *Dansk sundhedspolitik*. Copenhagen: Munksgaard, 2018.
——. “Sygehusstruktur: Fortid, nutid og fremtid.” *Økonomi og politik: Kvartalsskrift* 78, no. 1 (2005): 2–17.
Pedersen, Kjeld Møller, and Niels Christian Petersen, eds. *Fremtidens hospital*. Copenhagen: Munksgaard, 2014.
Pedersen, Ove Kaj. *Konkurrencestaten*. Copenhagen: Hans Reitzels Forlag, 2011.
Peters, Terri, ed. “Design for Health: Sustainable Approaches to Therapeutic Architecture.” Special Issue, *Architectural Design* 87, no. 2 (2017).
Regeringens ekspertpanel vedr. sygehusinvesteringer. Regionernes investerings- og sygehusplaner: Screening og vurdering I. Indenrigs- og Sundhedsministeriet og Finansministeriet, 2008. https://godtsygehusbyggeri.dk/media/7266/ekspertpaneles-screeningsrapport-i.pdf.
——. Regionernes investerings- og sygehusplaner: Screening og vurdering II. Indenrigs- og Sundhedsministeriet og Finansministeriet, 2010. https://godtsygehusbyggeri.dk/media/7267/ekspertpaneles-screeningsrapport-ii.pdf.
Region Hovedstaden. Region Hovedstadens anbefalinger for Helende Arkitektur, 2020. https://www.regionh.dk/nythospitalnordsjaelland/derfor-bygger-vi/inspiration/PublishingImages/Sider/Regionens-retningslinjer-for-nybyggeri/helendearkitekturmarts11.pdf.
Robinson, Sarah, and Juhani Pallasmaa, eds. *Mind in Architecture: Neuroscience, Embodiment, and the Future of Design*. Cambridge, MA: MIT Press, 2015.
Rockfon. “Helende arkitektur.” https://www.rockfon.dk/om-os/vores-tankegang/urbanisering/helende-arkitektur/. Accessed April 1, 2021.
Skouboe, Esben Bala. “Fremtidens Fødestue.” *Lys* 27, no. 2 (2015): 18–19.
Slaby, Jan, and Christian von Scheve. *Affective Societies: Key Concepts*. London: Routledge, 2019.
Social- og Indenrigsministeriet. “Lov om regioner og om nedlæggelse af amtskommunerne, Hovedstadens Udviklingsråd og Hovedstadens Sygehusfællesskab.” Retsinformation.dk, 2005. https://www.retsinformation.dk/eli/lta/2005/537.
Sonovision. “Helende arkitektur.” https://www.sonovision.dk/viden/helende-arkitektur/. Accessed April 1, 2021.
Sosa, Álvaro Valeta. “Healing Architecture and Evidence-based Design.” In Meuser, *Construction and Design Manual*, 27–51.
Spencer, Douglas. *The Architecture of Neoliberalism: How Contemporary Architecture Became an Instrument of Control and Compliance*. London: Bloomsbury Academic, 2016.
Sundheds- og Ældreministeriet. *SUU Alm.del 2017–18 Endeligt svar på spørgsmål 1212*. ft.dk: Folketinget, 2018.
Swenarton, Marc, Tom Avermaete and Dirk van den Heuvel, eds. *Architecture and the Welfare State*. London: Routledge, 2015.
Terkildsen, Pernille Weiss, ed. *Sundhedsarkitekturens ABC*. Copenhagen: ArchiMed A/S, 2015.
Troldtekt. “Tema: Helende arkitektur.” https://www.troldtekt.dk/nyheder/temaer/helende_arkitektur/. Accessed April 1, 2021.
Ulrich, Roger. “View through a Window May Influence Recovery from Surgery.” In *Science* 224, no. 4647 (April 27, 1984): 420–21. https://doi.org/10.1126/science.6143402.
Ulrich, Roger, Craig Zimring, Xuemei Zhu, Jennifer DuBose, Hyun-Bo Seo, Young-Seon Choi, Xiaobo Quan and Anjali Joseph. “A Review of the Research Literature on Evidence-Based Healthcare Design.” *Health Environments Research & Design* 1, no. 3 (2008).
Valck, Chris de, Jozien Bensing, R. Bruynooghe and V. Batenburg. “Cure-oriented versus Care-Oriented Attitudes in Medicine.” *Patient Education and Counseling* 45, no. 2 (2001): 119–26.
Vallgårda, Signild. *Sygehuse og sygehuspolitik i Danmark: Et bidrag til det specialiserede sygehusvæsens historie 1930–1987*. Copenhagen: Jurist og Økonomforbundets Forlag, 1992.
Verderber, Stephen, and David J. Fine. *Healthcare Architecture in an Era of Radical Transformation*. New Haven: Yale University Press, 2000.
Verderber, Stephen, Shan Jiang, George Hughes and Yanwen Xiao. “The Evolving Role of Evidence-Based Research in Healthcare Facility Design Competitions.” *Frontiers of Architectural Research* 3 (2014): 238–49. https://doi.org/http://dx.doi.org/10.1016/j.foar.2013.12.001.
Vidal, Fernando, and Francisco Ortega. *Being Brains: Making the Cerebral Subject*. New York: Fordham University Press, 2017.
Wagenaar, Cor. “Modern Hospitals and Cultural Heritage.” *Docomomo Journal* 62, no. 1 (2020): 36–43.
Wagenaar, Cor, Noor Mens, Guru Manja, Colette Niemeijer, Tom Guthknecht, Giuseppe Lacanna and Peter Luscuere, eds. *Hospitals: A Design Manual*. Basel: Birkhäuser, 2018.
Wallenstein, Sven-Olov. *Biopolitics and the Emergence of Modern Architecture*. New York: Princeton Architectural Press, 2009.
Wrønding, Tine, Aikaterini Argyraki, Jesper Friis Petersen, Märta Fink Topsøe, Paul Michael Petersen and Ellen C.L. Løkkegaard. “The Aesthetic Nature of the Birthing Room Environment May Alter the Need for Obstetrical Interventions: An Observational Retrospective Cohort Study.” *Nature; Scientific Reports* 9, no. 303 (2019): 1–7.

Notes

1 Danish Architecture Center, *Our Future Hospitals – Healing Architecture*, exhibition, 2018, https://dac.dk/en/exhibitions/our-future-hospitals-healing-architecture/, accessed November 1, 2020.
2 See, for example, Álvaro Valeta Sosa, "Healing Architecture and Evidence-based Design," in *Construction and Design Manual: Hospitals and Medical Facilities*, ed. Philipp Meuser (Berlin: DOM Publishers, 2019), 27–51.
3 On New North Zealand Hospital, see Jason Frantzen, "416 New North Zealand Hospital," Herzog & de Meuron presentation at Business of Design Week, Hong Kong, 2018, https://www.herzogdemeuron.com/index/projects/complete-works/401-425/416-new-north-zealand-hospital/video.html, accessed April 1, 2021.
4 Shipping and supermarket logistics were studied as exemplary models for hospital logistics by the planners of New Bispebjerg, according to New Bispebjerg communication consultant Louise Voss Bendixen. Personal communication at a study visit by the author to Bispebjerg Hospital May 18, 2018.
5 Nancy Fraser, "Crisis of Care? On the Social-Reproductive Contradictions of Contemporary Capitalism," in *Social Reproduction Theory: Remapping Class, Recentering Oppression*, ed. Tithi Bhattacharya (London: Pluto Press, 2017).
6 The theoretical proposition of "affective engineering" in Fremtidens Fødestue is previously explored in Runa Johannessen and Isak Winkel Holm, "Vi bygger for livet: Medikalisering af den danske hospitalsarkitektur," *K&K – Kultur og Klasse* 49, no. 131 (2021).
7 Godt Sygehusbyggeri, "Erfaringscase: Fremtidens sengestuer fødes i Herning," https://godtsygehusbyggeri.dk/inspiration/cases/fremtidens-sengestuer-foedes-i-herning, accessed January 3, 2021. All translations from the Danish by the author.
8 Esben Bala Skouboe, "Fremtidens Fødestue," *Lys* 27, no. 2 (2015): 18–19.
9 The trial is described in the study protocol, but the results are not ready yet. See Iben Lorentzen et al., "Study Protocol for a Randomised Trial Evaluating the Effect of a 'Birth Environment Room' Versus a Standard Labour Room on Birth Outcomes and the Birth Experience," *Contemporary Clinical Trials Communications* 14 (February 15, 2019), https://doi.org/10.1016/j.conctc.2019.100336.
10 Lorentzen et al., "Study Protocol for a Randomised Trial," 1.
11 Tine Wrønding et al., "The Aesthetic Nature of the Birthing Room Environment May Alter the Need for Obstetrical Interventions: An Observational Retrospective Cohort Study," *Nature; Scientific Reports* 9, no. 303 (2019): 1–7.
12 Godt Sygehusbyggeri, "Erfaringscase: Fremtidens sengestuer fødes i Herning."
13 Godt Sygehusbyggeri, "Erfaringscase: Fremtidens sengestuer fødes i Herning."
14 Interview with Esben Bala Skouboe, November 25, 2020. Interview by the author.
15 For the law of the reform, see Social- og Indenrigsministeriet, "Lov om regioner og om nedlæggelse af amtskommunerne, Hovedstadens Udviklingsråd og Hovedstadens Sygehusfællesskab," Retsinformation.dk, 2005, https://www.retsinformation.dk/eli/lta/2005/537. For the investments in hospitals, see Sundheds- og Ældreministeriet, *SUU Alm.del 2017–18 Endeligt svar på spørgsmål 1212* (ft.dk: Folketinget, 2018). For official recommendations to the government on the new hospital system, see Regeringens ekspertpanel vedr. sygehusinvesteringer, *Regionernes investerings- og sygehusplaner: Screening og vurdering I* (Indenrigs- og Sundhedsministeriet og Finansministeriet, 2008), https://godtsygehusbyggeri.dk/media/7266/ekspertpaneles-screeningsrapport-i.pdf.
16 The socioeconomic imaginary of the reform is described in Ove Kaj Pedersen, *Konkurrencestaten* (Copenhagen: Hans Reitzels Forlag, 2011). The scaling of the new Regions were based on a calculation of the (perceived) ideal population basis for fewer and larger hospitals; an operation much similar to the 1970 Municipal Reform's reduction of counties. See Kjeld Møller Pedersen, "Sygehusstruktur: Fortid, nutid og fremtid," *Økonomi og politik: Kvartalsskrift* 78, no. 1 (2005): 2–6; Kjeld Møller Pedersen, *Dansk sundhedspolitik* (Copenhagen: Munksgaard, 2018); and Kjeld Møller Pedersen and Niels Christian Petersen, eds., *Fremtidens hospital* (Copenhagen: Munksgaard, 2014).
17 The periodization of "the golden years" of welfare is according to Marc Swenarton, Tom Avermaete and Dirk van den Heuvel, eds., *Architecture and the Welfare State* (London: Routledge, 2015).
18 See Meuser, *Construction and Design Manual*; Stephen Verderber and David J. Fine, *Healthcare Architecture in an Era of Radical Transformation* (New Haven: Yale University Press, 2000); and Cor Wagenaar et al., eds., *Hospitals: A Design Manual* (Basel: Birkhäuser, 2018).
19 Sven-Olov Wallenstein, *Biopolitics and the Emergence of Modern Architecture* (New York: Princeton Architectural Press, 2009), 31–32.
20 Tuberculosis sanatoria were particularly influential for the stylistic ideals of hygienic modernism. See, for example, Beatriz Colomina, *X-Ray Architecture* (Zurich: Lars Müller Publishers, 2019), 94; and Giovanna Borasi and Mirko Zardini, eds., *Imperfect Health: The Medicalization of Architecture* (Zurich: Lars Müller Publishers, 2012), 24.
21 Signild Vallgårda, *Sygehuse og sygehuspolitik i Danmark: Et bidrag til det specialiserede sygehusvæsens historie 1930–1987* (Copenhagen: Jurist og Økonomforbundets Forlag, 1992).
22 The biological concept of illness within Danish hospital discourse was prevalent until the 1970s, according to Vallgårda, *Sygehuse og sygehuspolitik*, 272, 88. For the development of discourses on health and illness in a Danish context, see Lene Otto, *Rask eller lykkelig? Sundhed som diskurs i Danmark i det 20. århundrede* (Copenhagen: Komiteen for sundhedsoplysning, 1998).
23 Social science and social engineering became ideals in the 1930s. See Caspar Jørgensen, "Velfærdssamfundets bygninger – en introduktion," *Architectura* 35 (2013): 10.
24 Kim Dirckinck-Holmfeld, *Dansk arkitektur – Konkurrencer 1907–1968* (Nykøbing Sjælland: Bogværket, 2016).
25 The low-rise comb structure was introduced already in the 1930s with Aarhus Kommunehospital, for example, yet with significant changes in building methods with Hvidovre Hospital. On the development of general hospital typologies, see, for example, Cor Wagenaar, "Modern Hospitals and Cultural Heritage," *Docomomo Journal* 62, no. 1 (2020): 36–43.
26 Vallgårda, *Sygehuse og sygehuspolitik*, 29.
27 Medicalization as a sociological concept is a critique of the application of medical diagnosis on social phenomena; see Peter Conrad, *The Medicalization of Society: On the Transformation of Human Conditions into Treatable Disorders* (Baltimore: Johns Hopkins University Press, 2007); and Ivan Illich, *Limits to Medicine: Medical Nemesis: The Expropriation of Health* (London: Marion Boyars, 1976).
28 Victoria Bates, "'Humanizing' Healthcare Environments: Architecture, Art and Design in Modern Hospitals," *Design for Health* 2, no. 1 (2018); Pernille Weiss Terkildsen, ed., *Sundhedsarkitekturens ABC* (Copenhagen: ArchiMed A/S, 2015); Wagenaar, "Modern Hospitals and Cultural Heritage"; and "Ser på Hospitaler," *Åbne Øjne*, directed by Peter Olsen, 1994, on TV2.
29 The concept of "the patient in center" originates in service management theory. See Lisbeth Duus, "Kan man yde omsorg for patienten i centrum," *Sygeplejersken* 10 (1999).
30 Kurt Jacobsen and Klaus Larsen, *Ve og Velfærd. Læger, sundhed og samfund gennem 200 år* (Copenhagen: FADL's Forlag, 2017), 509–20.

31 By analogy to the well-known concept of evidence-based medicine, EBD denotes a practice in which design decisions are based on scientific facts established through empirical studies.
32 Roger Ulrich, "View through a Window May Influence Recovery from Surgery," *Science* 224, no. 4647 (April 27, 1984), https://doi.org/10.1126/science.6143402.
33 The concepts of somatic versus affective hospital architecture is proposed and discussed in Johannessen and Winkel Holm, "Vi bygger for livet."
34 Kirk D. Hamilton, "Evidence-Based Practice: Four Levels Revisited," *HERD* 13, no. 3 (July 2020), https://doi.org/10.1177/1937586720931064; Roger Ulrich et al., "A Review of the Research Literature on Evidence-Based Healthcare Design," *Health Environments Research & Design* 1, no. 3 (2008); Stephen Verderber et al., "The Evolving Role of Evidence-Based Research in Healthcare Facility Design Competitions," *Frontiers of Architectural Research* 3 (2014), https://doi.org/http://dx.doi.org/10.1016/j.foar.2013.12.001; and Wagenaar et al., *Hospitals: A Design Manual.*
35 Lars Heslet and Kim Dirckinck-Holmfeld, eds., *Sansernes Hospital* (Copenhagen: Arkitektens Forlag, 2007); Anne Kathrine Frandsen et al., *Helende arkitektur*, Institut for Arkitektur og Design skriftserie 29 (Aalborg: Aalborg Universitetsforlag, 2009); and Danish Architecture Center, "Our Future Hospitals – Healing Architecture." See also, for example, Christine Nickl-Weller and Hans Nickl, *Healing Architecture* (Salenstein: Braun, 2013); Stefan Lundin, "Healing Architecture: Evidence, Intuition, Dialogue" (Licentiate of Architecture, Chalmers University of Technology, 2015); Charles Jencks, "Maggie's Architecture: The Deep Affinities Between Architecture and Health," *Architectural Design* 87, no. 2 (2017); and Terri Peters, ed., "Design for Health: Sustainable Approaches to Therapeutic Architecture," special issue, *Architectural Design* 87, no. 2 (2017).
36 Nyt Hospital Bispebjerg, "Milliondonation skal give nyt liv til de fredede haver på Bispebjerg Hospital." 2018. https://www.bispebjerghospital.dk/nythospital/nyt-og-presse/nyheder/2018/Sider/Milliondonation-skal-give-nyt-liv-til-de-fredede-haver-på-Bispebjerg-Hospital.aspx, accessed September 8, 2020.
37 Suparna Choudhury and Jan Slaby, eds., *Critical Neuroscience: A Handbook of the Social and Cultural Contexts of Neuroscience* (Chichester: Wiley-Blackwell, 2012); Fernando Vidal and Francisco Ortega, *Being Brains: Making the Cerebral Subject* (New York: Fordham University Press, 2017); Jan Slaby and Christian von Scheve, *Affective Societies: Key Concepts* (London: Routledge, 2019); Sarah Robinson and Juhani Pallasmaa, eds., *Mind in Architecture: Neuroscience, Embodiment, and the Future of Design* (Cambridge, MA: MIT Press, 2015); Deborah Hauptmann and Warren Neidich, eds., *Cognitive Architecture: From Biopolitics to Noopolitics* (Rotterdam: 010 Publishers, 2010); and Harry Francis Mallgrave, *Architecture and Embodiment: The Implications of the New Sciences and Humanities for Design* (London: Taylor & Francis Group, 2013).
38 Heslet and Dirckinck-Holmfeld, *Sansernes Hospital.*
39 The research project was supported by Realdania and Danish Regions. See Frandsen et al., *Helende arkitektur*, 29.
40 See, for example, Godt Sygehusbyggeri's website, Godtsygehusbyggeri.dk.; Region Hovedstaden, *Region Hovedstadens anbefalinger for Helende Arkitektur* (2010), https://www.regionh.dk/nythospitalnordsjaelland/derfor-bygger-vi/inspiration/PublishingImages/Sider/Regionens-retningslinjer-for-nybyggeri/helendearkitekturmarts11.pdf; Healthcare DENMARK, *Sustainable Hospitals: New Hospital Construction – Future Hospitals in Denmark*. version 1, August 2000, https://www.healthcaredenmark.dk/media/trchcof1/hcd-whitepaper-future-hospitals-v1-2020.pdf, accessed December 29, 2021; Rockfon, "Helende arkitektur," https://www.rockfon.dk/om-os/vores-tankegang/urbanisering/helende-arkitektur/, accessed April 1, 2021; Troldtekt, "Tema: Helende arkitektur," https://www.troldtekt.dk/nyheder/temaer/helende_arkitektur/, accessed April 1, 2021; and Sonovision, "Helende arkitektur," https://www.sonovision.dk/viden/helende-arkitektur/, accessed April 1, 2021.
41 Regeringens ekspertpanel vedr. sygehusinvesteringer, *Regionernes investerings- og sygehusplaner: Screening og vurdering II* (Indenrigs- og Sundhedsministeriet og Finansministeriet, 2010), 24, https://godtsygehusbyggeri.dk/media/7267/ekspertpaneles-screeningsrapport-ii.pdf.
42 If your domestic, social, and economic conditions allow for it, that is. Home treatment is potentially a historical return to the time when hospitalization was for the poor, and the affluent were treated at home. On the anticipation of home hospitalization, see, for example, Godt Sygehusbyggeri, "Case: Et helt anderledes hospital," https://godtsygehusbyggeri.dk/inspiration/cases/et-helt-anderledes-hospital, accessed April 1, 2021.
43 Chris de Valck et al., "Cure-Oriented versus Care-Oriented Attitudes in Medicine," *Patient Education and Counseling* 45, no. 2 (2001).
44 Fraser, "Crisis of Care?," 21.
45 Fraser, "Crisis of Care?," 21–22.
46 Fraser, "Crisis of Care?," 34.
47 Fraser, "Crisis of Care?," 34.
48 Fraser, "Crisis of Care?," 34.
49 Sarah Leonard and Nancy Fraser, "Capitalism's Crisis of Care," *Dissent* (Fall 2016), https://www.dissentmagazine.org/article/nancy-fraser-interview-capitalism-crisis-of-care, accessed December 29, 2021.
50 Douglas Spencer, *The Architecture of Neoliberalism: How Contemporary Architecture Became an Instrument of Control and Compliance* (London: Bloomsbury Academic, 2016), 10.

2.36 Key events in Danish hospital development, 1990–2022

Medical concepts and diseases

"SOMATIC"
The body as distinct from the mind

Epidemic diseases

Lifestyle diseases

Organization and Structural changes

1909 National Health Authorities establish independent town and municipality hospitals

1933 Social reform and obligatory health insurance funds

1970 Municipal r

1946 First law on hospitals

1943 Invention of antibiotics

1970s "Patient in ce

1930s Gradual centralization and specialization

Architectural concepts and typologies

ARCHITECTURE AS CURE

ARCHITECT

Sanatorium

Pavilion

Matchbox on a muff

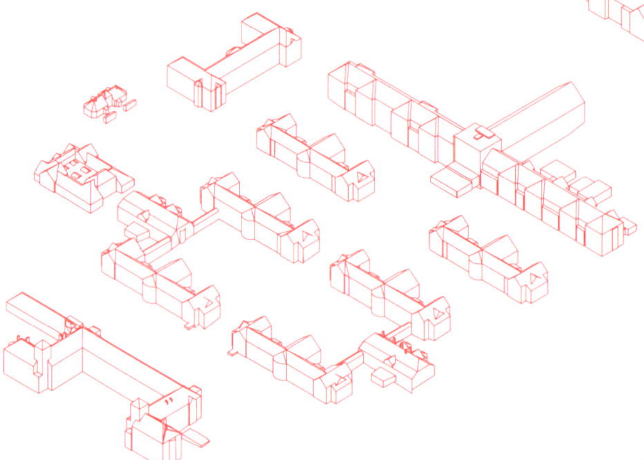

1913 Bispebjerg
Type: Pavilion with gardens
Architects: Martin Nyrop and Edvard Glæsel

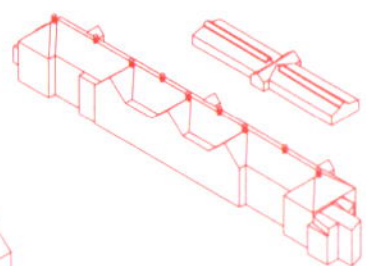

1958 Glostrup
Type: Compact core & wings
Architects: M. & R. Ypyä & V. M

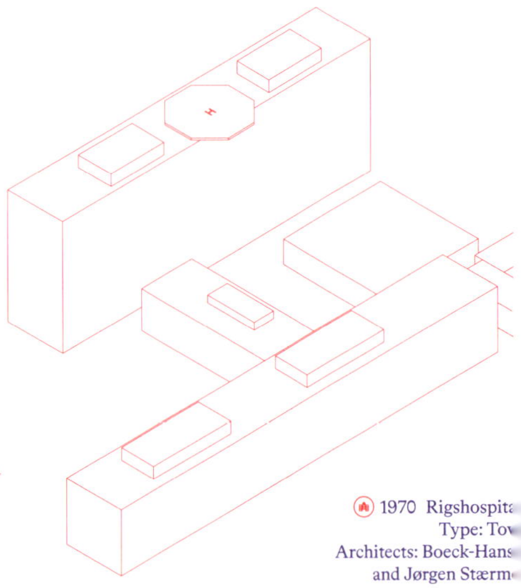

1970 Rigshospita
Type: Tov
Architects: Boeck-Hans
and Jørgen Stærm

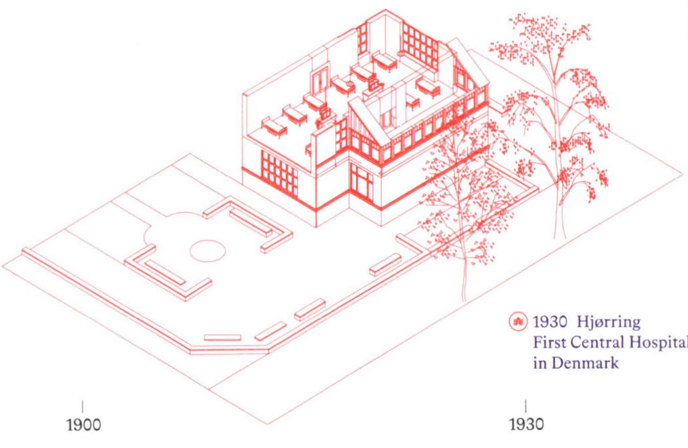

1930 Hjørring
First Central Hospital
in Denmark

1900

1930

1950

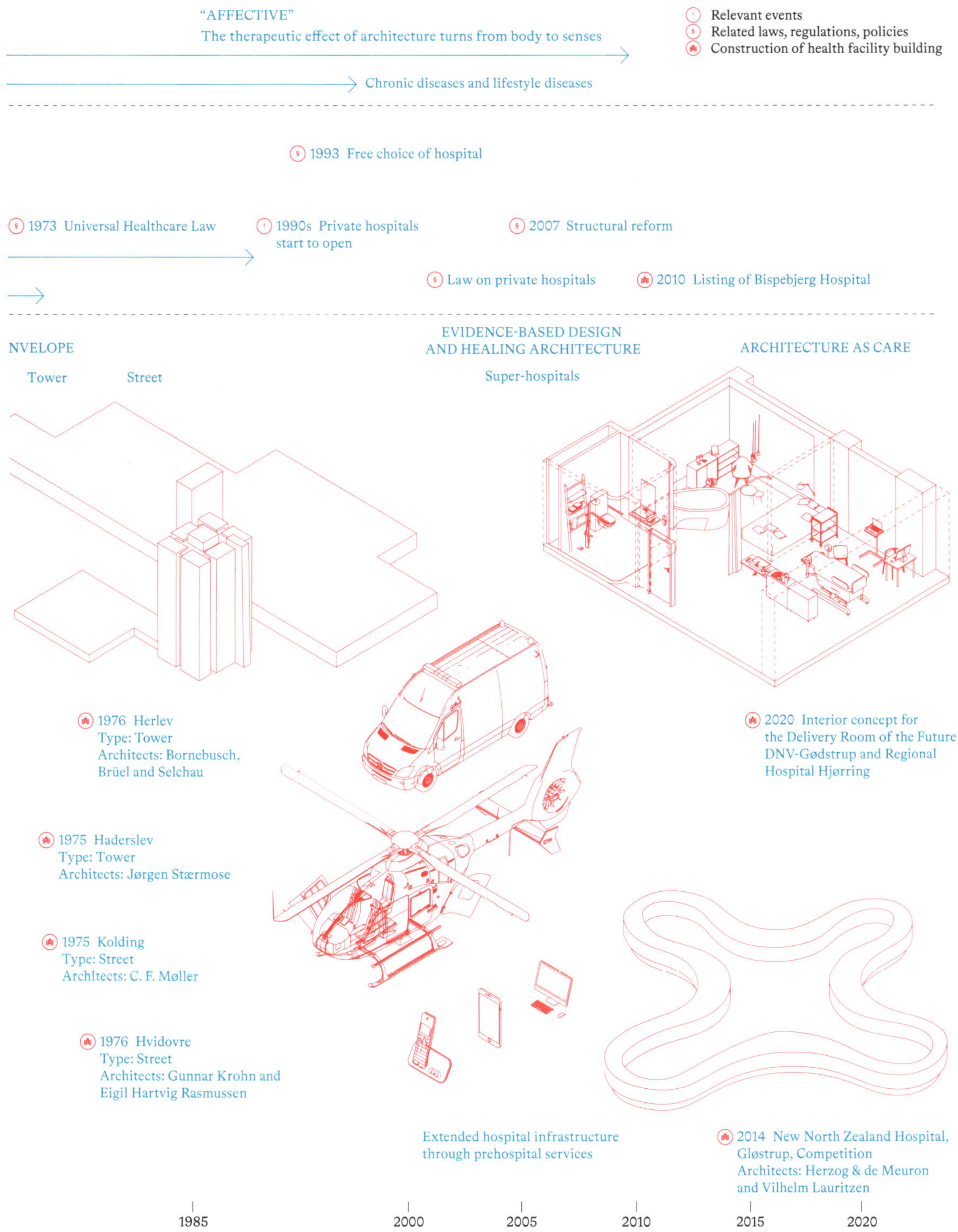

"AFFECTIVE"
The therapeutic effect of architecture turns from body to senses
Relevant events
Related laws, regulations, policies
Construction of health facility building
Chronic diseases and lifestyle diseases
1993 Free choice of hospital
1973 Universal Healthcare Law
1990s Private hospitals start to open
2007 Structural reform
Law on private hospitals
2010 Listing of Bispebjerg Hospital
NVELOPE
Tower
Street
EVIDENCE-BASED DESIGN AND HEALING ARCHITECTURE
Super-hospitals
ARCHITECTURE AS CARE
1976 Herlev
Type: Tower
Architects: Bornebusch, Brüel and Selchau
1975 Haderslev
Type: Tower
Architects: Jørgen Stærmose
1975 Kolding
Type: Street
Architects: C. F. Møller
1976 Hvidovre
Type: Street
Architects: Gunnar Krohn and Eigil Hartvig Rasmussen
2020 Interior concept for the Delivery Room of the Future DNV-Gødstrup and Regional Hospital Hjørring
Extended hospital infrastructure through prehospital services
2014 New North Zealand Hospital, Gløstrup, Competition
Architects: Herzog & de Meuron and Vilhelm Lauritzen
1985
2000
2005
2010
2015
2020

2.37 Multisensorial delivery room, DNV-Gødstrup, 2020

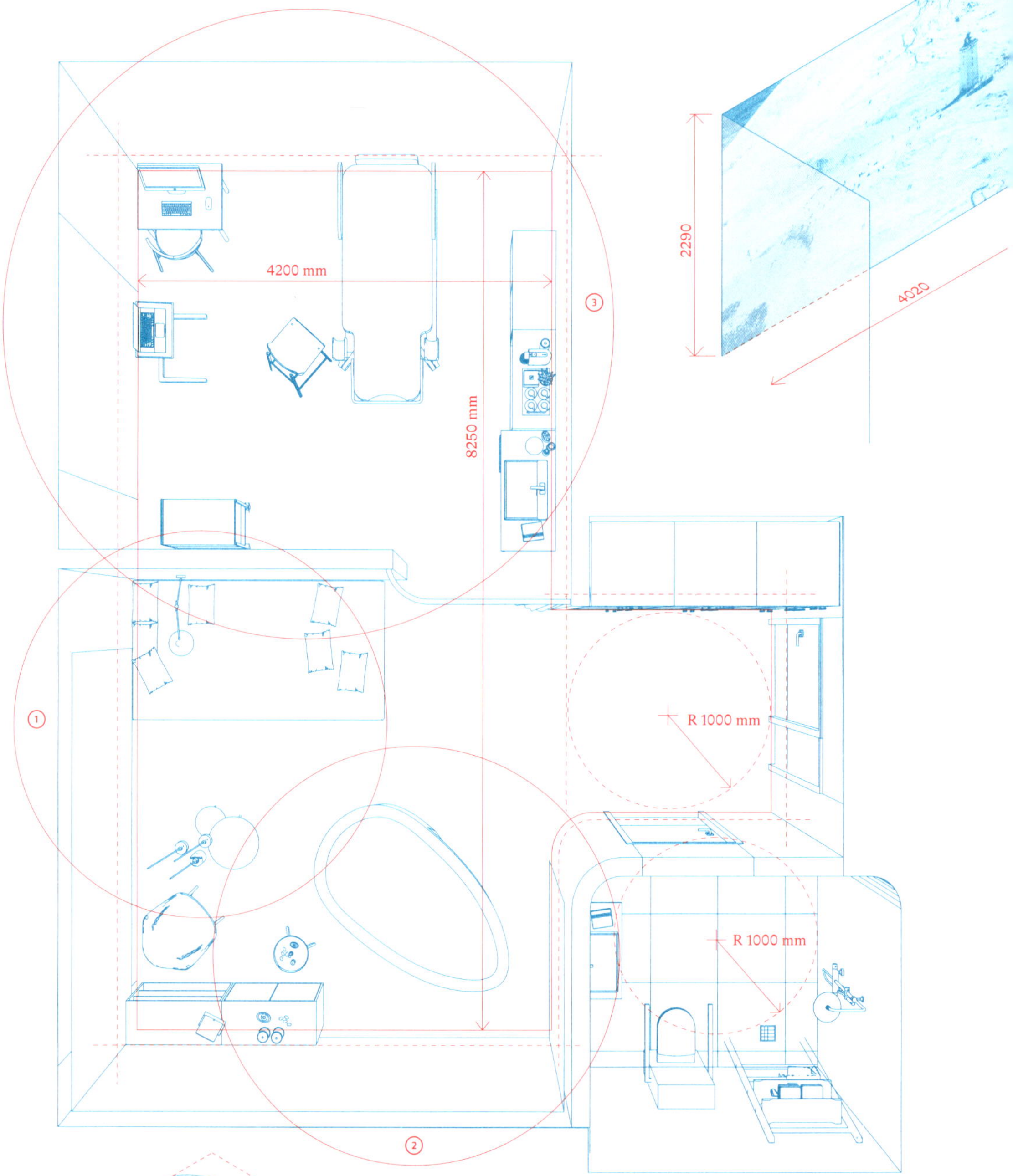

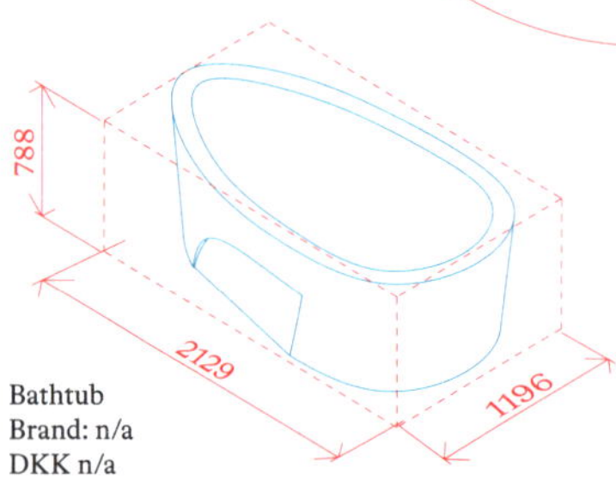

Bathtub
Brand: n/a
DKK n/a

Massage stones (Basalt)
Brand: n/a
DKK 30

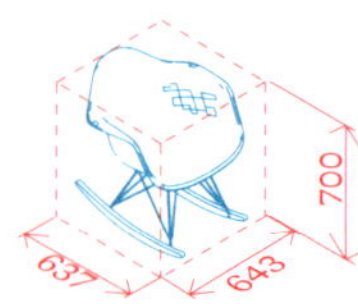

Rocking chair
Brand: Eames
DKK 3,600

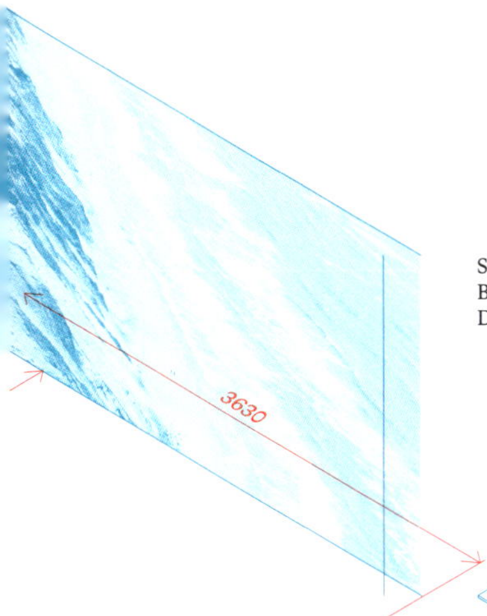

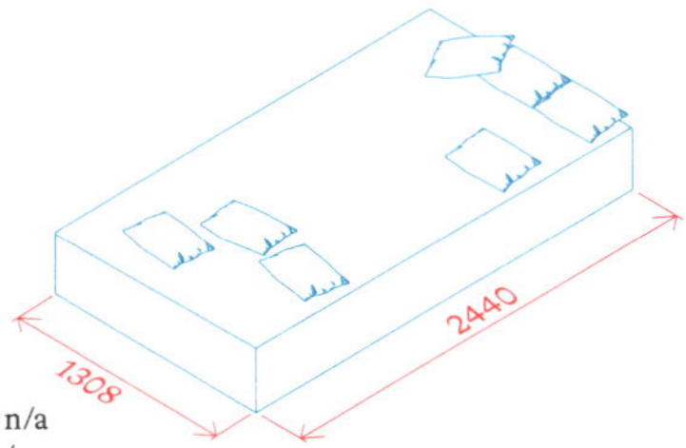

Sofa
Brand: n/a
DKK n/a

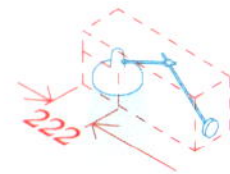

Wall lamp
Brand: Arigato
DKK 1,999

Coffee Machine
Brand: Nespresso
DKK 1,999

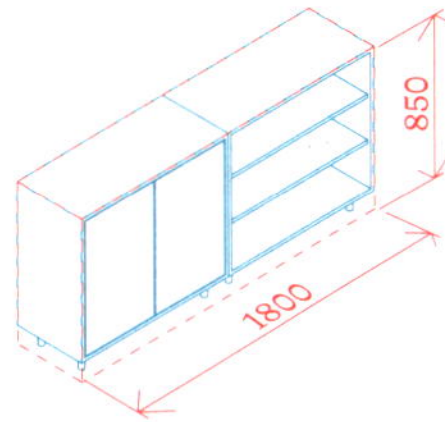

Family cupboard
Brand: My urban 1800
DKK n/a

Flip around table
Brand: Menu
DKK 1,699

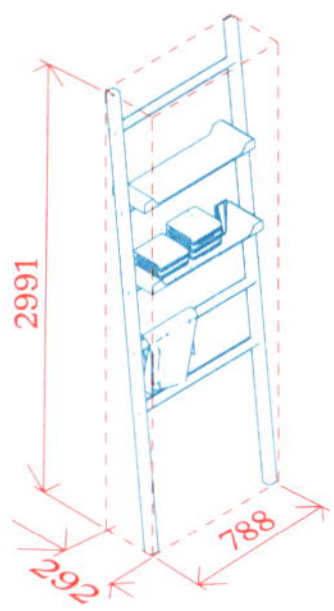

Bath rack
Brand: Trip trap
DKK 1,995

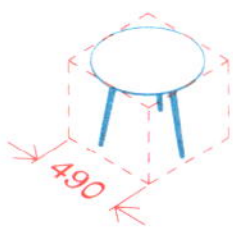

Coffee table
Brand: n/a
DKK 8,796

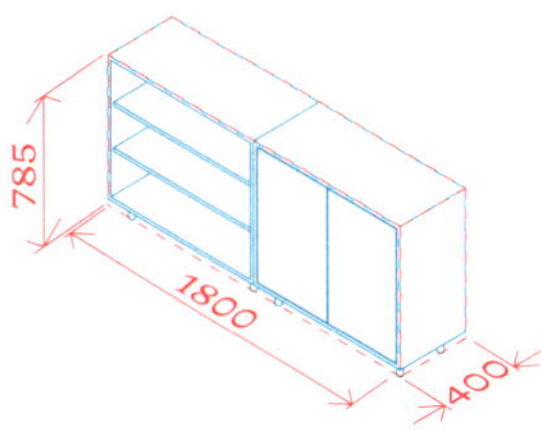

Family cupboard
Brand: My urban 1800
DKK n/a

Massage/ bathing oils and salt
Brand: n/a
DKK 80/dl

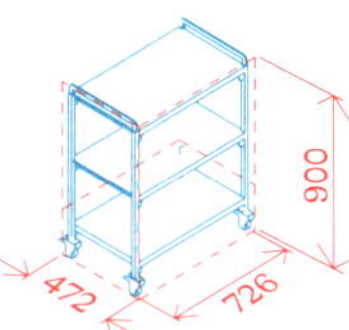

Rolling stool
Brand: IKEA
DKK 399

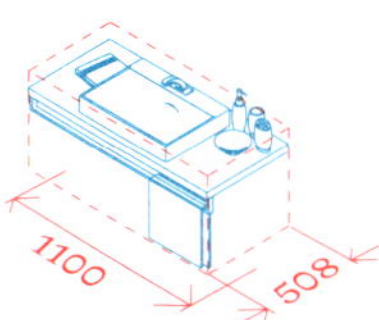

Wash basin
Brand: n/a
DKK n/a

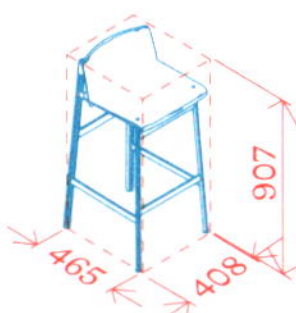

Bar stool
Brand: Muuto
DKK 2,995

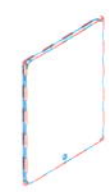

iPad Air -
projection and light control
Brand: Apple
DKK 4,999

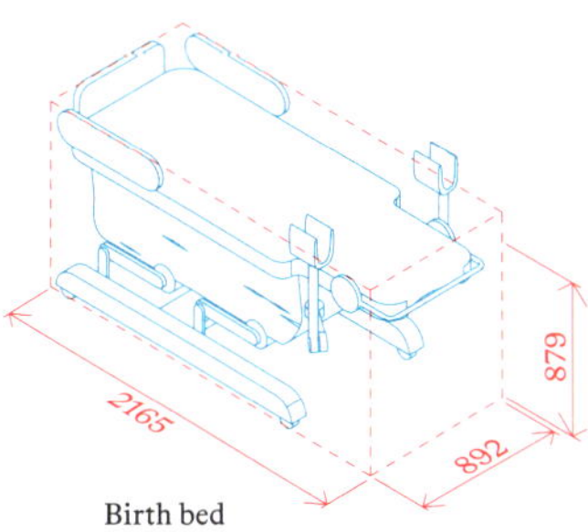

Birth bed
Brand: n/a
DKK n/a

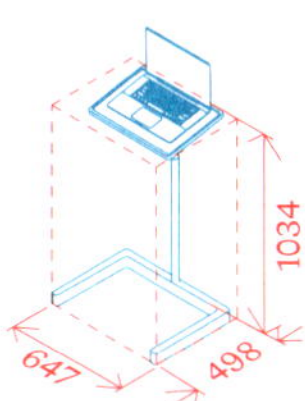

Laptop stool
Brand: Paustian
DKK 4,893

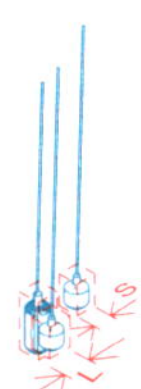

Lamp × 3
Brand: Norman Copenhagen
DKK 2,400

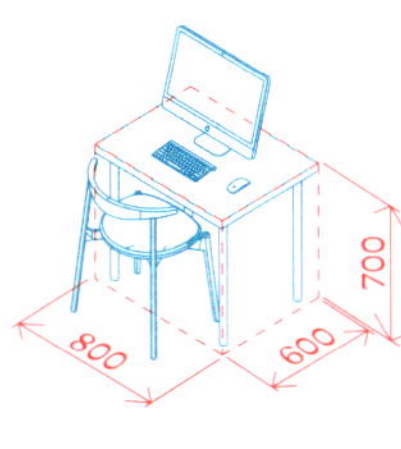

Computer Desk
Brand: n/a
DKK n/a

2.38 Conventional delivery room, Thisted, 2020

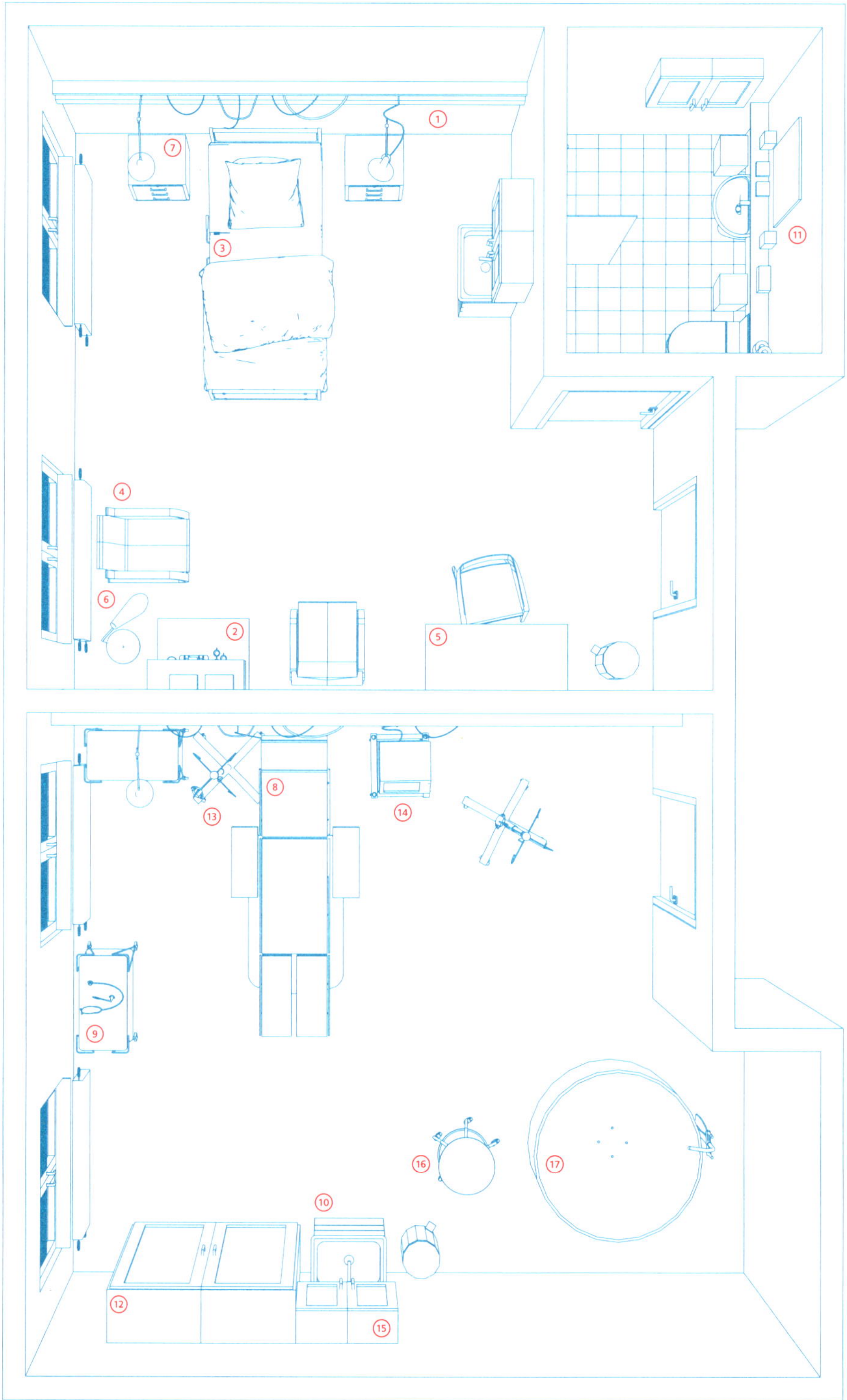

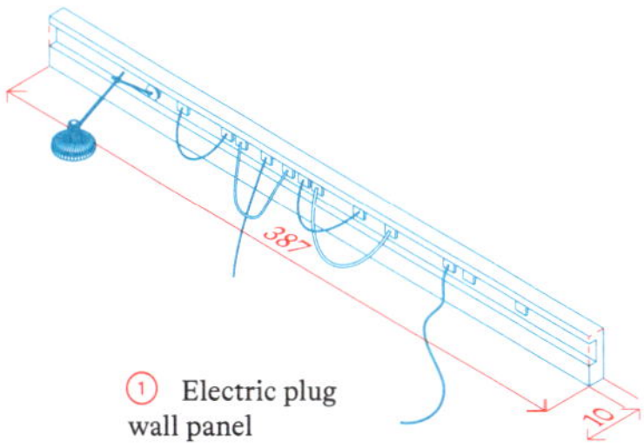

① Electric plug wall panel

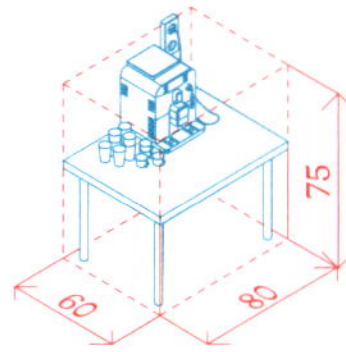

② Coffee machine

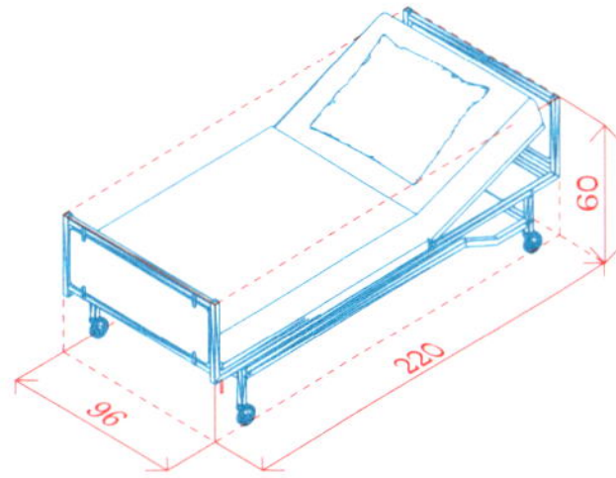

③ Hospital bed

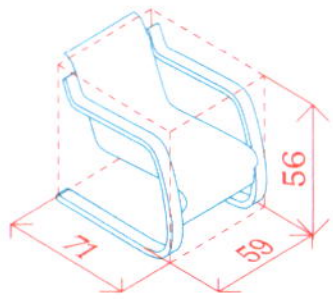

④ Armchair

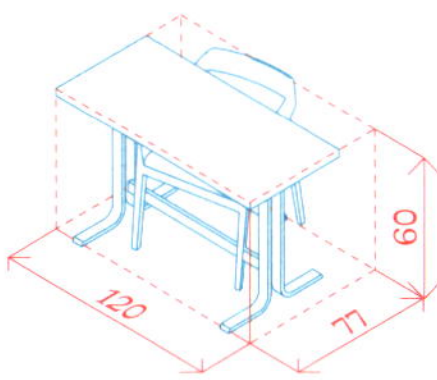

⑤ Desk station

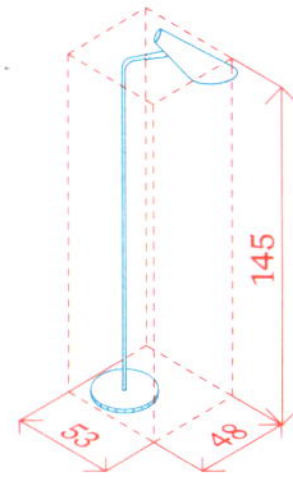

⑥ Standing lamp

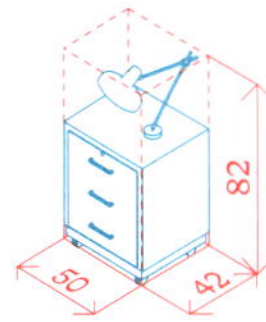

⑦ Bed cabinet/bed lamp

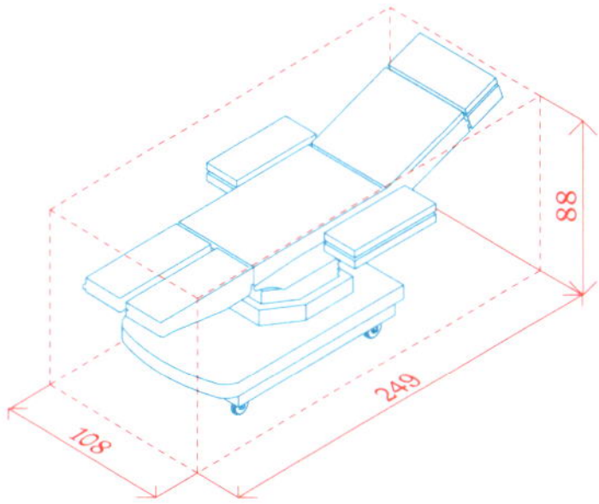

⑧ Birthing bed

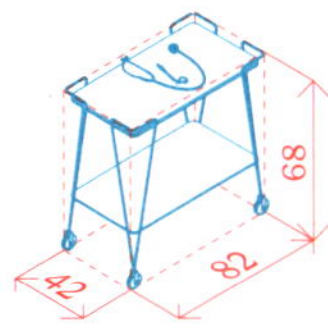

⑨ Stainless steel rolling cart/ stethoscope

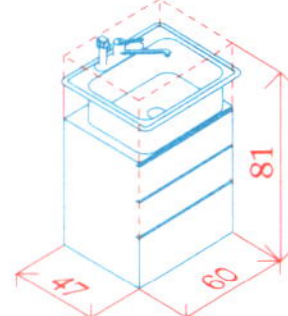

⑩ Sink

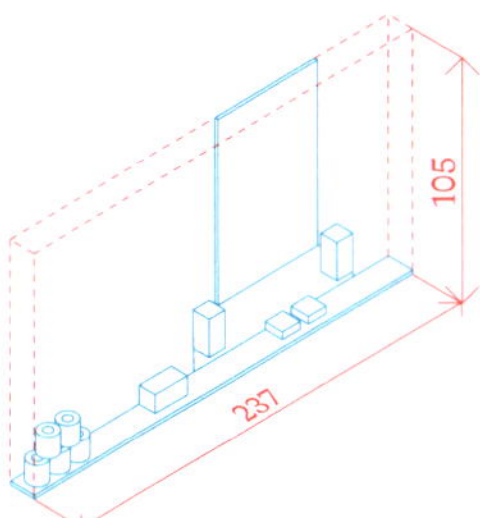

⑪ Cupboard

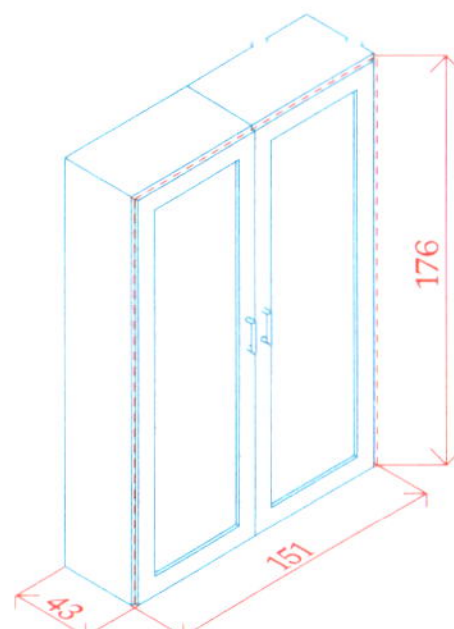

⑫ Bathroom mirror and shelf

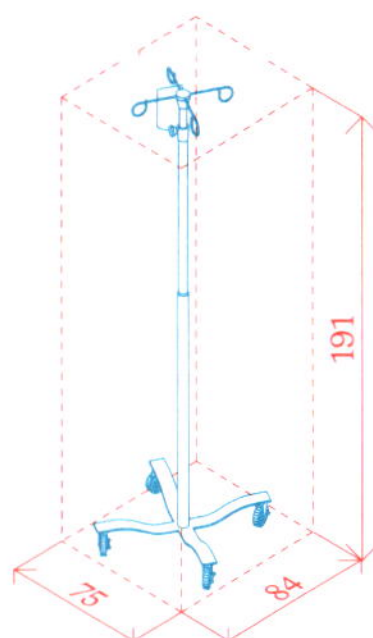

⑬ Infusion stand

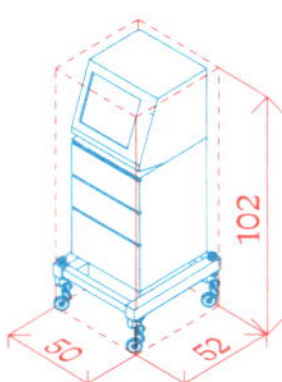

⑭ Cardiac monitor

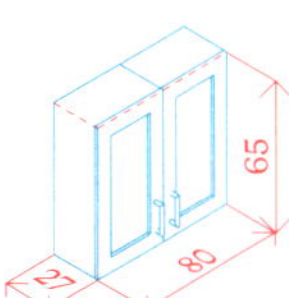

⑮ Cabinet above the sink

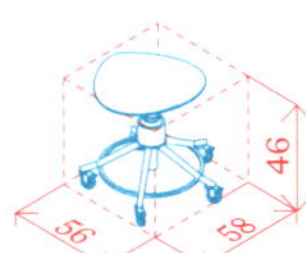

⑯ Metal stool

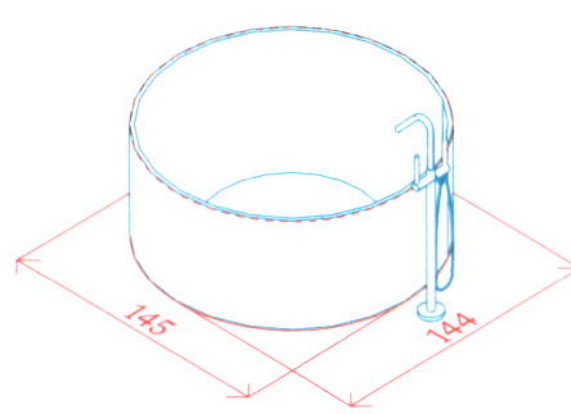

⑰ Birthing bathtub

2.39 Bed ward in pavilion, Bispebjerg Hospital, 1913

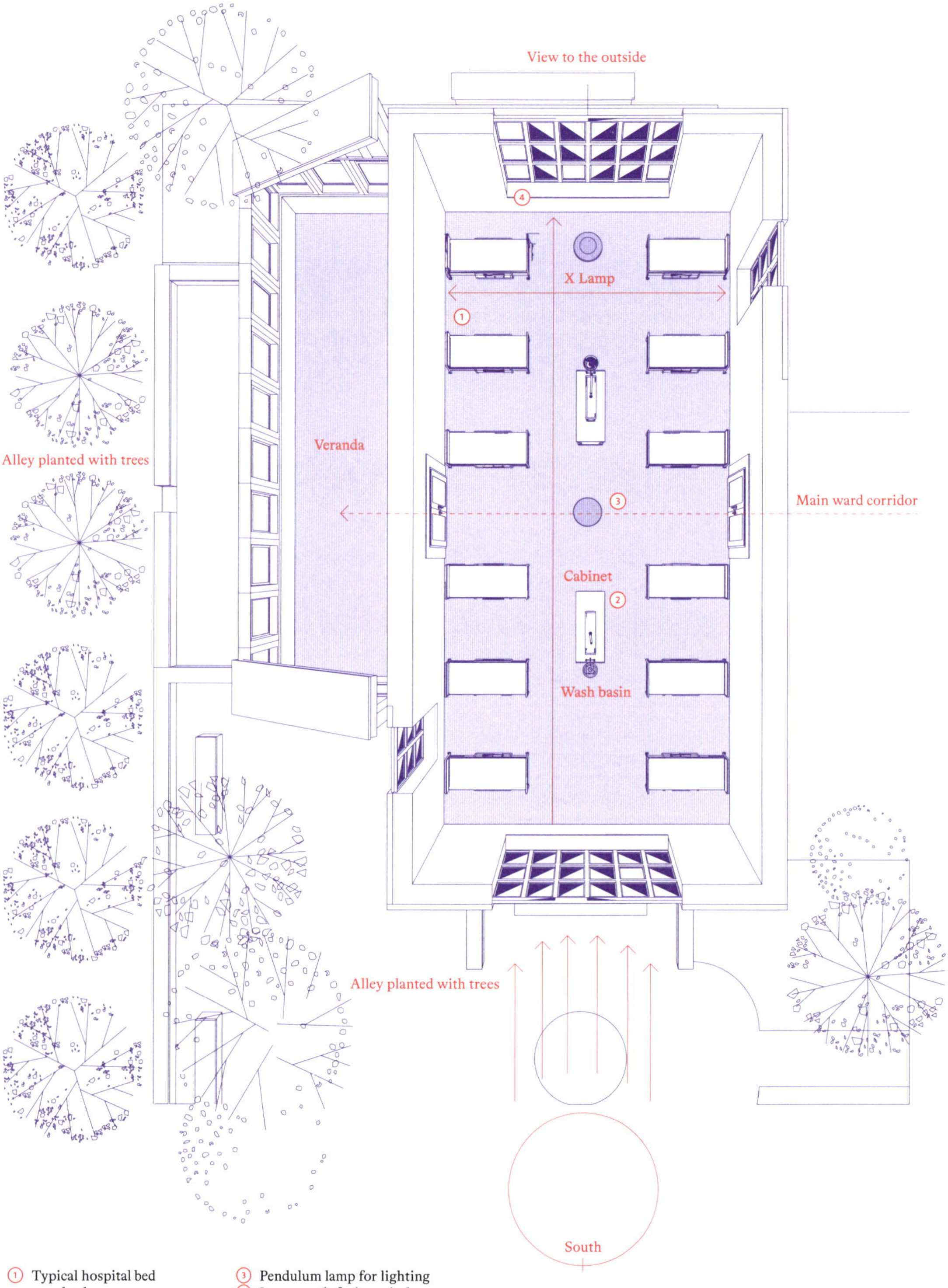

1. Typical hospital bed on wheels
2. Cabinet and wash basin station for the nurses
3. Pendulum lamp for lighting
4. Large south-facing windows ensured daylight and a view
5. Nurse/garden uniform

0 2 m

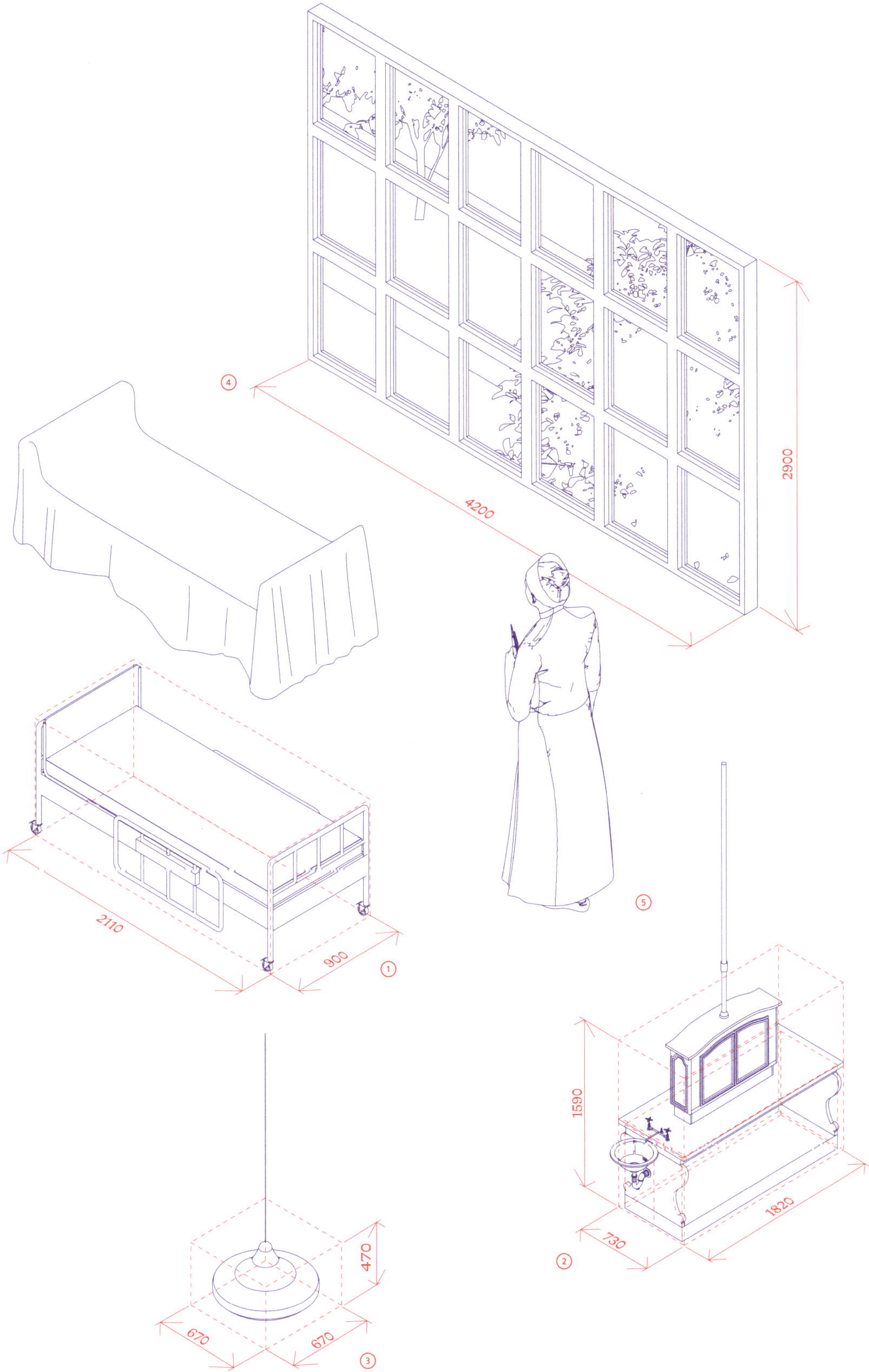
④
4200
2900
⑤
2110
900
①
1590
730
1820
②
470
670
670
③

2.40 Nature as a healing element: hospital garden (exterior), Bispebjerg Hospital, 1913

0 50 m

① Pavilions connected by bridges

② Main axis and green areas between pavilions

③ The hospital's location was originally an open field outside of the city of Copenhagen

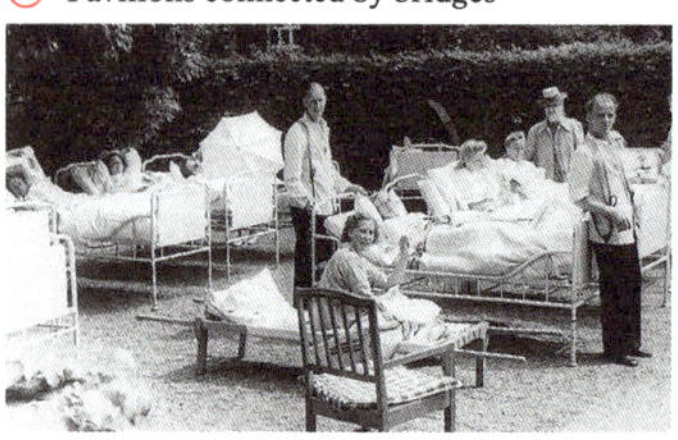

④ Beds moved to the garden

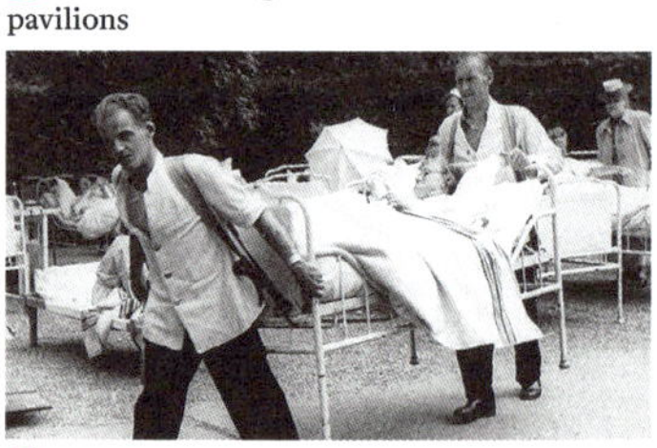

⑤ Hospital porters moving a patient in bed

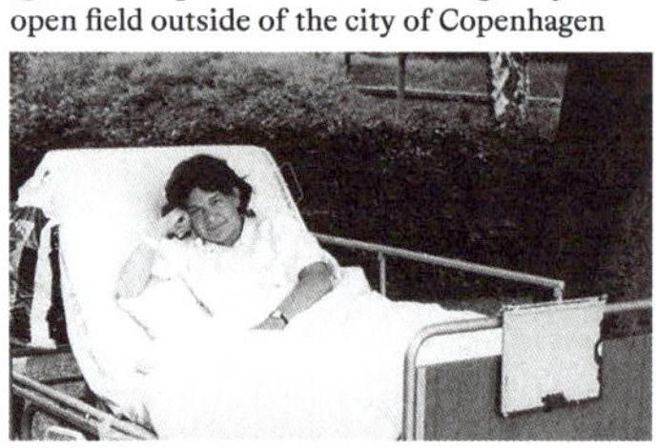

⑥ Patient in bed in the hospital garden

2.41 Nature as a healing element: visual projections (interior), DNV-Gødstrup, 2020

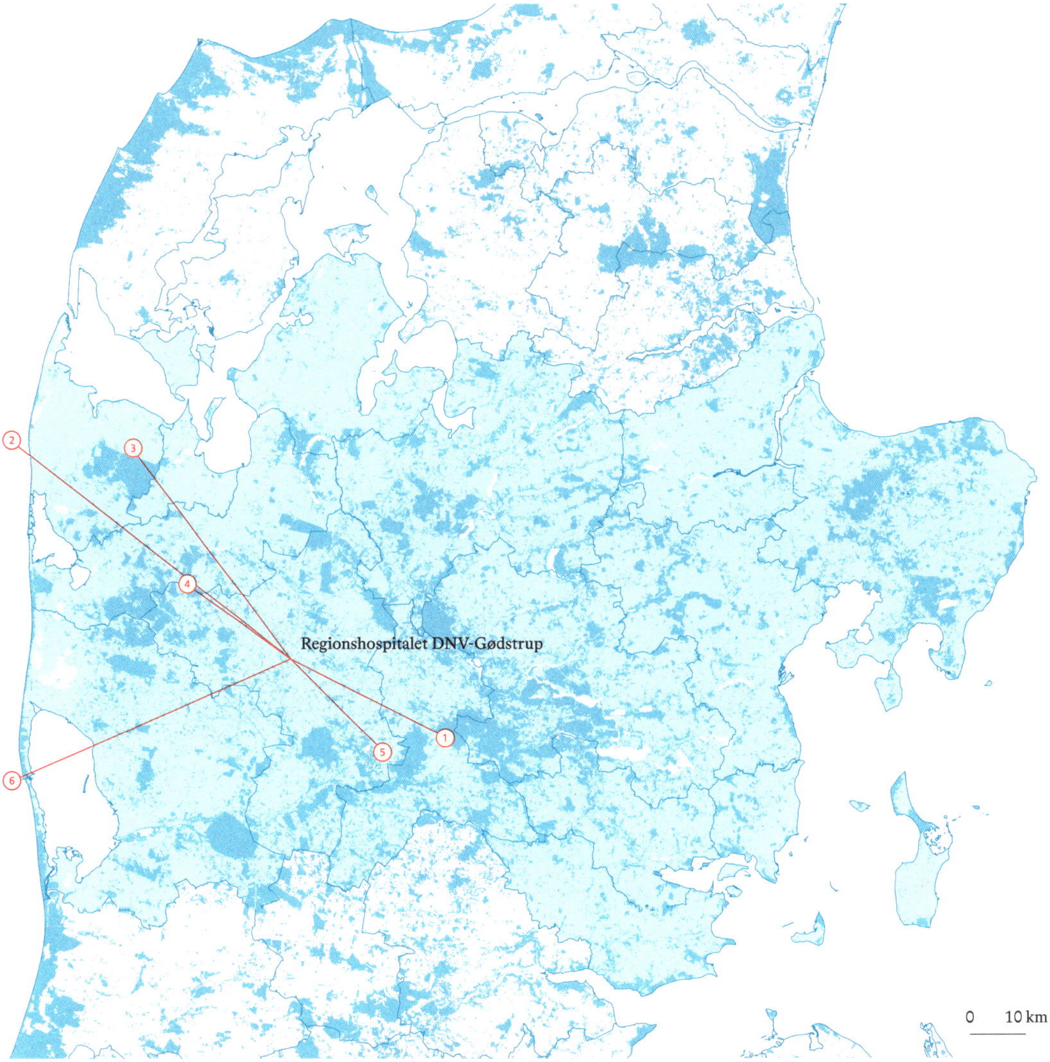

① Ikast-Brande

② Lemvig Bovbjerg Klint

③ Struer – Klosterheden

④ Holstebro – wood path

⑤ Herning – Harrild Hede

⑥ Ringkøbing-Skjern – Hvide sande

2.42 Geographical distribution of hospitals and number of beds, 1970

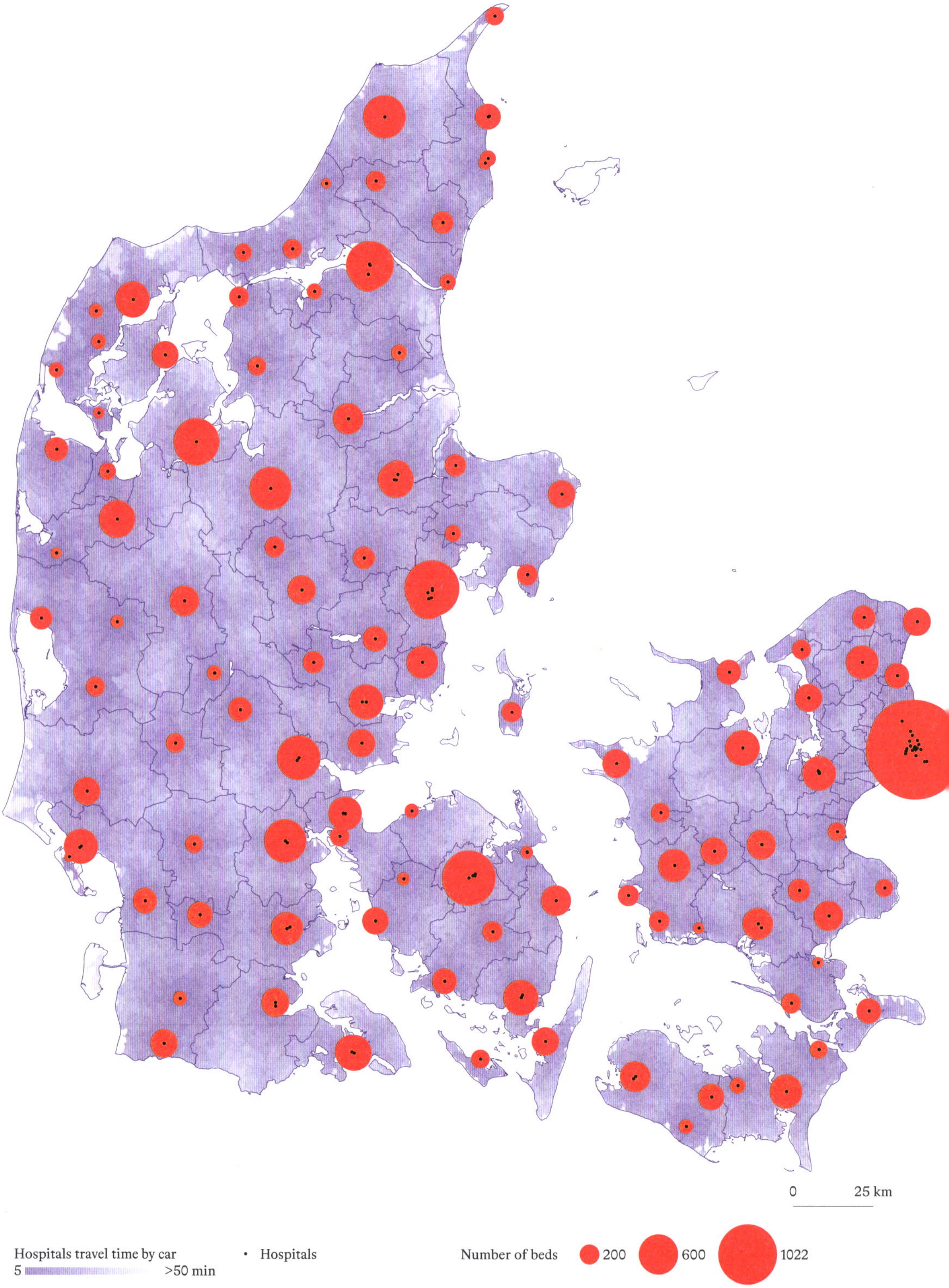

2.43 Geographical distribution of hospitals and number of beds, 2020

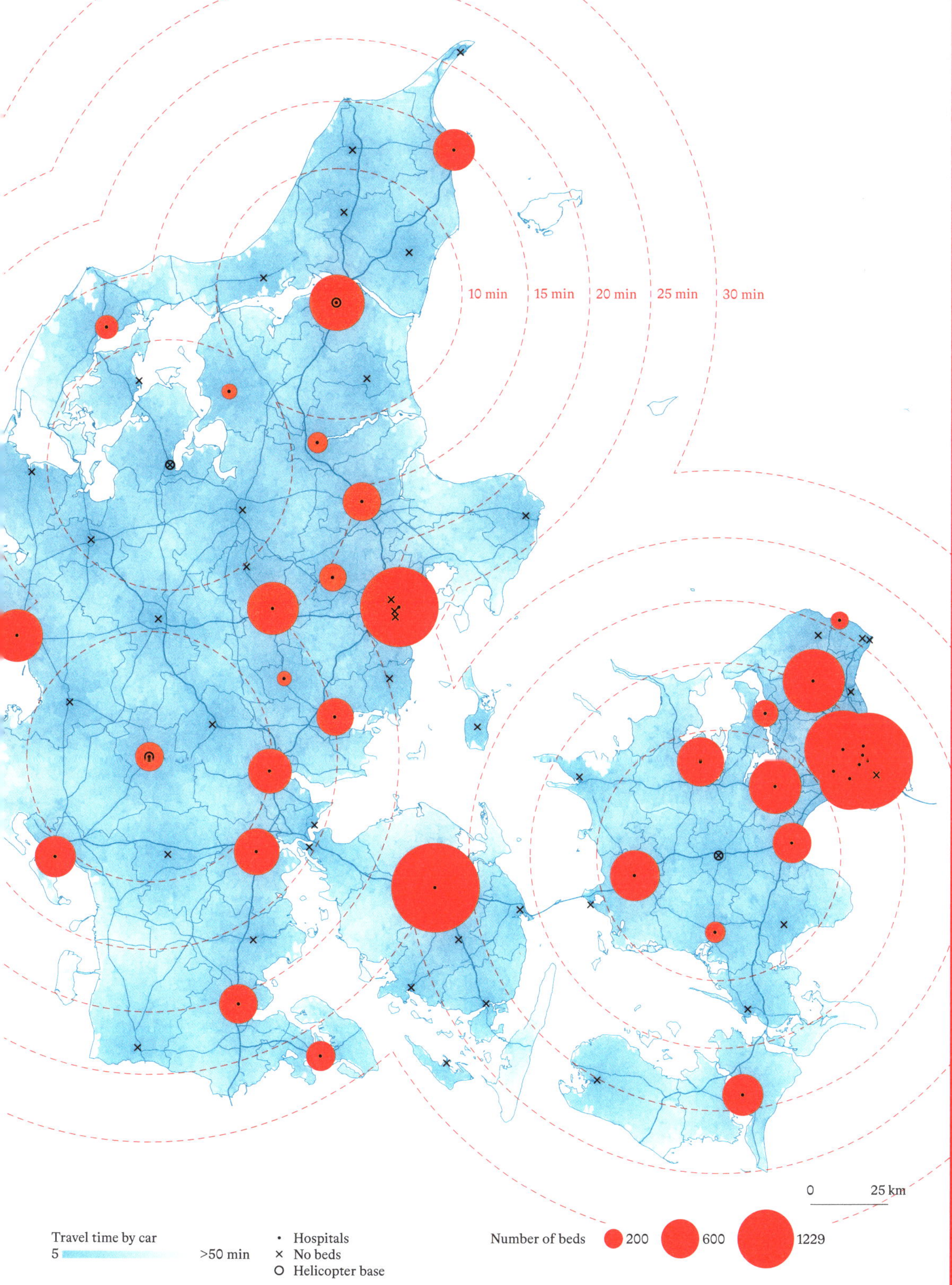

2.44 Extended hospital geography: pre-hospital transport and telemedicine

Utility helicopter
Eurocopter EC135 (Airbus Helicopter H135)
Variant: Air Ambulance

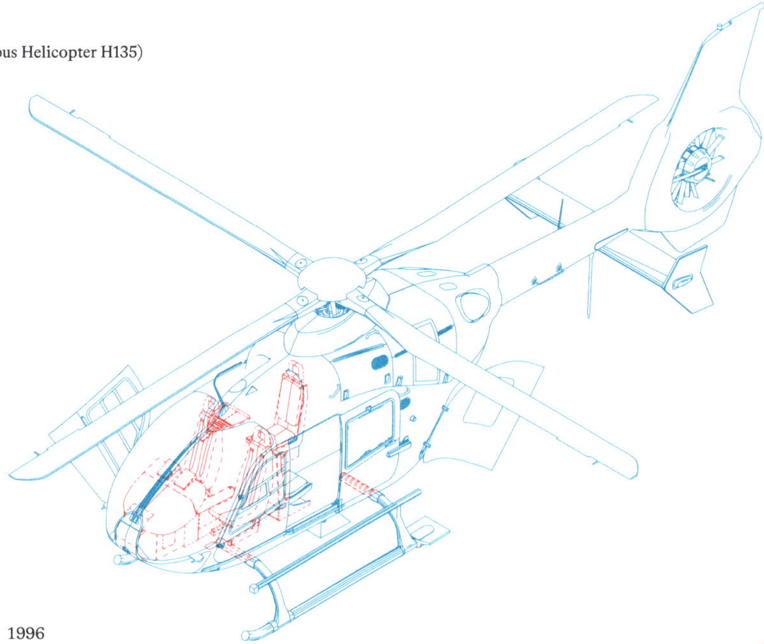

Introduction	1996
Produced	1995–present
Number built	1,400 (Sep. 2020)

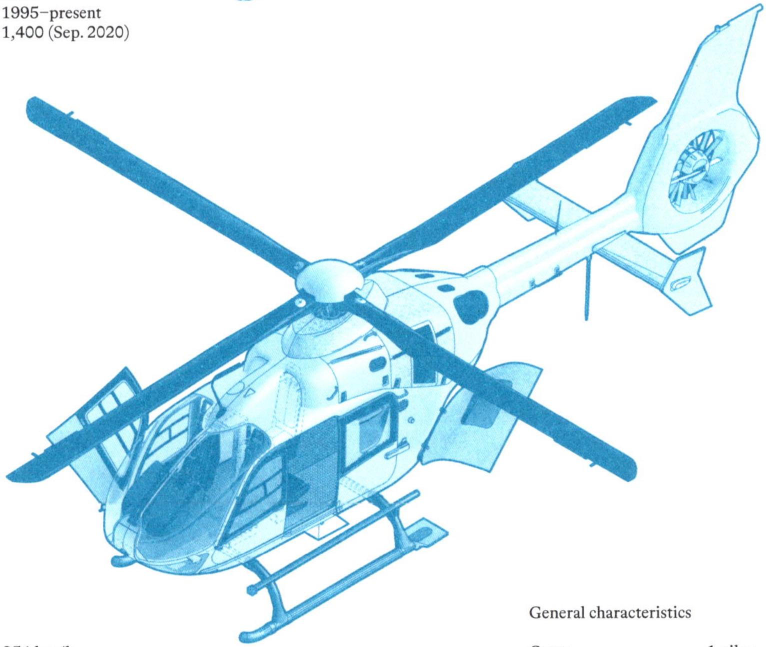

0 1 m

Performance

Cruise speed	254 km/h
Never exceed speed	287 km/h
Range	635 km
Service ceiling	6,096 m
Rate of climb	7.62 m/s

General characteristics

Crew	1 pilot
Capacity	2 crew and 2 patients
Length	10.2 m
Height	3.51 m
Empty weight	1,455 kg
Max takeoff weight	2,910 kg
Main rotor diameter	10.2 m
Main rotor area	81.7 m²

Computer

Mobile phone

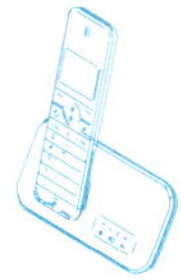

Phone

Ambulance
Mercedes Benz Sprinter
Body Type: Panel Van 324

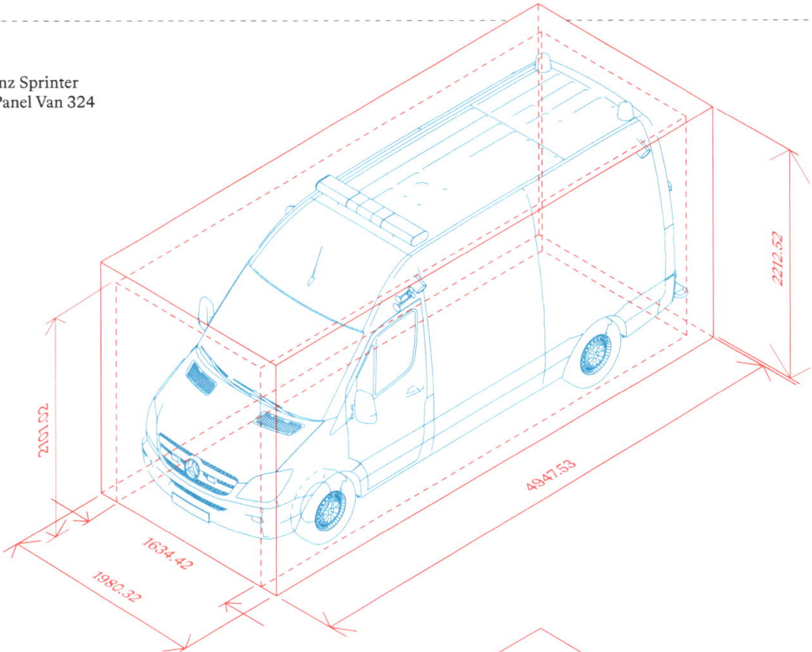

Produced 1995–present

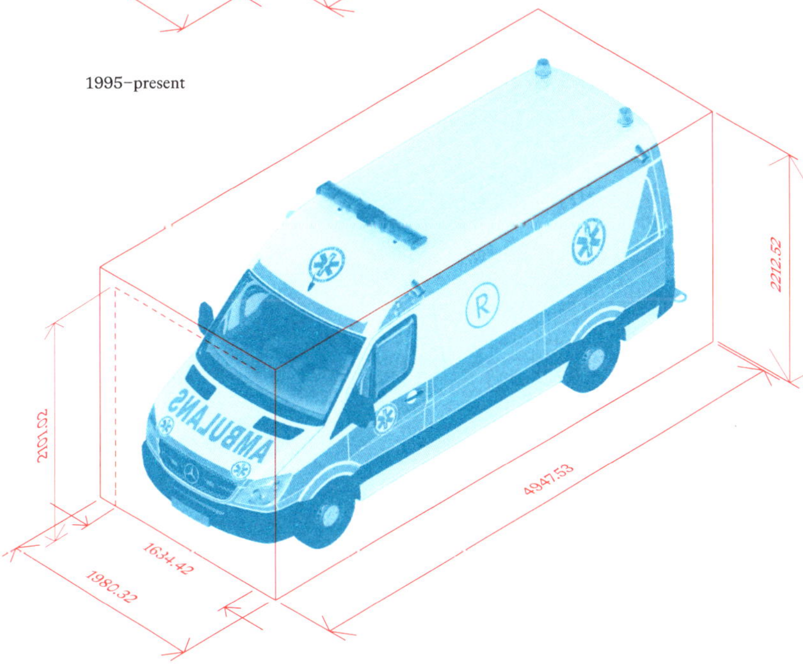

0 1 m

Performance	
Max speed	155 km/h
Range	680 km
Engine power	190 kW (258 PS)
	6 cylinder
	3,500 CC
	3.5 litre

General characteristics	
Crew	1 driver
Capacity	2 crew and 1 patient
Length	ca 3.49 m
Width	ca. 1,960 m
Height	ca. 1,975 m
Max. total weight	3,500 kg

2.45 Number of hospitals and beds, 1930–2020

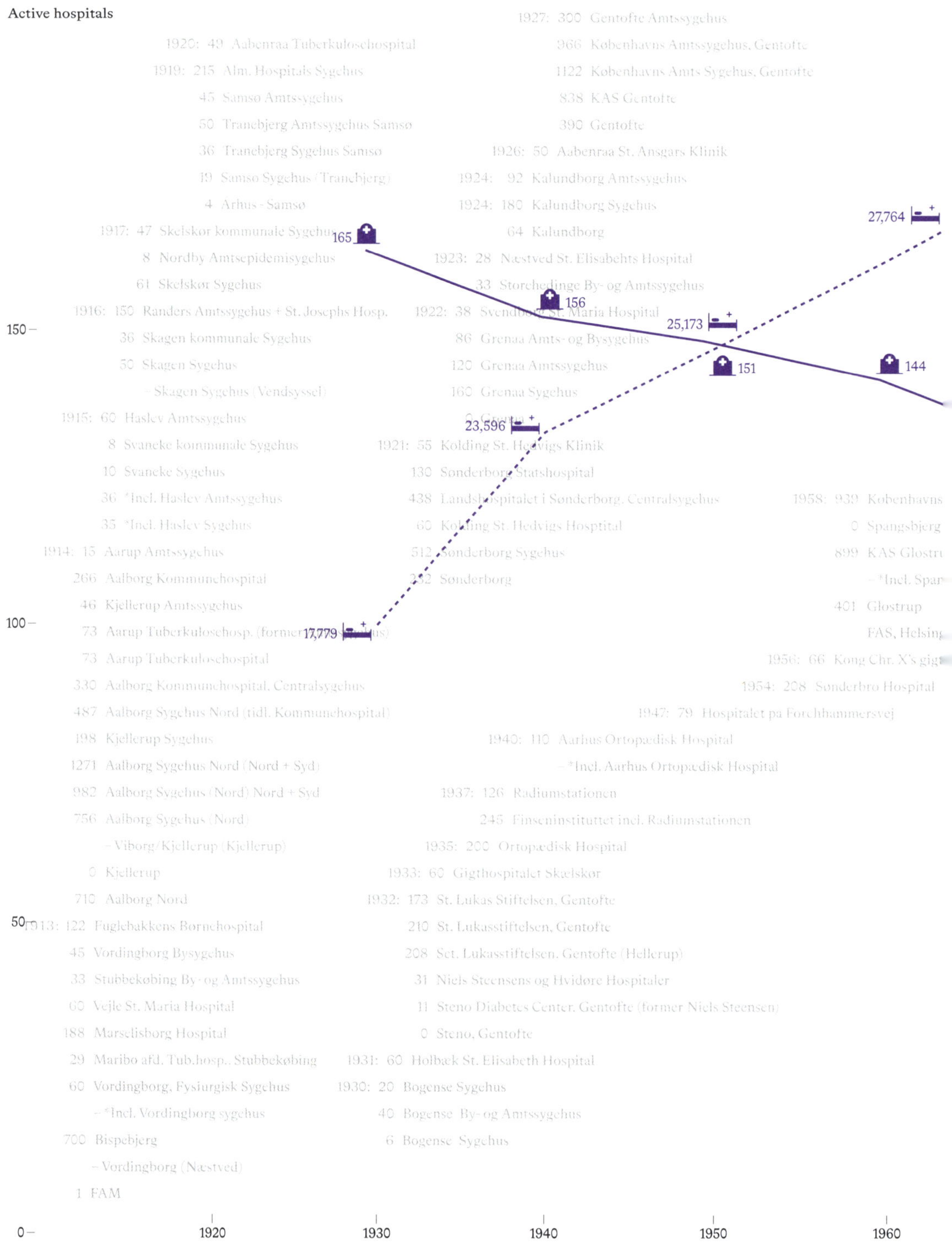

Active hospitals — Number of beds — Construction year of hospitals and bed counts

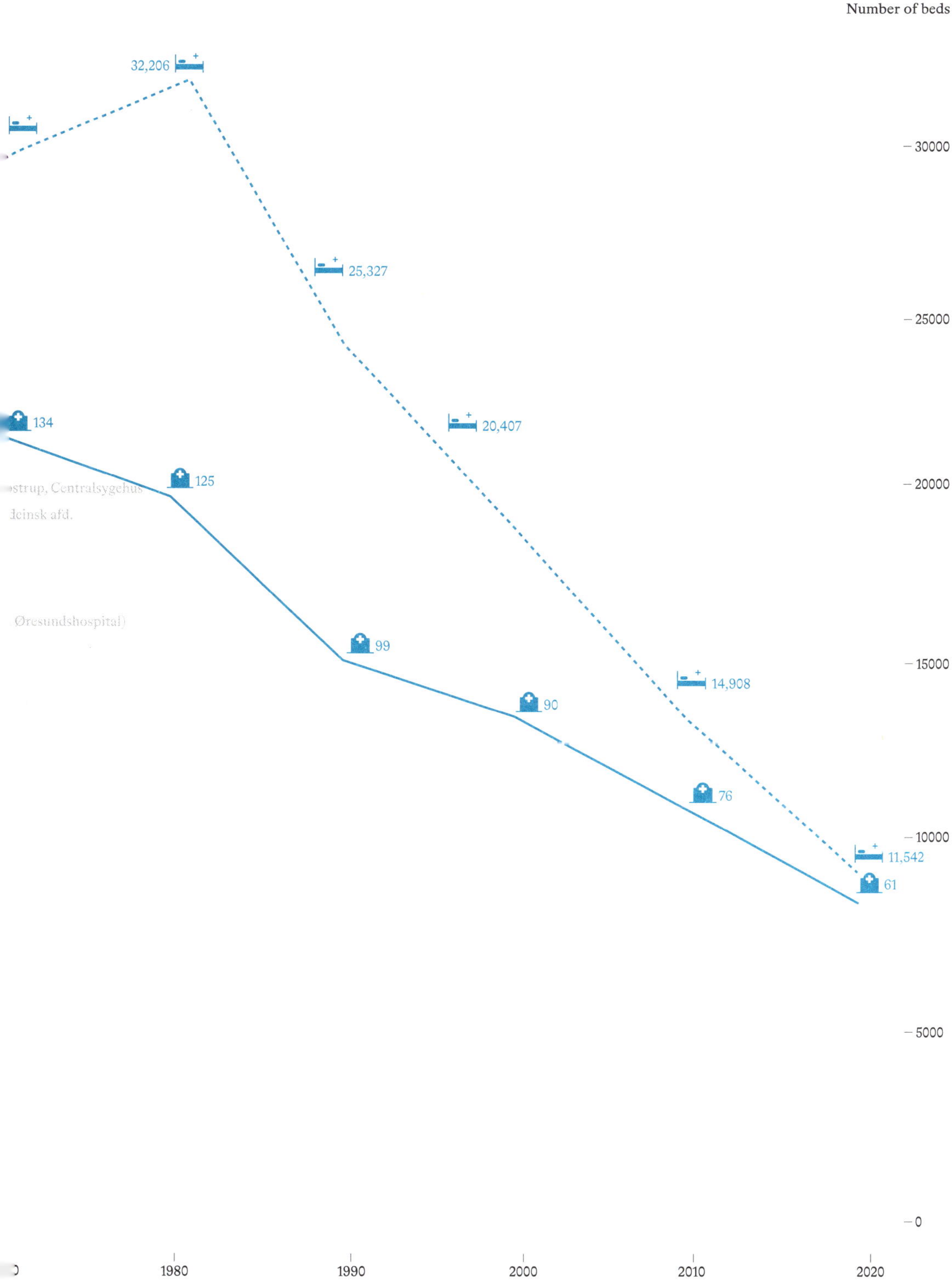
Number of beds
32,206
25,327
20,407
14,908
11,542
134
125
99
90
76
61
30000
25000
20000
15000
10000
5000
0
1980
1990
2000
2010
2020

Exploring Health Promotive Spaces of New Welfare
A Transdisciplinary Approach

Sten Gromark

Interviewed by Louise Dedenroth Høj and Max Pedersen

LDH Louise Dedenroth Høj
MP Max Pedersen
SG Sten Gromark

LDH + MP The number of elderly people is drastically increasing these years, both in Denmark and the Nordic countries, but also globally. Can you start by telling us what you consider to be the main challenges of the aging society in relation to welfare spaces?

SG The main objective is to ensure that the growing number of the elderly will be able to live a decent life. The challenge to modern society is to provide dignity in aging, and perhaps also a new kind of welfare for the elderly. This is a question very much related to housing, to the apartment, to the residential situation. This is because most future care actions will happen in apartments and not in institutions. That is a very important point, which we must address in this situation – how do we design apartments where it is possible for elderly to receive care in their homes? Due to technical achievements, in the future, more advanced medical services will be provided in the home. It is widely acknowledged that the feeling of being at home in your private dwelling contributes to the well-being of the elderly. It is even written into Swedish legislation that care institutions have to offer a home-like atmosphere. And that is a huge problem. Because how do you create a home-like atmosphere in an environment where many of the residents are in a fragile medical condition? In private homes, on the other hand, creating a home-like atmosphere is not part of the problem. Here, the challenge is to make them adaptable to medical care effectuated on-site. Doctors and health personnel have been saying for years that the only way to meet the challenge of the aging society within feasible economic limits is to move care support into the homes and to find residential solutions to make this possible, instead of building more institutions at huge societal costs.

LDH + MP So, the solution, you are saying, is not to build more care institutions, but to create flexible and adaptable dwelling spaces?

SG Absolutely. I think that is a main point concerning the future of dwellings: *alterability*, *adaptability* and *flexibility*. It is very important to be able to rearrange the crucial relation between spaces – the relation between the bedroom and the bathroom, for instance. Also, small technical things, like railings in the bathroom, are very important to preserve long-term quality of life in these situations. Another example from a compact living situation is where you have a wall with an opening between two rooms, and you have the whole wall movable from one side to the other, so you can seamlessly relegate the relation between one room toward another. Such a practical solution underpins the day-to-day, or even hour-to-hour change. I think that alterability is an important part of the future of residential production.

LDH + MP What implications does this have for welfare spaces?

SG I remember, while we were working on the book *Architecture for Residential Care and Ageing Communities*, we tried to imagine and initiate the realization of a new welfare.[1] This is quite important for me. The effect of the welfare state has been perceived as that of mass housing. I would like to exchange that for an adapted future housing provision of the specific realization of unfulfilled dreams and desires of people. For example, in the book *Ways of Residing in Transformation*, we have on the cover a family of clowns in Berlin.[2] They have taken part in the process of designing their own apartment, and designing it not only for domestic living, but also to be used as a training ground for acrobats, as you see in the picture. This symbolizes the concept of a new kind of welfare. Of course, this is a private property issue, but there is a construction company behind this which allowed them to take part in the design of their own reality in that way. That is an image for me that speaks about a new kind of welfare concerning qualities of dwelling, and I think that this is also relevant for making new care homes for the elderly – to bring them more dignity, a more homely atmosphere and make the exchange with others and the surrounding community easier, to avoid and to counter widespread loneliness. It is possible to initiate that kind of exchange, to bring in more quality and to make it possible to thrive also in these situations when you are not feeling altogether well. That is my idea of producing new welfare, or new preconditions.

LDH + MP Is reintegrating the elderly in the community a way of creating social cohesion in society?

SG Yes, I think we need to think more in terms of integrated ways of residing. That is important. To make a sort of transgression between different categories of housing and residents. And of course, we really want to avoid what has been happening in the care for the elderly, in the institutions that we have seen. Normally they are isolated, placed in a sort of excluded area, far from the center of the urban world. A main problem we see is unbearable loneliness. I remember that there was a thorough analysis of Swedish homes for the elderly done by the official social agencies on a national level, and they promoted one care home as the best example on almost every point. It was the best ever made in Sweden. But even in that situation, the residents still complained about the extreme loneliness they felt in the way they were residing in this building. That is perhaps the more difficult problem to address. Perhaps one solution is bringing more new categories of people in close vicinity, making these buildings more urban-like or integrated within the urban structure and to offer better opportunities for exchanges with other people. One extraordinary example of this approach can be found in Germany, the ASZ Eching, where several categories of people, of all walks of life, have united to form a sort of extended residential community across age differences and almost everything else.[3] I think that is the real future. That you mix as many categories as possible in such a situation. I often come across very different solutions for this integration, these integrative ways of residing. For example, students living next to the elderly in the same building or combining child day care with housing and care homes for elderly. I think there are a lot of valuable everyday exchanges going on in these situations, with the children enjoying being with the elderly and vice versa. These different situations and the symbolic transgression between categories in these different residential communities is apparently so rewarding for the people involved in them.

LDH + MP What you are talking about all relates to social aspects of architecture. Can you explain a bit more about your interest in this subject?

SG I hope my own contribution to architectural research could be labeled "studies on social sustainability." I wrote my dissertation back in the 1980s, where I pointed to a revolutionary project in Neubibergerstrasse in Munich by the architects Ralph and Doris Thut.[4] This pioneering project from 1974–77 has since been conceived as a sort of emblematic prototype for the whole alternative movement of sustainability from that time on, and is still valid in many aspects, because this was a building that was, among other features, done in self-construction. I think there were six households in the group that united and bought the terrain and built their cohousing on it. There is a pile of different recyclable materials used in the construction, apparent in the facade, early systems of solar energy were applied, and they were growing their own tomatoes in the common winter garden greenhouse and so on. The main notion here is the getting together and realization of new ways of residing in a very social way, so actually this really was the starting point of the whole alternative movement in residential and architectural terms. For me that was also the starting point of my research, the discovery of this kind of situation within the whole European and international context. And I have continued on that track up until today. Another important theme has been for me to study cases of the very opposite to compact living, the maximum of living in an abundance of square meters like the recent projects by French architects Lacaton & Vassal with Frédéric Druot. These have demonstrated that expanded apartments represent a basic, very-much-desired quality in many projects of social sustainable housing. So social sustainability, that is what I have been working around all the time.[5]

LDH + MP There is a recent project, the Viva collective housing in Chalmers. Could you tell us about your contribution to social sustainability in this project?

SG It was a transdisciplinary collaboration initiated under the title Positive Footprint Housing, PFH, between the Riksbyggen EF, a Swedish cooperative housing developer, and a team of researchers from Chalmers University of Technology and University of Gothenburg; I was fortunate enough to take part in almost the whole process. The company told us they knew all the technical aspects of sustainability, but they wanted us researchers to tell them what social sustainability could be in this situation. And what we agreed to focus on was the aspects of adaptability and the concept of integrative ways of residing. A realization of our influence was particular attention paid to the structural flexibility of the apartments, so they can be adapted to a specific way of life and adjusted seamlessly to different life situations. Whether you have one child or two children, then the apartments can adapt to these changes with time. Regarding the other aspect, the integrative residing, our contribution was the implementation of six small extra apartments for young professional people, who are paying a bit less but are still full members of the community. These young people are coming from the official municipality housing queue. Even though it is only a small part out of the total of 132 flats, I think it is an important step. That is how changes come about, a little tweaking in what is possible to be done. Björn Andersson, my colleague and academic partner, a professor of social work at the University of Gothenburg, said straight out to the company: you must do this to show that you are taking some social responsibility, making it possible for young people early in their careers and working life to have access to this type of community. And on the other hand, the Viva project has also been a great attraction and an occasion for many people to drastically change their lives, leaving their villas and two cars in the suburbs and moving into a city-like situation and a more sustainable way of living right on Chalmers's busy campus.[6]

LDH + MP How does the architecture stimulate social interaction in the Viva project?

SG In this project, the concept is that you take square meters from the private apartment and put them into shared common facilities. So it is a kind of compact living, but you get something extra added to your way of residing – in the case of Viva, for instance, a huge, giant bicycle garage instead of a normal car garage, several common meeting facilities, the extensive exterior garden areas and so on. That is also considered social sustainability, that people are getting together and doing things together. They are already having a lot of activities there, for example, the exchange of goods and recycling of materials, toys and bicycles. I think this is a good illustration of the concept of integrative ways of residing.

LDH + MP If you want to create these successful communities, do you then need a higher degree of user involvement?

SG Absolutely. I think that the building industry, the providers of housing should work in a different way and see how they can provide for open projects that can realize the dreams of people. Riksbyggen has done this to some degree in the Viva project. Here potential future residents were invited to meetings and had a chance to have an influence on the project beforehand and while waiting for access. In this way Riksbyggen is trying to create a culture of a tight residential community in order to make inhabitants come into the actual situation with an awareness of and predisposition for taking part in the residential community, which they eventually finally will be members of. I think that is a key question for the future. The possibility of taking part in an early cocreation process with others, together with professionals of construction and company administrators. The architects of course have a key role providing valid design options.

LDH + MP It seems that transdisciplinarity plays an important role in your scientific approach, linking the social with the spatial in architecture. Can you explain why this is important?

SG I think the realization of a socially sustainable architecture rests upon the transdisciplinary approach and the ability to exchange perspectives beyond the borders of academia. In the AIDAH project, which is the background for many of the projects I have worked on, initially we started a master's program with three studios: one on housing and dwelling, one on aging, and one on caring in hospitals, all organized as dedicated combined teams of researchers and teachers. When we started more than ten years ago, this was a big issue. The three groups all said unanimously: "we cannot work together; we have nothing in common." But in fact, I managed to get these three groups together, to seek common insights into the interrelationships between these different residential situations and to learn from one another, including master class students. In relation to Riksbyggen we developed a transdisciplinary way of unfolding a collaborative project during quite a long time span. My own main objective has been to try to exchange perspectives and views between sociology and architecture – but also to include, in the case of the wider AIDAH research environment, the medical sciences, designers and psychologists, medical doctors, nurses of care sciences and social workers. I think this transdisciplinary approach has been extremely rewarding for all partners. It has been a decisive attempt and unique occasion to rethink the social in architecture within the realms of a real design project process. The realization of what we could say is social sustainability.[7]

Bibliography

Gromark, Sten. *Boendegemenskap: En kritisk granskning av dess värden, villkor och förutsättningar samt exempel på praktisk tillämpning i ett västeuropeiskt sammanhang*. Gothenburg: Chalmers tekn. högsk., 1983.

Gromark, Sten, and Björn Andersson, eds. *Architecture for Residential Care and Ageing Communities: Spaces for Dwelling and Healthcare*. New York: Routledge, 2020.

Gromark, Sten, Björn Andersson and Anna Braide. "Explorations on Residential Resilience—brf Viva 2011–2019 [COST Intrepid publication]." In *Enabling the City: Inter- and Transdisciplinary Encounters*, edited by Josefine Fokdal, Liis Ojamäe, Olivia Bina, Prue Chiles and Katrin Paadam, 80–95. London: Routledge, 2021.

Gromark, Sten, Mervi Ilmonen, Katrin Paadam and Eli Støa, eds. *Ways of Residing in Transformation: Interdisciplinary Perspectives*. London: Ashgate/Routledge, 2016.

Gromark, Sten, Jennifer Mack and Roemer van Toorn, eds. *Rethinking the Social in Architecture: Making Effects*. Vol. 1 of *Architecture in Effect*. Barcelona: Actar, 2019.

Paadam, Katrin, and Sten Gromark. 2019. "Voices from the Inside: Residents' Experiences in the Bois-le-Prêtre Alteration Project, Paris, 2013." In Gromark, Mack and van Toorn, *Rethinking the Social in Architecture*, 213–31.

Notes

1 Sten Gromark and Björn Andersson, eds., *Architecture for Residential Care and Ageing Communities: Spaces for Dwelling and Healthcare* (New York: Routledge, 2020).

2 Sten Gromark, Mervi Ilmonen, Katrin Paadam, and Eli Støa, eds., *Ways of Residing in Transformation: Interdisciplinary Perspectives* (London: Ashgate/Routledge, 2016).

3 Gromark and Andersson, *Architecture for Residential Care and Ageing Communities*.

4 Sten Gromark, *Boendegemenskap: En kritisk granskning av dess värden, villkor och förutsättningar samt exempel på praktisk tillämpning i ett västeuropeiskt sammanhang* (Gothenburg: Chalmers tekn. högsk., 1983).

5 Katrin Paadam and Sten Gromark, "Voices from the Inside: Residents' Experiences in the Bois-le-Prêtre Alteration Project, Paris, 2013," in *Rethinking the Social in Architecture: Making Effects*, vol. 1 of *Architecture in Effect*, ed. Sten Gromark, Jennifer Mack and Roemer van Toorn (Barcelona: Actar, 2019), 213–31.

6 Sten Gromark, Björn Andersson and Anna Braide, "Explorations on Residential Resilience – brf Viva 2011–2019," in *Enabling the City: Inter- and Transdisciplinary Encounters*, ed. Josefine Fokdal, Liis Ojamäe, Olivia Bina, Prue Chiles and Katrin Paadam (London: Routledge, 2021), 80–95.

7 See the editors' introduction to Gromark, Mack and van Toorn, *Rethinking the Social in Architecture*, 8–35.

Design and Decolonization in the 1970s
Beyond Spaces of Danish Welfare

Alison J. Clarke

1 Stove from Jalisco, Mexico, anonymous design, ca. 1971, collected by John Frost, in Victor J. Papanek's collection. Photo by Roger Conrad/ Victor J. Papanek Foundation/University of Applied Arts Vienna.

Discourses around the dismantling and restructuring of Danish welfare spaces from 1970 onward are principally contextualized through national and pan-Scandinavian social, cultural and economic factors. In light of recent problematizations of the liberal welfare state model in relation to its intertwining with colonization and postcolonialization, this chapter uses the specific case of design in 1970s Denmark as a means of expanding beyond national and regional histories into the interstices of broader globalized histories.[1]

In August 1971 Denmark's leading design journal, *Mobilia*, featured on its front cover discarded automobile license plates refashioned into a portable stove on which, according to the editorial, a Mexican "family cooks all of their meals."⟨fig. 1⟩ Showcasing a range of similarly didactic artifacts of culturally appropriated technology (including a low-tech self-assembled, crank-powered refrigerator for distribution in the southern African country of Lesotho), the article, "What to Design and Why," used a Danish welfare state paradigm of design for the common good, extending it outward to address the needs of the Global South and its emerging independent nations.

This chapter explores how a newly imagined genre of socially responsible industrial design emerged in 1960s and '70s Denmark, offering a counterpoise to the dwindling enthusiasm for, and resistance to, "modernism's universalism and scale."[2] In Danish architectural discourse, the 1970s is often viewed as a period of national decline, a view summarized succinctly in the observation made by one historian that this was "the decade things started to go downhill when it came to social commitment, craftsmanship and architectonic quality."[3] By way of contrast, with the strictures of modernist rationalism cast aside and the dominance of architectural practice as the purveyor of social welfare functionalism and ideology waning, design began to take on a freshly radicalized, cutting-edge profile as a force for grassroots political change, tackling areas as diverse as the sensory environments of disabled children to cornmills for communities of the developing world.

Significantly, the ambitions for this newly forged brand of social activist design stretched far beyond the traditional spaces of the Danish and Scandinavian welfare state, tackling instead the geopolitical effects of ongoing late postwar processes of decolonialization. Buoyed by the conscious application of the Scandinavian and Nordic models to developing countries and by a substantial increase in the Denmark's per capita contribution to development aid, industrial design took on the form of quasi-anthropological social intervention that expanded national spaces of welfare outward to previously uncharted spaces of the Global South.

A Prescription for Rebellion: Design and Dissent in the Danish Academy

Nowhere was this transition from the primacy of architecture as the perceived purveyor of modernist social good to design as a transdisciplinary, culturally nuanced practice more obvious than in the inner machinations

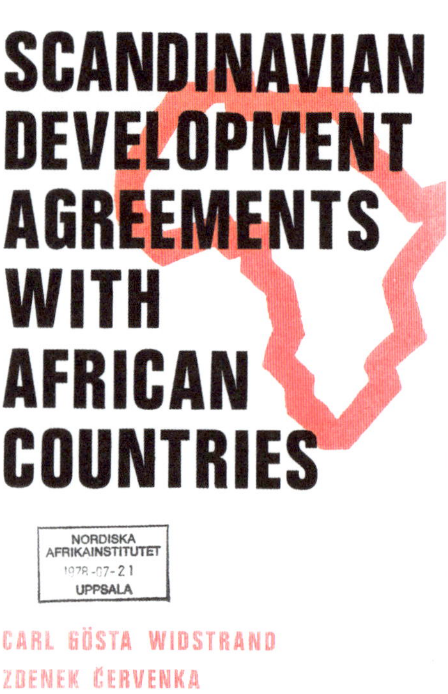

2 Front cover, *Scandinavian Agreements with African Countries*, 1978. Courtesy of the Nordic Africa Institute, Sweden.

of Det Kongelige Danske Kunstakademi (The Royal Danish Academy of Fine Arts) and Kunstakademiets Arkitektskole (The Academy's School of Architecture) itself. In 1971, the year of the *Mobilia* social design special issue, the Academy was in a state of upheaval, reeling from student protests directly challenging the institution's traditional nineteenth-century Beaux-Arts structure that placed architecture unequivocally at the top of an art-and-design hierarchy. These protestations revolved around the questioning of architects' overly prominent role in negotiating the politics of the Danish built environment and the national politics of welfare more generally. One former student of the art school during this period, Steen Juhler, recounted in an oral history interview how Danish design and architecture until this period had been controlled by an unspoken hierarchical structure whereby "only a few people and mostly people from architectural families made it into the Academy, and consequently the broader national Danish design scene."[4] As well as having a pedagogical remit, institutions such as the Academy essentially acted as state-sponsored gatekeepers, maintaining the status quo of the Danish architectural profession. To Juhler and his dissenting contemporaries, this professional nepotism was inextricably linked to the prolonged observance of an elitist Danish design culture of "good form," a culture that focused on design connoisseurship and the notion of good taste embodied in the oppressive strictures of midcentury Scandinavian modernist style. A group of disaffected would-be students – who had initially been rejected by the Academy after failing the architectural school entrance exams – envisaged a design culture of collaboration and social and political engagement that stretched beyond what they saw as superficial formalism and aesthetic dilettantism. In response to demonstrations, normal entrance policies were temporarily abandoned within at the establishment, with students able to move freely between studios. As a logistical response to the sheer size of the free-reigning student cohort, large-scale planning emerged across departments with cross-disciplinary platforms in urban planning, urban space and landscape and themes pertaining to the Global South. For industrial design students, in place of formalistic design exercises, socially immersive projects were instigated that required the minute observation of, and empathy with, the everyday practices and values of specific user groups – from illiterate women needing explanatory illustrative contraceptive packaging to self-built safety night lamps for "Third World" users.

At this point, Scandinavian and Nordic architecture had been fully instrumentalized in applying welfare-based models to the spatial and built environments of the newly imagined social democracies of the Global South. A detailed policy report of 1971, titled

Scandinavian Development Agreements with African Countries (produced by the Scandinavian Institute of African Studies, Sweden) noted the exponential increase of Danish aid expenditure from DKK 6,235 million in 1962–63 to DKK 47,186 million in 1969–70, with project agreements made with Botswana, Uganda and Kenya, to name but a few.[5] ⟨fig. 2⟩ Configuring what would become a well-rehearsed and rarely challenged discourse framing Scandinavia and the Nordic region's exceptional status vis-à-vis aid and development, the report flagged "the readiness of the African countries to enter into bilateral agreements with Scandinavian countries on account of their noncolonial past and above all their resolute stand in the decolonization of Africa and apartheid."[6]

Postcolonial Design Initiatives within a Noncolonial Paradigm

Over the past decade, the role of modern Nordic architects in promulgating the social democratic ideals of the 1960s development aid initiative has attracted renewed attention.[7] In 2014 the Venice Biennale exhibition *Forms of Freedom: African Independence and Nordic Models* (examining the role of Nordic architecture in fostering social welfare in countries such Tanzania, Zambia and Kenya) rehearsed the same noncolonial paradigm that had underpinned the Scandinavian Development Agreements report a full half-century earlier. As the curators themselves put it, leaders of the new African states "wanted partners without a murky colonial past and looked to emulate the progressive results achieved by the Nordic welfare states after WWII" with "solid bonds built on a mutual belief in progress."[8]

Postcolonial scholars working outside of architectural history, examining, for example, the intersection of gender, race and ethnicity in the Nordic region, have fundamentally challenged this absence of colonial discourse, arguing that despite managing to "retain an image of themselves as untouched by colonial legacies" in fact "antiracism and anti-imperialist movements, and academic commentary on issues of race and colonialism" have been integral to Nordic societies since the 1970s.[9] In architectural history (specifically the work of Tom Avermaete et al. in considering the *Colonial Modern*) there have been more nuanced explorations of the ways in which the aesthetic regime of modernism manifests itself in local settings as a form of negotiated modernism. However, in the Danish context the noncolonial paradigm largely persists in examining the modernist intervention of late postwar architects.[10]

One area of colonial architectural intervention that drew greater critical scrutiny early on centered on the material politics of the application of welfare models to Greenland. In the late postwar period, as Danish architects had been tasked with installing social housing on the expansive island located between the Arctic and North Atlantic oceans as an integral aspect of enhancing Greenland as a modern welfare society in keeping with its postcolonial status as part of the Danish realm (prior to the country's achieving full independence in 1979).[11] In the 1970s, the top-down installation of modernist, rationalist architecture planned by the Greenland Technical Organization (GTO), designed functionally to manage the hostile climatic setting, was the subject of much critical debate in the architectural press. According to architectural historian Kirsten Birk Hansen, this debate revolved predominantly around "the question of whether people would be able to adapt and tailor residential construction to the Greenlanders' needs and way of life."[12] How might a rationalist modernist welfare paradigm and aesthetic be adapted to respectfully and practically allow for indigenous practices and preexisting social worlds? A leading architectural design editor of the period, Poul Erik Skriver, in the highly regarded and longest-standing Scandinavian architectural journal, *Arkitekten*, called for a kind of user-participatory approach in a polemical article "Grønland i Focus":

> What could have been developed instead were forms of industrialized building, where lightweight components [...] could have been used for making new constructions and for the expansion of the original small homes. The education and training of Greenlanders to carry out this kind of industrialized construction would have been a more viable task than educating and training them to be participants in the construction of concrete buildings.[13]

Welfare Colonialism: Social Design as a Response

Critical debates around Greenland and the imposition of Danish social welfare spaces upon the inhabitants, including *Arkitekten*'s 1970 think piece "Grønland i Focus," coincided with the publication in Swedish of a groundbreaking book, *Miljön och miljonerna: Design som tjänst eller förtjänst?* (The Environment and the Millions: Design for Service or Profit?). Its author, Austrian-American designer Victor Papanek, proposed a radical rethinking of design's social purpose, challenging its commercial and corporate-driven infrastructure and sketching out a manifesto for a new generation of would-be design activists. By 1972 the head of design, Erik Herløw (affiliated with the School of Architecture) had invited Papanek to join the Danish Academy as a guest professor, in part to quell the student discontent within the institution and in part to address, through an emerging social design, the accusations of "welfare colonialism" taking place in Greenland.[14] Described as a "trendsetting" expert in the area of "design and environment," Papanek secured his post as guest professor on the back of his knowledge of Inuit material cultures and, most significantly, a proposal for a critical, cross-disciplinary study group exploring "Our Design-Based Influence in the Developing Countries."[15]

Released in English in 1971 as *Design for the Real World: Human Ecology and Social Change*, Papanek's best-selling book was also released in Danish as *Miljø for millioner: Design for behov eller profit* in 1972, the year of his arrival in Copenhagen. In fact, the tome was directly informed by the designer's interactions with Scandinavian designers and students, and more significantly, the role of design in welfare societies that ran counter to a US corporate capitalist profit-driven model of planned obsolescence. As a prominent voice advocating a user-based, culturally and anthropologically informed approach to design and the built environment, Papanek had first risen to prominence among Scandinavian student activists during his prolonged travels across the Nordic region from the mid-1960s onwards. His opening addresses, made at youth events from Finland to Norway, placed design students at the forefront of social progressive change:

> In the vanguard of revolutionary students are the design students. And this is true everywhere: the People's Republic of China, Czechoslovakia, Finland, Spain, Sweden and Tanzania. This is not surprising if we remember that in design we are planning the future and the place of man [*sic*] within it.[16]

The pivotal event leading to the instigation of the highly influential social design agenda Papanek would later bring to Denmark as a guest professor addressing issues of "welfare colonialism" took place in the summer of 1968, under the title "Industry, Environment, Product Design" on a small island in the port of Helsinki. The groundbreaking initiative of the newly founded Pan-Scandinavian Design Students' Organization (SDO) proposed a radical challenge to the status quo of conventional design culture, through the lobbying of national politicians, educators, and policymakers reaping support of a cutting-edge social design agenda.[17] The SDO had no qualms in spelling out their "Alternative Mission Statement" to the broadest mainstream design audience. "We oppose capitalism with every means at our disposal to attain a dynamic socialist system that will make total social justice possible," they declared in the Swedish design magazine *FORM*. Their published manifesto further clarified their position:

> We want to put an end to a system in which invented needs are satisfied at the expense of genuine needs. We want to carry out surveys of the genuine needs of people in different areas in the world. We want to analyze the results of these surveys and use them as a basis for participation in satisfying these genuine needs. We want to put an end to a system that misuses our shared resources on the globe. We want to support national liberation movements actively.[18]

The SDO's symposium audience and speakers consisted of a varied and interdisciplinary crowd, drawn from corollary design disciplines such as engineering and pedagogy, with the intention of carving out the possibility of a design practice that looked beyond the paradigm of the profit-driven market. Divisions among design, research, technology, architecture, social science and pedagogy were suspended. The UK-based Design Research Unit (a user-oriented design consultancy) spoke, for example, alongside architectural theorist Christopher Alexander, who addressed the audience with his lecture titled "The Organization of Design Pattern." Engineer Graham Whitehead considered the issue of "System Ergonomics: The Human Factor in Complex System Design" alongside world-renowned Finnish designers such as Kaj Franck and Antti Nurmesniemi, keen to support a transdisciplinary agenda.

But the most notable aspect of this event was the appearance, as keynote speakers, of well-known maverick architect and technocrat Buckminster Fuller alongside his lesser-known US compatriot and design activist Victor Papanek. At first glance, the event appeared to tune directly into late 1960s counterculture; taking place just months after the Paris student uprisings and the trashing of the 14th Milan Design Triennial in May 1968 in protest against design's role in driving environmental destruction and furthering social inequality. Rather than revolving around static hierarchical expert lectures, students mixed informally with the speakers in discussion groups, and crucially took part in practical cross-disciplinary projects aimed at highlighting the processual nature of social design – which was aimed as much at highlighting material and social politics as it was at creating finished products.

Papanek brought together a team of clinicians, designers and caregivers to create a prototype for portable play environment for children with cerebral palsy and other sensory disabilities, titled CP-1.[19] Buckminster Fuller's cross-disciplinary student team tackled the project of making a prototype for a portable reindeer abattoir very loosely adapted from Fuller's famous principles of geodesic structure. This was an audacious act – driven by the students rather than Fuller himself – to generate a political gesture rather than a practical design tool. Recent top-down government policy, devised in line with the increasing industrialization of meat production in the Arctic regions, had forced the Saami people (whose seminomadic reindeer herding underpinned their livelihood and traditional way of life) to adhere to unfeasibly strict regulations based on static methods of cattle slaughter. The design responded to the perceived erosion of the rights of indigenous Laplanders and homogenizing, dehumanizing effects of nation-states in historically defining Nordic ethnic-racial groups through colonizing scientific concepts such as "Lappology."[20]

The choice of Fuller and Papanek as keynote speakers for the SDO international event was undoubtedly inspired by intellectual curiosity, but it was also a calculatedly provocative gesture aimed at the Cold War sensitivities of the establishment. Fuller was already established as a visionary thinker and inventor of the biosphere, while Papanek was familiar to the organizers as an advocate of social design due to his attendance of Finnish cultural events in the mid-1960s. Most significantly, in soft diplomacy terms, Papanek and Fuller played the role of avant-gardists coming from an inherently culturally conservative nation, whose international reputation (particular among the European youth) had been harmed in particular by racial violence in the fight for desegregation.[21] Appearing in the most sensitive geopolitical region of the Cold War at the time, a northern European country poised precariously close to the Soviet Union, Finland had defiantly rejected aid from the US post–World War II Marshall Plan and ran a successful state welfare system whose collectivist ideologies stood in stark contrast to those of the free-market United States. But the overtly radical nature of this new Finnish-American relationship in the form of Papanek and Fuller's participation made a significant detour to an established trajectory – promoting a nation marred by its human rights record and resistance to racial desegregation – as a forward-looking world player.

Whether or not Papanek's involvement in student activism, as a self-defined socially responsible designer, was instrumental in assuaging socialist unrest and activism in the Nordic region is a moot point. But what is certain is that this period of late-1960s Cold War and decolonizing design politicking led directly to the creation of a highly influential, co-curated graphic design dubbed the "Copenhagen Flowchart" that spelled out the era's politics of design.⟨fig. 3⟩

The "Copenhagen Flowchart": A New Politics of Design

In the summer of 1969 Papanek had first been invited to Copenhagen as a keynote speaker for a follow-up SDO seminar; an invitation initiated by

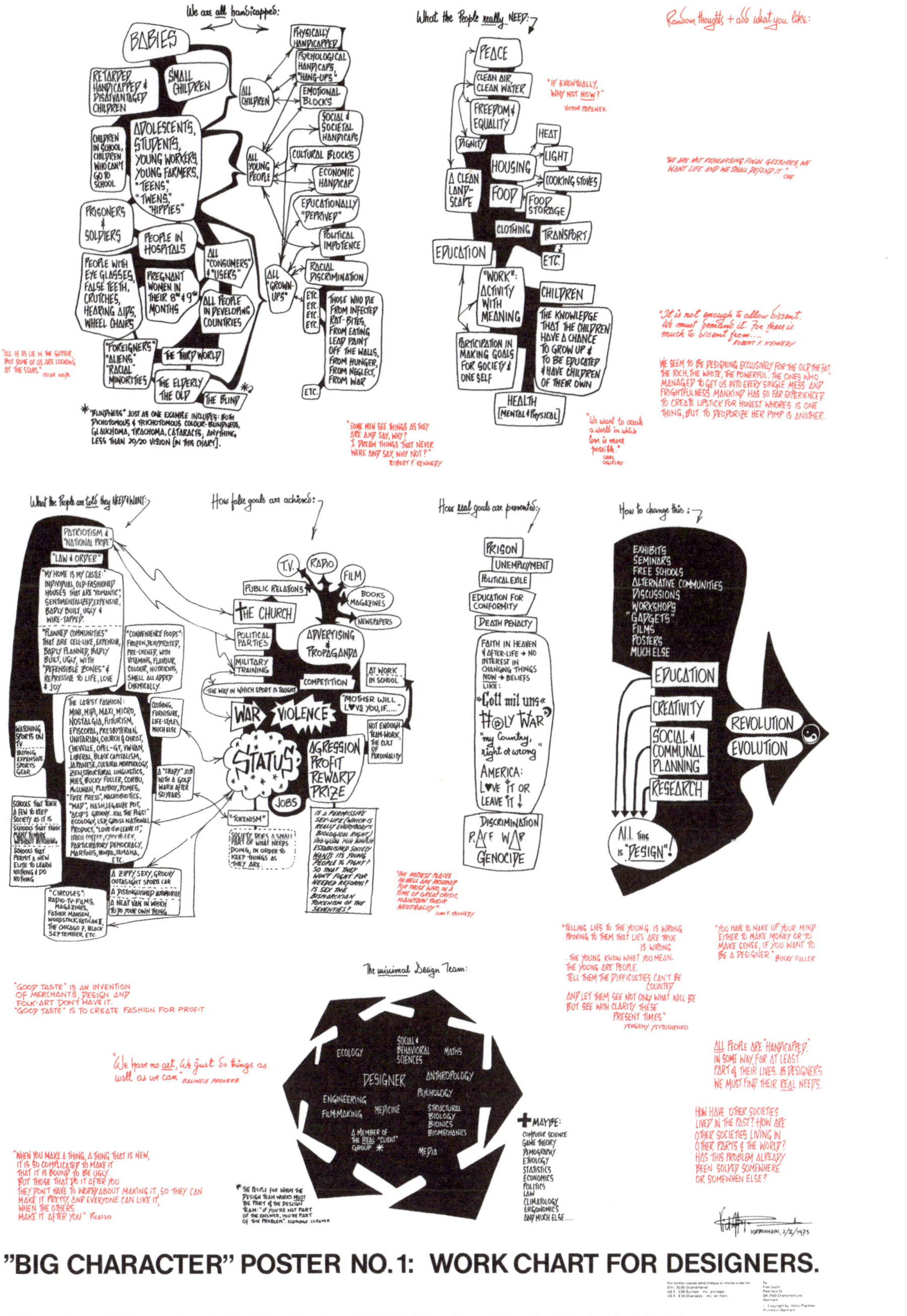

3 Victor J. Papanek, *Big Character Poster No. 1: Work Chart for Designers*, 1969 [1973]. © Victor J. Papanek Foundation, University of Applied Arts Vienna.

a group of Danish design students loosely tied to the Royal Danish Academy of Fine Arts. Building on his growing following in Northern Europe, the designer used the event and others to explore the politics of design and the future of design pedagogy with a specific emphasis on issues of disability and design. The seminar addressed five working groups held under the themes international solidarity, urban environments, health-care environments, working environments and future environments; an intellectually vibrant and fecund event, one of the Swedish students there, Susanne Koefed, engaging with the growing prominence of disability rights, sketched out a first draft of the wheelchair icon that would go on to become the international symbol for access.[22] Importantly, this event took place against a backdrop of disability rights and a focused support of disabled groups in the Global South that was specific to the Nordic region since the 1960s.[23]

In the atmospheric seventeenth-century academy building of Charlottenborg Palace, situated in the center of a 1960s capital city awash with alternative subcultural and community projects, the students helped the social design guru sketch out the first draft of a diagram dubbed the "Copenhagen Flowchart"; a visualization of the indices and intersections of power relations of design, mapped out as a hand-illustrated diagram, the central tenet of *Design for the Real World* reproduced, in 1973, as the purchasable *Big Character Poster No. 1: Work Chart for Designers*.[24] The intense gathering of like-minded designers gave rise to this iconic piece of graphic design, one that came to embody a new socially led politics of design that pushed notions of social welfare beyond a Nordic remit, addressing instead design's role in serving people in emerging countries, ethnic minorities and so-called foreigners, among others.

Three years later, in his role as guest professor at the Danish Academy, Papanek's proposed cross-disciplinary study group exploring "Design-Based Influence in the Developing Countries" had promoted design for decolonization as a serious, anthropologically informed practice – one commented on by leading Danish anthropologist Mette Bovin in the national press.[25] Yet despite the radical social design activism of the Nordic and Scandinavian students, and the apparent appeal to countercultural rebellion, this project was ultimately borne of a potent mixture of Cold War US politicking (in which design for development was instrumentalized as an overt postcolonial tool in decolonized nations) and the expansionist policies of Scandinavian welfare models. The national Danish press also expressed their reservations about an affluent, white American design professor preaching to the converted from his taxpayer-supported penthouse apartment in Nyhavn, in the picturesque center of the nation's capital.

Yet there were provable outcomes from this foray into development politics under the rubric of Danish social welfare. During his year-long guest position in Copenhagen, Papanek worked closely with an exchange student from the state-run Institut Teknologi Bandung (ITB) Indonesia, named Pak Imam Buchori. They worked together on the redesign of a kerosene stove and a dual-purpose lampshade used to trap insects; both projects were born of the close participant observations of local Indonesian domestic settings made by Buchori in his own community. The young designer's return to Bandung in 1973 coincided with a new, concerted modernization program under the government of President Suharto, with industrial design an integral part of the industrializing policy. Treading a thin line between the wholesale importation of Western ideas (and the model of a liberalized economy that went with it) and a vernacularized, community-based model of design, individuals like Buchori (who would go on to be a professor of industrial design at ITB) were admiring of the ambition of Papanek's "design for the real world" thesis – a thesis born of Scandinavian social welfare politics – ultimately surmising, however, that its critique relied on a Western model of design, production and consumption. "At that time," Buchori later recounted, "Indonesia had no experience of industrialization. [...] We had industry, but it was one that just copied and pasted from the West – when actually there was no Indonesian design involvement whatsoever. So we found it difficult – how does design survive as a profession if there is no industry?"[26] While the tin-can radio found favor with progressive Danish journalists keen to remedy the last vestiges of Western colonialism, Buchori himself found the recycled design faintly patronizing: "Papanek talked about designing a radio with some sort of used materials and lace [decoration]. I found it silly – sorry to say that – but the product is silly and not very good at all!"[27] Yet he and other international students did return to their homelands with alternative modes of design thinking that impacted far more positively than, for example, the postcolonial Bauhaus/Ulm School discourse of "good form" modernist aesthetic teachings exemplified by institutions such as the National Institute of Design in Ahmedabad, famously led by Ulm School alumni of Germany and impacted by Charles and Ray Eames's notorious "India Report" of 1958.[28]

Conclusion

The role of Danish architects in applying and expanding principles of social welfare to the development paradigm and the 1970s expansion of aid is well documented, with more recent codesigned initiatives challenging the historical power relations of that same phenomenon.[29] Less explored is the role of industrial design within this discourse. Yet arguably the most globally read and enduring publication emerging directly from the interstices of Danish spaces of social welfare, Papanek's *Design for the Real World* spawned a social design movement that would have direct implications for the policy of decolonizing nations in the 1970s. This book, and the ideas encapsulated in the "Copenhagen Flowchart" of the politics of design, impacted design schools across Europe and South Asia, ultimately leading to the pivotal 1979 UNIDO-ICSID Ahmedabad Declaration on Industrial Design for Development.[30] This late Cold War policy document, which advocated support for recently decolonized nations (with Western industrial designers deployed to advise indigenous communities how to harness growing consumer goods markets) proved far less progressive than the interventions Danish and fellow Scandinavian students had envisaged in their free-form seminars and cross-disciplinary creative platforms focused on the cultural values and incorporation of users themselves. And yet it is one of the most concrete historical legacies of this period of social design activism, born from the expansion of Danish spaces of welfare and expanding outward from national significance into the politics of decolonization in the global perspective.

Bibliography

Avermaete, Tom, Serhat Karakayali and Marion von Osten, eds., *Colonial Modern: Aesthetics of the Past, Rebellions for the Future*. London: Black Dog Publishing, 2010.

Balaram, Singanapalli. "Design in India: The Importance of the Ahmedabad Declaration." *Design Issues* 25, no. 4 (2009): 54–79.

Bendsen, Jannie Rosenberg, Katrine Lotz, Kjeld Vindum, Mette Jerl Jensen, Deane Simpson and Kirsten Marie Raahauge, eds. *Forming Welfare*. Copenhagen: Arkitektens Forlag, 2017.

Bhambra, Gurminder K., and John Holmwood. "Colonialism, Postcolonialism and the Liberal Welfare State." *New Political Economy* 23 no. 5 (2018): 574–87.

Cederstam, G. M., ed., *Vägen till människovärde: Några drag ur nordisk handikapphistoria åren 1945–1985*. Välingby: Nordiska nämndeerför handikappfrågor, 1990.

Clarke, Alison J. "'Actions Speak Louder': Victor Papanek and the Legacy of Design Activism," *Design and Culture* 5, no. 2 (2013): 151–68.

——. "Design for Development, ICSID and UNIDO: The Anthropological Turn in 1970s Design." *Journal of Design History* 29, no. 1 (February 2016): 43–57.

——. *Victor Papanek: Designer for the Real World*. Cambridge, MA: MIT Press, 2021.

Gerrard, Victoria. "What Did You Teach My Students?!" A narrated interview with Pak Imam Buchori. In Kries, Klein and Clarke, *Victor Papanek: The Politics of Design*, 172–79.

Guffey, Elizabeth. "Designing for Disability, Historical and Contemporary Perspectives." In Kries, Klein and Clarke, *Victor Papanek: The Politics of Design*, 193–209.

Hansen, Kirsten Birk. "The Danish Project: Developing Greenland into a Modern Welfare Society." In Bendsen et al., *Forming Welfare*, 92–109.

Kries, Mateo, Amelie Klein and Alison J. Clarke, eds. *Victor Papanek: The Politics of Design*. Weil am Rhein: Vitra Design Museum, 2018.

Lindahl, Gunilla. "SDO in Crisis," *FORM* 8 (1969): 372.

Mattson, Greggor. "Nation-State Science: Lappology and Sweden's Ethnoracial Purity." In *Comparative Studies in Society and History* 56, no. 2 (2014): 320–50.

Mulinari, Diana, Suvi Keskinen, Kuura Irni and Salla Tuori, "Introduction: Postcolonialism and the Nordic Models of Welfare and Gender." In *Complying with Colonialism: Gender, Race and Ethnicity in the Nordic Region*, edited by Diana Mulinari, Suvi Keskinen, Kuura Irni and Salla Tuori, 1–16. London: Routledge, 2020.

Osten, Marlon von, and Grant Watson, eds., *Bauhaus Imaginista: A School in the World*. London: Thames and Hudson, 2019.

Pagh, Jesper. "From the Common Best to the Common Market?" In Bendsen et al., *Forming Welfare*, 28–41.

Papanek, Victor. *Design for the Real World: Human Ecology and Social Change*. New York: Pantheon Books, 1971.

——. "Kymmenen ympäristöä." In *Ornamo Magazine* no. 2 (1970): 3.

Saleh, Nico. "Forms of Freedom: African Independence and Nordic Models." *ArchDaily*, June 15, 2014, https://www.archdaily.com/516338/forms-of-freedom-african-independence-and-nordic-models-the-nordic-pavilion-at-the-venice-biennale-2014, accessed December 28, 2021.

Skriver, Poul Erik. "Grønland i Focus." *Arkitekten* 72, no. 23 (1970): 541–42.

Widstrand, Carl Gösta, and Zdenek Červenka. *Scandinavian Development Agreements with African Countries*. Uppsala: Scandinavian Institute of African Studies, 1971.

Notes

1 Gurminder K. Bhambra and John Holmwood, "Colonialism, Postcolonialism and the Liberal Welfare State," *New Political Economy* 23 no. 5 (2018): 574–87.

2 Jesper Pagh, "From the Common Best to the Common Market?" in *Forming Welfare*, ed. Jannie Rosenberg Bendsen et al. (Copenhagen: Danish Architectural Press, 2017), 28–41.

3 Pagh, "From the Common Best to the Common Market?" 29.

4 Steen Juhler, personal interview with the author, November 12 2013, Denmark.

5 Carl Gösta Widstrand and Zdenek Červenka, *Scandinavian Development Agreements with African Countries* (Uppsala: Scandinavian Institute of African Studies, 1971), 71.

6 Widstrand and Červenka, *Scandinavian Development Agreements*, 18.

7 In 2014 the Nordic Pavilion of the 14th International Venice Architecture Biennale featured the exhibition *Forms of Freedom: African Independence and Nordic Models*, exploring the relationship between newly independent East African nations and modern Nordic architects in pursuing "noncolonial" models of architecture in the 1960s and '70s.

8 See Nico Saleh, "Forms of Freedom: African Independence and Nordic Models," *ArchDaily*, June 15, 2014, https://www.archdaily.com/516338/forms-of-freedom-african-independence-and-nordic-models-the-nordic-pavilion-at-the-venice-biennale-2014, accessed December 28, 2021.

9 Diana Mulinari, Suvi Keskinen, Kuura Irni and Salla Tuori, "Introduction: Postcolonialism and the Nordic Models of Welfare and Gender," in *Complying with Colonialism: Gender, Race and Ethnicity in the Nordic Region*, ed. Diana Mulinari, Suvi Keskinen, Kuura Irni and Salla Tuiri (London: Routledge, 2020), 2.

10 See Tom Avermaete, Serhat Karakayali and Marion von Osten, eds., *Colonial Modern: Aesthetics of the Past, Rebellions for the Future* (London: Black Dog Publishing, 2010).

11 See Kirsten Birk Hansen, "The Danish Project: Developing Greenland into a Modern Welfare Society," in Bendsen et al., *Forming Welfare*, 92–109.

12 Hansen, "The Danish Project," 103–4.

13 Hansen, "The Danish Project," 104.

14 Poul Erik Skriver, "Grønland I Focus," *Arkitekten* 72, no. 23 (1970): 541–42.

15 Tobias Faber, Rector of the Royal Danish Academy of Fine Arts, Copenhagen to Director Mr. A. Brøndum, The National Bank of Denmark, Copenhagen, February 25, 1972. Kind permission of The National Bank of Denmark archive.

16 Victor Papanek, "Kymmenen ympäristöä," *Ornamo Magazine* 2 (1970): 3.
17 The eight-day Suomenlinna design symposium took place in July 1968 as a two-part event spanning the month. The pan-Scandinavian Design Students' Organization began in Finland in 1965, was formally organized by 1967, and by 1969 began to face dissolution. See Gunilla Lindahl, "SDO in Crisis," *FORM* 8 (1969): 372.
18 Lindahl, "SDO in Crisis," 372, translation by the author.
19 See Alison J. Clarke, "'Actions Speak Louder': Victor Papanek and the Legacy of Design Activism," *Design and Culture* 5, no. 2 (2013): 151–68.
20 See Greggor Mattson, "Nation-State Science: Lappology and Sweden's Ethnoracial Purity," *Comparative Studies in Society and History* 56, no. 2 (2014): 320–50.
21 At the time of the symposium, Buckminster Fuller and Victor Papanek held positions at the Southern Illinois University, Carbondale, and Purdue University, Department of Industrial and Environmental Design, Lafayette, Indiana, respectively.
22 See Elizabeth Guffey, "Designing for Disability, Historical and Contemporary Perspectives," in *Victor Papanek: The Politics of Design*, ed. Mateo Kries, Amelie Klein and Alison J. Clarke (Weil am Rhein: Vitra Design Museum, 2018), 198.
23 See G. M. Cederstam, ed., *Vägen till människovärde: Några drag ur nordisk handikapphistoria åren 1945–1985* (Välingby: Nordiska nämndeerför handikappfrågor, 1990).
24 Victor Papanek, *Design for the Real World: Human Ecology and Social Change* (New York: Pantheon Books, 1971), 277.
25 See Alison J. Clarke, *Victor Papanek: Designer for the Real World* (Cambridge, MA: MIT Press, 2021), in particular chapter 9.
26 See Victoria Gerrard, "What Did You Teach My Students?!" A narrated interview with Pak Imam Buchori in Kries et al., *Victor Papanek: The Politics of Design*, 177.
27 Gerrard, "What Did you Teach My Students?!"
28 For an exploration of global expansion of the Bauhaus and Ulm principles, see Marion von Osten and Grant Watson, eds., *Bauhaus Imaginista: A School in the World* (London: Thames and Hudson, 2019).
29 See, for example, the exhibition *Africa: Rethinking Architecture and Design*, Royal Danish Academy, March 8, 2018–May 5, 2018, https://royaldanishacademy.com/calendar/africa-rethinking-architecture-and-design, accessed December 28, 2021.
30 See Singanapalli Balaram, "Design in India: The Importance of the Ahmedabad Declaration," *Design Issues* 25, no. 4 (2009): 54–79; and Alison J. Clarke, "Design for Development, ICSID and UNIDO: The Anthropological Turn in 1970s Design," *Journal of Design History* 29, no. 1 (February 2016): 43–57.

3

Community

Anthropological Perspectives on Housing as Welfare and Everyday Welfare Practices

Maja Hojer Bruun

Along with education, healthcare and pensions, housing can be considered a common public good and one of the main welfare services in the Danish welfare society, even though housing is not financed through the general tax system. Citizens have to rent or buy their dwellings in a market, but this market is highly regulated and planned, and a range of different private sector, state/municipal, civil society and market agents share the responsibility of providing housing for all. Although citizens are not allocated housing by the state nor is it free, the right to a dwelling is to be found behind the principles of the national housing policies. Some political scientists even argue that housing can be seen as a social right, because housing is a central concern for welfare state policies.[1]

In an anthropological perspective, the provision of housing can be seen as a larger moral economy where different institutions, expectations and reciprocal obligations are invoked, involving different economic and moral agents, from local or municipal to central state agents to individuals and families, banks, social movements and housing associations.[2] In the decades after World War II, during the height of the welfare state in Western democracies – the period that the French call "les trente glorieuses" (1946–75) – housing was part of a social contract between citizens and the state, wherein the state delivered housing in return for labor and citizenship.[3] By the 1970s, however, these glory days were largely over, and at different paces in various parts of the world, processes of structural adjustment, privatization and/or neoliberalization set in and gradually reduced the role of the state. Recent anthropological research has pointed to the multiple moral communities that exist today, making different claims to housing, whose demands are met in different ways.[4] During the heyday of the European welfare states, the right to housing was often achieved through citizenship and inclusion in society's and the nation-state's moral community, in return for labor, tax payments and other citizen duties. Moral communities also include families who inhabit owner-occupied housing but rely on well-functioning public infrastructures, both physical and financial, such as secure mortgage-lending systems and different arrangements of shared living and shared ownership with mutual obligations, as in cooperative housing.[5] Housing as welfare is thus provided by a range of different institutions and state and non-state agents, which is especially conspicuous in Denmark, where social housing is not owned or governed by the state but by civil society associations, which are in various ways connected to the state and municipalities; in addition there is a comparatively large third sector between state and market that counts as social housing and cooperative housing, as will be discussed below.

When it comes to welfare, the concept should not be limited to the transmission of resources and services or welfare benefits. This limited understanding of welfare is often implied in the differing "languages of welfare," as when welfare is defined quite materialistically as "the complex of financial assistance and in-kind goods that sustain those without income or savings."[6] Welfare can instead, in the broadest sense, be defined as "the process of normalizing or optimizing the well-being of dependent individuals, organizations and societies."[7] This broader definition of welfare, however, still entails that welfare is for dependent individuals, organizations and societies. This can be attributed to the Anglo-American context from which the definition stems, namely American and British anthropologists developing an "anthropology of welfare":

In countries with a liberal welfare regime, welfare is directed toward dependents and citizens in need. In a Scandinavian context, however, with a so-called universalistic or social democratic regime, welfare and welfare services are directed toward all citizens. This means that welfare benefits are for all, not just for those in need, as in liberal welfare regimes, or for those who have saved up for them, as in corporate welfare regimes.[8]

In regard to housing, this means that, in principle, all types of households should be able to live in all types of housing. Social housing is not reserved for the poor or deserving, although in fact there is a significant income difference between those who live in owner-occupied housing and those who live in social housing. In anthropological theories, the Scandinavian universalistic welfare regimes are often linked to cultural models of egalitarianism, equality and cultural norms of sameness and cultural conformity: According to the anthropologist Marianne Gullestad's influential monograph *Kitchen-Table Society*, Scandinavians have a tendency to identify themselves and their fellow citizens as the "same kind of people."[9] Feeling better or more high-class than others is socially prohibited, even though there may be objective social differences and class inequalities between people. People seek conformity, emphasize similarities and suppress differences in their everyday interactions; alternatively, they avoid and create symbolic fences between one another.[10]

It goes for all parts of the world that ideas and practices of welfare come together with social values, ethics, notions of care, social obligations and normative expectations of how institutions and citizens ought to interact, provide or receive services. In the second part of this chapter, I will approach housing through the lens of shifting and diverse welfare practices and "the embodiment of particular ethical orientations and normative expectations" conducted by citizens and communities.[11]

Throughout the chapter I focus on cooperative housing as an example of how housing and welfare are imbricated. In Denmark, cooperative housing is, however, a common, well-known and taken-for-granted form of dwelling, with 7.4 percent of all housing units being in cooperatives.[12] A large number of Danes either live or have lived in a housing cooperative themselves or know somebody who does. In Copenhagen, 27.9 percent of all residents live in housing cooperatives.[13] What makes cooperative housing an interesting case for a discussion of housing as welfare is that it originated before the incorporation of the Danish welfare state, and its development reflects the changes of the Danish welfare regime. Furthermore, due to the collective ownership and government, cooperative living entails many collective activities. Questions of management, maintenance, finance and aesthetics are discussed in common, open fora that lend themselves to ethnographic studies.[14] To explore the role of cooperative associations, and how it has shifted over time, I start with a brief historical account of cooperative and social housing in Denmark.

Association-Based Social Housing in the Danish Welfare Society

In the decades before the incorporation of the Danish welfare state, the labor movement, the cooperative movement and other civil society movements fought for social reforms and developed institutions and organizations to meet social needs. The first efforts to improve housing conditions in the industrializing cities and towns in Denmark came from a mix of philanthropic projects, mutual building societies and cooperative associations that together formed a social housing movement. The first social housing initiative was the medical association's row houses with small gardens. These houses were built with the capital that was left over from the relief funds that the medical association had disposed of during the cholera epidemic in Copenhagen in 1853. In the following decades more affluent workers joined the wave of new building societies that received state and municipality loans on the principle of self-help. These building societies were gradually dissolved, and the members became individual private owners when they had paid off their loans. By the way, some of these former building societies' row houses are among the most attractive and expensive dwellings in Copenhagen today. As a speculation-free alternative to the building societies, the first nonprofit cooperative housing associations were established in 1912. Here ownership of the property remained collective. Members only held a share of the building and got use-rights to their dwellings. Throughout the 1910s to '30s, hundreds of housing cooperatives were incorporated, and modern dwellings for workers and their families were constructed.

The first steps toward a Danish welfare state are usually attributed to the Social Reform Act of 1933, an extensive agreement between the Social Democratic and Radical Liberal government parties and the Liberal opposition party. As part of this agreement, the first large Danish social housing act was adopted and state subsidies for housing construction introduced. The Social Reform Act, however, meant that member-sponsored cooperative associations were largely replaced by state- and municipality-subsidized social housing schemes, and housing cooperatives lost their role in urban development. The labor movement had demanded that housing construction be a municipal responsibility and had for a long time been skeptical toward housing associations, but since the Social Reform Act was a compromise between the Social Democratic Party and the liberal parties, Denmark adopted an association-based and market-based model for social housing, unlike, for example, Sweden, where local councils own social housing today still.[15]

As a result, since the 1930s there are two different kinds of housing associations in Denmark. *Almene boligforeninger* (nonprofit housing associations) receive direct economic support from the state, are regulated by national social housing policies and place savings in a trust for new housing construction.[16] The residents are tenants of the housing associations that own the houses. Autonomous private *andelsboligforeninger* (cooperative housing associations) are governed in a decentralized manner by the local cooperative's members through general assemblies and local bylaws. Here residents are members who own shares of the association's common property, and they are allowed to sell for private profit under certain price-cap regulations. As we will see, this detail became important at the beginning of the twenty-first century in an overheated housing market during a period marked by neoliberal housing policies. Both kinds of housing associations have a strong tradition of participatory democracy with annual general assemblies and locally elected executive boards to control the day-to-day management of their housing. To sum up, social housing in the Danish welfare state, whether nonprofit housing associations or private cooperative housing associations, has never been state-owned but rather is owned and governed by civil society associations whose democratic practices and culture dominate still today.

Indeed, Danes more often speak about *velfærdssamfundet* (the welfare society) rather than *velfærdsstaten* (the welfare state), indicating that welfare permeates all of society.[17] As several ethnographers of Scandinavian societies have observed, the practical and conceived boundaries between the state and civil society are rather blurred in Scandinavia.[18] In political philosophy, from Alexis de Tocqueville to Jürgen Habermas, it is assumed that civil society has to stand apart, as a third sector of society, from both the state and the market for a modern democracy with free individuals to thrive. Individualization and political freedom are seen as freedom from the state, but in the Scandinavian context, the right to receive public welfare services from the state and other institutions considered public and to be part of society as a collective entity is seen as supportive of individuals' freedom.[19] Individual freedom and collective, communal and societal institutions are not in opposition but rather depend on one another in what Marianne Gullestad has called the Scandinavian version of "egalitarian individualism."[20]

In the second part of this chapter, I want to show how housing cooperatives have sought to balance individuals' and families' need for affordable and secure housing with collectives' maintenance of a public welfare good – but also how neoliberal housing politics have recently displaced this balance.

Caring for the Common Welfare Good

Traditional cooperative housing schemes had a revival after the adoption of another significant broad housing act in 1975. According to this act, tenants have the right of first refusal when landlords in private rental housing estates put properties up for sale. If a majority of tenants form a housing cooperative, they can buy the estate at the market price and take it over as a cooperative property. In the following years, many cooperatives were established in existing buildings as an alternative to privately owned rental housing. At the same time, old working-class neighborhoods in Copenhagen were undergoing urban renewal. Instead of having remote owners renovating the buildings, these newly formed cooperatives took charge of the renovation process, often with municipal financial support. Elsewhere I have argued that housing cooperatives became local stewards or caretakers of a public housing good that could also be seen as an urban common.[21] Cooperative members enjoyed the benefits of living in the commons, but had at the same time a duty to manage it and make sure that affordable and secure housing was available for all.

During the ethnographic fieldwork (2008–09) for my PhD project on social life and moral economies in Danish housing cooperatives I conducted interviews and participated in the daily life of eight different housing cooperatives, incorporated at different times and located in different neighborhoods in Copenhagen. One housing cooperative was incorporated at the beginning of the 1980s, when the municipal authorities had scheduled their six-story apartment building for a comprehensive renovation; the owner of the building, like many other private landlords at that time, did not have the capital to enter into a large regeneration project. One of the members of the housing cooperative looked back at that time during an interview rather nostalgically, telling me:

> We were really eager to take over the house, you know. This thought that this is *our* house and that we decide on our own! And, of course, we knew that it was a lot of responsibility too, because we have to make sure that the house is maintained properly. Moreover, we chose to manage the house on our own and have done so since then. Not without problems I would say, but out of the idea of "why not?" We were very community-minded at that time [*vi var meget fælles dengang*], so why not take care of the house together, have work weekends, collect rents and so on? And save something like, at that time, maybe twenty or thirty thousand kroner a year, which must be good for our economy? That was the main idea. To have a house together, and make sure it is good and cheap and that you are not dependent on some speculator who owns the estate, rents the flats and just makes those improvements that allow him to take more money from the tenants. Basically, it is about controlling our own house and not being controlled. It is about living in a communal way and supporting one another [*bo i fællesskab og støtte hinanden*].

It was during the 1980s and '90s, at a time when employment rates were much lower than when Copenhagen experienced an economic boom in the early 2000s, that the tradition of collective work parties started in many housing cooperatives. It became a common tradition in many housing cooperatives that members were summoned for a work party once or twice a year. Painting the staircases and cleaning up the courtyard, laundry room or basement were typical tasks. Such work parties, during which members work together to maintain their common living spaces, serve many purposes: They are seen as essential community-building activities that produce a sense of belonging among the members; they strengthen their neighborly relationships by spending time together, socializing and keeping up friendly associations; and they of course contribute to maintaining the material structure of the buildings and yards and the physical spaces for everyday living. The social and the material, the private and the public, and common good and individual interests blend together, practically and symbolically in such work parties, and in many ways they, and people's shifting attendance, became markers of community and solidarity in the housing cooperatives.[22]

Housing cooperatives are spaces where it is pronounced that welfare is not only about providing welfare benefits but also entails "the embodiment of particular ethical orientations and normative expectations."[23] Many ethnographic studies have focused on the Danish welfare state's interfaces, such as when social workers encounter welfare clients.[24] In regard to housing as welfare, such encounters certainly take place in the offices of social workers who allocate social housing units to vulnerable citizens; however, ethical orientations and normative expectations are also inherent in all of the other ways housing is distributed and reproduced in Danish society. During work parties in housing cooperatives, the social practices related to building maintenance, interpersonal relations and communal values are performed. The work done must not be too technically difficult or hard so that all members are able to participate, and when people work together, social and economic divides are brushed aside; "you cannot see if the person next to you is a garbage man or a manager," as members of housing cooperatives said to me. In this way, participants get an experience of unity, equality and community. While an egalitarian ethos dominates work parties in housing cooperatives it can be discussed how socially, economically and ethnically diverse these cooperatives in fact are, and especially have become during the last decades.[25] In the early 2000s the average household income of cooperative members lay between that of residents in owner-occupied housing and rental housing, and cooperatives constituted a middle-income group; but since the economic boom in the 2000s the prices of cooperative shares have gone up due to the deregulation of the price cap and housing credit facilities, so that members of cooperatives have gradually become more affluent.[26] The distribution of immigrants from non-OECD countries has always been lower in housing cooperatives than the national average.[27] This can be attributed to the time until around 2005 when shares in housing cooperatives were sold below market price and, as a result of that, mainly to family, friends and acquaintances of old-timers in the cooperatives rather than to immigrants and newcomers in Danish society.

When it comes to housing as a welfare good, the social meanings of home are important. Housing is about much more than a roof over one's head. The right to secure housing is at the same time a right to a proper home, a space for personal and domestic life, community, kin, family and reproduction that ties together social relationships, identities and materialities.[28] Again, from an anthropological perspective, the concept of the home should not just be seen as a social, symbolic or phenomenological counterpart to, and isolated from, the physical and material structures of houses and housing. Rather, housing as a welfare good and conceptualizations of what constitute a proper home are interwoven.

This is not least the case in Scandinavia, where middle-class ideals about family life, the organization of time and the design of interior home space became part of the constitution of the modern welfare state.[29] The home also constitutes a political arena, both from the perspective of socialization – that is, that the home is where political subjectivities are formed – and in the sense that politics are carried out in and through the home, for example through squatting and the anti-eviction movement or during the housing and mortgage crisis that started in 2008, and also in the feminist sense that the home is a site of gender domination and the reproduction of normative gendered roles.[30] Thus, instead of thinking about the home as a strictly private space, or a private sphere as opposed to a Habermasian public sphere, as in modernist political thinking, public and private spaces, and public and private matters are conjoined in housing and the home.[31]

Neoliberalization as a Risk to Housing Cooperatives as Welfare Spaces

In the early 2000s the civil society and association-based model of cooperative housing came under attack. When a Liberal-Conservative government came to power in 2001 it dismantled the housing ministry and presented its neoliberal housing policy as a "retreat of the state." As is characteristic of neoliberal political reforms, the changes to the housing cooperatives arrived through state institutions and yet, as a commitment to dismantle the state, delegated power to the market and private actors.[32] The changes were a combination of mortgage liberalization, the introduction of new mortgage products and the opportunity to mortgage cooperative members' individual shares – in short, a market orientation and commodification of cooperative housing.[33] The market orientation and commodification of housing cooperatives affected associations very differently: some of the most affluent associations increased their wealth even more, which has made the shares in these cooperatives very expensive, while some of the most vulnerable associations, located in the less attractive parts of Copenhagen and inhabited by poorer residents, have mortgaged their associations, some to the degree of bankruptcy, so that they no longer offer secure dwellings but rather have become debt traps. As a result, the ideology that cooperative housing should be for all, irrespective of income and social class, has suffered.

There is a certain irony in the fact that housing cooperatives, decentrally organized as they are, adopted these changes at annual general assemblies themselves. The state did not interfere directly in the management of the housing cooperatives, and the political culture of self-government and autonomy from the state has neither been formally nor legally violated. In practice, however, members' individual economic incentives undermined the civil society organizations' role in providing affordable social housing. Cooperative housing developed as a response to the lack of affordable and secure housing at the turn of the twentieth century. The incorporation of the welfare state constituted a settlement between citizens, state and capital, wherein the state and municipalities took a leading role in the provision of social housing, with civil society organizations parallel to the welfare state institutions, intertwining with them and offering social modes of government and participation. What we have seen in the beginning of the twenty-first century may be the beginning of a new era where housing is distributed in new ways, perhaps still as a welfare good or yet again, as before the social housing movement, as a market commodity where aspects of welfare are pushed into the background.

In 2019 a Social Democratic government came to power in Denmark and reestablished a ministry for housing – this time, however, as a combined ministry of housing and the interior. This ushered in a renewed focus on stabilizing housing prices and regulating the housing market. Cooperative housing does not have political priority, however. Housing politics is increasingly seen as a way to tackle questions of integration into the Danish welfare society in regard to counteracting a rural-urban divide; to the skyrocketing market prices of dwellings in Danish cities that increasingly expel low- and middle-income citizens and families from the city centers; and to avoiding a so-called parallel society of ethnic and religious minorities in the nonprofit social housing sector. As described at the beginning of this chapter, *almene boliger* (social housing) is regulated more directly by the state and by national social housing policies. By intervening in the housing market generally and more directly in this sector with proposals like the construction of new social housing or the conversions of private rental housing into social housing, the Social Democratic government seeks to take back housing as a common public good and a main pillar in a welfare society. These developments emphasize that housing, as welfare, always concerns much more than shelter.

Bibliography

Alexander, Catherine, Maja Hojer Bruun and Insa Koch. "Political Economy Comes Home: On the Moral Economies of Housing." *Critique of Anthropology* 38, no. 2 (2018): 121–39.

Bendixsen, Synnøve, Mary Bente Bringslid and Halvard Vike. "Introduction: Egalitarianism in a Scandinavian Context." In *Egalitarianism in Scandinavia: Historical and Contemporary Perspectives*, edited by Synnøve Bendixsen, Mary Bente Bringslid and Halvard Vike, 1–44. New York: Palgrave Macmillan, 2018.

Bengtsson, Bo. "Housing as a Social Right: Implications for Welfare State Theory." *Scandinavian Political Studies* 24, no. 4 (2001): 255–75.

Bruun, Maja Hojer. "Communities and the Commons: Open Access and Community Ownership of the Urban Commons." In *Urban Commons: Rethinking the City*, edited by Christian Borch and Martin Kornberger, 153–70. London and New York: Routledge, 2015.

——. "Egalitarianism and Community in Danish Housing Cooperatives: Proper Forms of Sharing and Being Together." *Social Analysis* 55, no. 2 (2011): 62–83.

——. "The Financialization of Danish Cooperatives and the Debasement of a Collective Housing Good." *Critique of Anthropology* 38, no. 2 (2018): 140–55. https://doi.org/10.1177/0308275X18761960.

Douglas, Mary. "The Idea of a Home: A Kind of Space." *Social Research* 58, no. 1 (1991): 287–307.

Edgar, Iain R., and Andrew Russel. *The Anthropology of Welfare*. London: Routledge, 1998.

Erhvervs- og Byggestyrelsen. *Analyse af andelsboligsektorens rolle på boligmarkedet*. Copenhagen: Erhvervs- og Byggestyrelsen, 2006.

Esping-Andersen, Gøsta. *The Three Worlds of Welfare Capitalism*. Cambridge: Polity Press, 1990.

Fourastié, Jean. *Les trente glorieuses ou la Révolution invisible de 1946 à 1975*. Paris: Fayard, 1979.

Greenhouse, Carol J. Introduction to *Ethnographies of Neoliberalism*, edited by Carol J. Greenhouse, 1–10. Philadelphia: University of Pennsylvania Press, 2010.

Gullestad, Marianne. *The Art of Social Relations: Essays on Culture, Social Action and Everyday Life in Modern Norway*. Oslo: Scandinavian University Press, 1992.

Gullestad, Marianne. *Kitchen-Table Society: A Case Study of the Family Life and Friendships of Young Working-Class Mothers in Urban Norway*. Oslo: Universitetsforlaget, 1984.

Habermas, Jürgen. *The Theory of Communicative Action*. 2 vols. Boston: Beacon Press, 1987.

Järvinen, Margaretha, and Nanna Mik-Meyer, eds. *At skabe en klient. Institutionelle identiteter i socialt arbejde*. Copenhagen: Hans Reitzels Forlag, 2003.

Jöhncke, Steffen. "Integrating Denmark: The Welfare State as a National(ist) Accomplishment." In *The Question of Integration: Immigration, Exclusion and the Danish Welfare State*, edited by Karen Fog Olwig and Karsten Pærregaard, 30–53. Newcastle upon Tyne: Cambridge Scholars Publishing, 2011.

Langer, Susanne, and Susanne Højlund. "An Anthropology of Welfare: Journeying towards the Good Life." *Anthropology in Action* 18, no. 3 (2011): 1–9.

Larsen, Henrik Gutzon, and Anders Lund Hansen. "Commodifying Danish Housing Commons." *Geografiska Annaler B* 97, no. 3 (2015): 263–74.

Löfgren, Orvar. "The Sweetness of Home: Class, Culture and Family Life in Sweden." *Ethnologia Europaea* 14, no. 1 (1984): 44–64.

Richman, Neal. "From Worker Cooperatives to Social Housing: The Transformation of the Third Sector in Denmark." In *The Hidden History of the Cooperative*, edited by Allen Dvaid Heskin and Jacqueline Leavitt, 143–62. Davis, CA: Center for Cooperatives, University of California, 1995.

Sabaté, Irene. "The Spanish Mortgage Crisis and the Re-emergence of Moral Economies in Uncertain Times." *History and Anthropology* 27, no. 1 (2016): 107–20. https://doi.org/10.1080/02757206.2015.1111882.

Vike, Halvard. "Likhetens natur." *Norsk Antropologisk Tidsskrift* 26, no. 1 (2015): 6–21.

Notes

1 See Bo Bengtsson, "Housing as a Social Right: Implications for Welfare State Theory," *Scandinavian Political Studies* 24, no. 4 (2001): 255–75.

2 Catherine Alexander, Maja Hojer Bruun and Insa Koch, "Political Economy Comes Home: On the Moral Economies of Housing," *Critique of Anthropology* 38, no. 2 (2018): 121–39.

3 Jean Fourastié, *Les trente glorieuses ou la Révolution invisible de 1946 à 1975* (Paris: Fayard, 1979).

4 See Alexander, Bruun and Koch, "Political Economy Comes Home."

5 Maja Hojer Brunn, "The Financialization of Danish Cooperatives and the Debasement of a Collective Housing Good," *Critique of Anthropology* 38, no. 2 (2018): 140–55.

6 Irene Glasser, cited in Iain R. Edgar, and Andrew Russel, *The Anthropology of Welfare* (London: Routledge, 1998), 2.

7 Edgar and Russel, *The Anthropology of Welfare*, 1.

8 For more on welfare regimes, see Gøsta Esping-Andersen, *The Three Worlds of Welfare Capitalism* (Cambridge: Polity Press, 1990).

9 Marianne Gullestad, *Kitchen-Table Society: A Case Study of the Family Life and Friendships of Young Working-Class Mothers in Urban Norway* (Oslo: Universitetsforlaget, 1984), 60.

10 See Marianne Gullestad, *The Art of Social Relations: Essays on Culture, Social Action and Everyday Life in Modern Norway* (Oslo: Scandinavian University Press, 1992).

11 Susanne Langer and Susanne Højlund, "An Anthropology of Welfare: Journeying towards the Good Life," *Anthropology in Action* 18, no. 3 (2011): 1.

12 Numbers from Statistics Denmark, 2021, www.statistikbanken.dk, tables BOL101 and BOL201.

13 Statistics Denmark, tables BOL101 and BOL201.

14 See, for example, Maja Hojer Bruun, "Egalitarianism and Community in Danish Housing Cooperatives: Proper Forms of Sharing and Being Together," *Social Analysis* 55, no. 2 (2011): 62–83; Bruun, "Communities and the Commons: Open Access and Community Ownership of the Urban Commons," in *Urban Commons: Rethinking the City*, ed. Christian Borch and Martin Kornberger (London and New York: Routledge, 2015), 153–70; and Bruun, "The Financialization of Danish Cooperatives."

15 See Henrik Gutzon Larsen and Anders Lund Hansen, "Commodifying Danish Housing Commons," *Geografiska Annaler B* 97, no. 3 (2015): 263–74.

16 For a more comprehensive account of the housing movement and the development from cooperatives to social housing, see Neal Richman, "From

Worker Cooperatives to Social Housing: The Transformation of the Third Sector in Denmark," in *The Hidden History of Housing Cooperatives*, ed. Allan David Heskin and Jacqueline Leavitt (Davis, CA: Center for Cooperatives, University of California, 1995), 143–62; and Larsen and Hansen, "Commodifying Danish Housing Commons."

17 See Steffen Jöhncke, "Integrating Denmark: The Welfare State as a National(ist) Accomplishment," in *The Question of Integration: Immigration, Exclusion and the Danish Welfare State*, ed. Karen Fog Olwig and Karsten Pærregaard (Newcastle upon Tyne: Cambridge Scholars Publishing, 2011), 30–53.

18 See, for example, Halvard Vike, "Likhetens natur," *Norsk Antropologisk Tidsskrift* 26, no. 1 (2015): 6–21; and Synnøve Bendixsen, Mary Bente Bringslid, and Halvard Vike, "Introduction: Egalitarianism in a Scandinavian Context," in *Egalitarianism in Scandinavia: Historical and Contemporary Perspectives*, ed. Synnøve Bendixsen, Mary Bente Bringslid and Halvard Vike (New York: Palgrave Macmillan, 2018), 1–44.

19 See Bendixsen, Bringslid and Vike, "Introduction: Egalitarianism in a Scandinavian Context."

20 See Gullestad, *The Art of Social Relations*.

21 See Bruun, "Communities and the Commons."

22 See Bruun, "Egalitarianism and Community in Danish Housing Cooperatives."

23 Langer and Susanne Højlund, "An Anthropology of Welfare," 1.

24 See Margaretha Järvinen and Nanna Mik-Meyer, eds, *At skabe en klient: Institutionelle identiteter i socialt arbejde* (Copenhagen: Hans Reitzels Forlag, 2003).

25 See Bruun, "Egalitarianism and Community in Danish Housing Cooperatives."

26 See Erhvervs- og Byggestyrelsen, *Analyse af andelsboligsektorens rolle på boligmarkedet* (Copenhagen: Erhvervs- og Byggestyrelsen, 2006).

27 See Erhvervs- og Byggestyrelsen, *Analyse af andelsboligsektorens rolle på boligmarkedet*.

28 See Mary Douglas, "The Idea of a Home: A Kind of Space," *Social Research* 58, no. 1 (1991): 287–307.

29 See Orvar Löfgren, "The Sweetness of Home: Class, Culture and Family Life in Sweden," *Ethnologia Europaea* 14, no. 1 (1984): 44–64.

30 See, for example, Irene Sabaté, "The Spanish Mortgage Crisis and the Re-emergence of Moral Economies in Uncertain Times," *History and Anthropology* 27, no. 1 (2016): 107–20.

31 See Jürgen Habermas, *The Theory of Communicative Action*, 2 vols. (Boston: Beacon Press, 1987).

32 Carol J. Greenhouse, introduction to *Ethnographies of Neoliberalism*, ed. Carol J. Greenhouse (Philadelphia: University of Pennsylvania Press, 2010), 1–10.

33 See Larsen and Hansen, "Commodifying Danish Housing Commons"; and Bruun, "The Financialization of Danish Cooperatives."

The Social Omnipotence of Neighborship

Max Pedersen

The development of modern retirement communities is often associated with the United States and enormous residential areas such as Sun City in Arizona from 1960.[1] However, Denmark too has a rather long tradition of housing environments that are reserved for senior citizens. The first Danish senior housing project thus dates back to 1952;[2] as of today, Denmark has more than 300 senior housing facilities with approximately 10,000 individual dwellings.[3]

3.02
Distribution of senior housing by ownership types, 2017

And these numbers are likely to rise in the years to come as the interest in spending the latter part of life in an age-restricted and "child-free" community has grown markedly within the last years. Thus, research made by VIVE (The Danish Center for Social Science Research) shows that one-third of all citizens over the age of fifty-two who are considering moving to a different dwelling wish to move to a senior housing facility.[4]

There is no single or simple explanation for the growing interest in age-restricted housing. On the contrary, most seniors will present you with a multitude of differing reasons when asked why they are considering moving to a senior housing facility.[5] However, one of the reasons that stands out in both interviews and surveys is the wish for being part of a strong neighborship.[6] Many seniors are convinced that being part of a small and tight community will exert a positive influence on their life quality in later life.[7] Thus you could say that moving to a senior housing facility is a strategic investment that aims at increasing your social capital in old age.

This conviction is widely shared by many politicians and professionals who view senior housing facilities as having a prophylactic effect on the challenges that may be associated with old age in a late modern society.[8] This applies in particular to the challenge of loneliness as the neighborship in senior environments is considered to be a remedy of social isolation. But it also applies in relation to many other challenges of old age, such as boredom, depression, insecurity and dealing with the practicalities of everyday life.[9] It has even been suggested that living in a senior housing facility is beneficial for the blood pressure of the elderly.[10] In other words: there is a tendency to view a strong neighborship as an omnipotent social resource that possesses the ability to absorb or mitigate a wide range of negative effects associated with old age.

Although the positive qualities of neighborship form an essential part of the argument in favor of senior housing environments, only a few Danish empirical studies have ventured into exploring the concrete benefits associated with neighborship in age-homogeneous environments.[11] Or to put it in a different way: it is widely acknowledged that neighborship in old age constitutes a significant social resource, but there is only limited empirical knowledge as to how the positive qualities of neighborship manifest themselves in everyday life and at what levels of everyday life they unfold. This chapter is a small-scale attempt to remedy this shortcoming by attempting to answer the basic question: How do residents in senior housing facilities concretely benefit from neighborship? In the following I will try to to explore this question based on a study of four collective housing facilities. The exploration will concentrate on three different levels of social interaction. The first level focuses on the random social interaction that takes place when neighbors coincidentally meet in the common areas of their property. The second level deals with organized gatherings in which neighbors participate in common activities.

And the third level of interaction deals with the personal relations that neighbors may develop. The purpose of this division is to examine how the benefits of neighborship manifest themselves in different spheres of everyday life, spanning from "simple" spatial copresence to residents' interpersonal relationships. As neighborship always unfolds within the physical structure of an architectural design, the last section will focus on the question of how the spatial layout of collective houses affect the formation of social relations among neighbors.[12]

This chapter is based on a mixed-methods study, which included interviews, anthropological fieldwork, a questionnaire survey and, to a lesser extent, archive studies. The anthropological fieldwork was carried out in four senior housing environments over a period of three and a half weeks. It was originally intended that the fieldwork would last four and a half months, but this plan had to be abandoned because of COVID-19. In addition to the abbreviated fieldwork, several semistructured interviews were conducted with residents and administrators in five additional senior housing environments.

The quantitative part of the survey consisted of a questionnaire containing 109 questions. The questionnaire was distributed to approximately 600 residents in the four facilities mentioned above. In many cases it was not possible to determine how many residents lived in each apartment, hence the approximation of 600. In all, 344 residents returned the questionnaires. The primary purpose of the survey was to identify residents' demographic characteristics and to explore to what extent they participated in a variety of common activities with neighbors. It was initially intended that the questionnaire should serve as a support tool to the anthropological fieldwork. Due to COVID-19, it turned out to be the other way around.

The Senior Housing Environments of the Study

The four facilities that have been studied for this chapter all belong to a subcategory of Danish senior housing environments that could be termed *collective housing for seniors* (kollektivhuse for seniorer). The conceptual role model of the facilities is the Swedish collective housing projects that were built for families in the 1930s and '40s, but in contrast to these the Danish facilities have been developed specifically to satisfy housing needs for the elderly and singles without children living at home.[13] Although the facilities are not exclusively aimed at seniors, residents older than fifty years of age make up more than 90 percent of the resident group.[14] Residents under the age of fifty will typically be in their late forties with no children living with them. Altogether, the collective housing facilities amount to between a fourth and a third of all senior housing environments in Denmark.

3.03
Overview of nineteen Danish collective housing projects

The collective housing projects primarily differ from other senior housing facilities in that they have a restaurant or cafeteria where residents can buy one or two daily meals.

The four housing environments selected for the study are all multistory properties with between five and fifteen floors. They are situated in the provincial towns of Holbæk, Vejle, Aarhus and Silkeborg.

Silkeborghus in Silkeborg has been used in several illustrations as a generic example of a collective house. However, Silkeborghus differs from most other projects by being attractively located close to both the city, nature, and cultural institutions.⟨fig. 1⟩

3.06
Silkeborghus and its immediate environment

Three of the studied housing environments have between 65 and 90 dwellings and the fourth a little more than 300. Apart from the restaurant, all four environments have a number of common facilities such as a laundry, guest rooms and one or more activity rooms. Three of the four housing environments were owned by local nonprofit organizations and the residents rented their apartments. Apartments in the fourth facility were owned by the residents themselves.

The residents in senior housing are often viewed as a homogenous group not just in terms of age but also in terms of lifestyle and behavioral values.[15] This is of course true when compared to the residents of multigenerational residential areas, but zooming in on the resident groups of the four facilities, a more nuanced pictured emerges.

3.09
Silkeborghus residents profile

For example, when regarding the fundamental criteria of age, all four facilities had residents who were at the most in their mid-fifties and residents who were at least in their early nineties. Thus, all facilities hosted residents who belonged to different historical cohorts with the behavioral implications hereof – one implication being that the youngest and the oldest residents often had conflicting preferences in food.

The age difference is but one of a series of significant differences that exist within the resident groups. For example, there are differences in residents' marital status. There are differences in health and support needs. And there are differing reasons for moving to a collective house, reasons that span from the proactive decision to relocate "in good time" to reactive decisions necessitated by the severe illness or sudden death of a spouse. These differences are to a large degree not visible to the homogenizing view of the outside world, but they exert an influence on social interaction within the resident group.

Random Encounters

The most widespread form of social interaction in the four senior housing facilities – and the only form of interaction in which all residents participate – is the random meetings between residents within their housing environment. In traditional residential complexes, meetings like these will most often take place in staircases, elevators or in the area just outside the building. This of course, is also the case in the collective houses, but in addition to this, the properties have several common facilities such as a library, gym, dining room and laundry. This means that the residents do not just meet when they have errands outside their environment. They also meet when they have in-house errands, and as a result they have a greater chance of encountering a neighbor by chance than if they had lived somewhere without common facilities.

1 View from the gallery of Kollektivhuset Silkeborghus. September 8, 2020, 2–3 pm. Camera settings: F3.5 SS 1/3200 ISO200.

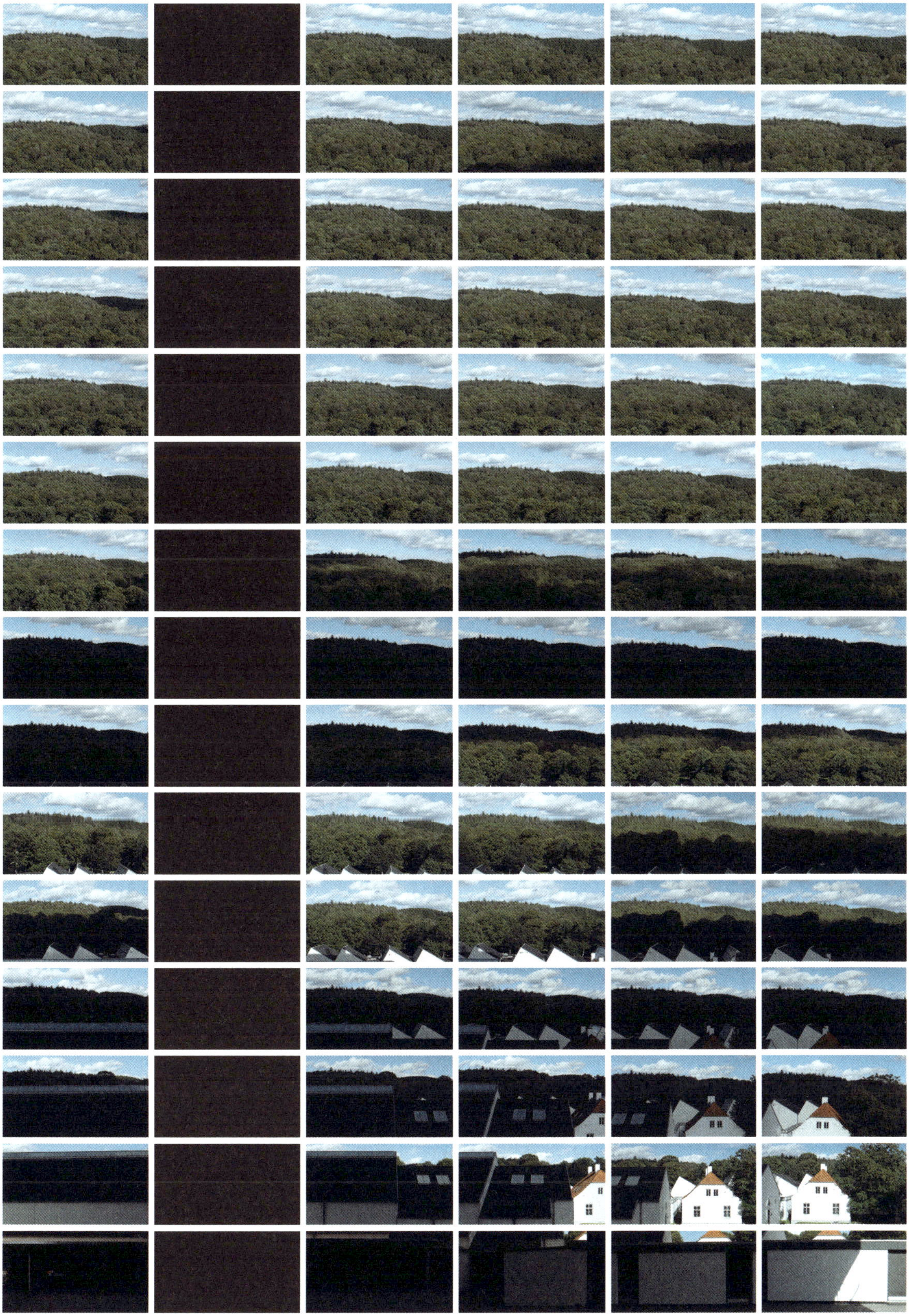

The collective houses also differ significantly from most traditional housing complexes in that the residents generally have more knowledge of one another. Not everyone knows one another by name, but especially in facilities with fewer than 100 dwellings – and this category includes the vast majority of the projects – most residents will at some point have participated in a joint activity where they have had some degree of personal contact with most of their neighbors. This means that it is neither strangers nor semianonymous neighbors whom residents meet when they move around their facility. It is people they know, thus adding a sense of social coherence to the sense of sharing the same physical environment.

The neighbors' mutual knowledge of one another permeates their random encounters in the common areas in a way that residents generally percieve as positive. It is thus the norm that residents verbally greet and look each other in the eyes when they meet by chance. And it is the norm to accompany these greetings with a smile. The mutual knowledge furthermore has the effect that the residents relatively often fall into conversation with the neighbors they happen to meet. The random conversations can happen everywhere in the building, but take place with the greatest frequency at the main entrance, in front of the elevators, in the corridors, at the entrance to the dining room and in common areas such as the library and the laundry. The chance of meeting a neighbor in these areas of the facility varies depending on the time of day. At the main entrance, for example, you are more likely to meet a neighbor from late morning until noon than at any other time.

In the laundry, on the other hand, there are good chances of meeting a neighbor all day. The laundry is also one of the places in the facilities where the residents most often fall into conversation with a neighbor because they stay for a longer period of time in the same room. About the meetings in the laundry a female resident in her seventies says:

> I like going to the laundry. It is nice because you always meet someone you can talk to. In fact, the laundry is a bit of a news center. It is often in the laundry that one hears if something has happened in the facility such as someone having been hospitalized or having returned from hospital. So just doing your laundry will keep you up-to-date with what is going on.

Like the quoted woman, most of the interviewees expressed their appreciation of the casual and informal conversations with their neighbors. Of course, the frequency of the conversations can vary greatly from person to person, but the questionnaire survey showed that 76 percent of residents had a conversation with a neighbor several times a week. And for just over half of them, it happened daily.

It is worth stressing that it was not only the residents who lead an active and outgoing life who tended to have coincidental conversations with the neighbors. The same was even more true for residents who at the most left the residential area twice a month. For this group of less-outgoing residents, 69 percent had at least one daily coincidental conversation with another resident, while 85 percent had conversations with other residents at least three times a week. In other words, the residents who were least likely to leave the facility were the ones who most often had a coincidental chat with a neighbor.

3.07
Major social hot spots in Silkeborghus

In conclusion, it can be mentioned that the study indicated a connection between the design of the buildings and the frequency of coincidental chats. The frequency of random conversations was thus significantly higher in the two facilities that had a common main entrance than in the two facilities with several entrances. However, it cannot be ruled out that other and undisclosed factors contributed to this result.

Organized Activities

Common social activities in Danish senior housing environments are as rule organized by the residents themselves and not by a professional activity manager. This is also the case with the four environments studied for this article. The most common activities in the four facilities are recreational activities such as card games, gymnastics, yoga, knitting clubs and coffee get-togethers with no other purpose than having a nice time. These activities typically take place once or twice a week in one of the common rooms. The number of participants fluctuates, but it appears to be rare that more than 10 percent of a resident group shows up. Attendance is generally significantly higher for larger events such as lectures, movie nights, bingo, excursions and crucial football and handball matches. For example, a third out of eighty-four residents participated in a bingo game held during fieldwork.

It was characteristic of most common activities that the female residents' level of participation was significantly higher than that of male residents. This applied both to the level of organizers and participants. Half of the female respondents answered that they regularly participated in common activities, while only a third of male respondents did. However, men were not the only category of residents whose level of participation was below average. Residents between fifty and sixty-nine also had a lower participation rate, while residents seventy and older were significantly more likely to participate in common activities than other age segments. Finally, divorced and unmarried singles also had a relatively low level of participation, which was probably a result of their being younger than the average resident and thus having a more active social life outside the collective housing facility.

The most frequent common activity in collective housing for seniors is the daily dinner, which typically takes place between 5:30 and 7:00 pm. As the specific organization and payment schemes varies from facility to facility, there is quite a big difference as to how many residents participate in communal dining.

3.10
Residents engagement in three types of social interaction

In two of the visited facilities, the majority of residents used the restaurant daily, while the use was much lower at the other two facilities. As is the case with the recreational activities, the group of residents above the age of seventy use the restaurant significantly more than do younger residents. Thus, many of the oldest residents eat in the restaurant almost daily.

Having dinner in the restaurant not only eases the practical challenge of cooking (and shopping for the meal). The dinner is also a social event that presents an alternative from eating alone in one's apartment and allows residents to have contact with their neighbors. However, at dinnertime contact is typically limited to the same three or four persons, because residents tend to eat with the same people every day, as a woman in her seventies explains:

> I eat in the restaurant every day unless I am invited home to one of my children. I have been dining with the same three people for the last couple of years, and we have gradually gotten to know each other really well and can talk about anything. And if we do not finish our conversation one evening, we will just continue the next.

The common dining also functions as a kind of daily census, in the sense that there is an informal registration of both the present and the absent residents. If one of the residents is suspiciously absent, one or more of the other residents will typically respond by investigating the reason for the absence. In other words, the dining situation works as a kind of alarm system that is activated in the event of an unexplained absence. Considered as an alarm system, the daily census has an arbitrary character, especially as it only includes those residents who attend the diners regularly. Nevertheless, fieldwork showed that the informal alarm system could work both quickly and efficiently. In the observed situation, it only took a few minutes from the moment it was established that a resident had not turned up for dinner until this person was found lying on the floor in his apartment – alive but unable to get up.

Interviews with the residents emphasized that the informal alarm system was a much appreciated source of security, especially for the elderly residents. It should be added that it is not only in connection with dinners and other common activities that residents react if they register some form of atypical behavior. For example, residents on the same floor will typically react if they notice any irregularity that could indicate a neighbor is ill.

Private Social Interaction

The abbreviated fieldwork left the impression that the majority of residents had a solid network among their neighbors and this impression was backed up by the questionnaire, which revealed that 77 percent of the residents considered at the minimum two of their neighbors as friends or "very good acquaintances," while 17 percent responded that they had no friends among their neighbors. The terms *friend* and *very good acquaintance* are of course open to individual interpretation, but the survey indicated that social relations between neighbors in many cases had genuine social and psychological depth. Thus, a little more than of half the respondents answered that they could talk about confidential subjects with at least one of the other residents. All in all, the collected data indicated that half of the residents had at least one close friend among their neighbors, while the other half had none.

Asked why they had no close friends among their neighbors, interviewees would give different answers. One would say that her need for contact was covered by the common dinner. Another answered that he felt no affinity with any of the other residents and thus had no urge to befriend his neighbors. And finally, a couple of the so-called young-old residents in their sixties explained that they had neither the time nor the need to engage in deeper relationships with their neighbors. One of the interviewees was a woman whose response was probably representative of the group of young-olds in the facilities:

> I have lived in this town since I was quite young and have many friends and acquaintances in the local area that I still meet with. I also have a daughter and two grandchildren whom I like to spend my time with. To cut a long story short, I have neither the time nor the need to cultivate close friendships among my neighbors, but I can well imagine that the urge may grow on me as I get older and do not get out so much anymore. I am just not at that point in my life right now.

Quite in line with the quoted woman's concluding remark, the questionnaire survey showed that there was a clear tendency that the residents over seventy years of age were more likely to meet with neighbors in their own homes. There was also a clear tendency for widows and widowers to have more meetings in private homes than residents who were married or cohabitating. The actual meetings in private homes could vary in form, but the interviews indicated that the most common kind of contact consisted of the residents meeting two on two. However, there were also several examples of residents meeting in small groups. This included a small group of single women who met regularly. One of them stated:

> There are five of us who meet once a week and have lunch together. You bring your own food, so our hostess does not have to make lunch for everyone. It really is a good tradition, and there are no limits to what we can talk about. But most of all we talk about the happy and sad things we have experienced in life. And then we talk a lot about our children and grandchildren of course.

The private interaction between the residents is not just limited to having lunch and drinking coffee. Other activities do take place. For example, it is not uncommon for friends and acquaintances to help each other with solving small practical tasks in everyday life.

3.11
Percentage of residents having helped neighbors within last month

Thus, just over 20 percent of the residents had given a neighbor a lift with their own car within the previous thirty days. The destination was often a local supermarket or shopping mall, but there were also examples of residents driving their neighbors to an examination at the doctor or to the hospital. Likewise, it was quite common for residents to do some shopping for a neighbor. All in all, 15 percent of the questionnaire's respondents had been shopping for a neighbor within the last thirty days. Likewise, 15 percent had taken care of a neighbor's apartment within the same period while he or she was away for several days.

There was a significant tendency for neighbors to be less likely to help one another in matters that were considered to belong to the realm of strict privacy. For example, only a few percent of the residents had helped a neighbor with contacting public authorities, and none had within the previous thirty days helped a coresident neighbor take a bath nor assisted with other matters concerning personal hygiene. It would thus seem that senior environments like collective housing for seniors do not have the potential of "unburdening" the welfare state in the sense that residents take over services that are provided for by the state so to speak. However, it should not be overlooked that some of the practical help – and transportation in particular – given by neighbors may overlap with public services. Also, it should be mentioned that a possible "unburdening effect" may be indirect and a consequence of some residents' experiencing enhanced life quality by having moved to a collective house, but this perspective lies far beyond the questions the study set out to investigate.

The Spatial Frame of Neighborship

It was originally intended that the study should include a sub study of the effect architectural design had on neighbor relations. The primary objective was to seek to identify the spatial configurations that either supported or inhibited the formation of an elaborate neighborship.[16] Due to the COVID-19 pandemic closure this part of the study had to be cut short, but the research did produce some results.

Unsurprisingly, field observations showed that common facilities such as living rooms, TV rooms and restaurants constituted the spatial premise of what could be called "the big neighborship." That is, the type of neighboring activities in which a larger group of residents take part. But the study also showed that organized activities in the common rooms had a mediating function and could serve as a stepping-stone to more private relations between residents. This, for example, was the case with two women who had gotten to know each other through participation in a needlework group and later became close friends.

Furthermore, the spatial layout of the collective houses seemed to have an influence on how often residents engaged in random conversations with their neighbors. Thus, the frequency of random conversations in the common areas was highest in the two collective houses which had a single main entrance and whose common rooms formed a coherent spatial conglomerate. The other two collective houses with a markedly lower frequency of random conversations both had several separate entrances, and their common rooms were situated in different places in the buildings. For example, in one property, the fitness room was located in the basement, the restaurant on the ground floor and the library on the top floor. It cannot be ruled out that other factors than the spatial layout could account for the variation in the number of random conversations, but it seems plausible that the spatial dispersion of entrances and common rooms has a reductive effect on the social interaction between the residents.[17]

Likewise, the layout of the apartments within the building seemed to affect the probability of forming strong social ties. Thus, the interviews indicated that residents often had the closest ties to a person living on the same floor or the same staircase as themselves. This is not to say that people from different corners of the housing complex could not form a close social bond. This is simply to say that the interviews indicated that the greater the distance between the apartments, the less likely it was that the residents would become friends.

2 In Silkeborghus there are common facilities for the residents on the ground floor that include a dining room with a professionally run kitchen, a shared living room, guest rooms, and various function rooms as well as the administration office and laundry. There are two elevators, an outside stair tower, and only one main entrance. The building originally had 80 apartments (1-bedroom, 2-bedroom, and 2.5-bedroom). Recently there has been a merging of apartments, so there are also 3-bedroom apartments now. Silkeborghus has a unique view over forest and city. All apartments have access to the gallery and a view from the living room to the west.

Town:	Silkeborg	Year of construction:	1960	Number of units:	68
Town population:	46,923	Ownership:	Nonprofit organization	Housing type:	Apartments
Name of collective house:	Silkeborghus	Number of floors:	15	Number of entrances:	1

The four collective houses of the research varied in size from 68 to 321 apartments. Despite this, or maybe because of this rather big variation, the study only provided an incomplete answer to the question of how the scale of the environments affected the social anatomy of neighborship. A much clearer picture emerges if one compares collective houses with smaller senior housing environments with twenty to thirty dwellings.[18] Thus a comparison between these two types of housing complexes shows that residents in the smaller senior housing environments have a stronger and more widespread social network among their neighbors. For example, in smaller senior housing projects 5 percent answered that they had no friends among the neighbors. In collective houses the number as noted above was 17 percent.

Conclusion

As mentioned in the introduction, neighborship in Danish senior housing environments tends to be viewed as an omnipotent social resource with an inherent capability to reduce loneliness, depression and a wide range of other more and less severe effects associated with aging. The study on which this chapter is based cannot substantiate that claim in all its complex totality. That would take a far larger study combining a multitude of scientific disciplines.

However, the study does indicate that neighborship in collective housing for seniors constitutes a multifunctional social resource that is likely to exert a positive effect at many levels of the residents' everyday lives, spanning from friendly greetings in the hallway to the possibility of forming deep friendships in later life. This overall favorable assessment of neighborship in collective housing is shared by the majority of residents. Thus, 89 percent of the respondents of the questionnaire answered that living in an environment with enhanced opportunities of different kinds of contact with the neighbors had increased their quality of life. But the research also showed that residents did not utilize the social resource of neighborship to the same degree. For example, women were more actively engaged with their neighbors than men; and residents seventy or older are more engaged than residents under the age of seventy.

It will come as a surprise to very few that neighborship in its benevolent incarnation has the potential to increase life quality in later life. This conclusion is in line with public wisdom and furthermore concurs with a large number of studies of the housing and living conditions of the elderly.[19] Nevertheless, there is reason to continue or even intensify the study of neighborship among the elderly. This is at least true in a strictly Danish context, where researchers only to a very limited degree have taken up essential questions such as What are the limits and potentials of neighborship as a social resource among the elderly? To what degree does neighborship in old age have the capacity to supplement the services provided by the welfare state? And how does neighborly interaction among the elderly in traditional residential areas differ from the interaction in spatially segregated environments like the four collective housing facilities?

Questions like these are not just of academic interest. Over the next thirty years the share of elderly will grow at an unprecedented rate and pose a wide range of challenges at both an individual and societal level. Neighborship is not a panacea, but it is a rich and complex social resource that may be instrumental in coping with these challenges.

Bibliography

Boll Hansen, Eigil, A. Dahl, Georg Gottschalk and Susanne Palsig Jensen. *Ældre i bofællesskab*. Copenhagen: Statens Byggeforskningsinstitut og Amternes og Kommunernes Forskningsinstitut, 2000.

Carrere, Juli, Alexia Reyes, Laura Oliveras, Anna Fernández, Andrés Peralta, A. Novoa, K. Pérez and C. Borrell. "The Effects of Cohousing Model on People's Health and Well-being: A Scoping Review." *Public Health Reviews* 41, no. 22 (2020): 1–28.

Choi, Jung Shin. "Evaluation of Community Planning and Life of Senior Cohousing Projects in Northern European Countries." *European Planning Studies* 12, no. 8 (2004): 1189–216.

Bohl, Kirsten, and Iben Hauschultz. "Hver 5. senior i vores spørgepanel føler sig rig." *SeniorBladet* 6, no. 4 (2018), 6–7.

Durrett, Charles. *The Senior Cohousing Handbook*, 2nd ed. Gabriola Island: New Society Publishers, 2009.

Gehl, Jan. *Life Between Buildings*. Translated by Jo Koch. Washington, DC: Island Press, 2011.

Glass, Anne P. "Sense of Community, Loneliness, and Satisfaction in Five Elder Cohousing Neighborhoods." *Journal of Women & Aging* 32, no. 1 (2020): 3–27.

Golant, Stephen. *Aging in the Right Place*. Baltimore: Health Professions Press, 2015.

Gómez, Daniel López, Mariona Estrada Canal and Lluví Farré Montalà. "Havens and Heavens of Aging-in-Community: Home, Care and Age in Senior Co-housing." In *Ways of Homemaking in Care for Later Life*, edited by Bernike Pasveer, Oddgeir Synnes and Ingunn Moser, 159–81. London: Palgrave Macmillan, 2020.

Hunt, Michael, et al. *Retirement Communities*. New York: Haworth Press, 1984.

Kolding Kommune. "Seniorbofællesskaber: En undersøgelse af borgernes ønsker og behov til fremtidens bolig." Kolding, 2019. https://det-gode-liv.dk/images/Seniorbofaelleskab_Kolding.pdf. Accessed December 20, 2021.

Kähler, Margrethe. *At bo er at leve*. Copenhagen: Høst and Søn, 1999.

Langkilde, Hans Erling. *Kollektivhuset: En boligforms udvikling i dansk arkitektur*. Copenhagen: Dansk Videnskabs Forlag, 1970.

Marants, Robert W., Michael E. Hunt and Kathleen L. Vakalo. "Retirement Communities." In *Elderly People and Their Environment*, edited by Irwin Altman, M. Powell Lawton and Joachim F. Wohlwill, 95–128. New York: Plenum Press, 1984.

Mumford, Lewis. "For Older People: Not Segregation but Integration." *Architectural Record* 119, no. 5 (May 1956): 191–95.

Nielsen, Kenneth T., and Max Pedersen. "Livskvalitet i seniorbofællesskaber." Copenhagen: Realdania, 2016. https://realdania.dk/tema/seniorbofaellesskaber. Accessed December 20, 2021.

Pedersen, Max. *Det store eksperiment*. Aalborg: Statens Byggeforskningsinstitut, 2013.

——. *Seniorbofællesskaber: Hvorfor og hvordan?* Copenhagen: Boligtrivsel i Centrum, 1999.

Scharlach; Andrew, and Amanda Lehning. *Creating Aging-Friendly Communities*. Oxford: Oxford University Press, 2016.

Simpson, Deane. *Generationsintegration*. Copenhagen: Udlændinge-, Integrations- og Boligministeriet, 2017. https://www.arkilab.dk/wp-content/uploads/2017/03/Generationsintegration_rapport_DK.pdf. Accessed December 20, 2021.

——. *Young-Old: Urban Utopias of an Aging Society*. Zurich: Lars Müller Publishers, 2015.

Siren, Anu, and Marlene Rode Larsen. *Ældres boligsituation og fremtidige boligønsker*. Copenhagen: VIVE – Det Nationale Forsknings- og Analysecenter for Velfærd, 2019. https://www.vive.dk/media/pure/13818/3096125. Accessed December 20, 2021.

Skodborg, Lene. "Kollektivhuset Høje Søborgs kollektive islæt." *Folk og Kultur: Årbog for Dansk Etnologi og Folkemindevidenskab*, edited by Tine Damsholt, Lykke Lafaque Pedersen, Iørn Piø and Birgitte Rørbye, 95–110. Copenhagen: Foreningen for Danmarks Folkeminder, 1997.

Sundheds- og Ældreministeriet. *Seniorer ønsker at bo midt i fællesskabet*. Copenhagen: Sundheds og Ældreministeriet, 2019. https://sum.dk/Media/637619509548572092/Seniorer%20%C3%B8nsker%20at%20bo%20midt%20i%20f%C3%A6llesskabet.pdf. Accessed December 20, 2021.

Transport-, Bygning- og Boligministeriet, Sundheds- og Ældreministeriet and Erhvervsministeriet. *Afrapportering: Fra det tværministerielle arbejde om seniorbofællesskaber*. Copenhagen, 2019. https://sum.dk/Media/637619509538689696/Afrapportering%20fra%20det%20tv%C3%A6rministerielle%20arbejde%20om%20seniorf%C3%A6llesskaber.pdf. Accessed December 20, 2021.

Unger, Donald, and Abraham Wandersman. "The Importance of Neighbors." *American Journal of Community Psychology* 13, no. 2 (1985): 139–69.

Vestbro, Dick. *Kollektivhuse från enkökshus til bogemenskab*. Stockholm: Statens råd for byggnadforskning, 1982.

Notes

1 Michael Hunt et al., *Retirement Communities* (New York: Haworth Press, 1984); Deane Simpson, *Young-Old: Urban Utopias of an Aging Society* (Zurich: Lars Müller Publishers, 2015).

2 Hans Erling Langkilde: *Kollektivhuset: En boligforms udvikling i dansk arkitektur* (Copenhagen: Dansk Videnskabs Forlag, 1970).

3 The numbers are based on the author's own registration of Danish senior hosuing projects.

4 Anu Siren and Malene Rode Larsen, *Ældres boligsituation og fremtidige boligønsker* (Copenhagen: VIVE – Det Nationale Forsknings- og Analysecenter for Velfærd, 2019).

5 Max Pedersen, *Seniorbofællesskaber: Hvorfor og hvordan?* (Copenhagen: Boligtrivsel i Centrum, 1999), 45, 61, 76.

6 Pedersen, *Seniorbofællesskaber*; and Kenneth T. Nielsen and Max Pedersen, "Livskvalitet i seniorbofællesskaber" (Copenhagen: Realdania, 2016), 9ff.

7 Danske Seniorer, *Seniorbladet* 6, no. 4 (2018), 6ff.

8 Transport-, Bygnings- og Boligministeriet, Sundheds- og Ældreministeriet and Erhvervsministeriet: *Afrapportering: Fra det tværministerielle arbejde om seniorbofællesskaber* (Copenhagen, 2019), 3.

9 Margrethe Kähler, *At bo er at leve* (Copenhagen: Høst and Søn, 1999), 51–52.

10 Transport-, Bygningnings- og Boligministeriet, Sundheds- og Ældreministeriet, and Erhvervsministeriet: *Afrapportering*, 3.

11 See Eigil Boll Hansen et al., *Ældre i bofællesskab* (Copenhagen: Statens Byggeforskningsinstitut og Amternes og Kommunernes Forskningsinstitut, 2000); and Max Pedersen, *Det store eksperiment* (Aalborg: Statens Byggeforskningsinstitut, 2013).

12 See Jan Gehl, *Life Between Buildings*, trans. Jo Koch (Washington, DC: Island Press, 2011).

13 See Langkilde, *Kollektivhuset*; Dick Vestbro: *Kollektivhuse från enkökshus til bogemenskab* (Stockholm: Statens råd for byggnadforskning, 1982); and Lene Skodborg, "Kollektivhuset Høje Søborgs kollektive islæt," in *Folk og Kultur: Årbog for Dansk Etnologi og Folkemindevidenskab* (Copenhagen: Foreningen for Danmarks Folkeminder, 1997), 97–98.

14 Langkilde, *Kollektivhuset*, 119.

15 Deane Simpson, *Generationsintegration* (Copenhagen: Udlændinge-, Integrations- og Boligministeriet, 2017), 9ff.

16 Gehl, *Life Between Buildings*.

17 See Gehl, *Life Between Buildings*, 83ff; and Anne P. Glass, "Sense of Community, Loneliness, and Satisfation in Five Elder Cohousing Neighborhoods," *Journal of Women & Aging* 32, no. 1 (2020): 8.

18 Pedersen, *Det store eksperiment*, 105.

19 See Donald Unger and Abraham Wandersman, "The Importance of Neighbors," *American Journal of Community Psychology* 13, no. 2 (1985): 139–69; Andrew Scharlach and Amanda Lehning, *Creating Aging-Friendly Communities* (Oxford: Oxford University Press, 2016); and Juli Carrere et al., "The Effects of Cohousing Model on People's Health and Well-being: A Scoping Review," *Public Health Reviews* 41, no. 22 (2020): 1–28.

3.01 Distribution of senior housing by building types, 2017

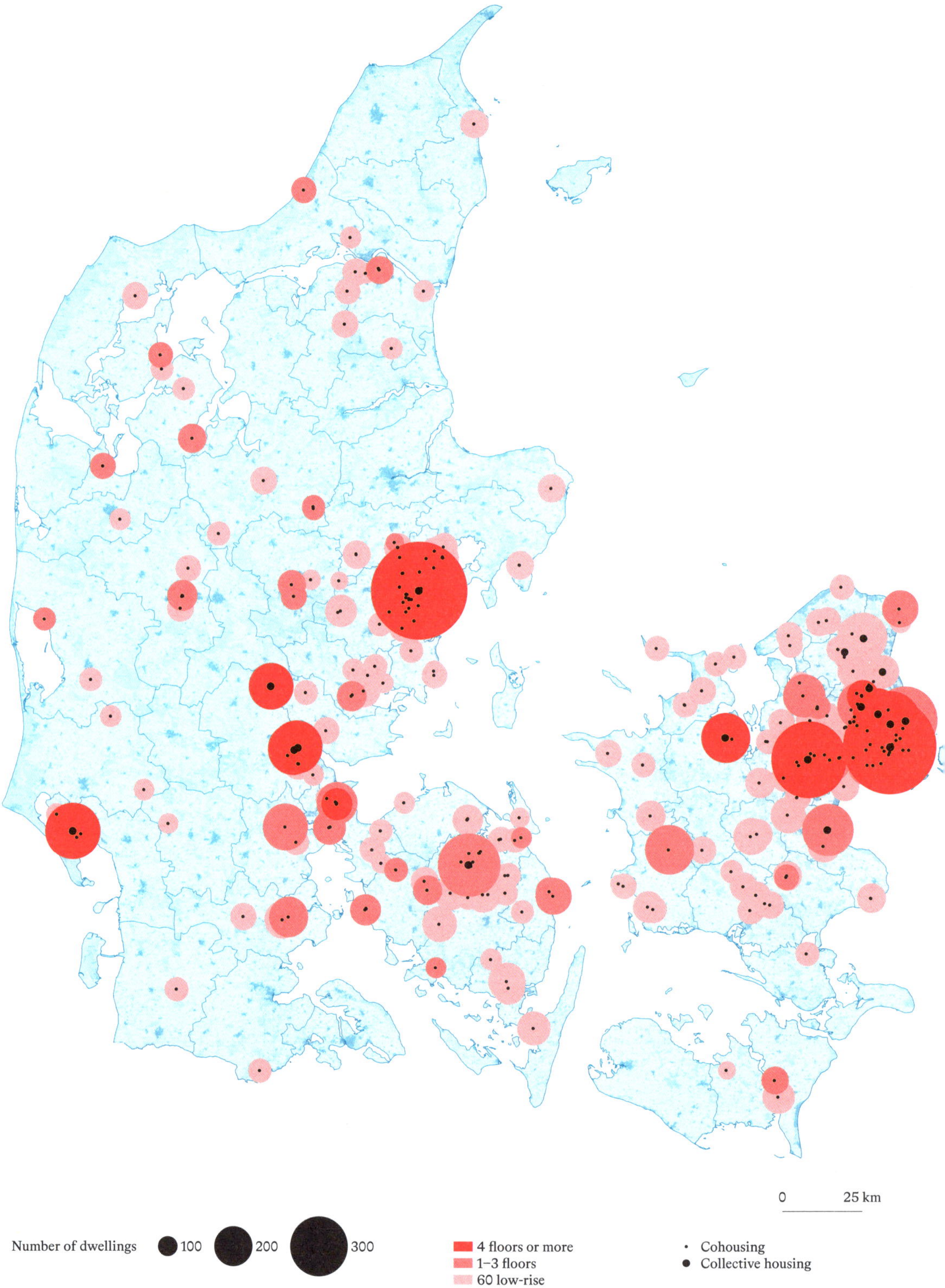

3.02 Distribution of senior housing by ownership types, 2017

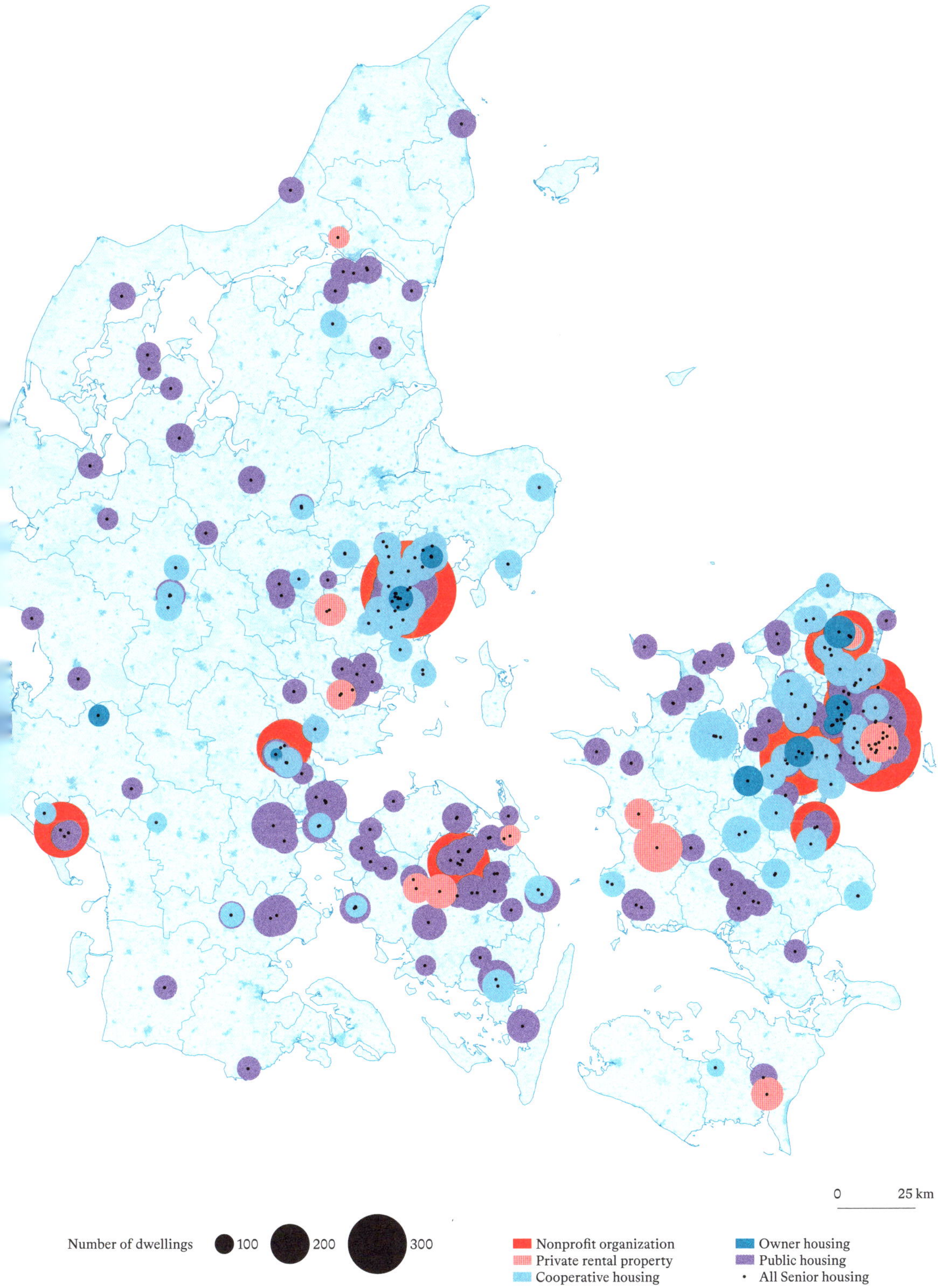

3.03 Overview of nineteen Danish collective housing projects

Town	Birkerød	Hillerød	Holte-Nærum	Charlottenlund/Gento

● Location near town (1:500,000)

Town population 2020	20,823	33,391	19,953	74,830 (municipality)

■ Building footprint (1:20,000)

Name of collective house	Lions Club Birkerød	Lions Club Hillerød	Lions Park Søllerød	EGV Strandlund
Year of construction	1971	1969	1966	1977–80
Ownership	Nonprofit organization	Nonprofit organization	Nonprofit organization	Nonprofit organizatio
Number of floors	–	–	–	2
Number of units	100	90	103	144
Housing type	Apartments	Apartments	Apartments	Rowhouses/Apartmer

	Værløse	Århus	Roskilde	Køge	Silkeborg

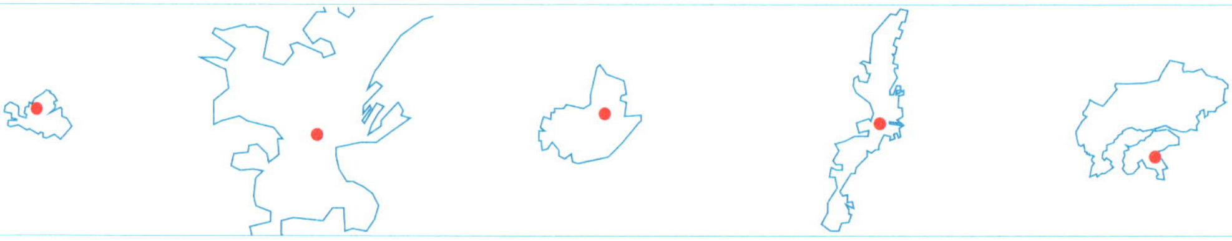

	12,926	280,534	51,262	37,754	46,923

	Kollektivhuset Ryetbo	Langenæshus + Langenæsbo	Margrethegårdens K.hus	Sandmarksbo Køge	Silkeborghus
	1970	1961/67	1969	1971	1960
	Nonprofit organization	Nonprofit organization	Nonprofit organization	Nonprofit organization	Nonprofit organizatio
	3	15	7 + 4	3	15
	68	321	192	84	68
	Apartments	Apartments	Apartments	Apartments	Apartments

Surrounding city context

Søborg/Gladsaxe	Esbjerg	Fredensborg	Frederiksberg	Bagsværd/Gladsaxe

69,262 (municipality)	72,037	8,769	104,305	69,262 (municipality)

Kollektivhuset Høje Søborg	Esbjerg Kollktivhus	Fredensborghusene	Frederiksgården	Hareskovbo
1951	1967	1963	1959	1959
Public housing	Nonprofit organization	Nonprofit organization	Nonprofit organization	Nonprofit organization
6	10 + 6	1	9	4
132	99	77	306	70+
Apartments	Apartments	Rowhouses	Apartments	Apartments

Frederiksberg	Odense	Vejle	Vejle	Holbæk
	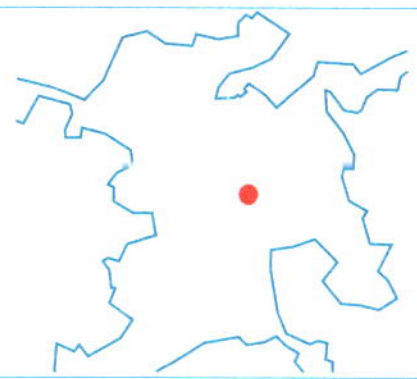	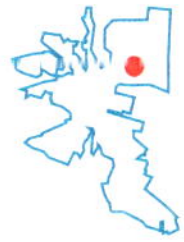	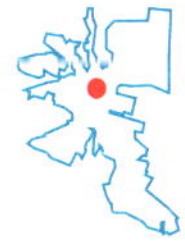	
104,305	180,302	57,655	57,655	28,833

Sophie Amalie Gården	Odense Kollektivhus	Kollektivhuset Nørrevænget	Toftegården	Vesterled
1965	?	1959	1977–80	1963
Nonprofit organization	Foundation	Nonprofit organization	Nonprofit organization	Co-operative housing
8	4	7	8	9
215	127	88	82	77
Apartments	Apartments	Apartments	Apartments	Apartments

3.04 Number of apartments, 1950–2021

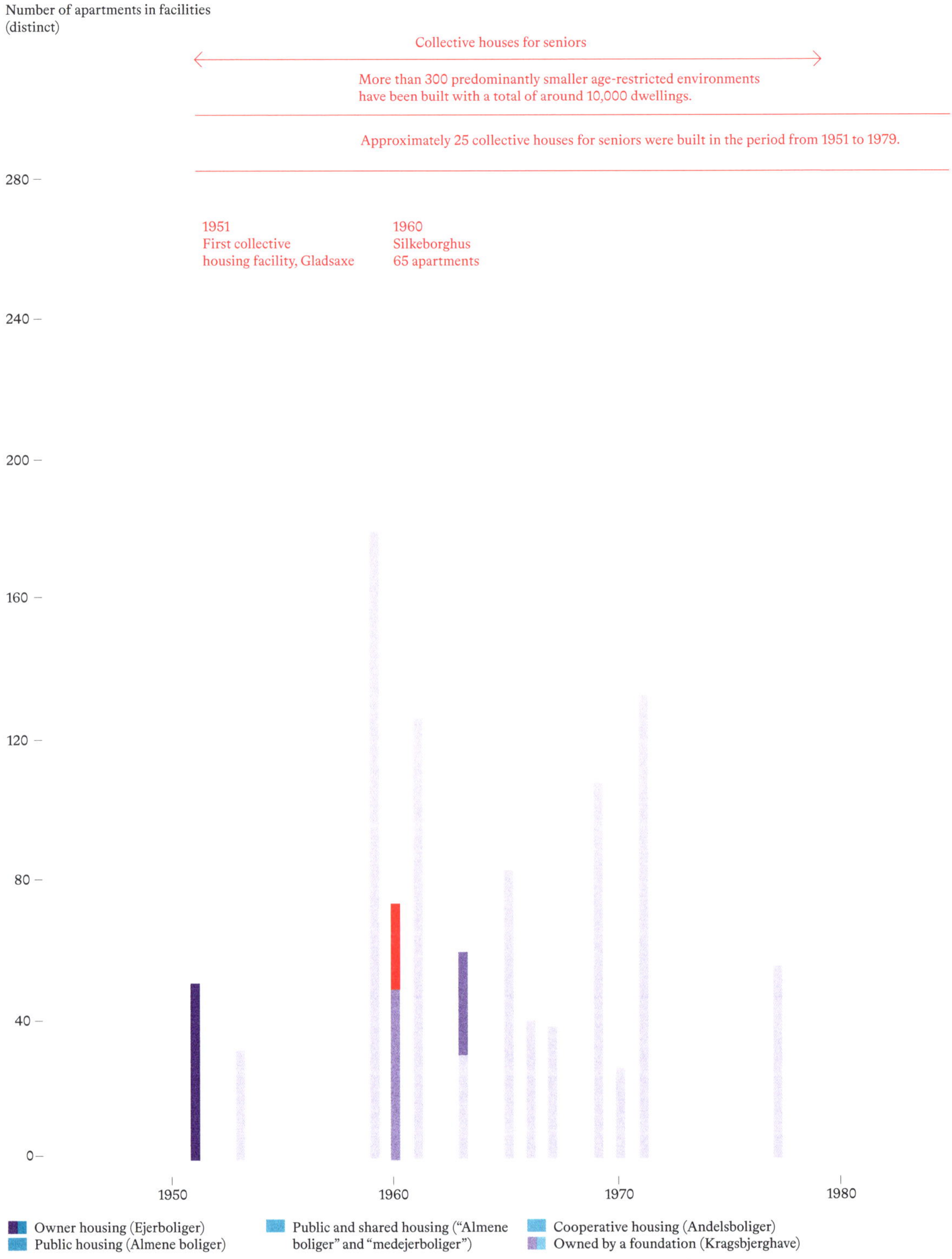

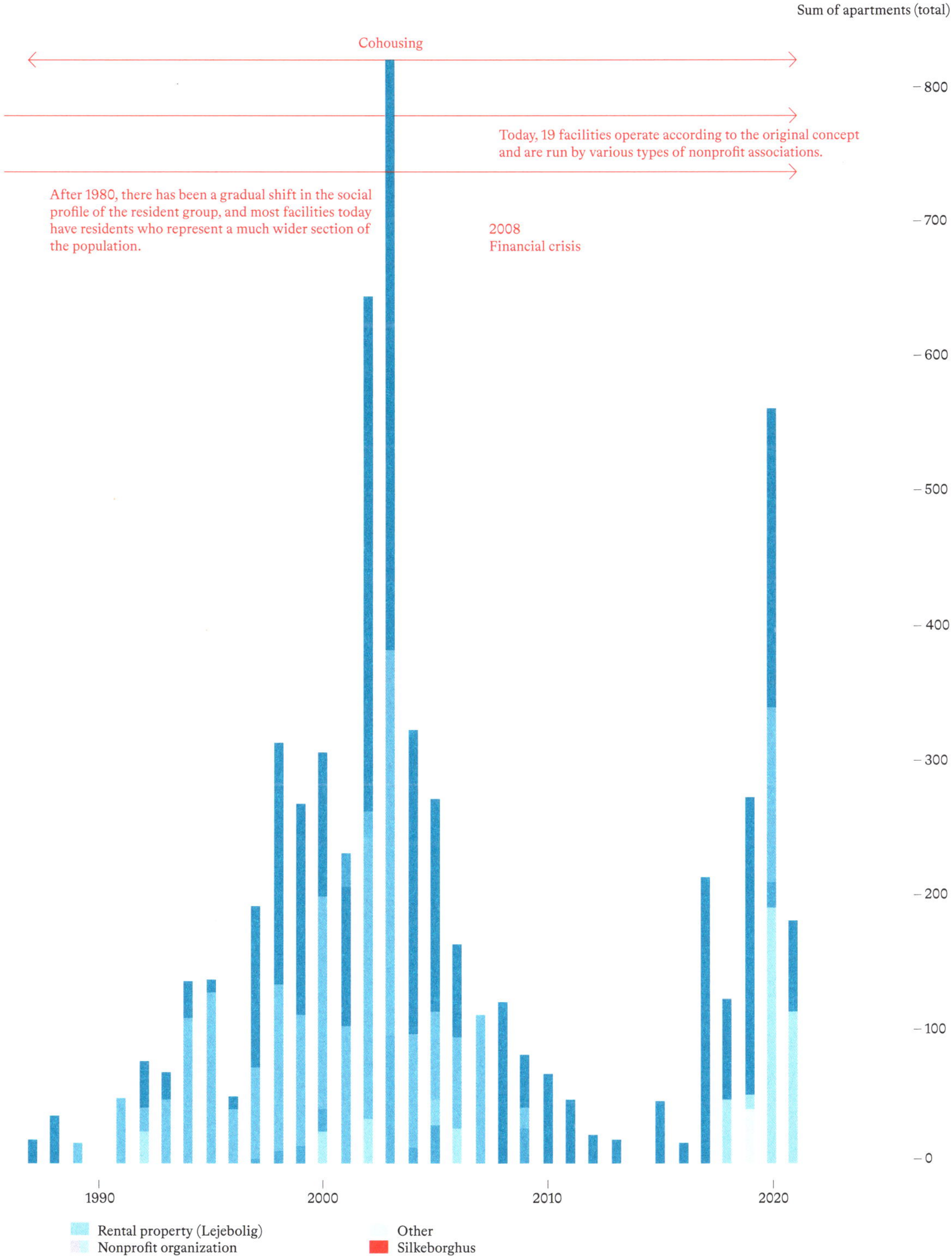
Sum of apartments (total)
Cohousing
Today, 19 facilities operate according to the original concept and are run by various types of nonprofit associations.
After 1980, there has been a gradual shift in the social profile of the resident group, and most facilities today have residents who represent a much wider section of the population.
2008
Financial crisis
800
700
600
500
400
300
200
100
0
1990
2000
2010
2020
Rental property (Lejebolig)
Nonprofit organization
Other
Silkeborghus

3.05 Number of apartments in collective housing projects, 1950–80

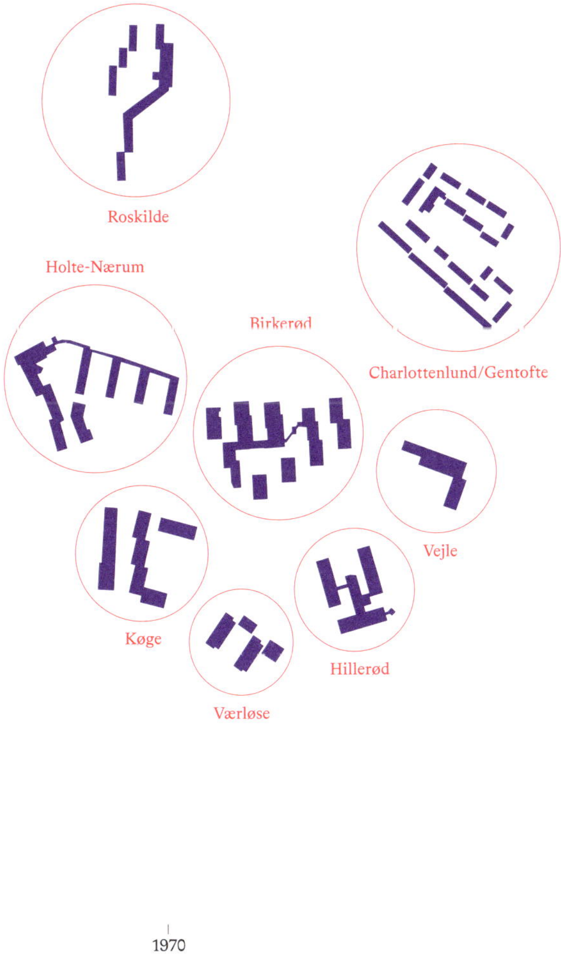
Roskilde
Holte-Nærum
Birkerød
Charlottenlund/Gentofte
Vejle
Køge
Hillerød
Værløse
1970
1980

3.06 Silkeborghus and its immediate environment

① Single family houses, local neighborhood
② Art museum Jorn, Silkeborg
③ Retirement home
④ Silkeborg Efterskole, boarding school
⑤ Summer houses, private garden areas

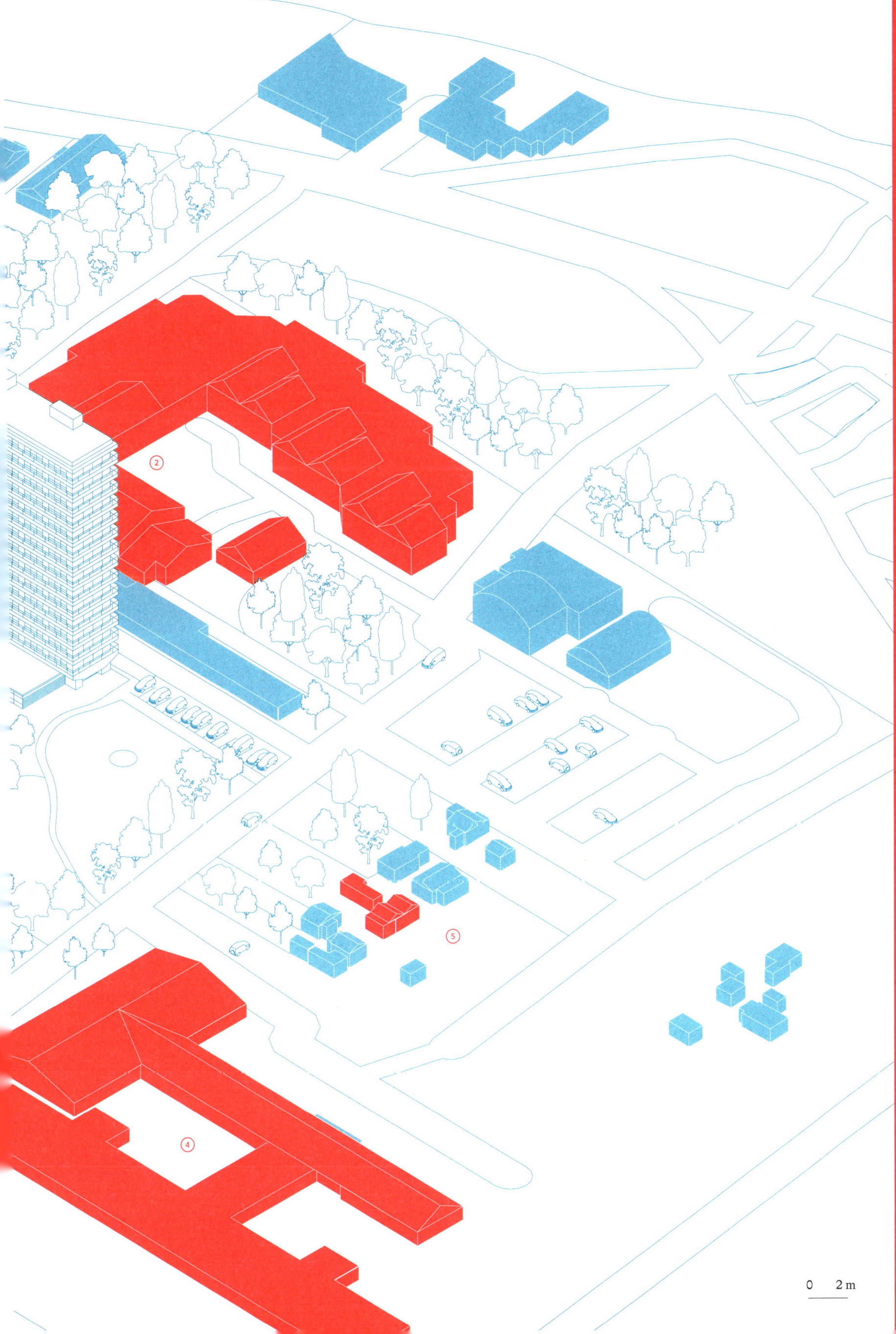

2
5
4
0 2 m

3.07 Major social hot spots in Silkeborghus

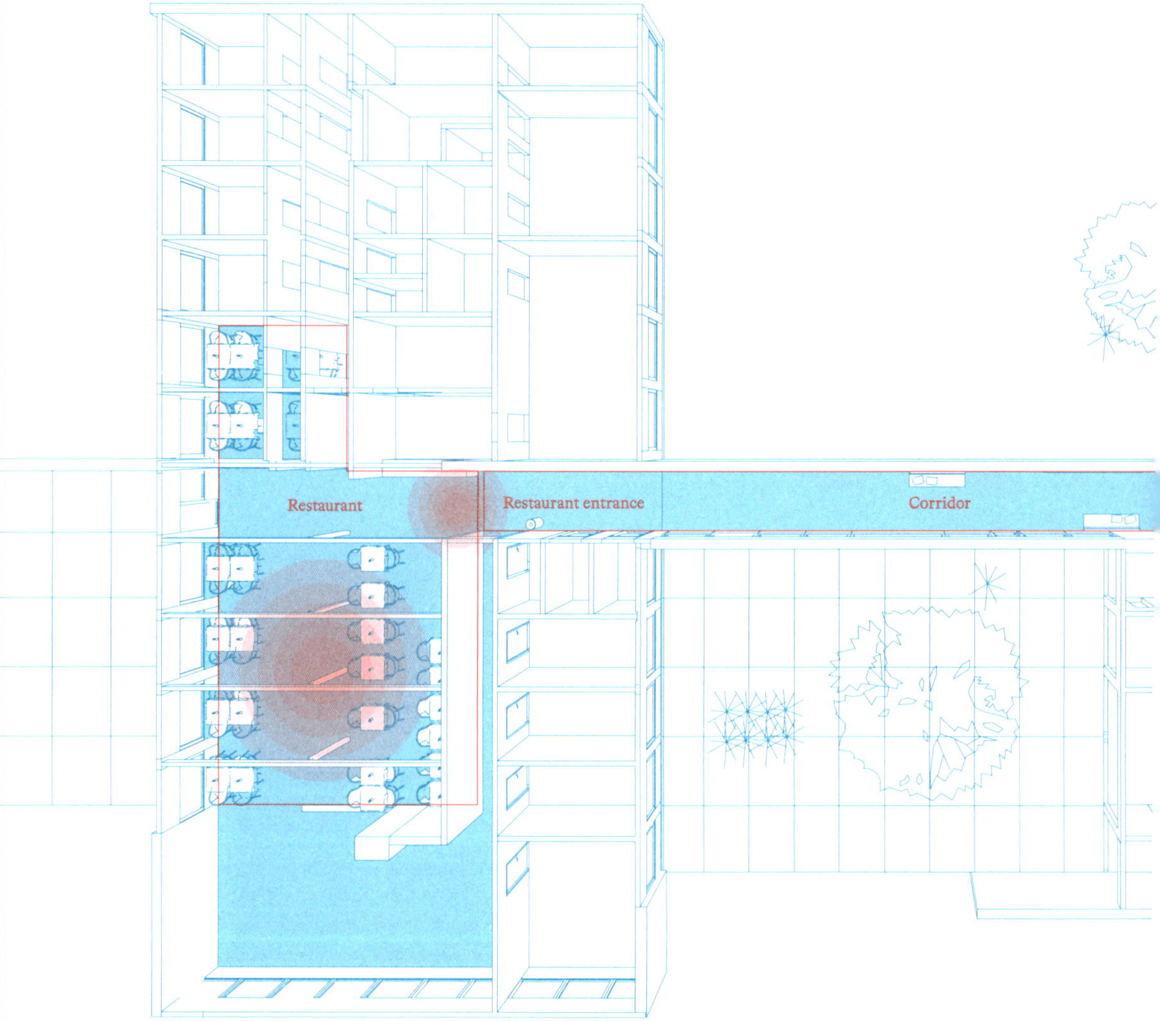

Ground floor

The collective houses differ significantly from most traditional housing complexes in that the residents generally have a more knowledge of each other. Especially in facilities with less than 100 dwellings residents will at some point have participated in a joint activity where they have had some degree of personal contact.

The neighbors' mutual knowledge permeates their random encounters in the common areas. It is the norm that residents verbally greet and look each other in the eyes when they meet by chance. The mutual knowledge furthermore has the effect that the residents relatively often fall into conversation with the neighbors they happen to meet.

The random conversations can happen everywhere in the building,but take place with the greatest frequency at the main entrance, in front of the elevators,, in the corridors, at the entrance to the dining room and in common areas such as the library and the laundry. The chance of meeting a neighbor in these areas of the facility varies depending on the time of day.

A special hearse with room for four coffins will take the dead person together with (up to) three other dead persons to the crematorium.

Resident about the laundry as a social hot spot:

"I like going to the laundry. It is nice because you always meet someone you can talk to. In fact, the laundry is a bit of a news center. It is often in the laundry that one hears if something has happened in the facility such as someone having been hospitalized or having returned from hospital. So just doing your laundry will keep you up to date with what is going on."

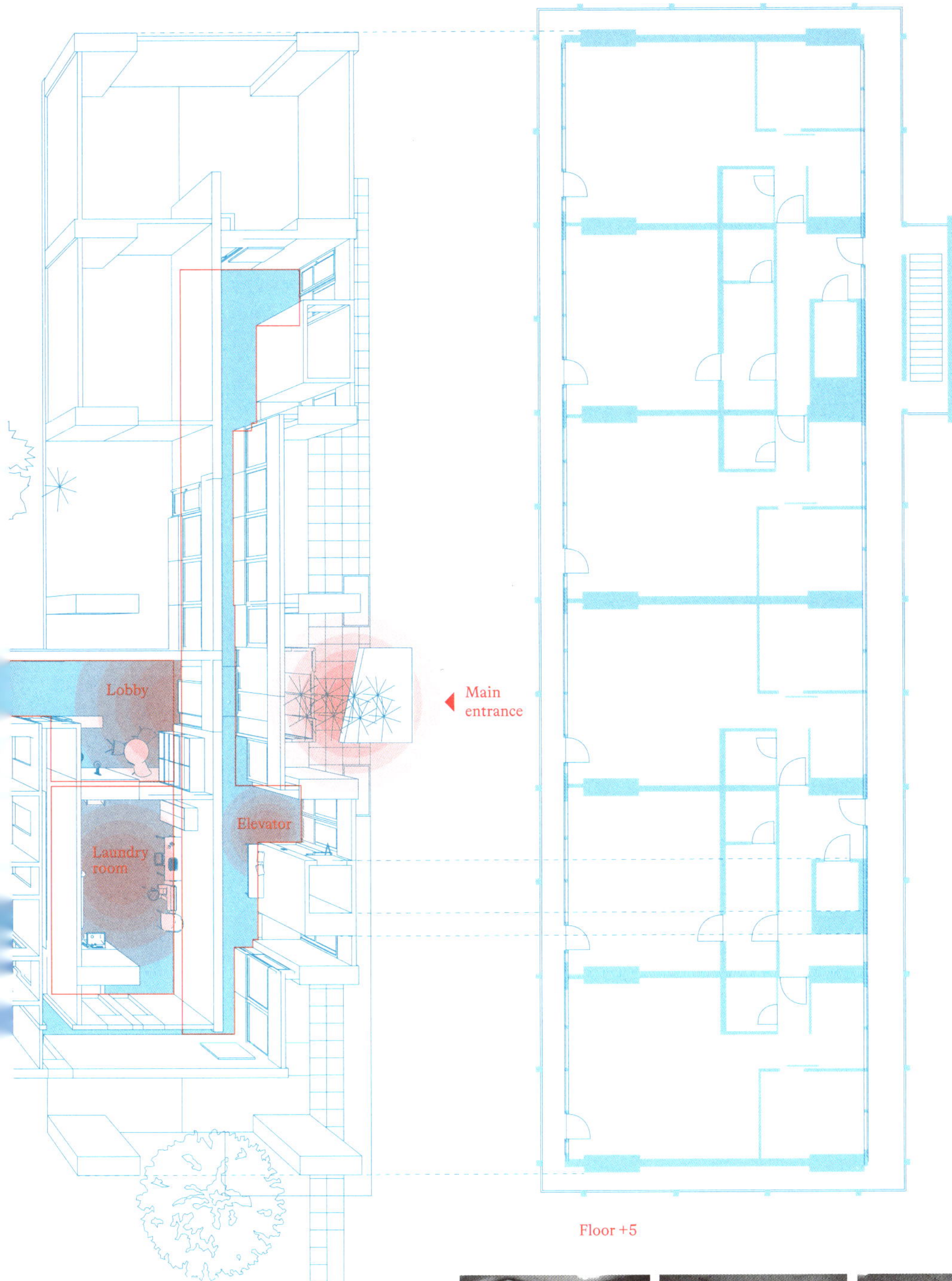

Floor +5

3.08 Silkeborghus space allocation

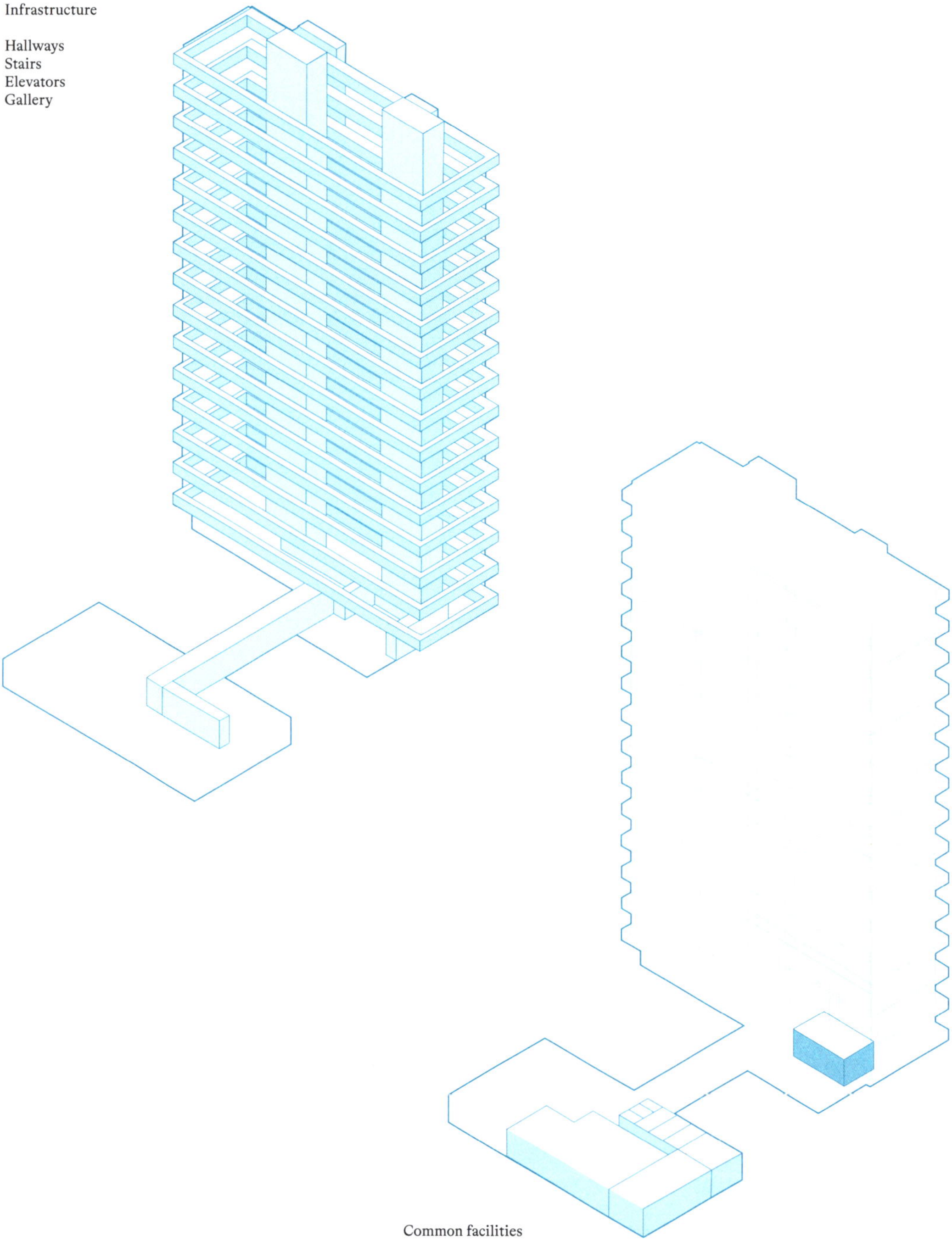

Staff facilities

Offices
Workshop
Kitchen
Changing rooms
Bathrooms
Storage
Hallway

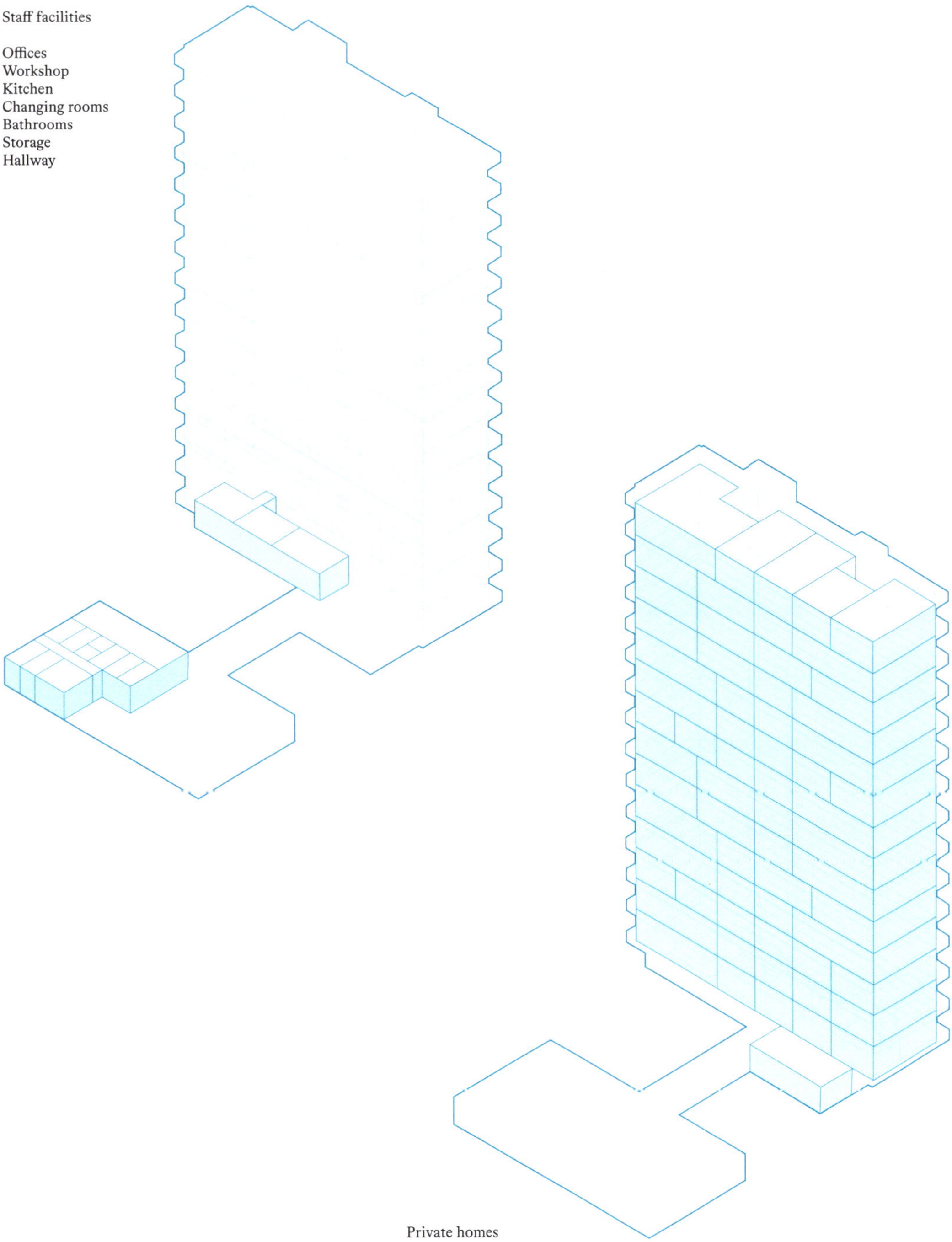

Private homes

12 × 1-bedroom apartments
36 × 2-bedroom apartments
8 × 2.5-bedroom apartments
12 × 3-bedroom apartments
1 × 2-bedroom ground-floor apartment
(used to be for the caretaker)

3.09 Silkeborghus residents profile

Gender distribution

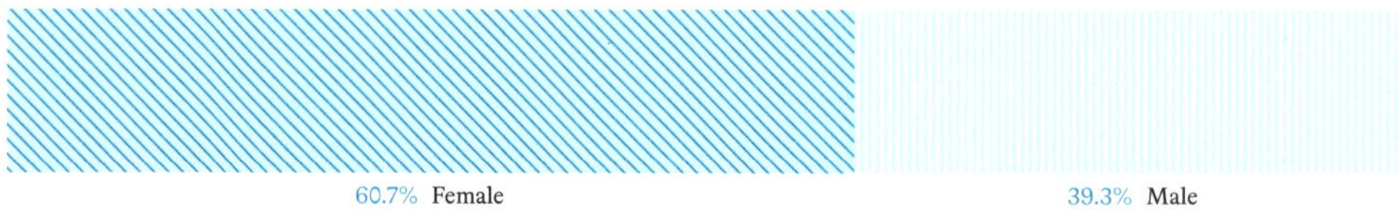

Age at the time of moving in

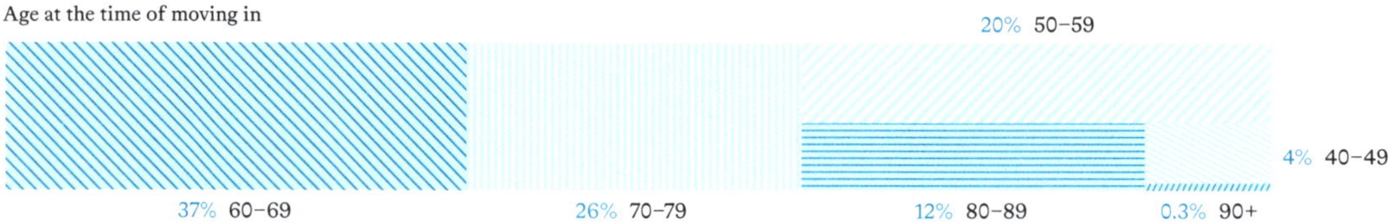

Age at the time of survey

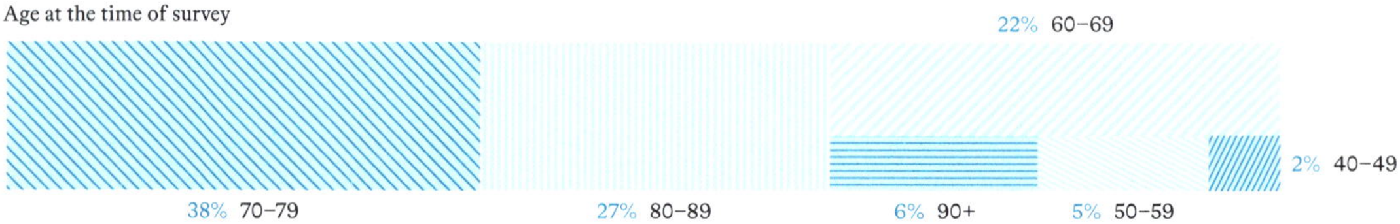

Marital status

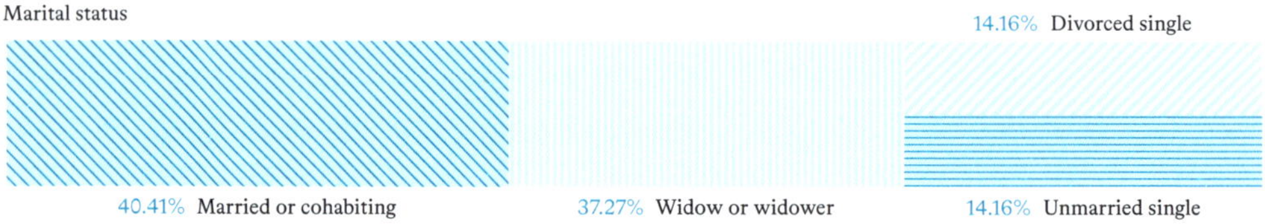

Health

Leaving the building

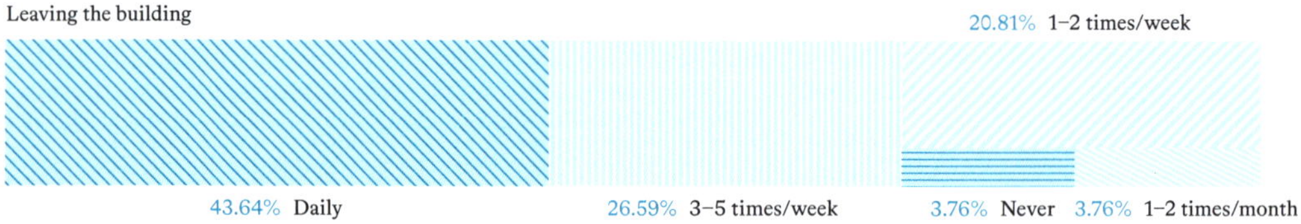

3.10 Residents engagement in three types of social interaction

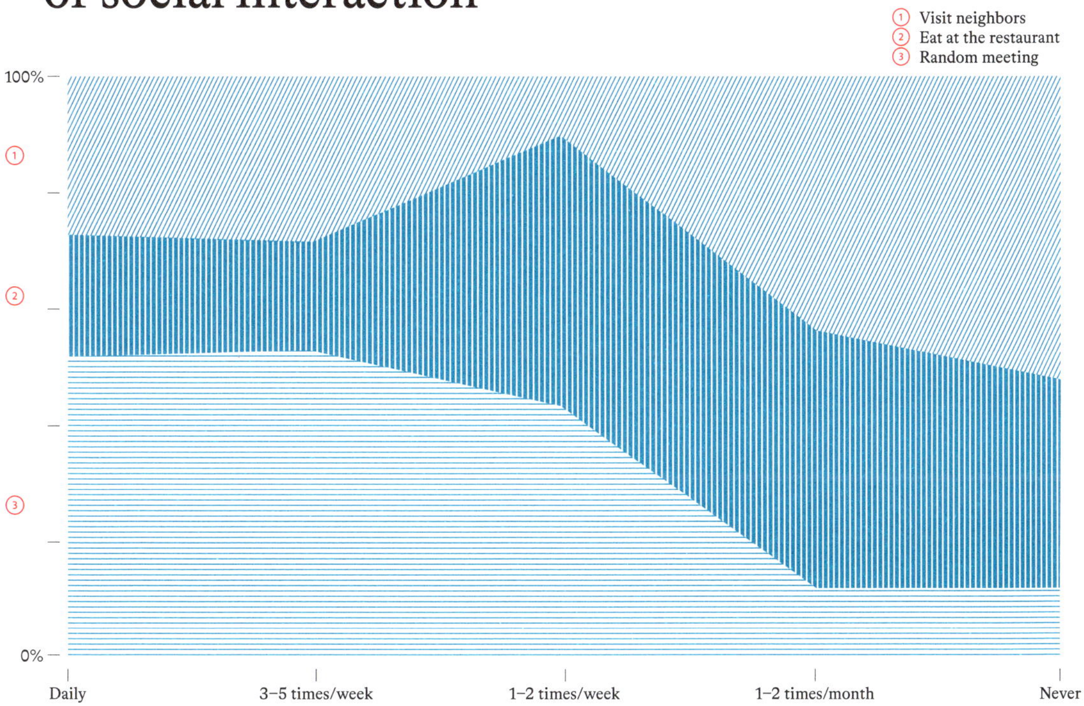

3.11 Percentage of residents having helped neighbors within last month

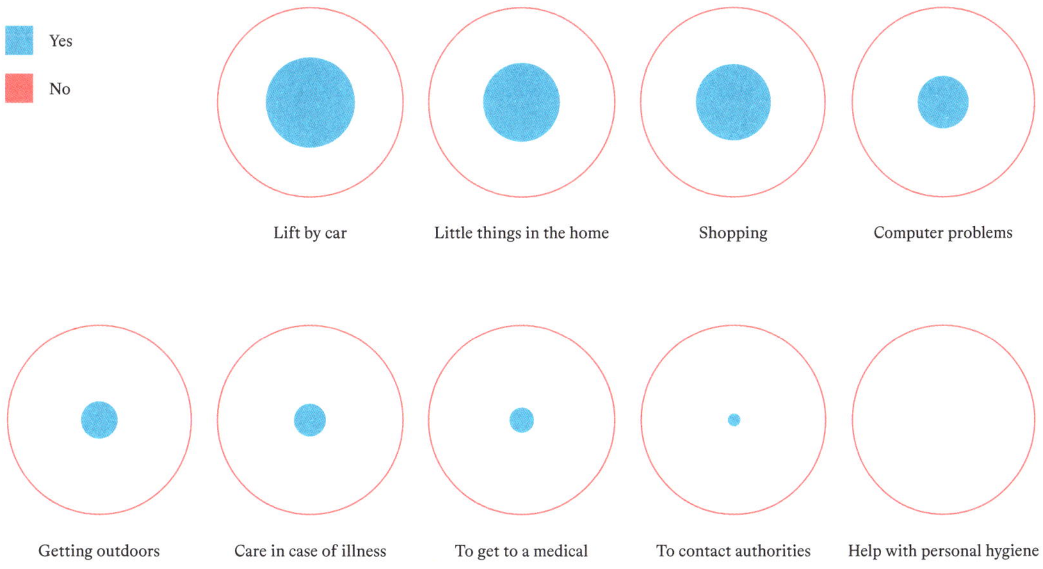

Ideology of the Welfare State in Solidified Concrete for Housing

Claus Bech-Danielsen

Housing construction has been a vital instrument in the development of the Danish welfare society. In the early twentieth century, housing shortages and unhealthy housing conditions were a contributing factor to tuberculosis and other serious diseases,[1] and the struggle for better housing conditions was a natural part of the class struggle.[2] When the Social Democrats came to power in Denmark in 1924, housing construction also became an important political issue, particularly during the economic downturn of the 1930s, when housing investment (even then) was considered an instrument to create an economic boost.[3] With Social Democrat Thorvald Stauning[4] as Prime Minister, several bills on housing support were implemented.

In Denmark, two housing types especially received support. One housing type was the privately owned single-family home. The scheme Laan til Boligbyggeri (Loans for Housing Construction, later known as Statslånsordningen) was established in 1938 and worked until 1958. It significantly boosted the construction of small privately owned single-family homes.[5] The second housing type was social housing. With a political agreement in 1933,[6] the ideas behind social housing in Denmark were enshrined into law (the first law on state support for housing construction in Denmark was however passed in 1887, and the first Danish social housing associations were established in 1912).[7] Unlike many other countries, where social housing is only meant for residents in the lowest rung of the societal hierarchy, social housing was intended for a broad section of Denmark's population. Today, social housing in Denmark is called *almene boliger*, with approximately 580,000 homes, which amounts to 20 percent of all Danish homes.[8]

The focal point of this chapter is social housing in Denmark. The societal conditions that formed the basis for the construction, as well as the intentions behind the development of social housing in the Danish welfare society are described, and a number of basic physical and architectural conditions in the constructed housing areas are pointed out. Subsequently it is described how the residential areas, despite good intentions, have run into a large number of different problems. In that light, the extensive physical transformations that are planned to be carried out in the postwar housing areas up to the year 2030 are discussed.

Danish Social Housing in the 1940s and '50s

When World War II ended in 1945, Denmark had a significant shortage of housing. A report in 1946 from the Ministry of the Interior indicated an acute housing shortage of 50,000 homes in Denmark, and the report pointed out that the real need for new construction was even greater because 130,000 to 150,000 homes were not suitable for habitation.[9] The housing shortage grew further in the following years, as the Danish population grew by 741,000 people (from 3,844,000 to 4,585,000) from 1940 to 1960.[10]

Urbanization also led to a growing need for new construction, as the existing homes were not necessarily located where they were needed the most: in urban areas. In the postwar period, however, urban growth occurred in the suburbs. The population in the City of Copenhagen started to decline in 1950 and continued to decline until 1990. More than 300,000 citizens left Copenhagen during this period in favor of suburban

1 Creating housing for the working class was a significant task of modern Danish architects. The Danish functionalist architect Edvard Heiberg wrote the book *2 Vær. straks* (2 Rooms Now) in 1935. In the book, Heiberg stated that in parts of 1930s Copenhagen, there was an average of only 1.6 square meters of housing available per person.

municipalities. In the suburbs, progress was experienced in postwar Denmark, whereas the old city collapsed into a mix of poor and outdated housing, deteriorating infrastructure and dilapidated industrial areas.[11]

In the postwar years, the emerging welfare state kick-started housing construction, and social housing gained strong political support. A 1945 government report concluded that the construction of social housing ought to be promoted, and with the Housing Support Act and Building Support Act in 1946, a financial basis was established for the construction of new housing. Moreover, the state pushed for the development of industrialized construction.[12] In 1947 the Ministry of Housing[13] was established, and in the same year, the Danish Building Research Institute was established to support the industrialization of construction.[14] With industrial construction, the bottleneck of the lack of skilled craftspeople had to be overcome, and through rationalization and systematization, the way had to be paved for the mass production of housing.[15]

The architect Svenn Eske Kristensen was among the pioneers in the development of industrialized housing construction in Denmark. With two social housing estates in Hvidovre – Engstrands Allé (1952–54) and Strandhavevej (1953–55) – he designed the first Danish multistory buildings built with prefabricated concrete elements.[16] Another landmark was Milestedet (1953–58), with more than 2,500 dwellings, which approached the scale of the 1960s housing developments. Thus, in the housing policy and experimental buildings of the 1950s, some features like prefabrication, industrialization and scale point to the large assembly constructions of the 1960s.

However, most social housing areas from the 1940s and '50s were built as park estates and constructed in traditional masonry, and only some elements like balconies and stairways were constructed in concrete. From an architectural point of view the most successful of the period's housing areas were designed organically based on conditions at the specific site, and the level differences due to hills or uneven ground on the site were often used to establish a landscape quality with fluid spatial connections. The green landscape surface reaches the plinths of the buildings, and the buildings appear as sharply cut elements of burnt brick pressed down into a soft bottom of clay.[17] The interplay between buildings and landscape is fundamental to the architectural design, and the landscaping testifies that the outdoor spaces were shared and meant for the housing community. The closest the private homes came to outdoor spaces was through the experience on the balconies.

Health is a fundamental ideal that was the basis of architectural design. The housing areas are for instance organized according to daylight; living rooms are oriented toward the south or west, and the bedrooms and kitchens to the north or east.[18] If some apartment blocks were desired to be oriented differently for spatial and design reasons, serious consideration was given to the lighting conditions to argue for this. A leaflet to the first residents moving into the Tingbjerg residential area in 1957 stated the following:

> The largest part of the apartment blocks is oriented so that the rooms faces east and west, respectively. It is estimated that most residents mainly use their living rooms in the afternoon and evening most of the week and can therefore enjoy the sun the most if they have living rooms facing west. An exception, however, is

2 Svenn Eske Kristensen, Bredalsparken, Hvidovre, 1949–59. Bredalparken presents the housing ideals of the 1950s at their best. A hilly terrain was used to create fine spatial transitions in the landscape between the buildings, and there was plenty of life in the outdoor spaces. In 1950 60 percent of Danish households consisted of families with children (two adults and at least one child). Today, they make up only 18 percent.

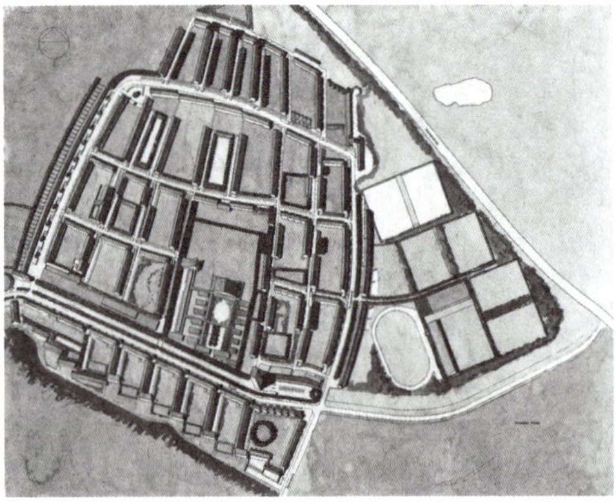

3 Steen Eiler Rasmussen and C. Th. Sørensen, Tingbjerg, Brønshøj, 1957–75. Tingbjerg is a special version of postwar housing areas playing on the contrast between landscape and urban qualities. The area consists of an open-block structure, where homes face relatively narrow streets on one side and green outdoor spaces on the other. Reflecting the ideal of "new towns," Tingbjerg is well equipped with the functions needed to meet the needs of everyday life: shops, church, school, and institutions. Paradoxically, Tingbjerg is today referred to as hopelessly isolated – surrounded by protected natural areas.

> the housing that is planned for the old-age pensioners, who must be at home even in the middle of the day. Here the living rooms are located directly to the south.[19]

Although families with children were the primary target group of Tingbjerg, several generations and household types were thus considered in the design of the housing area. A total of 240,000 dwellings were built in Denmark from 1945 to 1959, and about 120,000 of these were social housing.[20]

Industrialized Housing Construction in the 1960s and '70s

As described, many efforts were made to promote housing construction in the 1950s. However, housing construction did not reach 24,000 dwellings/year until 1957, corresponding to the years before World War II. The housing shortage was not overcome. The population grew significantly, and in the early 1960s, the high birth rates from the years around the war led to even more housing applicants. The need for new construction grew further as individual households generally became smaller due to changing family patterns.[21] In addition, urbanization continued to lead to migration from the country to the city regions.[22]

In the 1960s, the industrialized mass production of housing took off, and production grew steadily, reaching 50,000 homes per year in 1969.[23] The many regulations and legislative changes implemented through the 1950s to push for industrialization culminated with the introduction of Montagecirkulæret (The Assembly Construction Act) in 1960.[24] Housing was required to be built using prefabricated elements in order to obtain financial support. In the introduction to the Assembly Construction Act, the aim is to design and arrange residential buildings as much as possible as follows:

> Assembly construction with prefabricated elements and building parts for thereby achieving the greatest possible savings in the hours worked and quantities of material spent and, in general, as high productivity as possible. [...] The Act also presupposes that the design of the individual buildings is organized in such a way that, to the greatest extent possible, it is possible to use series-produced, generally usable building parts provided by a continuous production. This requires for example that the construction program is simple, that the design is carried out on the basis of modular schemes, that there is as

> much repetition as possible, such as by using uniform (standardized and typified) building components, that the chosen floor plans are thought through and generally applicable, and that the buildings are given an uncomplicated design.[25]

The state made massive demands on housing construction: new architectural, technical and logistical ideas were to be considered, and the development of rational workflows was to be considered in the design.

With Montagecirkulæret, the construction of 7,500 dwellings over four years was guaranteed, creating a basis for standardized construction investments, which contributed to realizing the intended mass production of homes. The largest construction boom in Danish history became a reality in 1960–79. In the same period, the total urban area in Denmark more than doubled, an expansion that primarily occurred in the suburbs.[26]

In contrast to the 1950s buildings, which were placed in a soft landscape and shaped in relation to the local topography, the buildings in the housing areas of the 1960s and '70s were typically placed as cubic blocks on a surface. The housing developments were planned as universal, so site-specific differences, such as topographic conditions, were minimized. The optimal building site for housing in the 1960s and '70s was a flat field where the contractor could easily roll out the crane tracks in the same way as the previous construction. Any variations in the terrain were typically smoothed out, and the paths in the outdoor spaces followed the rectilinear course of the crane tracks. The scale was large, which applies to the size of the individual housing areas and the apartment blocks and the spaces between them.

> The outdoor areas were planned with rational gardening in mind with – in contrast to the inner cities' dense courtyards – large lawns that provided a euphoric experience of light, air and open space. As was the case with 1950s housing areas, the outdoor spaces were common areas shared by residents, and it was seen as the physical manifestation of the solidary community. Although the ground-floor apartments had living rooms at the lawn level, they did not have direct access to the common lawns. Equality was an essential ideal in architectural design; in a welfare society, everyone should have equal access to the same qualities, and no one should have more or less than their neighbor, which also applied to the green outdoor spaces. Thus, none of the residents should have individual ownership of such spaces.[27]

Safety was another important issue. The International Congresses of Modern Architecture (CIAM), an organization founded in 1928 to spread the concept of modernism on architecture and planning, pointed out the

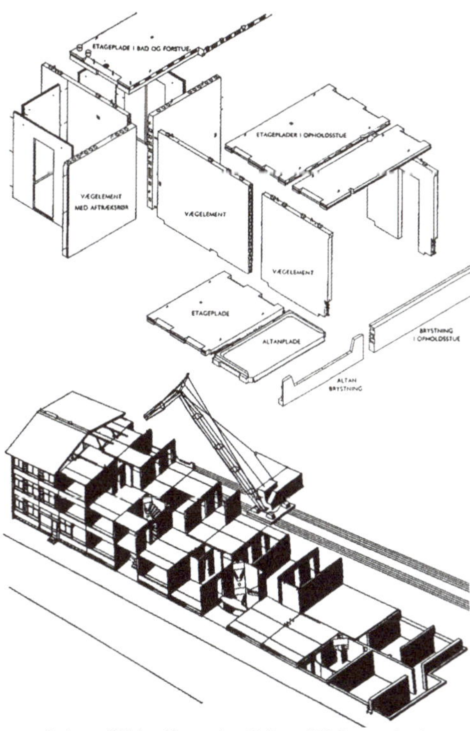

4 Larsen & Nielsen, Torveparken, Gladsaxe, 1955. Construction along crane tracks with use of prefabricated concrete elements – here in Torveparken. The engineering company was responsible for the construction design based on experience from their previous housing constructions.

problematic of planning housing side by side with busy roads, and inspired by this, industrialized housing areas were organized with a separation between soft and hard road users to create calm and safe conditions for children in residential areas.[28] Therefore, traffic was directed in an arc around residential areas, and cars were parked in the periphery. As the residential areas were simultaneously designed with a distinctive and homogeneous architectural expression, they often stood out from the surrounding city. This distinction was strived for as a quality that provided each housing area with a strong identity and a good basis for developing a sense of community in the area. From 1960 to 1979, approximately 818,000 dwellings were built in Denmark, of which more than 200,000 were social housing.[29]

The 2020s – The Parallel Society Act

Measured by the goals of the welfare state to improve the housing standard and eliminate the housing shortage that characterized the years after World War II, postwar construction was a success. In a few years, construction was revolutionized. Traditional craftsmanship and traditional building materials were replaced with industrial forms of production and completely new building materials. It succeeded in creating a mass production of homes that has not been seen similarly before or since. In that light, postwar housing construction can be regarded as the largest full-scale construction experiment in Danish history. Therefore, it is thought-provoking that many of the housing areas of that time are now the subject of several physical transformations that can be regarded as the largest social housing experiment in Danish history.

The background is that the postwar social housing areas are associated with several serious challenges with an interplay of economic, constructional, social and architectural problems, which have led to these areas' being stigmatized and given a bad reputation. Many postwar large-scale housing areas have ended up at the bottom of the hierarchy in the local housing markets, and those who can choose for themselves settle in other housing types.[30] Although Danish social housing is intended for a broad section of the population, many postwar housing areas have become home to disadvantaged residents.

Problems in the social housing area are not new. Already in the wake of the energy crisis in 1973, many new housing associations reported financial troubles, and in 1976 a report warned that a concentration of disadvantaged residents was developing in large-scale social housing areas.[31] In the 1970s, the first constructional problems appeared.[32] In the following decades, numerous physical and social efforts have been implemented in virtually all large-scale housing areas of the postwar period. Nevertheless, the residential areas are still dealing with the same social problems today as they did forty to fifty years ago.[33] Although issues of ethnicity and integration have gained greater focus over the years, they primarily draw the same problems that have plagued residential areas throughout the years.[34]

That was why the Danish Parliament in 2018 passed the *Parallel Society Act*, which requires extensive physical transformations in fifteen particularly disadvantaged housing areas. The areas were defined in the legal text as *hårde ghettoer* (hard ghettos), housing areas that have been on the Danish ghetto list for four years in a row. The ghetto list is based on five criteria for residents in the housing areas: (1) the proportion of residents with non-Western backgrounds; (2) residents' connection to the labor market; (3) residents' education level; (4) residents' income level; and (5) the proportion of residents with a judgment for a crime. Only social housing areas with more than 1,000 residents can be included in the ghetto list.

As the five criteria show, the Parallel Society Act primarily focuses on ethnic and socioeconomic conditions in disadvantaged housing areas. Physical efforts are considered a means of changing these conditions. The overall objective is that the proportion of social family housing, which today typically amounts to 100 percent in the fifteen residential areas, must be reduced to 40 percent by 2030.[35] This reduction can be achieved by reducing the number of social family homes through demolition or divestment, but it can also be achieved through densification (that is, by building new housing types, such as owner-occupied housing, and new commercial buildings). The Parallel Society Act requires major physical transformations in the fifteen areas, and the benchmarks for the transformations are the ghetto list's socioeconomic criteria.

The overall goal of the Parallel Society Act is to create more socially mixed neighborhoods. Thus, it can be argued that it is a matter of rediscovering the idea behind Danish social housing, which was intended for a broad section of the population at its starting point. As I will get into, however, in other areas the planning concept and housing ideals of the postwar period were significantly compromised, which is expressed, among other things, through several physical transformations based on a changed view of safety.

Ideological Battlefield

The changed view on safety contributes to the fact that the postwar ideals of housing areas as independent units standing out from the surroundings are being dismantled. The safety that was originally created for the residents and their children (by leading roads around the housing areas) is understood differently when the areas are linked to other forms of danger. Politicians now link physical isolation with the development of "parallel societies," where cultural and social norms are established without connection to the surrounding society. As a bridge to surrounding neighborhoods, inspired by Jane Jacobs's call to have "eyes on the street,"[36] new roads and paths are being constructed into areas to bring down crime and norm-breaking behavior[37] among the area's children and youngsters. This situation may seem paradoxical: in the 1970s, roads were led in a large arc around housing areas to create safety. In the current transformations, roads are led right through the middle of the same residential areas, again to create safety.

Admittedly, many residents still appreciate the areas' traffic separation and experience greater safety and security by having car-free outdoor spaces.[38] Today, however, the focus is not only on the safety of the residents. The middle class in the surrounding city needs to be attracted to disadvantaged housing areas; therefore, to a large extent, the focus of the current transformation is on the insecurity in the surrounding neighborhoods, and here the insecurity is often related to the

5

6a

5 The South Jutland Plan, designed by Børge Kjær in collaboration with ten South Jutland housing associations and constructed in suburbs in several Danish provincial towns during the 1960 and '70s. The blocks are constructed as standardized element buildings in concrete and have horizontal window bands and flat roofs. The blocks are relatively deep, with load-bearing partition walls, and all of the homes are well-equipped and have access to a balcony. A total of 24,000 dwellings of this type were built.
6 a) Povl Ernst Hoff and Bennet Windinge, Søndergård Park, Bagsværd, 1949–50; b) Povl Ernst Hoff and Bennet Windinge, Høje Gladsaxe, Gladsaxe, 1960–64. The differences between these housing estates by the same architects are indicative of the revolution that the building industry underwent in the early 1960s.

6b

7 The fifteen disadvantaged housing areas defined as "hard ghettos." Judging from socioeconomic data, they are very much alike, but their urban location and scale are drastically different.

8 Architects: Skaarup & Jespersen, Avedøre Stationsby, Avedøre, 1972–82. Location: Avedøre. When suburban housing areas were established in the postwar period, the city was a dystopia against which was the dream of housing close to green landscapes in suburbia. Today, the situation is the opposite: green outdoor spaces are described as empty and unsafe, while urban qualities and busy city life are considered a means of increasing security. The euphoria has left the experience of the open outdoor spaces in postwar areas, and it is thought-provoking that these spaces, previously considered a shared common area and a symbol of the community, are today described as a "no-man's land."

appearance of groups of children and youngsters in the disadvantaged neighborhoods. In the 1970s, the aim was to create a feeling of safety for the children and young people in the housing areas by protecting them from the surrounding city. Today, the aim is to create a feeling of safety in the surrounding city by protecting it from children and young people in the housing areas.

New residents and new users are meant to be attracted to disadvantaged housing areas through constructing owner-occupied homes and new infrastructure with functions that open to the surroundings and invite the surrounding neighborhoods inside. However, the physical structures and social life of the surroundings are not the only aspects invited into these areas. The market forces that characterize urban development in the surrounding city also penetrate social housing areas. Along with market forces come capitalism, privatization, and increased individualization, which is observed when parts of the social housing areas are sold off to create space for private investment. This is observed when private gardens are laid out to create personal ownership of the green outdoor spaces originally planned as common spaces shared in solidarity. Moreover, this is also seen when social housing associations enter the housing market competition. Furthermore, this is reflected in introducing new rental rules that favor resourceful middle-class residents on the waiting lists for social housing.

The welfare state was built on a political ideology, and in the large social housing areas, the ideology was realized and cast in concrete. The apartment blocks stand as monuments of when equality, community and solidarity were fundamental values. When apartment blocks from these years are demolished and transformed, it symbolizes that these values are deteriorating. The current transformations in the welfare state's large social housing areas from the postwar period are regarded as an ideological battleground.[39] This issue is also experienced by residents who find that their housing area has been politicized and has increasingly become a battleground for various political views and factions.[40] Residents deal with those who come from the outside, telling them that their housing area should be demolished or that they should protest. Many residents find both views frustrating. They desire to be heard themselves.

Bibliography

Andersen, Hans Thor, and Hans Skifter Andersen. "Fra provinsen til forstæderne – vandring og bosætning i København." In *Har forstaden erobret byen?* Edited by Hans Kristensen, 19–30. Copenhagen: Dansk Byplanlaboratorium, 2017.

Bech-Danielsen, Claus. *Moderne arkitektur – hva er meningen?* Aarhus: Systime, 2004.

Bech-Danielsen, Claus, and Gunvor Christensen, *Boligområder i bevægelse: Fortællinger om fysiske og boligsociale indsatser.* Copenhagen: Landsbyggefonden, 2017.

Bech-Danielsen, Claus, and Marie Stender. *Fra ghetto til blandet by.* Copenhagen: Gads Forlag, 2017.

Bech-Danielsen, Claus, Mette Mechlenborg and Marie Stender. *Vollsmose: Arbejdsrapport – baselineundersøgelse 2019 – SBI; Nr. 2020:07.* Copenhagen: Aalborg University BUILD, 2020.

Bendsen, Jannie Rosenberg, and Dorthe Bendtsen. *Drømmen om eget hus – Statslånshuse 1933–1959.* Copenhagen: Strandberg Publishing, 2021.

Bertelsen, Sven. *Bellahøj: Ballerup: Brøndby Strand: 25 år der industrialiserede byggeriet.* Hørsholm: Statens Byggeforskningsinstitut, 1997.

BL – Danmarks Almene Boliger. "Boliger." https://bl.dk/politik-og-analyser/fakta-og-tal/boliger/. Accessed May 17, 2021.

Braae, Ellen. "Welfare Landscapes and Communities." In *Forming Welfare*, edited by Jannie Rosenberg Bendsen, Katrine Lotz, Kjeld Vindum, Mette Jerl Jensen, Deane Simpson and Kirsten Marie Raahauge, 34–49. Copenhagen: Arkitektens Forlag, 2015.

Danmarkshistorien.dk Aarhus Universitet. "Danmarks befolkningsudvikling 1769–2015." https://danmarkshistorien.dk/leksikon-og-kilder/vis/materiale/danmarks-befolkningsudvikling/. Accessed May 17, 2021.

Dansk Bygningsarv, ed. *1940'erne og 1950'ernes murede boligbebyggelser: Renoveringsguide. Kvaliteter, udfordringer og anbefalinger.* Copenhagen: Realdania, Landsbyggefonden, Grundejernes Investeringsfond and Kulturstyrelsen, 2015.

Frost, Esben Dannemand. "Boligmassen og bygningskulturen." In Dansk Bygningsarv, *1940'erne og 1950'ernes murede boligbebyggelser,* 10–27.

FSB. *Velkommen til Tingbjerg!* Copenhagen: Foreningen Socialt Boligbyggeri, 1957.

Heiberg, Edvard. *2 Vær. straks.* Copenhagen: Mondes Forlag, 1935.

Høi, Arne, and Troels Østergaard. "Bevaringsværdier." In Dansk Bygningsarv, *1940'erne og 1950'ernes murede boligbebyggelser,* 42–57.

Jacobs, Jane. *The Death and Life of Great American Cities*. New York: Random House, 1993 [1961].

Kristensen, Hans. *DAB – 75 år med almene boliger*. Frederiksberg: DAB, 2017.

The Athens Charter. New York: Grossman Publishers, 1973. Originally published as *La Charte d'Athènes* – an edited version of *Constatations de IV Congrès,* 1942.

Lilja, Elisabeth. *Den ifrågasatta förorten. Identitet och tillhörighet i moderna förorter.* Stockholm: Byggforskningsrådet, 1999.

Lind, Olaf, and Jonas Møller. *Bag hækken. Det danske parcelhus i lyst og nød*. Copenhagen: Arkitektens Forlag, 1996.

——. *FolkeBolig. BoligFolk. Politik og praksis i boligbevægelsens historie*. Copenhagen: Boligselskabernes Landsforening, 1994.

Skriver, Poul Erik. *Byerne langs Køge Bugt.* Copenhagen: Dansk Byplanlaboratorium, 1984.

Tietjen, Anne. *Forstadens bygningskultur 1945–1989: På sporet af velfærdsforstadens bevaringværdier.* Copenhagen: Dansk Bygningsarv, 2010.

Weatherall, Cecilie Dohlmann, Bence Boje-Kovacs and Aske Egsgaard-Pedersen. *Et historisk tilbageblik på de særligt udsatte boligområder udpeget i 2014 Udviklingen i tilflyttere, fraflyttere og fastboende*. Copenhagen: Kraks Byforskning, 2016.

Notes

1 The housing conditions in this period were also linked to alcoholism, prostitution, and mental illness. See, for instance, Elisabeth Lilja, *Den ifrågasatta förorten. Identitet och tillhörighet i moderna förorter* (Stockholm: Byggforskningsrådet, 1999), 4–5.

2 Claus Bech-Danielsen, *Moderne arkitektur – hva er meningen?* (Aarhus: Systime, 2004), 57–60.

3 Olaf Lind and Jonas Møller, *Bag hækken: Det danske parcelhus i lyst og nød* (Copenhagen: Arkitektens Forlag, 1996), 79.

4 Except for a single break (1926–29), Thorvald Stauning was the prime minister of Denmark from 1924 to 1942.

5 To be granted one of the advantageous state loans, the house had to meet several requirements for price, size, interior design, equipment, and insulation. Initially, the house had to be a maximum of 85 square meters. During the 1940s and '50s, housing could be built a bit larger; see Jannie Rosenberg Bendsen and Dorthe Bendtsen, *Drømmen om eget hus – Statslånshuse 1933–1959* (Copenhagen: Strandberg Publishing, 2021).

6 The agreement is titled "Kanslergadeforliget," one of the best-known political agreements in Danish politics from the twentieth century; see Olaf Lind and Jonas Møller, *FolkeBolig: BoligFolk: Politik og praksis i boligbevægelsens historie* (Copenhagen: Boligselskabernes Landsforening, 1994), 92.

7 Lind and Møller, *FolkeBolig*, 64.

8 Boligselskabernes Landsforening, BL. *Boliger*. https://bl.dk/politik-og-analyser/fakta-og-tal/boliger/, accessed December 21, 2021.

9 In 1950 50 percent of the apartments in Copenhagen and 70 percent in the provinces were without a bath. Moreover, 60 percent of the apartments in Copenhagen and 75 percent in the provinces were without central heating and hot water. In rural areas, many homes were without electricity (for example, only 38 percent of the homes on Bornholm had electricity).

10 Aarhus University, *Danmarks befolkningsudvikling 1769–2015*, https://danmarkshistorien.dk/leksikon-og-kilder/vis/materiale/danmarks-befolkningsudvikling/, accessed December 21, 2021.

11 Hans Thor Andersen and Hans Skifter Andersen, "Fra provinsen til forstæderne – vandring og bosætning i København," in *Har forstaden erobret byen?*, ed. Hans Kristensen (Copenhagen: Dansk Byplanlaboratorium, 2017), 21.

12 Hans Kristensen, *DAB – 75 år med almene boliger* (Frederiksberg: DAB, 2017), 26.

13 It was first established with the name Ministeriet for Byggeri og Boligvæsen.
14 Lind and Møller, *FolkeBolig*, 127.
15 The welfare state supported development with a number of legislation and support schemes. For instance, in 1947, the Danish Parliament passed Elementhusloven (The Element House Act), which provided economic state aid for housing built with a construction technique requiring less use of skilled labor; see Esben Dannemand Frost, "Boligmassen og bygningskulturen," in *1940'erne og 1950'ernes murede boligbebyggelser: Bevaringskultur og bevaringsværdier*, ed. Dansk Bygningsarv (Copenhagen: Realdania, Landsbyggefonden, Grundejernes Investeringsfond and Kulturstyrelsen, 2015), 10–27. In 1951 the Ministry of Housing set up a committee to boost research and development projects in housing construction; see Sven Bertelsen, *Bellahøj: Ballerup: Brøndby Strand: 25 år der industrialiserede byggeriet* (Hørsholm: Statens Byggeforskningsinstitut, 1997), 36. In 1953 the Ministry of Housing published an act on state loans for nontraditional construction; see Bertelsen, *Bellahøj: Ballerup: Brøndby Strand*, 30–31). With the pamphlet "Modulordningen" (The Module Arrangement) from The Danish Association of Engineers, a standard for modular rules was introduced in construction in 1956 to pave the way for rational series production; see Frost, "Boligmassen og bygningskulturen." With Landsbyggeloven (The National Construction Act) in 1960, modular design became a prerequisite for all residential construction for rent; see Bertelsen, *Bellahøj: Ballerup: Brøndby Strand*, 60–63. With Montagecirkulæret (The Assembly Construction Act) in the same year, it also became a prerequisite for all financially supported housing construction; see Bertelsen, *Bellahøj: Ballerup: Brøndby Strand*, 60–64).
16 In the earlier concrete buildings, the load-bearing walls were commonly cast on-site, whereas story decks, non-load-bearing partitions and facades were made in an assembly fashion. See Poul Erik Skriver, *Byerne langs Køge Bugt* (Copenhagen: Dansk Byplanlaboratorium, 1984); and Bertelsen, *Bellahøj: Ballerup: Brøndby Strand*, 41–43.
17 Ellen Braae, "Velfærdslandskaber og fællesskaber," in *Forming Welfare*, ed. Jannie Rosenberg Bendsen et al. (Copenhagen: Danish Architectural Press, 2017), 54.
18 Arne Høi and Troels Østergaard, "Bevaringsværdier," in *1940'erne og 1950'ernes murede boligbebyggelser: Renoveringsguide. Kvaliteter, udfordringer og anbefalinger*, ed. Dansk Bygningsarv (Copenhagen: Realdania, Landsbyggefonden, Grundejernes Investeringsfond and Kulturstyrelsen, 2015), 48.
19 FSB, *Velkommen til Tingbjerg!* (Copenhagen: Foreningen Socialt Boligbyggeri, 1957), 4. All translations from the Danish by the author.
20 Kristensen, *DAB – 75 år med almene boliger*, 26.
21 For instance, the number of divorces grew, and young people did not necessarily stay with their parents until they were married.
22 Anne Tietjen, *Forstadens bygningskultur 1945–1989: På sporet af velfærdsforstadens bevaringværdier* (Copenhagen: Dansk Bygningsarv, 2010), 24–25.
23 Frost, "Boligmassen og bygningskulturen," 23.
24 In the same year, for the first time, a (almost) nationwide construction law, Landsbyggeloven (The National Construction Act) was passed in Denmark, which was to support increased standardization. Thus, the nationwide construction law paved the way for the industrialization of construction, as it could be difficult to work with standardized construction across parishes, each with its own building regulations. However, the National Construction Act did not initially apply to the whole country, as Frederiksberg first joined in 1972 and the City of Copenhagen joined in 1977; see Bertelsen, *Bellahøj: Ballerup: Brøndby Strand*, 55.
25 Bertelsen, *Bellahøj: Ballerup: Brøndby Strand*, 60–61.
26 Tietjen, *Forstadens bygningskultur 1945–1989*, 37, 41.
27 Bech-Danielsen, *Moderne arkitektur – hva er meningen?*, 76–78.
28 This was for instance done in *The Athens Charter* §16 (original published as *La Charte d'Athènes*), developed at the 4th CIAM conference in 1933 and published in 1943.
29 Claus Bech-Danielsen and Gunvor Christensen, *Boligområder i bevægelse: Fortællinger om fysiske og boligsociale indsatser* (Copenhagen: Landsbyggefonden, 2017), 20.
30 Claus Bech-Danielsen and Marie Stender, *Fra ghetto til blandet by* (Copenhagen: Gads Forlag, 2017), 14–21.
31 Bech-Danielsen and Christensen, *Boligområder i bevægelse*, 20–23.
32 Tietjen, *Forstadens bygningskultur 1945–1989*, 44–45.
33 Cecilie Dohlmann Weatherall, Bence Boje-Kovacs and Aske Egsgaard-Pedersen, *Et historisk tilbageblik på de særligt udsatte boligområder udpeget i 2014 Udviklingen i tilflyttere, fraflyttere og fastboende* (Copenhagen: Kraks Byforskning, 2016), 12–25.
34 Weatherall, Boje-Kovacs and Egsgaard-Pederson, *Et historisk tilbageblik*, 16–25.
35 In some of the housing areas larger transformations and refurbishments are already far advanced, yet in others only the initial planning is done.
36 Jane Jacobs launched the concept "eyes on the street" and discussed it in her famous book *The Death and Life of Great American Cities* (New York: Random House, 1993 [1961]).
37 The term describes noisy groups of children and young people not following the code of good behavior of the elderly population.
38 This has been evident in a current research at Aalborg University in a research project titled: Regeneration of Danish Disadvantaged Neighborhoods: Long-term Evaluation, 2019–29.
39 Bech-Danielsen and Stender, *Fra ghetto til blandet by*, 21–22.
40 Claus Bech-Danielsen, Mette Mechlenborg and Marie Stender, *Vollsmose: Arbejdsrapport – baselineundersøgelse 2019-SBI; Nr. 2020:07* (Copenhagen, Aalborg University BUILD, 2020), 47–48.

New Housing Economics

Silje Erøy Sollien

1 Hogslätts Vänboende, Gerlesborg, Sweden. Photo by Per Pixel Petterson.

Housing today is, to a large extent, considered first a financial product and then a place to dwell for human life. Housing and real estate is the world's preeminent asset class, with urban housing considered one of the safest investments possible. This is the case both for the middle classes and for billionaire-owned investment funds.[1] One of the characteristics of financially designed products is that they lead to streamlining, standard solutions and monoculture, as we see in the (urban) housing markets today. Privileged locational spaces concentrate a certain type of housing product and a certain type of socioeconomically profiled customer, resulting in both social and architectural monoculture.

This chapter points to aspects of housing development, which ten years ago could have been considered beyond architecture to deal with and of the same nature as a "natural disaster" which we cannot control and what Marie Stender calls "unintended design."[2] However, as the housing affordability crisis has been spreading in European cities and driving increasing inequality, the role of land, money creation and finance in relation to housing is receiving more attention as part of the architectural creative and political agenda.[3] Housing welfare is here considered on the one hand as part of the "right to the city" movement inspired by (among others) David Harvey, where groups marginalized on the standard housing markets are literally carving out spaces in the city through new collectives, alliances and democratic engagement, securing land and financing for housing. On the other hand, there is an agenda of adapting housing forms and qualities of housing for the different needs of diverse types of real families and individuals, ignored by the standard real estate agents' spreadsheet families.[4] Alternative development models may be used to develop projects focusing on these qualities and show innovative ways of approaching more individualized housing needs.

In this chapter I link these housing movements to new forms of economic value and present a brief introduction to how some alternative housing development models relate to land, financing, management and standardization mechanisms in the building industry. I thus draw on the work of economists, architects, urbanists and other social scientists. It may be seen as a form of agenda for further research into aspects of housing welfare, focusing on architecture's and urbanism's providing alternatives to an increasing housing monoculture and thus pointing toward more robust mixes of housing forms and social diversity.

A New Economics

Principles of a new economics and a new housing economics have been emanating to the surface over the last decade or more. This directly relates to the economic concept of the welfare state in terms of evaluating what definitions of value should determine economic redistribution. Calls for new ways of measuring economic wealth, moving towards an economics of distribution and regeneration, of biophysical and social measures, instead of GDP and monetary measures, is no longer fringe leftist critique.[5] For example environmental economist Inge Røpke recently wrote an article outlining how to redesign "Econs 101," the introductory university economics course, to focus on biophysical and social measures.[6] Economics of care offer a feminist critique of neoclassical economics, and various degrowth parameters for a different way of seeing economic value are currently being discussed.[7] Several observers have elaborated how in the 1980s the Chicago School of Economics redesigned a new political economy favoring corporate capitalism, which now is out of date.[8] We are currently at a point where economics is being reconceptualized again, in order to account for the real world of limited resources and increasing social inequality.

The role of housing and land in the reversal of the relative success of the redistributive welfare states is very important and has until recently been underplayed in economic theory and policy. Thomas Piketty's seminal work on inequality due to capital gains' overtaking wages as a share of the economy didn't put a particularly explicit emphasis on housing.[9] This has been updated by the work of Josh Ryan-Collins and others, showing how the financialization of land and housing plays a big part in this transfer of wealth returns from wages to capital.[10] The continued widening of house prices to income ratio is creating rapidly increasing differences in income between owners and renters on the housing market in big cities, including Copenhagen. At the same time, the difference between urban and rural housing markets ensures that if you leave the city, it is difficult to reverse the decision again, due to the difference in capital gains in the two markets.

2 Genossenschaft Kalkbreite, Zürich, Switzerland.

There are increasingly calls for "alternative housing" projects to find new ways of doing housing to counter these trends of increasing inequality and financially motivated monoculture. Beyond the big issue of affordable housing in general, part of the debate is concerned with designing the type of housing people really need today and which is not met by the ordinary housing market.[11] This may regard changing family structures and needs for more sharing and community in housing, other forms of architectural and urban quality or minimization of natural resource use. It may regard the inclusion of vulnerable groups on the housing market, a concern with social mix in general or democracy and user involvement in the design and development. All these issues may not necessarily be addressed in the same way, but they may all be part of the complex web of solutions forming an emerging housing economics that is more welfare-oriented.

Following are some European examples of ways to target parts of the value chain in the provisioning of housing and to open up spaces for humans making decisions rather than mainly spreadsheets calculating profits. The examples generally focus on a form of collaborative approach to new housing solutions, also called hybrid forms, that emphasize co-creation between different actors such as citizens, municipalities and commercial entities instead of following older divisions into municipal, private and commercial housing provision.[12]

3 Genossenschaft Kalkbreite, Zürich, Switzerland.

Land

The main variable in the equation of exponentially rising property prices is land. Access to land is often the biggest issue for realizing community-driven housing projects, at least in big cities. Different countries and cultures have different urban land tenure systems, including nationalized or municipal land where you mainly sell long-term leasehold rights but not freehold ownership of the land. In Switzerland, cooperative housing projects are often built on land leased from the city for a sixty-year leasehold, as in the case of the highly publicized flagship project Kalkbreite, which opened at a central location in 2014. Kalkbreite shows how to build a modern cooperative in the middle of the city with no car ownership, an almost extreme variety of apartment types supported by a good number of flexible use rooms, community services and commercial space.

What we see in some of the places most severely affected by housing unaffordability and some areas needing upgrading and revitalization are new forms of community land trusts (CLTs) with new legislation supporting these. A CLT is generally a grassroots initiative and is governed in collaboration between local residents, other stakeholders and the municipality in order to develop long-term affordable housing. In Switzerland and Germany, we see Stiftungen (Foundations) buying up land in order to remove it from speculation and offer leaseholds for long-term affordable housing developments or experiments in radical sustainability or new types of apartment configurations.

When municipalities control the allocation of land and are not counting on land sales for maximum profit, they can be more concerned with long-term values in the urban development than short-term monetary ones. The sale of smaller plots of land at fixed prices specifically to small private cooperatives, where competition for the plot is based on quality criteria instead of price competition, is a strategy adopted in some German cities focusing on ordinary citizens' taking charge in developing their own housing. Tübingen pioneered the model in the 1990s, while Hamburg today has a strategy of 20 percent small private cooperatives in new development areas. This allows the municipality to be strategic in selecting projects that offer types of apartments the large commercial developers don't offer and to focus on groups with strong local ties and initiatives that involve the neighborhood in general. In order to ensure long-term affordability, profit on onward sales of the property must be restricted. German law only allows a ten-year index-regulated cap on profit from onward sales. This has in fact led to Tübingen's experiencing the same affordability problem as elsewhere today. The cooperative neighborhoods may have achieved an exceptional long-term urban quality, but they are today also becoming unaffordable. As we see in the next section, this has, however, also led to a culture of very innovative solutions for affordable housing where citizens themselves literally own the development process as codevelopers together with the municipality and private companies.[13]

La Borda cooperative housing in Barcelona has been a pioneer in Catalunya, achieving a building site after a long activist fight for new community-driven housing in the city. However, in return for receiving privileged access to the central brownfield site, the cooperative has accepted adhering to the local social housing regulations. This means that the original members of the cooperative had to leave the project, as their incomes were too high to live in Catalan social housing.

4 Byfællesskabet Thomas B., Odense, Denmark.

5 Byfællesskabet Thomas B., Odense, Denmark.

Today in Denmark, there is legal warrant for reserving land for nonprofit housing associations only in new development plans. There is a lot of potential for fresh collaborations involving nonprofit housing associations, as they have some access to land and an interest in developing innovative ways of housing. This we already have seen since the introduction of Almen+ in the first decade of the twenty-first century and new forms of coliving and cohousing.[14] For other types of smaller and alternative organizations, access to building land in the capital are currently bleak, as public land has been pledged for maximum-profit sales in order to finance infrastructure for the foreseeable future.[15] Outside the big cities, however, cohousing projects are often good business, whether grassroots-driven or not, at times achieving up to 30 percent higher prices than standard housing. This is attracting a different type of resident, and that way may in some contexts potentially create a form of positive gentrification and a new social mix.

Financing

The second most important hurdle challenging alternative housing projects is financing, as banks generally want to lend to organizations which already have money and to organizations with a legal set-up they can tick off in existing spreadsheets. In Germany today, where private building cooperatives are a well-known housing development form, banks see it as a nonspeculative and less risky form of loan, because people have invested their own private savings in homes for themselves.

In Denmark today – after five years of a great resurgence of interest in cohousing developments, a private cooperative with all apartments reserved, an attractive building site as collateral, a professional and trustworthy organization and an architectural project, plus 20 percent equity, should also be able to find a bank financing partner. Byfællesskabet in Odense found a bank that accepted the shared solution of ca. 20 percent equity and a very attractive plot as collateral. The nine families formed a limited company in order to fit better into the spreadsheet boxes of the bank.[16]

What we see in some of the most innovative and socially inclusive alternative housing projects from Germany, but also with examples from Sweden, Spain and elsewhere, are forms of crowdfunding where the community surrounding the project contributes to the housing project, as it clearly has a societal welfare value beyond finding housing for the specific housing project members. For the small but quite remarkable grassroots project Hogslätts Vänboende in Bohuslän in Sweden, neighbors helped secure the money for buying the building plot, the municipality changed their policy for social housing loan guarantees and the local entrepreneur himself lent the all-female cooperative DKK 1 million in order to secure the loan from the local bank. The fact that the construction project came home DKK 3 million less than budgeted makes it even more remarkable. This was probably due to the mostly sixty-year-old+ cooperative members helping on the building site and a building process of complete trust and openness.

The Mietshäuser Syndikat, operating in Germany, originated out of Freiburg at about the same time as the system of small private cooperatives. The syndicate is established in order to take housing properties off the speculative market, and its structure ensures that the sale of the property will always be vetoed by the syndicate as coowner, in order to ensure long-term affordability and self-management by the tenants' association. The housing projects depend on direct private loans from friends and community to meet the equity required by the banks for a housing project. In return the projects show a remarkably social and inclusive makeup, often also incorporating community spaces that invite the public in. The syndicate contributes with small financial subsidies and resources in the form of know-how for new members. The legal form of the syndicate is interestingly a limited company (GmbH), supporting a highly social and at times quite left-wing activist organization.[17]

What we saw in Tübingen in 2015 when more than a million refugees were coming to Europe from Syria and elsewhere was that the city got together and collectively crowdfunded new-build housing for their new citizens, called Neue Nachbar*innen KG. The community formed a Kommanditgesellschaft (limited partnership), where more than 100 citizens bought shares of a minimum € 2,500 up to a maximum 5 percent of the equity of the project, so that nobody could dominate the project. The Bürger*innen-Wohnbau-Gesellschaft ("citizen-housing-company") is thus owned by the citizens, who rent it to the municipality to manage as refugee housing with a couple of cohousing apartments for nonrefugees.

La Borda used two crowdfunding platforms and a bank for finance – in the end involving an extremely large number of what they call "participatory funding" opportunities for the project with a high political and architectural profile. From Sweden there is an example of a commercial news corporation which decided to crowdfund more environmentally sustainable building with a large online crowdfunding platform for ordinary people to save up with a fixed interest rate in ETC Bygg shares. Collective financing can take on many forms and involve very different types of actors.

Construction

The contracting forms and industry standards in the building industry are part of the system favoring established actors and design solutions. This also needs to be challenged when developing a new welfare-based housing economics of difference and regeneration. What we saw in the Danish pioneer project Fællesbyg, a private building cooperative inspired by the Tübingen model, was that when alternative guarantees for the financing finally were secured, there were a lot of challenges in the way the project was translated by the contractor into a building. New risk premiums on the wooden building system outlined in the early proposals and forming the base for the original price estimate made wood too expensive after all. The standard process of the contractor filling in the blanks in the project and making everything else into "extras," as is the

6 Fællesbyg Køge Kyst, Køge, Denmark.

case with turnkey contracting without much involvement of the cooperative, made one future resident describe it as feeling like "we were caught in a net."[18]

As already mentioned, projects in cities with a significant proportion of developments with small private cooperatives exist as a form of structured coproduction between municipality, private cooperative and professional building sector actors. Process leadership roles, efficient communication and milestone checks are central. A good, efficient and transparent process, in which large price and time deviations are avoided, is central to a project where ordinary people and their life savings are the main ingredients. This is especially important when innovative building systems are used and ambitions for radically reduced climate footprints are part of the values motivating a building cooperative, as there are numerous examples of.

An important element here is the economics of trust, which is important in order to support an economics of social and environmental qualities. Experienced developer Anette Krarup argues that the savings that can accrue from a process ran by trust, good leadership and generosity can save DKK 1,500 per square meter.[19] The building industry is to a large extent based on the legal avoidance of responsibility and the avoidance of risk instead of trust and collaboration, which can turn out expensive for everyone except the lawyers involved. Högslätts Vänboende mentioned above came in under budget due to a process of complete trust and openness. The cooperative also saved a lot compared to the estimated work hours due to help from the generally 60+ all female cooperative members in unskilled work like painting cladding boards, cleaning and bringing waste to the recycling station.

The economics of trust can be seen in all forms of development processes in the building industry, not just cooperatives. One large pension fund that Vandkunsten Architects is working with to develop senior cohousing projects states that in the projects where the future residents are highly involved from the start, apartments are much easier to rent out. This is also a form of economics of trust, where a sense of ownership capital is being created, even if technically the projects are private rental housing with no particular collaborative tenure or even management elements.

Management

The last phase in taking control of housing welfare economics occurs when the building is finished and the inhabitants have moved in. This may be a continuation of a collaborative project, which started with the end aim being an alternative way of living together and sharing everyday spaces, meals, maintenance and household decisions. This is, however, not necessarily always the case. Many of the building cooperatives in German-speaking countries are cooperatives only in the building phase and don't put so much emphasis on shared dinners and other activities common in the Danish cohousing model developed in the 1970s and '80s.

Some of the new cohousing projects only start as the building is finished, as it has been developed by an actor not necessarily knowing the future residents during the construction phase. If highly motivated residents move in, it is still possible to create a cohousing project with a lot of social support and sharing even if the residents didn't "own" the development process, either figuratively or legally. There is also an interesting example at Vandkunsten, where the process with a developer was so frustrating for the future inhabitants that they formed their own association uniting against the developer in order to protect their housing project with their own lawyer, in the end developing a highly engaged and united group with their own innovative democratic procedures. There are some new housing models, like Almen+ in the Danish nonprofit housing sector, where part of an equation producing more affordable rent is that the maintenance of the buildings is managed by the residents themselves. This is also causing new forms of community, as people work together to solve necessary practical challenges independently from the housing association.

The tenure form will influence to what extent the inhabitants actually make decisions influencing the future of the housing economy in terms of financial decisions related to the property. Whether a sharing economy is sharing economic decision-making or just sharing space may be important. When sharing space is coupled with economic decision-making power, there may on the one hand be a potential for more radical solutions. But at the same time there is the risk that in a highly financialized context with rising land values, too much control to determine the price setting for cooperative shares may tempt most cooperatives to win the potential profits for the group instead of making affordable entry to cooperative housing in the future a priority.[20] The insiders want to be able to share in the incredible rises in urban land prices instead of taking part in a fight against those same rising property prices to keep entry thresholds low. In the Mietshäuser Syndikat we see an outside element hinder speculative sales to avoid this. This very clearly illustrates how a cooperative housing project in some contexts can be termed democratic if a group of owner-residents in the intermediate term can decide what happens with the increased land value, according to some measures. On the other hand, in order to promote more socially inclusive housing projects in the future, the price on the shares could be kept low, which may be termed more democratic in other contexts, focusing also on the wider community outside the cooperative residents.

A New Housing Economics of Difference and Democracy

This chapter has presented some very concrete examples of ways to insert more inclusive and inhabitant-driven decision-making and collaborative processes in housing development projects. These are ways of taking control of the economics of the project and opening up ways of inserting a more diverse architecture of difference, trust and social mix. We call this a new housing economics, focusing on social measures and community instead of profit and speculation. The big focus is to shift from exchange value to use value or from housing as a financial product to a dwelling space with architectural and social qualities, focusing on welfare in a broader sense.

The complexity of the building industry calls for much longer analysis and far-reaching new research, as in fact much of the inertia in the housing market lies with the organization of the building industry and the very large amounts of money involved when mistakes happen. There is a need to develop new partnerships in order to regenerate the housing industry with more welfare for everyone, measured both in more equitable distribution of resources and a more democratic way of designing and developing housing for varied needs. Opening up more areas of collaborative development and true housing commons may be a fundamental part of this way toward more housing welfare, both in terms of redistribution of housing wealth, different measures for housing quality and a more diverse and inclusive city.

The chapter is based on research from the industrial postdoctoral project *Diversify Now!*, a collaboration between Vandkunsten Architects and Aalborg University.

Bibliography

Bech-Danielsen, Claus, Søren Nielsen and Silje Erøy Sollien. "Fleksibilitet, fællesskab og social bæredygtighed: Inspirationskatalog med 20 boliger fra udlandet og 15 fra Danmark." Working paper. Copenhagen: Realdania, December 2018.

Bortel, Gerard van, ed. *Affordable Housing, Governance and Finance: Innovations, Partnerships and Comparative Perspectives*. Abingdon: Routledge, 2019.

Czischke, Darinka. "Collaborative Housing and Housing Providers: Towards an Analytical Framework of Multi-Stakeholder Collaboration in Housing Co-Production." *International Journal of Housing Policy* 18, no. 1 (January 2018): 55–81.

D'Alisa, Giacomo, Federico Demaria and Giorgos Kallis, eds. *Degrowth: A Vocabulary for a New Era*. Abingdon: Routledge, 2014.

Dasgupta, Partha. *The Economics of Biodiversity: The Dasgupta Review*, London: HM Treasury, 2021.

Frank Hansen, Marianne, and Danish Research Institute for Economic Analysis and Modelling. *Demografi, socioøkonomi og boligstruktur i danske kommuner: En fremskrivning med mikrosimulationsmodellen SMILE på et opdateret datagrundlag*. Copenhagen: DREAM; in cooperation with the Boligøkonomisk Videncenter, 2021.

Id22, Michael La Fond and Larisa Tsvetkova, eds. *Co-Housing Inclusive: Self-organized, Community-led Housing for All*. Berlin: Jovis, 2017.

KAB. "AlmenBolig+" Accessed January 28, 2022. https://www.kab-bolig.dk/boligsoegende/boligformer/almenbolig.

Mazzucato, Mariana. *The Value of Everything: Making and Taking in the Global Economy*. London: Penguin Books, 2019.

Mietshäuser Syndikat. "Der Projektverbund." Accessed January 28, 2022. https://www.syndikat.org/de/.

Neue Nachbar Tübingen. Accessed January 28, 2022. https://www.neue-nachbarn-tuebingen.de/.

Piketty, Thomas. *Capital in the Twenty-First Century*. Cambridge, MA: Harvard University Press, 2014.

Raworth, Kate. "A Safe and Just Space for Humanity: Can We Live Within the Doughnut?" Oxfam Discussion Papers. Oxford: Oxfam, February 2012. https://oxfamilibrary.openrepository.com/bitstream/handle/10546/210490/dp-a-safe-and-just-space-for-humanity-130212-en.pdf;jsessionid=93BAB9CCE5403B39EE2B756346346E24?sequence=13.

——. *Doughnut Economics: Seven Ways to Think like a 21st-Century Economist*. London: Random House Business Books, 2017.

Ryan-Collins, Josh. *Why Can't You Afford a Home? The Future of Capitalism.* Medford, MA: Polity Press, 2019.

Ryan-Collins, Josh, Toby Lloyd, Laurie Macfarlane and John Muellbauer. *Rethinking the Economics of Land and Housing*. London: Zed, 2017.

Røpke, Inge. "Econ 101 – In Need of a Sustainability Transition." *Ecological Economics* 169 (March 2020): 106515.

Simpson, Deane, "Copenhagen under the Metric Regimes of the Competitive and Attractive City." In *Atlas of the Copenhagens*, edited by Deane Simpson, Kathrin Gimmel, Anders Lonka, Marc Jay and Joost Grootens, 17–53 Berlin: Ruby Press, 2018.

Söhlke, Cord. "Small-Scaled, Urban, Diverse: The Tübingen Development Strategy." Accessed January 28, 2022, https://www.byplanlab.dk/sites/default/files/4%20Short%20Cord%20version%20for%2004.10.19.pdf?0.7747483201438867.

Sollien, Silje Erøy. "Byggefællesskaber: Grundlag for udvikling af en dansk model." Working paper. DiversifyNow! Copenhagen: Tegnestuen Vandkunsten, May 2020. https://vandkunsten.com/content//2020/06/Vandkunsten-Byggefaellesskaber-Arbejdspapir-spreads.pdf.

——. "Some people play football. We developed a house." In *The Welfare City in Transition: A Compilation of Texts and Images 1923–2020*, edited by Pernille Maria Bärnheim, Signe Sophie Bøggild and Kristoffer Lindhardt Weiss, 148–50. Copenhagen: Danish Architectural Press, 2020.

Sollien, Silje Erøy, and Søren Nielsen. "Constructing Community? A Collaborative Housing Development Process Meeting Credit and Concrete." In *Architectural Anthropology: Exploring Lived Space*, edited by Marie Stender, Claus Bech-Danielsen and Aina Landsverk Hagen, 224–36. London: Routledge, 2021.

Stender, Marie. "Man-Made Mountains and Other Traces of a Fluctuating Market: An Anthropological View on Unintended Design." *Ardeth* 2 (Spring 2018): 76–95.

Sørvoll, Jardar, and Bo Bengtsson. "Mechanisms of Solidarity in Collaborative Housing: The Case of Co-Operative Housing in Denmark 1980–2017." *Housing, Theory and Society* 37, no. 1 (2020): 65–81.

Thörn, Hakan, Henrik Gutzon Larsen, Pernilla Hagbert and Cathrin Wasshede, eds. *Contemporary Co-Housing: Towards Sustainable Cities?* London: Routledge, 2019.

Notes

1 Some types of investors, like pension funds, often balance a requirement for regular returns with other values.

2 See Marie Stender, "Man-Made Mountains and Other Traces of a Fluctuating Market: An Anthropological View on Unintended Design," *Ardeth* 2 (Spring 2018): 76–95.

3 See, for example, Hakan Thörn, Henrik Gutzon Larsen, Pernilla Hagbert and Cathrin Wasshede, eds., *Contemporary Co-Housing: Towards Sustainable Cities?* (London: Routledge, 2019).

4 See, for example, Id22, Michael La Fond and Larisa Tsvetkova, eds., *Co-Housing Inclusive: Self-organized, Community-led Housing for All* (Berlin: Jovis, 2017).

5 See Partha Dasgupta, *The Economics of Biodiversity: The Dasgupta Review*, published by the British Government in February 2021. "Doughnut economics" have been adopted by some cities to govern policy.

6 See Inge Røpke, "Econ 101 – In Need of a Sustainability Transition," *Ecological Economics* 169 (March 2020): 106515.

7 Giacomo D'Alisa, Federico Demaria and Giorgos Kallis, eds., *Degrowth: A Vocabulary for a New Era* (Abingdon: Routledge, 2014) offers an overview of many of these movements and the terminology used.

8 See Mariana Mazzucato, *The Value of Everything: Making and Taking in the Global Economy* (London: Penguin Books, 2019).

9 See Thomas Piketty, *Capital in the Twenty-First Century* (Cambridge, MA: Harvard University Press, 2014).

10 See John Ryan-Collins, Toby Lloyd, Laurie Macfarlane and John Muellbauer, *Rethinking the Economics of Land and Housing* (London: Zed, 2017).

11 See, for example, Marianne Frank Hansen and the Danish Research Institute for Economic Analysis and Modelling, *Demografi, socioøkonomi og boligstruktur i danske kommuner: En fremskrivning med mikrosimulationsmodellen SMILE på et opdateret datagrundlag* (Copenhagen: DREAM; in cooperation with the Boligøkonomisk Videncenter, 2021); and Claus Bech-Danielsen, Søren Nielsen and Silje Erøy Sollien, "Fleksibilitet, fællesskab og social bæredygtighed: Inspirationskatalog med 20 boliger fra udlandet og 15 fra Danmark," working paper (Copenhagen: Realdania, December 2018).

12 See, for example, Darinka Czischke, "Collaborative Housing and Housing Providers: Towards an Analytical Framework of Multi-Stakeholder Collaboration in Housing Co-Production," *International Journal of Housing Policy* 18, no. 1 (January 2018): 55–81; and Gerard van Bortel, ed., *Affordable Housing, Governance and Finance: Innovations, Partnerships and Comparative Perspectives* (Abingdon: Routledge, 2019).

13 See the presentation of the Tübingen model by mayor Cord Söhlke and the website of integration project Neue Nachbarn KG: Cord Söhlke, "Small-Scaled, Urban, Diverse: The Tübingen Development Strategy," accessed January 28, 2022, https://www.byplanlab.dk/sites/default/files/4%20Short%20Cord%20version%20for%2004.10.19.pdf?0.7747483201438867; Neue Nachbar KG, accessed January 28, 2022, https://www.neue-nachbarn-tuebingen.de/.

14 See "AlmenBolig+," KAB, accessed January 28, 2022, https://www.kab-bolig.dk/boligsoegende/boligformer/almenbolig.

15 This is especially critical in Copenhagen, where the profits from sales of municipal- and state-owned land is pledged to finance the building of the new Metro and sold by a company established especially for this purpose only. Discussed in Deane Simpson, "Copenhagen under the Metric Regimes of the Competitive and Attractive City," in *Atlas of the Copenhagens*, ed. Deane Simpson, Kathrin Gimmel, Anders Lonka, Marc Jay and Joost Grootens (Berlin: Ruby Press, 2018), 17–53.

16 See Silje Erøy Sollien, "Byggefællesskaber: Grundlag for udvikling af en dansk model," working paper, DiversifyNow! (Copenhagen: Tegnestuen Vandkunsten, May 2020), https://vandkunsten.com/content//2020/06/Vandkunsten-Byggefaellesskaber-Arbejdspapir-spreads.pdf.

17 See "Der Projektverbund," Mietshäuser Syndikat, accessed January 28, 2022, https://www.syndikat.org/de/.

18 Silje Erøy Sollien and Søren Nielsen, "Constructing Community? A Collaborative Housing Development Process Meeting Credit and Concrete," in *Architectural Anthropology: Exploring Lived Space*, ed. Marie Stender, Claus Bech-Danielsen and Aina Landsverk Hagen (London: Routledge, 2021), 224–36.

19 Interview with author, November 6, 2020.

20 See Jardar Sørvoll and Bo Bengtsson, "Mechanisms of Solidarity in Collaborative Housing: The Case of Co-Operative Housing in Denmark 1980–2017," *Housing, Theory and Society* 37, no. 1 (2020): 65–81.

On the Battle for Amager Common

A Power Play of Housing Politics in Copenhagen

Jesper Pagh

In early spring of 2021 protesters chained themselves to the fence around a construction site on Amager Fælled (Amager Common) in Copenhagen, blocking access to the site for the landowner, the publicly owned partnership By & Havn (Copenhagen City and Port Development) and its contractors. To some they were Green fanatics infringing on property rights and opposing the efforts of creating affordable housing in Copenhagen; to others, righteous rebels on behalf of nature and future generations. Eventually the police removed the protesters. The conflict and arguments from both sides have been heavily covered in the press, but how did it ever get this far?[1]

For decades, urban development in Copenhagen was a rather dry and apparently highly successful undertaking with very little public attention and next to no protests in the public realm over either specific projects or overall strategies. A shift in planning politics from the postwar paradigm of predict-and-provide into long-term strategic planning has been key in the city's resurrection from postindustrial decline in the 1970s and '80s to an acclaimed position as one of the world's most livable cities in the 2010s. Simultaneously, this has meant a significant shift in relations and interactions between stakeholders and actors in the field of urban planning and development.[2] As this chapter points out, this change in relations and interactions has in turn led to a change in the structuring or emergence of welfare spaces as they are construed and constructed.

Methodological Approach

The chapter is based on a comprehensive study of contemporary urban politics and planning in Copenhagen. The case opens in mid-September 2017 and moves in two directions: One is to follow events as they take place, another is to study the *longue durée* and *conjuncture* of events that went before to create a fruitful discussion of what this is a case of.[3]

I am interested in the relation between the formal, the real (or the actual) and the realized planning. The formal planning I understand as that which is described in the bureaucracy of the planning system and in the body of planning legislation, which can be studied as law and public administration.[4] In the realm of the realized planning, we find the material and spatial structures of architecture and infrastructure, which again can be studied, analyzed and understood in so many ways.[5] Somehow connecting these two perhaps most concrete aspects of planning, the real or actual planning takes place as a professional activity from knowledge to action.[6] For Bent Flyvbjerg, these three realms of planning – the formal, the actual and the realized – can also be understood as relating primarily to each of Aristotle's three intellectual virtues: *episteme* (concerning theoretical know-why – the formal planning), *techne* (denoting technical know-how – the realized planning) and *phronesis* (emphasizing practical knowledge and practical ethics – the actual planning).[7]

The Structure

In this chapter the main focus is on the latter – the real or actual aspects of planning. I am interested in what happens, why it happened, and the consequences of what happens – addressing what Flyvbjerg has called four "value-rational questions" at the core of *phronesis*.[8]

1 Where are we going with planning?
2 Who gains and who loses, and by which mechanisms of power?
3 Is this development desirable?
4 What, if anything, should we do about it?

These four questions inform the structure of my analysis. Before this – as the empirical starting point – I describe some of the context around the plans to build on Amager Fælled, which eventually led to the blockade in 2021.

Saying No to Green Narrow-Mindedness

Early in the morning on Sunday September 17, 2017, the Lord Mayor of Copenhagen, Frank Jensen – of Socialdemokratiet (The Social Democratic Party) – spoke at his party's annual congress in his native town of Aalborg. Back home in Copenhagen in Borgerrepræsentationen (City Council), he was under pressure by The Green Wing, a coalition between Enhedslisten (The Red-Green Alliance), Radikale Venstre (The Danish Social-Liberal Party) and Socialistisk Folkeparti (The Socialist People's Party). They had joined forces with the newly formed self-declared Green party and movement of Denmark, Alternativet (The Alternative), not yet represented on the Borgerrepræsentationen, demanding a full stop for By & Havn's plans to develop 260,000 square meters of housing on Amager Fælled – the so-called Ørestad Fælled Kvarter (Ørestad Common District).

Since 1995 the area had been planned as the last stage of the new town Ørestad, and the realization of the development rights on the lot were factored in as a part of the financing of the Copenhagen Metro.[9]

1 Then Lord Mayor of the City of Copenhagen, Frank Jensen speaking at the Socialdemokratiet (The Social Democratic Party)'s annual congress in Aalborg on Sunday September 17, 2017.

The Green wing received popular support for their cause, which they had been promoting through the NGO Amager Fælleds Venner (Friends of Amager Common) since the spring of 2016, when the winning proposal for Ørestad Fælled Kvarter, designed on the principles of Nature-based Solutions (NBS) by a team led by the architectural office Vandkunsten was announced.[10] The project was planned to be realized as a joint venture between By & Havn and PensionDanmark, the largest noncommercial pension fund in Denmark administering pensions for more than 750,000 people primarily employed as skilled and unskilled workers within most industries.

2 Illustration from the winning proposal for Ørestad Fælled Kvarter, designed by Vandkunsten on the principles of Nature-based Solutions (NBS).

The weekend before the Socialdemokratiet's annual congress, thousands of citizens had gathered on the then future construction site on the occasion of Naturens Dag (Nature's Day) – an annual event arranged by the Danmarks Naturfredningsforening (Danish Society for Nature Conservation) – to express their dissatisfaction with the plans. The celebrity chef Nikolaj Kirk, who has his own weekly show on national television, addressed the protesters; Anne Dorte Michelsen sang with a reunited version of her 1980s pop band Tøsedrengene (literally: The Sissies); while the reality star Linse

3 The celebrity chef Nikolaj Kirk at Naturens Dag (Nature's Day) on Amager Fælled, Sunday September 10, 2017.

4 Reality star Linse Kessler (left) dancing at Naturens Dag (Nature's Day) on Amager Fælled, Sunday September 10, 2017.

Kessler danced to the beat – everything thoroughly documented by the daily press.[11]

In Borgerrepræsentationen, however, Frank Jensen's Socialdemokratiet – which has held the Lord Mayor's office since 1904 – with the right-wing parties maintained the majority to carry on with the plans; thus, at the congress Jensen told his fellow party members:

> We must say no to the Green narrow-mindedness and stand by our sustainable, green-and-red vision for town and country; people and nature. Lately there has been a lot of talk about threatened species in my city. Let me say it loud and clear: The species I fear for the most in my city; the species I reckon to be threatened most of all – threatened by the right-wing's belief in the market and the left-wing's brick allergy – is the common working-class family with two or three children, who just wants an attractive, affordable apartment.[12]

The threatened species the Lord Mayor was referring to (apart from the working-class families), were plants growing and smaller animals living in the area zoned for urban development as Ørestad Fælled Kvarter. Prominent in the public debate were several sorts of orchids, the northern crested newt and the moor frog, identified by Danmarks Naturfredningsforening as having the site as their habitat. Together with the newly formed Amager Fælleds Venner, Danmarks Naturfredningsforening had dubbed the area *Strandengen* (The Salt Meadow), with reference to its biological characteristics and topographic provenance.

3.19
Amager Common demonstration, 2021

Hence, all three corners of what Scott Campbell describes as the "Planner's Triangle" representing three diverging interests of urban planning and development: "to 'grow' the economy, distribute this growth fairly [equity], and in the process not to degrade the ecosystem [environment]" were put into play. The diverging interests at each corner of the triangle lead to three fundamental conflicts described by Campbell as "The Property Conflict" (economy vs. equity), "The Resource Conflict" (economy vs. environment) and "The Development Conflict" (equity vs. environment). Integrative, sustainable development planning, Campbell says, is reached through the reconciliation of these conflicts.[13]

Listening to the Heavy Criticism

Sunday morning at the Socialdemokratiet's congress, Frank Jensen focused on reconciling the property conflict between equity and economy, stating that the working-class families' desire for an attractive, affordable apartment could be reached by steering clear of "the right-wing's belief in the market and the left-wing's brick allergy" and keeping the project on track. Simultaneously the project would contribute an estimated total of DKK 1.9 billion (approx. € 256 million) to By & Havn.

This did not satisfy the demands for meeting the environmental interests put forward by the Green wing and their allies however, and on Monday Det Konservative Folkeparti (The Conservative People's Party) in Copenhagen announced their support for the idea to look for alternative locations for the 2,500 housing units planned in Ørestad Fælled Kvarter. Now the Lord Mayor suddenly had to add his own majority for the development plans in Borgerrepræsentationen to the list of threatened species in his city. With polls indicating that Socialdemokratiet might lose the Lord Mayor's office after the local election only two months away, Venstre (The Liberal Party) too sensed the dawn of better things and declared their support for the proposal from Det Konservative Folkeparti that the right-wing parties joined the Green wing. Hence, the Lord Mayor was left more or less alone in his support for By & Havn's desire to carry on with the project. With more than twenty-five years of experience at the top tier in politics, the Lord Mayor knew when to fold, and on Wednesday, September 20, he announced his retreat from the plans on national television:

> I too – of course – have listened to the heavy criticism among Copenhageners around the city to build on exactly this lot. [...] Now we don't plan to build where we had planned. Now we plan to build somewhere else.[14]

Planning to Build Somewhere Else

After the decision to cancel the plans to build at Amager Fælled, the Lord Mayor was faced with at least two immediate problems. First, he needed to win the local election in November in order to remain Lord Mayor, which he did. Second, he needed to find somewhere else to build.

Two weeks after the decision not to build on the original site, the Borgerrepræsentationen passed a resolution on October 5, 2017, to screen for alternatives. Based on this initial vetting, the Borgerrepræsentationen resolved at a meeting on May 31, 2018, to further screen a selection of the alternatives presented, including some specifications regarding possible combinations of identified alternatives – and (at least partly) reimbursing By & Havn for the loss they suffered due to the cancellation of the original plans.[15]

This further screening – presented in a thirty-eight-page report with twenty-six appendices (including the confidential appendix 26 – "Assessment of Possible Compensation Claims from By & Havn") – then formed part of the political negotiations over the city's budget for 2019 resolved late in the night between September 6 and 7, 2018. From this followed the agreement that is the foundation for today's developments in four different places in the city.[16] Instead of developing 260,000 square meters of floor space in Ørestad Fælled Kvarter, the alternatives in figure 5 were agreed upon.[17] ⟨fig. 5⟩

A total of 384,500 square meters during the planning process regarding Bådehavnsgade East (later referred to as Stejlepladsen) increased to a total of 392,000 square meters, or 50 percent more than originally planned. Why should 260,000 square meters be replaced with 392,000? Because the assignment was not to replace the number of homes (approx. 2,500) that was planned for Ørestad Fælled Kvarter – nor was it to replace the 260,000 square meters of floor space. Rather it was to reimburse By & Havn for the loss of market value of the original plot (DKK 1.3 billion) and the anticipated profit from the project development (DKK 0.6 billion) – a total of DKK 1.9 billion. Hence, we need to look at the total in the third column of figure 5, showing a total of DKK 1,263 million. To top it up, the City of Copenhagen paid DKK 37 million in cash plus an additional DKK 17 million to compensate for the loss of profit from the project development from these DKK 37 million. From the budget agreement it appears that this total of DKK 54 million in cash money is raised by cutting the annual budget for renovation of courtyards with DKK 13.5 million – from 26.2 to 12.7 million – over a period of four years. Hence, with respect to the budget for the City of Copenhagen, the operation is considered *cost neutral*.

As far as the formal planning requirements go, in the municipal plan at the time, the new development areas were not zoned for development, and thus were not included in the plan for the order of development.[18] Stejlepladsen was actually zoned as an environment fragile to future developments in the area. As a natural consequence of the majority behind the budget, however, this was changed in the following regular revision of the municipal plan, paving the way for the later district plans.[19] Further – like the Camping Site and Selinevej North – Stejlepladsen had a status as a protected nature area. Hence, the Folketinget (The Danish Parliament) had to get involved to lift the protection of the three nature areas by force.

At the time of writing, teams led by CCO Architects and Henning Larsen Architects respectively have won new master plan competitions for Stejlepladsen and Vejlandskvarteret. The results have been used as the outset for district plans passed by the Borgerrepræsentationen on the basis of the revised municipal plan, the lifted nature protection status and a revision of the Act on Ørestad. Protests from local citizens (specifically in the area around Stejlepladsen) and others with an interest in nature conservation have been significant, and as indicated in the introduction has led to physical confrontations between protesters and the police.

Vejlandskvarteret has been renamed Fælledby (Common Town) by By & Havn and Lærkesletten (The Lark Plain) by DN, indicating that the decision to build elsewhere is not exactly fulfilling everybody's idea about planning for a green, growing and just city.

In March 2021 the Danmarks Naturfredningsforening and Amager Fælleds Venner filed a complaint with Planklagenævnet and Miljø- og Fødevareklagenævnet (the appeal boards for planning and environmental issues) arguing that the project did not in a satisfactory manner take into consideration the future conditions for the northern crested newt and should therefore be stopped. In July the appeal board ruled in favor of the organizations and added that development would be stayed until the case had been resolved "by the end of 2021."[20] On December 14, 2021 the appeal boards decided in favour of the Ciy of Copenhagen, overruling the complaints from Danmarks Naturfredningsforening and Amager Fælleds Venner. Hence the project can continue as planned by By & Havn.

Because of something completely different – accusations of repeated instances of sexual harassment – Frank Jensen was forced to leave the Lord Mayor's office on October 19, 2020. With little more than a year to the 2021 election, Socialdemokratiet then had to promote a new candidate for the office: the now former chairman of the Capital Region, Sophie Hæstorp Andersen, who ran in the recent local election. With support from the right-wing parties, she barely kept the office. Disputes over urban development heavily dominated the election, and Socialdemokratiet went from 27.6 percent to 17.2 percent of the vote, losing their position as the largest party in the Borgerrepræsentationen to Enhedslisten (working to stop the project), which went from 18.4 percent to 24.6 percent. The battle for Amager Fælled goes on.

Where Are We Going with Planning?

Instead of abandoning the idea of green-field development altogether and reconsidering the land value capture strategy behind By & Havn as suggested by Danmarks Naturfredningsforening and others, the decision from the Lord Mayor to "plan to build somewhere else" was more one of a strategic pullout to regroup. As soon as the local election was secured, new plans for realizing the originally planned profit were developed. What the focus of the analysis that formed the basis of the decisions specifying how to "plan to build somewhere else" reveals is that the municipal plan for a city like Copenhagen is as much a business plan as anything else. It is the column adding up the land value and expected profit ⟨fig. 5⟩ that is the decisive factor in the political process directly linked to the negotiations over the general budget, not considerations in favor of the environment or social justice. If politicians favored the "Green City" or the "Just City" over (or in a balance with) the "Growing City," as Scott Campbell puts it, they might favor the long-term development of the city and society in general but fail their immediate responsibility as majority owners of By & Havn.[21]

Who Gains and Who Loses?

If again we consider the three positions the Lord Mayor presented in his congressional speech: Socialdemokratiet's "sustainable, green-and-red vision for town and country; people and nature," the right-wing's "belief in the market" and the left-wing's "brick allergy" – it is hard to point out a winner. With 392,000 square meters now being developed instead of 260,000 in order to make sure the planned profit will be realized, it might appear that the market won. However, considering the uncertainty created with the Lord Mayor's decision to build somewhere else, the prolonged schedule of development and the continuing popular protests (which with the ruling from the appeal boards on planning and environmental issues once again rocked the boat), it is not fair to declare the market a winner per se. On the other hand, as all documents containing information about the economic consequences for the investors involved are classified and we have no access to the internal considerations in these multinational corporations whatsoever, we actually do not know. Moreover, this was not what the Lord Mayor meant anyway. With "belief in the market," he pointed to the economically liberal notion that left to its own devices, the market would find a natural equilibrium and take care of the housing supply by itself. So far, it has not, and nothing indicates it ever will.

As far as nature goes, the revised plans in short have led to more green-field development than the original plan, which had also carefully considered the importance of station proximity – supporting the use of public transport over private car-ownership – which the new plans don't. By all regular standards, in terms of environmentally friendly (or at least "less harmful") urban development, the original plans were considerably "better" than the new ones.

What about the other endangered species, then – "the common working-class family with two or three children, who just wants an attractive, affordable apartment," as the Lord Mayor put it in his congressional speech? In short, under the present political economic regime in a city like Copenhagen, increasing housing prices cannot be solved by building more housing. The housing market simply does not work this way. Housing is not a commodity like toothpaste, and many other factors than this supply and demand-relation impact the development of the housing prices.

Is This Development Desirable?

As Bent Flyvbjerg concludes in his work on *Rationality and Power* (and not least: *rationalization*):

> In open confrontation, rationality yields to power [...] where power relations take the form of open, antagonistic confrontations, power-to-power relations dominate over knowledge-power and rationality-power relations; that is, knowledge and rationality carry little or no weight in these instances. As the proverb has it, "Truth is the first casualty of war."[22]

The debate has been heavily laden with far-from-rational arguments from both sides: The housing shortage argument is but one example; it is also notable that nowhere in the discussion about building on the original site was Vandkunsten's work with Nature-based Solutions (NBS) taken into serious consideration.

Rather than engaging in a conversation and contributing to enlightening the public and informing the process, the parties have engaged in an open, antagonistic confrontation with the purpose of winning. But winning what? More or less everyone involved has lost.

What, if Anything, Should We Do about It?

Long-term planning and strategic urban governance as a means to strengthen investor security and make decisions in planning more transparent to the public and thus more democratic have been advocated for decades.[23] The long-term plans make it evident to the public what they can expect from future developments, and for investors to know where to put their money. Copenhagen has excelled in this for decades now.[24] The problem is, of course, that if the circumstances change, the plans need to change, too. More than a problem, this is perhaps rather an intriguing paradox: How can one make a long-term plan and stick to it while being open to changes as we go along? In a market-dependent model like By & Havn, it goes without saying that the plans adapt to the mood of the investors or the market. And since the profits have already been factored in as a part of the financing of the Copenhagen Metro, doing something else than keep attracting new citizens and continue green- and brown-field development is not an option. Hence, changing circumstances based on environmental or social issues like the ones occurring in Amager Fælled are difficult to address. There is simply no way of planning for a growing, green and just city under the present urban political regime.

Since the spring of 2016, much has been said about politics and planning in Copenhagen, and many alternatives to the present situation have been put forward by citizens, organizations, local politicians, the government and others. However, the main problem in the current debate is that the antagonistic relationship between the parties has created a situation where – as Flyvbjerg puts it – knowledge and rationality carry little or no weight.

Nevertheless, addressing the issues put forward in the analyses above based on the case of The Battle for Amager Common, here are three open suggestions for what could be done to address issues within the economy, planning and politics:

1 *Adjust the model for By & Havn.* Public ownership of a development corporation that can act on market terms has proven to be an extremely effective model on its own terms. The legal framework of the corporation has been adjusted several times to fit changing circumstances and catch new opportunities or provide cheaper building rights for the housing associations.

2 *Look beyond the envelope of the municipal borders.* The economic model for By & Havn creates a situation where the City of Copenhagen is effectively competing with its neighboring municipalities to attract new citizens and hence get the opportunity to develop new urban areas and sell off building rights. The administrative system and the planning system that follows this is designed to enhance competitiveness between municipalities on behalf of a more comprehensive, sustainable planning in general.

3 *Engage in a new political culture.* As a political leader, the Lord Mayor must put forward her vision for possible futures for the citizens and take upon herself the responsibility to realize these visions in collaboration with the other political parties, organizations and the public. Or she could invite the citizenry to participate in an actual collaborative process about the future of the city and take upon herself the responsibility to work for the realization of this. There can be more radical versions of this and many positions on the sliding bar between them, but sneaking around can never be a viable political practice in an advanced democracy where decisions – also political ones – must be based on rationality and knowledge and not solely be the result of a power play.

Location	Surface (m²)	Value (DKK)
The Camping Site (Vejlandskvarteret)	219,000	841,000,000
Bådehavnsgade East (Stejlepladsen)	64,500	262,000,000
Selinevej North	81,000	110,000,000
Densification in Ørestad	20,000	50,000,000
Total	392,000	1,263,000,000

5 Floor space and land value in the alternative plan from the 2019 budget.

The construction and operations of By & Havn (Copenhagen City and Port Development) is an example of the practical implications of the shift in relations and interactions between stakeholders and actors in the field of urban planning and development from the 1970s "managerial" into the present-day "entrepreneurial" urban governance, as David Harvey puts it in his 1989 article on the matter.[25]

Managerial urban governance in the era of predict-and-provide planning would be characterized by:

- a focus on management and administration;
- the distribution of resources and provision of welfare benefits;
- a clear distinction between the interests of municipal actors and the interests of private businesses; and
- focus on urban space as primarily for use rather than for exchange on the market.

Entrepreneurial urban governance, on the other hand, would be characterized by:

- urban governance instead of urban administration;
- urban development instead of urban planning;
- business-led development in public-private partnerships;
- a high degree of speculation of risk with the public sector hedging the risk for the private partners to reap the gain;
- a focus on the political economy of space, flagship projects and urban space as an asset for exchange on the market; and
- business strategies and inter-urban competition for resources and investments.

The history of By & Havn goes back to the original construction of Ørestadselskabet (Ørestad Development Corporation) in 1993.

In the 1970s and '80s, Copenhagen experienced a heavy economic decline because of deindustrialization and depopulation. The Conservative-Liberal national government and the left-wing supported Social Democratic led City Council in Copenhagen, were at odds with each other and for years did not manage to agree on a plan for the city. As global politics changed during the latter half of the 1980s toward a new focus on cities as the powerhouses of economic growth and prosperity, however, so did the focus on the importance of the condition of the Danish capital. In 1990 an historic alliance formed between Prime Minister Poul Schlüter of the Conservative People's Party, the Social Democratic Party's leader, Svend Auken, and the newly elected Social Democratic Lord Mayor of Copenhagen, Jens Kramer Mikkelsen, to plan for the resurrection of Copenhagen. Some of the results of this alliance were the decisions to build a bridge between Copenhagen and Malmö, Sweden; to expand the airport; and to finance the construction of an underground metro through the development of publicly owned land on Amager Common into a new town, Ørestad.

To accomplish this, Ørestadselskabet was established as a publicly owned, privately run corporation, co-owned by the Danish State (45 percent) and Copenhagen Municipality (55 percent). The state and the municipality provided the company with land assets they owned within the municipal border, and the municipality became responsible for rezoning the land from industrial and recreational purposes into commercial, educational, business and housing purposes. The first part of this land was an area of 1.2 square miles on the island of Amager that became Ørestad.

The explicit goal of Ørestadselskabet was to create revenue through asset management and development of the land the company now owned, and to use this revenue to service the debt it was obliged to assume to develop the new metro line, which in turn increased the value of the land owned by the corporation. Meanwhile, the municipality as a planning authority provided the necessary rezoning for the area, which was supposed to attract new businesses and inhabitants. In this way, the corporation and the municipality entered into a mutually beneficial alliance.

In 2007 Ørestadselskabet was split into the two corporations: By & Havn and Metroselskabet (The Copenhagen Metro). While the latter is responsible for establishing, maintaining and running the metro lines, By & Havn is responsible for the continuous development of the areas in and around Copenhagen Harbor and runs the harbor through its subsidiary Copenhagen Malmö Port (CMP). The tasks, construction and ownership of the corporation has since changed several times, and today the company is owned 95 percent by Copenhagen Municipality and 5 percent by the Danish State.

The inspiration for the corporation originally came from development corporations like London Docklands Development Corporation (LDDC), which used the same land value capture model for developing the Docklands and the Docklands Light Railway (DLR) in the 1980s. While LDDC and similar corporations have been established on a project basis with a limited amount of land assets and a time frame, By & Havn is now in practice an eternity machine trusted with all major strategic urban development projects within the municipal borders of Copenhagen in the foreseeable future. No other Danish municipality has a development corporation like it.

Bruce Katz and Luise Noring describe the business model for urban development through By & Havn in seven steps:

1. National and local government transfer assets to By & Havn.
2. Local government rezones the land for residential and commercial use.
3. The land increases in value.
4. By & Havn borrows (generally with loans on favorable terms from the Denmark National Bank) based on the (increased) value of the land.
5. This capital is either transferred to the metro construction company for broader transit investments and/or used by By & Havn to pay for local infrastructure that enables the development of the land.
6. By & Havn facilitates development through a variety of mechanisms, including land sales to or lease agreements with developers and, in a limited number of cases, development by the corporation itself.
7. This generates revenue that is used to service debt.[26]

6 Urban Governance and By & Havn.

Bibliography

Abbott, Andrew. "What Do Cases Do? Some Notes on Activity in Sociological Analyses." In Ragin and Becker, *What Is a Case?*, 53–82.

Andersen, Hans Thor, and Lars Winther. "Crisis in the Resurgent City? The Rise of Copenhagen." *International Journal of Urban and Regional Research* 34, no. 3 (September 3, 2010): 693–700.

Anker, Helle Tegner, *Planloven med kommentarer*. Copenhagen: Jurist- og Økonomforbundets Forlag, 2013.

Bisgaard, Holger. *Københavns Genrejsning 1990–2010*. Copenhagen: Bogværket, 2010.

By & Havn. "Ørestadshistorien." https://byoghavn.dk/orestad/historie/. Accessed October 12, 2020.

Campbell, Scott. "Green Cities, Growing Cities, Just Cities? Urban Planning and the Contradictions of Sustainable Development." *Journal of the American Planning Association* 62, no. 3 (1996): 296–312. https://doi.org/10.1080/01944369608975696.

Flyvbjerg, Bent. "Five Misunderstandings About Case-Study Research." *Qualitative Inquiry* 12, no. 2 (April 29, 2006): 219–45. https://doi.org/10.1177/1077800405284363.

——. "Phronetic Planning Research: Theoretical and Methodological Reflections." *Planning Theory & Practice* 5, no. 3 (September 2004): 283–306. https://doi.org/10.1080/1464935042000250195.

——. *Rationality and Power: Democracy in Practice*. Chicago: University of Chicago Press, 1998.

Friedmann, John. *Planning in the Public Domain.* Princeton: Princeton University Press, 1987.

Hajer, Maarten A. "Doing Discourse Analysis: Coalitions, Practices, Meaning." In *Words Matter in Policy and Planning – Discourse Theory and Method in the Social Sciences*, edited by Margo van den Brink and Tamara Metze, 65–74. Utrecht: Koninklijk Nederlands Aardrijkskundig Genootschap, 2006.

Hajer, Maarten, and Wytske Versteeg. "Performing Governance through Networks." *European Political Science* 4, no. 3 (2005): 340–47. https://doi.org/10.1057/palgrave.eps.2210034.

Harvey, David. "From Managerialism to Entrepreneurialism: The Transformation in Urban Governance in Late Capitalism." *Geografiska Annaler. Series B, Human Geography* 71, no. 1 (1989): 3–17.

——. "Use Value, Exchange Value and the Theory of Urban Land Use." In *Social Justice and the City*, rev. ed., 153–94. Athens: University of Georgia Press, 2009.

Jensen, Thomas Klose, Per Bang Thomsen and Stig Haaning Thøgersen. "Frank Jensen i kovending: vil flytte udskældt byggeri på Amager Fælled." *Danmarks Radio*, September 20, 2017. https://www.dr.dk/nyheder/regionale/hovedstadsomraadet/frank-jensen-i-kovending-vil-flytte-udskaeldt-byggeri-paa#!/.

Jørgensen, Marianne Winther, and Louise Philips. *Diskursanalyse som teori og metode*. Frederiksberg: Roskilde Universitetsforlag, 1999.

Katz, Bruce, and Luise Noring. *The Copenhagen City and Port Development Corporation: A Model for Regenerating Cities*. Brookings Centennial Scholar Initiative. Washington DC: Brookings Institution, 2017.

Københavns Kommune. "Undersøgelse af alternative byggemuligheder til Ørestad Fælled Kvarter," 2018.

——. "Yderligere undersøgelse af alternative byggemuligheder til Ørestad Fælled Kvarter," 2018.

Lov om Ørestaden m.v. (LOV nr 477 af 24/06/1992) (1992). https://www.retsinformation.dk/eli/lta/1992/477.

Nygaard, Erik. *Arkitektur Forstået*. Copenhagen: Bogværket, 2011.

Nævnenes Hus. "Planklagenævnet og Miljø- og Fødevareklagenævnet har tillagt klager over etablering og drift af bydel på Amager Fælled, Vejlands Kvarter, opsættende virkning." naevneneshus.dk, 2021. https://naevneneshus.dk/nyhedsarkiv/2021/juli/planklagenaevnet-og-miljoe-og-foedevareklagenaevnet-har-tillagt-klager-over-etablering-og-drift-af-bydel-paa-amager-faelled-vejlands-kvarter-opsaettende-virkning/.

Økonomiforvaltningen Københavns Kommune. "Budgetaftale for København 2019." Copenhagen, 2018.

Pagh, Jesper. "Copenhagen: A Metropolis for People." *Twentyfirst* 1, no. 3 (2014): 44–49.

——. "En bolig er ikke en købmandsvare." *Altinget*, October 21, 2020. https://www.altinget.dk/hovedstaden/artikel/arkitekt-og-adjunkt-en-bolig-er-ikke-en-koebmandsvare.

——. "Strategic Urban Governance." *Twentyfirst* 1, no. 3 (2014): 6–9.

Ragin, Charles C., and Howard Saul Becker, eds. *What Is a Case? Exploring the Foundations of Social Enquiry.* Cambridge: Cambridge University Press, 1992.

"Se billederne: Tusindvis af københavnere kæmpede og festede for Amager Fælled." *Berlingske*, September 11, 2017. https://www.berlingske.dk/kultur/se-billederne-tusindvis-af-koebenhavnere-kaempede-og-festede-for-amager-faelled.

Simpson, Deane, Kathrin Susanna Gimmel, Anders Lonka, Marc Jay and Joost Grootens, eds. *Atlas of the Copenhagens*. Berlin: Ruby Press, 2018.

Socialdemokratiet. "Frank Jensens tale ved Socialdemokratiets kongres 17. september 2017." https://www.youtube.com/watch?v=ovpvREM2Y5g.

Vandkunsten. "Team Vandkunsten Wins Master Plan Competition for Amager Fælled Neighborhood." https://vandkunsten.com/en/news/wins-amager-faelled. Accessed November 12, 2021.

Wieviorka, Michel. "Case Studies: History or Sociology?" In Ragin and Becker, *What Is a Case?*, 159–72.

Notes

1 Since 2017 students at The Royal Danish Academy, School of Architecture and Roskilde University have contributed to the work on the research project this paper is a part of. Some have participated in workshops as a part of courses on planning practices and on case study methods where they have researched into the course of events and key stakeholders before reenacting central parts of the conflicts. Others have worked with the case or related issues in their project reports and have shared and discussed their work with me along the way. In both cases, they have contributed with valuable insights, details and reflections without which this work would not have been the same.
2 See Hans Thor Andersen and Lars Winther, "Crisis in the Resurgent City? The Rise of Copenhagen," *International Journal of Urban and Regional Research* 34, no. 3 (September 3, 2010): 693–700; Holger Bisgaard, *Københavns Genrejsning 1990–2010* (Copenhagen: Bogværket, 2010); Deane Simpson, Kathrin Susanna Gimmel, Anders Lonka, Marc Jay and Joost Grootens, eds., *Atlas of the Copenhagens* (Berlin: Ruby Press, 2018); and Jesper Pagh, "Copenhagen: A Metropolis for People," *Twentyfirst* 1, no. 3 (2014): 44–49.
3 See Bent Flyvbjerg, *Rationality and Power: Democracy in Practice* (Chicago: University of Chicago Press, 1998), 8, 235; Bent Flyvbjerg, "Phronetic Planning Research: Theoretical and Methodological Reflections," *Planning Theory & Practice* 5, no. 3 (September 2004): 299; Michael Wieviorka, "Case Studies: History or Sociology?" in *What Is a Case? Exploring the Foundations of Social Enquiry*, ed. Charles C. Ragin and Howard Saul Becker (Cambridge: Cambridge University Press, 1992), 159–72; Andrew Abbott, "What Do Cases Do? Some Notes on Activity in Sociological Analyses," in Ragin and Becker, *What Is a Case?*, 53–82; and Bent Flyvbjerg, "Five Misunderstandings About Case-Study Research," *Qualitative Inquiry* 12, no. 2 (April 29, 2006): 219–45.
4 See Helle Tegner Anker, *Planloven med kommentarer* (Copenhagen: Jurist- og Økonomforbundets Forlag, 2013).
5 See Erik Nygaard, *Arkitektur Forstået* (Copenhagen: Bogværket, 2011).
6 See John Friedmann, *Planning in the Public Domain* (Princeton: Princeton University Press, 1987).
7 Flyvbjerg, "Phronetic Planning Research," 287.
8 Flyvbjerg, "Phronetic Planning Research," 302.
9 Lov om Ørestaden m.v. (LOV nr 477 af 24/06/1992), 1992, https://www.retsinformation.dk/eli/lta/1992/477; and By & Havn, "Ørestadshistorien," https://byoghavn.dk/orestad/historie/, accessed October 12, 2020.
10 Vandkunsten. "Team Vandkunsten Wins Master Plan Competition for Amager Fælled Neighborhood," https://vandkunsten.com/en/news/wins-amager-faelled, accessed November 12, 2021.
11 "Se billederne: Tusindvis af københavnere kæmpede og festede for Amager Fælled," *Berlingske*, September 11, 2017, https://www.berlingske.dk/kultur/se-billederne-tusindvis-af-koebenhavnere-kaempede-og-festede-for-amager-faelled.
12 Socialdemokratiet, "Frank Jensens Tale Ved Socialdemokratiets Kongres 17. September 2017," https://www.youtube.com/watch?v=ovpvREM2Y5g.
13 See Scott Campbell, "Green Cities, Growing Cities, Just Cities? Urban Planning and the Contradictions of Sustainable Development," *Journal of the American Planning Association* 62, no. 3 (1996): 296–312. https://doi.org/10.1080/01944369608975696.
14 Thomas Klose Jensen, Per Bang Thomsen and Stig Haaning Thøgersen, "Frank Jensen i kovending: vil flytte udskældt byggeri på Amager Fælled," *Danmarks Radio*, September 20, 2017, https://www.dr.dk/nyheder/regionale/hovedstadsomraadet/frank-jensen-i-kovending-vil-flytte-udskaeldt-byggeri-paa#!/.
15 Københavns Kommune, "Undersøgelse af alternative byggemuligheder til Ørestad Fælled Kvarter," 2018.
16 Københavns Kommune, "Yderligere undersøgelse af alternative byggemuligheder til Ørestad Fælled Kvarter," 2018.
17 Økonomiforvaltningen Københavns Kommune, "Budgetaftale for København 2019" (Copenhagen, 2018).
18 A part of the municipal plan is a map with three signatures indicating in which order areas designated for future development will be zoned, planned and ready for development: in the first half of the twelve-year period of planning; in the latter half; or "later."
19 A regular revision of the municipal plan (which has an outlook of twelve years), must take place every four years, according to the Danish Planning Act.
20 Nævnenes Hus, "Planklagenævnet og Miljø- og Fødevareklagenævnet har tillagt klager over etablering og drift af bydel på Amager Fælled, Vejlands Kvarter, opsættende virkning," *Nævnenes Hus*, July 7, 2021. https://naevneneshus.dk/nyhedsarkiv/2021/juli/planklagenaevnet-og-miljoe-og-foedevareklagenaevnet-har-tillagt-klager-over-etablering-og-drift-af-bydel-paa-amager-faelled-vejlands-kvarter-opsaettende-virkning/.
21 See Campell, "Green Cities, Growing Cities, Just Cities?"
22 See Flyvbjerg, *Rationality and Power*.
23 See Jesper Pagh, "Strategic Urban Governance," *Twentyfirst* 1, no. 3 (2014): 6–9.
24 See Bruce Katz and Luise Noring, *The Copenhagen City and Port Development Corporation: A Model for Regenerating Cities*, Brookings Centennial Scholar Initiative (Washington DC: Brookings Institution, 2017) and Pagh, "Copenhagen: A Metropolis for People."
25 For further reading see, for example, Andersen and Winther, "Crisis in the Resurgent City?"; Bisgaard, *Københavns Genrejsning 1990–2010*; Simpson et al., *Atlas of the Copenhagens*; Pagh, "Copenhagen: A Metropolis for People"; Katz and Noring, "The Copenhagen City and Port Development Corporation"; and David Harvey, "From Managerialism to Entrepreneurialism: The Transformation in Urban Governance in Late Capitalism," *Geografiska Annaler: Series B, Human Geography* 71, no. 1 (1989): 3.
26 See Katz and Noring, "The Copenhagen City and Port Development Corporation."

3.12 Amager Common, key events, 1990–2021

Ⓢ 24 Jun 1992
The Folketinget passes Lov om Ørestad (Act on Ørestad) as the legal foundation for the future development of the areas on Amager owned by the Danish state and the City of Copenhagen, the provision and financing of a metro line as well as the organization of the development process through a series of publicly owned private companies.

Ⓘ 11 Mar 1993
The Ørestadsselskabet (Ørestad Development Corporation) is established.

Ⓘ 13 Apr 1994
An international competition for a master plan for Ørestad is announced. The competition runs until September 27 and after a process with public debate and further assessment of four first-prize projects, a project from the Finnish firm APRT is chosen as the one to develop into the final master plan. To oversee the development and detailing of the master plan, APRT forms Arkki as a joint venture with the Danish architecture firm KHR. In the winning proposal, Ørestad Fælled Kvarter (Ørestad Common District) is planned as the last stage of the development of Ørestad.

Ⓢ 21 Dec 1995
Folketinget passes a revision of Lov om Ørestad paving the way for the Ørestadsselskabet's realization of the master plan for Ørestad which is later reflected in the municipal plan for the City of Copenhagen. Ørestad Fælled Kvarter is described as an "ecological neighborhood" – the last stage of the development process.

Ⓘ 19 Oct 2002
The first stage of the metro opens.

Ⓘ 1 May 2004
The first people move into Karen Blixen Parken in Ørestad.

Ⓘ 1 Oct 2007
The Ørestadsselskabet is reconstructed and By & Havn (Copenhagen City and Port Development) and Metroselskabet (The Copenhagen Metro) formed.

Ⓘ 15 Dec 2015
By & Havn announces a call for participants for the competition to develop a master plan for Ørestad Fælled Kvarter. Five teams are selected to participate in the competition, which runs from April 11 through June 27, 2016.

Ⓘ 1 Mar 2016
Amager Fælleds Venner (Friends of Amager Common) is established as a "group of citizens" on the initiative of Klaus Mygind, a representative of SF (The Socialist People's Party) in the Borgerrepræsentationen. The purpose is to protect Amager Common in general and from the development of Ørestad Fælled Kvarter in particular. They dub the area "The Salt Meadow."

Ⓘ 18 Sep 2016
Amager Fælleds Venner and Danmarks Naturfredningsforening (Danish Society for Nature Conservation) together with other NGOs arrange the first of many protest events on Amager Fælled: Several thousands of people gather, holding hands in a "human ring" around the project area.

Ⓘ 13 Oct 2016
Team Vandkunsten's winning proposal for a master plan for Ørestad Fælled Kvarter is announced by By & Havn. Protests from Amager Fælleds Venner, Danmarks Naturfredningsforening and others gain momentum immediately after the announcement. The Green wing, a coalition between Enhedslisten (The Red-Green Alliance), Radikale Venstre (The Danish Social-Liberal Party) and SF is formed with the promise of stopping the development plans if they gain the majority in the Borgerrepæsentationen after the local election in 2017.

Ⓘ Relevant events
Ⓢ Related laws, regulations, policies

1990 1992 1994 1996 1998 2000 2002 2004 2006 2008 2010 2012 2014 2016

10 Sep 2017
Thousands of citizens gather on the then future construction site on the occasion of Naturens Dag (Nature's Day) – an annual event arranged by the Danmarks Naturfredningsforening – to express their dissatisfaction with the plans. The celebrity chef Nikolaj Kirk, who has his own weekly show on national television, addresses the protesters; Anne Dorte Michelsen sings with a reunited version of her 1980s pop band Tøsedrengene (literally: The Sissies); while the reality star Linse Kessler dances to the beat.

17 Sep 2017
Lord Mayor Frank Jensen speaks at the Socialdemokratiet's congress in Aalborg, emphasizing his intentions of moving ahead with the project.

18 Sep 2017
Det Konservative Folkeparti announces their support for the idea to look for alternative locations for the 2,500 housing units planned in Ørestad Fælled Kvarter.

19 Sep 2017
Venstre declares their support for the proposal from Det Konservative Folkeparti that the right-wing parties joins the Green wing.

20 Sep 2017
Lord Mayor Frank Jensen announces his retreat from the plans.

5 Oct 2017
The Borgerrepræsentationen passes a resolution to screen for alternative sites for development.

31 May 2018
The Borgerrepræsentationen resolves at a meeting to further screen a selection of the alternatives presented, including some specifications regarding possible combinations of identified alternatives – and (at least partly) reimbursing By & Havn for the loss they suffered due to the cancellation of the original plans.

7 Sep 2018
The Borgerrepræsentationen resolves the municipal budget for 2019 through an agreement that is the foundation for today's developments in four different places in the city: The Camping Site (Vejlandskvarteret), Bådehavnsgade East (Stejlepladsen), Selinevej North and densification in Ørestad (fig. 5).

19 Mar 2019
A majority in Folketinget consisting of SF, Socialdemokratiet, Radikale Venstre, Konservative, Venstre, Liberal Alliance and Dansk Folkeparti lifts the nature protection of the areas selected as alternative sites for development and passes a revision of the Lov om Ørestad in accordance with the new plans.

27 Nov 2019
Team CCO wins By & Havn's competion for a master plan for the alternative site in Bådehavnsgade East (Stejlepladsen) with the proposal Her det gror (Here it grows).

5 Dec 2019
Henning Larsen Architects wins By & Havn's competition for a master plan for the alternative site The Camping Site (Vejlandskvarteret) with the proposal Fælledby (Common Town).

27 Feb 2020
The Borgerrepræsentationen passes Municipal Plan 2019 providing the planning framework for further planning and developing the alternative sites.

4 Aug 2020
Klaus Mygind leaves Amager Fælleds Venner after continuous disputes over whether on one hand he can be a member of the protest organisation and on the other be a representative of SF in Borgerrepræsentationen, supporting the further development of projects to build on Amager Fælled.

19 Oct 2020
Frank Jensen leaves the Lord Mayor's office after accusations of repeated instances of sexual harassment.

4 Feb 2021
A majority in the Borgerrepræsentationen consisting of Socialdemokratiet, Radikale Venstre, SF, Venstre, Konservative and Dansk Folkeparti passes the district plan for the Camping Site (aka. The Lark Plain) to realize the project Fælledby.

24 Feb 2021
The project company Fælledby P/S, co-owned by By & Havn and Pension Danmark begins construction works on the Camping Site.

25 Feb 2021
Amager Fælleds Venner organizes protests around the construction site while Extinction Rebellion and others begin to block access to the construction site.

10 Mar 2021
The Danmarks Naturfredningsforening and Amager Fælleds Venner files a complaint with Planklagenævnet and Miljø- og Fødevareklagenævnet (the appeal boards for planning and environmental issues) arguing that the project did not in a satisfactory manner take into consideration the future conditions for the northern crested newt and should therefore be stopped.

16 Mar 2021
Police remove the blockade and protesters from the construction site.

Throughout 2021
Amager Fælleds Venner, the Danmarks Naturfredningsforening, Extinction Rebellion and others organize various protests and events around Copenhagen.

7 Jul 2021
Planklagenævnet and Miljø- og Fødevareklagenævnet rules in favor of the Danmarks Naturfredningsforening and Amager Fælleds Venner and adds that development should be stayed until the case had been resolved "by the end of 2021."

16 Nov 2021
Socialdemokratiet goes from 27.6 percent to 17.2 percent of the vote in the local election, losing their position as the largest party in the Borgerrepræsentationen to Enhedslisten (working to stop the project), which went from 18.4 percent to 24.6 percent.

14 Dec 2021
Planklagenævnet and Miljø- og Fødevareklagenævnet decides in favor of the Ciy of Copenhagen, overruling the complaints from Danmarks Naturfredningsforening and Amager Fælleds Venner. Hence the project can continue as planned by By & Havn.

2018 2020 2022

3.13 Copenhagen urban development areas, metro lines and natural areas, 2017/2020

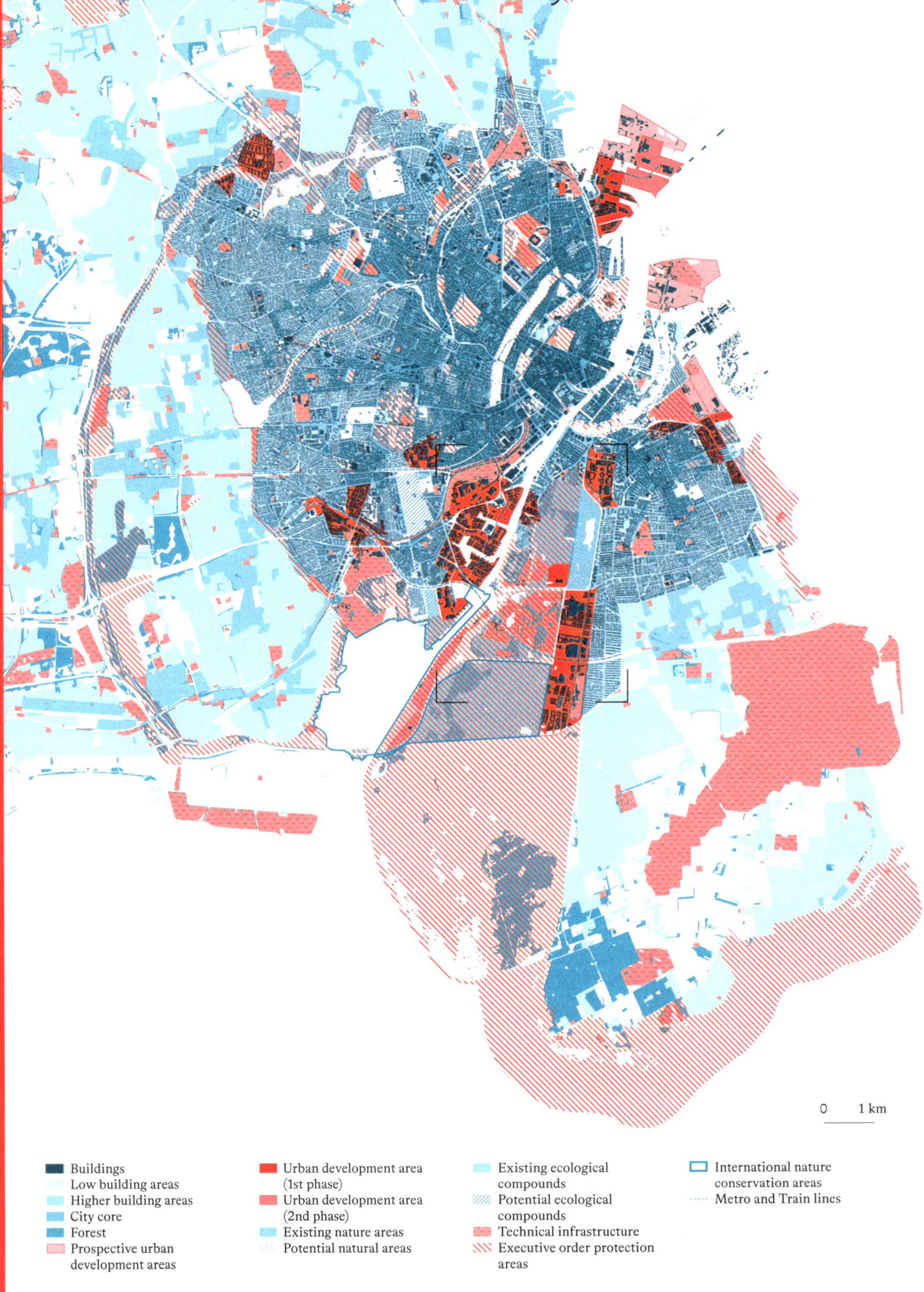

3.14 Ørestad Fælled Kvarter and replacement sites, size and anticipated profit, 2017/2020

3.15 Ørestad Fælled Kvarter and replacement sites, size and anticipated profit, 2017

3.16 Ørestad Fælled Kvarter and replacement sites, size and anticipated profit, 2020

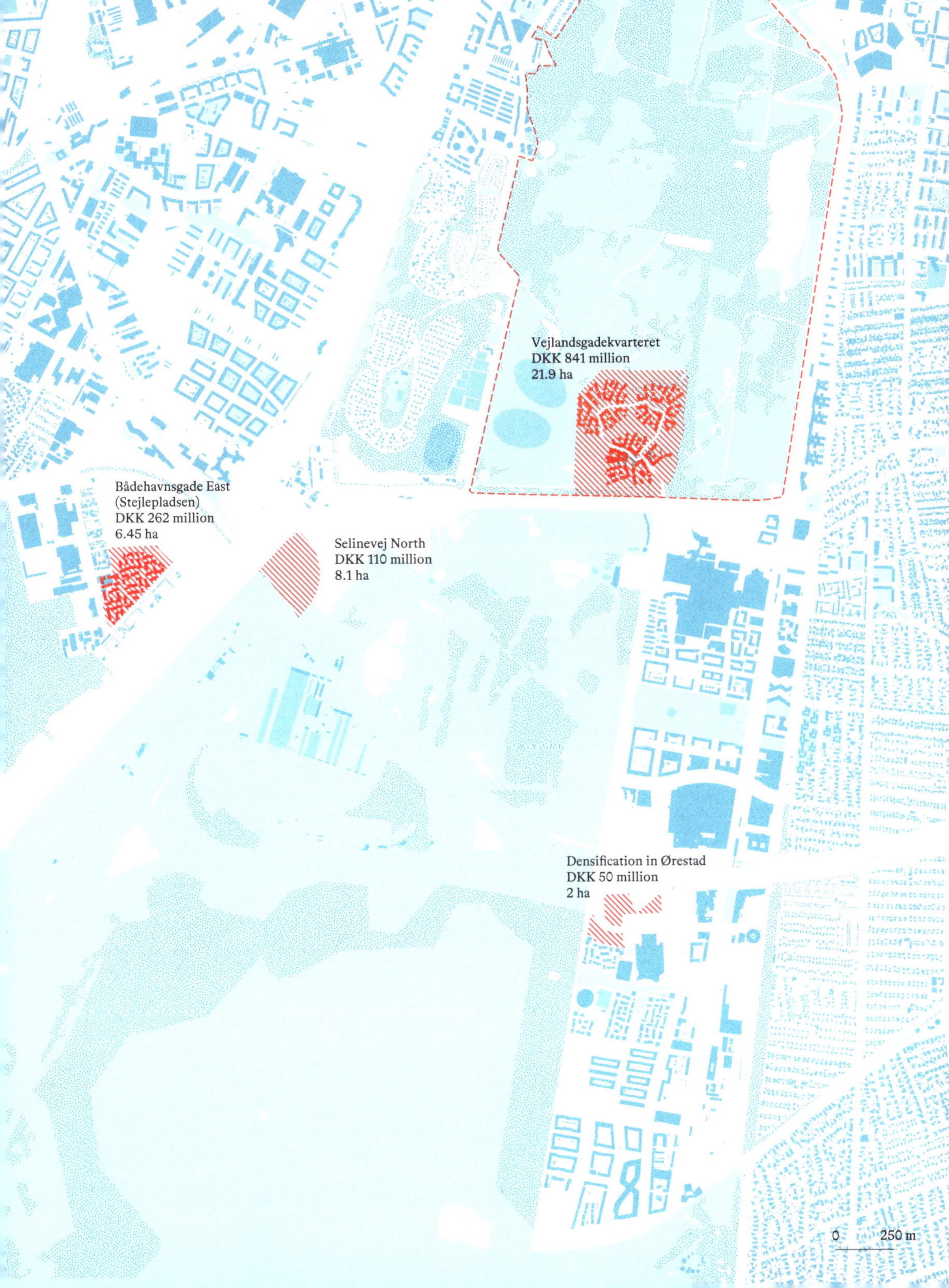

3.17 Søringen protest signs, 1970s

Søringen protest:
We are building adult playground here.

Søringen protest:
Søringen a scandalous engine plague ring

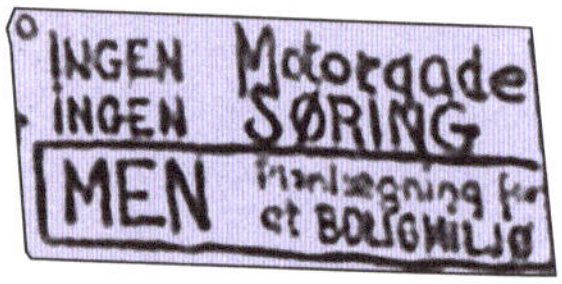

Søring protest:
No motorway. No Søringen. But planning for a housing environment.

Søringen protest:
Remove the pest around my neck Søringen.
Thank you to Alternativ Stad Stockholm.

Sydhavnen freight railroad protest:
The worlds longest coffee table

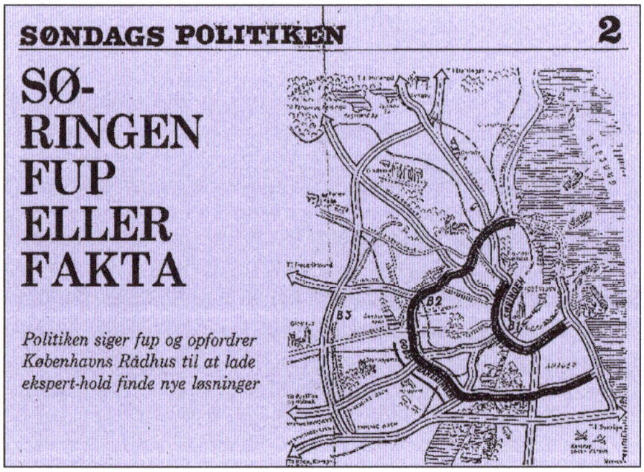
SØNDAGS POLITIKEN 2

SØ-
RINGEN
FUP
ELLER
FAKTA

Politiken siger fup og opfordrer Københavns Rådhus til at lade ekspert-hold finde nye løsninger

Politiken article about Søringen:
"Søringen false or facts"

Sydhavnen freight railroad protest:
Stop the bridge

3.18 Amager Common protest signs, 2018–21

50,000 demand public vote!!

Common about the Common

Preserve Copenhagen's green lung!!

Conservation is not for sale

Preserve Amager Common

Toad brigade defend the Common

Nature is not trading goods

Saying meaning I swear

Preserve Amager Common

3.19 Amager Common demonstration, 2021

Homeless salamander.
Extinction Rebellion protests in front of By & Havn and Pension Danmark

Nature activists dressed as larks in the Ministry of the Environment Building

Wild orchids

Tote bag (with a sign Amager Fælleds Venner)

Policeman on a horse

High-visibility vest (with a sign Amager Fælleds Venner)

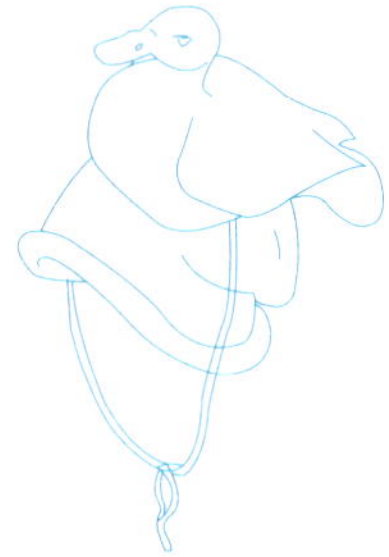

Hat with a rubber duck figure attached

Beak masks

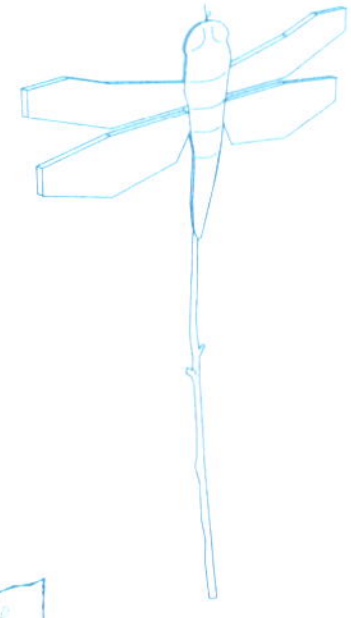

Stick with a dragonfly

Torch

Stick with a nightingale

Police car

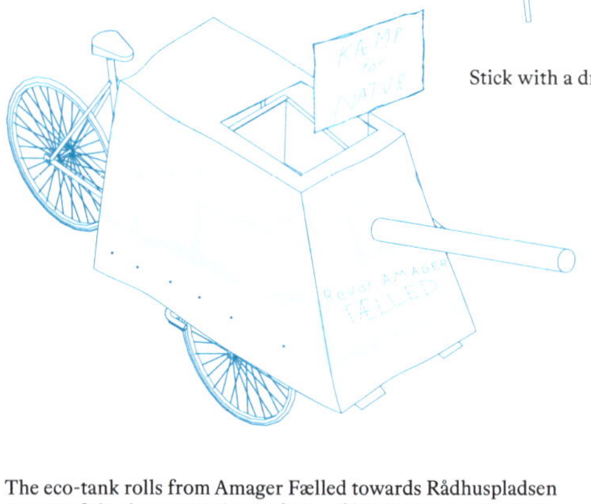

The eco-tank rolls from Amager Fælled towards Rådhuspladsen as part of the demonstration in favor of biodiversity and nature conservation on Amager Fælled

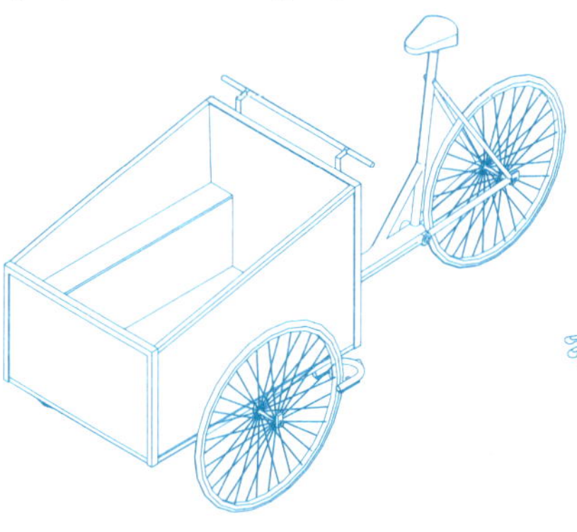

Frog

Nikolaj Kirk speaks at the Amager Fælled demonstration

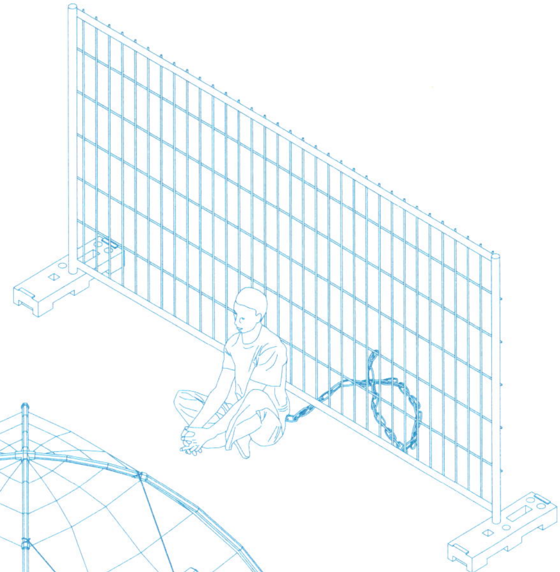

Demonstrators bound to a fence

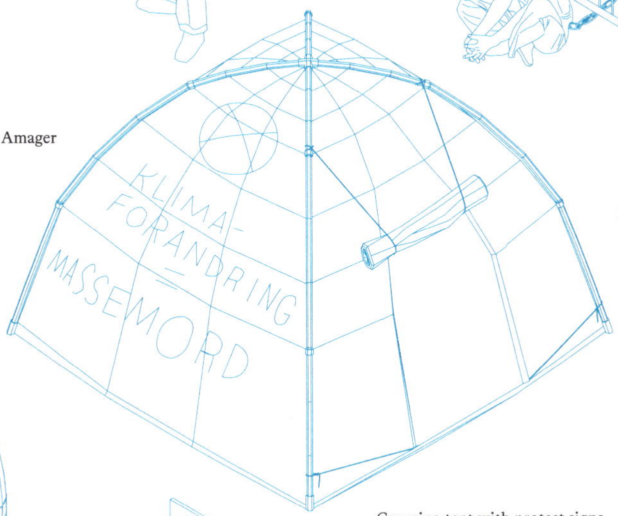

Camping tent with protest signs

Metro sign

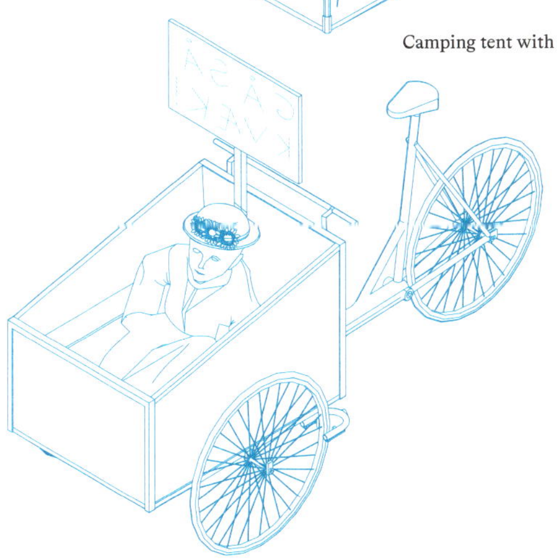

Nightingale

Christiania bikes adapted for the purposes of the protest. From demonstration on May 16, 2021, against the developments on Amager Fælled and Stejlepladsen

People holding letters forming a sign "Bevar Amager Faelled" (Protect Amager Faelled) during torch demonstration for nature at Amager Fælled on Amager, Saturday February 6, 2022

Megaphone

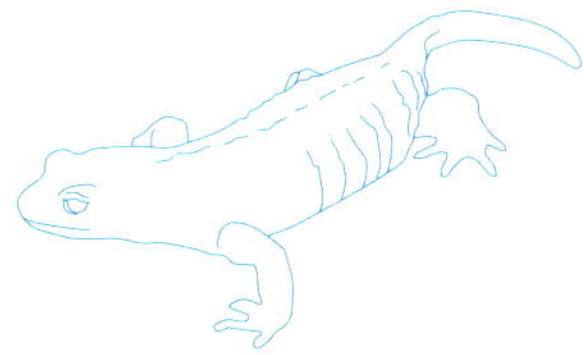

Northern crested newt

Postscript

Niels Grønbæk, Runa Johannessen,
Katrine Lotz, Kirsten Marie Raahauge,
Deane Simpson, Martin Søberg

At the completion of the more than five-years-long Spaces of Danish Welfare research project, a series of thematic threads stand out. These themes point toward trajectories for future research.

Clearly, the range of case studies exploring the transformation of welfare spaces does not collectively point to a singular picture of transformation from one condition to another. Nor do the cases confirm a coherent portrait of a Nordic welfare utopia, let alone reality, as oftentimes presented in various international formats post-2008 such as world happiness reports, indexes on urban livability, etc. Rather, the chapters collectively sketch the contours of a more complex and sometimes contradictory set of spatial developments. In the research process, what turned out to be a constant is the simultaneous dismantling and restructuring of Danish welfare spaces and the ensuing continous reinterpretations and changes in the related practices.

In the following, we sketch out some of the most powerful thematic threads of our studies, and some of the questions that could be asked in order to move further. Three aspects will be unfolded addressing these themes and questions, namely taxonomies, distribution and topographies. Since the three aspects fold in and out of one another, the questions of each section also echo the other aspects.

Shifting Taxonomies

The "Five Pillars of Welfare" suggested in the William Beveridge report in 1942 have been a productive point of departure in the overall project. However, the wider understanding of the relationship between welfare and space that has emerged out of the studies points to a finer-grained reading of complex and uneven taxonomies of spatial conditions, spatial practices, spatial relations and spatial models of welfare that far exceeds this division of the tasks of the welfare state. Thus, the studies have shifted their center of gravity from a concern for welfare spaces as entities (typological formats of architecture, taxonomic formats of welfare provision, specific formats of sociospatial conditions, etc.), toward an increased curiosity concerning the relations between spatial frameworks or elements and their effect in supporting practices of welfare as well as practices in everyday life. These extend to include architecture; landscape; urban space; infrastructure; neighborhoods; interiors of institutions, homes and shops; design objects and programmatic conditions; as well as images and media representations as they present themselves in the discourses on welfare in politics and economy.

Furthermore, welfare spaces have shifted from comprehending the institution as embodiment of a benevolent welfare state to partly becoming virtual networks. The transformation of relations between elements is impacted by new virtual connections between spaces of various scales, virtual digital spaces in themselves and spaces situated in different localities. In other words, the space-welfare transformations happening become yet more complex, intertwining new hybrids of the welfare-space-combination through still new kinds of virtualization, actualization, scaling and distribution of welfare amenities happening simultaneously yet in different paces.

The studies have also drawn attention to the shifting character of who commissions, produces and controls spaces of welfare, as well as the implications this has on how space is experienced and used in the everyday. Through the analytical lens of space, we see the outcome of welfare shifts between the three main welfare providers; state, market and civil society, as the state has extracted itself from some settings and expanded into others. These shifts have lead to a diversification of actors and their roles and to a diversification of the performativity of space. Across initial perceptions of political discourses on what the role of the welfare state is or should be, the studies point to more complex, concrete friction lines between the three realms of welfare providers. The distributions of roles concerning welfare provision is under transformation: Some cases show the expansion of the role of the market in production of welfare spaces, others point to expansions of civil society produced welfare space, yet other cases point to renewed expansion of state-produced space.

Political decisions on changes in the conditions for economic distribution, distribution of institutions and distribution of decision-making itself has an impact on both concrete local configurations and national geographies of welfare spaces, as well as the idea of welfare as universal. When analyzed over time, space reveals itself as a kind of "political plastic" of a highly composite character, in which the "cause and effect" logics seem insufficient. Often, the impact of policies are not to be anticipated, sometimes contrary to the intent, always affecting everyday life in multiple ways. These complexities are only to be unraveled by way of concrete case studies and an explorative attitude toward new theoretical perspectives, revealing in higher detail how space, politics and economy are interrelated. Drawing on our studies, we suggest that new trajectories of importance for future research on the shifting taxonomies of welfare spaces can be guided by questions like:

- What role does the rapidly increasing digitalization of welfare amenities have on our spatial taxonomy and on our ideas and understandings of welfare?
- How can the exploration of the "political plastic" of welfare spaces be methodologically and theoretically developed to further understand the situated distributions of welfare and its decision-makers?
- How can the frictions and connections be explored when dealing with welfare in its double-sidedness of ideally universal and spatially situated?

Shifting Distributions

The notion of universality of welfare provision, equally accessible to all citizens, has been a central concept in the Scandinavian welfare states. By international standards, Denmark has maintained this as evident, supposedly connected to the relatively low inequality. For example, the state maintains a somewhat strong and decommodified health system along with an education system that supports one of the highest rates of intergenerational social mobility. However, our studies show that the perspective of shifting time-space geographies plays a major role in the dismantling and restructuring of welfare: Increasing unevenness in the distribution of, and access to, welfare spaces give rise to an unevenness concerning the access to welfare. This dismantlement of welfare in the provinces is related to the restructuring of welfare connected to the continued growth of urban centers. Geographical unevenness of welfare accessibility at the national level follows from peripheralization eroding equal universal access.

Shifts in universality of the welfare subject do not only stem from geographical unevenness and inequalities of access across the national map; shifts concerning universality are also implicit in various kinds of inequality within large cities. Studies presented in the anthology show that the acting out of the concept of universality and the related concept of inclusion is far from straightforward. Spaces of exception are made from the ideal of universality at the level of governmental policymaking. Behind this lies contrasting political agendas toward realizing or *not* realizing the universality of the welfare subject due to matters of integration and inclusion. Furthermore, as the shifts in universality are affected by spatial localization, the spatial dynamics that become drivers of these shifts are both intended and unintended. These spatial changes have an impact on who in practice is deemed worthy or unworthy of welfare, when it is possible to distribute welfare, where and how it is distributed, and to what extent it can be provided.

Spatial dynamics also play a role in the normativities of welfare distribution. In our studies, there is a tendency for interiors of welfare institutions to be in transformation. In hospitals, the design moves towards a more homey, less institutionalized aesthetic that mirrors the preferences of some groups of society more than others. In schools, the simple logics of distance between rooms and connections between them serve as including and excluding mechanimsms.

As seen from a spatial point of departure, the state, whether at a national, regional or municipal level, plays a major role as part of the spatial transformations that are happening, retracting itself from some settings and expanding its influence over others. Across initial perceptions of political discourses on what the role of the welfare state is or should be, the studies point to concrete, but, again, also more complex friction lines, to breaches in coherence, mismatches between policies and practice, and to uneven distributions. These shifts suggest not only shifting actors and roles, but also different levels of associated responsibility. Based on our studies' recognition of such shifts in the distribution of welfare provisions – manifest in spatial dispositions – we suggest that new trajectories could be unfurled from a set of questions like:

- How can the study of spatial networks, sites, accessibility and distribution further qualify studies of welfare spaces as well as welfare in a broader and more common sense of the concept?
- What spatial elements and relations are involved and which modes of inclusion and exclusion are at work when studying who is encompassed by welfare provisions?
- How can we unravel the normativities of welfare spaces and the dominance of some groups over others as exclusive markers in welfare spaces?

Shifting Topographies

The perspectives of anthropology, architecture and art history have made it possible to point to shifts in the topographies of welfare. This is a key aspect in the studies, pointing to the abovementioned shifting spatial distributions as well as the concrete allocations of welfare. The cases explored in this anthology testify to the emergence of a geography of centralization and consolidation of some institutions, while other welfare spaces have been decentralized. To a large extent both centralizations and decentralizations are the result of new public management logics of efficiency and rationalization related to the intentions behind the Danish municipal reforms of 1970 and 2007.

The centralizations have been justified by and large according to the ideas of increasing the quality of services through streamlining and concentration rather than pursuing an even distribution of resources, whereas decentralizations in turn have been justified by the idea of lifting quality through allocating decisions of welfare distribution to local actors. These transformations have specific impacts on the structuring of space at a national level, but also on the everyday lives of citizens. It expresses itself in distances and time spent on getting to a doctor, to attend school, to visit a relative in hospital, and it shows where decisions on welfare distribution and assesments of eligibility for welfare benefits are made. Differentiated topographies are similarly evident on an urban scale within the larger cities in terms of spatial living conditions and the geographical access and provision of welfare between one housing area and another, or one neighborhood and another. Yet beyond the topographies of spaces that are purposefully understood as connected to welfare, welfare spaces are always located in a wider environmental ecology: this means that welfare as both analytical and empirical object cannot be taken out of the equation of our intensified crises of climate change on a planetary scale. Thus welfare becomes not only a matter of human social welfare, it becomes a matter of a larger and more holistic scale, implying more than human agents of all sorts.

By resting on anthropological and architectural studies of everyday life while simultaneously addressing events and actors impacting situated space, our studies show a friction line between situated everyday life on the one hand and policies and planning on the other. The misunderstandings, problems and disproportions of welfare distribution are manifest and to be pointed out in the topoi of the concrete sites while they often stay hidden when seen from a planning gaze. Therefore, we suggest a potential in addressing this issue, pointing to space as the important factor when understanding the consequences of political decision-making processes; a concern for the effects of changing welfare topographies is crucial in order to understand the impact of policies on society at large and on everyday life. New trajectories for exploring these areas could be guided by questions like:

- In what ways can the spatial gaze into shrinking and expanding welfare spaces contribute to further qualification of the double nature of welfare as universal and specific?
- Which new spatial models can be developed to better grasp how welfare is being redistributed, practiced and imagined?
- How can we, based on an understanding of welfare topographies, develop a more nuanced understanding of how welfare is embedded in climate change, loss of biodiversity and environmental degradation?

From certain perspectives the transformations of the last five decades have led to the supposed "death of welfare as we knew it," at least according to narratives from many Western European, Nordic and North American contexts. Collectively, the books's contributions – from a spatial perspective – explore the ongoing relevance of welfare when studying the current changes in the Danish context, supplemented by cases from Sweden. Danish politics has shown the full political spectrum embracing "the welfare state" in a variety of understandings, and thus also in relatively different ways of conceiving what constitutes the political necessities for its continuation. In light of – and in spite of – this, it is our hope that these studies hold wider relevance in the context of the broader questioning of the ideal of the welfare state and welfare society internationally.

The big jumps from state to region to municipality to the actual small office within the municipality offer very different spatial insights into the everyday organization of the Danish welfare system. If there are cracks in the confidence in the welfare system by its citizens, these are likely to become visible in its discrete spatialization rather than through the abstract modeling of it favored by shifting governments. Owing to this, there is all the more reason to pursue further research trajectories into spaces of welfare – in Denmark as well as in broader contexts. We acknowledge that we run the risk, via our spatial point of entry, to have pointed out a new efficient way to look for weak spots to optimize by centrally located actors. However, we dare to suggest that our research might also contribute inspirations for how to think about decentrally situated welfare policymaking and at the same time stay with the discussion on what "universality" might entail in the concrete and different spatial contexts. First and last, it is our hope that these studies may offer points of departure for a renewed concern in addressing space as a factor when studying how practices, rationales and realities in welfare systems change.

Author Biographies

Claus Bech-Danielsen, architect MAA, professor, PhD. Works as a housing researcher at BUILD, Aalborg University. Bech-Danielsen has been head of research at Danish Building Research Institute, head of the Center for Housing Research and chair of governmental think tanks. Bech-Danielsen has published books on housing trends, modernism, postwar housing and suburban transformation. Bech-Danielsen is currently the project manager of a long-term evaluation (2019–28) focusing on physical transformations in fifteen disadvantaged social housing areas. As part of this his research team are developing the interdisciplinary research field architectural anthropology. Bech-Danielsen has received several awards for his research work.

Maja Hojer Bruun is associate professor at the department of Educational Anthropology, Aarhus University, convenor of the Danish Research Network for the Anthropology of Technology (AnTech) and coeditor of the forthcoming *Palgrave Handbook of the Anthropology of Technology* (2022). Her PhD work (degree received in 2012 from the University of Copenhagen) focused on the social life and moral economies of Danish housing cooperatives. Her current research centers on emerging digital technologies, spanning robots, drones, urban living labs and data encryption infrastructures, and in her work she explores collaborative, interventionist and experimental ethnographic methods.

Alison J. Clarke is chair of Design History and Theory and director of the Papanek Foundation at the University of Applied Arts Vienna. As a trained historian and social anthropologist her research highlights the crossovers in history, design and anthropology; her work has been supported by major awards and fellowships from organizations including the Arts and Humanities Research Council, the Smithsonian Institution and the Graham Foundation. Clarke directs the biennial Papanek Symposium exploring the legacies and futures of alternative design cultures through critical multidisciplinary approaches. A regular broadcaster and international speaker, her most recent monograph, *Victor Papanek: Designer for the Real World* (MIT Press, 2021) explores the contentious history of the social design movement.

Bastian Feltgen studied architecture at the University of Stuttgart and graduated in the Spatial Design master program at the Royal Danish Academy – Architecture. His research focuses on the interdependent effects of spatial and social change over time through which he codeveloped visualization methods for this anthology, capable of communicating the complex spatial transformations of the Danish welfare system. Prior to starting at the Royal Danish Academy, Bastian worked for a number of years in various architecture firms in Copenhagen, New York City and Hamburg.

Sten Gromark, dr, professor em; architect SAR/MSA, Chalmers University of Technology ACE, department of Architecture and Civil Engineering, Gothenburg, Sweden. His research profile is on critical interpretations of contemporary residential architecture based on humanistic and social science-oriented perspectives. In 2020 Gromark coedited publications on rethinking the social in architecture and on architecture for residential care and aging communities. In 2021 he edited a collection of texts on architectural anthropology and published an analysis of an explorative residential case of transdisciplinarity as part of EU COST Actions research. He is recently appointed editor in chief of the *Nordic Journal of Architectural Research* (NJAR).

Niels Grønbæk is an associate professor and head of the Political Architecture – Critical Sustainability international master program at the Royal Danish Academy – Architecture. Among Grønbæk's research interests are subject didactics within architectural education, entanglements between architecture and politics – currently seen through the lenses of "welfare" and "Critical Zone architecture" – as well as topics such as "stasis" (civil war) in relation to the Greek *polis* during the Classical period, and architectural analysis of mannerist architectures as cosmological constructs. Grønbæk is a member of the research cluster Architecture, Strategy and Politics at RDA.

Louise Dedenroth Høj is an architect and PhD student at Friis & Moltke Architects and the Royal Danish Academy – Architecture. Her research focuses on the development of housing and care models for elderly people in a historical perspective, and how the architecture of current care home environments is influencing the use and daily life in these facilities.

Runa Johannessen, PhD, is an assistant professor at the Royal Danish Academy – Architecture. Johannessen is specialized in the political instrumentation of architecture in sites of societal transformation and conflict. They have pursued their postdoctoral research on the Danish hospital system as part of the research project Spaces of Danish Welfare.

Heidi Svenningsen Kajita, PhD, is an architect, educator and researcher. She is also assistant professor at the Section for Landscape Architecture and Planning, University of Copenhagen. Her research deals with how architecture and planning can (re)produce social processes focusing on the history and transformation of welfare state large-scale housing. Kajita draws on emerging ethnographic-architectural methodology to combine knowledge of users' everyday practices; normative frameworks for the built environment and architects' drawn and written work.

Lars Bo Kaspersen is a professor at the Copenhagen Business School; formerly he was head of the department of Political Science at the University of Copenhagen. He is the author of, among other publications, *Anthony Giddens: An Introduction to a Social Theorist* (Blackwell, 2000); *Does War Make States?*, coedited with Jeppe Strandsbjerg (Cambridge University Press, 2017); and *War, Survival Units, and Citizenship* (Routledge, 2021). Kaspersen's research areas are state formation processes in Europe, the transformation of the welfare state, the sociology of war, civil society (including the idea of associative democracy), social theory and in particular relational theory. He is the codirector (together with Liv Egholm) of the research project CISTAS.

Katrine Lotz is an architect, PhD, associate professor and head of the Institute of Architecture, Urbanism and Landscape at the Royal Danish Academy – Architecture. Her research takes a point of departure in the nexus between the architectural profession, spatial practices and the welfare state, both historically and in terms of contemporary changes and challenges. She is coeditor of the anthology *Forming Welfare* (Danish Architectural Press, 2017) and among the initiators of the Scandinavian research-network for architecture and welfare, https://architectureandwelfare.net/.

Jennifer Mack is associate professor and docent at the KTH Royal Institute of Technology. Broadly, Mack's work links theories and methods from architectural history and anthropology to investigate questions of equality, power, ecology and social change in the built environment. Her current research focuses on the design, use and renovation of late modernist landscapes. She is author of *The Construction of Equality: Syriac Immigration and the Swedish City* (University of Minnesota Press, 2017), which received the 2018 Margaret Mead Award (SfAA/AAA), and coeditor of *Rethinking the Social in Architecture* (Actar, 2019) and *Life Among Urban Planners* (University of Pennsylvania Press, 2020).

Mette Mechlenborg holds an MA in literature and modern culture. She is a senior researcher at the Department of the Built Environment, Aalborg University, and has profound knowledge of everyday life practices, homemaking and place development.

Her interest is in theories on space and the entanglement of the physical, social and cultural aspects of everyday life. Mette Mechlenborg has more than seventy publications, including several books, and has been enrolled in various international and national projects within housing culture, place transformation and residential practices. She is part of the national research project Regeneration of Danish Disadvantaged Neighborhoods: Long-term Evaluation (2019–28), where she has developed media analysis methods, among other things.

Aleksander Nowak is an architect, urban planner and a strategic designer working with data visualization, spatial and system mappings. His main area of research at the Royal Danish Academy, as well as practice, focuses on how visual approaches could deal as research tools for breaking down the complexity of contemporary society's dynamic conditions. Aleksander combines a wide-ranging expertise including data processing and visualization, network-, systemic- and GIS-mapping, among others. In his recent work, within Dark Matter Labs, he has been involved in projects which work with the Nordic food system resilience as well as potentials of alignment of biodiversity's needs with the financial system.

Jesper Pagh holds an MA in architecture from the Royal Danish Academy and a PhD from Roskilde University, where he was an assistant professor in urban planning from 2019 to 2021. From 2017 to 2019 he was a research assistant at the Royal Danish Academy. Since 2021 he is the City Architect in Rødovre Municipality, a suburb to Copenhagen. His research focuses on the relationship between the social, political, economic and material aspects of the built environment as it emerges in the intersection between the formal, the real and the realized planning, in particular in contemporary projects in and around Copenhagen, which he follows through close case studies. Pagh is former director of the Danish Association of Architects and a former editor at The Danish Architectural Press.

Max Pedersen is a social anthropologist and PhD student at the Royal Danish Academy – Architecture, Design, Conservation. His field of research is alternative housing for elderly citizens, mainly senior cohousing and collective housing for seniors. Max has conducted studies about senior cohousing for nonprofit organizations, municipalities and private companies. He has published two books on senior cohousing, one of them, *Det store eksperiment* (2013) in cooperation with the Department of the Built Environment, Aalborg University. Max has also done research on senior housing in the USA, Sweden, the Netherlands and Spain.

Kirsten Marie Raahauge, professor wsd, PhD in anthropology. Principal Investigator of the research project Spaces of Danish Welfare; Raahauge's contemporary project is the outskirts. She is head of the Center for Interior Studies. Her field of research is the anthropology of space and materiality; her fieldwork includes the outskirts, houses and homes, neighborhoods, urbanity, landscapes and haunted houses. Raahauge has worked at several universities, since 2009 at the Royal Danish Academy – Architecture, Design, Conservation.

Svava Riesto is an associate professor in the Section for Landscape Architecture and Planning, University of Copenhagen. Linking critical heritage studies and architectural history, she examines questions of sustainability, equity and power in cities and landscapes. Riesto has written on how historical narratives and cultural imaginaries are used in the renovation, preservation and climate adaptation of welfare-state landscapes. Her publications include *Biography of an Industrial Landscape* (Amsterdam University Press 2017); *Vademecum: 77 Minor Concepts for Writing Urban Places* (NAi, 2021, coedited); *European Mass-Housing Welfare Landscapes* (Landscape Research, 2021, coedited); and *Public Space in European Social Housing* (collaborative research exhibition HERA 2019–21).

Meike Schalk is an associate professor in Urban Design and Urban Theory at the KTH School of Architecture in Stockholm. Her research combines critical inquiry into discourses of sustainability, democracy and inclusion in urban planning and design with practice-oriented research methods. She has explored historical and contemporary shifts of welfare spaces and policies in housing in the Nordic countries and Vienna, often in collaborative projects. She has coedited several books and journals, including *Dimensions of Architectural Knowledge* 3, *Species of Theses and Other Pieces* (2022); *Caring for Communities* (2019); and *Feminist Futures of Spatial Practice: Materialisms, Activisms, Dialogues, Pedagogies, Projections* (2017).

Deane Simpson is professor of architecture, urbanism and planning at the Royal Danish Academy – Architecture, where he leads the master program Urbanism and Societal Change. His research addresses contemporary urban and architectural problematics such as the securitization of public space; the spatial transformation of welfare systems; the spatial implications of demographic transformation; problems of the informational and "smart" city; and questions of urban social and environmental sustainability. He is author of *Young-Old* (Lars Müller Publishers, 2015); and coeditor of *The City between Freedom and Security* (Birkhäuser, 2017); *Forming Welfare* (Danish Architectural Press, 2017); and *Atlas of the Copenhagens* (Ruby Press, 2018).

Silje Erøy Sollien, cand. arch., PhD, moves between practice-based research and research-based practice. Sollien earned a PhD in architecture about integrated urban heritage planning in a UNESCO World Heritage slum area in Mozambique and has wide experience from research on self-organized housing and urbanism in mainly African cities and from architectural and urban practice in mainly European cities. Until recently Sollien was a housing researcher at Vandkunsten Architects focusing on alternative housing forms. Sollien is currently an architect and urban planner at Roskilde Municipality in the department of Planning and Urban Development, attempting to help implement some of the research about alternative housing forms in local urban projects.

Marie Stender is an anthropologist and senior researcher in the department of the Built Environment at Aalborg University. She is the head of the research group Transformation of Housing and Places and is the founder and project manager of the Nordic Research Network for Architectural Anthropology. Her research focuses on place-making, disadvantaged neighborhoods, social sustainability and the relationship between social life and built environments. Marie is enrolled in the research project Regeneration of Danish Disadvantaged Neighborhoods: Long-term Evaluation (2019–28), where she has developed a qualitative study of residents' experiences, among other things.

Martin Søberg is an art historian and associate professor of architectural theory, artistic research and poetics at the Institute of Architecture and Culture at the Royal Danish Academy. He is author of *Kay Fisker: Works and Ideas in Danish Modern Architecture* (Bloomsbury, 2021); and coeditor of *The Artful Plan: Architectural Drawing Reconfigured* (Birkhäuser, 2020); *What Images Do* (Aarhus University Press, 2019); *Refractions: Artistic Research in Architecture* (Architectural Publisher B, 2016); and of special issues of *Architecture and Culture* ("Spaces of Welfare," 2022); *Artifact Journal* ("What Images Do," 2017); and *Nordic Journal of Architecture* ("Forming Welfare," 2015). He is chair of the Danish Association of Art Historians.

Acknowledgements

Thank you to all the institutions who have granted and supported this book and the research project that it is connected to, *Spaces of Danish Welfare*. The Independent Research Fund Denmark have generously supported the research project with a large grant; The Innovation Fund Denmark and the Danish architectural office Friis & Moltke Architects have supported the Industrial PhD. Foreningen Realdania, Dreyers Fond and Beckett-Fonden have supported the publishing of this book; the Royal Danish Academy has supported the artistic research that is part of this book and funded scientific assistants over the years.

Thank you to all the researchers and others that have supported the research project and the book: Our advisory board have patiently engaged in constructive discussions and critical, inspiring comments on our projects and papers during the period of the research project. Our advisory board consists of distinguished researchers within their fields: Claus Bech-Danielsen, Maja Hojer Bruun, Alison J. Clarke, Sten Gromark, Steffen Jöhncke, Lars Bo Kaspersen, Helena Mattson and Clare Melhuish. Our visiting researchers and our colleagues and friends have continuously kept us alert through their critical comments and great inspiration. Among others we are grateful to the researchers from The Nordic research network for Architecture and Welfare; the research project Reconfiguring Welfare Landscapes at University of Copenhagen; and the research group Aesthetics of Institutions, The University of Southern Denmark. Along the way, workshops have given us inspiring input, among others with Joost Grootens, Birgitte Louise Hansen, Masashi Kaijita, Lasse Horne Kjældgaard, Thomas Max Martin, Lydia Jørgensen and Peter Scharff Smith. Thank you to Kjeld Vindum for continuous inspiration. The collaborations with our visualization team and our scientific assistants have been invaluable, particularly Susanne Eeg, Bastian Feltgen and Aleksander Nowak, but also Desmond Man-Kit Choi, Alice Haugh, Durita Hojdal, Mikkel Lux Larsen, Anne Katrine Røien and Camille Tygesen. At our conference *Spaces of Welfare* (2021) we had the great pleasure of being able to present a large number of interesting studies by the delegates, along with the fantastic keynote lecturers Tom Avermaete and Daniel Miller.

The subprojects have prospered from the assistance and sparring of local actors. Thank you to Tønder Municipality, to Birgitte Thomsen, head of the Historical Association for Old Tønder municipality, the historical archive; thank you to Esben Bala Skouboe, Lene Bjerg Kristensen, special consultant and leader of Terror Security at TMF, Copenhagen Municipality; Ingeborg Degn, head of Sikker By, Copenhagen Municipality; Martin Dinesen, Jesper Laisen, Emilie Lyngsaae Nielsen and Henrik Riis Stawicki, PET; Søren Astrup, journalist, *Politiken*; Lars Bo Kaspersen, CBS; Stine Ilum, anthropologist and PhD student, University of Copenhagen; Marie Christine Skammelsen, PhD student, Aarhus University; Camilla Van Deurs, Gehl Architects, City Architect of Copenhagen; Hans Scheving, Bertelsen & Scheving; Jan Gehl, architect; teachers and children at the Svend Gønge-School in Vordingborg, and Grethe Top and Kamilla Hyldebo Toft from the municipality of Vordingborg; the residents, managers and staff at the collective houses Vesterled, Nørrevænget, Silkeborghus, Langenæshus and Langenæsbo; Tom Olsen, head of *Fælleskrematoriet* (The Common Crematorium) in Ringsted; and senior architect at Henning Larsen Architects, Peter Munch.

Our deepest gratitude, however, is directed toward all the people who were willing to tell us about their lives in and between the multiple welfare spaces.

Image Credits

Unless otherwise noted, all visualizations are drawn by the visualization team: Aleksander Nowak, Bastian Feltgen and Susanne Eeg.

Visual Introduction
1–16

fig. 1 Photo by Hakon Nielsen/Ritzau Scanpix
fig. 2 Photo by Lars Hansen/Ritzau Scanpix
fig. 3 Photo by Morten Langkilde/Ritzau Scanpix
fig. 4 Photo from the C. Th. Sørensen Collection/Det Kongelige Akademi – DOCS
fig. 5 Photo by Jens Dresling/Ritzau Scanpix
fig. 6 Photo by August Fischer/Arkitekturbilleder.dk
fig. 7 Photo by Peter Klint/Politiken/Ritzau Scanpix
fig. 8 Photo by Sandra Gonon/Arkitekturbilleder.dk
fig. 9 Photo by Sandra Gonon/Arkitekturbilleder.dk

Children as Symbolic Figures in Welfare Space Photography
50–71

All photos in this chapter are published with kind permission from *Arkitekten.*
figs. 1–12, 15–19, 22, 24–36 Photographer unknown
fig. 13 Photo by Poul Erik Skriver. Published with kind permission from Peter Skriver
fig. 14 Photo by Erik Gleie/Ritzau Scanpix
fig. 20 Photo by Lundhans © Helmer Lund Hansen/VISDA
fig. 21 Photo by Palle Hestbech. Published with kind permission from Palle Hestbech
fig. 23 Photo by Henrik Fog-Møller. Published with kind permission from © Henrik Fog-Møller

Global events, 1970–2022
72–73

1973 First Oil Crisis. Photo by Zuma/Ritzau Scanpix
1978 First child, in vitro fertilization treatment. Photo by AFP/Ritzau Scanpix
1980 Ronald Reagan is elected US President. Photo by Gerald Penny/AP/Ritzau Scanpix
1986 The Chernobyl disaster. Photo by Vladimir Repik/AFP/Ritzau Scanpix
1987 Stock market collapse. Photo by Kathy Willens/AP/Ritzau Scanpix
1989 Tiananmen Square. Photo by Jeff Widener/AP/Ritzau Scanpix
1989 Fall of the Berlin Wall. Photo by Gerard Malie/AFP/Ritzau Scanpix
1996 Dolly the sheep. Photo by Jeremy Sutton Hibbert/Shutterstock/Ritzau Scanpix
2001 September 11 Terror Attacks. Photo by Seth Mcallister/AFP/Ritzau Scanpix
2010 Arab Spring begins. Photo by Ben Curtis/AP/Ritzau Scanpix
2014 US-led coalition invades Iraq. Photo by Eric Feferberg/AFP/Ritzau Scanpix
2015 So-called European Migrant Crisis. Photo by Robert Atanasovski/AFP/Ritzau Scanpix
2016 BREXIT. Photo by Toby Melville/Reuters/Ritzau Scanpix
2017 #MeToo movement. Photo by Erik Mcgregor/Zuma/Ritzau Scanpix
2021 Glasgow Climate Pact. Photo by Paul Ellis/AFP/Ritzau Scanpix

Events in Denmark, 1970–2022
74–75

1971 Freetown Christiania. Photo by Pedersen Peer/Ritzau Scanpix
1973 National building activity peaks. Photo by Erik Gleie/Ritzau Scanpix
1979 Greenland obtains hjemmestyre. Photo by Ebbe Andersen/Ritzau Scanpix
1989 Same-sex civil partnership. Photo by Morten Langkilde/Ritzau Scanpix
1997 Storebæltsbroen. Photo by Michael Eisenberg/Ritzau Scanpix
2000 Øresundsbroen. Photo by Lars Laursen/Biofoto/Ritzau Scanpix
2005 So-called Muhammed Crisis. Photo by Binsar Bakkara/AP/Ritzau Scanpix
2007 Structural reform. Photo by Jens Dige/Ritzau Scanpix
2008 Copenhagen, the World's Most Livable City. Photo by Carsten Snejbjerg/Ritzau Scanpix
2015 Terror attack at Krudttønden. Photo by Lars Krabbe/Jyllands-Posten/Ritzau Scanpix
2017 Ban of wearing face-masking garments in public. Photo by Per Rasmussen/Ritzau Scanpix

1 Security

From Architecture of the Architect to the Architecture of *Salus Populi* and the Architecture of Security
78–93

fig. 1 Photo from the C. Th. Sørensen Collection/Det Kongelige Akademi – DOCS
fig. 2 Photographer unknown/Svendborg Byhistoriske Arkiv
fig. 3 Photo by Jens Cederskjold/Wikimedia Commons
fig. 4 Photographer unknown/Dansk Sygeplejehistorisk Museum
fig. 5 Photo by Frederik Riise/Wikimedia Commons
fig. 6 Photographer unknown/Stadsarkivet
fig. 7 Photo from vestvolden.info
fig. 8 Photographer unknown/Krigsmuseet
fig. 9 Photo by Per Munkgaard Thorsen/Arkitekturbilleder.dk
fig. 10 Photo by Per Munkgaard Thorsen/Arkitekturbilleder.dk
fig. 11 Photo by Andreas Trier Mørch/Arkitekturbilleder.dk
fig. 12 Photo by Sandra Gonon/Arkitekturbilleder.dk
fig. 13 Photo by Helene Høyer Mikkelsen
fig. 14 Photo by Emilie Koefoed
fig. 15 Photo by Karlsson Arkitekter
fig. 16 Photo by Andreas Trier Mørch og Henning Ørbæk/Det Kongelige Akademi – DOCS
fig. 17 Photo by LYTT Architecture A/S
fig. 18 Photo by Martin Toft Burchardi Bendtsen/Arkitekturbilleder.dk

Spaces and Measures Between Welfare State and Security State
94–147

fig. 1 Photo by Google Streetview
fig. 2 Photo by Liselotte Sabroe/Ritzau Scanpix
fig. 3 Illustrations by Troels Vorre Olsen,Viatrafik/Sanne Slot Hansen,Schønherr
fig. 4 Ekstra Bladet/Internet magazine Inspire
fig. 5 PET
fig. 6 Danish Government/Justitsministeriet
fig. 7 1) Eva Ring/Billedskolen; 2) Søren Bidstrup/Ritzau Scanpix; 3) Simon Læssøe/Ritzau Scanpix

fig. 8 Illustration by Simpson/Gimmel/Lonka/Jay/Grootens/Atlas of the Copenhagens
fig. 9 Photographer unknown/Forstadsmuseet
fig. 10 Photographer unknown/Københavns Museum
fig. 11 Photo by Erik Petersen/Ritzau Scanpix
fig. 12 Photo by Strüwing/Københavns Museum
fig. 13 Realdania
fig. 14 Video stills by Alison Withers/Steve Bloomfield/Jakob Ohrt Nielsen/Monocle
fig. 15 Illustration by Gehl Architects
fig. 16 Screenshot TV2/Lorry. Photo by Katrine Emilie Andersen/Ritzau Scanpix
fig. 17 Drawings by Carl Røgind. 1) Aalborg Stadsarkiv; 3) Assens Lokalarkiv
fig. 18 3D scan/Aleksander Nowak and Bastian Feltgen
vis. 1.14 Photographer unknown/Associated Photographers/Københavns Stadsarkiv
vis. 1.17 photo by Lennard/VISDA/photo by Tage Rugaard/Københavns Museum
vis. 1.20 1) by Ole Woldbye/Københavns Museum; 2) photographer unknown/Københavns Museum
vis. 1.23 1) by Ellen Thoby/Københavns Museum; 2) Mogens Falk-Sørensen/Stadsarkivets fotografiske Atelier/Københavns Museum

Between Technologies of Power and Notions of Solidarity: A Response to the Danish *Ghetto Plan* and Swedish *Vulnerable Areas* Documents
148–59

fig. 1 Regeringen
fig. 2 Riksrevisionen, photo by Joachim Nywall
fig. 3 Migrationsverket
fig. 4 Regeringen
fig. 5 Regeringen
fig. 6 Regeringen
fig. 9 Migrationsverket

Holes in the Spaces of the Welfare State: Media Coverage and Residents' Responses in the So-Called Hardest Ghettos in Denmark
160–73

fig. 1 Photos by Claus Bech-Danielsen/BUILD/Aalborg University
fig. 2 Photos by Claus Bech-Danielsen/BUILD/Aalborg University
fig. 3 Photos and diagrams Claus Bech-Danielsen and Mette Mechlenborg/BUILD/Aalborg University
fig. 4 Diagram by Claus Bech-Danielsen and Mette Mechlenborg/BUILD/Aalborg University
fig. 5 Diagram by Mette Mechlenborg/BUILD/Aalborg University
fig. 6 Diagram by Mette Mechlenborg/BUILD/Aalborg University

Are We Caring? Dilemmas Between Home and Institution in Architectures for the Elderly
174–215

fig. 1 Photo by Peter Elfelt/Københavns Stadsarkiv
fig. 2 Photographer unknown/Medicinsk Museion
fig. 3 Photographer unknown/*Arkitekten*
fig. 4 Photographer unknown/*Arkitekten*
fig. 5 Photographer unknown/*Arkitekten*
fig. 6 Photographer unknown/*Arkitekten*
fig. 7 Erik Ejlers & Henning Graversen/*Arkitekten*
fig. 8 Erik Ejlers & Henning Graversen/*Arkitekten*
fig. 9 Frederiksen & Knudsen A/S Arkitekter
fig. 10 Frederiksen & Knudsen A/S Arkitekter
fig. 11 Photos by Louise Dedenroth Høj
fig. 12 Photos by Louise Dedenroth Høj
fig. 13 Photos by Louise Dedenroth Høj
fig. 14 Photos by Louise Dedenroth Høj
fig. 15 Photos by Louise Dedenroth Høj
fig. 16 Photos by Louise Dedenroth Høj
vis 1.41 Photos by Louise Dedenroth Høj
vis 1.42 Photos by Louise Dedenroth Høj
vis 1.43 Photos by Louise Dedenroth Høj

2 Adaptability

A Welfare Situation in Tønder
218–49

fig. 1 Photo by Kirsten Marie Raahauge
fig. 2 Photo by Kirsten Marie Raahauge
vis 2.05 1) Neue Photographische Gesellschaft, Museum Sønderjyllands Mediearkiv: Tønder Banegård, Marsch-Bahnhof; 7) Tonhalle Foto, Museum Sønderjyllands Mediearkiv: Tønder Handelsgymnasium & Handelsskole, Martin Hammerichsvej 2, Tønder; 14) H.C. Davidsen, Museum Sønderjyllands Mediearkiv: Ribe Landevej i Tønder, Hedeselskabets ejendom, tidligere landbrugsskole; Where nothing else is mentioned: Photographers unknown/The Historical Association for Old Tønder municipality, the historical archive.
vis 2.06 Photos by Kirsten Marie Raahauge

From Purgatory to District Heating: Extending the Last Journey within the Danish Welfare State
250–81

fig. 1 Photo by Niels Grønbæk
fig. 2 Photo by Niels Grønbæk
fig. 3 Photo by Tom Olsen, Director of Fælleskrematoriet
fig. 4 Photo by Tom Olsen, Director of Fælleskrematoriet
fig. 5 Photo by Tom Olsen, Director of Fælleskrematoriet
fig. 6 Photo by Tom Olsen, Director of Fælleskrematoriet
fig. 7 Photo by Tom Olsen, Director of Fælleskrematoriet
fig. 8 Photo by Peter Andersen
fig. 9 Photo by Anders Sune Berg/Henning Larsen Architects
fig. 10 Photo by Anders Sune Berg/Henning Larsen Architects
fig. 11 Photo by Niels Grønbæk
fig. 12 Photo by Niels Grønbæk
fig. 13 Photo by Jennie Lorentsson
fig. 14 Photo by Niels Grønbæk

Are We All Here? Inclusion and Spatial Restructurings in the Danish Primary School 1993–2020
282–309

fig. 1 Photo from Lokalhistorisk Arkiv for Korsør og Omegn
vis. 2.32 Photos by Aleksander Nowak

Healing Architecture and the Crisis of Care
310–39

fig. 1 MODOS & Regional Hospital West, Herning
fig. 2 Herning Hospital
fig. 3 Hilllerød Hospital
fig. 4 Hospitalsenhed Vest, Herning
fig. 5 Dansk Sygeplejehistorisk Museum

fig. 6 Erik Brandt Dam Arkitekter & Charlotte Skibsted Landskabsarkitekter
fig. 7 Herzog & de Meuron
fig. 8 Dansk Sygeplejehistorisk Museum.
fig. 9 Aalborg Hospital
fig. 10 JWR Architects
vis. 2.40 Archival photos from Bispebjerg Hospital
vis. 2.41 Photos by Kulturregion Ikast-Brande, Visit Nordvestkysten, Nicolas Jægergaard/Sol og Strand Harrild Hede, Dansk Vandrelaug Holstebro, Randbøldal Camping Hvide Sande, Struer Lydens By

Design and Decolonization in the 1970s: Beyond Spaces of Danish Welfare
346–57

fig. 1 Photo by Roger Conrad/Victor J. Papanek Foundation/ University of Applied Arts Vienna
fig. 2 Nordic Africa Institute, Sweden.
fig. 3 © Victor J. Papanek Foundation, University of Applied Arts Vienna

3 Community

The Social Omnipotence of Neighborship
370–99

fig. 1 Photos by Susanne Eeg
fig. 2 Drawing by J. K. Schmidt and Kaj Schmidt
vis. 3.07 Photos by Karl Erik Jensen

Ideology of the Welfare State in Solidified Concrete for Housing
400–11

fig. 1 Photographer unknown/Københavns Bymuseum
fig. 2 Photo by Claus Bech-Danielsen
fig. 3 Drawing by Steen Eiler Rasmussen/Danmarks Kunstbibliotek
Fig. 4 Kaj Agertoft and Juul Møller, image from Arkitekten Ugehæfte, volume 48
fig. 5 Photo by Michael Varming
fig. 6 a–b) Photo by Claus Bech-Danielsen
fig. 7 Illustration by Bech-Danielsen & Sørensen
fig. 8 Photo by Claus Bech-Danielsen

New Housing Economics
412–21

fig. 1 Photo by Per Pixel Petterson
fig. 2 Photo by Silje Erøy Sollien
fig. 3 Photo by Silje Erøy Sollien
fig. 4 Photo by Silje Erøy Sollien
fig. 5 Photo by Silje Erøy Sollien
fig. 6 Visualization by Vandkunsten

On the Battle for Amager Common: A Power Play of Housing Politics in Copenhagen
422–43

fig. 1 Photo by Henning Bagger/Ritzau Scanpix
fig. 2 Visualization by Vandkunsten
fig. 3 Photo by Michael Bonnevie
fig. 4 Photo by Jens Astrup/Ritzau Scanpix

Visualization Index

0.01 22–23

0.02 24–25

0.03 72–73

0.04 74–75

1 Security

Spaces and Measures between Welfare State and Security State

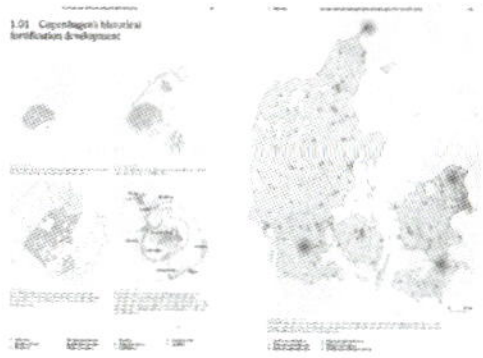
1.01 118–19

1.02 120–21

1.03 122

1.04 123

1.05 124

1.06 125

1.07 126

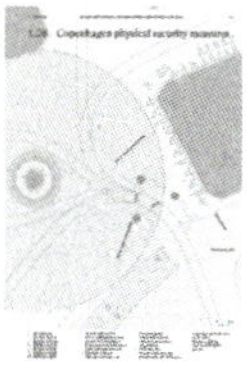
1.08 127

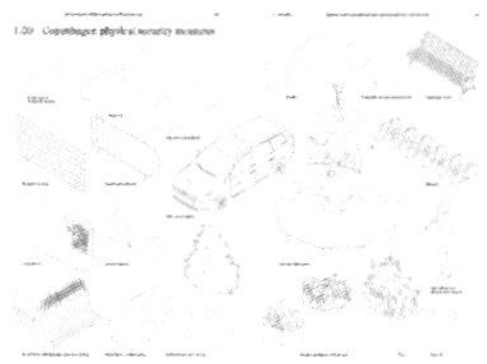
1.09 128–29

1.10 130

1.11 131

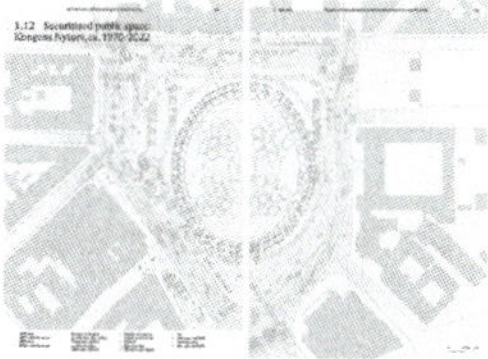
1.12 132–33

1.13 134

1.14 135

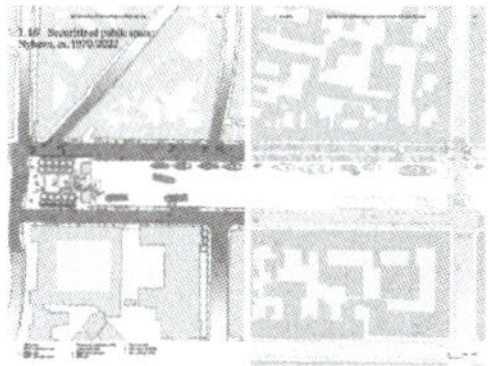
1.15 136–37

1.16 138

1.17 139
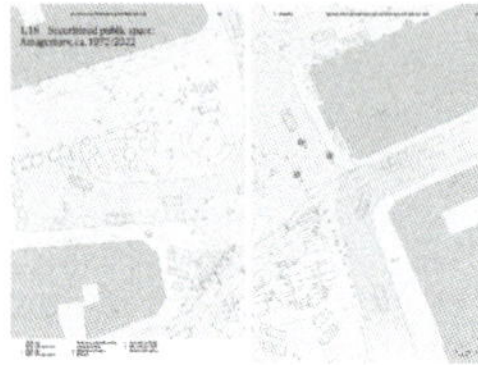
1.18 140–41

1.19 142

1.20 143

1.21 144–45

1.22 146

1.23 147

Are We Caring? Dilemmas Between Home and Institution in Architectures for the Elderly

1.24 188

1.25 189

1.26 190

1.27 191

1.28 191

1.29 192

1.30 193

1.31 194

1.32 195
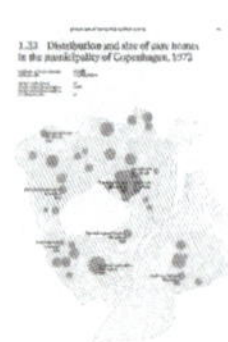
1.33 196
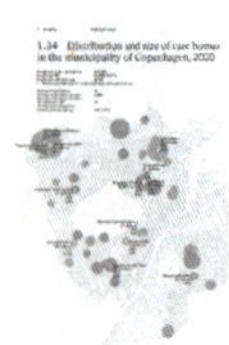
1.34 197

1.35 198

1.36 199
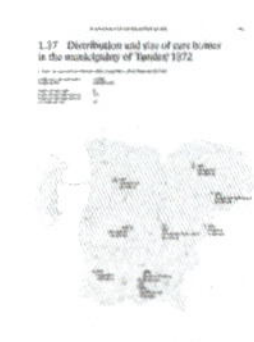
1.37 200
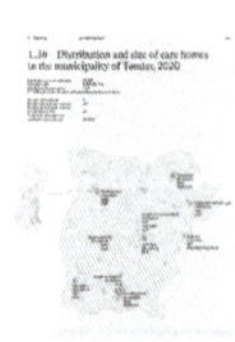
1.38 201
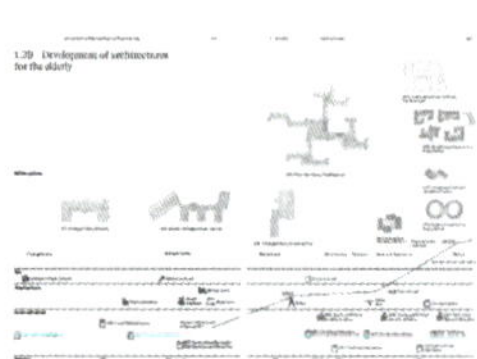
1.39 202–03

1.40 204–05

1.41 206–07
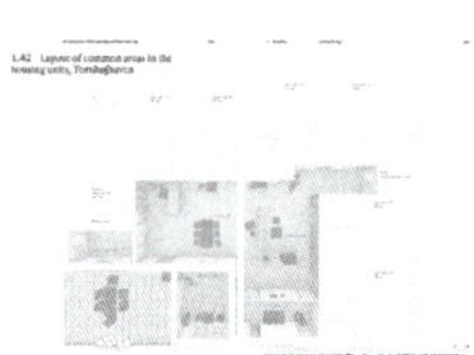
1.42 208–09
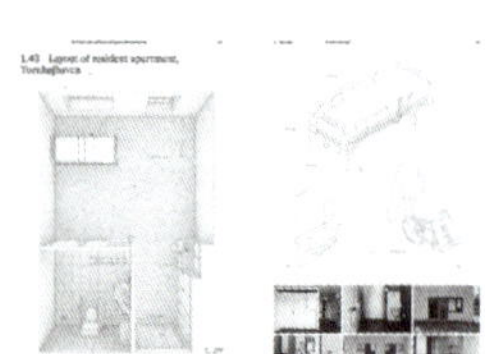
1.43 210–11
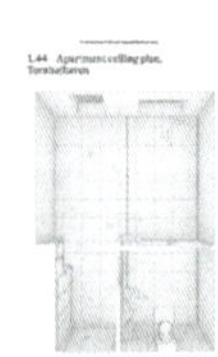
1.44 212
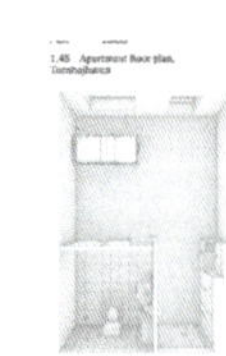
1.45 213
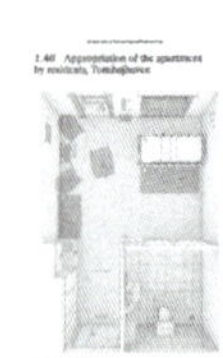
1.46 214
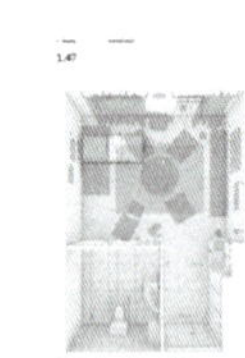
1.47 215

2 Adaptability

A Welfare Situation in Tønder

2.01 233

2.02 234

2.03 235

2.04 236–37

2.05 238–39

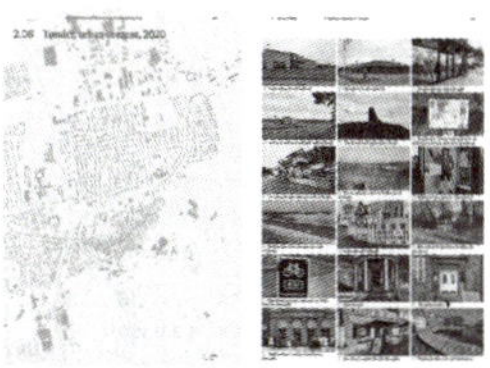
2.06 240–41

2.07 242

2.08 243

2.09 244–45

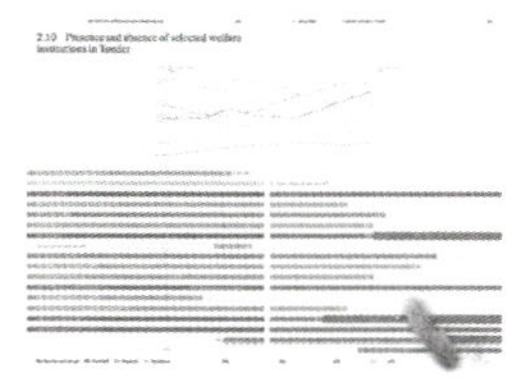
2.10 246–47

2.11 248

2.12 249

From Purgatory to District Heating: Extending the Last Journey within the Danish Welfare State

2.13 265

2.14 266

2.15 267

2.16 268

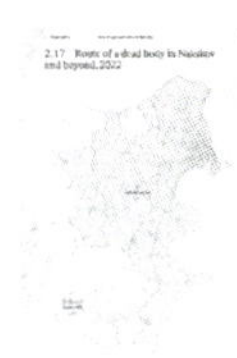
2.17 269

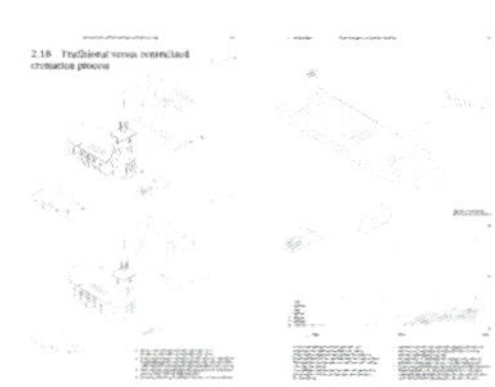
2.18 270–71

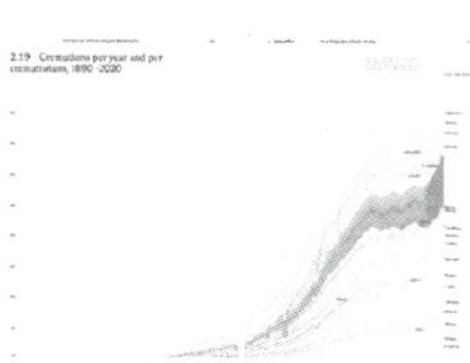
2.19 272–73

2.20 274

2.21 275

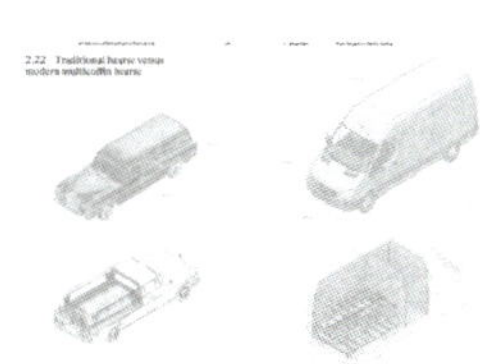
2.22 276–77

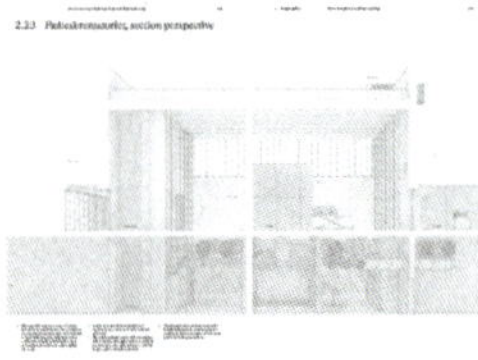
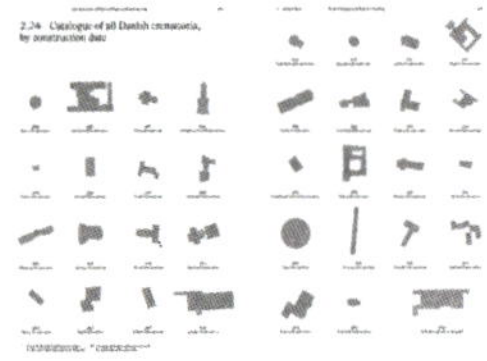

2.23 278–79
2.24 280–81

Are We All Here? Inclusion and Spatial Restructurings in the Danish Primary School 1993–2020

2.25 295
2.26 296
2.27 297
2.28 298
2.29 299
2.30 300
2.31 301

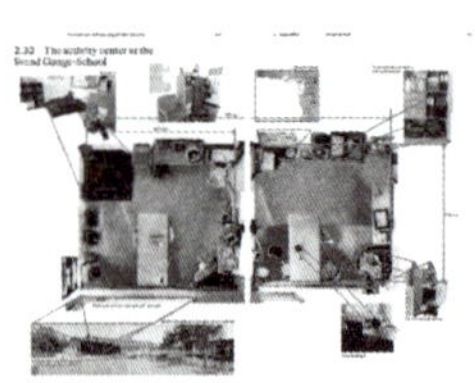
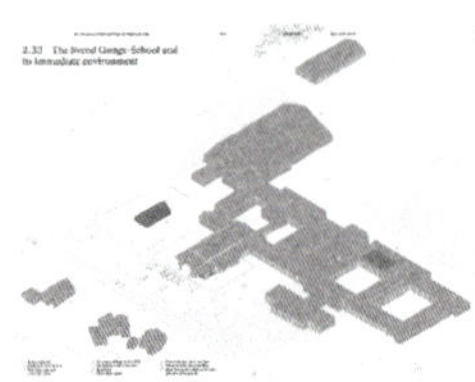
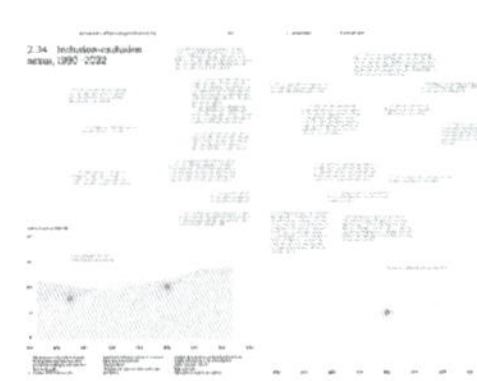

2.32 302–03
2.33 304–05
2.34 306–07
2.35 308–09

Healing Architecture and the Crisis of Care

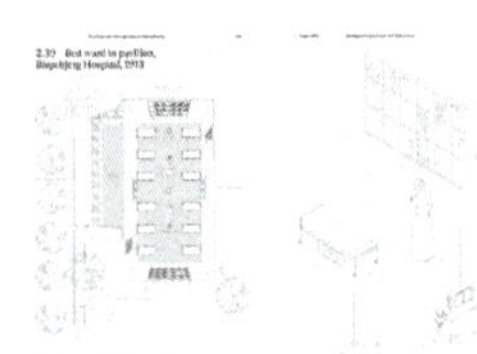

2.36 324–25
2.37 326–27
2.38 328–29
2.39 330–31

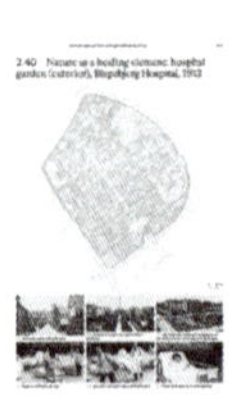

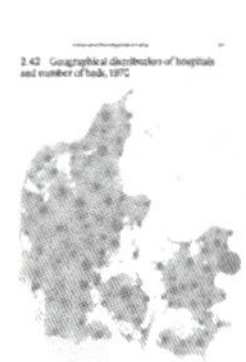
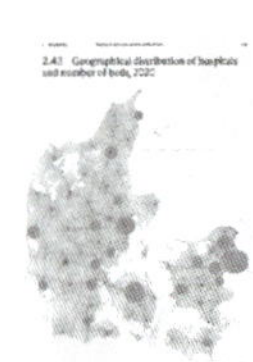
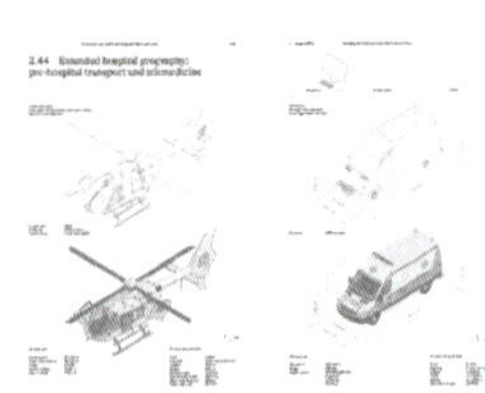

2.40 332
2.41 333
2.42 334
2.43 335
2.44 336–37
2.45 338–39

3 Community

The Social Omnipotence of Neighborship

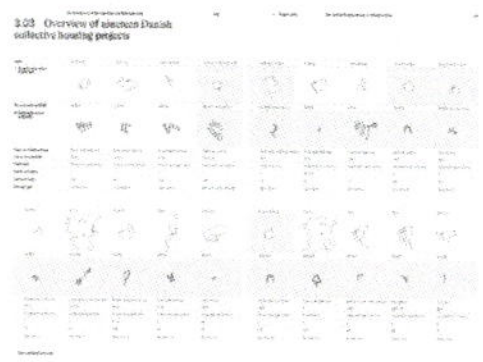
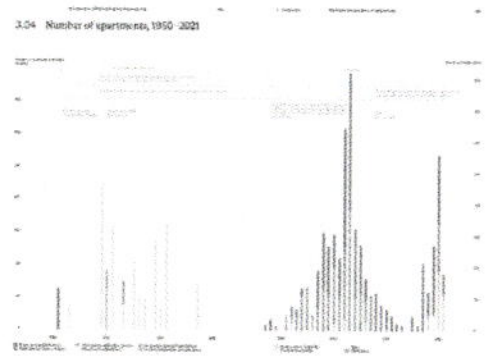
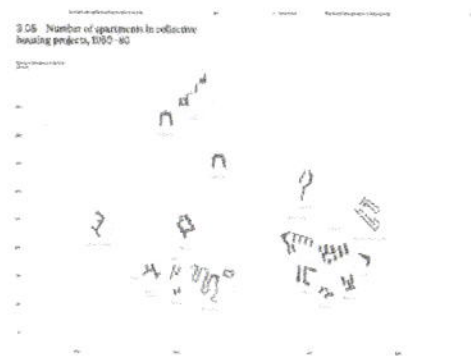

3.01 384
3.02 385
3.03 386–87
3.04 388–89
3.05 390–91

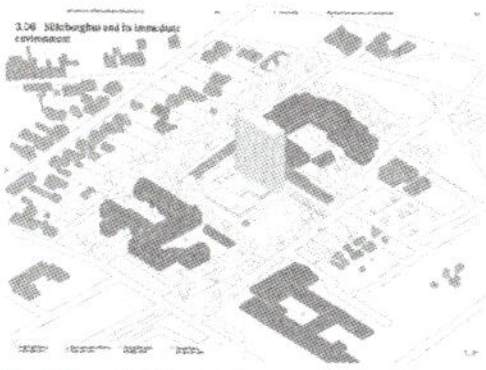
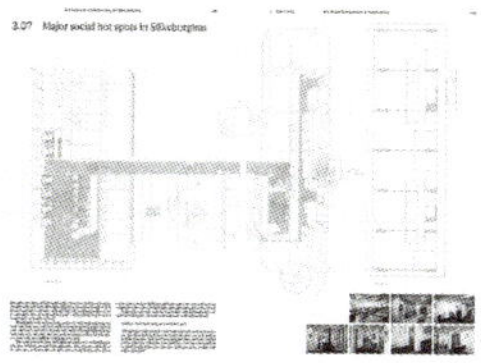

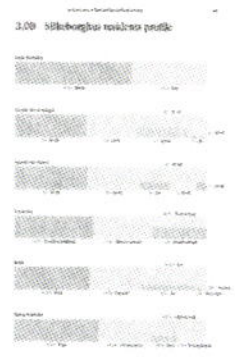

3.06 392–93
3.07 394–95
3.08 396–97
3.09 398

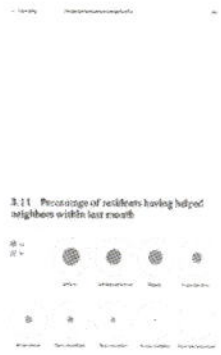

3.10 399
3.11 399

On the Battle for Amager Common: A Power Play of Housing Politics in Copenhagen

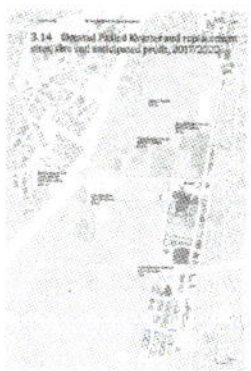

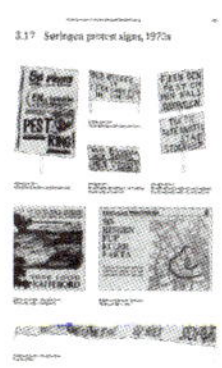

3.12 434–35
3.13 436
3.14 437
3.15 438
3.16 439
3.17 440

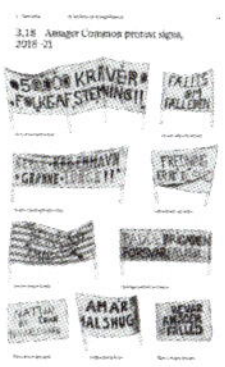
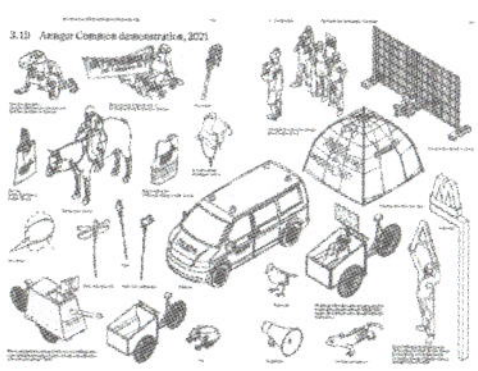

3.18 441
3.19 442–43

Editors	Kirsten Marie Raahauge, Deane Simpson, Martin Søberg, Katrine Lotz
Production editor	Sandra Gonon
Editorial team	Susanne Eeg
Copyediting and proofreading	Keonaona Peterson
Visualizations	Aleksander Nowak, Bastian Feltgen, Susanne Eeg
Design	SJG / Joost Grootens, Dimitri Jeannottat
Design visualizations	SJG / Joost Grootens, Philipp Doringer, Julie da Silva, Dimitri Jeannottat
Lithography	Marjeta Morinc
Printing and binding	Wilco Art Books

Lars Müller Publishers is supported by the Swiss Federal Office of Culture with a structural contribution for the years 2021–24.

Lars Müller Publishers
Zurich, Switzerland
www.lars-mueller-publishers.com

ISBN 978-3-03778-691-8

Distributed in North America by ARTBOOK | D.A.P.
www.artbook.com

Printed in the Netherlands

PEER REVIEWED

The certification means that an independent peer of at least PhD level has made a written assessment justifying this book's scientific quality and original contributions.

This book is supported by

DANMARKS FRIE FORSKNINGSFOND
INDEPENDENT RESEARCH FUND DENMARK

BECKETT-FONDEN

DREYERSFOND

Realdania

Royal Danish Academy
Architecture Design Conservation